Praise for *It's No Wonder Kids Don't Learn—Just Look What They Teach Teachers*

"How well students learn is reliably predicted by how well their teacher scores on a math or verbal test. Education schools fail to enhance teacher's knowledge, and then compound the problem by indoctrinating teachers with anti-intellectual slogans—the very opposite of what our schools need. Complaints about low school performance are routinely dismissed by ed-school insiders as a 'manufactured crisis' invented by the 'right wing.' But Konstantine Turkalo, an ed-school insider, has broken ranks to report what it's really like in there. May he lead the way to more palace revolts—our best hope for improving education schools from within."

—E. D. Hirsch, Jr.
Professor of English, University of Virginia
Author, *Cultural Literacy: What Every American Needs to Know*

"I had a chance over the weekend to read your material and admire it greatly. It tells the truth about the real root problems in secondary education in words that, amazingly, seldom ever get spoken aloud. Will it help? Who knows, but it at least sets the record straight and describes what is actually happening, rather than the gruel of lies and half-truths that are fed to us by the media and the unions."

—Alvin B. Kernan
Professor of English, Princeton University
Author, *In Plato's Cave*

It's No Wonder Kids Don't Learn—Just Look What They Teach Teachers

Konstantine Turkalo

VANTAGE PRESS
New York

FIRST EDITION

Published by Vantage Press, Inc.
419 Park Ave. South, New York, NY 10016

Manufactured in the United States of America
ISBN: 0-533-15185-6

Library of Congress Catalog Card No.: 2005901631

0 9 8 7 6 5 4 3 2 1

For my children

Contents

Preface

As time goes on, it is becoming clear to me that books such as this are becoming useless. This is so because no one really cares anymore. Hardly anyone who graduates a modern high school reads much beyond TV listings anyway, so what difference does it make whether schools know how to teach reading, or much of anything else?

Ever more frequently we strange and ascetic few who do read at least occasionally, come across statistics that do not seem to concern very many, though are disturbing to us. Such facts as the *Wall Street Journal* reported in March of 1989 that told us that only 10 percent of applicants for mail room jobs in Chicago could pass the literacy standard, or that 80 percent of all applicants for jobs at Motorola failed English tests set at the 7th grade level and math tests set at 5th grade.

You may ask, in a time touted as the Information Age, why would these things be of concern to us? All is as it should be. Our educational system is busy preparing us for the future. Isn't it?

Introduction

Have you noticed that the American public school system is failing? That is not surprising. It has been in all the papers. In fact you could ask almost anybody, except an American 'educator.'

My opening paragraph is not entirely fair, of course. If you speak with public school teachers, especially experienced old-timers, you will discover that the educational wagons are not all tightly circled. I have heard experienced teachers advise people loudly to take their kids out of the public school system and to pay whatever private schools ask. I have asked other teachers what they thought of the Special education revolution and the response is remarkable, although not very surprising. What I often saw was a quick glance around, to see who might be listening, and a lowering of the voice even if no one was nearby. Identifying oneself as 'against Special ed', or even questioning the validity of the Special ed precepts, is dangerous in our age of militant niceness. Yet, one of the things I hope to show with this book is why you too should want to see the practices of Special education, which have come to dominate all modern public school activities, contained to appropriate levels. Nevertheless, the folks who clasp their hands over their hearts, trying to look beatific while repeating the mantra, "It's for the children," often cow genuine teachers into a sullen silence.

Other indicators that all is not well include reports over the past several decades about dramatic increases in child abuse, spousal abuse, recreational drive-by shootings, road rage, date rape, teenage pregnancy, childhood obesity (and the diseases that come with it), deadbeat parent sightings, mothers killing their own children for sexual liberation, a massive decrease in integrity (both personal and governmental), rudeness and even insolence as a virtue (attitude), an astonishing decrease in sexual mores (and the increase of the diseases that come with it), an increase in gangs, drug use, and unrepentant child killers (both 'youthful offenders' and killers of children, often both at once), millions of normal kids identified as having 'Special needs,' victimology, a national obsession with self esteem, and a disastrous decrease in academic achievement at all levels, to name just a few.

Periodically, however, as with our ever increasing gasoline prices, when, after some frightening new peak is reached, such as the Columbine High School shootings, the reports diminish for a time, we heave a sigh of relief, and tell ourselves, "We can live with that." Yet the 'peak' engenders new adjustments to our ways of doing things which would once have been unthinkable. These modern, Progressive 'improvements' to our way of life are interconnected, and we will discuss the connections as we go along.

Ask old-timer teachers what has changed the most over the course of their careers and we almost invariably get a litany, prominently featuring lack of classroom (and self-) discipline, sometimes genuinely frightening rudeness, lack of pupil respect for anybody (including themselves) or for institutions (including school), lack of perseverance, and a lack of a willingness to work which, if not reversed quite early in life, lead almost inevitably to an arrogant lifelong ignorance, and the occupational limitations inherent in ignorance. Even new teachers notice the decrease of study habits and average competence over time. All these good things have waned while other bad things have increased.

Among those things that have increased are unreasonable demands from parents (including demands to teach less, so as to allow more time for after-school activities), administrators administering a dizzying array of programs and 'interventions,' and demands for even more nonacademic interventions. We are asking teachers to be all things to all people—babysitters, activity facilitators, bureaucratic report filers, policemen, surrogate parents, and almost every stripe of social services workers.[1] We are asking teachers to do almost everything but teach.

I will very shortly begin to prove that last statement, but while in many schools my descriptions would be considered understated, we should not take it to mean that every teacher is abiding by every syllable of what I will tell throughout the book at all times. If that were literally true, our educational system would have imploded fully long ago. Of

---

1 I suspect that you have all noticed that Special educators now almost never speak of any sorts of instruction at all. They mainly speak in terms of "providing services."

course, it has imploded fully in some places. Those places tend to be precisely where the Progressive ideology intends doing the most good, the "at risk" schools, because that is where the Progressive techniques are used in their purest forms, and may have been imposed over the objections of sensible teachers and parents. Of course, when the community notices a profound lack of learning in the school's graduates, they then blame "the times we live in," lack of parental involvement, a lack of money to install still more intervention programs, and any other factor they can think of other than their teaching practices. Nevertheless, enough of the practices and techniques detailed here are thought to be required by law and are taught as 'appropriate' in Ed schools and in teacher in-service training,[2] so that what I say is true enough, often enough that our kids and our society are suffering for it. Some schools try very hard to abide by *all* the Progressive requirements however, and think of themselves as successful, and innovative, simply because of it. For example, some years ago a cover story in the National Education Association magazine (*NEA Today*) featured a school that "Has everything!" The characteristics that the NEA was so proud of included <u>no</u> tests, <u>no</u> age-appropriate class organization, <u>no</u> homework, and, unfortunately, little or no learning.

Happily, the instructional solutions to our educational problems are simple, though setting up the solutions would engender considerable bureaucratic angst. This is largely true because the ones who are asked to fix the mess are the ones who are most committed to the mess, and have the most to lose if the mess were fixed.

I am a recently trained and certified teacher, too. That is one reason I can write this book. Among the reasons that I underwent the teacher training is that I was concerned about the decades of news reports that said that the American educational system was failing. Now that I have young kids of my own, I wanted to see whether the reports were justified. They were. Oh, boy, were they ever! Here is only one reason. One lesson, perhaps the fundamental lesson, from my educational training was that: *"Teaching subject-matter content is the least important thing that teachers do."*[3]

---

2 Though I have recently (2005) read that these are beginning to change as a result of the No Child Left Behind Act, and, of course, that 'educators' are complaining.

3 Educators espoused this idea at least as early as 1915 when Abraham Flexner, working for the General Education Board, one of the Rockefeller philanthropic trusts, said, "The education offered [to] students should be 'the least of the services rendered . . . More important would perhaps be its influence in setting up scientific as against dogmatic educational standards.' " What turned out to be 'scientific', however, was the "project-method" which, like today's 'activities methods,

'Subject-matter content' is educational jargon for the facts and ideas of every subject; history in history class, math in math class, and science in science class, etc. Go back and read the italicized sentence again. In an age that calls itself the 'Information Age' and proclaims that 'knowledge is power', this is an extraordinary idea for the teachers of teachers to profess. Think about it for a moment, and its implications for 'academic excellence'. Academic excellence is the product promised us, in exchange for continually increased funding. Yet, this excellence, like the Emperor's new clothes, is quite invisible. We have been promised a beautiful result since the current Progressive educational revolution began in the mid-1960s, and have dutifully increased funding to achieve it many times since. We have tried innumerable techniques and procedures touted as 'critical' in the expert journals and before every governmental body in the nation. Yet, our bloated system has not improved its results. The educational experts, we are still told, require still more funding to get it right. Not surprisingly, neglecting subject matter content is also at the heart of the debate about 'standards', but more on this later.

If the teachers of American teachers find that teaching is an unnecessary burden upon a teacher's time, is it any wonder that our educational system is failing? Is it any wonder that we have obliged America's colleges to require very basic remedial composition or 'speech' and math classes of *all* incoming freshman, since colleges can be well assured that too many high school graduates can barely write or speak a coherent sentence? Is it any wonder that our technology companies have to go offshore to employ enough qualified engineers, though this is the Internet generation?

Unfortunately, the above abbreviated list of concerns is no impediment to Progressive thinking. For instance, Berliner and Biddle, in their strange but honored book, *The Manufactured Crisis. Myths, Fraud and the Attack on the American Schools* (1995), positively revel in the dumbing-down of American schools, though they deny that it is happening at all. In their second chapter (p. 28), which attempts to dispel the 'myth' of falling achievement, they write this:

> ... the jobs of the future may actually require fewer, not more, high-level skills. In an unusual display of agreement, dozens of economists

---

stem from the kid's stated interests rather than from what educated (i.e., successful and educationally experienced) adults consider important to teach and learn. In essence, the children would write the curriculum.

have predicted that growth is likely in the *service* sector of employment—and this means more jobs for janitors, limousine drivers, word processors, sales clerks, and the like. We've also seen estimates that the hospitality industry—e.g., tourism—is now employing more people than any other and that the Wal-Mart chain will soon be the largest single employer in America. But most jobs in hospitality and retail sales do not require high-level mathematical skills. So if schools do not prepare everyone to perform high-level mathematics, perhaps it is because students and their teachers are responding sensibly to the looming job market.

This, however, is an odd argument coming from those who insist that *all* pupils must go to college to qualify for "good" jobs.

Berliner's next paragraph begins with, "Such musing may also be off the mark, however." Yes, I would say it is off the mark. What we see is a strange and contradictory, but common, amalgam of ideas. Dumbing-down is not happening, but even if it is, it is a good thing. We will find many such confused inconsistencies in the things that Progressive educationists tell the public as opposed to what they teach teachers to do in the classroom.

For instance, when questioned, educationist bureaucrats (sometimes called educrats) and school administrators, etc., routinely tell us that their ideas lead to educational excellence, but we will see many twists in logic similar to the above example as we go along. We will also see many samples of what Progressive thinkers accept as high-level or quality work. After reading them, try to imagine surviving life in the future knowing even less than the Progressive idea of what is good enough (because less is what they typically achieve). This is true whether the subject matter is mathematics or anything else, including their stated ideal of universal harmony.

One example of what is accepted as 'quality' is suggested by modern report cards. On my kids' grammar school reports, the highest level of achievement is labeled a subjective 'Satisfactory'. Even if we accept the subjective label, as opposed to an objective grade based on a percentage of correct answers given for many hundreds of questions asked, it seems odd that modern school policy apparently does not recognize 'Excellent' as a category of achievement. 'It's good enough', we are told. Still, when we look at the work brought home, all of it looks as if it were intended for much younger students.

As I said, I am a recently certified teacher. I realize, however, that the word 'recently' may conjure images of a young man only just weaned academically and without the experience to make bold pronouncements about anything. I also realize that I am completely unknown and that I do not have the cachet of a doctorate from school of education. On the other hand, after reading this book, you may not feel that having a degree of any kind from a modern American school of education is as impressive as it ought to be. You may even feel that such a degree is a positive detriment because of what is learned there.

Nevertheless, for those reasons I offer this mini résumé: I am retired from a career in the U.S. Army, where I served both as an enlisted man, two years of which were spent as an instructor, and as an officer in the Medical Service Corps. I hold three Bachelor degrees (psychology + mass communications (dual major), microbiology, and secondary education). I was certified to teach biology, chemistry, and general science in my current home state in 1997. I also have a Master's degree in Health Services Management, and what is essentially the Army's equivalent of a second Master's degree. For those in-the-know about these things, I graduated from all of the Army officer professional development schools through the Command and General Staff College (CGSC). I consider the Officer-Basic course and the Officer-Advanced course, along with the years of field experience that go with them, as the Army's version of a bachelor's degree, while CAS[3] (read 'cass-cubed', the Combined Arms and Services Staff School) and the CGSC, with its additional associated years of field experience, to be the Army equivalent of a Master's degree.

Additionally, I have young children[4] and was concerned enough about their educational prospects to undergo the teacher training. I wanted to see what the fuss was all about, from the inside. When I started Ed school I fully intended teaching to be a second career, but my experiences in the classroom as a teacher's aide, student teacher, and substitute teacher convinced me that it would be too frustrating to try to earn tenure while keeping my concerns to myself. I also didn't want to spend my life doing daycare. Ironically, I have now spent time as a substitute teacher which has allowed me to see modern educational practices on an extended basis and in several school districts, including a Catholic school district. With local variations, what I see is similar everywhere. I have no doubt that the similarities extend nationwide.

---

4 At the time that I originally completed this book in 1998, my kids were 4, 5, and 9 years old.

The newspapers and TV and radio news programs have been filled with passionate political debate regarding schools over the years. Nevertheless, it seems all too frequent that we hear another report about how poorly American kids stack up against the rest of the world or against long-established standards. As I began writing this book in 1997, the most recent of these reports said that United States kids managed to beat only South African and Cypriote kids in basic academic skills. In 2004, after American kids were again beaten handily by most other nations' kids, the Brookings Institution's Brown Center Report on American Education evaluated the latest tests given by the National Assessment of Educational Progress (NAEP), and found that they are designed for well below grade level, as compared with the rest of the world.

Yet many parents still seem to agree that while the problem is profound and widespread, it does not reach as far as their own school. This is true with parents in my children's school district, and even with politicians who may want to close the U.S. Department of Education but profess deep satisfaction with their neighborhood schools. Apart from a politician's desire not to insult his constituents, this satisfaction may be predicated on the perception that the local teachers are deeply committed to the welfare of their pupils. There are many teachers who, for instance, buy school supplies with their own money and perform other such acts of dedication (I did, too). However, our national academic results have become, and remain so poor on average, that it seems clear that teacher dedication is not the problem. Academic results would be considerably improved if teachers did their natural acts of dedication within a system that worked, rather than in one that does not. Therefore, while we should honor their heartfelt dedication, bureaucratically requiring teachers to flounder with faulty academic prescriptions is why the results are so poor.

Though an important reason for the problems we see in education, teaching is not about bureaucratic decision making. It is about what happens in the classroom. Yet, the parents who are likely to read a book such as this find it difficult to perceive a problem behind the nice, smiling faces of teachers, administrators, and counselors, and the clean, relatively safe schools that their own kids attend—until some kids shoot up the place. Even then, many demand more of what we have tried in the past several decades, to achieve 'closure', etc. For many it seems unnatural to consider the possibility that what we are doing now caused, or exacerbated the problems in the first place, and that the problems are growing and widening the longer we do them. Unaccountably, the parents of kids in the worst schools, with the most serious problems with violence and even lower achievement, still listen to the 'experts' who recommend precisely the wrong solutions and ridicule or denigrate, any suggestion that works.

The currently acceptable solutions have now been tried for generations with little, if any, positive effect, yet they are sold as social progress that cannot be reversed without serious social consequences. The fact that we have already seen very serious social consequences precisely because of the currently used recommendations, is vehemently denied by those who market themselves as experts and should, therefore, know better.

Looked at objectively, the Progressive arguments are as faulty as the solutions proposed, yet reality is difficult to separate from the political spin. Part of the reason is that it has now been a long time since the Progressive philosophy has again achieved its stranglehold on schools. As a rule, today's parents had only recently graduated from the same school districts where they have enrolled their kids, and are convinced that Education, as practiced there, is as it should be, since that is what their own teachers did (i.e., it is traditional). Furthermore, parents have been trained to think that the patchwork of social programs and services, layered over those teaching practices, is the answer to the social problems spilling in from 'the streets' or from 'the media'. We refuse to acknowledge that the truth is more like a two-way street. In a large and growing measure, the kids *are* the streets since our young adults take the ideas they learned in school with them into the streets, and when they enter the media and other forms of adult life. Thinking themselves wise and good, newly minted adults then perpetuate the attitudes they learned in school. These attitudes include another Progressive teaching, that genuine, traditional education is a bad thing, causing the problems that have grown only recently. As a result, all is not well in American schools today, and we have very good, systemic reasons to think so.

All of this being true, to understand why our schools are failing, my method will be less an erudite survey of legislation and the high-level musings of professional organizations and think tanks than a look from inside the classroom. The sorts of general information mentioned above (e.g., high-level musings) are very useful, and I will quote several of them, but what happens in the classroom is what the pupils experience.

Politicians may argue about who gets to waste our money, but the classroom is where the kids are found. That is where our kids are learning what, to them, becomes common sense. That is where our kids develop, and modify, what becomes our American culture. That is where the 'times we live in' are mutated.

My intention is to take the reader through a brief synopsis of my experiences in the Ed school classroom, and in the public and private school classrooms where I taught, with commentary to translate the education jargon, etc., used in the 'research' articles said to support the Progressive point of view. In the end, you may become confused, or perhaps outraged, at the unsupportable opinions that pass for research and the contradictory arguments that pass for logic.

My method will involve concentrating on the average kid, rather than the exceptional. If we can get the average pupil to achieve at least at an average level (i.e., age- and grade-appropriate), we will again have an educational system based on common sense and proven procedures. Then we will also produce more kids who can truly be called 'excellent' and fewer kids with problems.

I also intend to sprinkle the narrative lightly with some of my experiences as a parent attending Board of Education meetings, speaking with and listening to principals, teachers, and other parents at site-council meetings, etc. The point of this exercise will be to show what kinds of things are being done in the classroom, as opposed to what ought to be done, in the name of promoting learning and academic excellence.

If I am right, then the Progressive rhetoric that tells us how well prepared our kids will be, if we follow their prescriptions, must be wrong. I want to give people a better perspective on what all of this might mean for their kid's development and future prospects. I hope to show that what is currently being done may actually be designed to accomplish something quite different than what we are told is intended.

This last statement is somewhat difficult for me to write because, of the teachers that I have met, I can find very few hints that they are deliberately trying to harm the kids or the society. With few exceptions, they seem to believe sincerely that they are doing the 'right' things for the right reasons. Of course, probably every one of them has graduated from a public school and from Ed school, and has been duped from an early age along with the rest of us. This may be so because teachers sign on to be teachers, not researchers, so they generally take the word of the 'experts', along with the rest of us. Unfortunately, the experts often ignore, or 'reinterpret' their own research results in favor of a nonfunctional, though apparently easy to sell, ideology.

Nevertheless, the direction that our society has taken over the last forty years or more, speaks for itself. Education is too important to be left in the hands of 'educational professionals' with political agendas, utopian notions of human nature, and a disdain for reality. Incidentally, I am not trying to put the blame for all of our social ills on the educational system. Our social problems are more complex than that, and I will try to establish at least part of the etiology of those problems in Chapter 2, but the schools, as one of the first-line developers of kids' opinions and attitudes, are deeply responsible for enhancing and perpetuating the problems we see today. That is the ultimate point of this book.

I will try to limit the use of technical and rhetorical jargon, or to translate the gobbledygook where necessary, to make the arguments accessible for anyone. We will see that ordinary words are being reinterpreted in extraordinary ways, without telling us. This practice confuses the issue when we think that one thing is being said, which we agree with, while something very different is meant. In this way we are convinced to vote for things we would never consider ordinarily. I believe this exercise should be instructive and useful to parents because most of us do not truly understand what is being passed off as appropriate educational theory and practice today. The words used to describe educational recommendations, and the promised results, sound good to parents and others. Unfortunately, as with most political rhetoric, we are promised results we want to hear, but are not told how those results will be attained. Look under the surface of the promises, and you may see why the results we have are not the results we have been promised. When the results are less than acceptable, excuses are made, and everything under the sun is blamed. Everything, that is, except their own faulty recommendations.

Recently, for instance, a favorite scapegoat has been a lack of 'parental involvement'. The reason that your 9th grader cannot read very well, we are told, is that *you* did not read to him enough when he was four, because *you* did not take him to the zoo or did not sign her up for soccer activities early enough in life. The question remains, however: if kids, even 'at risk' kids with the reported worst record of parental involvement, can learn to read in only a few weeks (this is well documented in the professional and popular literature, as we will soon see), why won't our 'educators' use those proven methods? Another question is:

How was it that kids with fully illiterate parents, being taught in one-room schoolhouses with virtually no resources, could learn the three Rs? Other questions follow closely behind: if kids today do not learn how to read, add, or think, despite multiple, expensive programs and decades of innovative attempts to facilitate learning, what are the kids actually doing in school? Can what we are doing in school affect the attitudes of our kids and, what might be the long term result of these learned attitudes? If, after a decade or more of Progressive teaching, kids eventually graduate (or, as huge numbers now do, drop out) and enter life as adults, can we tie what was done to them in school to the growing litany of problems that the nation faces today?

If we allow the educational system to continue as it is practiced now, we will continue to accomplish exactly the opposite to what most of us expect to accomplish. Progressive educationists, however, may be accomplishing precisely what they intend, though they use rhetoric to lull us to complacency and convince us that they are after educational, and social excellence. Yet, the failure of the educational system can be equated with the other substantial failures achieved by our most bureaucratic attempts at achieving social justice. We are told, for instance, that multiculturalism will bring us closer together, but racist groups, from all sides, are alive and well. The War on Poverty was intended to reduce poverty, but the relative distance between the haves and have-nots has increased enormously. The War on Drugs was intended to eliminate the use of drugs, but more, and younger kids are using them than ever before, and psychoactive drugs are being prescribed to millions of normal kids, and demanded by millions of parents, though no physical disease can be found to justify it. Bicultural education was intended to prepare other-than-dominant-culture kids for life in America but has only managed to help create conditions in parts of America from which emigrants have always tried to flee. Sex education was intended to reduce teen pregnancy, abortions, and the spread of venereal diseases, but we are currently in a decades-long epidemic of these ills with no end in sight. In fact we now argue loudly that these are not bad things at all, they are merely lifestyle choices that either, 1) are nobody else's business or 2) can be mitigated by still more drugs so are nobody else's business, or 3) should be subsidized by taxes. Special education was supposedly designed to help kids with 'special needs' but has only managed to dumb down the whole system, helping few while hurting many. Relevance theory was intended to instill a lifelong love of learning in our kids, but more kids than ever are dropping out of school saying that school is irrelevant. Self-esteem theory was intended to help prepare our kids to succeed but has only managed to insure that more kids fail, or consider gunplay as an option to rectify their despair. The list goes on and on and I intend to back up these statements with examples from theory and practice.

Compare this with what Merry White tells us about Japanese school kids based on her decades-long study of Japan (*The Japanese Educational Experience: A Commitment to Children*, 1987, p. 73). During a discussion of the Japanese record in international comparisons of scholastic achievement, after telling us that 94 percent of all Japanese children graduate from high school, and 34 percent finish college[5] she says:

> . . . The children also, in greater numbers than elsewhere, report that they *like* school.
>
> The curriculum—the courses taken and the material covered—is so rich that a high school diploma in Japan can be said to be the equivalent of a college degree in the United States. In math and science particularly, Japanese children receive a broad and comprehensive education. *It has recently been shown that the lowest math and science scores in fifth grade classes in Japan are higher than the highest test scores in comparable American schools.*
>
> *Significant also is the fact that there is less variation in performance across the population than in most other societies* [my emphasis—we'll also discuss the concerns, and achievements, of the multiculturalists in Chapter 5]. Indeed it is the source of some wonder in Japan that children elsewhere do not perform as well and that standards and incentives in other advanced nations are so low.

White goes on to say:

> The effects of this situation are evident well after the end of formal schooling. For widespread literacy is accompanied by widespread engagement in all forms of knowledge-enhancing activities across all sectors of the population [i.e., life-long learning]. There is a high level of cultural engagement as well: blue collar workers submit original classical verse to newspaper columns. Moreover, the national media use highly sophisticated technical vocabularies,[6] and it is assumed everyone can read music.

---

5 The American national average, according to the Census Bureau, was 80.4 percent high school and 15.5 percent college graduates, as of the 2000 census: //censtats.census.gov/cgi-bin/pct/pctProfile.pl/

6 While our politicians and advertisers, etc., are constantly looking for the simplest way to try to explain things to us.

Many Americans, on the other hand, even after graduation from high school, cannot read at the 7th grade level, nor compute at the 5th grade level, and their cultural lives often peak with afternoon television.

Despite their self-styled 'moderate' and 'inclusive' labels, many modern American classrooms flounder in ignorance also because the Progressive educators who dominate our schools refuse to acknowledge that the traditional side has anything useful to say. Even John Dewey, the Father of American Progressive Education, noticed this tendency in his followers at least as early as 1938.[7] He called it the principle of "either-or," and noted that Progressive workers are so ideological in their thinking that if they disagree with any part of an argument, they refuse to accept all parts of that argument. This is so even when the parts disagreed with are proven to be true, and the parts acceptable to the Progressives are proven to be untrue, or are unprovable.

Unfortunately, the authors to be mentioned who argue against Progressive theory and practice, are largely ignored by the education community, with the exception of Dewey, of course, who they deliberately misinterpret. This is probably because the principle of either-or is alive, well, and still flourishing. Perhaps the sorts of research being done in education today, as well as in the other social sciences, should be brought to the public debate, and not left to molder in books seen as stodgy and irrelevant to the Modern Age. When parents and legislators see what is actually being published, and used as justification for a growing number of intervention programs, they might sit back and re-think their support. Ideally, this reading would also be true of many who think they agree with the Progressive side, for political reasons.

Most classroom teachers, for instance, signed on to be teachers, not researchers. Typically, teachers, and perhaps especially grade school teachers, don't read the supposedly scholarly journals. Instead, they take the word of the Ed.D.s and Ph.D.s, whom they think of as experts. Many teachers are disappointed in their own performance, yet they don't know why their performance is less than they would like. They have dutifully followed all of the Progressive prescriptions, which promise such wonderful results, yet can see that our litany of social problems is not getting any better and is, in fact, growing.[8] They can also see that

---

7 Dewey, John (1938), *Experience & Education*, Touchstone, New York, 1997.

8 Aside from our well-known litany of social woes, from teen pregnancy to the seeming death of morality, as of this writing, the most recent reports tell us that kids spending a lot of time in daycare, where Progressive dictates are used (e.g., 'time-out', in place of discipline, etc.), are more aggressive than their parents, and that the percentage of violent crime committed by girls has been rising alarmingly of late.

their pupils are graduating without seeming to have learned very much.[9] If classroom teachers knew what was being passed off as research, and if they knew that relatively simple changes would be needed to improve their own performance and the achievement of their pupils significantly, they might reconsider the unswerving support that is expected of them. As taxpayers, knowing that they could improve their performance for a fraction of the current cost, thereby freeing up money to improve salaries and repair buildings, etc., teachers might be moved to change the way they do things.

Many historians of education and many political commentators, however, have noted that the Progressive theorists and practitioners are never discouraged by an abject failure of their philosophy to describe reality, or by their techniques to produce promised results. In fact, many problems we are debating today may have been caused, or at least exacerbated, by Progressive solutions to previously perceived problems. This is one reason that the debate so far has not been very fruitful and is one of my motivations for writing this book.

As an example, we need go no further than *The Academic Achievement Challenge: What Really Works in the Classroom* (2002) by Jeanne Chall. Chall was an emeritus professor of education at Harvard University until her death in 1999. On page 180, she writes:

> In various research studies I have been a part of over the past fifty years,
> I have found that many popular, respected practices were not supported

---

Another recent report tells us that there is yet another national epidemic brewing. This one is an epidemic of type II (adult) diabetes in our increasingly obese children. An apparently unaddressed factor in these results may be that many children are given their child-centered choices in all things, as recommended by mental-health professionals (including special educators) and as practiced by educators and daycare workers. Given a choice, children choose fatty snacks over a balanced diet, and in many schools, such as my children's school, they can even choose not to participate in phys. ed. activities, in school. This argument is fairly intuitive in regards to our national weight problem, but is a bit more complicated regarding the rise of aggression. A shortened version of it goes like this: Kids' choices + never being asked to say you're sorry (self-esteem training) + never learning from mistakes (more self-esteem training and rubric-grading) + lack of historical and moral context (revisionist and multiculturalist history) about what is acceptable behavior and what has 'worked' in the past (Don't pour facts on their heads)—leads to → arrogant ignorance (I can do no wrong—teacher told me so) and selfishness (I matter and you don't).

9 Allow me a short personal aside to illustrate this point. Recently, when my two oldest children were sixth and second graders, respectively, I gave them a short, "knowledge-based" test of basic facts (see Gross, p. 255). Both kids achieved virtually identical scores. Later, as a seventh grader, the older one took the ACT exams as a participant in the Duke University "Talent Identification Program (TIP)." She earned a composite score at the 56th percentile, and reached the 77th percentile in some categories. She scored better than the average college-bound high school senior, yet didn't know any more than the second-grader. There seems to be something fundamentally wrong with a result such as that.

by research. Indeed, *practice often went in a direction opposite from the existing research evidence* [original emphasis] ... Although research evidence from the early 1900s found benefits for a structured, systematic teaching of phonics and other skills, practice went in the opposite direction—toward a progressive, student-centered approach (Chall 1967, 1983a, 1996a).

Chall also references many other studies and reviews of literature that individually and collectively discredit and repudiate virtually every Progressive idea now extant, from testing, to whole language, science, math and social studies instruction, to how we view the 'learning disabled', and others. If the genuine scientific literature, including some of the stuff developed by the Progressives themselves (as we will see), says that the Progressive ideas don't work, and you are confused when you hear an educator or education professor say, "We know from research that . . . ," think of Chall's next words:

> There is also a tendency [by social sciences researchers] to forget earlier research findings on a particular question—to treat each study as a new phenomenon unrelated to those done earlier.

Under normal circumstances, if an idea has failed repeatedly over a century of trying, most reasonable people would conclude that the idea should be set aside. Yet, no matter how often the Progressive theory fails, it can be resurrected because if the previous failure is recalled at all, the conditions 'this time' are said to be new, even unique. Of course, they are not new, and certainly not unique. The situation that all teachers have faced anywhere and anytime in the long history of humanity, and in any culture, is a cadre of untutored children in need of instruction in the basics of what is considered important for advancement and survival. Only the topics selected for instruction have changed over the years, as have some of the modes of presenting them. However, the needs of children to be taught, and to learn, are unchanged—and never will change.

However, it is this tendency of Progressive educators to ignore the evidence of research and to ignore experiential reality generally (i.e., the evidence of millennia of teaching people to do things they did not know how to do, which is to say: Tell them how, show them how, then let them practice, and finally, test their mastery). This tendency to ignore the essential simplicity of genuine education, allows Progressive educators to dominate the ongoing education debate by reaffirming their own simple-sounding, ideological class-struggle-dominated philosophy loudly and often, until many of their tenets have taken on a life of their own in pop philosophy and psychology. Even though we know them to be invalid. Oddly, they continue to profess that their views are all based on research and data. Yet, stripped of all the erudite sounding proclamations, in brief the Progressive recommendations amount to: Let the kids figure it out for themselves. Instruction is not only not optional, but is to be avoided. It is too boring, you see, and does not develop higher-level thinking skills.

Common sense and experience require a balance between theory and practice. Yet 'balance' has never been one of the Progressive's most salient qualities. For instance, the argument that says that 'life requires more than mere book learning', resonates as deep wisdom with many people. It resonates because the statement is literally true. On the other hand, it is most assuredly not true that book learning is of no use, yet this is an assumption of the most committed Progressive educators, and can be seen in their recommended practices.

Finally, the education debate is made more confusing for many because all sides often use the same words. All sides argue that their philosophy will ensure 'excellence' in schooling and will accomplish this by, 'challenging' kids with academic, and social excellence. These words, 'excellence', 'challenge', etc., are the right words to use if you want parents (and voters) to agree with you. We *want* our kids to 'think like a scientist'. We *want* our kids to use 'higher-level thinking skills', because we know that the world that our kids will enter demands it, and because 'intelligence' virtually defines our species. However, many of us view the results of the last several decades, including the directions taken by the society as less than excellent, while others are mollified when they hear the words 'challenge' and 'excellence' and 'We are not satisfied with the system and will work hard to improve it', coming from the mouths of educators and administrators. Then, when the system takes credit for a few brilliant kids with high achievement, who would have succeeded in any case, as evidence that the system works, people vote to send more money.

A recent annual national-average education budget was about $7,000 spent per pupil.[10] This equates to about $140,000 per 20-pupil

10 The 2000 census revealed that the spending per pupil averages $6,835 nationally and was raised by $477 per pupil since 1999 or 5.8 percent in that year (raised $9,540 per 20-pupil classroom). The increase per pupil was about as much as we spent per pupil in total in the 1950s.

classroom per year. Under this budget, an elementary school with 450 kids would receive $3.08 million each year. We have to wonder what they do with all that money, and why they think they need more. Gross (1999, p. 30) tells us that some schools in some grades spend more than $10,000 per child per year. Beyond even that, a letter to the editor in my local newspaper, written by the President of the State Public Policy Institute, said that the money spent per pupil per year in this state averaged $7,699, and ranged from $5,396 to an incredible $12,914 ($258,280 per 20-pupil class per year; $5,881,300 per 450-kid grammar school per year). Yet the average results are as awful in that school system as anywhere else, and may be worse. The letter also stated that a survey of 'hundreds of studies', revealed in testimony at the Kansas City, Missouri, school desegregation trial, that: "There is no link between education spending and education quality." Yet the political debate in this state, as I am sure is true of all others, revolves around the argument that even those who do not argue for decreasing spending, but merely want to limit increases in spending, are horrible people, because "we know from research" that wasting money is the right thing to do.

Other methods of mollifying nervous parents include releasing local news reports describing some indoctrinated kid's comments regarding his self-esteem and how it has helped him achieve success. The educators who credit themselves with this success then smile, pat themselves on the head, and speak about the wisdom of children. 'Parenting' classes and websites are established or weekly 'Helpful Minute' type reports are broadcast during local news programs, dispensing psychologically unwarranted advice, identical to that which schools use, thereby pseudovalidating, maintaining, and strengthening pop philosophy. Even worse, national evening news programs will occasionally broadcast 'What can we do about education?' segments which decry the results achieved over the past few years, then propose the latest unsupported educational innovation (read 'fad') as the answer to a parent's dreams. The justification for the innovation is how much fun the kids have while doing the latest hands-on activities, or a thoroughly unsubstantiated claim about how creativity and 'higher-level thinking skills' will be developed in the academic sandbox. This system is then tied to a hope that kids might learn more if they are 'engaged' and allowed to discover the great truths of life for themselves. Not surprisingly, to accomplish these great things, schools are organized primarily as 'activity' centers (read daycare centers) rather than as places where teachers teach lessons. The educators who work there hope that a bit of learning occurs incidental to the fun. Since very little does, however, they must continually search for new innovative ways of preparing kids for the realities of their future, because today's ways are continually being discredited.[11]

Yet, we cannot redirect money budgeted for a practice that even the educators no longer support if it had been authorized as a part of some legislation. As we know, we cannot dismantle social legislation this side of the River Styx. That would require dismantling the bureaucracy developed to administer the bad idea. Hence the call for additional funding.

Because politically correct pop philosophy is now everywhere, the results that our schools achieve are poor, despite emotional assurance that we are 'doing the right thing'. It is well past time that those results are evaluated against the techniques used and understood by average folks. The idea of 'an informed citizenry' demands that we must judge those techniques for ourselves, and to do that we must see what is being taught in Ed schools to have the information upon which to base an informed judgment. Unfortunately, the teachers, and their representatives, will not tell us.

Yet there are, and have been, profound indicators published over the years. For instance, in 1984 a now frequently quoted excerpt from *A Nation at Risk,* written by the National Commission on Excellence in Education, stated that:

> If an unfriendly foreign power had attempted to impose on America the mediocre educational performance that exists today, we might well have viewed it as an act of war. As it stands, we have allowed this to happen to ourselves.

I hope to help explain how we have done, and continue doing, this to ourselves. For example, the debating points we hear regarding education, and many other issues, often revolve around some esoteric philosophic point (or 'practical' political point) or another, often in support of one or another current technique. Take the recent Congressional hearings (Summer 1998) about teaching 'eubonics' as an example. Ask black parents whether they want to teach their kids eubonics or

---

11 See, Jeanne Chall, *The Academic Achievement Challenge,* Guilford Press, 2000, as a start.

standard English, and most will opt for English. Only the 'professionals' who have a personal stake in eubonics (i.e., they make a living as a consultant, school administrator, teacher-union officer or community 'leader' of some sort) espouse this damaging and divisive notion. Despite the lip service given for wanting what is best for children, when we consider the long-term results 'helping kids' may not be what they are after at all. Techniques, methods, and philosophy would have changed long ago if that were it, because our kids and our society are clearly being harmed, not helped.

Periodically we hear of some 'brave and visionary' principal from a school in an inner-city slum who has forsaken the Progressive agenda in favor of a more traditional education. The decidedly low SES (socio-economic status, [read 'poor' or 'at-risk']) kids then easily turn in compar-atively astonishing results, showing that the Progressive philosophy may be what was holding them back. Then, in order to continue to receive funding from the School Board, the visionary school reverts to Progres-sive requirements, and sinks back into educational mediocrity. Yet the 'professionals' keep recommending the ideas that do not work and schools continue to use them, to validate their modern, Progressive and 'innovative' credentials. Since most (all?) State education bureaucracies are dominated by graduates of Ed schools, school funding is also often tied to adherence to those nonfunctional ideas.

It was very gratifying to see that Californians have recently decided to stop using bicultural education in their schools. Once self-styled as the 'land of fruits and nuts', California has long led the nation in trying the latest fad and philosophy. However, since they may have had the longest experience with our current brand of educational philosophy, and with the awful results that it brings, we could do worse as a nation, than follow their lead back to sanity and common sense (if it lasts). It was particularly gratifying to hear that those who voted against the practice included most Hispanic parents, the supposed beneficiaries of that failed technique. California voters have voted it out, and evidence is accumu-lating that the decision was the right one, yet many California 'educa-tors' continue to press for it. It is 'the right thing to do'.

I should specify what I mean by some words, especially words like 'Progressive' and 'traditional' (as in Progressive vs. traditional education). This is important since these same words are used by different people to mean very different things. For instance, the dictionary defines 'tradition' as that which is passed down from one generation to the next. However, many of us now dilute that definition merely to mean 'old' or 'obsolete', as opposed to 'modern' or 'progressive' which are new and, as advertisers have trained us to believe, invariably better. The dictionary definition is more useful since in practice most of us think of traditional things as those we remember from our own childhoods, including what school was like. This is the meaning I use, and since my own childhood and my precollege schooling spanned the mid 1950s to the late 1960s, for me this period is 'traditional'. That is also, at least partly, the period before the latest surge of negative effects, based on the 'reforms' of the Great Society became evident in the mid to late 1960s. Another benefit of this basic idea is that the practices of education in the late 1950s and early 1960s are still within the living memories of many of us.

Even so, historians of education will not necessarily remember the 1950s and 1960s as a golden age in teacher education. In fact, in 1959 Jacques Barzun, historian and former Dean of Columbia University, described our public school system as in a "ridiculous" state of "paralysis." Also, in 1962 James Koerner, President of the Council for Basic Education, and author of *The Miseducation of American Teachers*, characterized American education as "remorselessly fragmented, subdivided and inflated," with subject matter marked by "intellectual impoverishment" and suffused by a jargon he calls Educanto[12] that ". . . masks thought, supports a specious scientism . . . and repels any educated mind that happens upon it."[13]

---

12 Barzun calls educational jargon, "a flatulent Newspeak," and even as early as 1929 John Dewey called it "pedagese."

13 Here is the example of "Educanto" that Koerner gives us. He took it from a " . . . report of an expert in educational guidance at one of our most prestigious universities."

Responsibility is being manifested in the evolving *attitude* toward self in world which each person is affecting. This attitude forms successively in relation with a person's accomplishments of his identities as person, child, friend, boy or girl, student, player, husband or wife, parent, citizen and man. Effects of the resolution of these several identity crises are cumulative. Together the resulting identities and the accumulating attitudes toward self in world form the personality of a man. Guidance attempts to maintain productive character in emerging personality.

I have puzzled over this pedantic sentiment. I think it means that 'guidance counselors' try to help kids understand themselves. How understandable is this counsel, do you think? A question implicit in Koerner's book is: Would you want this 'expert' guiding *anything* that concerned your kids? It is a good question.

That is strong language, but while the U.S. Office of Education (the precursor to today's Department of Education) recommended the ideas Koerner and most genuinely educated people reject, in the early 1960s the schools that were fully committed to them were still fairly few,[14] though growing in number. Also, I suspect that despite prophetic and alarmed pronouncements from many regarding the educationists' reach, the 1960s still had many older members of local School Boards, who were educated academically, and had the good sense not to subscribe to the worst of the excesses.

Therefore, you the reader may not recognize the ideas that will be presented here as in your own tradition and might find them hard to believe. That is part of the problem. The very people who must now fight to reverse our pernicious educational trends may not know what is on the minds of today's educators beyond their stated and formulaic concern for additional funding, special education, equity, and so forth. Yet these ideas slowly became more common as Ed schools and teacher unions made adherence to them (or at least the practice of them) a criterion of graduation, certification, and tenure. Today, these doctors of education dominate all levels of the education system. The system includes state and federal departments, school district superintendants and school administrators, the teacher's unions, regulatory and accreditation agencies, textbook publishers, and standardized-testing companies. Also, of course, it includes a growing percentage of an under- and uneducated population 'educated' by the educators trained by the system.

As already stated, our educational disputes are difficult to follow for most folks, unless dollars-per-student is your only concern, with no regard for the results. In fact our ongoing arguments, often defined as mere ideological and political battles between those who love children and the rich (defined this way by those who say they love children), are hardly understood by the participants. This seems to be true because the two sides of the argument seem to be speaking two separate languages. The words used do not hold the same meanings for each side, so the arguers often speak past each other, and are not understood by the other side. Words once common, are redefined and take on new meanings as jargon. As educational jargon, even terms as common as

---

14 At least it had not yet made a significant impact in the school district that educated me, until the late 1960s.

'education' have changed their meaning. While it is obvious that the outcome of education expects someone to learn something they do not know, for Webster, as for most of us, the process of education, especially early on, requires that someone teach something.

Here is the definition of *educate* taken from Webster:[15]

> **ed•u•cate** (ĕj'ə•kāt') *v.* **-cat•ed, -cat•ing, -cates** [ME (Middle English) *edu-caten* < Lat. *educare.*] —*vt.* **1. a.** To provide with training or knowledge, esp. via formal schooling: TEACH. **b.** To provide with training for a specific purpose, as a vocation. **2.** To provide with information: INFORM. **3.** To stimulate or develop the mental or moral growth of. —*vi.* To teach or instruct another or others.

Webster, however, feels the need to include a rare explanation for the misuse of this word. They add:

> A <u>word history</u>: It has often been said that *educate* means "to draw out a person's talents as opposed to putting in knowledge or instruction. This is an interesting idea, but it is not quite true in terms of the etymology of the word. *Educate comes from the Latin educare,* "to educate," which is derived from a specialized use of Latin *educere* (from *e,* "out," and *ducere,* "to lead") meaning "to assist at the birth of a child."

I suppose that the 'we love kids more than you do' folks would embrace this misuse of the word, but my purpose is not to be an etymological purist, it is rather to simplify the educational debate, but using words in ways understandable to both sides.

For the Progressive theorist, then, education can proceed *without* teaching. Instead, each kid is expected to recreate the sum of human knowledge for themselves and the 'educator's' job is to merely provide 'activities' that will, it is said, spark the scholar's imagination resident within each kid, and thereby draw out the knowledge and learning to be found in each kid's genetic memories. You will recognize this idea also from Jeanne Auel's *Clan of the Cave Bear* series of novels. Mrs. Auel attributed this capability to her Neanderthal characters, but, perhaps significantly, not to her Cro-Magnon (modern human) heroine.

This knowledge-from-within idea can now be seen in the most common recommendations for teaching the various academic subjects.

---

15 Webster's II, New Riverside University Dictionary, 1984.

For instance, we are told that we should not teach the basic arithmetic skills, but should concentrate on 'problem solving' which ask kids to solve problems often without significant and ongoing instruction in arithmetic and mathematical techniques, such as multiplication or working with fractions. Instead, the use of calculators rather than brains begins as early as Kindergarten. Likewise, we are told that we should not teach the facts inherent in the various sciences, but should facilitate Discovery or Inquiry Learning activities. Neither should we teach phonetic reading nor the basics of grammar, but should allow the child to be immersed in a Whole Language experience, because, we are told, teaching the rules of punctuation, etc., quells natural creativity.

As you probably know, 'Developing great communicators' is a stated 'Outcome' typical of many school systems. Toward that end, it seems necessary to know a common language if communications are to be possible. Yet, allowing, or more to the point, requiring every kid to develop his or her own personal language, as Whole language does, doesn't seem compatible with the idea of enhancing communications.

Expanding this idea to all forms of learning, it would seem obvious that only after ideas are understood can creativity allow new combinations of known ideas to describe some hitherto unknown concept. We can describe this as the building-block theory that says that complex ideas are built up from combinations and modifications of simpler ideas. Likewise, it would be difficult for the rest of us to have some chance of understanding the creative new idea, if we did not understand the older, smaller ideas from which it was derived. This can be seen by reference to any idea that was considered ahead of its time. This does not mean that the new idea was incorrect when it was first proposed, but only that it was not understood by those who did not know what the pioneer knew.

Not teaching, on the other hand, is often described, and occasionally defined, as providing kids the *opportunity* to learn, which actually means, 'Don't say anything. Maybe he'll think of it himself'. But facilitation does not work well as the only method for providing the opportunity to learn science, for instance. This was obvious to me even during my student teaching days. Nor do hands-on 'assessments' work as well as a mode for standardized testing, but that is another story, to be discussed later.

So, though the education of the 1950s and 1960s, that I will tout as 'excellent', is probably no such thing, but only a spotty approximation of the real thing (with the spots losing ground), if most of the schools of the day could maintain and improve such indicators as rising SAT[16] scores, it would be a step in the right direction to use those pre-Progressive techniques and practices as a recent benchmark of relative excellence. If we can at least get back to there, theoretically and practically speaking, beginning to move forward again in improving schools would be much easier.

Unfortunately, teacher education today is even worse than Koerner thought in 1962, and its effects are made more pervasive by mere longevity and the retirement of those sensible people formerly in charge.

I mention this definition of 'tradition' for two reasons. First, everybody who is interested in education today has a different tradition upon which to draw. This was made clear to me at a local school board meeting not long ago. Though not unique, I am something of an anomaly at such meetings, because of my age. Most of the parents of today's grammar school kids went to high school in the 1990s or 1980s, long after Progressive education began to take hold again. This description applies to many of today's educators as well. Unfortunately, this timing is also used by some to denigrate any recent idea that has been found not to work. We often hear news reports, for instance, that detail the mistakes inherent in some technique designed by Progressive educators several years previously, that labels it as 'traditional', thereby equating tradition with failure.

The particular school board meeting to which I refer, featured a presentation by several parents and pupils. In an attempt to improve their kids' reading, etc., a district elementary school had bought and experimented with a system of 'phonics' instruction. This system was said to extend beyond early language instruction into arithmetic and other areas.[17] The parents liked the results. One by one, they and their

---

16 Scholastic Aptitude Test. Universities and colleges commonly require this standardized test, administered by the Educational Testing Service of Princeton, NJ, or, alternatively, the ACT exam, administered by the American College Testing Foundation of Iowa City, IA, as entrance examinations. The average score recorded each year for the SAT, continued to rise until 1963, then dropped to its low in 1980. With only minor variations, it has stayed at, or near, the 1980 level ever since. This span of time (17 years) that it took our system to reach its nadir, brings up another question. Assuming the impossible, that we reverse all the mistakes of the past several decades today, and begin teaching appropriately today, would it take another 17 years before we raised our national averages to where they should be? The answer is almost certainly 'Yes'. This is so because the "new" traditional system would not be fully effective to those infected by Progressive ideas, but would be best when begun in Kindergarten, and used by teachers trained exclusively by these methods.

17 How phonics extends to mathematics, etc., was not explained, but commercial marketing is not always very logical. It is designed to sell something, not to be an erudite explanation of linguistic nuances.

kids stood up to describe the results achieved and to ask the School Board to use the program permanently.

What struck me (apart from the no-longer-surprising idea that we need commercially prepared programs to do for us what our Ed schools are paid to do, that is, teach our teachers how to teach), was that the parents were asking the School Board to change routine instructional policy from our local version of Whole Language instruction back to a system that featured phonetic instruction because, as one parent said, "It works much better, and my kids learned much more than I did under the 'traditional' way of teaching that I remember."

For me, Whole Language types of systems are new, experimental, and dismal failures. For these younger parents they are traditional, and dismal failures. Since the nation saw a rapid and pronounced decline in academic achievement with the introduction of Progressive education (see Chapter 2) and sees a rapid and pronounced improvement when Progressive techniques are dropped, we have hope that common sense may still return to schools. Nevertheless, for that to happen sooner rather than later, we must expose the sources of the theoretical absurdities that are holding our kids back.

Second, specifying these two definitions in particular is important because students of the history of American education tell us that there were other Progressive periods dating back into our history. An excellent summary of the most recent emergence, other than the current, can be found in *The Troubled Crusade: American Education 1945–1980,* by Diane Ravitch, former Assistant Secretary of Education. After describing the dogmatic dumbing-down recommendations of educationists and the alarmed responses of academics and others, she says that Progressive education died in 1955 due to a concerted onslaught of academics, parents, and business leaders. We have hope, then, that we can kill off this latest resurgence as well. Still, it will again take a concerted effort by all of us. It will be much more difficult now than it was then, however, because the Progressive educational leadership is far more deeply entrenched now than it was in 1955.

Though never stated explicitly, among the reasons that this summary (Ravitch, 1983) is so useful is that it shows the idea that Progressive rhetoric is intellectually, politically, and ethically very fluid. Progressive educationists seem to have no problems equating their ideas with any argument, if it 'sells' at the moment, persuading people of the goodness of their intentions. Reading Ravitch's summary, we note that the stated political and social reasons to use Progressive ideas seem to have changed dramatically. Yet, since teaching history is said to be nothing but a recitation of boring and unrelated facts, it matters not at all to educationists that in different periods the very same procedures were said to reform precisely opposite social ills. For instance, once upon a time Progressive education argued that since most kids *should not* go to college, they could see no need to teach anyone college prep courses. This included those who were preparing for college. Instead, we should develop child-centered courses, formerly called life-adjustment training, that considered only what the kids wanted to know. After the mid 1960s, however, when college-is-for-everyone became a battle cry, these selfsame child-centered techniques reappeared and are now being used to push every kid *toward* college, and argue that they will improve success in college and in life. As we go along, we will see many similar examples of this relativistic tendency to say whatever is fashionable to promote Progressive techniques. These sorts of arguments continue although the evidence of the past few decades shows clearly that the promised educational and social goals have not been achieved.

Incidentally, I have recently seen life-adjustment training touted as the solution for people who remain part of the hardcore unemployed. Unfortunately, it may be that these folks are the hardcore unemployed at least in part because they, and their parents, were educated this way. It did not work for them as kids and it does not work for them as adults, but the idea keeps coming back because it is based upon a Progressive ideology that does not consider its own results.

Among the less ridiculous, though still faulty curricular suggestions, was one put forth by Charles Prosser. In fact, Prosser's ideas might almost be a restatement of Benjamin Franklin's ideas on education (see Chapter 8), though taken to unsupportable extremes. Quoting from Ravitch:

Prosser, who had begun his career as a lobbyist for vocational education, had spelled out his educational values in a 1939 lecture, in which he insisted that every subject taught in high school must be judged by its utility for everyday living. He claimed that "business math was superior to plane or solid geometry; learning ways of keeping physically fit to the study of French; learning the technique of selecting an occupation, to the study of algebra; simple science of everyday life to geology; simple business English to Elizabethan classics." If school subjects were judged by utility, he believed, all mathematics and foreign languages would be dropped as required studies. He saw no point in "a system of education-for-more-education," other than to select out students for higher education and to keep certain faculty employed.

Continuing Ravitch quotes B. L. Dodds in *That All May Learn* (1939).

The trouble with the academic curriculum, was that if "fostered and definitely encouraged" unrealistic ambitions had made too many "unselected" [not college bound] youth aspire to enter managerial and professional jobs for which they are not fitted. Too much time, effort, and money was wasted to teach the conventional subjects to the "educationally neglected."

These kids were designated as educationally 'neglected' because they were forced to learn English and math rather than the life-adjustment courses which were judged more suitable. Courses called such things as Living Skills are still being offered.

Therefore it was argued that, one way to correct the "unrealistic" philosophy of traditional education, with its troubling emphasis on "mere knowledge," was to ask the kids what concerned them. Surveys were taken which discovered that the true needs of youth were, "how to find a job, how to make friends, how to behave on a date, how to protect one's health, how to get the most for one's money, and how to make life worthwhile." Paul R. Mort and William S. Vincent, in *A Look at Our Schools: A Book for the Thinking Citizen*, said:

It is vain and wasteful to take a girl who would make a fine homemaker and try to fit her into the patterns of training which make a lawyer, or to take a boy who would be successful in business and try to fit his training to that which produces doctors.

Based on these kinds of conclusions, courses were developed around the nation that tried to accommodate the true 'needs' of kids (sound familiar?). These were some results, again from Ravitch:

Denver, Colorado offered a course (which included English, social studies, guidance, health, "democratic living, personal and social growth, intergroup education, human relationships," and "general living units"), as did most of the schools in Wichita, Kansas; Springfield, Missouri; Albuquerque, New Mexico; Eugene, Oregon; Long Beach and Pasadena, California; Minneapolis, Minnesota; Grand Rapids and Detroit, Michigan. The schools of Garrett County, Maryland, organized the curriculum for grades seven through twelve entirely around adolescent "needs," with no reference to subject matter; the curriculum for grade twelve, for example, consisted of "family living; role of education; making a living; health and safety; consumer problems; and technology of living." The schools of Hartford County, Maryland, had no curriculum selected in advance, since teachers "are free to select from or reject them in light of the needs of pupils as they discover them."

Not every school district in the nation subscribed to these ideas, of course. The districts that did, however, produced pupils who were as unfit for adult life as many of today's graduates are, as noted by Bestor (1953), and others. Nevertheless, although such a discrepancy in achievement was evident between the 'innovative' few and the stodgy, but instructive many,

> These districts were cited by the U.S. Office of Education as examples of advanced educational practice which were meeting "the imperative needs of every youth." (Ravitch)

Thomas Toch, in his book *In the Name of Excellence* (1991), details the history since the early 1900s, of the various educational reform movements. His method was a survey of laws passed around the country and of the political battles fought, featuring the role that teacher's unions played in destroying any hope for reestablishing genuine education into the schools. Toch also delves into the bureaucratic morass of teachers union-dominated personnel rules that allow, and even mandate, a variety of counterproductive actions. These actions include allowing unqualified, though senior, teachers to fill plum vacancies, teaching subjects they know little about, while junior teachers who had knowledge of, and expertise in, the plum-assignment subjects are forced to teach classes *they* know little about. Toch quickly and concisely (particularly in Chapter 2) gives us a greater understanding of why the notion of: "Most of you have no chance of getting ahead anyway, so you do not need to learn how to think," apparently made sense to many people, and was used to justify child-centered and life-adjustment techniques. Since the second half of the 20th century, and especially after 1970, college-is-for-everyone sells, and is used to justify modern child-centered and life-adjustment technique that, in essence are unchanged since 1910.

No matter the justifications used, the Progressive educational techniques continue to reemerge, like the 'undead' of bad horror movies. Then as now, however, Progressive teaching leaves much to be desired. While Toch may be generally supportive of the Progressive agenda (in the end he recommended the innovation of the day—magnet schools), he still concludes that for minority pupils, for instance, "The civil rights movement may have won a place for minority and disadvantaged pupils in the nation's high schools; it didn't win them a good education."

John Dewey, the educational theorist of the early 20th century, is often touted as a founding light of Progressive education. Needing historical, and at least scientific-sounding, justifications, reinterpreted versions of Dewey's ideas are presented to modern student-teachers, without elaboration, as the rationale for what is called experience-based education. This is a cornerstone of the various child-centered practices. His influence is said to have inspired such modern techniques as 'Whole language' instruction and 'Discovery' or 'Inquiry' learning, among others. (We will discuss these ideas as we go along, and I will present several quotations from Dewey's writings so that you may judge whether all of his ideas are fairly represented by the educationists. The modern techniques all stem from the same idea, though applied to various subject areas.) Dewey defines the differences between Progressive and traditional education by saying that Progressive thinkers believe that all learning comes from within each of us and traditional thinkers assume education to require instruction by someone who knows the subject. A very quick shorthand of this distinction could be that educationists think we can ultimately do without 'teachers' altogether and traditionalists know this idea to be unworkable at best. An ideal Progressive educational system would have no teachers at all, only activities-*facilitators* and social services providers.

Think back to your own education. If you think that you became fully qualified, even for entry, for your job by merely playing with your friends and casually observing life around you, you may agree with the Progressive ideals. On the other hand, if you need math, specialized knowledge in any field, an ability to think and to deal with facts and/ or the ability to express yourself clearly and persuasively, you are well on your way to understanding educational common sense. My assumption is that the latter description is more accurate, even for the No-experience-necessary jobs, such as manual laborer and garbage truck worker. Even garbage truck workers may be citizens, authorized to vote.

Another reason to define the terms 'progressive' and 'traditional' is that we have seen reform movements even within the Great Society reforms touted as new reforms. Other reforms have been developed to counteract the Progressive reforms. Yet even if your favorite reformer advocated a return to the practices of the past, not one deliberately called themselves a 'throwback' or 'reactionary'. On the contrary, they depicted themselves as moving into the future. All these new, innovative reforms, reforming previous reforms have collectively been characterized as 'tinkering' with the system. All these ideas, however, have individually been championed very forcefully, effectively pulling education in conflicting directions, bogging it down with dense layers of bureaucracy, and adding to the general confusion of terminology, while dramatically increasing costs, in the American system.

Perhaps worst of all, even the reforms that make some sense have then been left largely to the education establishment to set up. The current establishment is where the teachers and administrators can be found, after all. Unfortunately, that is where the Progressive educationists are, too. Also unfortunately, Progressive ideologues (such as the NEA) hold great sway over the classroom teachers, and great influence over the political and bureaucratic processes. For instance, for any proposed change to be legitimized, laws must first be passed and then carried out. Implementation requires that regulations be written. However, regulations written by those who are rabidly opposed to the parent law do not always abide by the letter, or the spirit of the law. Nor does the eventual practice used in the classroom. Even John Goodlad said as much. In *A Place Called School* (1984, p. 16), he wrote.

> Principals and teachers who do not want what others seek to impose on them often are extraordinarily adept at nullifying or diffusing practices perceived to be in conflict with prevailing ways of doing things. The result may be the appearance of change, but no change.

For instance, even modern phonics instructions is dumbed-down to accede to the notion of 'preparing kids to learn',[18] as opposed to teaching

---

18 Kindergartners are already 'ready to learn' by virtue of being five-year-old humans with developing brains.

them to read. This is done by facililtating activities *about* letters, rather than affirmatively teaching kids the sounds that letters represent and recognizing combinations of those sounds.

I would like to offer this 'tinkering idea' as a partial proof that *something* must be done about the educational system, as everyone seems to know. Americans have traditionally (see what I mean) been practical folks who had to make-do only with what they had on hand. On the frontier, which is our collective tradition even if we did not immigrate here until much later, pioneers[19] did not have many extras or manufactured luxuries. Nor could they easily get 'store bought' items, at least until mail-order catalogues became common. In any case, we are a people who did not have the leisure to redo and fine-tune basics and for whom, 'Don't fix it if it ain't broke' frequently qualifies as deep wisdom. Today however, we have so many fixes, discussions, debates, proposed reform programs and legislation that clearly many of us consider that today's schools are 'broke'. The idea that something must again be done is clearly shown by the breadth, depth, and intensity of the ongoing debate, about education and about the very wide range of social ills that beset the U.S. The subject of all those debates is what should be done, not whether something should be done, and we see a very wide range of opinions voiced and options proposed.

We also see a few folks who argue that there is nothing wrong with the educational system, and that it is doing a sterling job of preparing our kids for the future. If you read their arguments, such as *The Manufactured Crisis* mentioned earlier, however, be prepared to scratch your head bloody as you wind your way through the presented logic. It is difficult to find an argument presented by these authors that passes the 'reasonable person' test. Yet there they are, and they are praised by other Progressive leaders. These *un*reasonable ideas then find their way into what our teachers are taught and the authors are among the unnamed 'experts' referred to in college education textbooks and in political rhetoric.

My own opinion is that further tinkering with a system that has clearly failed will do nothing but add more confusion and get very little accomplished. Instead, politically unrealistic as it undoubtedly seems, I believe we should go back to a system that was getting the job done,

---

19 In a sense every immigrant is a pioneer. Anyone who uproots himself and his family to seek a better life is a pioneer moving onto the frontier, even if that frontier turns out to be a modern city, rather than an uncharted territory.

relatively speaking, as in the early 1960s. What we should do is clear away the layers of bureaucracy and ideology currently weighing education down. We should then let the dust settle for several years on the changes needed to reestablish the 'new' system before working to fine-tune a system that works, rather than tinkering with a system that does not. This can be done in part by finding retired teachers and principals who were active and already experienced in the early 1960s, and asking them, "What textbooks did you use back then?", and "What techniques did you use, and why did you use them?" We could also research school board and State Department of Education archives to see what sorts of policies were in place at the time. We might even want to see which states and school districts consistently produced the highest average SAT or ACT scores, and distribute those policies around the nation. This would not be as a mandatory set of rules imposed from above, but as a practical resource for ideas that produced educated citizens.

Additionally, until the teaching colleges can be retooled to operate under the precepts of common sense and scientific evidence, it would be a good use of a school administrator's time to research whether there are teaching systems available with proven track records for producing graduates whom we can legitimately graduate. What we have now are many empty promises, much intellectual angst and the conviction that we can make things better while ignoring the reality of objective data. Teaching is both an art and a science. There must be specific things that we can do and other things that we must not do, if educated ideas are to find a home in pupils' heads. Progressive teachers say they want these things too, but using methods that teach mere pattern recognition (e.g., word search games), or using coloring and cut-and-paste activities in a history, literature or science class seems an odd way of going about it.

Instructional ideas and systems are available that can teach our current cadre of Progressively trained teachers the how-to of teaching, and also what to teach, to produce genuine, broadly founded understanding in pupils. We should find and use them, even if their baseline ideology is not as pretty or romantic as some of us would like. The primary criterion for the adoption of an educational policy should be increased learning among our children, not scientifically unsubstantiated utopianism.

Therefore, to the extent that there is a mismatch between what we did when America assumed that the role of its schools was to educate rather than indoctrinate, and what we do now, we should trash what we do now and go back to go forward. In reality, however, we would not be 'going backward' at all (Again. See what I mean?). We would merely be releasing ourselves from the bondage of an ideology that is holding us and our kids back. The 'ship of education' has been encrusted so thickly with bureaucratic and ideological barnacles for so long that we are left fouled and aimlessly circling. If we would go forward again, we must scrape the hull clean and free the rudder for sensible course adjustments.

The place to start is in the Ed schools.

As a start, the idea that the faculties of our schools of education are the only ones who understand the requirements of instruction should be carefully examined. The evidence shows that many Ed school professors are bereft of any genuine understanding regarding the needs of pupils, the nature of learning, or the place that schools occupy in a democracy, as this book will show. These wayward intellectuals need to be guided firmly back to reality and common sense, or dismissed. What is needed is someone who can read the 'research' said to support Progressive recommendations, and say, "Hey guys. This research says precisely the opposite of what you say it says, and negates completely your conclusions *and* the recommendations based on your conclusions. Why are we presenting this as educational wisdom?" We also need someone who can say, "This stuff is nothing but unsupported opinion based on faulty assumptions, and it clearly does not work. We *will* stop teaching this." Theoretically, this is what a governmental department of education could be used to do (since the Ed schools cannot be trusted to do it themselves). However, to get a position on the staff of a department of education, whether at the state or federal level, seemingly logical personnel practices require an advanced degree in education from a modern Ed school. Considering what we know about the workings of Ed schools, however, at the moment this requirement may be characterized as the blind leading the blind.

A possible way to restructure Ed schools, and ultimately the whole system, might be to transfer academic specialists from other university colleges and departments into the Ed schools. Another is to establish departments of pedagogy directly in the various colleges, eliminating the insular Ed schools altogether. For instance, historians, geographers, economists and others may be assigned to work in departments of social studies instruction; mathematicians and perhaps engineers and physicists should be involved in mathematics curriculum development and instruction; and scientists ought to develop science instruction curricula, etc. This would refocus instruction in each subject back to the subject and away from indoctrination in mere political correctness, activity facilitation, and utopian dreams. A genuinely realistic perspective (i.e., based on reproducible evidence) is needed because realists move forward by seeing the results of what they have done. They realize that a failure of an idea to accomplish its end requires a change in technique or a new approach. Progressive theories never change, no matter the results and whatever their protestations to innovation.

This idea was already tried at least once. Charles H. Judd, John Dewey's successor at the University of Chicago after 1909, ". . . ended all undergraduate programs, placed the training of secondary school teachers under the control of a university-wide committee that could strengthen work in the subject matter teachers were preparing to teach . . ."[20] Judd concentrated the work of the 'education school' on research, and on the preparation of administrators who could use the research. Unfortunately, this idea did not flourish, at least in part because nationally 'education' was attempting to establish a separate identity and validity as a profession worthy of the name, apart from its roots (at the university level at least) in philosophy. They did this by aligning themselves with the then new and burgeoning disciplines of psychology and sociology. Politics and personal ambition played a part then as now to reduce good ideas to positions that could not be countenanced if they contained aspects of the enemy's ideas. Ironically, Judd played a part in aligning the university study of education with psychology and the social sciences, and therefore helped to plant the seeds of destruction of his good idea. The destruction occurred when the study of educational psychology took a turn away from the quantitative, behaviorist perspective of Edward L. Thorndike at the Teachers College of Columbia University, to the psychiatric, sociological, and more explicitly unprovable perspective we see today.[21]

An excellent and very readable discussion of the early history of 'the education movement' in American universities can be found in

---

20 Lagemann, p. 68.

21 This does not mean that I would necessarily recommend a return to strict behaviorism. On the other hand, since Progressive education is rabidly against this idea, and since Progressive education can be shown to be wrong about almost everything, perhaps behaviorism deserves another hard look. The fact that it is much more difficult to understand than supermarket psychology should not be an impediment to its use if it can be shown to predict behavior better. Modern physics is virtually undecipherable to most of us, but that doesn't stop us from using the machines and toys built using those ideas.

Ellen Lagemann's book, *An Elusive Science*. Since my book is not primarily a history of education, I will not deal with all of the twists and turns that university politics have taken over the years in any great detail, yet this next quotation may begin to show how staking out extreme positions keeps our kids as philosophic pawns, to their detriment. Lagemann discusses the means by which Dewey's holistic ideas were covered with scorn and derision in Judd's Chicago, then says (p. 69), " . . . the fulfillment of Judd's professional aspirations seemed to require denial of the possibility that the study of education might have become 'scientific' in a very different way [than Thorndike's]. That may not be surprising in light of the fundamental differences that existed between Dewey and Judd. Although both thought experimentation was necessary in education, Dewey saw the school as the laboratory of education, whereas Judd saw the school as primarily the place for the implementation of real laboratory findings."

If we thought about them, for most of us a combination of these ideas would probably seem logical, until rhetoric pushed us in one direction or the other. While we do not want our kids to be guinea pigs in grand social experiments (especially ones that quickly prove to be harmful to the society), we understand that teaching and learning are not rigid, inflexible, and monolithic enterprises. On the other hand, if a 'system' of teaching labels itself as scientific, many of us wrongly assume that the system has already discovered all of the answers and, to be effective, must merely fit all the different 'subjects' within the framework of the system. Neither end of this spectrum is completely correct, but both say things that make some sense. Schools must be laboratories in which intelligent and insightful teachers continually use their experience to fine-tune instruction in their specialties. Schools must also be willing to use ideas developed, proven, and consolidated from multiple other sources, if the ideas advance the pupil's academic (i.e., "thinking") education and community feeling. The question is, how should Ed schools achieve this theoretical and practical balance?

Perhaps universities can make several years spent on the faculty of their School of Education a condition of promotion or tenure for some faculty members of other academic departments. Unfortunately, being deeply interested in pursuing the cutting-edges of their own chosen fields and not wanting to be distracted from that pursuit by academic assignments in mere pedagogy, young university scholars would probably reject the idea vehemently. Another possibility might be for professor emeritus types, or senior academics generally (especially those with scientific or statistical training), to be asked to keep an eye on, or chair, our Ed schools and arbitrate when damaging, unprovable philosophical silliness begins to creep back in.

With due consideration for updating the specific concerns voiced, a sensible and far more extensive set of recommendations can be found in Arthur Bestor's book, published in 1953. One idea that bears consideration has been put forth by the Holmes group of graduate schools of education, of which Michigan State is one,[22] in their 1986 report, *Tomorrow's Teachers*. Their idea would also eliminate our current schools of education. Since it is clear that teachers who do not know very much are little more than daycare workers, prospective teachers would first be required to fulfill the normal requirements for a baccalaureate degree in the field they propose to teach, then embark on a year of graduate study/internship culminating with a Master's degree in teaching. Those intending to teach at the elementary level would be required to earn a General Studies-like degree, which covers the range of subjects that elementary schools teach. It would probably consist of many surveys courses, but also concentrate on such things as English grammar, American and world history, general science, music, and art. A program of this kind would increase the professional standing of teaching to a level somewhat approaching medicine or the law, or at least to the level of medical technology or paralegal for elementary teachers. It would do this by vastly improving the average subject-matter knowledge-base of working teachers. Teachers' salaries may have to rise to match the qualifications, too. Other sets of recommendations can be found in Koerner and in Sowell, and my own recommendations are in Chapter 8. Undoubtedly there are other sensible ideas available as well.

Of course, the traditional educational system of earlier times was not perfect. Nothing is. Yet it was head-and-shoulders better than today's confused mess. Getting to a system that teaches *and* is more equitable for everybody would be very much easier from a position where most of the problems are already solved (since they did not yet exist), than from a position that increases, or even causes, new problems without solving the old.

---

22 Kramer (1991), p. 73.

Therefore, for me, Traditional Education means the general way it was around 1960, after the Sputnik scare when math and science education were temporarily reemphasized, and before the Great Society restarted dumbing-down American education. I define the time since the Great Society programs began as the current Progressive period.

Since this essay is at least partially a personal memoir more than a broad study of schools generally, my experiences may be better or worse than those of other teachers or parents. The schools I will describe may be better or worse than the schools in your neighborhood. While individual teachers there may be trying mightily,[23] the school district where I did my student-teaching, for instance, achieves genuinely awful results, but, undoubtedly, there are schools that are worse. Also, the school district where I have my kids enrolled is almost certainly the best in this city, but it is very far from good enough. This last point is my ultimate motivation for writing this book now. We are talking about *my* kids now. They are alive now and in school *now*. I want to add my voice to the chorus of folks of common sense who deplore conditions as they are now. Perhaps I can convince some who can make a difference quickly to affect positive changes so that my kids have a better than fighting chance of getting a good education.

Of course I know that, short of a genuine revolution, out-of-control juggernauts cannot be stopped on a dime. Reestablishing sensible cultural constants, not to mention public policy, will likely take a while. Still, it will never happen if we do not start.

I should end by saying that any factual inaccuracies that are found in this book are entirely mine.

---

23 The literature however (e.g., Toch) recognizes that many teachers have essentially given up. Many have succumbed to the Progressive reality that teaching is essentially unnecessary, and act as much as Soviet workers did. There was a saying among Soviet citizens that summed up the realities of working in a system dedicated to the sameness of individuals and to the dogmatic leveling of expected results. They said, "They pretend to pay us, and we pretend to work." Many of today's teachers are merely marking time. As a result, many of our kids are merely marking time with them.

It's No Wonder Kids Don't Learn—
Just Look What They Teach Teachers

1   What's the Problem?

Everywhere I go I am asked whether the university stifles writers.
My opinion is that they don't stifle enough of them.
There's many a bestseller that could have been prevented by a good teacher.
—*Flannery O'Connor*

That the American public education system is a disaster has been said more than once. Yet how can we say that? Don't we still win the occasional Nobel Prize? Don't the National Merit folks still give out their awards every year and aren't more people than ever going to college? What's the problem then? What are the clues that there is a problem at all?

One set of clues is in the various published studies and reports, such as *A Nation At Risk*. Other clues can be found in the State Governor's Council on Education's reports and the periodic reports from the National Center for Educational Statistics. Also, the Third International Math and Science Study (TIMSS) speaks about the evidence of falling scholarship and America's dismal recent record in academic comparisons with other industrialized nations. We have all seen or heard about these and many others, so I will not dwell on them.

Surprisingly, however, these reports do not seem to alarm many educational professionals. Why not? They are the ones who continually tell us that what they do will prepare our kids for the future, provided we give them more money. Don't they know how hard a life a functional illiterate lives? We hear many speculations about how poverty affects everything, including success in school. We have to wonder what is going on in the Progressive mind. Why do school districts release upbeat marketing brochures several times per year when many of their graduates can barely read the brochures? With a virtual monopoly on all things educational, why should a public school system need marketing brochures at all?

Other indicators of the general problem are the blurb-type news reports about how well our kids are doing and how much they seem to know as a group. For instance, recently NBC News reported on one question out of a survey that the National Science Foundation[24] asked of pupils. The question asked how long it takes for the Earth to orbit once around the sun. Only 48 percent of the pupils taking the survey knew what a 'year' is. Only 48 percent! A result such as this makes one wonder what percentage of those who got the answer right, guessed.

Another result of the same type was found by the National Geographic Society a few years ago. As I remember it, the Society gave college freshmen a geography quiz and an astonishingly high percentage of them could not locate the Atlantic Ocean on a map. Other authors, including myself, have interviewed high school pupils who do not know where the Atlantic Ocean is or what is the definition of 'peninsula'. I even recall sitting in a restaurant and overhearing a conversation between several adults in which one was describing his astonishment and delight over just having discovered that some books actually include a list pairing subject items with the page numbers on which those items could be found. One would have thought that the existence of an index would have been pointed out to pupils sometime during grammar school, and used throughout their subsequent educations. Apparently not so in the Progressive world.

Of course in the year 2000, the U.S. Department of Education told us that the state of American education is as good as it has ever been, and is getting better. So, who do we believe? Perhaps we should believe comedians, such as Jay Leno, who frequently asks man-in-the-street questions regarding what should be common knowledge. He asks questions such as, "How many Senators are there in the U.S. Senate?", and "What is a *Homo sapiens?*" The answers he gets can only be the stuff of comedy routines, or a genuine teacher's nightmares. The fact that he found a 6th grade 'teacher' in Los Angeles who did not know on what continent the United States could be found, says as much, or more, than all the *Nation At Risk*-style reports we could name.

By my opening, you may have guessed what the thrust of my general argument will be, and you may think that you disagree with me at this point. Please read on even if you think that you will not agree with me as a rule. You may be surprised to learn that we agree on more points than you thought. Those of you who think that we *will* agree on all

---

24 As a portion of a report titled *Science and Engineering Indicators, 1998.*

things may also be surprised to see that we do not. That is the cross any genuinely centrist[25] idea must bear. Nevertheless, I intend to ridicule few besides those who should know better but continue to profess a damaging philosophy,[26] but it is possible that you may be unintentionally insulted because you think that you agree with the Progressive side on a particular issue. I cannot help that in the short term. While what I have to say may, on the surface, seem like the same old polemic noise, if you read carefully you will discover that I am trying to balance the worst of the excesses (by elimination) and dampen the wildest exaggerations (by exposing the wasteland of unsupported ideas used as theory). Balance means that we consider both sides of an issue and use the parts that make sense and can be demonstrated as valid. Validity is the key. Unsupportable rhetoric is not enough, no matter how much we think we want it to be so. It may be that courses in Education, as such, hold no magic in preparing teachers at all. Perhaps the main qualifications needed of teachers are knowledge of the subject they intend to teach and enjoyment, or at least a benign toleration, of the company of pupils.

My own preference in deciding whether a philosophy is worthwhile is to judge whether the actions taken in the name of that philosophy do harm or do good in the long term. Since I am a member of this society as well as an individual, and since I have to live here (and raise my kids here), I also like to see whether the society as a whole benefits, or whether it is hurt by the actions taken in the name of a philosophy.

One purpose of this book is to describe and give examples of the actions that the folks of a Progressive inclination recommend. I will also attempt to match the examples given with results in school and in the wider society to see whether the recommendations 'work', or to suggest why they do not. Political debate, and the media's coverage of that debate, have given us the idea that only two, diametrically opposed views are possible on any question. Yet we have another possibility. One that considers what both sides say, uses the good and workable ideas from each and rejects the faulty ideas of each. So, whatever your current political views, you may surprise yourself by discovering that you may

---

25 For the record: Since I recommend a merging of the recommendations of the two polar extremes, I consider myself somewhere in the middle. One of the things that disturbs me is the irrationality and dishonesty of Progressive arguments that are based not upon research, which results they ignore anyway, but upon a political world view which may be congenial to their political sensibilities, but does not match reality (i.e., research results).

26 As with any comment of this sort, the standard proviso applies: Broad, sweeping comments regarding named groups (e.g., teachers) do not necessarily apply to every individual in that group.

not have to give up your ideals if you see another path that will get us where you think your kids, and our society, should be.

Before I begin to develop my arguments, however, I must say a word about my assumptions. This book consists of some thoughts regarding schooling and society in America today. It is possible (perhaps likely) that you will disagree with some views expressed. So, for this book to have use for *all* readers, we should try to come to some middle ground if we are to have any chance of rediscovering the kinds of school systems and educational techniques that allowed America to rise to the top of virtually every field of endeavor you care to name. To do this, our first step is to agree on *something*.

I hope that everybody reading this book will agree on this basic definition: A teacher is someone who helps parents to prepare their children for adulthood.

You may want to add the official bureaucratic or union-driven modifiers that this is a specifically trained and certified person paid by a school system, or that a parent can (and must) also be a teacher, or that the teacher is a specialist in academic matters, etc., etc. All of that is OK, but if we cannot at the very least agree with the fundamental definition of a person who helps kids grow up by teaching things that the kids don't already know, then you might as well put the book down now.

If, however, we accept this description (as I assume most will), the next step is to begin to evaluate our educational system, to see whether it accomplishes what it promises to accomplish. An important part of that evaluation should include the realization that the system *is* a system, and that its results affect the wider society. As in all systems, changing one part of it inevitably changes the functioning of other parts of the system. For that reason, before we can hope to achieve any sensible reform, the system must be evaluated as a whole. One reason that the education debate has been so fruitless of late is that many of the controversial aspects to today's system are evaluated separately. Proposed solutions are often designed for one perceived problem without reference to other, related problems. This approach allows a proliferation of programs to be designed. These solutions then overlap, pull in conflicting directions and confuse the issues. Solutions are proposed and set up that cause (possibly) unintended negative effects in other areas of the system. Then, instead of cancelling the program that caused the negative results, especially if the positive results intended do not appear, we merely add new intervention programs to address the newly perceived problems, which result from the original intervention program. This may have the result of undermining, or destroying, the intent of the original program. Yet no program can be changed, and certainly not eliminated, because, despite obvious problems, each individual program takes on the mantle of political sacred cow, and cannot be touched without political consequences. Furthermore, if the achieved systemic change is perceived by some as social degeneration (for example, sex education leading to a growing acceptance of pornography as an honorable lifestyle) but is perceived by others as social progress (e.g., increasing freedom of speech), we have an obvious problem. Additionally, the debate is usually couched in the political rhetoric of a group most interested in a particular issue, redefining common ideas to their own needs, as in the examples just above. This is how we get many new programs proposed for government action and funding. Often these same problems are addressed at many levels of government simultaneously. However, since many of the programs essentially address the same problems, but propose contradictory and overlapping solutions, the bureaucracy inevitably becomes overburdened and ineffective (i.e., too many cooks spoiling the broth).

Another word about current results, and the interpretation of those results, before we begin. As we examine the evidence, we will see many examples of Progressive educators' interpretations of data. We can also see, and hear, the same kinds of arguments in the political debate. For instance, one argument used to counter traditional complaints of the reduction of learning in our kids, is that learning is not being reduced at all. The main piece of evidence for this is that standardized test scores have 'at worst' remained flat for the past several years. That is true, but it is a very short-term look at things that only considers the record of the past few years and does not look as far back as the start of the systemic decline in the mid to late 1960s.

In any case, since the education system is a system, we would expect that there are limits to what it can accomplish. Upper and lower limits. Reaching an infinity of education or producing an adult who has learned literally nothing at all, are not possible. The upper limit might be every kid individually learning everything that humanity has ever learned over the millennia, and then proposing advances. Even the best system imaginable is likely to fall a bit short of that. The bottom limit, on the other hand, is what we might see if no one was exposed to systematic education at all, and learning was left to individuals 'picking things up' as they 'hung out' together. Unfortunately, you will soon see that average results for high school standardized tests approach this lower limit. Therefore, if things have fallen to a point where they *cannot* get any worse, then not getting any worse is quite a hollow victory. Also, the obvious first step in any systematic solution to a systemic problem, is to stop doing the things that got us to this state. (Incidentally, 'hanging out' learning depends on those kids finding things relevant to their lives [so that they might want to think about them, if only briefly], and as you probably know, 'relevance' is one of the fundamental precepts of Progressive theory.)

Finally, we must see whether the recommendations designed to achieve excellence and made in the name of a philosophy accomplish what is promised and we must judge whether the results achieved are truly excellent. We must also recognize that, as in other systems, changing one part can affect all other parts of the system. If one change causes multiple negative effects, the solution is not to change the parts newly affected. Instead, we should either modify or eliminate the original change that caused the multiple problems, then perhaps try something else. Setting up multiple bureaucracies aimed at multiple, but inter-twined, problems inevitably creates an intractable bureaucratic quag-mire that cannot easily be resolved.

Each philosophy tries to teach something. Each philosophy has its treasured assumptions that it equates with 'common sense'. I do that too. Each philosophy uses these assumptions to justify its policies and its actions. Each of us either agrees with or disputes the assumptions of the other, if they are different. However, if you have had even a short introductory unit in 'logic' sometime during your own schooling, you will know that the most preposterous ideas can be internally very 'logical' and, if presented well, can superficially make sense. The use of fallacious logic is known as sophistry, and more recently as 'spin'. Therefore we must constantly examine the assumptions used by any system, against their effects in reality.

If a philosophic idea has some verifiable validity, it may be used to promote a practical recommendation. However, if the proponents of that idea refuse to acknowledge its limitations, and refuse to acknowl-edge the verifiable validity of opposing ideas, then sensible, balanced policy decisions become impossible to achieve. This is where we find ourselves today. Therefore, all is not well in River City. The far ends of each side in the debate can be equally wrong in their approach. Since the end that currently has a stranglehold on the laws, and especially on the practices regulating education, is the self-styled Progressive end of the spectrum, and since this is the end of the spectrum that has recently (since the mid 1960s, at least) been responsible for our current mess, I will concentrate on trying to rebalance the seesaw we call educational theory and practice to what the majority might recognize as common sense. Keep in mind that the majority includes people of relatively different political stripes.

We must also not forget that maintaining a balance means not going too far to the other end of the spectrum when fixing mistakes. Political pendulums swing to opposite extremes because people often consider that if some change is good, more must inevitably be better. This reaction has played a very large part in our current troubles. We will see the Progressive tendency to ignore everything their opponents say, if they disagree with any part of it. Even John Dewey, the reputed patron saint of Progressive education, recognized this tendency in the early part of the 20th century. Progressive rhetoriticians, of course, tout themselves as open-minded and accuse their opponents of tunnel vision.

Nevertheless, the point here is not merely to win a political debate, it is to prepare our kids for a future in which we would be happy for our kids to live. This happiness must consider human nature if it is to succeed; and human nature is not entirely Utopian. We all have warts and bumps, strengths and weaknesses that must be considered, not merely ignored or treated with psychoactive drugs. That being said, the balance we are attempting to establish and maintain will never be perfect, no matter what we consider to be perfection. We have no magic bullets that work with every kid every time under every situation. The best we can reasonably hope to achieve is that most of us grow up as happy, productive members of our collective society, and identify strongly with that society and with the other members of it. Also, we will always see 'bad' people in the world, no matter what we think is bad for people to be. Also bad acts can be done by otherwise good people, if we teach that the sensible, culturally defined, traditional limits to behavior are themselves bad (No Limits!). Under these conditions, the options chosen can be dangerously inappropriate. Witness the recent epidemic of school shootings. We have to deal with that truth too, or we will certainly continue to fail.

Another way to try to puzzle out the truth among the conflicting reports is to quote the many debates, on C-SPAN and on the floor of Congress, etc., that lay out this or that philosophy in broad rhetorical terms. Proponents of each philosophy or teaching technique say that their way will save the day. Yet, why must the day be saved at all, if everything is wonderful?

This debate can also be very confusing to the public since everybody uses the same words when speaking about their pet 'way'. Proponents of every position insist that their way will lead to excellence and that they are very concerned with challenging pupils to do their best. No one says that they *want* kids to be as ignorant as modern technology will allow. The problem is, however, that in order to see through the political posturing and to sort through the rhetorical noise, we have to know a good deal of the technical education jargon. You also have to know how these sensible sounding promises will be kept. What will actually happen in the classroom?

Another problem that few consider is, how do we speak to one another if the opposing camps define the same seemingly common words in opposite ways. We will see that this is a much bigger problem than most of us imagine.

The conflicting rhetorical noise is exacerbated in some cases by the media who, inadvertently or otherwise, give the public little more than superficial summations and short sound bites when reporting education (or any other) news. Since this is not a political treatise, I will largely avoid the common complaint that 'the media' does not present the range of ideas in a balanced way, but tends to show the ideological left end in a favorable light, but this may be part of the problem as well.

I do not intend to blame the media for everything. I intend to quote several news reports, etc., in my favor, and in at least one very significant case we must give the media credit for a positive social result. Yet typically using only the most controversial statement as a sound bite (to sell air time) rather than something that might be genuinely informative (and potentially reflect reality more broadly), helps to solidify ideologically polemic positions that ignore common sense. So while the debates are occasionally interesting as political theater, they do not illuminate the problem for many of us, unless we feel that solidifying ideologically dogmatic positions further is a good thing.

The general philosophy invoked, in debates or written pieces, has to be considered when discussing education. If everybody says that they stand for excellence, then we have to see what each side in the debate defines as excellent. We must also see what each side recommends and what they do to achieve this hoped-for excellence. These things are not always the same.

As already stated (in the Introduction), Progressive marketing efforts have, in recent iterations, used diametrically opposed ideas to justify their favorite techniques. In the early part of the century the cry was, 'Most kids do not need college'. Today we hear, 'College is for everybody'. Yet the classroom recommendations designed to achieve both these ideals remain essentially unchanged. Somehow, 'child-centered' techniques continue to be touted as the answer to all educational problems.

It is, however, one part of human nature to believe that those who should know more about a topic than we do, should be left to construct systems that help us, while we attend to our own business. Unfortunately, while leaving the experts to their own devices is human nature, it is misguided human nature if the experts ignore the evidence that would normally qualify them as experts. So *you* must consider the possibility that you have been taken in by the rhetoric of the folks who profess social justice above all else. You have heard the rhetoric for so long that it just sounds like the 'right thing to do'. However, what folks say and what they do is sometimes very different, as is what people wish for, as opposed to what the evidence shows.

Leo Tolstoy described a character in *War and Peace* in a way that might be used for many Progressive educational theorists. Tolstoy's character, a German military theorist named Pfühl in Tsar Alexandr's court, could never see failure in his theories despite the evidence of lost battles and dead soldiers:

On the contrary, to his mind it was the departures from his theory that were the sole cause of the whole disaster, . . He was one of those theoreticians who so love their theory that they lose sight of the theory's object—its practical application. His passion for theory made him despise all practical considerations and he would not hear of them. He positively rejoiced in failure, for failures resulting from deviations in practice from the theory only proved to him the accuracy of his theory.[27]

---

27 Leo Tolstoy, *War and Peace*, Signet Classic, p. 771. (1968).

Like Pfühl, Progressive educationists cannot see the results of their practices despite decades of complaints that many graduates manifest profound ignorance, to the point of functional illiteracy. Neither can educationists connect their recommendations with the progressively deteriorating 'times we live in'. So I hope that you will give me a chance to connect the gentle, loving words professed with the awful, damaging results achieved by the 'socially compassionate'.

I intend to provide many more examples that put politically correct educational theory and practice into perspective, yet perhaps my experience is not common. Perhaps I am just a disgruntled student with a chip of my shoulder. Why should you consider anything that I say? We do have many distinguished, school-trained educators who are lifelong specialists in the instruction of children, don't we? Surely they have the problems well in hand and are pursuing practical solutions to our common problem. Aren't they?

Certainly we have some educators with a genuinely research-based perspective that spend their time testing new methods to learn what works and what does not. That is true, but unfortunately, these educational researchers are systematically ignored and vilified, in favor of the untested theories of cloudy-headed idealists with their fingers in the public cookie jar. However, the evidence shows that those in charge of the cookie jar may be as deluded as those we ask to carry out our reforms.

Here is one very large, very significant example of what I mean.

The fact that Progressive teaching modifications do not teach very much is not news of course, though it is often a topic in the news. For instance, several years ago, the ABC News *20/20* program aired a segment called *The Philosophy of Teaching*. In this segment John Stossel examined reading and arithmetic teaching techniques such as Whole Language instruction, and compared the results against Direct Instruction. Direct Instruction is a technique developed more than 30 years ago by Zig (Siegfried) Engelmann, who was at the University of Illinois then, but is at the University of Oregon now.[28] Direct Instruction systematizes 'old-fashioned' learning techniques (not very different from, but much more detailed than what I will recommend). He discovered that what works the best for teaching the most basic skills to early learners, even with young 'at risk' kids, was drill. Just do it over and over for a few days or weeks, and it soon sinks in. Doing 'homework' is an extension

------

28 1998.

of this simple idea. It works because the system insists that we *teach* the fundamentals, and requires kids to prove that they have learned those fundamentals, before moving on. In other words, you cannot start at the top of the ladder. You must move up the ladder one rung at a time to reach the top. These skills include such rudimentary things as reading, writing, and arithmetic. The most basic skills are, of course, learned in a very short amount of time, and once they sink in, we can move on to something a bit harder that builds on the basics that we already know. There is certainly more to teaching than that, but as a start knowing that learning the basics of reading takes mere weeks, not years, is important. It should be no surprise to note that reading for meaning (i.e., reading comprehension [a higher-level thinking skill]), even at the first grade level, is difficult if the pupil cannot read at all.

In any case, the Stossel report told us that the U.S. Office of Education (the precursor to today's Department of Education) conducted a large study in the late 1960s. The study was called the *Follow Through Project,* cost us $1 billion (in late 1960s money), and pitted various instructional and 'learning preparation' systems, such as 'Whole Language,' Headstart, and others, against each other. The *Follow Through Project* intended to learn which system produced the best academic results. The results of the study were to provide the basis for instructional recommendations for the entire nation. Besides the Direct Instruction system, the other competitors:[29]

> . . . consisted of 12 other major sponsors (each of which had more than two sites) [i.e., schools participating in the study. Engelmann, for instance, sponsored 20 sites with a total of around 9,000 students] and a lot of self-sponsored sites. The competition presented the range of prejudices of the day, which is the same range that is present today. Most of the sponsors were "child developmentalists" who rallied around theories like those of Piaget.[30] There was the Open Classroom model that believed in the natural ability of children to make choices and intelligent decisions if given space and opportunity [i.e., relevance and child-centered theory]. There were projects like the Tucson Early Education Model that promoted "language experience" reading (which is all but identical to the

---

29 Engelmann, 1992.

30 Jean Piaget, a Swiss psychologist who deduced several stages in the mental development of children. His conclusions regarding the existence of various 'stages' of learning (brain) development led Progressive educators to delay the introduction of various items of instruction, until kids were thought to be 'developmentally ready' for them. This was a major component of the ideas that we now call 'dumbing-down'.

"whole language" approach that is currently in vogue) and Cognitively Oriented Curriculum, which focused on social development. Some of the sponsors stressed "discovery learning" and problem solving of the type that is popular today.

The 'competition' started in 1968 and followed the kids from Kindergarten through the 4th grade. The results showed that kids who were taught by Engelmann's Direct Instruction methods attained:

First place in reading
First place in arithmetic
First place in spelling
First place in language
First place in basic skills
First place in academic cognitive skills

and, most interestingly, considering the fundamental emphasis placed on self-esteem training by the Progressives,

First place in positive self image

In Engelmann's words:

> . . . our kids took first place in just about everything measured—first for urban sites, first for English speakers, and first for non-English speakers.
> Our disadvantaged kids performed near the 50th percentile (average) in the various subjects.[31] The Title 1 programs typically turned out kids who performed around the 20th percentile. Some of the [other programs] beat the 20th percentile, but most didn't. *The ones with the sweetest rhetoric about children's self-image, discovery learning, and cognitive processes did the worst. Some kids had* [on average] *below the 15th percentile* [my emphasis].

Not surprisingly, the *Follow Through Project* concluded that Direct Instruction was the most effective method evaluated for teaching basic skills to young kids. Despite being the most effective method available by far, it is not in use much today because Progressive educators do not

---

31 The same as dominant-culture kids. That is, he closed the so-called 'Achievement gap', at least for the most basic of skills.

like it, the Office of Education did not recommend it, and Ed schools typically ignore it, unless they want to say that it is not recommended because it is too rigid and inflexible. On the other hand, the 'innovative' systems with the sweetest rhetoric about children's self-image, discovery learning, and cognitive processes, and are beloved of educationists, are still going strong. It is for these ineffective programs that we are constantly being asked to increase funding.

Direct Instruction's 'failure' was that it was not 'innovative' enough. Innovation, in this sense, is defined as abiding by the dogmatically romantic view of children that characterizes the Progressive vision. Engelmann concluded that the reason that his method was swept aside was that lobbyists for the newly retrenched educational professionals convinced the Office of Education, and the School Boards in the districts where the various instructional experiments were conducted, that it would be embarrassing to announce to parents that the systems promoted with such fanfare and used for the previous several years, were a total bust.

That sounds quite reasonable, from a political CYA[32] point of view. Yet what was the point of doing an experiment, especially one that cost us a billion dollars, if we then refuse to use the results that the experiment provides? Ignoring reality makes sense if we love our theory more than the results. My own feeling is that Direct Instruction failed because educationists at all levels of our education system just did not care that it worked. Direct Instruction does not abide by Progressive assumptions, so it was ideologically unacceptable, and failure to adopt this major Great Society program would have jeopardized the arguments for others.

Still, what about the education of kids? The original point was to find the most useful and reproducible techniques to educate kids. What ever happened to that goal? It is a shame that the kids were ignored in the scramble to prevent embarrassment, though the Progressive rhetoric redoubled its emphasis regarding their concern for the kids and the rightness of their recommendations. Today, even moderate recommendations to gently edge away from the current system are met with various counter arguments that say that the recommendations are right wing attempts to 'leave poor, working kids behind', etc. The basic, publically stated reason for rejecting any traditional educational technique is that,

---

32 Cover your a**.

whether learning occurs or not, individual achievement is still 'inequitable' (i.e., variable), maintaining the Achievement gap. It does not matter that average achievement may rise impressively in all groups. Since the Progressive ideology assumes that everyone is the same as everyone else, the conclusion is that we should see no variations in achievement at all.

The problem is that we do see variations. It matters not at all who designs the instruction. It matters not at all what the instruction tries to teach. It even matters not at all how we define our achievement standards. If there are more than one pupil involved, there will be a variation of results. Progressive folks say that this is not only unacceptable, but that there are no explanations possible for this variation other than racism, elitism, or a philosophy that honors merit, as if this last reason is a bad thing.

In the end, however, the lesson the Progressive educational establishment learned from the *Follow Through Project* was that they were in the driver's seat and could get away with educational fraud, if their ideas sounded superficially plausible and were supported by erudite sounding (they use a lot of big words) psychological opinions that could be camouflaged as 'research'.

People believed them because the 'experts' said it was so. Very few people checked the details of what was told to the public, and those that did could be ridiculed as extremists who were 'against education'.

Apart from highlighting the differential results between these other systems and Direct Instruction, the 20/20 segment was largely about why school systems generally refuse to use the Direct Instruction method. Of course, some schools have tried it, improved results by leaps and bounds, and then discontinued its use in favor of receiving State and Federal money, only to slump back into the same perpetuation-of-ignorance mode that makes Progressive education infamous.

The 20/20 report quoted the Superintendent of the San Diego schools saying that Whole Language instruction was 'better', because Direct Instruction was too regimented. By insisting that teachers learn the details of teaching, in fact by insisting that *instruction* means that information is dispensed, Direct Instruction did not allow the pupils' natural creativity to shine through. (We will see examples of this creativity throughout this book and in Chapter 7 we will discuss genuine instructional flexibility). Yet when asked why San Diego's upper grade school and Middle school kids could not read and were dropping out at alarming rates, while at-risk Kindergartners under Direct Instruction learn to read, to do arithmetic, and to like doing it, her explanation was that San Diego public education was, "still in transition." San Diego preferred innovative techniques (read, 'the latest Progressive fad'). Unfortunately, San Diego's kids have the disconcerting habit of getting a year older every year, and a year farther behind. They cannot afford to wait until San Diego gets its act together.

Why is it so hard to teach Progressive theorists that one will never become a creative writer if he cannot read, and one will never do algebra, much less become an engineer, physicist, astronaut, or grocer for that matter, if she cannot add? All of the modern techniques that attempt to 'motivate' kids to learn, or to 'encourage' creativity' simply fall flat if used much beyond Kindergarten. Happily, Californians have now officially trashed Whole Language instruction, along with Bicultural education (but some of their educators have not noticed).

Usually, we array and judge educational 'excellence' along a continuum. This excellence is often equated with a vision of society that the individual philosopher likes. The continuum stretches from rigid political correctness and even anarchy (in the name of freedom and democracy) and ethnic and cultural separatism on the left (i.e., Unity through Diversity—a recent NEA slogan), through traditional academic excellence and 'justice for all', etc., in the center, to rigidity and ethnic and cultural separation on the right. In lay terms this continuum stretches from absolute, unrestricted individual freedom and 'anything goes' on one end to 'You must agree with me on all things or you are a traitor' on the other. Oddly enough, both of those ends often meet on the left, with treason being recast as being 'against education' or as 'racism', or in politically correct terms generally. A healthy society with a healthy, happy, and productive citizenry and healthy, happy kids trying to emulate their parents whom they love, lies somewhere between the extremes.

Will this 'healthy, happy' society ever be perfected? No, not ever. The range of human behavior does include considerable latitude for individual experience and for individuality ("I'm just doing my own thing, Man"), and extends far into madness. Also, individual happiness in the short term, is a fluid thing based on ongoing experience. Even Rousseau[33] understood this. On page 80, he tells us:

---

33 Jean-Jacques Rousseau, 1712–1778, in *Emile or On Education*, 1762. This book has been called an early 'bible' to Progressive theory.

We do not know what absolute happiness or unhappiness is. Everything is mixed in this life; in it one tastes no pure sentiment; in it one does not stay two moments in the same state. The affections of our souls, as well as the states of our bodies, are in a continual flux. The good and the bad are in us all, but in different measures. The happiest is he who suffers the least pain; the unhappiest is he who feels the least pleasure. Always more suffering than enjoyment; this relation between the two is common to all men. Man's felicity on Earth is, hence, only a negative condition; the smallest number of ills he can suffer ought to constitute its measure.

That means that 'happy, healthy' is a relative thing and that we will never be able to include everyone under its mantle all of the time. The very best we can ever hope for, is to try to achieve the positive side of 'the smallest number of ills he can suffer'. This is called 'the greatest good for the greatest number'. Nothing looms on the horizon that is likely to fix everything, not even Soma,[34] but if we try to do things with basic common sense, it will be better than the society we have been moving toward at least since the mid 1960s.

Unfortunately, what we think of as common sense correlates highly with what we are taught. This fact is another of the motivations for this book. What our children are being taught, and what our teachers are being taught to teach, may sound pleasing to some, but exacerbates the very problems it is designed to solve.

Parts of this book may seem quite confusing at first. The reason for this is that so many competing ideas are pulling in conflicting directions that it will sometimes sound as if we are spinning our philosophic wheels. You should be delighted with this realization, because we are currently spinning our wheels. At times you will read arguments that imply that everyone is the same as everyone else, so we have to treat everyone uniquely. You will read arguments that say that everybody is unique, so we have to treat everyone identically. You will read arguments that say that some kids have no interest in, or aptitude for, learning much beyond individual job skills, but that we owe it to them to send them to college. You will read arguments that insist that objective tests are faulty because the results should not be used to compare pupils, even if the tests have been taken by millions of pupils. This is said to be so because no one, other than the pupil himself, can judge what a pupil has learned. The

______

34 The psychoactive, dulling drug in Aldous Huxley's *Brave New World*, the modern equivalents of which may be Ritalin, Valium, and Prozac, etc.

solution to this dilemma is to allow the pupils to make up and act out their own dramatic plays, so that everyone, including those not present for the performance, will immediately recognize what each pupil can do. (I am not making this up.)

The result of this twisted reasoning, and many more like it, is a system that gets normal kids to produce average test scores at the approximate level of cabbages at least partly by assuming that there must be evil intent at play when some kids do not keep up with others.

We will also find some repetition of argument. This is unavoidable under the circumstances since the same arguments are often used by Progressive educationists to justify a variety of theories and techniques, although many fundamental Progressive ideas fully contradict other fundamental ideas. This is done because those same arguments are politically convincing, whether they have any basis in reality or not. Either way, they must be answered repeatedly because we are trying to understand the 'education problem' as a whole.

I will eventually argue that theoretical simplicity and consistency are good things and that teaching lessons, as opposed to facilitating activities or developing new 'focused programs,' will produce what we all say we want. That is, literate, educated, creative, and socially responsible citizens. If we can get kids to learn the simple things well (and we can, easily) then harder things become possible (and in their turn become seen as simple). Yet before we go on to the hard things we must first learn the simple things (i.e., you must walk before you can run). The corollary of this homely bit of wisdom is also true. We cannot run if we have not learned to walk (i.e., higher-level skills are difficult if the lower-level skills have not been mastered or if the supposed higher-level thinker does not know very much). Furthermore, if a pupil is to go beyond the simple things, learning the hard things requires work. Since kids are different, they will learn at different rates and some will move on to the harder things sooner than others. (This is revolutionary stuff, isn't it?) In fact, some kids may never catch up to the fastest runners at all, and that is OK too, because reality is what it is, not what we want it to be.

What Is a 'Good' School?

I would like to begin by trying to deal with the real-world problem of how to try to find a good public school. What is a 'good' school anyway? This question is at the heart of the debate between the two major philosophical camps and we must decide which one makes the most sense to us. Unfortunately, our problem with schools is now so widespread and so deep that down looks like up. Did you read, not too very long ago, that the SAT math scores actually rose a point or two for the first time in twenty or thirty years?[35] Jubilation! Rejoicing!! "We're on the right track!!!"[36] What caused this remarkable event, apart from again making the tests easier several years ago? Forty years ago we spent just a little money per kid,[37] relatively speaking, and we had arguably the best public education system in the history of the world. It seemed that more of our kids eventually won Nobel prizes every year than the rest of the world combined. Today we spend thousands on each kid and we are a laughingstock. What was the difference? Forty years ago we expected kids to study and learn, and they did. Today we *ask* kids what they think is relevant to them, and many of them tell us to go punt (or words to that effect). Do we need a Nobel winner to help us understand?

At the time I started writing this book (Summer 1997), I had recently moved to a new city so I had at least one advantage over many longtime residents who generally have to settle for whatever school is designated for their area. The advantage is that I had the option of moving to an area that has the 'best' public schools, so I tried to find the best school system in or near the city where my wife and I had jobs.

Still, what is a good school? I had to solve this problem for myself and my family. My own assumption is that a good school is a combination of many things. It is safe, clean, and well maintained, where kids

---

35 Possibly due to the fact that the SAT scoring system was 'renormed' recently (i.e., artificially readjusted upward). If you access collegeboard.com (as I did in January 2005), [under the "educators" section, click on the hot button labeled 'College bound seniors 2004', then on 'National and State reports', and finally on '1996 National Report', you will discover that data are presented only as far back as 1972, and that the averages posted are not the "original" scores. A footnote in the "Mean SAT/SAT I Scores, 1972–1996" page says: "For 1972–1986 a formula was applied to the original mean and standard deviation to convert the mean to the recentered scale. For 1987–1995, individual student scores were converted to the recentered scale and then the mean was recomputed. For 1996 most students received scores on the recentered scale. (Any score on the original scale was converted to the recentered scale prior to recomputing the mean.)" Comparing scores currently posted to the scores reported previously, (see footnote 48 on page 42), scores were raised approximately 75 points.

36 Of course verbal scores continue to fall, but, "Hey. You can't have everything."

37 It is difficult to tell where Martin Gross (*The Conspiracy of Ignorance*, 1999, p. 30) gets his data since he does not provide specific references but merely lists sources for each chapter in the general order of their use, but his list includes the Organization for Economic Cooperation and Development (OECD) and the National Center for Education Statistics of the U.S. Department of Education for his statistics. He says that we spent $375 per pupil in 1960 and more than $7,000 per pupil in 1999.

are happy and teachers like to work. It is also a place that produces many kids with good scholastic achievement. An indication of that achievement means good standardized test scores, but it also means more than that. It means that kids can read and use learned information in making informed decisions. It is a place that helps parents raise good citizens and decent future leaders. So far so good, you say? Everybody wants these same things. Maybe so, but we see one item on that list that is of great philosophic concern: standardized test scores. We will get deeper into that argument later in this chapter and again in Chapter 7, but for now, just grant me the assumption that having good standardized test scores is important, if for no other reason than that they help a parent find a school that stands out on some objective, scholastic measure. Without an objective measure we must depend on some of the other ideas I mentioned (e.g., safe, clean) and on a subjective evaluation of how well your prospective school system stacks up. Incidentally, some of those subjective ideas have been formalized as 'exit outcomes'. We will discuss that in Chapter 3.

There is one more thing. Good schools are staffed by good teachers who know how to teach things worth knowing, whether those things be 'good' or 'bad'. Amazingly, this too is very controversial, but what I have in mind is very much akin to what Rita Kramer[38] described when she said:

> We are talking about the age-old process by which someone who is grown-up, experienced, and educated imparts knowledge to the young—skills and facts, how to use them, what to make of them—eventually wisdom. A familiarity with the world, past and present, and a sense of one's place in it.

What must be understood from the outset however, is that, as Kramer puts it:

> Teaching is an activity that can be successfully conducted in a basement room with meager furnishings. About all that is required are books and writing materials. The rest is trimming.

The bulk of this book will be used to help explore these ideas, and why today's schools do not (cannot) live up to them. The short version

---

38 *Ed School Follies: The Miseducation of America's Teachers*, p. 2.

is that today's educators have elevated the trimmings to the level of essentials and have seemingly forgotten what genuine education is. And the trimmings cost us $billions each year.

Before I started to look for a place to live, I began the process of finding a school district. In this effort I did some things that one would expect. I visited various schools, spoke with principals, counselors, school district superintendents and teachers to get a feel for how things are in specific schools. However, I also got the School Building Report Card data from the State Department of Education. This was a large database, originally only available in cryptic form, that listed the individual schools' average[39] scores on a variety of State-sponsored tests. The tests are administered to kids in specified grades, and results are reported to the State and compiled into a database that was then made available to anyone who asked for it. Its current format is now also available on the Internet. The data consisted of some demographic information and the average scores, reported by school building and specific test, in several categories for every school in the State. This data is also presumably used by State officials for the purpose of 'accountability' and also to make further educational and bureaucratic decisions.

I looked at several private and parochial schools too, but I found the parochial schools typically had some requirements I was not willing to meet. Usually, those included a catechism to which I did not fully subscribe, or they included teaching Creationism, occasionally to the exclusion of science.[40] In addition, after being surprised during my first day as a student-teacher that some of my 9th grade pupils could not spell words as simple as "they" and "on," I asked principals whether all of their 9th graders could spell "they." Several said that they could not guarantee it. Keep this in mind when you think about the 'voucher' issue. Merely being a private school does not insure excellent academic results. Also keep in mind that new teachers, even those who are eventually hired by private and parochial schools, are typically trained by Ed schools. We might also keep in mind that the record of those who prefer vouchers is very instructive. In general parents of 'at risk' kids from depressed neighborhoods are the greatest supporters of plans that might

---

39 The statistical *mean*.

40 I will comment further about this debate in Chapter 4, but since I can reconcile the differences in the Creationism—Evolution controversy quite easily in my own mind, I would see no real need to make a fuss about this issue if it did not affect education as much as it does in some communities.

allow them to send their kids to schools elsewhere, rather than the schools run by the local public school board. What I cannot understand is why many others of these same parents, and their 'community leaders', still support the establishment. We have done virtually everything our educational professionals have asked, and implemented virtually every program and reform that our Progressive brethren have demanded, and have done so since the mid-1960s at least, and we see no improvement. Rather than improvement, we have seen a swift and disastrous decline in academic achievement and in society's general well-being. Apparently the rhetoric of the class struggle is more compelling than seeing their own kids prosper. I must admit to some profound confusion on that score.

Therefore, I find it unsatisfactory to have to pay the equivalent of college tuition every year for each of my kids, from Kindergarten through college, and still pay taxes to support the public schools. Especially if the private school also produces pupils who cannot spell "they" by the time they enter high school. Granted, "they" is a tough word, but I think that by the ninth grade *all* pupils should have moved on to more formidable challenges.

Another problem is that the denizens of some secular private schools can also be quite snooty, and I do not want my kids to be socially elitist. For example, during my interview with one 'Headmaster', the great man looked up and down at me and my off-the-rack clothing, and with one eyebrow raised said, "You know, XYZ Academy is not for everybody." Yet, if we think of their attitude as, 'successful people's realization of what is needed for success', and insisting on it for their children, sending your kids there by using vouchers may be an acceptable alternative.

The optimum solution, then, is to find a place that teaches kids the things they will need for their professional and civic lives, without going bankrupt in the process. That is what Thomas Jefferson had in mind when he championed the idea of publicly funded schools in the late 1770s. He suggested that it might be good to teach *all* kids things. Jefferson knew that a democracy required that its citizens understand the issues of the day, and that those same citizens be professionally competent. I think old Tom would be disappointed with what we have done to his ideas.

Are You Ready for This?

From the School Building Report Card database I found fifteen school districts across six counties within easy driving distance from downtown. In all, the school districts contained eighteen high schools, twenty-six junior-high and middle schools, and sixty-two grammar and elementary schools. I pulled out the individual reported scores for each school building from each of these school districts and summarized the academic achievement of the nearly 36,000 pupils represented (see pages 28 to 33).

I then compiled the reported data for those 106 schools into a series of spreadsheets and ranked the schools by achievement (as expressed by their reported average scores) to try to find a good school. Some schools scored better than others, but the final tally shows that, academically at least, there are no 'good' public schools in and around this city at all.

Since hearing this kind of thing upsets people (as it should), I camouflaged the identities of these schools and of this city. Finding which city I live in may not be too difficult, but in truth there is little point to trying. This city's record is certainly not very different from your city. The indications are that a very similar result is common in the rest of America, too. Therefore, I have no intention of embarrassing anyone in particular and many people I will tell about are genuinely trying to do a good job. They cannot do a good job, however, because they are shackled by the rules that have become mandated by law and the regulations of several levels of educational bureaucracy, and they are held back and led astray by the philosophy that prevails in education today. They cannot do a good job because they literally do not know how. Many may never have attended a class conducted in any way other than as a facilitated activity, except perhaps in college, and because their Ed schools taught them that activities are the only acceptable way to conduct a class.

I cannot leave with, "There are no good schools in town," and not show what I mean. So I have reproduced the spreadsheets that led me to these disturbing conclusions, so that *all* can judge for themselves.

As you know, most educational professionals argue that the sort of comparison I made is invalid on its face because each school is a unique mix of characteristics, and so forth. However, this 'uniqueness' argument is disingenuous at best, because the fact that all schools are unique is the best reason to do comparisons. If all schools were identical there would be no need for a comparison at all. Besides, people are rarely willing to highlight their warts, and the educationists just do not want objective data to sully their glowing news releases. They know that this kind of comparison is necessary, and they do not like it.

Though few want to admit it anymore, this kind of comparison is one reason that standardized tests were designed in the first place. To that end, the standardized testing industry has maintained itself over the long term by being useful.[41] Done correctly, their results go a long way in predicting eventual success in college and in life.

Even those who argue the loudest against standardized scores, however, know the value of them, which is why we see a strong effort to redesign and/or to 're-norm' the tests and to use 'percentile rankings' in place of absolute pupil achievement. These efforts at redesign, etc., and the reinterpretations of achievement results are meant to render the tests useless, or to confuse the reader with incomplete data. I will give many examples of these efforts as we go along, but here is a typical one as a start. *Literacy at the Crossroads*, by Regie Routman, a 'language arts resource teacher' from Ohio, is rife with this sort of thing. To convince us that spelling—one of the language arts—has not been degraded over time, she tells us (p. 8) that; "According to the NAEP (National Assessment of Educational Progress), students in grades 4 and 11 show no change in the percentage of misspellings in their writing between 1984 and 1992." Unfortunately, she neglects to tell us that by 1984 the damage had been done, and spelling skills had nowhere to go but up, but have not improved, despite Progressive efforts.[42] If she had referenced research that compared typical pupil spelling skill between 1960 and 1992, if any such exists, I suspect that she would have noticed a significant change for the worse.

---

41 The College Entrance Examination Board, publishers of the Scholastic Aptitude Test (SAT), frequently change their exams in an effort to keep their customer base happy. Yet they still say, in their latest Internet release (*The New SAT*, [www.collegeboard.com/about/newsat/history.html], accessed June 27, 2002 (shortly after the newest changes were announced), that:

National SAT scores rose to their highest levels in 1963. In the 1970s, the College Board conducted 38 studies and assembled a panel to learn the causes of the subsequent steady decline in scores. The Board's conclusions noted the changing composition of the college-bound population, lower school standards, and changing mores that affected students' motivation to learn.

42 Progressive reforms of this period consisted largely in attempting to dilute whatever improvements were made by the back-to-basics efforts.

Superficially at least, the educational professionals are right, however. Each school and school district is a unique blend of strengths and weaknesses and any direct comparison is not an absolute thing at all, any more than an intelligence 'score' is an absolute thing. I am not arguing, for instance, that a school ranked 12 is necessarily superior in all respects to a school ranked number 17, or even 45. Much of a school's worth to a family involves subjective evaluations. For instance, an academically acceptable school may be a perennial cellar-dweller in sports, or may have no orchestra, which may taint its reputation. Nonacademic criteria are a legitimate issue for many and I will be the last to say that they are not important. I participated in three sports, chorus, and several extracurricular activities every year, and loved (almost) every minute of it. I learned a lot about the value of persistence, the value of hard work, and teamwork among other things, too. There are probably as many subjective reasons for picking a particular school as there are people picking, but one reason (I submit it is the most important reason) to fund, staff, and maintain a school, is academic learning. If we organize an institution for any other reason, it is not a school. It may, or may not, be a good thing to have, but it is not a school (as defined by the laws which say that every kid is required to attend).

For these reasons I make no absolute claims about these relative rankings. Nevertheless, I feel that a system of standardized testing, including the one shown here, gives much valuable information that correlates well with eventual 'success', and is therefore ultimately valid.

However, many educational professionals also argue that the standardized tests themselves are invalid because they do not assess a child's ability accurately. They say that the kid 'could' do better, but that they just do not think that the tests are important enough to be taken seriously. Since kids pick up their attitudes from what they are taught, that sort of statement says more about the school, and the kind of academic culture the school maintains, than about the kid, and convinces me that using standardized tests is even more important than it otherwise would have been.

The first year for which I got these data was school year 1995–1996, which by coincidence is the first year for which these particular data sets were compiled. Apart from being fundamentally changed periodically, the database is also a work in progress since the items reported change year by year.[43] In 1995 for instance, two separate reading scores were reported, along with three math scores plus a 'Math Power' score, that is an average of the other three. Six separate writing scores were reported as well. Subsequently the reports were modified by including summary scores in each category, not just for math. For instance, the various 'Writing' scores were averaged into a 'Composite' score and the 'Reading' scores into an 'Index' score. Also, new tests were being developed for science, etc. The 'three Rs', however, have been systematized and averages are reported by School District and by individual school building (see pages 32–33 for the 1997–1998 district averages).

As previously stated, the data were available on the Internet, too, for all years since 1995–1996, but I present the scores for all the individual schools only for the school-year during which I had to select a district for my kids. Subsequently, I show the district averages only, and only for the most recent year (as of this writing) since reporting reams of similar data will add little that is new.

I present these charts on pages 28 through 33. You may study the charts and work out for yourselves what the charts mean without referring to my descriptions, in which case you can skip the section printed in a sans-serif font below. Nevertheless, the descriptions are presented here as a guide. After the descriptive section is done, I will examine some points that seem pertinent to me. I will not do an exhaustive evaluation since that would take too long, so you may want to look some more to see whether you can notice any peculiarities. There certainly are peculiarities, such as the school (Eleven-E) that ranks first in several categories, and one place shy of dead last in another.

These data detail the 'Building Report Card' data reported by each school to the State Department of Education (DoE). The DoE then compiles this data and makes it available for whoever wants to see it. My guess is that they get few requests.

To camouflage the schools involved, I changed the actual School District (SD) number designations and renamed each

---

43 The data for school year 2000–2001 was based on new tests and is also reported differently. What can be found on the State's official education website now [2002] are a series of charts detailing the percentage of the State's pupils who are evaluated, based on the percentage of questions answered correctly on the standardized tests, as falling within five broad, subjective categories. These categories are, Unsatisfactory, Basic, Proficient, Advanced, and Exemplary. Unfortunately, according to the State's standards, acceptable percentages of correctly answered questions begin at around 35 percent.

school. The School District numbers are now listed as 'One' through 'Fifteen', shown on the left side of each chart. Each school is also named according to its district and level. School levels are given a letter designation, "H" for high schools, "M" for middle or junior high schools and "E" for elementary or grammar schools. If a district has more than one school at a particular school level, each school is also numbered after the level designation. For instance, school "Twelve-H" is the only high school in school district Twelve while school "Fifteen-E16" is the sixteenth elementary school in district Fifteen.

The column headings are fairly self-explanatory, although I will comment on some of them shortly.

Tests were given to specific grade levels rather than to all of the kids in each school and the numbers listed in each category column are generally percentage figures depicting the school average at that grade level on a particular test. For instance Math Problem Solving was not administered to every pupil in the school system but only to fourth, seventh and tenth grade pupils, or one grade per school level. The Reading and Math scores are all percentage scores (number answered correctly out of 100 questions asked). On the other hand, Writing was scored using a subjective *rubric* score of 1 through 5 (more on this later).

The school rankings are the numbers in **bold** type shown just to the right of each school average score, and show how each school average compared with the other schools. I list the rankings in reverse order. That is, the lowest rank number represents the highest average score. Therefore, I rank the highest scoring school in each category as #1, and so forth. I base the Final Rank (at the far left in **bold** type after the school name) on the sum of the rankings in all the other categories (Total points) and again reverse the result. The school with the lowest ranking sum (sum of the individual category ranks) is the "best" and is ranked #1 overall.

If a school did not post all the scores (e.g., school "Nine-E4" in the 1995–1996 Elementary School Rankings), it could not be included in the Final Rank and was therefore segregated from the other school data in an area above the main chart. The scores that were available, however, are shown and those individual scores are ranked with the other category scores.

The number listed under the category 'Total Enroll'[ment] in the row marked 'State average' is merely the number of the kids enrolled in the schools shown, not a State average.

The first thing to notice about the charts is that all of them are simply buried in black areas. These more darkly shaded data cells show that the individual school average on that measure was below the State average for that measure, which is shown near the top of each category column. More than half of all the scores reported are below the State average and several schools score below the State averages in all categories. 'Average' here implies that, statewide, half the scores should be above the average and half should be below. However, in the 1995–1996 High School chart for instance, several Writing categories show thirteen of eighteen schools below the State average and the Math categories generally have ten or eleven out of eighteen below the State average. That is still nothing to get too excited about. There is bound to be some variation after all. This relatively low showing may merely show the common finding that city schools often score worse than other schools. Also, there are bound to be some schools that regularly do better than others (one hotly debated political point). So let us try to find a school that never falls below the State average on any measure. In 1995–1996, all elementary or high schools fell below the State average on some measure. Every school. Even the ones ranked #1 overall. I hope that many would say that is not an acceptable result. On the other hand, if we agree with the Progressive equity assumption that everyone is exactly like everyone else, we would be annoyed at implying that some kids are 'better' and would expect all scores to be about the same. Since 'rich guys get all the breaks', all we need do is remove the breaks and *all* can then score identically.

These two arguments do not quite mesh comfortably however. What is wrong with this picture? We are peeking into the murky world of the Nature–Nurture debate, and there will be more on this throughout the book. For now we should know that Progressives generally come down foursquare on the side of Nurture. Pure Nurture. No inequitable contribution from Nature at all. In other words, some kids do worse than others only because, for instance, their parents earn less money than the parents of other kids. Even if correlations can be made between parental income and academic success, is this a reasonable argument? Are there no differences in people at all? We see some kids who actually learn things, even while enrolled in public schools, and there are some

1995–96 Area High School Rankings*

High School	Final rank	Total points	SD no.	Total enroll	% low SES	% white	Expository	Narrative
Standards of Excellence							**81.0**	**84.0**
State average				9852	30	83	57.4	66.6
One-H2	1	77	1	200 **15**	14 **6**	98 **2**	60 **5**	68 **4**
Eleven-H	2	89	11	317 **9**	9 **2**	97 **6**	62 **1**	70 **1**
Two-H	3	91	2	179 **16**	21 **13**	93 **11**	60 **5**	69 **2**
Nine-H	4	97	9	367 **7**	19 **11**	96 **8**	59 **7**	68 **4**
Fifteen-H3	5	104	15	1239 **3**	19 **11**	74 **16**	61 **3**	67 **7**
Twelve-H	6	120	12	1419 **2**	13 **4**	90 **13**	55 **15**	64 **15**
Four-H	7	122	4	298 **10**	13 **4**	98 **2**	57 **9**	67 **7**
Eight-H	8	125	8	259 **13**	25 **14**	97 **6**	62 **1**	66 **10**
Five-H	9	128	5	253 **14**	28 **15**	85 **15**	56 **11**	69 **2**
Seven-H	10	135	7	276 **11**	14 **6**	98 **2**	59 **7**	65 **11**
Thriteen-H	11	139	13	470 **6**	8 **1**	89 **14**	57 **9**	65 **11**
Fifteen-H2	12	147	15	1882 **1**	41 **17**	63 **17**	56 **11**	65 **11**
Ten-H	13	150	10	805 **5**	10 **3**	94 **10**	52 **16**	65 **11**
Fourteen-H	14	163	14	366 **8**	15 **8**	98 **2**	56 **11**	68 **4**
Six-H	15	179	6	265 **12**	28 **15**	100 **1**	58 **11**	67 **7**
Three-H	16	188	3	158 **18**	16 **10**	95 **9**	50 **18**	63 **16**
One-H1	17	214	1	163 **17**	15 **8**	93 **11**	61 **4**	63 **17**
Fifteen-H1	18	248	15	936 **4**	56 **18**	49 **18**	52 **16**	61 **18**

*Based on 1995-96 Building Report Card data - DoE

1995–96 Area Junior High and Middle School Rankings*

Junior High Middle School	Final rank	Total points	SD no.	Total Enroll	% low SES	% white	Expository	Narrative
Standards of Excellence							**81.0**	**84.0**
State average				9344	30	83	57.4	66.6
One-M1		55	1	295 **15**	40 **20**	74 **20**		
Two-M3	1	60	2	62 **26**	29 **15**	97 **5**	83 **1**	74 **1**
Two-M1	2	91	2	247 **19**	29 **15**	96 **7**	65 **5**	61 **14**
One-M4	3	118	1	260 **18**	28 **13**	95 **10**	73 **2**	70 **2**
Two-M2	4	119	2	79 **25**	19 **7**	90 **17**	66 **3**	70 **2**
Twelve-M	5	126	12	842 **1**	21 **8**	93 **15**	57 **16**	62 **11**
Nine-M	6	130	9	163 **23**	18 **5**	99 **2**	60 **11**	62 **11**
One-M3	7	133	1	309 **14**	18 **5**	96 **7**	58 **14**	61 **14**
Eleven-M	8	139	11	317 **13**	9 **1**	97 **5**	65 **5**	70 **2**
Thirteen-M	9	143	13	618 **2**	17 **4**	87 **18**	59 **12**	64 **8**
Ten-M2	10	154	10	457 **9**	9 **1**	95 **10**	63 **8**	65 **6**
Three-M	11	164	3	289 **16**	24 **9**	94 **14**	55 **18**	62 **11**
Four-M	12	189	4	246 **20**	27 **12**	95 **10**	63 **8**	63 **9**
One-M2	13	191	1	88 **24**	41 **21**	98 **3**	50 **23**	57 **21**
Fourteen-M	14	207	14	416 **11**	15 **3**	96 **7**	58 **14**	61 **14**
Eight-M	15	219	8	194 **22**	29 **15**	95 **10**	66 **3**	67 **5**
Fifteen-M3	16	222	15	581 **4**	42 **22**	63 **23**	64 **7**	65 **6**
Six-M	16	222	6	265 **17**	28 **13**	100 **1**	49 **24**	59 **19**
Fifteen-M4	18	239	15	542 **6**	36 **19**	73 **21**	56 **17**	61 **14**
Fifteen-M5	18	239	15	613 **3**	29 **15**	70 **22**	61 **10**	63 **9**
Seven-M	20	241	7	224 **21**	24 **9**	98 **3**	55 **18**	55 **23**
Five-M	21	257	5	321 **12**	45 **23**	81 **19**	59 **12**	61 **14**
Ten-M1	22	261	10	426 **10**	25 **11**	93 **15**	54 **21**	58 **20**
Fifteen-M6	23	312	15	546 **5**	56 **24**	58 **24**	52 **22**	57 **21**
Fifteen-M1	24	315	15	467 **8**	77 **26**	51 **25**	55 **18**	51 **25**
Fifteen-M2	25	340	15	477 **7**	66 **25**	49 **26**	46 **25**	52 **24**

*Based on 1995–96 Building Report Card data - DoE

1995–1996 High, Junior High, and Middle Schools

1995–96 Area High School Rankings continued*

	Math				Writing				
Problem solving	Commo	Reason	Math power	Idea/content	Org	Voice	Word choice	Sentence fluency	Convention
80.0	80.0	80.0	80.0	3.70	3.70	3.70	3.70	3.70	3.70
43.4	47.4	41.0	43.9	3.58	3.46	3.42	3.42	3.44	3.39
43.0 9	51.2 3	35.6 17	43.3 9	3.99 1	3.99 1	3.93 1	3.61 1	3.74 2	3.78 1
43.8 7	50.6 4	41.6 4	45.3 4	3.49 9	3.48 5	3.39 16	3.19 12	3.33 6	3.53 3
47.8 2	56.7 1	48.1 2	50.9 2	3.47 11	3.45 6	3.69 5	3.39 6	3.44 4	3.43 5
42.1 10	46.8 9	38.1 12	42.3 10	3.85 2	3.75 2	3.83 3	3.51 3	3.48 3	3.42 6
46.9 3	50.2 5	43.0 3	46.7 3	3.53 7	3.30 10	3.67 6	3.28 9	3.26 9	3.16 9
42.0 11	44.8 12	37.1 14	41.1 13	3.69 3	3.32 9	3.79 4	3.55 2	3.78 1	3.72 2
39.3 16	40.1 17	37.4 13	39.0 16	3.62 4	3.68 3	3.63 9	3.49 4	3.44 4	3.50 4
43.7 8	43.6 14	38.4 11	41.9 12	3.59 5	3.55 4	3.86 2	3.42 5	3.29 7	3.01 13
53.3 1	54.7 2	52.0 1	53.3 1	3.36 16	3.30 10	3.54 14	3.32 8	3.23 11	3.34 7
36.6 17	48.0 6	38.7 10	44.6 6	3.51 8	3.22 15	3.59 11	3.37 7	3.25 10	3.22 8
44.8 6	46.4 10	41.4 5	44.2 8	3.41 13	3.28 12	3.63 9	3.16 13	3.15 13	3.16 9
45.8 5	47.3 8	40.8 7	44.3 7	3.48 10	3.28 12	3.64 8	3.25 10	3.23 11	3.06 12
40.9 13	42.2 13	39.0 9	40.7 15	3.44 12	3.34 7	3.67 6	3.24 11	3.28 8	3.13 11
41.9 12	44.4 15	39.6 8	42.0 11	3.40 14	3.26 14	3.59 11	3.07 15	3.05 15	2.94 15
39.7 15	41.1 16	36.3 16	39.0 16	3.56 6	3.34 7	3.51 15	3.07 15	3.10 14	3.01 13
46.0 4	47.7 7	41.0 6	44.9 5	3.40 14	3.03 16	3.57 13	3.08 14	2.77 18	2.67 18
40.2 14	45.1 11	37.1 14	40.9 14	3.01 18	2.75 18	2.98 18	2.85 18	2.99 16	2.89 16
31.2 18	34.9 18	33.7 18	33.3 18	3.12 17	2.99 17	3.29 17	2.90 17	2.93 17	2.81 17

Reversed numbers = below State average | Lightly shaded = above standard of excellence

1995–96 Area Junior High and Middle School Rankings continued*

	Math				Writing				
Problem solving	Commo	Reason	Math power	Idea/content	Org	Voice	Word choice	Sentence fluency	Convention
80.0	80.0	80.0	80.0	3.70	3.70	3.70	3.70	3.70	3.70
43.4	47.4	41.0	43.9	3.58	3.46	3.42	3.42	3.44	3.39
71.0 1	68.5 2	56.6 2	65.4 1	4.45 1	4.30 1	4.75 1	4.30 1	4.21 1	4.19 1
63.4 2	73.8 1	59.2 1	65.2 2	3.70 6	3.49 6	4.37 2	3.74 4	3.79 4	3.79 3
50.6 8	61.4 7	47.3 8	53.1 7	3.51 7	3.41 8	3.46 10	3.32 8	3.47 6	3.71 4
50.5 9	60.4 9	48.1 4	53.0 8	3.71 5	3.71 5	4.08 5	3.43 6	3.46 7	3.55 7
54.5 4	65.8 3	48.1 4	56.2 3	3.35 14	3.31 11	3.60 7	3.29 9	3.36 10	3.25 10
49.3 13	54.7 19	45.1 11	49.7 13	3.98 3	3.79 4	4.11 4	3.93 2	3.89 3	3.60 6
53.6 6	59.8 10	50.6 3	54.7 4	3.45 10	3.38 9	3.47 9	3.18 12	3.46 7	3.32 9
60.3 3	50.6 22	41.6 17	45.3 21	3.49 8	3.48 7	3.39 11	3.41 7	3.40 9	3.40 8
54.5 4	64.1 5	45.6 10	57.7 4	3.36 13	3.25 1	3.38 12	3.13 14	3.19 13	3.23 11
48.2 16	59.6 11	41.8 16	49.7 13	3.41 11	3.29 12	3.57 8	3.21 10	3.22 11	3.20 12
45.8 18	58.8 13	41.1 20	48.6 17	3.73 4	3.80 3	3.71 6	3.53 5	3.60 5	3.66 5
49.4 12	57.7 14	43.0 13	50.1 11	3.47 9	3.24 14	3.36 13	3.07 15	3.03 16	3.07 13
48.6 15	50.6 22	27.4 25	42.2 23	4.16 2	4.29 2	4.24 3	3.82 3	4.16 2	3.88 2
50.3 10	55.1 17	41.4 18	48.9 16	3.37 12	3.10 15	3.25 17	2.96 18	2.93 18	2.87 17
44.6 20	63.0 6	43.2 12	50.3 10	3.00 21	3.01 18	3.17 22	3.02 17	2.92 19	2.79 19
51.5 7	59.2 12	48.1 4	53.0 8	2.99 22	2.91 21	3.08 25	2.91 20	2.87 20	2.69 21
49.3 13	55.0 18	42.2 15	49.9 12	2.94 24	3.36 10	3.27 15	3.19 11	3.20 12	2.85 18
49.8 11	64.8 4	47.7 7	54.1 6	2.99 22	2.90 22	3.14 23	2.83 22	2.80 23	2.63 22
46.2 16	60.7 8	40.3 21	49.1 15	3.12 17	2.95 19	3.24 18	2.87 21	2.85 22	2.59 23
45.5 19	52.7 21	42.8 14	47.0 19	3.18 16	3.09 16	3.22 19	3.17 13	3.15 14	2.93 16
41.4 22	54.5 20	39.5 22	45.0 22	3.28 15	3.06 17	3.30 14	3.04 16	3.07 15	3.05 14
42.1 21	55.4 16	41.4 18	46.3 20	3.04 19	2.93 20	3.26 16	2.83 22	2.95 17	2.98 15
37.8 24	46.5 25	36.4 23	40.2 24	3.02 20	2.90 22	3.22 19	2.94 19	2.87 20	2.70 20
40.8 23	55.5 15	45.9 9	47.4 18	2.90 25	2.75 25	3.14 23	2.65 25	2.58 25	2.35 25
37.4 25	48.1 24	33.4 24	39.6 25	3.05 18	2.87 24	3.21 21	2.74 24	2.64 24	2.57 24

Reversed numbers = below State average | Lightly shaded = at or above standard of excellence

1995–1996 High, Junior High, and Middle Schools

1995–96 Area Elementary School Rankings*

Grammar Scl	Final rank	Total points	SD no.	Enroll	(rank)	% low SES	(rank)	% white	(rank)	Expository	(rank)	Narrative	(rank)
Standards of Excellence										77.0		80.0	
State average				17871		30		83		57.4		66.6	
Five-E		128	5	395	23	40	40	74	39	65	19	69	7
Nine-E1		195	9	83	59	17	14	99	2	66	16		
Nine-E4		504	9	88	58	31	29	100	1	64	22		
Two-E3	1	175	2	56	62	11	7	98	4	65	19	69	7
One-E1	2	182	1	73	61	30	27	77	37	70	5	74	2
One-E2	3	205	1	309	21	18	17	96	13	55	48	59	35
Thirteen-E1	4	207	13	532	5	11	7	91	26	67	13	63	21
One-E4	5	227	1	260	33	28	25	95	17	66	16	66	13
Two-E1	6	248	2	247	36	29	26	96	13	60	36	63	21
Thirteen-E2	7	249	13	451	7	12	9	91	26	70	5	70	6
Nine-E2	8	267	9	180	50	22	19	99	2	69	8	65	18
Seven-E	9	268	7	439	8	24	21	98	4	61	28	61	29
Four-E	10	269	4	253	34	33	33	97	9	63	25	66	13
Twelve-E2	11	273	12	498	6	2	1	94	20	68	11	76	1
Nine-E3	12	291	9	228	40	30	27	98	4	61	28	59	35
Fifteen-E15	13	299	15	315	20	46	46	57	51	69	8	72	3
Six-E	14	302	6	231	39	26	24	98	4	55	48	54	46
Fifteen-E17	14	302	15	237	38	38	37	84	34	64	22	66	13
Fourteen-E	16	310	14	762	1	24	21	97	9	61	28	67	11
Ten-E6	17	334	10	289	25	14	12	93	23	62	26	63	21
Thirteen-E4	18	345	13	402	12	13	11	90	28	70	5	72	3
Ten-E2	19	346	10	173	53	10	5	97	9	63	24	61	29
Fifteen-E26	20	349	15	371	14	32	30	67	46	56	46	56	42
Ten-E5	21	364	10	185	49	17	14	94	20	62	26	58	38
Fifteen-E5	22	366	15	217	43	32	30	72	41	58	42	64	19
Fifteen-E20	23	374	15	426	9	36	35	69	45	59	39	58	38
Twelve-E3	24	382	12	591	3	6	3	88	30	68	11	68	9
Thirteen-E3	25	396	13	419	11	37	36	80	35	61	28	59	35
Eleven-E	26	399	11	379	13	15	13	95	17	72	1	67	11
Ten-E8	26	399	10	293	24	7	4	96	13	60	36	63	21
Twelve-E5	28	405	12	561	4	12	9	87	32	67	13	68	9
Fifteen-E22	29	414	15	249	35	51	48	65	47	67	13	63	21
Two-E2	30	433	2	79	60	19	18	90	28	72	1	62	27
Fifteen-E2	31	455	15	196	46	39	39	62	49	55	48	57	40
Three-E	32	472	3	289	25	24	21	94	20	61	28	66	13
Twelve-E1	32	472	12	422	10	17	14	93	23	60	36	62	27
Fifteen-E4	34	473	15	242	37	34	34	79	36	56	46	54	46
Fifteen-E14	35	486	15	351	15	47	47	70	43	66	16	55	43
Twelve-E4	36	493	12	742	2	44	44	88	30	61	28	60	33
Ten-E7	37	495	10	273	27	4	2	96	13	61	28	61	29
Fifteen-E13	38	517	15	325	18	22	19	71	42	55	48	54	46
Ten-E3	39	533	10	177	52	10	5	95	17	72	1	72	3
Fifteen-E1	40	534	15	187	48	88	60	49	57	47	57	47	57
Fifteen-E16	41	535	15	266	31	38	37	70	43	61	28	55	43
Fifteen-E23	42	549	15	266	30	70	54	56	52	57	45	54	46
Fifteen-E24	43	563	15	268	29	41	41	65	47	59	39	55	43
Fifteen-E12	44	565	15	222	41	59	49	73	40	58	42	64	19
Fifteen-E18	45	566	15	266	31	86	57	76	38	43	60	41	59
Fifteen-E21	46	609	15	269	28	64	51	45	59	53	53	51	51
Fifteen-E10	47	643	15	179	51	42	43	50	56	55	48	52	50
Fifteen-E11	48	645	15	346	17	69	52	60	50	51	55	50	54
Ten-E4	49	649	10	165	54	45	45	93	23	69	8	66	13
Fifteen-E19	50	651	15	208	44	81	56	51	54	43	61	46	58
Eight-E	51	656	8	350	16	32	30	97	9	59	39	61	29
Ten E1	52	703	10	304	22	59	49	85	33	71	4	63	21
One-E3	53	716	1	88	57	41	41	98	40	65	19	60	33
Fifteen-E6	54	740	15	317	19	69	52	51	54	48	56	49	55
Fifteen-E7	55	775	15	198	45	87	58	42	60	45	58	61	51
Fifteen-E25	56	815	15	195	47	87	58	54	53	58	42	57	40
Fifteen-E3	57	834	15	139	55	94	61	32	61	53	53	49	55
Fifteen-E9	58	843	15	222	41	96	62	29	62	44	59	41	59
Fifteen-E8	59	861	15	128	56	79	55	46	58	43	61	51	51

*Based on 1995–96 Building Report Card data - DoE

1995–1996 Elementary Schools

| Math | | | | Writing | | | | | |
Problem solving	Commo	Reasoning	Math power	Idea/content	Org	Voice	Word choice	Sentence fluency	Convention
75.0	75.0	75.0	75.0	3.60	3.60	3.60	3.60	3.60	3.60
43.4	47.4	41.0	43.9	3.58	3.46	3.42	3.42	3.44	3.39
				3.54 5	3.47 6	3.35 19	3.05 32	3.28 14	3.07 28
43.6 52	49.6 49	39.7 54	44.3 52	3.21 25	3.08 29	2.99 42	2.90 42	2.92 41	3.39 8
71.2 2	63.6 16	55.0 18	63.3 8	3.63 4	3.49 5	3.63 5	3.48 3	3.33 9	3.50 6
69.4 3	81.0 1	70.4 2	73.6 2	3.25 20	3.43 8	3.65 4	3.40 5	3.60 3	3.85 2
53.4 31	66.6 10	61.4 7	60.5 15	3.93 1	3.71 1	4.00 2	3.57 2	3.83 1	4.09 1
59.2 17	66.7 9	58.0 11	61.2 12	3.32 15	3.26 13	3.33 21	3.20 15	3.31 11	3.32 11
61.2 10	70.0 7	62.1 6	64.5 6	3.49 7	3.12 23	3.46 8	3.19 16	3.26 16	3.12 24
60.6 12	64.0 14	59.2 9	61.2 12	3.33 13	3.40 9	3.43 12	3.23 10	3.34 8	3.23 17
60.0 15	63.3 17	55.8 15	59.7 16	3.16 32	3.16 20	3.07 36	3.09 23	3.29 13	3.37 9
64.1 6	71.6 4	58.0 3	67.9 3	3.25 20	2.83 44	3.33 21	3.08 25	3.53 4	2.92 40
59.0 18	57.9 34	53.6 21	56.8 25	3.40 9	3.36 11	3.37 17	3.29 7	3.22 20	3.25 16
54.3 28	57.0 37	52.8 25	54.7 28	3.53 6	3.52 4	3.47 7	3.30 6	3.38 7	3.43 7
62.7 7	72.0 3	67.4 4	67.4 4	3.00 42	3.00 32	3.10 34	2.98 36	3.02 33	2.92 39
53.1 33	55.9 39	50.0 33	53.0 34	3.75 2	3.58 3	4.17 1	3.92 1	3.42 6	3.59 5
62.3 9	65.5 12	57.2 14	61.6 10	3.24 22	3.24 15	3.32 23	3.21 14	3.15 23	3.06 29
49.2 44	61.1 23	52.1 26	54.1 32	3.75 2	3.65 2	3.94 3	3.40 4	3.78 2	3.69 3
62.7 7	62.6 20	53.6 21	59.6 17	3.36 11	3.29 12	3.46 8	3.17 18	3.12 24	3.16 20
56.4 23	58.0 33	51.7 28	55.3 26	3.22 24	3.14 21	3.32 23	3.12 21	3.18 22	3.18 19
59.9 16	58.3 30	53.6 21	57.3 22	3.20 26	3.13 22	3.12 31	2.97 38	3.31 11	3.35 10
55.0 25	63.9 15	59.9 8	59.6 17	3.02 41	2.89 41	2.71 53	2.90 42	3.06 30	3.26 14
60.4 13	69.1 8	55.1 16	61.5 11	3.08 35	2.99 34	2.87 47	3.07 28	3.26 16	3.20 18
60.3 14	63.3 17	54.8 19	59.5 19	3.33 13	3.25 14	3.32 23	3.22 12	3.25 18	3.14 22
50.8 38	57.1 36	50.3 31	52.7 36	3.32 15	3.18 18	3.25 27	3.28 8	3.46 5	3.69 3
67.7 4	60.1 26	57.7 13	61.8 9	3.28 18	3.11 24	3.43 12	3.08 25	3.05 31	3.06 29
53.6 30	60.9 25	49.3 35	54.6 30	3.35 12	3.20 17	3.45 10	3.23 10	3.23 19	3.16 20
67.3 5	65.4 13	66.6 5	66.4 5	2.72 53	2.61 53	2.82 49	2.81 49	2.88 46	2.78 48
51.1 36	61.8 22	57.8 12	56.9 24	3.16 31	3.09 25	3.22 29	3.10 22	3.12 24	3.10 26
74.1 1	78.0 2	71.9 1	74.7 1	2.67 55	2.54 55	2.46 61	2.51 58	2.52 55	2.53 55
52.6 35	50.4 47	47.7 39	50.2 40	3.17 29	3.09 25	3.03 40	3.17 18	3.28 14	3.26 14
57.2 22	71.2 5	54.5 20	61.0 14	2.81 48	2.73 50	2.93 44	2.82 48	2.90 43	2.86 44
57.7 19	58.2 31	49.1 36	55.0 27	3.17 29	3.39 10	3.39 16	3.15 20	3.08 29	3.00 33
53.3 32	61.9 21	48.7 37	54.6 30	2.58 57	2.86 42	3.41 14	3.09 23	3.22 20	3.13 23
55.6 24	58.9 27	49.4 34	54.7 28	3.26 19	3.23 16	3.35 19	3.27 9	3.11 26	3.03 31
50.7 39	58.5 28	51.8 27	53.7 33	2.87 45	2.77 47	2.92 45	2.87 45	2.90 43	3.27 13
57.7 19	63.2 19	53.6 21	58.2 21	2.85 46	2.76 48	2.75 51	2.87 45	2.82 49	2.88 43
54.2 29	52.4 45	47.2 41	51.3 39	3.38 10	3.17 19	3.45 10	3.19 16	3.09 28	2.93 37
54.8 26	61.1 23	55.1 14	57.0 23	3.06 38	2.93 38	3.06 37	2.93 41	2.94 40	2.90 42
61.0 11	70.1 6	59.1 10	63.4 7	2.68 54	2.54 55	2.75 51	2.59 57	2.64 54	2.73 51
51.1 36	55.0 41	44.5 44	50.1 41	3.14 34	2.79 46	3.01 41	3.00 34	2.97 39	2.90 40
54.8 26	58.4 29	44.6 43	52.6 38	3.24 22	2.96 37	3.36 18	3.07 28	2.80 50	2.68 53
45.1 51	54.2 42	47.3 40	49.0 44	2.87 44	2.72 51	2.78 50	2.70 50	2.84 47	2.95 36
48.9 46	48.1 52	40.3 53	45.7 50	3.46 8	3.44 7	3.59 6	3.22 12	3.33 9	3.31 12
52.7 34	55.4 40	50.1 32	52.7 36	3.03 40	2.93 38	3.20 30	3.06 31	2.98 37	2.96 35
48.5 47	53.7 43	41.6 49	47.9 46	3.29 17	3.09 27	3.40 15	3.08 25	3.11 26	3.08 27
50.1 41	58.1 32	50.4 30	52.9 35	2.99 43	3.00 32	3.09 35	2.96 36	3.01 34	2.84 46
50.5 40	51.6 46	44.1 46	48.8 45	3.19 28	2.97 36	3.06 37	2.94 40	3.03 32	3.12 24
57.6 21	66.6 10	51.7 28	58.6 20	3.08 35	2.85 43	3.06 37	2.97 38	2.91 42	2.83 47
50.0 42	49.8 48	41.4 50	47.1 48	3.20 26	3.07 30	3.32 23	3.07 28	3.00 35	2.93 37
45.1 50	48.0 53	40.5 52	44.5 51	3.16 32	3.09 27	3.23 28	2.99 35	3.00 35	3.02 32
49.0 45	53.0 44	48.1 38	50.0 43	3.05 39	2.98 35	3.11 33	2.90 42	2.83 48	2.74 50
46.4 48	49.4 50	46.4 42	47.4 47	2.77 50	2.64 52	2.47 59	2.63 54	2.80 50	2.65 54
49.4 43	57.3 35	43.5 47	50.1 41	3.08 35	3.04 31	3.12 31	3.02 33	2.98 37	2.85 45
41.0 54	45.9 56	36.0 58	41.1 56	2.64 56	2.59 54	2.71 53	2.67 52	2.89 45	2.77 49
38.4 57	48.7 51	40.7 51	42.9 55	2.52 61	2.46 59	2.56 58	2.41 61	2.37 60	2.18 61
40.7 55	56.5 38	42.5 48	46.5 49	2.56 59	2.92 40	2.47 59	2.42 60	2.33 61	2.50 57
42.0 53	46.2 55	44.3 45	44.1 53	2.83 47	2.75 49	2.89 46	2.69 51	2.70 53	2.69 52
39.8 56	44.5 58	33.5 59	39.3 58	2.78 49	2.80 45	2.83 48	2.87 45	2.78 52	3.00 33
35.1 60	36.5 60	31.6 60	34.4 60	2.74 52	2.47 58	2.65 56	2.63 54	2.51 56	2.33 59
36.4 59	44.2 59	37.7 56	39.4 57	2.77 50	2.49 57	2.97 43	2.65 53	2.46 57	2.48 58
46.0 49	47.9 54	38.2 55	44.0 54	2.57 58	2.45 60	2.63 57	2.48 59	2.43 28	2.51 56
36.5 58	44.9 57	36.2 57	39.2 59	2.55 60	2.31 61	2.70 55	2.63 54	2.42 59	2.30 60

Reversed numbers = below State average   Lightly shaded = at or above standard of excellence

1995–1996 Elementary Schools

1997–98 Area Elementary School Ranking, by District*

District	Final rank	Total points	Total Enroll		% low SES		% white		Demographics / Reading: Expository		Narrative		Index	
Standard of Excellence									77		80		77	
State average			35794		30		83		66.6		64.1		65.4	
Nine	1	76	1120	6	20	6	97	3	72.4	4	68.2	3	70.3	3
Three	2	84	441	15	25	10	93	11	64.6	11	69.8	2	67.2	5
Four	3	89	1092	7	27	11	96	4	72.5	3	70.5	1	71.5	2
Seven	4	95	968	9	18	5	98	2	68.5	7	64.9	12	66.7	7
Eleven	5	102	712	12	14	1	96	4	73.0	2	60.3	14	66.6	8
One	6	108	1090	8	23	8	94	10	70.4	5	65.0	11	67.7	4
Two	7	112	597	13	29	12	96	4	65.8	9	65.7	7	65.7	11
Fourteen	8	128	1528	5	20	6	96	4	65.1	10	66.9	5	66.0	9
Twelve	9	146	5092	2	17	4	89	12	68.8	6	65.1	10	67.0	6
Ten	10	147	3317	4	16	2	95	9	64.5	12	65.3	8	64.9	12
Six	11	150	482	14	23	8	100	1	77.2	1	67.4	4	72.3	1
Thirteen	12	162	3512	3	16	2	88	13	66.5	8	65.2	9	65.9	10
Eight	13	179	801	11	30	13	96	4	63.6	13	64.0	13	63.8	14
Fifteen	14	214	14144	1	55	15	60	15	58.5	15	57.4	15	58.0	15
Five	15	218	898	10	39	14	80	14	62.3	14	65.9	6	64.1	13

1997–98 Area Junior High/Middle School Ranking, by District*

District	Final rank	Total points	Total Enroll		% low SES		% white		Demographics / Reading: Expository		Narrative		Index	
Standard of Excellence									81		84		81	
State average			35794		30		83		65.2		63.8		64.5	
Nine	1	45	1528	5	20	6	96	4	77.1	2	70.0	3	73.6	2
Three	2	95	1120	6	20	6	97	3	72.3	3	69.6	5	70.9	3
Four	3	97	1090	8	23	8	94	10	70.3	4	67.6	7	69.0	4
Seven	3	97	597	13	29	12	96	4	64.6	11	70.0	3	67.4	8
Eleven	3	97	482	14	23	8	100	1	69.2	6	68.7	6	68.9	5
One	6	102	801	11	30	13	96	4	80.2	1	75.2	1	77.7	1
Two	7	117	3512	3	16	2	88	13	68.1	7	66.5	8	67.3	9
Fourteen	8	126	5092	2	17	4	89	12	70.1	5	66.4	9	68.2	7
Twelve	9	141	441	15	25	10	93	11	68.5	9	64.1	11	65.3	11
Ten	10	142	968	9	18	5	98	2	64.1	13	61.8	13	62.9	13
Six	11	146	712	12	14	1	96	4	64.4	12	72.0	2	68.2	6
Thirteen	12	181	3317	4	16	2	95	9	67.4	8	63.7	12	65.6	10
Eight	13	186	1092	7	27	11	96	4	65.5	10	60.3	15	62.9	13
Fifteen	14	220	14144	1	55	15	60	15	58.3	15	61.4	14	59.9	15
Five	15	227	898	10	39	14	80	14	64.0	14	65.9	10	65.0	12

1997–98 Area High School Ranking, by District*

District	Final rank	Total points	Total Enroll		% low SES		% white		Demographics / Reading: Expository		Narrative		Index	
Standard of Excellence									81		84		81	
State average			35794		30		83		59.8		67.8		63.8	
Nine	1	63	597	13	29	12	96	4	65.3	4	70.4	3	67.8	4
Three	2	73	1528	5	20	6	96	4	63.1	5	68.6	8	65.9	6
Four	3	88	482	14	23	8	100	1	66.9	3	71.3	2	69.1	2
Seven	4	94	5092	2	17	4	89	12	61.1	7	72.3	1	66.7	5
Eleven	5	104	1092	7	27	11	96	4	59.8	8	69.9	5	64.8	8
One	6	115	712	12	14	1	96	4	69.3	1	69.7	6	69.5	1
Two	7	119	1090	8	23	8	94	10	61.6	6	69.4	7	65.6	7
Fourteen	8	126	3512	3	16	2	88	13	58.9	9	68.3	9	63.6	9
Twelve	9	152	1120	6	20	6	97	3	67.7	2	70.1	4	68.9	3
Ten	10	156	3317	4	16	2	95	9	54.7	14	67.8	11	61.3	11
Six	10	156	968	9	18	5	98	2	56.0	13	65.4	13	60.7	13
Thirteen	12	162	441	15	25	10	93	11	47.5	15	52.3	15	49.9	15
Eight	13	200	14144	1	55	15	60	15	57.3	10	68.2	10	62.7	10
Fifteen	14	201	801	11	30	13	96	4	56.3	12	65.5	12	60.9	12
Five	15	212	898	10	39	14	80	14	56.7	11	62.7	14	62.7	14

* Based on the 1997–98 District Building Report Card data - State DoE

1997–1998 Scores Averaged by District

| Math | | | | Writing | | | | | | |
Problem solving	Commo	Reasoning	Math power	Idea/content	Organization	Voice	Word choice	Sentence fluency	Convention	Composite
75	75	75	75	3.6	3.6	3.6	3.6	3.6	3.6	3.6
60.55	63.62	54.91	59.69	3.20	2.84	2.98	3.06	2.93	3.25	3.03
70.9 2	72.8 1	67.1 2	70.3 2	3.40 7	3.33 6	3.31 8	3.18 6	3.35 5	3.29 6	3.32 6
63.2 5	67.5 5	59.7 4	63.4 4	3.72 3	3.79 1	3.67 4	3.74 1	3.79 1	3.86 1	3.74 1
57.1 11	62.6 10	51.7 12	57.1 12	3.83 1	3.71 2	3.87 1	3.65 2	3.49 3	3.31 5	3.71 2
59.7 10	68.1 4	53.7 11	60.5 8	3.78 2	3.68 3	3.65 5	3.51 3	3.52 2	3.58 2	3.64 3
78.8 1	69.0 3	77.0 1	74.9 1	3.33 8	3.20 9	3.36 6	3.13 7	3.18 7	3.04 11	3.23 7
60.5 8	62.2 11	55.9 7	59.6 9	3.81 4	3.51 5	3.76 3	3.44 4	3.47 4	3.57 3	3.57 4
62.6 7	65.5 7	57.8 6	62.0 6	3.52 5	3.67 4	3.79 2	3.34 5	3.35 5	3.53 4	3.56 5
69.5 3	69.8 2	64.0 3	67.8 3	3.26 9	2.89 14	3.29 9	3.00 13	2.97 13	3.13 8	3.09 12
63.9 4	65.5 7	58.8 6	62.8 5	3.00 14	2.94 12	3.10 14	2.96 14	3.02 10	3.16 7	3.01 14
62.9 6	66.5 6	55.0 10	61.5 7	3.23 11	3.11 10	3.19 12	3.10 9	3.12 9	3.10 10	3.16 10
51.3 15	56.9 15	47.8 15	52.0 15	3.21 12	3.29 7	3.33 7	3.06 10	2.99 12	2.99 13	3.19 9
59.9 9	64.6 9	55.1 9	59.9 9	13	2.94 12	3.14 13	3.05 11	3.00 11	3.13 8	3.06 13
56.8 12	57.8 13	48.2 13	54.3 13	3.43 6	3.21 8	3.24 11	3.12 8	3.13 8	3.02 12	3.23 7
54.4 14	57.3 14	48.1 14	53.3 14	3.25 10	3.03 11	3.28 10	3.05 11	2.95 14	2.87 15	3.11 11
56.8 12	60.9 12	55.2 8	57.6 11	2.88 15	2.88 15	2.85 15	2.93 15	2.90 15	2.94 14	2.89 15

| Math | | | | Writing | | | | | | |
Problem solving	Commo	Reasoning	Math power	Idea/content	Organization	Voice	Word choice	Sentence fluency	Convention	Composite
80	80	80	80	3.7	3.7	3.7	3.7	3.7	3.7	3.7
47.49	60.52	41.42	49.81	3.45	3.28	3.49	3.20	3.27	3.32	3.35
57.4 1	70.8 3	47.9 3	58.7 2	4.17 1	4.00 2	4.04 3	3.83 1	3.75 3	3.83 2	3.99 2
48.3 8	63.9 9	44.6 8	52.3 7	3.66 5	3.56 5	3.58 7	3.57 4	3.42 7	3.76 4	3.60 5
46.4 11	64.6 7	45.1 5	52.0 9	3.89 4	3.81 4	4.22 2	3.56 5	3.61 4	3.86 1	3.83 4
50.8 5	62.5 10	42.9 9	52.1 8	4.12 3	4.04 1	4.43 1	3.68 3	3.78 2	3.81 3	4.03 1
55.3 2	73.6 1	51.6 1	60.2 1	3.60 6	3.44 7	3.72 5	3.33 8	3.29 9	3.20 10	3.48 7
52.5 3	72.8 2	50.8 2	58.7 2	3.26 12	3.44 7	3.20 14	3.30 9	3.44 6	3.72 5	3.36 9
51.8 4	65.2 5	45.0 6	54.0 5	3.54 8	3.41 9	3.55 8	3.36 7	3.39 8	3.50 7	3.46 8
50.2 6	67.5 4	44.8 7	54.2 4	3.41 9	3.30 10	3.51 9	3.16 10	3.29 9	3.28 9	3.34 10
44.8 14	49.8 14	39.4 12	44.7 15	4.17 1	4.00 2	3.89 4	3.77 2	3.81 1	3.66 6	3.94 3
45.0 13	64.7 6	40.9 11	50.2 10	3.57 7	3.47 6	3.63 6	3.43 6	3.51 5	3.16 11	3.49 6
49.3 7	64.4 8	45.5 4	53.1 6	3.21 14	3.10 14	3.38 11	2.99 14	3.15 11	3.45 8	3.19 12
46.1 12	58.8 11	41.4 10	48.8 11	3.22 13	3.11 13	3.25 13	3.02 13	3.05 13	2.95 13	3.13 14
46.6 10	56.3 12	38.7 13	47.2 12	3.36 10	3.25 11	3.32 12	3.11 11	3.10 12	3.00 12	3.23 11
44.1 15	47.4 15	35.6 15	45.0 14	3.29 11	3.12 12	3.46 10	3.04 12	2.98 14	2.87 14	3.17 13
47.0 9	52.6 13	37.9 14	45.9 13	2.79 15	2.73 15	3.02 15	2.84 15	2.78 15	2.87 14	2.83 15

| Math | | | | Writing | | | | | | |
Problem solving	Commo	Reasoning	Math power	Idea/content	Organization	Voice	Word choice	Sentence fluency	Convention	Composite
80	80	80	80	3.7	3.7	3.7	3.7	3.7	3.7	3.7
35.09	48.57	36.30	39.97	3.46	3.33	3.55	3.30	3.40	3.35	3.40
41.7 3	60.9 1	39.4 2	47.3 2	3.85 3	3.74 4	4.24 2	3.77 2	3.86 1	4.06 1	3.89 2
42.4 2	57.1 2	46.4 1	48.6 1	3.84 4	3.69 5	4.21 3	3.66 3	3.52 7	3.43 7	3.77 4
42.7 1	51.2 3	38.5 5	44.1 3	3.66 7	3.61 8	3.83 5	3.54 7	3.58 4	3.37 8	3.62 7
33.8 7	50.3 5	33.3 9	39.1 7	3.72 5	3.63 6	3.71 7	3.57 5	3.61 3	3.67 3	3.66 6
34.4 6	48.3 8	38.9 4	40.6 5	3.69 6	3.79 3	3.73 6	3.60 4	3.49 8	3.49 6	3.67 5
38.9 4	50.6 4	39.2 3	42.9 4	3.41 11	3.21 12	3.37 14	3.14 12	3.15 10	3.53 5	3.29 11
27.1 15	43.7 13	33.1 10	34.5 12	4.04 2	4.00 1	3.89 4	3.53 8	3.76 2	3.86 2	3.88 3
32.5 11	46.3 9	35.0 7	37.9 9	3.61 8	3.63 6	3.70 8	3.55 6	3.57 5	3.59 4	3.61 8
33.4 9	46.0 10	32.8 12	37.4 10	3.37 12	3.27 11	3.29 15	3.18 11	3.09 14	3.10 11	3.25 13
32.7 10	50.1 6	35.9 6	39.6 6	3.48 10	3.28 10	3.68 9	3.07 13	3.13 12	3.02 13	3.33 10
36.1 5	49.0 7	32.4 13	39.1 7	3.54 9	3.31 9	3.42 12	3.28 9	3.13 12	3.22 9	3.36 9
27.8 14	39.2 15	30.1 15	32.4 15	4.15 1	3.92 2	4.37 1	3.90 1	3.55 6	3.11 10	3.95 1
33.6 8	45.7 11	33.1 10	37.4 10	3.23 14	3.08 15	3.42 12	3.06 14	3.04 15	2.91 15	3.15 15
28.4 13	40.9 14	31.9 14	33.7 14	3.30 13	3.20 13	3.57 11	3.20 10	3.18 9	2.97 14	3.26 12
32.1 12	44.5 12	34.9 8	37.2 12	3.21 15	3.14 14	3.64 10	2.95 15	3.14 11	3.06 12	3.20 14

Reversed numbers = below State average

Lightly shaded = at or above standard of excellence

1997–1998 Scores Averaged by District

poor kids who get to go to Ivy League schools, yet those are other parts of the argument. For the moment it is enough to say that the average kid is not more stupid in this generation than in previous generations. We could not have devolved that far in only two generations. The problem lies elsewhere than with the kids.

So the question is: Why can't the educational system that promises to 'level the playing field' by giving everyone the same benefits that rich kids enjoy, teach perfectly ordinary kids enough to know that the Earth takes a year to go around the sun once? Since we have been hearing the equity arguments for many years now, and funding nearly every Progressive program asked of us, why is it that average kids now seem so terribly ignorant, rather than being 'richly' competent?

Let us leave the Nature–Nurture argument for the moment and grant the assumptions about Nurture. If we do, we can examine the schools whose pupils are primarily the children of highly educated, well-paid professionals living in upscale suburban neighborhoods. These are the families who can afford to have computers in the home and can also afford to pay for school facility upgrades with bond issues, pay for music lessons and sports camps and trips to museums, etc., and perhaps pay private tutors to escape the systemic dumbing-down effect seen everywhere.[44] While not a 'pure' upscale district, School District Twelve may be the best candidate within this metropolitan area for such a designation. However, in the 1995–1996 data, the best elementary school in SD Twelve (Twelve-E2—ranked #11) shows below State-average scores in all of the writing categories and the high school, Twelve-H, reported below State-average scores in all the math and reading categories and in one writing category. In fact, Elementary school Twelve-E2 ranked number one overall the next year, but their raw scores were lower than the year they ranked #11. So much for pure Nurture. (For a very good discussion of the silliness of the worst of the Nature–Nurture debate given from the genetic point of view, see *The Agile Gene: How Nature Turns on Nurture* by Matt Ridley (2003).)

When we attempt the same evaluation of the 1995–1996 Middle and Junior High Schools, we find that two schools achieved scores that

---

44 This is why I included the demographic rankings in the final ranks. These items may seem politically incorrect to include, but since it is the politically correct who continually remind us that correlations with these items are important, I figured that anything that helps me find a 'good' school for my kids is OK with me.

are above the State average on all measures. These schools were ranked #1 and #4. The schools that ranked #2 and #3 fell short on at least one measure, as do all of the rest of the schools. Notice that the Middle school rated #1 overall ranked #1 on 10 of the 15 measures. How did they manage it? Also, how did they manage an average score that is higher than the State's 'Standards of Excellence' on all of the Writing measures? Let us leave this surprising achievement for a discussion of grading 'rubrics', but in all fairness, achieving relative excellence on these measures should be easy, by just insisting that the kids write often and by grading their efforts using genuinely high standards. The same applies for learning basic arithmetic. This astonishing philosophic construct (if we teach things, kids will learn things) is predicated on the ancient observation that if we practice, we get better. In other words: Only those who have been taught to do simple things well will ever acquire the ability to do difficult things easily.

Why have we forgotten this simple truth? If kids are asked to 1) read something, 2) think about what they read, 3) commit their thoughts to paper in essay questions, short essays, book reports, etc., in virtually all of their classes (not just English), and 4) have the essays graded for content, grammar, spelling, syntax, etc., should we be surprised that the kids might become competent writers and analyzers of written ideas? It is surprising to the Progressives, because they recommend that we not ask kids to do these things. 'Too confining', they say. Teaching rules of grammar, etc., 'limits their creativity', they tell us.

Also, teaching rules of any sort implies that we must pick a set of rules to teach. We are all supposedly confused about whose rules to teach, since American kids come from so many cultures. Apparently following the rules of standard English while facilitating 'language skills' means that we are not trying to teach language at all. We are really trying to enslave other-than-dominant-culture kids[45] to maintain the scholastic superiority of white kids. Why then do Asian kids consistently beat white kids on scholastic measures on average, and why can children across the world learn English, in addition to their native languages? Oops. Oh well. But then inconsistencies never seem to bother the Progressive rhetoriticians. I do not know about you, but being limited to the 'F word' as all parts of speech and saying, "I was, like, ________" (fill in the blank), ". . . You know," and "Like, Duh," as the main weapons in

---

45 Called such despite the fact that many of them have been Americans for many generations.

an arsenal of potential explanatory devices does not sound remarkably creative to me.

Yuh Should Dance wit' dah One What Brung Yuh

If there is a question about whose rules to teach and follow, it seems to me that Western Civilization may be a good choice. If Western Civilization was not the leader in the development of modernity, and in looking for new ideas wherever they could be found, and in the systematic development and promotion of social equality, we would not be having this pointless ongoing argument. After all, immersion in the American Melting Pot has done more for the acceptance of diversity than any other system yet created. Many cultures contributed to America, but none so much as 'the West'. Also, with its scientific tradition going at least as far back as Aristotle, the West has done much of the basic research and development of the ideas, technologies, and institutions that are the basis of American dominance and culture. If that ever changes, as many insist it is changing, it will be because we forgot how to think, thanks to slovenly instruction and Progressive, downwardly redefined academic standards.

I should comment on the 'Standards of Excellence' at this point (shown lightly shaded) at this point. These scores are apparently set arbitrarily by the State, as an objective goal for individual pupils to shoot for. Perhaps they are statistically set at, or close to, the 1st standard deviation above the mean of all scores, but I doubt it. In any case, since the Standards of Excellence are intended as an incentive goal for each individual pupil, we would not expect whole schools to beat those levels on average. In fact, it would be remarkable if a school could achieve these levels as an average.

Yet, look at the scores deemed excellent. Does an individual math score of 80 percent sound excellent to you? How about 75 percent, which is the level of excellence set for grammar schools? What can we say about a State's educational standards if they accept 80 percent as excellent? I have to use my own experiences as my guide, of course, and I recall some of my friends achieving very high 90s as their four-year high school math averages, under the standards in place before the Progressive revolution started in the mid 1960s. 'Those' were excellent results. I can assure you that those of us who floundered in the 80 percent to low 90 percent range did not consider ourselves to be 'excellent' math pupils at all.

Yet, even if the 'Standards of Excellence' are meant to pertain to a whole-school average, rather than as individual goals, these still seem low. In my experience, this was approximately the level that the average kid attained in the early 1960s. This 'average' was expected, and routinely achieved, not deemed extraordinary.

Here is an indication of the problem. On October 4, 2000, a local newspaper reported that a high school in the state was considering tightening the graduation requirements in math.[45a] Currently they require only two years of what passes for 'math,' for graduation. [The school from which I graduated required three years and most kids took four.][46] An Assistant Principal (with an education doctorate to his name) was interviewed for the article. He was against raising the standards because, "Some of these ('borderline') students are struggling and if they are required to take a third year they could struggle even more. They may not be interested in going on to a Regents school." Translation: "Poor Babies. We cannot ask kids to learn anything beyond simple arithmetic, even if they will need the knowledge to survive in college and beyond. If we do, the ones who would rather be bartenders, secretaries, construction workers, and flight attendants might not want to go to college."

Given their results, the average kid in the district is not likely to qualify for college now (the 1997–1998 math Power score was 39.1 percent [below the State average]). An average score below 40 percent suggests that the classes they teach are not up to snuff as it is. A score below 40 percent suggests that we are teaching our 10th graders at roughly the 5th-grade level. Yet, requiring only two years of 'math', that may be presented as little more than simple arithmetic games, is considered enough to prepare kids for college, and for adult life, because the kids might not like more.

Another method of reporting pupil achievement that is gaining popularity is converting all scores to a 'percentile ranking'. This method is not reported in the data that I reproduced, but I include this short discussion because your school may try to pull the wool over your eyes using this technique, so you should be aware of it. My children's school does report their standardized scores to parents using this technique.

45a Reprinted by permission of the *Topeka Capital-Journal*.
46 We took four years of math because we had not dropped out.

What 'percentile ranking' means is that the grade earned by an individual pupil is compared with the other pupils in a relative manner, rather than as a percentage of questions answered correctly. The question asked in developing a percentile rank is, "Is this score higher or lower than the other scores earned?" For instance, assume there are 100 pupils in your kid's grade-level and your kid earned the 10th best score. This would mean that there were 9 scores that were higher than hers, and 90 scores that were lower. Her score would therefore be higher than 90 percent of the other scores and would then be reported as 'at' the 90th percentile.

Superficially, this sounds as if it would be acceptable to traditional-minded teachers and parents since it compares kids in terms of achievement. The problem with it, however, is that it has no reference whatever to the subject tested, but merely distributes kids along a relative grade-continuum. In a district where the average pupil scores less than 40 percent on exams, a 90th percentile ranking cannot be equated with answering 90 percent of the questions correctly.

Just as with the 'percentage' grades that concern us in this section, educationists rejoice, and encourage parents to rejoice, when a pupil scores 'in the upper half'. Yet just as with the other scores we are discussing, scoring in the upper half, or at the 90th percentile for that matter, is less than impressive if the average learning of ninth graders, for example, is at the fourth grade level. How happy should you be with your kid's achievement, even if he has a high percentile ranking, if the best score in your ninth grader's class is a dismal 55 percent correct, for instance, even when taught at a sixth or seventh grade level, or lower.

Yet another common score-reporting method used to fool parents is the 'grade equivalent' method. This is sold to parents as describing the relative grade level at which a kid is achieving. In other words, if your 3rd grader gets a grade equivalent of 4.2 on an exam, parents are told that their kid knows as much as a fourth grader in the second month of school. Of course no test of 3rd grade-level knowledge can actually determine such a thing. Telling us that a test can determine that our kids 'know" answers to questions that will not be asked until some time in the future, seems questionable at best. The grade-equivalent measure is nothing more than a variation of the percentile ranking method, and is saddled with the same problems. The grade-equivalent score is determined by some arbitrary conversion factor applied to the percentile rank. So, a '4.2 grade equivalent' on a 3rd grade test may mean merely that the pupil tested at the 80th percentile on that test. Furthermore, if the basic '3rd grade' test measured understanding of 1st grade-level instruction, a 4.2 grade-equivalent score loses even more of its luster.

Other technical problems with standardized test score–reporting techniques exist because school systems that deliberately limit the teaching of subject matter content, are being asked to administer the very tests that would prove their incompetence. Yet, we will not delve into that morass now. We will, however, touch on it when we discuss the significant differences between objective testing and Progressive 'authentic assessments' in Chapter 7.

The Report Card data showed no elementary or high schools in this area that surpassed all of the State averages. Is this a bad thing? Could it be that the State is so educationally outstanding that the State averages are virtually insurmountable? Apart from what we just said about the States' standards of excellence, and what we will shortly say about national achievement, that question does not make sense if we understand the meaning of 'an average'.

So, we are back to the everyone-is-the-same-as-everybody-else argument. Yet, maybe this argument is right, and maybe we should not expect wide variations in academic achievement. Unfortunately for the prediction, we do have wide variations. Still, what about the averages themselves? How high are they? The most objective measures that we have to work with are, of course, the math scores. Though some of us may act as if it is not so, two plus two still equals four in standard, base-10 arithmetic.

Look at the State Average Math 'Power' score, which is an average of the other math scores. The State average is 43.9 percent[47] correct. *Forty*-three point nine percent. Out of one hundred. Is a State average almost 20 percent below 'F' and almost 40 percent below 'passing' ('C') acceptable to you? Remember this is an average. Roughly half of all the schools in the State score lower than this. Some score considerably lower. Some schools score so low on average that their average kid scored at, or just barely above, what they would have scored had they closed their eyes and marked-in answers randomly.

---

47 Forty-three point nine percent was the 1996 high school State average. In 1998 the average recorded was 39.97 percent.

What we have then, is that by the time of graduation, the average pupil in our public schools has learned only marginally better than someone who did not go to school at all and half of a school's pupils score lower than the school average. This is the result of the hanging-out, personally-relevant learning mentioned earlier. How much 'learning' should we think is done in these lowest-scoring schools and how much credit should our educational professionals take for that result?

By this time, you may believe me that my State's results are poor, but that these results do not apply to your own school, district, and State. If you do, you should know that my State is ranked above the National average on some measures by the U.S. Department of Education and other federal panels, such as the National Assessment Governing Board, and the National Educational Goals Panel that is " . . . charged with monitoring and speeding progress toward the eight National Education Goals." These groups produce such reports as the National Education Goals Report and the National Assessment of Education Progress (NAEP). These are some of the National results published in 1997 by the Goals report. See if you are pleased.

- The U.S. ranked number three in the world in fourth grade science achievement in 1995. Our eighth graders only managed a 17th place, however.
- In 1992 only 52 percent of American adults ranked above Level 3 (functionally literate) on the National Adult Literacy Survey.
- In 1991, 24 percent of 10th graders reported using illicit drugs. The National Goal was to reduce that to 0 percent by the year 2000. Yet by 1996, 40 percent of 10th graders reported using illicit drugs, an increase of 67 percent.
- In 1991, 10 percent of teachers reported that they were threatened with physical injury. Again, the goal was to reduce that to 0 percent by 2000, but in 1994 teachers reporting threats increased by 50 percent to 15 percent.
- In 1994, 17 percent of fourth graders, 14 percent of eighth graders and only 11 percent of twelfth graders met the Goals Panel's performance standard for history. That means, of course, that 83 percent of fourth graders were below the standard, and the percentage of failures increases the longer pupils stay in school.

- Only 12 percent of high school seniors managed to match the Panel's math standards in 1990. That percentage rose to 16 percent by 1996, but the goal was to have reached more than 60 percent of seniors by then.

The published report is almost 340 pages long, so I will not reproduce everything here. My point is that the results achieved in this State, and by my local schools, are not an anomaly.

"Oh, but these results are invalid anyway and should not be used," the educational professional might say. "All standardized tests must be 'renormed' before they can tell us anything."

Renorming is an idea that is dear to the hearts of those who think that whatever effort a kid is willing to give is OK, if the pupil feels good about himself. This is a subset of the 'relevance' and 'self-esteem' theories that we will discuss later. To accept this renorming idea, however, we must accept the Progressive notion that it is the teacher's responsibility, as stated by my education professors, to "... insure that *all* kids succeed." Notice that there is no provision for the kid's effort or capability in this statement. Note also that it is considered the teacher's responsibility to insure success despite the idea that kids should not be taught 'mere' facts, but must be allowed to discover them for themselves and develop their own reality.

'Success' is defined as getting passing grades. Get a passing grade, whether you earned it or not, and you are a success and can feel proud. Unfortunately, passing grades are the rule in many schools, whether they were earned or not, under the policy of 'social promotions', because 'getting left back' would make you feel bad about yourself. My Ed school classmates and I were told this remarkable idea (teachers must insure success) in so many words, by an education professor who also said that if we do not agree with him (i.e., if we expect kids to earn their grades), we should find another line of work, because we are "not suited to teaching." This professor, who in the year of my graduation, was given the College of Education Excellence in Graduate Teaching Award, is also considered the local expert in school law.

Do you find it strange that a man thought to be an expert at something, (i.e., has learned more about a subject that anyone else) can argue that learning is not necessary for others? As that hokey old aphorism tells us: The dictionary is the only place where we can find success before work.

The idea behind renorming assumes that since the original 'passing' grade (70 percent) was decided upon in New England in the seventeenth century, it is outdated and no longer valid. This ancient decision was undoubtedly based upon extended public [private] school practice in England reaching even further into antiquity. This is bad because, for some, being of 'Anglo' origin is, as if by definition, racist. The logic goes like this: Since school was mainly for rich white boys in colonial New England, the passing scores are unfair and should be changed to reflect the 'new' America.

Renorming might just take one of these abysmal State average scores mentioned above, and accept it as a passing grade, much as the SAT did in 2000,[48] or they might accept an even lower score as 'passing' since we want *all* kids to succeed, not just the upper half. Imagine graduating with a four-year high school academic average score of 30 percent or so. We do not have to imagine it. It is happening all over the country right now, and some of these pupils even get accepted to college.

The problem is, of course, obvious. The longtime standard 'passing grade' of 70 percent was not decided upon by reference to the kids and their self-perceived needs, whoever they might have been. The passing grade was a reflection of what was deemed the minimum level of *knowledge* the pupil had to master to have a fighting chance of understanding the material in the next unit, the next grade, college, or postsecondary occupation. If it is a knowledge-based occupation with requirements that cannot be taught by mere training (e.g., attach widget A to sprocket B and tighten to torque x), then to 'pass' (read, be hired) into that occupation, we must define the minimum knowledge required of those who would seek such employment. Since it is impossible to develop a test which can be given to *all* pupils, and which can specify precisely the entrance requirements of every potential occupation available now and in the future, some general standards are required. We must use the general standard, therefore, to determine which graduates have mastered the presented knowledge at a level that shows their capacity to understand the requirements of as many potential occupations as possible. When we do this (rate the achievement of all pupils), the reality of

---

48 The average SAT score had dropped to 424 by 1995 (on a scale of 200 to 800, or 37 percent of the total [224/600]). So this unacceptable low score was officially recorded as 500, an artificial rise of about 34 percent. My guess is that this fact is the basis of the U.S. DoE's announcement, in 2000, that our schools are as good now as they ever were, and sometimes even better.

life is that the higher our overall achievement, the more opportunities await us. (This is also why colleges use standardized college entrance exams.) High-school graduation requirements once reflected this idea too.

In effect, potential future employers (and colleges) want to limit the number of applicants to whom they must say, "If you have not yet learned at least 'this' much, you are not yet ready to learn what we teach. Sorry, we cannot accept you because you just won't 'get it'."

A high school curriculum tries, or should try, to determine what that minimal knowledge is, and then tries, or should try, to set its minimal standards to that level, or slightly higher. In this way, those who significantly surpass the minimum standards can be judged best qualified to advance to higher education or to 'high end' jobs. However, even those who do not qualify for higher, specialized education, are still better off, more fully educated, and better prepared for whatever job or occupation they subsequently undertake, than if they merely hung-out and played games for thirteen years. Since the various future knowledge-based occupations, as represented by the various colleges and departments in our universities and colleges, will not settle for those who have not demonstrated academic mastery beyond a minimal general level, they will set their own requirements for entry into their world. Seventy percent math scores are not enough, when applying to an engineering college, especially if the highest level of math class attended was 'pre-algebra'. Nor will a 70 percent English score, nor a 500 SAT 'verbal"[49] score likely be good enough if you plan to study Literature or Journalism. If mere high school passing grades and these low SAT scores are considered enough by a college to warrant acceptance, that college may not be worth attending. They may not be in the 'higher education' business at all.

Therefore, to prepare pupils for additional, beyond-the-minimum requirements, our schools must also teach at higher than minimal levels. In some cases, much higher. Hence, some form of academic ability-tracking must also be reinstated, but more on that later.

---

49 As of June 2002, the SAT calls this 'critical reading' instead of 'verbal'. Their explanation for what prompted the change sounds a bit like double-talk. In the question and answer section of their web site, accessed June 27, 2002, was this: "Critical reading, which the SAT I has emphasized since its last set of changes in 1994, involves a higher level of reading than simple comprehension. It is rather, the complicated process of acquiring meaning from text."

The new SAT has also dropped its use of analogies. That is a pity. Perhaps they could have used this one: Acquiring meaning from text: reading comprehension :: acquiring critical thinking skills : ??

For now let's see another example of what our modern educational system achieves. The University of Iowa administers and sells a series of tests nationwide known everywhere simply as the Iowa Tests. The 2004 results for 8th graders (based on tests given in October 2003) were lying about on the desk of a teacher that I subbed for one day.[50] Here are some of the national averages that Iowa reported [Note: "%C" is the Iowa abbreviation meaning "percent correct"]: 'Math estimation,' 46%C; 'Problem solving' (probably the flagship promise given by math educators), 51%C; 'Approaches and procedures,' 57%C; 'Data interpretation' (mostly reading simple bar graphs, etc.), 63%C; 'Read amounts,' 62%C. I suppose we should be pleased that 'Compare amounts' (?Does 2+8=5+5?) got a 70%C. It was the only passing grade that I saw. 'Relationships and trends' scored 59%C nationally. Even 'Compute with whole numbers,' 'taught' at least since the first grade, scored a dismal 55%C. 'Add or subtract fractions' scored 43%C but 'Multiplying' and 'Dividing fractions' each scored 35%C. Even placing decimal points was too much for our 8th graders. 'Adding and subtracting decimals' scored 56%C, 'Multiplying' scored 51%C, and 'Dividing' scored 39%C. Remember that calculators are used as critical components of an educator's manipulative arsenal.

Other subjects fared no better. 'History' scored at 49%C, the 'Geography' score was 44%C, and 'Economics' scored 49%C. There were others, but this is just too depressing to continue.

Among the reasons that our kids do so poorly might be all the open book and open notes tests they take. With no reason to memorize anything, they don't take the time to learn much and, therefore, don't take the time to think about what they should have learned. No thinking leaves them with little understanding. As a result, even our sub-minimal Progressive standards are too much for our educators to achieve, yet they continue to give each other awards for 'teaching excellence'.

The nation also has a stake in instructing its citizens to some minimal level. If we allow millions of citizens to be ignorant of facts such as upon which continent our nation can be found, or how many feet there are in a yard, how much confidence can we have that their votes on complex social and political issues are well-considered? The higher-level thinking skills that Progressive education promises are impossible

---

50 You can probably get these results by going to http://www.education.uiowa.edu, though the link to those standards was nonfunctional when I tried.

under conditions of profound ignorance, unless our definition of higher-level thinking is little more than an adherence to ideological pronouncements.

While the level of acquired knowledge required for competent citizenship is more general than that which the specialized occupations will require, it may or may not be higher. Nevertheless, whatever the specifics, whether for adulthood, citizenship, or a specialty occupation, they are much higher than our schools provide today.

The ultimate objective of any school is to graduate their pupils into a world that expects a certain level of competence of them. It is that level of academic or literate competence that the minimum passing grade is set to measure, not a pupil's ancestry. [The civilized world also expects a measure of moral and ethical competence, but that is another, though related, story.] To develop literacy and academic competence, we must teach enough stuff to complete the basic job no later than the end of the 10th grade. This date, tied to our child labor laws, was set long ago to account for those pupils who need to start earning a living early. For those kids who are not going to college and do not have emergency reasons for dropping out, the last two years of high school can be thought of as a final transition to full, independent citizenship. The last two years of high school for college-bound pupils are a sort of enrichment phase that continues to prepare them for the rigors of college work. Therefore, the curriculum for college-bound pupils should begin to mimic the sorts of expectations that colleges once required.

To accomplish these different requirements, we must push *all* our pupils so that their learning matches the knowledge dispensed. We must do this so that they get to the finish line just when their teachers run out of breath. This academic 'pushing' is required because to be considered competent to stand democratic adulthood, the knowledge each of our citizens requires is more than many kids can easily, or willingly, digest (i.e., given the choice, most kids would not choose to work that hard nor to study those subjects). The pushing is also instrumental in developing the moral competence adults need, by teaching perseverance, the value of hard work, and honesty. Progressive prescriptions, readjusting the pace of knowledge dispersal so that no one is taught any more than anyone else, and grading 'equitably' (i.e., dumbing-down), would require several more years of schooling before a kid could be considered competent for adult responsibilities. Under this proposal, a college degree would be the equivalent of a barely passing 10th grade education, as taught at a 5th grade level.

We have another problem with our rich-white-boy-passing-grade idea, but we must read between the lines to catch it. Everybody is exactly like everybody else, but the passing grade set specifically for rich white guys (RWGs) is racist and unfair to nonwhites and females. How can that be? Even if it were true that RWGs invariably do better than all others, why is the passing level racist? This assumption says that no one is capable of achieving at the level of the target audience. More than that, it says that no one other than RWGs could pass a standard test, even if those others are sitting in the same class and listening to the same lesson. This assumption is not true of course and does not account for those pesky Asians, many females, the hordes of nonwhite guys (rich or otherwise) who do measure up. Nor does it account for the many RWGs who are academic dolts, but we have to follow the logic as it is presented.

Is the accusation of racism a tacit acknowledgment that no minority kid or any girl, etc., could possibly achieve at the level required for minimal success? With friends who think this of so many of our citizens, is it any wonder that education for *all* kids is so poor? Slippery slopes win when we stop moving uphill. Slippery slopes are especially slick when we grease the hands and feet of the climbers. In our case, Progressive educationists, and their buddies, have even decided that the act of moving uphill is somehow evil (honor mediocrity, not merit; competition is bad), so they redefine sliding down the slope as social progress. Where do you suppose we will end with leadership like that?

The stated reason that the traditional passing standard of 70 percent is considered unfair is because the rich guys tried to keep 'secret' knowledge and teaching techniques away from everyone else, so that they could keep power for themselves, then raised the bar so high that only they could learn enough to pass.

Let us assume for the moment that this idea is true and we have just discovered the conspiracy, and have the power to correct the injustice. What would *you* do if you were faced with such an inequitable-distribution-of-knowledge dilemma? Would you immediately set out to teach everyone that the ones who were getting the knowledge are social vermin, and very little else? This is what is routinely recommended and is being done, to a greater or lesser degree, everywhere. We call this idea Multiculturalism (see Chapter 5). On the other hand, if we truly wanted to level the playing field for *all* pupils, wouldn't it make more sense to teach everyone the 'good stuff' that previously had been taught only to the lucky few? Of course it would, unless our political agenda were more important to us than the education of our kids.

The preceding may be the most maddening aspect of this whole strange controversy. Recall that publicly funded schools were created to help give all of our children access to the knowledge that expensive private schools gave their pupils. If there was ever an institution developed to promote equal opportunity, the public school was it. Yet, modern educational professionals are willing to 'improve', by subversion, the very institution designed to give everyone, including their own kids, access to the opportunity for success. That is a shame. To do it merely to make political points, is a tragedy. To do it while telling your constituency that it will lead to academic and social excellence, is political spin of the worst sort. The fact that the knowledge dispersal was sometimes less than perfect is a reason to widen the dispersal, not to assault learning itself. While Progressive theorists define 'educational opportunity' as funding their nonsensical programs, genuine educational opportunity means access to the same intellectually uplifting instruction that produces leaders of others. <u>No</u> instruction means no opportunity. Nevertheless, educationists are ready to destroy this genuinely democractic, playing-field-leveling system to maintain an ignorant, dependent constituency.[51]

I can see how the whole Progressive movement got started in the 1960s, but I do not understand how they can continue to advocate these ideas now, with so much evidence available that the ideas are damaging their own kids? We must admire their lemming-like dedication to their 'ideals,' but not their higher-level thinking skills.

Relevance Theory

A common idea used all over the nation to make learning more 'equitable', is to try to make learning easier by having kids relate what they think they should learn more closely to their own experience. The

---

51 As stated previously, 'political spin', as a label, is only a variation on a very ancient practice. Sophistry is attributed to the ancient Greeks and implies, as Webster defines it as, "a plausible but misleading or fallacious argument." What is it they say? The more things change, the more they stay the same.

idea is that a pupil can understand the things that are familiar more easily than those that are unfamiliar. Sounds right on the surface? What is wrong with this idea? What is wrong is at least two things.

The first thing wrong with the relevance idea is that one of the most important reasons for having a school is to expose kids to ideas to which they would not otherwise be exposed. School was once designed as a broadening and uplifting experience. In Chapter 7, however, we will see that today's educationists expect learning to be more "... in depth than in breadth." Yet, limiting learning to what naïve kids already know, or think they want to know, severely limits a kid's exposure to the perspectives and requirements of many potential future interests and careers, and, in any case, can hardly qualify as in-depth.

Additionally, limiting the scope of instruction to the kid's self-determined 'needs' defeats another of the most important purposes of school, which is transmission of our common culture. Of course 'multiculturalism' is here to fill the gap, isn't it? We will deal with that idea later because it is a different part of the peculiar patchwork of political ideas that Progressives have adopted to build a coalition, and is intended to fill a different, though related, need than 'relevance' theory.

The second thing wrong with the relevance idea is the way it is done. Relevance theory says that we should ask the kids what they think they would like to learn, since if they choose it they will have a greater stake in learning it. I am sure that what a six-year-old might have thought was relevant was not even considered by the colonial town elders who started our first schools, nor by school boards in traditional communities of yore. Nor was it considered relevant by the father of relevance theory, John Dewey. Here is what he wrote.[52]

> ... the gulf between the mature or adult products [lessons produced by genuine teachers] and the experience and abilities of the young is so wide that the very situation forbids much active participation by pupils in the development of what is taught.

Despite the self-confident pronouncements of modern kids and our educational professionals, the evident ignorance of modern kids, as shown by average school achievement, disqualifies even most high school seniors from a seat at curriculum planning sessions. Sensible

---

52 *Experience & Education*, p. 19.

adults know that kids have little notion of what might be required of them in the future. Kids only begin to understand what is expected of them by being taught by the adults, and by experience that is then interpreted by adults. Such was the thinking during the ancient, traditional times when kids actually asked advice of their parents. The idea was that until the kids became adults, it was the adults' (i.e., parents', etc.) responsibility to teach, and in so doing (and depending on what is being taught) show the kids the variations in behavior deemed acceptable and honorable by society. In this way we may teach not only reading, writing, and arithmetic, but transmit and extend our common culture, including the community standards of integrity, ethics, morality, and faith. When the kids become adults themselves, was considered soon enough to allow them adult choices. Of course, these sensible notions are now considered indications of racism and of the repression of creativity.

Do you remember the cute self-admonishment of the 1960s and early 1970s that said: "Don't trust anyone over 30"? This saying had some moment at the time because kids began to notice that as people approached 30 years of age, they would start to change their attitudes and their assumptions about life. It often took several years past legal adulthood, after experience molded the kid's natural idealism and previous learning into something like an adult's practical sensibility. The realities of earning a living (including the necessities of knowing things to qualify for particular jobs), raising kids of your own, paying taxes, mortgages, daycare, and the myriad of other limitations and hurdles that life places before us, begin to temper the idealism of youth.

Ironically, the "natural idealism" of youth is born of the ideas taught to them by adults. Kids were typically taught a variety of society's rules, such as the Golden Rule along with "Don't kill," "Don't steal," "Don't lie," etc. These rules are taught simply to very young children, without relativistic variations. Psychological developmentalists then discovered that kids learn these rules simply and expect everyone to abide by them absolutely. These absolute expectations of inexperienced children are the basis of youthful idealism. Eventually, as newly minted adults begin to realize that life is not quite as simple as they expected, they also begin to realize that 'the old man' might have been right about the reasons for the rules they previously found unfair. These unfair rules could include such simple rules as: Kids have a curfew imposed on them but adults may set their own curfew, and kids should not see certain movies that adults may. At the point that we begin to see the wisdom of differential rules, and when we choose to get some sleep rather than partying the night away, we begin to 'become' our parents and are no longer fully accepted in kid society. At that point, folks begin to understand that life will not, and cannot, be as sweet as the utopians would like. Hence the admonition. Policy decisions made from the perspective of the naïve kid (i.e., just make it fun and do not expect me to earn my keep) or even of the nominal but inexperienced adult (i.e., a college student away from home for the first time) produce the kind of system we have now.

So, how do we get kids who would rather play, to work hard enough to earn genuinely passing grades and prepare for adulthood? We force them to learn by requiring work and by presenting grades as a goal that everyone should strive to achieve. *Force* them? Use grades as a *goal*?? (The thump you just heard was educationists hitting the ground as they fainted dead away.) The answer is, of course, that if we ever want to approach the ideal of universal educational excellence, it is not possible to achieve it in any other way. Very few kids will find the 'arbitrary' rules of grammar or the lessons of what seems like dim and distant history relevant on their own. Try to remember yourself as a 2nd grader. Would you have asked to study more arithmetic if you were placed in a room with twenty kids your own age? Me neither.

Another thing to remember is that, done correctly, 'force', in the sense that most of us would hate, would be necessary in few cases and at few times. Even now we have national debates about such things as mandatory random drug testing, guns in the schools, character training, anger-management training, etc., and many people argue that the percentage of kids involved in the worst of our litany's offenses are few. They may be relatively few, but 40+ percent of 10th graders using illegal drugs even occasionally, and 15+ percent of teachers reporting physical threats, represents a very significant increase when compared with 50 years ago. Beyond that, there are still more kids who may not actually cross the line to illegal behavior, are encouraged to, and revel in, 'pressing the edge' of the acceptability envelope. This is so despite the fact, or perhaps because of the fact, that what is defined as acceptable behavior is now much looser than 50 years ago. Fifty years ago we were outraged by juvenile delinquents who might cruise down Main Street and roll cigarette packs in the sleeves of their T-shirts. Today we worry about random massacres perpetrated by children, children having children, and Middle school kids smoking 'crack' cocaine, rather than about kids passing notes in class.

Of course kids still pass notes to each other (when they don't merely shout their questions or comments across the room or just go to the classmate's desk whenever they choose, even during exams), but the character of at least some of those notes has changed. An example from my own experience is telling. Apparently a friend of a kid in a class I was teaching called the school office and dictated a pornographic message to whoever answered the phone. I know this happened because, astonishingly, the note was delivered.

Nevertheless, most pupils would accept a teacher's forceful efforts in the sense of what John Dewey called 'direction'. "Direction [Dewey writes] . . . suggests the fact that the active tendencies of those directed are led in a certain continuous course, instead of dispersing aimlessly," as we would expect under the leaderless child-centered facilitation that modern educationists favor. We know this because sensibly raised kids have always accepted direction, from parents and teachers. It is only since we embraced the dictates of unrestricted individual choice at all ages that kids have increased in anarchist tendencies, and been rewarded for doing so.

Naïve children have always questioned tradition. That is natural. They base their objections to traditional rules on an incomplete (childish) understanding of reality and on a dedication to their own convenience. Yet the fact that chronological adults are now forcefully challenging sensible rules, in the name of 'democracy', is a problem. That those adults then teach kids a modern common sense that says that anarchy is a good thing (redefined as democracy or personal freedom), is another problem our civilization must solve, or collapse.

Force, then, would correspond more exactly to what Dewey called "control (which is) . . . an energy brought to bear from without and meeting some resistance from the one controlled." In this sense force, or control, is the less favorable variation of what teacher's responsibilities require of them. Yet, because of the normal variations among human personalities, force can never be eliminated completely, even under the best of conditions. If we must fight our way back from the brink of educational disaster to something more closely approximating ideal conditions, you can be sure that whether we call it force or control or anything else, there will be some resistance from those controlled. We should, of course, expect more resistance from those who have been in our anarchic system the longest.

Ironically, today's kids would be morally right to resisting this redirection (relativistically speaking). This is so because they had been trained and led to believe that their ignorant and selfish way of doing things is OK. When we then tell them that they are not the whole universe, but only a small part of it and that they must work merely to achieve their rightful place in the universe, the kids will not understand why we are so anti-traditionalist and mean. If we can, however, reestablish a system that recognizes and honors adult responsibilities in directing our children's futures, we would eventually get back to something that looked more like most schools, and the society, of the early 1900s, both in pupil conduct and achievement, though expanded to wider swaths of our population than was possible then. We would not have to lose the hard-fought advances in racial equity, etc., of the past few decades to do it, either. Our neighbors would not allow that. Yet consider the alternative of not fighting to reestablish common decency as within the bounds of acceptable behavior. If we allow children's unrestrained selfishness to remain a fundamental part of our curricula, we might see an increase in corporate scandals of integrity and executive greed, not to mention television shows that celebrate debauchery and anonymous license. You say that has increasingly become a problem in recent years? Who'd a thunk it?

Does forcing pupils work? It certainly seems that it has in the past. Remember the number of Nobel prizes won by Americans, etc. It seems to have worked at least partly because most kids thrive on challenges and are always looking for ways to prove themselves. A simple example of this is the young kid who insists on putting on her own car seatbelt stating emphatically, "I will do it myself!" This is not an example of a kid 'choosing' to learn about standard seatbelt operations. It is an example of a kid who, having been told that seatbelts are necessary, wants to prove that she can do it as well as the adult. Therefore, 'forcing' must include attempts to motivate pupils to want to learn, to earn good grades, and does not merely imply setting up an academic salt mine, as the Progressives would have us believe. Force, or more precisely 'direction', also involves guiding pupils by successive approximations, from incorrect or flawed habits to systematically more perfect renditions of whatever is being taught. This is so whether the incorrect usage is in the pronunciation of words, shooting free throws, balancing chemical equations, or personal conduct. In this sense direction also requires the teacher to make encouraging noises at times when performance is less than excellent, and congratulatory noises when it is.

Either way, however, it is the instructed *practice* required of pupils that teaches and perfects performance. Just ask any coach—or any parent with sense. If we asked a coach, "Do you think you could bring your team to the championship without practicing?", the coach would probably drop his mouth open, stare at you for a few moments, then walk away shaking his head and wondering how anyone could have made it to their adult years and still ask questions such as that. Unfortunately, when we strip away all the erudite sounding folderol, that is precisely what Progressive facilitation recommends. It gets the results we would expect, too.

Additionally, forcing (directing) does <u>not</u> imply that the child's thoughts and needs are never considered. Common sense and traditonal good teaching practice always consider the kid and her inexperienced confusion. Inexperienced confusion is what we pay teachers to help dispel, with explanations, examples, and forced practice. So the horrific disciplinary scenarios expected by Progressive rhetoriticians do not arise. If particular horror stories are exposed in individual classes, we should have no hesitation in reprimanding, or dismissing, the teacher(s) responsible.

More formal treatments balancing kids' expectations with teachers' requirements can be found in the literature. For instance, William Damon (1995) calls the commonsense balance between the permissive-at-all-costs and the authoritarian teaching styles *authoritative*. Mortimer Adler also reminds us that 'authority' is rightly considered the voice of reason, not the forceful imposition of alien might. This implies that while there is a balance required between kids' wants and society's needs, that the balance sensibly tends toward what adult life will require of kids. It also implies that the teacher has been hired because she knows things that the pupils do not, and is, as far as the kids are concerned, an authority in those things. The teacher's job is to pass on that knowledge, not merely hope that the kids might choose to glance at it occasionally.

This is as it should be. Kids are important. In fact kids are why we have teachers in the first place. What we expect teachers to do is to help us guide the kids toward adulthood. We need these genuine educational specialists because life is no longer such that average parents can adequately prepare their kids themselves. No longer can a child be taught all he needs to know while on a routine hunting trip or while watching the fine points of cultivating the ground with a digging stick.

At this point Progressive educationists would probably tell us that they know, and have recommended for years, that parents should be more involved in their kids' educations, including the teaching of technical subject matter. While this sentiment is superficially true, just consider the dynamics of their version of this exchange. The way this works is that teachers send homework home for the parents, under a heading such as, 'Things to do with your children'. These things are almost certainly some sort of 'activity' such as exercising, going to the museum, etc., and are presented as if it is they, the teachers, who need our help in training our kids, rather than the other way around. This turnaround is made worse since, other than the obvious examples of reading with the kids, the recommendations sent home are usually variations on the activities-facilitation techniques that do not work in school. This is true even though the activities may be good things in and of themselves, such as going to a museum. For example, my daughter's 6th grade class took a trip to the city zoo. Unfortunately, the instructional content of this trip consisted of a teacher reading the names of the animals from the placards posted in front of the cages, and apparently little else. This was a social outing, not an educational experience. Incidentally, the placard reader had proudly announced, when we first met, that she had 'gifted experience'. She knows how to get the best out of kids.

If teaching consisted of little beyond asking kids how they feel about things, and doing unscramble-the-letters and word-search games (as is currently the norm), parents potentially *could* do that. (You *do* believe that unscrambling 'nmaail" into "animal" is a significant biology skill, don't you?) It is unreasonable, however, to expect parents to teach chemistry, world history, world literature, trigonometry, and all the rest. Do you consider yourself qualified to teach your kids these things, after supper? If you do, you are certainly not among the millions of modern American parents who never read any books at all. Yet, whoever you are, you are expected to do the actual instruction of your kids, because the 'educators' are too busy facilitating superficial activities to bother, and because many don't know the subjects they are hired to teach.

After a full day on the job (maybe two jobs) a parent does not have the time or the facilities necessary to research, prepare, and deliver lessons, test and grade his kids on all the 'core' subjects, much less the extracurricular things, for twelve years or more. Doing this is impossible for the working parent with only one kid in the 1st grade. How much more so is it if you have several of them, all in different grades? Add to this fact that many modern, Progressively educated parents are now among the group that does not know the definition of a year or think that Babylon is a luncheon meat, and the need for genuine teachers becomes obvious.

Incidentally, have you ever wondered whether our modern emphasis on 'skills' has anything to do with the reduction in learning we have seen in recent decades? Modern schools do not speak about 'acquiring knowledge' anymore. It is all 'math skills' and 'language skills' and 'higher-level thinking skills'. To hear our educational professionals speak, you would think that getting an education is all about learning certain simple tricks, which will then propel us to the Ivy League and beyond. Based on their results, thinking that the educationists may have strayed from reality just a bit, might not be too far-fetched. Maybe learning to think requires practice in thinking, and a wide variety of subjects to think about, not mere sleight-of-mind tricks.

Ironically, there was a time early in the modern education wars, and in particular in relation to the phonics–whole language debate, when traditionalists railed against Progressive techniques by saying that learning was waning in American schools because the Progressives did not teach the simple skills (such as adding and decoding the letter symbols to their language-specific sounds), but instead let kids flounder without specific instruction (we will argue the same things). To confuse the arguments, however, Progressive educators then started to say that their techniques do teach skills, all sorts of skills. Unfortuantely, the techniques did not change, and the poor results did not improve. Only the rhetoric changed, because parents wanted their kids to learn. The word 'skills' had been appropriated, because complaints could be deflected when people were told what they wanted to hear. Other examples of the rhetorical spin-cycle include appropriating many words, including 'academically challenging', 'high standards', 'critical thinking', 'we must use what works', 'morality', even 'at risk', and others, while never deviating from the techniques whose results prompted the complaints in the first place.

To continue with a homey, feeling-focused at-home curriculum, however, all that parents might need to do would be to read the newspaper and canvass everyone's feelings regarding the issues of the day around the supper table. Of course, kids, and parents too, would still need to know the details of the topics to which the paper was referring. Facts are important for any competent discussion of the economy, space exploration, crime, politics, third-world agriculture, national holidays, the environment, nuclear devices, religion, or the thousands of other topics whose surfaces are scratched by newspapers and the electronic media today.

In any case, for force, or social direction à la John Dewey, to be effective we have to begin instruction during the kid's earliest days, so that the force used is gentle and routine and is therefore quickly rendered non-emotional most of the time. It also helps if it is consistent, with similar polite, respectful, and directed behavior expected at home, at school, and on the streets.

As for helping (forcing) kids to learn, however, an example might be that if a kid expects to have to write regularly in class (or at home at night), then he writes. At first, he might just be doing it to get the ordeal over quicker, but he does write, and learns something in spite of himself. As he writes, and as he systematically uses more complex ideas in his writing, he also learns to become more creative in the use of ideas. It may be surprising to some, but teaching and grading the old-fashioned way achieves the most modern, Progressive goal of individual creativity much more easily than the way educationists try to do it. Trying to achieve higher-level thinking skills from a base of profound ignorance, is decidedly unrealistic.

Starting now to reorganize curricula is essential if we are to save at least some of our kids, but it will cause a considerable commotion at first. Kids may not like it (especially those who are close to exiting the system and have never been expected to think). As stated earlier, making fundamental changes in the way that things are done, and especially in such things as the depth of understanding that would now be required and the amount of homework assigned, would cause 'moral' outrage until the new reality became fully established. I see this outrage in microcosm frequently even now. As a substitute teacher I am considered to be a strict teacher, expecting attention and punishing disruptions by referring them to the office. Some might say that sending kids to the office for being a kid (i.e., carefree and full of life) is cruel and unusual punishment, but my feeling is that there is a time and a place for everything. The classroom is not intended as a playground, but rather as a place to dispense knowledge. That purpose is seriously compromised with continual disruptions, but I can understand the kids' point of view. After all, I was a kid once too.

However, despite being normally restless and often bored as a school kid, I can remember nothing like the resistance to authority and the refusal to cooperate I see routinely in the modern child-centered environment. It is clear that some of the teachers for whom I substitute have no control whatever, and have apparently given up trying to control their kids. This is evident by the fact that the kids in these classes know almost nothing[53] and use their class time merely for socializing. Nor is this merely the kids in 'substitute teacher mode', since 'regular' teachers have told me that they have identical problems.

Nevertheless, adults who mistakenly equate traditional teaching with repression would also howl. I recall a conversation with a high school principal who proudly proclaimed that 'almost nobody' assigns homework anymore and that this is a good thing, proven by the fact that his college-bound kids averaged a 23 on the most recent ACT. To put this into perspective, you should know that once upon a time, it was generally accepted that to demonstrate readiness for college-level work at a college of decent standards, a pupil had to score at least a 26 or 27 out of 36 on the ACT. I'm not sure whether ACT scores can be equated to percentage scores, but a 23 out of 36 equates to about 64 percent (D), while a 26 works out to 72 percent (C minus). Therefore, a school's college-bound population should average 30 (83 percent; B minus) or higher. Of course, this principal was also proud of the fact that 80 percent of his graduates went to college and that almost 50 percent of those actually graduated. He also denied that he had unusual discipline problems in his school (he was right about that; behavior in his school was routinely disgraceful), and suggested that if I didn't like it there, I didn't have to work there. Within two or three weeks I received a letter from an assistant superintendent saying that my services would no longer be necessary.

On the other hand, I have been surprised at who gave thanks for my efforts. When I finished my student-teaching stint, and was about to depart for the last time, one of the kids, who was on Ritalin, told me that she would miss me because I was the only teacher who genuinely "tried to get me to learn anything." I have also received surreptitious thanks from a few kids after attempts to keep a classroom's normal state

---

53 I have met many high school aged kids who simply cannot add without a calculator, cannot spell or even read grammar school–level books fluently, and who stare blankly when asked to answer questions about what they have just read.

of chaos to a dull roar. There are kids in the schools who want to learn and who find it difficult to concentrate under the unrelenting disruptions allowed by Progressive educators, and by those teachers who have given up trying to maintain civility and courtesy.

Happily, the worst of these classrooms are fairly rare, though the rest cannot be described as anything like ideal, but even one is too many. Nevertheless, even taking into account that the way kids act with a substitute teacher is worse that with the full-time teacher (like I said, I was a kid once too), a 'normal' classroom features continual disruptions. Many classes allow kids to get out of their chairs to converse at will, extended public address announcements, and even automatically programmed television transmissions, may be made during normal class time rather than during homeroom periods, messengers from the office or from other teachers come into classrooms to deliver messages directly to pupils with no acknowledgment that a teacher is there. Naturally, those messengers don't hesitate to have extended conversations with other kids, too. Ask one kid a question and half a dozen may answer, then feel put-upon when told to be quiet. Many kids find it difficult to restrain themselves from commenting about anything at any time and many of those comments are designed to be rude or insulting in order to elicit laughter, etc. Kids leave to visit lockers or toilets almost at will and stay out for extended periods, kids frequently take several minutes to 'settle down' at the start of classes and begin to pack up several minutes before the bell, wasting perhaps 20 to 25 percent of scheduled class time daily. Some of the schools I work in can only be described as 'zoos', and the educators smile benignly, thinking that anarchy fosters creativity.

This talk of 'forcing' has probably brought forth another idea for some. Would forcing sometimes require paddling, or other corporal punishment? It's up to you: "You pays you' money. You takes you' choice." Which is better, an occasional sore butt or a national debate about whether to treat our Progressive epidemic of youthful unrepentant killers, abusers, and date rapists (of both sexes) as adults? Which is better, enforcing the community standard of decency or wringing our hands over what to do because our children are having children and those children are born already addicted to drugs? Which is better, teaching self-control and social expectations or filling our children with psychoactive drugs? Which is better, expecting our kids to exhibit common courtesy, or being afraid to take a walk in the neighborhood even in the daytime? Which is better, having a kid get to college ready for college, or wasting time with remedial classes while in college?

It is just possible that some corporal punishment may not be such a bad thing. Ideally, parents would routinely be responsible for this chore, of course. It should also be no surprise that kids, whose parents take this responsibility seriously, and do it responsibly, are rarely a problem at school, and are rarely prescribed behavioral medications.

On the other hand we must be cognizant that this is the age of personal rights. Kids have a right not to be made self-conscious in front of their peers, don't they? Maybe. But who says so? The kids? Is it the adult's responsibility to eliminate all embarrassing situations from the kid's experience, or the kid's responsibility to do what it takes to avoid them? Maybe a little potential embarrassment would act as a deterrent for modern kids, as it did in days of old. Maybe knowing that inappropriate behavior will likely cause embarrassment, or a sore butt, would induce kids not to engage in that behavior ('Don't do the crime if you can't do the time,' or, as Poor Richard reminds us, " 'Tis easier to prevent bad habits than to break them.") Maybe early practice in controlling themselves in the small, childish things would help kids to develop lifelong self-control? Maybe if they did, we would not be having our society-is-falling-apart debates.

Are individual rights that much more important than living peacefully with your neighbors? Individual rights are important. In fact they are essential, but so are societal responsibilities. Not so much society's responsibility to individuals, as the individual's responsibility to society, to their families, and to themselves. "Ask *not* what your country can do for you! . . ." Remember?

There is no question that both rights and responsibilities are essential, but they are currently badly out of balance. What happened to the idea that we must earn the respect of others at least partly by showing respect to others, rather than by merely demanding it, as a gang member might do? Not coincidentally, gangs have been a problem again recently, too. Under our current system kids no longer have to develop their own self-esteem by doing things for which they can be individually proud. Today we are told that someone in authority is responsible for dispensing self-esteem, like kibble to performing dogs. However, the fact that unrelenting praise is harmful to self-esteem had been known for a very long time. As William Shakespeare put it in *Sonnet LXXXIV*, lines 13–15 (*circa* 1595):

You to your beauteous blessings add a curse,
Being fond on praise, which makes your praises worse.
[Translation: When you do nothing but praise, your praise means less than nothing.]

Not all that long ago we had a grade for 'conduct' on our Report Cards. Good conduct was expected, and was common, not considered a medical emergency or a matter of personal choice. Now the balance between rights and responsibilities has been thrown out of whack, and the results are exactly the opposite to what we say that we want.

One other part to this puzzle, and a reason that the debate on this 'paddling' issue is so irresponsible and unproductive, is that the 'socially compassionate' side seems to see everything in extremes. I will point out other examples of this along the way, but if we even hint that we might on occasion support the idea of negative reinforcement, we are almost immediately accused of one of two things, and often both. First, we are seen as recommending that schools set up torture chambers where trivial infractions of arbitrary rules are dealt with harshly. Otherwise we are told that we should never strike anyone as a solution to a problem because the children will only learn that: 1) 'Might makes right', 2) we love 'things' more than we love them, or 3) their personalities will devolve to cringing neurotics or criminals if we try to maintain some behavioral standards.

Keep in mind that talk of an occasional paddling to get the attention of a particularly egregious miscreant should not imply that whipping is the only disciplinary technique used. It is the method of next-to-last resort. The methods of last resort are expulsion, or incarceration. If we raise our kids to a traditional standard of decency, and if we start with gentle but consistent and firm discipline in the earliest grades (and most especially if parents started it from birth), very little actual paddling is required. Our legal system would not be overwhelmed either, so visions of Dickensian charnel houses need not arise. For example, I have three kids. As of this writing, their combined ages total more than thirty years. During those 11,000+ days of their combined lives, I have had to spank them a total of perhaps a dozen times, and most of those spankings consisted of a single firm swat on a rump. That is less than one swat each per 7+ years. That can hardly be considered extreme, cruel, or inhuman. Not so incidentally, I have gotten compliments nearly everywhere I have taken these kids, regarding their cheerfulness and good behavior. Also, our former daycare sitter had just about given up on kids generally, and was ready to quit the business, until she met mine.[54] Yet, although I think they are the best kids in the history of the universe, they are not remarkable kids, not really, and I am no paragon. In fact, I am often thought of as a grump. I mention this to explain that you need not be perfect to raise excellent kids, any more than you have to strive for utopian perfection to have an excellent school. You only need be a responsible adult who looks at the world as an adult, bases actions on experience (including history), and expects kids to become responsible adults, too. I will shortly expand on this idea when I discuss child-centered teaching.

The truth is that one of my most serious concerns is that raising my kids will become more difficult as they have regular, extensive contact with Progressively raised kids (and educators). Another is the alternative that many educationists and mental health professionals recommend. That is the increased use of psychoactive and sedative drugs to control perfectly normal kids. Drugging is apparently the solution of choice of our Government too, who have released a report, just before Christmas 1999, saying that upwards of 20 percent of the American people are mentally ill and in need of therapy. Keep this bit of wisdom in mind when you read about how Special education sees your kids, in Chapter 6.

On the other hand, here is a quiz: What recent period in our history has seen an explosion of suicides—both attempted and successful—and of convictions and jailing for violent crimes and crimes against self (e.g., drug related crimes)?

Meanwhile, here is another example of how the mere threat of paddling works. The principal of my grammar school, in the 1950s, kept a wooden paddle on a wall behind his desk. As far as I know, he never used it, but we kids thought he could, and that is what counted. We also knew that there would likely be another iteration of the experience once we got home, and we did not want that either. Later, in the high school, there was no hint that paddling would ever be needed. In fact the only incident that came close during my first six years beyond grammar school was a fist fight. It is the only schoolyard fight I can recall and the combatants had enough respect for the school that they did

---

54 After the kids were old enough that I no longer needed her services, she did quit the business.

not go after each other in the hall, where the dispute flared, but attended all of their classes for the rest of the day. Only then did they fight in the back parking lot, after school. I doubt if anyone ever thought that bringing a gun to school was a choice they had—much less a necessity—and platoons of 'counselors' were not considered necessary to settle our quaking nerves. 'Closure,' as an emotional notion, was still for the future.

However, we were speaking about academic grades.

When I was in high school, even the kids who eventually dropped out of school, and there were very few of those,[55] got non-dumbed-down grades in the 70s and 60s (C's and a few D's). Now we have a State average math score of near 40 percent and schools pat themselves on the head when they score marginally above that. The schools accept scores that only the most generous person might even call 'mediocre' and then smile complacently when their pupils beat it, because in their minds they 'have done the right thing' with recent policies. What is that 'right thing' exactly and why are schools spending money on armed, uniformed policemen, video surveillance cameras and metal detectors, teaching 'conflict resolution' seminars, and even recommending that teachers take up the martial arts? Are these kids being prepared for adulthood in our civilized, multinational, and increasingly technological society, or are we preparing for the second-coming of Attila the Hun?

Perhaps worse than that, it also seems that the longer a kid is subjected to our school system, the more ignorant he becomes. For instance, in this State in 1998, 4th grade math problem-solvers scored 60.55 percent on average, 7th graders scored 47.49 percent, and 10th graders scored 35.09 percent on average. This means that, for those deemed nearly ready to step into life as adults, out of every 100 questions asked, 65 are missed. Sixty-five percent *correct* was once considered a failing grade but now the average 10th grader is in the blind-guessing range and we are told that we should not be concerned. As if the averages are not bad enough, locally the top-ranked grammar school scored a failing 63 percent (D minus) on the summary (Power) math score while the top-ranked high school scored a 43 percent (F minus).

---

55 I have tried very hard but I cannot recall a single case from my high school, though there may have been some. On the other hand the recorded graduation rate for 1996–1997 for the school where I did my student-teaching was only 76.1 percent. That means that almost one of every four kids that started the ninth grade, did not graduate. A dropout rate of *only* 24 percent would be considered a miracle in some of the worst schools today.

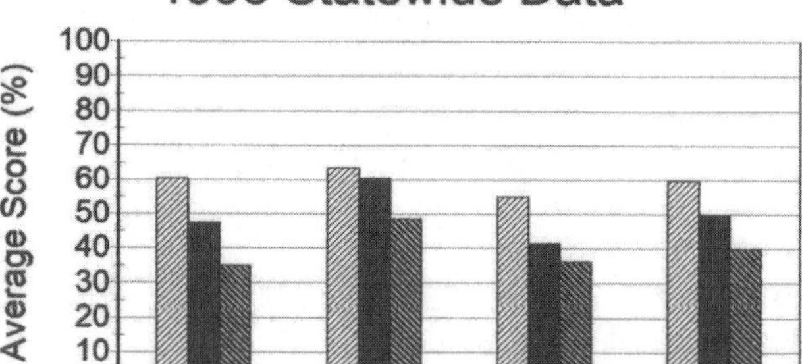

Figure 1 From 1997–1998 District Data

Therefore, since high school–level testing is done early in the 10th grade, what we have, at least for math, is that by less than three years prior to graduation, average pupil achievement has dropped to a point that is little better than guessing. As a result, we can be justified to think that most pupils might be better off had they not gone to school at all. With a record such as this, how can we accept the Progressive definitions of 'excellence'? With such chronically damning examples of their professional incompetence available in the public record, we can easily understand why our 'educational professionals' protest whenever objective tests are mentioned? (See Chapter 7.)

The two 'Reading' tests recorded in 1995–1996 are quite similar, except that they use a different emphasis in the materials read. 'Expository' reading involves reading short essays about something and then answering questions relating to the information contained in the essays. The topics that might be used include such things as aspects of the Civil War, Egyptian hieroglyphics, the poetry of Walt Whitman, the Industrial Revolution, how to identify cloud types, the symbolism of Indian headdresses, and an almost limitless range of other topics. These are the familiar multiple-choice reading comprehension tests that we have all come to love. The basic idea is to read about something that may or may not be familiar to us, and then to see how well we have understood what was written in the short amount of time allotted. The questions are designed to test reading skills including knowledge of vocabulary, understanding, short-term memory, and perhaps fact- or concept-analysis (i.e., 'thinking'). The State average was 57.4 percent (F). Locally, the top-scoring grammar school scored at 65 percent (D) and the best high school scored at 60 percent (D minus). Should we be satisfied that our top schools only make it into the failing D range on average? The overall State average, however, even in this most basic of 'language arts' skills is still an F.

An F is what the average kid at the 50th percentile scored. Some Progressive thinkers also tell us that it is a good thing that more than 60 percent of our kids go on to college. This 60 percent reaches down below the 40th percentile or so, in academic achievement. What does this say about the sorts of adjustments we force our colleges to make? Can we still call college 'higher' education?[56]

The 'Narrative' reading tests are also multiple choice in nature, but the stories are typically easier to follow, because they are stories. These narratives may detail a series of events in the life of someone. For instance, "John woke up and then he ate breakfast and then he brushed his teeth," and so on. I do not mean to imply that all the stories are necessarily that simplistic, but at the 4th grade level they might be. For instance, my daughter's 4th grade 'Accelerated Reading' list included a book about a cricket who was accidentally taken to the city and was befriended by a cat and a dog. [We're not talking Rudyard Kipling here, either, Best Beloved.]

Remember that after more than 30 years of Progressive education the latest Federal plan merely expects to have kids reading by the <u>end</u> of the 3rd grade. So we may ask: What are the kids doing during the four years of schooling prior to the end of the 3rd grade?

In any case, the Narrative test-taker is asked to follow a verbal trail and then remember some events along the trail. Even here, while trying to read at only slightly beyond the equivalent of 'Dick and Jane' stories, the State average only manages to make it up into the D range, and only a very few schools score, on average, in what was once the expected passing range of C or higher.

Let us say that all this is disturbing to you, but you remember hearing educators, etc., say that using multiple choice tests is a bad

---

56 For a fuller treatment of this problem, read Alvin Kernan's *In Plato's Cave.*

thing. Why would they say that? One of the arguments against multiple choice and other 'objective' tests generally, is that they supposedly do not test a kid's ability to think, being based entirely on fact regurgitation. In fact, nowadays if you are a teacher who teaches facts, you are considered a bad teacher and not innovative enough in your approach. I will deal with this silly argument in greater detail in Chapter 7, but, naturally, nothing could be further from the truth. As usual, this argument is merely another example of a Progressive prediction that is not supported by reality. We will discuss why throughout the book.

Why should we use multiple choice tests? First, if you remember your Piaget and developmental child psychology generally, most children are thought not to have the capacity for true inductive reasoning (the ability to take facts and details to construct larger conceptual systems) until roughly the time of puberty (perhaps ages 12 to 14). Before that time, children's brains have not developed the neuronal connections, hormonal involvement, or whatever is required to achieve true reasoning. To convince ourselves of this, we need only to ask a young kid to read a story, then ask him what the story "is about." (However, do not use a story that had already been discussed, since we might get an adult's explanation, rather than the child's original thoughts. This would be much like cocktail party discussions of books not actually read, but only read about, as from reviews, etc.) If we do this experiment with a kid, chances are excellent that what we will get is a mere chronology of events. Even if we try to describe possible themes and symbolic devices (i.e., Harry Potter symbolizes the never-ending struggle of good versus evil), we will likely get confused looks and blank stares. We are unlikely to get any sort of literary analysis beyond, "I liked it" or "It was funny." Commonly, even getting the kid to explain why he liked it is a serious and unproductive struggle.

The point is that kids are not merely miniature adults in their ability to think. The necessary 'mental machinery' has not been installed yet.

If young kids are physiologically incapable of true reasoning (higher-level thinking), why would we want to send them to school at all, and would doing superficial activities supposedly designed to develop higher-level thinking skills make any sense? If Piaget was right, trying to teach very young kids to 'think' is the equivalent of throwing a newly hatched eagle chick out of its clifftop aerie and expecting it to soar gracefully. Given time and appropriate development, both eagles and children can do wonderfully well, but not until they are ready. Yet even if Piaget was wrong in his conclusions, if even small kids have a greater capacity for reasoned thought that Piaget thought, they still need things to think about, and at the beginning, they need them in relatively small doses, so as not to overwhelm them. (Old-timers used to say that we have to build a foundation before putting up the house. New-timers are having trouble building a house with no foundation, and cannot understand why. Working on 'higher-level thinking skills' in the first grade is like trying to put up the roof before the walls are built—and trying to do it on uneven ground.)

We'll discuss the claims of Discovery or Inquiry learning in more detail later, but if the conclusions of the psychological developmentalists are correct, 'thinking' may be the one thing that is truly discovered by each individual pupil rather than the 'concepts' that Progressive educationists promise. Even Rousseau explicitly, and repeatedly, warned that ". . . purely speculative knowledge is hardly suitable for children, even those nearing adolescence."[57] Rousseau insisted, repeatedly, that if you want a child to understand ideas, his education should advance by small steps. If these ideas are accurate, not having something to think about, and not having practiced how to think about it if we did, may be the fundamental legacy of Progressive education that helps to cause the other problematic legacies of our litany of woe (see pages xi and 135).

Does that mean that the schools can do nothing until kids are teens? Of course not. Besides sending the kids to learn the basics of readin' and writin' and 'rithmetic, we send them to learn to get along with many different kids and adults, to help learn our collective histories, and to internalize and practice our cultural and community standards of truth, justice and the American way.[58] At least we did once upon a time. Nevertheless, we also send them precisely to accumulate facts about the basic subjects, so that when they can finally truly begin to think for themselves, they will have the basic facts needed to begin an educated, competent analysis. Not teaching facts lays no academic foundations and may essentially limit kids' knowledge of the world to old wives' tales, and to what the multiculturalists (or MTV) might have told them.

Kids will need new facts first when they are asked to answer school questions, of increasing complexity, and then when they start making

---

57 *Emile, or On Education*, p. 177.
58 This too is, of course, terribly controversial nowadays. Three cheers for multiculturalism!

adult decisions. Therefore, giving them facts and ideas is necessary, in simplified form, to practice with. (If you practice, you get better—and remember more.) Practice in handling facts and ideas is practice in thinking. How can we possibly expect to make reasonable decisions about anything, if we do not know what the thing is about? Even making as 'simple' a decision as what career to pursue requires data from many sources. Furthermore, kids need to discover what kinds of stuff (e.g., words, numbers, science) they are capable enough with, and interested enough in, to which to dedicate a lifetime. Though choice in all things is another of the Progressive ideals, if we do not teach facts, we limit our kids' eventual choices severely.

If all of this sounds a bit circular, you may be right. Facts lead to ideas and expanding ideas often require more, or more complex, facts. That is why we need years to prepare for high school-level work, and years more to prepare for college. Contrary to Progressive ideals, learning subject matter content along the way is not only occasionally useful, it is essential. If the description of what schools should do (i.e., teach and test for learning, identify and correct mistakes then teach more, and more complex, stuff and test again) sounds like enforcing practice in 'thinking,' you are certainly right. Ask yourself: Does not doing these kinds of exercises actually retard our kids' development and creativity? I believe that most would agree that if we start by practicing with the easy facts and ideas, eventually we will learn to handle more complicated facts and ideas. Contrary to Progressive hopes and recommendations, the opposite does not.

Educationists recommend that we concentrate on concepts, rather than mere facts in teaching thinking skills. Progressive science teachers call it Discovery learning. Under present conditions, it does not work (see Chapter 7). To understand why, we must think about the Progressive methods of teaching thinking skills for a moment. First, we do not teach facts, so that the pupil has no basis upon which to develop a higher-level concept. Instead, we merely identify an observation or two about a topic. This might be done with a standard 'gee whiz' demonstration, or merely by using an introduction. Of course, introducing a topic is certainly a necessary preliminary, and demonstrations, of themselves, are valuable techniques. However, after a period of uninformed speculation, often labeled as a 'brainstorming'[59] session, we might tell the pupil

---

59 Brainstorming is an idea used in business and in strategic and tactical planning sessions generally. The term implies that a group of experienced workers collectively applies their varied expertise to solve a new problem of common interest. Frequent brainstorming among baby neophytes is unproductive at best.

what cutting-edge concept is appropriate, again perhaps without mentioning the facts upon which it is based. Then we move on to the next topic, expecting Junior to have understood everything and to be creative in the use of that concept.

Under this scenario Junior has merely learned the concept *as* a mere fact, rather than as a concept, and isolated facts are quickly forgotten, just as the Progressives argue. Therefore, once again the old-fashioned version of fact-based schooling supports their stated ideals better than the Progressive recommendations. Old-fashioned schooling does this by being simpler, less expensive, more equitable, and by approaching children's mental characteristics and capabilities as they are, not as the Utopians wish they were.

Starting with hard, complex ideas, while telling ourselves that we are teaching at the cutting edge, mainly confuses and discourages pupils since they cannot understand why the ideas apply. If that is true, they would probably end up hating school altogether. This is precisely the result that educationists say they are working to avoid, yet my 9th graders fit that description, and descriptions of pupils nationwide seem to fit it as well. Based on what I see in the classroom, my conservative estimate is that perhaps 50 percent of pupils, at or beyond, the Junior High school level, have concluded that school is totally irrelevant to them, other than as a social institution. National dropout rates and the lack of effort shown by many of those who stay support this conclusion.

What we need in place of this depressing silliness is stated very well in a mail-order advertisement for a magazine that I received recently. The ad was begun as a question and answer session:

Q: What's wrong with magazines today?
A: The print media ape the manners of television, and on television form precedes content, emotion replaces reason, legend substitutes for history, fiction dictates to fact.
Q: What's right with XYZ magazine?
A: At XYZ, we still celebrate substance over style. Reason over emotion. Good prose over pabulum. We're so far gone on this subject that we actually believe that *clear writing spawns clear thinking, and that clear thinking engenders right actions* (my emphasis).

It is good to see that there are some people in America who seem to understand the reasons for education. It would be nice if this included our education establishment.

Rubrics and Standardized Tests

The last of the three major areas, Writing, as reported in the School Report Card data, is not tested using an 'objective' test at all. The Writing group of tests is scored using a subjective 'rubric' system. Rubric scoring is done by reference to a subjective 'criterion'. This means it is a 'performance based' assessment, and what <u>that</u> means is, if a teacher feels that a pupil has done well enough at some specified component of a task, the pupil gets full credit for that portion of the task. We will see an example of this scoring system in the next chapter when I show a 'project' assignment in a modern biology text. The point to understand, however, is that the grading system often awards full credit for the *lowest* performance considered acceptable (by a Progressive grader), rather than encouraging kids to reach for their best effort.

The 5-4-3-2-1 rubric system used by my home State in scoring writing efforts can be equated essentially to the old A-B-C-D-F system and is not necessarily a bad thing by itself. Teachers who have had to score creative writing efforts have used variations on this system for a very long time. 'Creative' here is not necessarily meant to imply a fully original piece, but rather a pupil's personally developed explanation on a theme that is generally known to the pupil (i.e., "Do it in your own words"). Writing essay-test answers or book reports are two common examples. The idea is to display competence in the various mechanics of writing and in the formulation of explanations or persuasive arguments. The mechanics of writing include the use and organization of ideas, grammar, synonyms and antonyms, sentence structure, paragraph organization, and so forth. These are all examples of the sorts of traditional rules said to limit creativity.

Though other forms of rubrics are possible, the rubric used in the State-sponsored standardized tests is a five-stage subjective evaluation made by the grader, typically an educator from the same school as the pupil. Each grader may use very different standards and a grade of 3 from one grader may earn a 4 from another, or a 2 from a third. Thus, this system is too haphazard for a test graded by many different graders, as in state-wide tests, but is perfectly OK within an individual classroom where the kids are graded all year by one professional teacher with high standards who makes it quite clear what her standards are. Kids adjust to those standards. We once called that adjustment 'learning from your mistakes'.

Using subjective standards as a grading scheme for a statewide standardized test though, is quite problematic.[60] Just as each grader within a single school faculty may have different standards, entire school districts may have different standards regarding how strictly to grade punctuation mistakes, for instance, if they are graded at all. Keep in mind that these statewide tests are graded locally. Only the whole-school average results are sent to the State for compilation. In our current atmosphere of self-esteem-as-king, however, we may expect that most test-graders are quite lax and most grades are seriously inflated.

One reason that schools may inflate grades is to make themselves look good. In the age of 'accountability', this is not a trivial concern. To demonstrate that subjective scoring is a genuine problem we need look no further than the charts on pages 28 to 33. As stated, the math and reading tests are objectively graded, so the only way to affect the results is by adjusting the difficulty of the tests, and, of course, by using better or poorer teaching techniques while preparing kids for the tests. It is a curious coincidence, therefore, that virtually all of the scores reported to be above the state's standards of excellence can be found in the area of Writing; the area graded subjectively. How is it that kids who prove themselves to be so incompetent at the basics of addition and can read only so poorly that they cannot answer simple questions about what they read, manage to develop such extraordinary writing skills? To quote the King of Siam, "It is a puzzlement." Or maybe it's not. Maybe the addition of a subjectively graded writing portion was an effort to introduce an instance of Progressive grading with low standards into standardized tests, thereby diluting the credibility of tests generally, while giving schools something to crow about.

In any case, are you old enough to remember how proud some kids were when they worked their tails off and earned a grade they did not expect? Maybe you had been one of them, as I was. For instance, I recall how happy I was upon being told by my 10th grade math teacher, "Congratulations. I didn't think you had it in you," after nearly 'maxing' an end-of-year, New York State Regents geometry test. This sort of thing

---

60 This is even more of a problem for a national test such as the new SAT, which has just added a writing test to its format. Almost 1.5 million kids take the SAT yearly. Grading all those essays consistently will be a problem, even though, perhaps especially because, the CEEB plans to have each essay read by at least two graders. The ACT institutes a similar system starting in 2005.

should be impossible under current theory. It was once, however, quite common.

In an idealized grading rubric, a score of '5' may be the relative equivalent of reaching grade-level literary perfection. The ideas are clear, interesting and convincing, and they answer the question posed. The spelling, punctuation, and grammar are virtually flawless. The facts and ideas used are organized in a way that makes the conclusion reached seem inevitable. Each paragraph has one idea that follows directly from the one before and leads into the next. Transitions are clear and interesting. Word choice is appropriate, elegant, and beautifully descriptive. There is a beginning, a middle, and an end and each part leaves us wanting more. In short, it is wonderful. An 'A' effort.

A score of '4' is also good, but not quite as flawless as '5'. Perhaps the difference is that the ideas, arguments or descriptions do not quite convince us. If the general explanation advanced is good, perhaps something important is missing, or is not well explained. The mechanics may be a bit casual with minor mistakes or omissions. Perhaps using a different word here (e.g., replace 'good' with 'wonderful'), and reordering several sentences or paragraphs there, would improve the structure or readability. Perhaps the writer's spelling, punctuation, or use of facts is not quite as it could be. A good effort though. A 'B'.

A '3' is a bit less impressive than a '4'. The mechanics are less elegant and the argument may be less convincing or complete. Spelling and punctuation mistakes, etc., may be common and perhaps exasperating, but not yet alarming. The facts used to advance thematic explanations and arguments are less than convincing but still on the right track. If the facts are there, perhaps they are not fully explained or well organized. The whole effect is workmanlike but not stellar. It leaves us with the impression that this was a good try, but that the writer does not quite know his subject. In any case it still needs work. A passable effort. A 'C'.

Earning a '2' is not worthy of celebration. There are enough flaws in all aspects of the piece to elicit a frequent "Huh?" reaction from the reader. Spelling and punctuation may be decidedly informal and the 'answers' these pieces formulate may be somewhat independent of the questions asked. After reading it, and frequently during the reading, this piece makes you think, "This kid doesn't have a clue." A poor effort below what you would expect of someone who had attended classes. A 'D'.

A '1' falls well below grade- or age-appropriate expectations. An 'F'.

If the 'rubric' system is basically the same as the old A-B-C-D-F system, why did we change? My guess is that we did it to camouflage the similarities. We also consider it unthinkable to give one kid an 'A' and another a 'C'. The kid with the 'C' will probably be 'devastated' and have her life ruined. Besides, since a modern teacher's primary goal is to insure that everyone passes, a kid's record featuring virtually nothing but 'F's,' would make that goal difficult to attain but earning a '1', as opposed to an 'F', may have some positive emotional overtones, as in "I'm number one!"

Finally, the rubric system is considered an 'assessment' rather than a 'test,' and as such does not imply passing or failing. Assessments are equitable while tests are racist, or at least unfair, we are told. This is so because tests assume that someone will do better than someone else while assessments are simply trying to determine each pupil's 'individual learning level' (everyone is the same as everybody else, so we have to treat them uniquely). This distinction does not exist in reality, of course, but it is used as an ongoing indication that dumbing-down (teaching at a 'developmentally appropriate' level) is warranted. Later you will be amused (or perhaps enraged) by what educationists consider acceptable individual assessments of a pupil's knowledge and understanding.

This form of evaluation is also sometimes known as 'authentic' assessments to imply that objective grading has nothing to say about the achievement of individual kids. Tests, you see, compare the pupil to other pupils while assessments concentrate on the pupil alone, with no regard to how others are doing.

Considering that among the most common, and vocal, complaints regarding equity revolves around the differential achievements of various groups of kids, did you just have a 'Huh?' reaction? How do we determine whether the 'achievement gap' is closing unless we can compare kids with each other?

Because of the subjectivity of rubric grading, I cannot comment directly on the Writing results as recorded by the State Department of Education, since I was not one of the graders. I was, however, a grader of the work of normal high school Freshman during my time as a teacher. I will say that judging from the papers I saw, the results reported by the

State are within the range of what I would expect. This is to say that I am not too surprised at the grades recorded. I would, however, be very surprised if the grades accurately reflected the kid's literary achievement, because many of the 9th graders I taught could not complete a sentence coherently. Also, for the kids at least, attitude[61] is more important than good style. One young scholar, for instance, proudly announced one day that she, ". . . does not *do* periods."

I was not satisfied with the results I was getting with my pupils, of course, and since I was The Teacher, I figured it was my job to try to improve the kids' performance. Ninth grade is high school after all, and the kids were presumably beginning their final push toward graduation, adulthood, and independence. To try to force a bit more thought into my pupils' answers, I tried to require that my short essay answers be at least two sentences long.

Imagine. Two whole sentences. The resulting lamentation was something to hear, however. Continue this flight of imagination to the point where the teacher says, "OK. I'm wrong. You're right. Don't bother with that. It's OK not to answer the question at all if you don't want to." If you do this (I was told that my standards are impossibly high), you will begin to understand the ideal Progressive pedagogical philosophy. We may describe this as the inmates in charge of the asylum.

Many pupils, perhaps 30 percent, simply did no work at all. They never bothered to bring a book, a piece of paper, or a pencil to class. I rarely saw the faces of one or two of them. These young scholars simply arrived in class (sometimes), laid face down across their assigned desks, and stayed that way until it was time to leave. Obviously, the fire of lifelong learning did not burn very brightly in their Progressive souls, as their parents were promised. These pupils did not suddenly stop handing in assignments because they were rejecting my unfamiliar and repressive teaching style. They arrived at the 9th grade with no intention of handing in assignments, having just graduated from a Middle School whose principal's proudly stated objective was to run a school where no one could fail. They had rejected learning several years previously and looked at me simply as their caretaker while they served their 9th grade biology sentence. My demands did not affect these do-nothing kids, but were an outrageous surprise to the rest.

---

61 "Attitude" has become a positive end to itself, and the idea is found everywhere. Today even kitchen appliances are marketed as having attitude, a positive example of the sort of creativity that Progressive education promises.

To see whether I truly was demanding more than was reasonable, I got a copy of the State's science curriculum standards and tried to match performance exhibited by my pupils to the published standards. The standards are divided into multiple year groupings by detailing what kinds of 'outcomes' are expected for Kindergarten through grade 2, grades 3 to 5, 6 to 8, and 9 to 12. I began to worry when I saw this breakdown, even before I got to the details. Was there nothing that could be expected of a 5th grader that a 3rd grader could not do? Why bother going to the last three years of high school, if one could achieve the State's highest standards by the 9th grade? Something seemed wrong. I was convinced of that fact when I noticed that the best overall match that I could make for my high school Freshmen was the expected performance described for the 3rd through 5th grade 'outcome'. These kids were only in their ninth year of school and already they were about half a decade behind official expectations.

I mentioned this observation to my academic advisor and he angrily told me, "Don't ever say that!" Apparently kids' actual achievement had to be interpreted before it could be explained to the public.

Apart from their literary incompetence, this result (i.e., 9th graders working at the 4th grade level, on average) was evident in large part because the kids in my biology class did not have even a rudimentary understanding of natural systems and processes. For instance, the perfectly basic concept of 'diffusion' (fluid molecules spreading out to fill a space evenly) was perfectly unknown to them. Another example is that, during a brainstorming session trying to figure out what 'being alive' meant biologically, no pupil had any suggestions beyond, "You can move." As previously stated, brainstorming is a favorite classroom activity of Progressive educationists, at least it was taught in my Ed school as being frequently appropriate. Brainstorming is expected to teach higher-level thinking skills. It is said to inspire "thinking outside the box," which is a euphemism for creativity. The above example, however, shows clearly that knowing a fact or two from inside the box is useful if we are going to "press the edge of the envelope." [Knowing not to mix metaphors requires additional instruction.]

Also, my pupils could not reason through the simplest situations. For instance, one activity that our textbook asked the kids to do resulted in all of them deciding to cut pictures out of a magazine to display their understanding of human evolution. When asked what a particular picture used represented, however, I got virtually identical blank stares from all of them. They managed the 'activity' of cutting and pasting, but had no notion why they had done it.

Also, of course, they could not read at all well.

Lest you are still tempted to think that this awful result was a school specific phenomenon, read this next example. Shortly after graduation, I worked as a substitute teacher in a different school district where 60 percent of the kids were listed on one Honor Roll or another (there were at least three). My assignments that day was a mixed 10th–11th grade Social Studies class, and the activity I was assigned to oversee involved cutting pictures out of a magazine. This activity was designed to advance the pupil's understanding of the effect of various climates on societies. For instance, could the prevailing weather (Nordic vs. tropical) have any effect on the development of cultural traditions? Among the pictures selected were images of snow-covered trees and palm-shaded beaches, etc. Though none of the pupils could explain to me the symbolism of their choice of pictures, the pictures of trees did induce one pupil to ask another, "Are trees plants?"

Most of my pupils could not construct a simple sentence without help. For many of them a complete paragraph seemed entirely out of the realm of possibilities and writing a short essay was not even contemplated. Without basic writing skills that allow the structure for the formulation of an argument more complex than " . . . Like, duh!", thinking skills are unrealistic, and without thinking skills the contemplation of 'academic success' reaches the realms of science fiction.

The school where I taught 9th grade biology would have ranked in the bottom half of the schools I recorded here, but it was within the range of these schools. Nevertheless, this school ranked above the State average, according to its marketing brochure. The administration was proud of that.

If you are reading this book, chances are that your kids attend schools that score in the upper half of the range and that things may not be quite as awful in your kids' schools. Do not lull yourself into thinking your school is immune, however. Look back at the achievement levels of the top schools in the area (i.e., 35 percent in math reasoning) and ask yourselves if that is good enough.

To put that 35 percent into perspective, remember that the typical standardized test question is a four-answer multiple choice question.

This means that you have a 25 percent chance of guessing the correct answer, even if you do not recognize the language in which the test is written. So, to say that 35 percent is an acceptable result after perhaps a decade or more of Progressive 'education', constitutes educational spin of the worst sort.

Education Research: Who Do You Trust?

While engaged on our seemingly endless and frustratingly fruitless national education debate, one phrase is heard again and again. Actually many phrases are repeated interminably, since the debate has taken on the aspect of a ritual, ideological dance, but one phrase is a particular roadblock to further progress. That phrase is (and variations certainly exist), 'For every study you quote, I can show you another that says the opposite'. Given this phrase, it is quite surprising that there have not been more comparative evaluations of the quality of the Progressive educational research examined in the popular press. We seem to act as if research is research, and each published article means as much as any other, is as well done, and whose conclusions are as valid as any other.

To determine whether this is in any sense true, we need to ask ourselves several questions. Some of them are: Are the researches that support each polar position in the debate good enough to perfectly counterbalance the other side? Are the polar positions truly as polar as argued, and if they are not, why haven't the genuinely moderate similarities entered the debate, and why haven't the congruencies been highlighted?

Answering the last question, highlighting the useful compromises, is the easiest question to answer. The answer is that the polar spokesmen are making a good living keeping the pot boiling. It's a shame that the education of the kids is being shorted, and the society is racking up new national epidemics on a regular basis, but hey, at least the politics are fun to watch, and more fun to report than dull reality.

Actually, the phrase mentioned above is most often heard from the Progressive side. Adherents to the more traditional side of the debate have used another category of phrase, though not often out loud. Seeing the results attained by the adherents to Progressive educations' tenets (i.e., the appalling dropout rate, the multiplicity of social problems extant and growing, the easily demonstrable and burgeoning ignorance of some of our citizens as opposed to the just as easily demonstrated educational advances of perfectly ordinary kids who are actually taught subject matter content, etc.), they look at each other and say, "These guys (Progressive educators) just don't have a clue." I suspect that attempting to maintain a sense of courtesy, even while engaged in a shouting-head debate on late-night TV, keep many from saying what they want to say.

The Progressive side has been much more vocal in their public condemnations, however, while arguing that we should always maintain a civil dialog. It is not at all unusual to hear traditional thinkers called such things as, "mean-spirited," "ideological," "against education," "against children," and their reform and other legislative proposals characterized as "hateful," "a sham," "fraud," and "racist," or even "meritocratic," as if recognizing excellence were a bad thing.

Yet we were speaking of the believability of modern educational theory, and its supposedly research-based underpinnings. If the opinions of their academic colleagues are valid, what effect do these doctors of education have on the direction of education generally, and what sort of research do they produce?

Incidentally, I will not be dealing with the dueling think-tank researches that interpret, misinterpret, and spin state and federal education statistics. It should be noted that the statistics represent the combined effects of a goulash of state and federal educational programs, and various techniques, both 'innovative' and otherwise, being tried in individual classrooms around the nation. Trying to come to legitimate conclusions regarding individual ideas, much less the best approach to educating everyone, based on this mish-mash of results, may not be possible. Since even individual teachers may try a variety of approaches during the course of single day, even a year's academic results for a single school may not reflect the full effect of a philosophy, either good or bad. Therefore, we will deal with the sorts of research that are said to demonstrate the usefulness of particular strategies in the classroom, and the spin-off ideas that are making their way into far-flung corners of our society (i.e., the stuff the think-tanks—not to mention education departments—ought to be thinking more about).

The authors mentioned throughout this book all cited research in the course of their writings, and while some described the sorts of examples I will relate, few have concentrated on the kinds of research currently referred to as informative and important. There are two authors that have looked at the general run of research being done, and both published in 2000. They are Jeanne Chall and Ellen Lagemann. Lagemann wrote a carefully worded general history of educational, and its related psychological, research[62] and concentrated upon the 'classic', seminal research that influenced the broad sweep of the movements that education has followed since the start of the last century. Chall, on the other hand,[63] has done several broad reviews of the more mundane educational literature over the past half century. Based on the hundreds of studies reviewed, as well as on her own research, she has concluded, and quoted other broad reviews of literature as concluding, that the activities-based, child-centered teaching techniques, championed by Progressive education, and widely used in American schools, simply don't work as well as advertised. Their research also concludes that traditional, fact-based, systematic, lecture-and-testing style of instruction is better for *all* pupils, but *especially* for 'at-risk' children. Yet, despite the fact that extensive research, not to say the experience of centuries, concludes that teachers would do best to *teach* rather than facilitate day camp style activities, teaching genuine lessons is precisely the sort of technique that horrifies Progressive educators, especially for at-risk students. Even so, Chall is very gentle in her language and circumspect in her conclusions. As an honorable academic, she was obliged to mention that there is some evidence that says that child-centered techniques are not perfectly useless. The research shows that an activities-based curriculum can work to a certain degree, but that it works better with advanced pupils (who have already mastered a large and growing body of knowledge) than with the less talented and less well informed. Progressive education insists upon precisely the opposite conclusions.

Though she never says it outright, and does not speculate as to reasons, a full reading of Chall's book leads to a conclusion that a flexible combination of the teacher- and child-centered approaches, tied to the average capabilities of each classroom, would likely benefit most pupils more than either style alone. The way this combination of styles should work would be to begin each lesson with a dispensation of pertinent facts (i.e., teaching new stuff the kids do not yet know), probably by some variation of a lecture, which could, and often should, be spiced

---

62 Lagemann, Ellen C., *An Elusive Science: The Troubling History of Education Research*, U. of Chicago Press, Chicago, 2000.

63 Chall, Jeanne S., *The Academic Achievement Challenge: What Really Works in the Classroom?*, Guilford Press, New York, 2000.

up by demonstrations and discussions, etc. The lecturer should certainly encourage the questions of the students, and should strive mightily to place facts in context, whether that context is scientific or historical, etc. Therefore lectures are, or should be, generally lively things, contrary to the descriptions of lectures by Progressive educators as miserly and boring recitations of irrelevant facts (i.e., "Pouring facts onto kids' heads."). The 'activities' component of a sensible curriculum would allow pupils to explore the presented topic in greater depth, but would still require the topic to be thoroughly and soundly introduced. Then the pupils' learning (mastery and understanding) of the facts and context should be routinely tested, so that the pupils' speculations would not flounder in the activities-based ignorance that characterizes many modern classrooms.

This teach-and-test regimen is the point that most Progressive educators find so troubling, however. While attempting to develop the higher-level thinking skills, the most purely Progressive curricula merely concentrate on making things easy and fun. Learning, and therefore genuine teaching (i.e., dispensing information), is a tertiary, or lower, consideration. ("Teaching subject-matter content is the least important thing that teachers do.") This advice is justified largely upon the notion that kids don't like facts and lectures and that building self-esteem is more important than learning. In child-centered classrooms, the pupil's wishes are foremost. Child-centered philosophy is the educational equivalent of asking kids whether they would prefer ice cream or a balanced diet for supper.[64] The kids say "ice cream" and the educators give it to them, and our decades of slumped academic results, rising drop-out rates, and school violence speak for themselves.

Thinking Like a Scientist?

While a student-teacher, I was also involved in conducting the new State sponsored 10th grade science assessments, saw what the kids did, and was at least peripherally involved in grading. (I attended the departmental meetings where grading was discussed and helped to proctor

---

64 The kids get pizza, soft drinks, and fatty snacks from the school cafeteria and from vending machines too, despite rhetoric that touts the teaching of healthful living styles. When asked to remove the vending machines, Progressive administrators say that they need the money, regardless of the results.

several pupils while they took the test.) The work done by the pupils, however, was apparently so poor statewide, that even Progressive educators could not use the results. Please keep this 'assessment' in mind when we discuss how modern science instruction has been teaching kids to "think like a scientist" more fully in Chapter 7. Also keep in mind that the kids I knew have probably now all graduated, or dropped out. All are now parents and voters, helping to decide our collective futures. These are also some of the parents that Progressive educators want to depend upon to help with their own kids' educations, under the heading of 'parental involvement'.

The science assessment was not required of all pupils, and several—perhaps 30 percent of the chosen, chose not participate (with no negative consequences, as far as I could tell). I suppose that not making the test mandatory of all pupils makes some sense, since this was the first time this assessment was tried. Testing the test, to work out the logistical bugs, is not necessarily a bad idea. On the other hand, it should have been apparent to those writing it that attempting this sort of assessment on a statewide basis, would have its problems. Also imagine the logistics of doing this for every 10th-grader in the State.

The assessment was designed to see how well pupils had learned the scientific method. It asked them to choose a question to investigate, from a list of possibilities provided, then design and conduct a simple experiment based on the question chosen. To complete the assessment, it required the pupil to write a report explaining the details of their experimental design, and of the results. In effect, the pupils had to write a simple scientific research paper.

This is really hot stuff. We can easily sell this to an unsuspecting public as an indication that we are preparing kids for the 21st century. However, it is often said that if you love the law, or sausages, you should not watch either being made. It might be best if people did not know how things actually went with the science assessment as well. But if you like horror stories, here goes . . .

Logistically, the assessment was scheduled to be completed in three class periods over several days, insuring, no doubt, that each assessment would be individual and not the result of collaboration (read, 'cheating'). All of the kids who showed up to participate in this assessment chose to try to solve the "quicker picker-upper" question. This question tested which brand of paper towel could soak up the most liquid. As such, the experimental design could have included a simple comparison of the various brands of paper towels provided. An acceptable result could have included an experimental design such as: 1) Cut various paper towels into similarly sized pieces; 2) weigh each piece of towel while dry; 3) expose each sample to measured volumes of water; 4) weigh again; 5) compare the wet weight of the various towel brands to their dry weight.

Not one of the kids I proctored had the vaguest notion of how to begin. After half an hour of giving them increasingly specific suggestions, to no effect, we proctors had to set up the experiment for them. Also, the kids (10th grade) seemed to have no idea how to use a balance (a scale for weighing things) and had to be prompted to zero the balance before use (make sure that the balance showed zero weight when empty). Unfortunately, they did not know how to do that either, so the proctors did it. Experimental controls were nonexistent in any of the pupils' designs. For instance, paper towel pieces were merely ripped off a larger piece so that there was no uniformity of size. Also, none of the pupils thought to label their samples or to keep records of the data collected, until prompted. Next, pupils waited until the proctor suggested that they might want to weigh the pieces of toweling and standardize the volumes of water to be used. Several of these future scientists waved this standard procedure off as unnecessary busywork. Doing so will hardly have mattered, however, since the scales were never dried between samples, even after new suggestions from proctors. That meant that samples of toweling placed onto the wet scale were recorded as dry weight. Then the 'dry' sample was soaked with an undetermined volume of water and, while still dripping excess water onto the scale, lab tables, and floor, reweighed. The balances could determine mass to 1/10th of a gram, but most of the kids were satisfied with measurements to within 3 to 5 grams—I think. It was hard to tell exactly, since the swinging three-beam balance was never allowed to come to a full stop. Still, the fact that the data gathered was perfectly useless did not matter much either, since no pupil had the foggiest notion how to prepare a report of their 'findings' or what sorts of information should have been included, nor what sort of format to use.

The State is currently redesigning its science assessment, though not its instructional criteria. The new version was due in 2001.

As I have said, I have no doubt that some schools got better results than the school district where I did my teaching, but the district also had a goodly pupil turnover. As the primary high school in a military community, many kids came in from many parts of the country, stayed a few years and moved on. The new pupils were not noticeably more, or less, proficient than the lifelong residents. This fact, and the fact that this State is often listed among the upper tier of States academically, makes me bold enough to suggest that the problems I encountered are quite general.

Let me explain the grading scheme I was allowed to use.

When I started my stint as a teacher, I gave assignments and graded according to my best traditions (i.e., correct answers earn accolades). The average grade, for those pupils who submitted their assignments, was near 10 percent. The papers were purely awful, almost invariably incomplete, and frequently incoherent. My 'co-op' (i.e., cooperating teacher—the experienced teacher who agrees to take on and supervise a student teacher) was quite concerned about the grades I recorded and told me to stop it. He said he would have to live with those grades after I was gone. He was right about that of course. However, though I could not reverse years of bad practice in ten weeks, I did see some minor improvement in the week or two before I was asked to readjust my grading scheme. Answers given in class discussions and homework assignments began to show a bit more care and thought. The results were moving toward merely atrocious and away from totally abominable.

There was, however, another reason that I was told to change my grading scheme. The co-op told me that it was "my job" to make sure that I passed as many pupils as possible, and that he, ". . . did not care how I did it." I quickly developed a new grading scheme which was approved:

- Only those who turned in nothing at all, even after a week or two of make-up opportunities, got 0 percent. Many zeros were still awarded even though the assignments amounted to something like, "Read four pages and answer the seven questions at the end." Assignments were posted at least a week before they were due and we also regularly gave the pupils time during class to complete them. In fact, this extra time often consisted of entire block-schedule class periods (90 minutes each) devoted to homework, during which no new material was presented.
- Next, *anything* submitted with a decipherable name, got 50 percent no matter the content (i.e., an otherwise blank page with a

legible name got 50 percent. 'Legible,' of course is also a relative term, but by that time I was beginning to associate individual scribbles with individual kids.

- Next, papers with at least some questions answered got 60 percent. These acceptable answers were not necessarily accurate enough to be considered 'in the ballpark', of course, but were at least sometimes within the same county as the ballpark. Sixty percent was a passing grade in our school.
- Also, since I could not in good conscience announce my new grading policy, I continued to give lip service to my two-sentence-per-essay writing requirement, but, to abide by my new scoring scheme, I had to forgo it as a grading criterion entirely.

A few of my pupils even got good grades without answering any questions at all. They simply copied the questions out of the book, which was not required, leaving the answers blank. I was told that merely copying those questions was a "major effort" for a 9th grader, and to grade them poorly would "discourage" them to the point that they would do no work at all. (Would that I had known that doing-no-work-at-all was an acceptable option when I was in the 9th grade). Evidently the kids set the standards no matter what the State publishes. I eventually awarded A's to some pupils who would have flunked in my high school. They would have failed not because they were so much dumber than my own classmates, but because their modern school system was.

The State writing assessments, as reported in the Building Report Card data, were almost certainly graded to similar, though not necessarily identical, criteria, no matter what the rubric expected. For instance, the grading instructions for the State-sponsored tests included a provision that each teacher should grade the work of pupils not currently assigned to his or her own classes. The rules expect each teacher to grade the work of kids who were unfamiliar to them. This was done, presumably, to avoid exactly what happened. At the department meeting called to discuss grading the science assessments, one educator argued, and others agreed, that it would be best if he could grade the papers of his own pupils, because he would be able to, ". . . figure out what (the pupil) *meant* to say," whereas anyone else might not understand the written answer, and therefore might not give an "appropriate" grade.

Although the school's exit outcomes promised to create effective communicators, the educators agreed that it takes time to develop individual kid-to-English dictionaries to be able to decipher individual kids' uses of our common language.

I was a student teacher at the time, of course, so I was also being evaluated for a grade. Since my faculty advisor could not witness my performance in the public school classroom on a daily basis, he periodically sent a graduate student to sit in on a class that I conducted. My advisor also stopped by once or twice. After each visit we discussed my performance and suggestions for improvement were made. Typically the suggested improvements merely included more games and group activities, changing the seating arrangements to resemble gathering around a campfire, and so forth.

During those sessions I showed my grader some of the papers that my pupils handed in. I showed the question asked from the text, and the answers provided by the pupils. I would hold up a paper and say, "Look. These answers are incoherent." Often I could not guess which question the pupil was attempting to answer. Of the questions that I could legitimately grade, many responses were so badly written that the evident answer intended was not the actual answer written. I had to be very generous in what I would accept.[65]

I continued to point out these things to my advisors until the graduate student finally asked me in an exasperated voice, "Why are you concerned?" Now (this is the scary part) the graduate student who evaluated my work was a 'science educator' with nearly a decade of classroom experience.

For me that was a big clue.

The graduate student has since earned a doctorate. This, too, concerns me.

Therefore, it did not surprise me to see State Writing averages in the "C" range and some whole-school scores in the "B" range. In fairness to the schools that recorded B-range average scores, they might have achieved them honestly since teaching competent writing is not supremely difficult. It is not difficult, but it is a long process that requires much instruction and practice. To teach competent writing, after instruction and mastery of the basic rules of grammar, spelling, and sentence structure, etc., we should simply require kids to write a lot, and

---

65 I was refused permission to keep the papers after the kids saw their grade or I would have reproduced some of them to prove these things.

then grade their efforts according to the rules of standard English. From the earliest grades we should ask pupils to write very short pieces as answers to questions of progressively increasing difficulty. A sentence, a phrase or even a word at a time, will do by the end of the Kindergarten, but we need questions and written responses in every subject area. We should grade these answers for content and grammatical correctness, in every subject area, not just in English class. Other-than-English teachers need not be as detailed in their language grading (e.g., pointing out split infinitives or dangling participles), but they can make it clear, by reducing an assignment grade by half a letter grade, for instance, that persuasive communication requires the writer to, at least, sound competent. This sort of exercise, along with doing math problems in class, etc., is ridiculed as grey and dreary seat-work that should be avoided. This, we are told, is mere training, not education. On the other hand, doing math and language skills activities is education, not training. We all see the differences and the wisdom of these pronouncements. Don't we?

The following is an example of a typical requirement in one 8th grade English class that I witnessed. The class is broken up into small groups called 'Lit circles'. Each group is instructed to read a portion of a book that is written at, at best, a 5th grade level. Then they are given the following worksheet, which is printed on a half sheet of paper.

Discussion Topics (wonderings)
1.
2.
3.
Interesting/Difficult Words with Definitions
1. ______________.
2. ______________.
3. ______________.
Literary Highlights (best part of what you read)
1. *pg.____paragraph #____*   2. *pg.____paragraph #____*

This was an assignment for a class of kids who are now presumably capable of true inductive reasoning. Do you see any requirement for any of the kinds of discussion topics you would expect to see in a Junior High 'literature' class? Such items as discussions of major themes, of character development, or of the symbolism(s) intended by the author? Instead, the 'literary highlights' consist of page and paragraph references for the kid's favorite parts, and nothing else. Not even an explanation of why those parts were considered particularly interesting was expected, much less required. You should know that these literary circles are conducted with the minimal cooperation of the educator, who must do little to facilitate this intellectual activity beyond, perhaps, defining "wonderings." As such, this activity can be conducted by someone who had not read this bit of literature at all, such as a substitute facilitator, but is clearly a routine activity since the kids went right to it and needed no prompting at all.

Another 8th grade Language Arts class was busy writing one-page comic books; an assignment that could easily be completed in about an hour or less, especially considering the level of inspiration evidenced by the work. When I was there, however, the original due date for this assignment had been the Friday of the week before. I was there on a Wednesday and the kids were being given time in class to work on their creative masterpieces, with no new due date set. Evidently, the kids didn't bother to do the assignment, so class time was being given to complete an overdue homework assignment. But, no! This was not a homework assignment at all. Writing a comic book cannot be done alone. This assignment was being done in groups, and some of the groups could not finish theirs, since the kid with all the materials was absent, or being counseled in the office for a disciplinary problem.

If this level of accomplishment is all that is expected of 8th graders, do you wonder what could they possibly ask of 2nd graders? The answer would be, 'Pretty much the same thing'. Developing higher-level thinking skills, like creativity, requires open-ended assignments such as these. We will come back to these ideas again, but it is clear that Progressive education does not progress at all in the sense of building on previously acquired knowledge or understanding. It merely does things over and again, expecting different results with each try.

Instead of an unrelenting diet of these sorts of trivial, pointless, and non-progressive assignments, we should require longer, more detailed written answers to essay questions in each subject area. Complete paragraphs should be routine probably by the beginning of the 2nd and certainly by the middle of the 2nd grade, though introduced early in the 1st grade. Obviously this implics that kids begin to read early in the 1st grade at the latest, not by the end of the 3rd grade, as under current Federal guidelines. Later still, book reports, essays, and eventually term papers, or research reports, in every subject area could be added. These efforts need not be very long at first. I recall 250 words being a common requirement in the 5th grade. Two hundred fifty words might seem unreasonable to a 5th grader (I remember moaning and groaning, too), but we eventually discover that to do a decent job of explaining something even moderately complex, 250 words will hardly get us started.[66] That is why the average book may be 250 pages, not 250 words long, and why organic chemistry textbooks are so thick and their print so small.

Besides, other than not learning how to write (or think) coherently if we are never asked to write, what kind of stress will we feel when a college professor requires a 40-page term paper, or an employer requires some detailed analytical report, if we have rarely written one complete paragraph at a time.

Asking kids to write should also insure that the kids read materials that are well written, and write about what they read. We should grade these papers for content and grammar, etc., *in every subject area*. If you practice, you get better. *Not* reading and writing leaves kids illiterate and stunts creativity by limiting access to a limited set of simple, not to say childish, ideas.

How would the teachers find the time to grade all of this written work?[67] Admittedly, a transition of this sort would cause a greatly increased workload for today's teachers as they researched and developed coherent year-long lesson plans (a workload that many modern educators reduce by allowing the kids to grade their own papers). Still, once the plans were written (preferably at least in draft outline form as a major requirement in Ed school), only minor adjustments and updates would be required as they used their basic plans repeatedly, year after year. After all, each new class of pupils knows as little of the, for them, new material as the class before. There is no need to continually develop innovative new approaches only to drop them, when they prove to be ineffective, for new, even more innovative, but equally noninstructive activities. With an, at best, slowly changing but thoroughly familiar curriculum, the teachers would have time to fine-tune their presentations, and to add timely, new materials (i.e., staying near the cutting

---

66 When I mentioned this 250-word requirement to one 6th-grade teacher, who said she had "Gifted experience," she literally gasped and was left speechless for a time.

67 This method would also have the added benefit of letting the teacher know how well each individual student is doing (as in a Progressive assessment). Additionally, use of a sane, traditional grading method that focuses on learning, would eventually allow legislatures to modify, or eliminate, the massively bureaucratic "accountability" requirements, and the requirements of QPA (Quality Performance Accreditation), 'outcomes alignment', No Child Left Behind, etc., placed on teachers in recent years, freeing up still more time that could be used to better purposes.

edge), and to grade assignments. Teachers would do this by thinking of several ways to get the point across, or by trying various media and techniques to see what works best. Over time, they would have an idea about what works best with classes of differing personalities, while still focusing on the subject.

An example of this comes from my time as an instructor in the Army's veterinary technician school. One of my lessons, related to cell membrane function, required me to teach the idea of the 'semipermeable membrane' for which I used my standard explanations that had worked for me in the past. For one class however, my standard explanation, a description of the physical properties of living cells, was not getting through. Suddenly, I thought of an analogy to a window screen, which allows small things through, such as air molecules and tiny bugs, but does not admit larger things, such as houseflies. Almost immediately lights began to go on all around the classroom. Brows began to unfurrow and smiles of understanding bloomed on many faces. After the class one pupil asked me why I had not said that in the first place. I frankly just had not thought of it until I was on the spot. I knew I could not just let it go though, since the pupils needed the idea of semipermeability to begin to understand the functions of cell membranes and why certain lab procedures worked in some cases but not in others. Of course, while the new analogy proved useful, I continued to use my former, more biologically accurate description, too, since it had more of the specific detail that was needed for a fuller understanding. The quick parallel got the descriptive ball rolling, while the facts and detail were needed to develop the correct concept more completely.

Maybe the schools with high recorded averages did require routine writing, and graded the papers professionally with good results, as opposed to the way that I had to grade my pupils' papers. For those kids' sake, I hope that is true because handing out high grades for shoddy work makes a kid question the worth of the whole process. This idea was brought home to me in a different venue when I was in the 8th grade (*circa* 1965). The school's athletes were being honored at a sports awards assembly. It surprised us seeing team 'managers' (the kids who helped the coaches by retrieving equipment after practice, etc.) get a 'Letter' and a sweater to go with it. Those of us who worked out persistently and competed successfully started to look askance at the 'Letter' we had just been awarded. Suddenly the Letter lost some its meaning.

Please note, this innovation was first introduced to our school in the mid 1960s. Shortly afterwards, the traditions of the Letter sweater, and eventually the merit-based valedictorian, were discontinued on the assumption that honoring excellence left other kids with a low self-esteem.

Another complaint of many parents, and others, is the relative lack of school spirit shown by modern pupils. I wonder whether Progressive precepts can be blamed for this, too. We are told that among the foremost of the Progressive ideals is to make school fun. A typical attempt can be seen from the local Middle School attended by my oldest daughter. Late in the year, the school tried to generate school spirit by sponsoring a "Wacky Hair Day." With few exceptions, anything anyone wanted to do to their hair that day would be allowable, just for the fun of it. This activity was permitted to allow a morale-building break from what, we were told, was the daily grind of hard work that is expected typically. This idea was a continuation of the innumerable reasons for having a party that had been a part of my daughter's grammar school experience. While finding the whole notion of a Wacky Hair Day rather silly (though she was not yet 13), but being a good pupil, my daughter participated in a modest way. Then she discovered that she was among only three pupils in the school to do so.

The fact that the Rah-Rah is dying along with academic competence should get the attention of even the most committed educationist. Yet, they seem to have failed in even their most basic endeavor, making school fun, and do not notice.

Well. What About the Teachers?

Even if the teachers find the time to teach and grade pupils' work professionally, do they know what they are talking about and are they even qualified to grade anything? Some are, but then again, many are not. Recently, Massachusetts required its teaching students to take that great bugaboo of the teacher's unions, a test of basic skills. Fifty-nine percent of these 1,800 16th graders (college seniors) on the verge of graduation and 'educational professional' status failed, although the tests were written only at the 10th grade (high school equivalency) level. Among other things, the teachers had trouble writing, coherent sentences and spelling common words such as 'burned' and 'abolished'. Since it is quite clear that the Massachusetts Ed schools were not concerned with their students' competence with subject matter content, nor with competence in basic communication, we can infer from the college requirements listed below, what they did consider important for their graduates to know. The following is a partial list of courses offered at the University of Massachusetts-Amherst (as provided to John Leo, *U.S. News and World Report*, August 3, 1998):

Leadership in Changing Times, Social Diversity in Education (four different courses), Embracing Diversity, Diversity & Change, Oppression & Education, Introduction to Multicultural Education, Black Identity, Classism, Racism, Sexism, Jewish Oppression, Lesbian/Gay/Bisexual oppression, Oppression of the Disabled, and Erroneous Beliefs.[68]

Leo concludes from this list that, "Our schools of education have been a national scandal for many years, but it is odd that they are rarely front-and-center in our endless debate about failing schools. The right talks about striving and standards, the left talks about equal funding and classroom size, but few talk much about the breeding grounds for school failure—the trendy, anti-achievement, oppression-obsessed, feel-good, esteem-ridden, content-free schools of education."

One of my hopes is to bring the educational silliness of an Ed school education more onto center court, and we will touch on the dangers of drilling the teachers of our nation's young in little beyond ideological hatred in Chapter 5. Yet, for most people, having a college education still implies that the graduate has learned some useful things. Furthermore, we give any college professor the benefit of the doubt with regards to knowledge about educational matters. We do this because we expect colleges to hire and retain instructors and professors based on their academic acumen rather than merely on how pleasant they are, or on their blind adherence to an ideology. After reading this book, I hope you will see that trusting an Ed school professor to know much about education is often an erroneous belief.

Morris Berman, in his book *The Twilight of American Culture* (2000), gives a good example of the kind of thing that I mean. As you read this extended quote, you should know that Dr. Berman is a proud, self-proclaimed liberal who blames much of America's woe on big business and commercialism. Yet, he is also an educated man and can recognize slumping standards as well as anyone. His primary educational

---

68 This seems to account for 68 credits in a 120-credit curriculum, or about 57 percent of graduation requirements.

concern is the adjustments deemed to be necessary by our colleges in an everyone-needs-college world, rather than primary and secondary education per se, but his experience is appropriate for our purposes, as an indication of what Progressive educational philosophy spawns [Note: Parenthetical comments are Berman's, while my comments are in brackets]. He writes [beginning on page 121]:

> Universities retain an aura of elitism (positively conceived) [i.e., it's a good thing to be educated]; they are seen as the loci of the most advanced thinking in the land, places where men and women are free to pursue the sciences and the humanities and thus imbibe the highest elements of culture. Latin mottoes adorn the crests of many of these schools, Boasting of "light" and "truth." The reality, however, is something very different, as thousands of these have literal or *de facto* open admissions policies in the name of "democracy." The democratization of desire means that nearly everyone can go to college; the purpose being to get a job; and in an educational world now subsumed under business values, students show up—with administrative blessing—believing that they are consumers buying a product. Within this context, a faculty member who actually attempts to enforce the tradition of the humanities as an uplifting and transformational experience, who challenges his charges to think hard about complex issues, will provoke negative evaluations and soon be told by the dean that he had better look elsewhere for a job.

Then on page 123, he continues:

> I had an opportunity to see these tendencies at their worst when I was unexpectedly hired by a trendy "distance learning institute" a few years back. On the face of it—that is, from its published study guides—"Alt. U," as I shall refer to it, sounded quite reputable, and that was what originally drew me in [much like my teaching college]. As I soon discovered, however, the actual educational practice was something else . . . Alt. U had no real identity; it was a kind of corporate creation driven by popular rhetoric and content to identify itself with whatever was academically avant-garde. A large percentage of the students were corporate employees trying to advance their careers by adding Ph.D. after their names, and because the school was 100 percent tuition-driven [student's academic credentials were not relevant], these students effectively called the shots. It was thus impossible for Alt. U to enforce (assuming it even cared about) real academic standards, because that would have threatened its academic base. Hence, an ideology prevailed that *any* academic authority

was an "abuse of power," and an instructor who had any notion of serious academic accountability was quickly dropped by the students in favor of one—and there were many—who made very few rigorous intellectual demands. Since mentors had to attract "mentees" in order to survive, it behooved them not to demand too much. As far as I could make out, most applicants were accepted, and the screening interviews were bogus: In the case of the two students I did reject (and this meant they were *really* bad), one was admitted anyway, and the other was reinterviewed twice. Grades for study units completed were basically Yes and Not Yet, so the student who just kept at it, no matter how inadequate, eventually obtained a Ph.D.

As for the faculty it was not clear how they had been hired, beyond the fact that they seemed to fit in with the group. Merit was at best a secondary consideration, and a good number of them were embarrassingly unqualified: not only breathtakingly ignorant but aggressively anti-intellectual in their outlook, and contemptuous of any individual expression that violated the group mind. Thus I was ridiculed for using the word *desultory*, and attacked for reading George Steiner. When I once referred to Francis Bacon at a faculty meeting, my colleagues seemed to have no idea whom I was talking about. These "retreats" as they were called, contained large doses of traditional-institution bashing and had the flavor of cult rituals, binding the group together [much as teacher in-service days do in the grade and high schools]. The dean took me aside at one point and told me that I would do a lot better at the place if I were to start publicly praising the institution at the retreats—a suggestion reminiscent of the Chinese Cultural Revolution. Reading over student work, I was amazed at how feeble most of it was, how little effort was required of these doctoral candidates, and how easily their work received a passing grade . . . The protocol was never to call students "students"; rather, they were "co-learners," and in an odd sense, this was accurate, because Alt. U was a classic case of the blind leading the blind.[68a]

Unfortunately, Berman's book is profoundly sad since he has concluded that we can do nothing to prevent the ongoing decay and ultimate fall of our culture. His hope is that a few of us, quietly and unobtrusively, try to remember how to read, so that after the next inevitable and imminent Dark Age, there might be small patches of learning left that might, if we are lucky, eventually allow civilization to flower

---

68a From *The Twilight of American Education* by Morris Berman. Copyright © 2000 by Morris Berman, Used by permission of W. W. Norton & Company, Inc.

again. This is another remarkable opinion in a time that proudly proclaims itself as The Information Age. I hope he is wrong about this. My kids are alive now. I do not want them living in his predicted *Blade Runner* world.

That the traditional frustration with the direction of education generally, and with reform efforts specifically, may be more heartfelt than is heard in public, can be deduced from the way that this frustration occasionally spills out. A number of authors have over the years, allowed themselves to say things in print that is generally unheard of in collegial circles. For instance, in the quote above, Berman has gone so far as to say that some of his faculty colleagues are "breathtakingly ignorant."

Opinions such as Berman's are not new, of course, and many authors discuss the state of American Schools of Education specifically. These books are well known in academic circles, and go back at least as long ago as 1953. In that year Arthur Bestor published *Educational Wastelands: The Retreat from Learning in Our Public Schools.*[69] In it he described the growing educational inadequacies in American public schools and put the blame squarely on the shoulders of the growing numbers of "professional educationists," the anti-intellectual intellectuals that had been systematically transforming American education at least since the days of Edward Thorndike and John Dewey. What later became known as Progressive educational theory may have had its origins circa 1650 with the writings of the Czech thinker Jan Komensky (Barzun, 2000, p. 18). In the 1950s, however, Bestor's book, along with the collective concerns of traditional teachers, business leaders, and parents halted the spread of progressive education to the point that Diane Ravitch (*The Troubled Crusade: American Education 1945–1980*, [1983][70] concluded hopefully that, for a time at least, Progressive education seemed dead. Yet that description was clearly premature.

Other authors, notably James Koerner,[71] Rita Kramer,[72] Jacques Barzun,[73] and even Lynne Cheney[73a] published accounts that, to a

---

69 Bestor, Arthur (1953), *Educational Wastelands: The Retreat from Learning in Our Public Schools*, University of Illinois Press, Urbana, 1985.

70 Ravitch, Diane, *The Troubled Crusade: American Education 1945–1980*, Basic Books, New York, 1983.

71 Koerner, James D., *The Miseducation of American Teachers*, Penguin Books, Baltimore, 1963.

72 Kramer, Rita, *Ed School Follies. The Miseducation of Teachers*, Excellence in Education Series, John M. Ashbrook Center for Public Affairs, Ashland University, Ashland OH, 1992.

73 Barzun, Jacques, *The House of Intellect*, Harper Books, New York, 1959.

73a Cheney, Lynne V. *Telling the Truth*, Touchstone, New York, 1995.

greater or lesser degree, excoriated modern educators. These authors have been joined by Allan Bloom,[74] Alvin Kernan,[75] Thomas Sowell,[76] Martin Gross,[77] and others. Some of these authors went so far as to quote research that looked at the scholastic records of the candidates for the various professions, and described the very low academic entrance standards used by schools and graduate schools of education. Koerner, for instance, noted that the average candidate for admission to our schools of education was only marginally more qualified for college than art students and secretarial candidates. Since schools of education supply us with our teachers, administrators, and educational bureaucrats at all levels, it can be no surprise what has led to the plummeting standards that continue to concern us.

Berman spoke of Alt. U., a "trendy distance-learning" institute, and the previous section decried the qualifications of classroom teachers, but what about our "real" universities? Can Berman's concerns be extended to them? What standards do they use when qualifying educators? To answer this question, I looked at *Dissertation Abstracts* under the general heading of "Education." The Abstracts are available now on the Internet through a library database subscription. While there may be many intelligent, thoughtful, and committed scholars represented there as well, we have already mentioned the general preparedness of education majors, including our doctoral candidates. You should know that the rest of the academic community has some concern that our educational tradition is eroding in Ed schools,[78] however.

Traditionally, doctoral degrees require that, besides completing all course work satisfactorily (no less than a 'B' in any course), some original work must be done that significantly advances understanding in the field. This original work should be nontrivial and, of course, it should be new, not a mere rewording of previous work. Apart from the candidate's own research, the academic advisor should help to insure that these standards are met, since sponsorship of a candidate to a doctoral committee implies that the advisor is aware that the quality of the dissertation presented is at least minimally sufficient and important enough

---

74 Bloom, Allan, *The Closing of the American Mind*, Touchstone, New York, 1987.

75 Kernan, Alvin, *In Plato's Cave*, Yale U. Press, New Haven, 1999.

76 Sowell, Thomas, *Inside American Education: The Decline, The Deception, The Dogmas*, The Free Press, New York, 1993.

77 Gross, Martin I., *The Conspiracy of Ignorance: The Failure of American Public Schools*, Perennial, New York, 1999.

78 Bestor, 1953, Murray, 1984; Kramer, 1991; Sowell, 1993; Kernan, 1999, and others.

to present to the academic world. An indication of the standards of our Ed schools can be gotten from reading the titles and abstracts of dissertations that were accepted, and for which the degrees of Ed.D. or Ph.D. in education, were awarded.

There are many education doctorates awarded now. By some measures, there are as many Ed.D.'s and Education Ph.D.'s awarded as all of the other academic fields (e.g., physics, chemistry, literature, etc.) combined, and have been for a long time.[79] That fact seems to say that a great deal should now be known about education and about learning, since so many are seemingly working so hard to learn it. Some of this stuff is probably relevant, too. On the other hand, *A study of the readability of on-screen text* won a Ph.D. from the Virginia Polytechnic Institute and State University. The study's 'discovered' and concluded that since 8-bit onscreen text is more readable than 1-bit onscreen text, onscreen text ought to be of the 8-bit variety. The author also encourages a future quest for knowledge designed to conduct a "further exploration of the readability of onscreen text (and to) examine more fonts and screen display variables." Since this dissertation was published in 1999, not 1959, we have to assume the computer industry had passed on to other challenges long since.

Harvard University awarded a doctorate for *In the words of girls: The reading of adolescent romance fiction.* This study, based on only 20 subjects, discovered that adolescent girls identify with characters in romance novels, which they read "for instruction in how to live." It also discusses the "educational implications" of the *Sweet Valley High* series of books no longer being available through school book clubs.

A new doctor from The Union Institute, wrote *Zoos in the twenty-first century: Can't we find a better way to love nature?* This scholar creatively argues that creating a 'New Zew', that does not display living animals, is a conceptually better way to love nature. Apparently live animals get in the way of fully appreciating nature. This is a very modern notion to say the least, and the dissertation abstract goes on to tell us that kids learn more about the environment, ecology, and the 'universal plight of animals' while wandering through nonliving natural history museum exhibits. The relative advantage of reading a bit first, before going to visit either a museum or a zoo, is not mentioned.

---

79 Barzun, 1959.

A doctoral candidate at the University of Sarasota discovered, according to his dissertation abstract titled, *A research conducted to study the effect of accelerated reader designed to help increase reading levels in a third-grade class of at-risk students*, that if we give kids a computerized reading test at the start of the school year, then periodically (parameters were not specified) ask them to read for an hour, and test again, they achieve better reading scores at the end of the school year. Considering the groundbreaking information uncovered (as we practice a thing, we get better at doing that thing), we will not quibble that the new doctor could not tell that even her title was ungrammatical, and incomplete. We would expect that from a recent high school graduate. Why should a doctoral candidate do any better?

Some doctoral candidates did field research that took them all over the globe. For instance, a candidate from Teachers College, Columbia University went all the way to Ghana to discover that the more that librarians learn about libraries, and the longer they work in libraries, the more they understand how libraries affect the people that use them, and that some people appreciate it. This discovery was described in *Ghanian volunteer librarians: Transformative participation in communities of practice.*

The University of Memphis awarded an Ed.D for *Newsroom technology: Form, style, and content* that examined a computer training class for newspaper reporters, organized by the newspaper. It concluded that since the trainers had no organized training plan, "The results point to a need for a training program for trainers to enhance their skills in this critical area."

Even divinity schools are not immune to this inane stuff. *Formative educational experiences of leaders as factors influencing innovation in organizations*, from Trinity Evangelical Divinity School, tells us that life experiences help leaders to learn to lead, and that different life experiences affect different people differently. Furthermore, it "confirm(ed) the literature of *innovation in organizations* (emphasis in the original) as to the importance of leadership, relationships, trust, scope, low power distance and low risk avoidance to innovation." I guess we must read the literature to sort it all out.

The University of Maryland, College Park is undoubtedly proud of its contribution to the sum of human knowledge with the acceptance of *Validation of a simulation to evaluate instructional consultation problem identification skill competence.* Unfortunately, there is no telling what this is about. The abstract is almost as incoherent as the title, though this study seemed to use sample set sizes ranging all the way up to 27 people. Ironically, the final sentences put forward the opinion, that "results suggest need for refinement of rating criteria and rater training before replication with larger, more heterogeneous samples. implications (*sic*) for training are discussed." I think this means that he (the researcher) should have known what he was talking about before he started writing, and should have used larger samples if he had intended to actually prove anything. If that is it, it is hard to disagree. However, "refinement of rating criteria and rater training" is a cause for concern. We will soon see that much of what passes for research is, in fact, little more than subjective evaluations of subjective surveys rated by people trained to give the responses needed to support the author's contention. Apparently, our budding researcher had not yet mastered this technique. The fact that "implications" was not capitalized may have been a publisher's error.

Maybe our educational professionals do not know as much about education as we like to think. While these are certainly not the sum of all doctorates awarded, and I am sure that some dissertations are better than these, there certainly seem to be a lot of folks busily studying irrelevant and trivial aspects of the field. All of these folks earned their doctoral degrees in 1999. Many, perhaps all, of them are now respected members of the education establishment, lending their dubious expertise to promoting learning and to reaching for academic excellence. The fact that any dissertations of this quality had been accepted at all, however, speaks volumes about the standards of at least some of our graduate schools of education.

But what do all of these scholars do after graduate school? Many, of course, are in the schools or in the educational bureaucracy at all levels. Their contributions and inability to evaluate reality have caused the national educational debacle that we can't seem to resolve. And the beat goes on, though there is some question about the competence of at least some of our modern band leaders.

I should mention that the pool of qualified candidates available to Education has shrunk considerably since women began entering other professions. Several decades ago qualified, ambitious women were largely restricted to either nursing or teaching. Today they can train for and enter any profession they choose. Nevertheless, dropping standards to the extent detailed here is unforgivable.

However, we should get back to the public schools. With this sort of standard set for doctoral candidates, it is no wonder that the teacher's unions are against the competency tests for mere Ed school graduates. Remember, tests of 10th-grade understanding and expertise are racist instruments that degrade anyone taking them by forcing us to submit to the oppressive influences of dead white guys. One Massachusetts teacher, who presumably failed the initial test the previous year, was interviewed as a part of an ABC News piece that reported that Massachusetts will soon retest the teachers who failed the initial test.[80] The almost-educator forcefully argued that a written test cannot completely prove her skill as a teacher. True enough, but they also interviewed a test administrator who said, "We are not asking (educators) to be able to write like Shakespeare, only a little better than Daniel Boone." If we recall our American history, Daniel Boone is credited with carving something like, 'D. Boon kilt a bar on ths tre', on a tree as a young man. He was describing an encounter with a bear.

The State Board of Regents in my own State was recently presented with a proposal that used the same argument as the angry educator-candidate above. This proposal was given as a complaint. 'Why', they asked, 'were education schools accepting only those applicants with the highest academic credentials?' Other high school graduates, even those who had not proven that they understood the subjects they proposed to teach, could also make good teachers, they said. Taking only the applicants with the highest academic credentials available was unfair. Teaching is as much an art as a science, and book learning is only a part of the total person who stands in front of a class.[81]

That is quite true of course, and in a perfect world each teacher would have the sagacity of Cicero, the eloquence of Pericles, the realistic compassion of Gandhi, and the force of personality of MacArthur. Of course in a perfect world we would also pay teachers enough to attract qualified graduates away from other careers that fund the 'good life', as expressed in advertising. In a perfect world the intricacies of the Krebs

---

80 I understand that 50 percent of the teachers also failed the retest.

81 I'm afraid that I did not clip this article when I read it prior to deciding to write this book, but I believe it was the State chapter of the NEA (National Education Association), which markets itself not as a trade union but as a 'professional association', that argued that ignorance in their members is a good thing.

Cycle or the trigonometric functions would fascinate kids more than gossip, fashions, social cliques, and sexy music videos. And, in a perfect world educational professionals would know something about education.

Unfortunately there are precious few Ciceros or MacArthurs in the world, and few of these want to be public school teachers. So, short of a perfect world it is probably best that teachers prove they have mastered their subject (so they can explain things clearly and answer detailed questions) if the kids are going to have any chance of understanding much. Just imagine being instructed in the quadratic equation by someone who confuses the square-root symbol for the division symbol. Are average kids still asked to struggle with quadratic equations? I wonder.

I sat in on some of my 9th graders' other classes, to see whether they are merely having trouble with biology, or whether their ignorance was more general. As I witnessed a 'pre-algebra class', the educator was reviewing a test the kids had taken the previous day. Sadly, one question that more than 50 percent of the kids had missed was:

$$-k = 7 \qquad \text{Solve for k.}$$

Incidentally, 'pre-algebra' is a Middle School euphemism for re-hashed 6th or 7th grade mathlike material. Considering that many of my 9th graders thought that 1,000,000 was three times 1,000 (because it has three more zeros), it is not surprising they had to be 'left back' (while being promoted) and redo the pointless activities that had failed to instruct them the year before, and the year before that. Remember, my biology pupils were generally exhibiting a 4th grade level of knowledge and understanding.

Being 'left back' was once a disgrace to be avoided at all costs. A little embarrassment goes a long way as a motivator with humans. In my student-teaching school though, it was not at all uncommon for parents to demand that their kids be left back. The only problem is that these modern parents were trying to keep their kids back because they had become convinced that even the dumbed-down classes were too much for their kids. The principal in my own kid's grammar school tells me that he has parents come in to complain that the Kindergarten-level work is too much for their kids. Three cheers for Progressive expectations.

I wonder whether the following influenced those parents: During the annual "Kindergarten Parents" information night, a Kindergarten educator stood up to caution parents that they must seriously consider whether their children are "ready" for the rigors of Kindergarten. Parents must be sure that Junior can handle the onslaught of new ideas and the stressful emotional trials that await their little pumpkin. Subjecting Junior to these tribulations before he is ready to color pictures while sitting alongside other kids, might render him as a cauldron of seething, self-destructive emotions, destined for the ministrations of mental-health professionals and Special educators.

I am not the first to have noticed a lack of substance in American educational standards and I have no interest in insulting anyone specifically, yet the run of everyone involved in American education is not good. Aside from Berman, mentioned previously, both Koerner in 1963 and Sowell in 1993 have surveyed the question of professional qualifications, and their conclusions are the same. American teachers, administrators, education professors, and all the education 'doctors' in state and federal agencies and teachers' unions, on average, have proven themselves to be of lower quality, intellectually and academically, than the graduates of virtually every other discipline represented in American universities. In fact, American schools of education, at both the undergraduate and graduate levels, are similarly held in contempt by their academic peers. For example, the street in front of Columbia University's Teachers College, probably the single most influential Ed school in our history, was called, the "widest street in the world, because it separates Teacher's College from the rest of the university." As early as 1933, even the Harvard University School of Education was described by Harvard's own retiring President, as "a kitten that ought to be drowned." The schools have been called "academic slums" that repel the intelligent applicant. Sowell describes the situation as, "Darwinism stood on its head, with the *unfittest* being most likely to survive as public school-teachers."

Some of this contempt was based on the educationists' retreat from an academic study of education and its purposes, toward what was called more "practical" training for school superintendents and other administrators. For instance, among the recommendations for training included more business-oriented training. While facility with budgets and the esoterica of building maintenance are necessary sets of skills for administrators, they were not viewed as subjects fit for study at the graduate level, nor for the awarding of advanced degrees. These skills were thought to be little better than vocational training. Another factor found contemptible was the intellectual direction that the educationists took, starting at least by 1910, away from subject matter, and toward the "project method," which is virtually indistinguishable from today's activities-based curricula. The project method, "originated among teachers of agriculture and domestic science" but was proposed as the method of choice for all classes and all subjects to promote "social utility."[82]

However, another of the factors leading to the contempt was, ironically, the standardized tests that educationists had themselves begun to develop earlier in the century.[83] National statistics show that applicants to schools of education often have lower academic credentials (i.e., lower SAT scores) than applicants to other programs.[84] With the obvious proviso that the motivation for becoming a teacher does not apply to everyone, because of the lower pay, teaching is often seen as a career to enter if you cannot qualify for something better. This is not to say that the people who are teachers are invariably stupid or unconditional losers. Far from it. It only says that many of them are not those whom corporate "head hunters" or rigorous graduate schools would pursue. Even the professors in Berman's example above were not necessarily stupid, only "breathtakingly" ignorant.

In 1959 Jacques Barzun described American education professors as having a, ". . . colossal ignorance and conceit which makes modern 'experts' impervious to criticism." He said, "After listening to parents, to conscientious teachers, as well as to young scholars and professional men, one is tempted to conclude that our present 'approach' . . . turns out with certainty only two products—complaints and (intellectual) cripples."

Additionally, one of my manuscript reviewers, a teacher with twenty-six years of classroom experience, told me that in her experience, some prospective primary school teachers major in 'elementary' education only after rejection from the 'secondary' programs, that are often unworthy of the description of institution of higher education. That was a personal observation that had been validated several times by extensive

---

82 Lagemann, p. 110.

83 The Educational Testing Service (ETS), the test writing group within the College Entrance Examination Board (CEEB), publishers of the SAT and other standardized tests, was established in 1947 with the help of the Carnegie Corporation and the Carnegie Foundation for the Advancement of Teaching. (Lagemann, p. 130).

84 From Gross, 1999, pp. 43–44. *General Test Percentage Distribution of Scores within Intended Broad Graduate Major Field,* Educational Testing Service.

comparisons of the degree candidates from various fields. As Richard Murnane, an economist from Harvard, said, "College graduates with high test scores are less likely to become teachers, licensed teachers with high test scores are less likely to take jobs, employed teachers with high test scores are less likely to stay, and former teachers with high test scores are less likely to return."

You have probably heard the none too complimentary, yet descriptive, ditty about teachers that says; "Those who can't do, teach." While in Ed school, I heard the ending to this poem. It goes: "And those who can't teach, teach teachers."

But then all of the incompetent student teachers are in Massachusetts, not in *my* State. Right?

Unfortunately, American education is still pursuing the same 'approach' that inspired despair in the educated a century ago. One would think that American parents would, at long last, find this condition unsatisfactory.

In the mid 1980s, Albert Shanker, longtime President of the American Federation of Teachers, shocked his members by championing fundamental teacher professional-development reforms, along with hierarchical teacher testing, akin to Board Certification for physicians, to increase public confidence as well as to improve the perception, of the public and of teachers, of the professionalism of teachers. He went so far as to say that teacher testing was necessary because, "there are teachers teaching in this country who are illiterate and who should not be in the classroom."[85] Apparently, Mr. Shanker was also considered to be 'against education' since his idea did not survive for very long.

So now, although many well-qualified people deliberately choose teaching (and then leave when the realities of bureaucracy—not to mention the burgeoning rudeness of progressively raised kids and the working conditions in schools dedicated to the pursuit of mediocrity—become intolerable), we often start with some of the least qualified applicants, on average, graduate the low end of this group, and they still ask us to drop the standards.

Don't Teach, Facilitate

So what characteristics would our school teachers need to exhibit, if not academic competence? They would simply have to be pleasant

---

85 Toch, p. 144.

and, of course, willingly follow Progressive dictates. The following is an example of what I mean.

The Teacher as Facilitator, a book by Joe Wittmer and Robert Myrick, describes the required characteristics of 'good' teachers.[86] They expect all modern teachers to model themselves after this ideal form. A facilitative teacher is one who does not 'teach' in the traditional sense of explaining and leading discussions about subject topics. Nor do educationists consider it important for the kids to know and prove that they understand things by testing for mastery of the information presented. Instead, facilitators, ". . . provide learning situations" [how bureaucratic sounding] that are:

- Personally meaningful
- Positive and nonthreatening
- Self-initiated
- Self-evaluated
- Feeling-focused.

In other words, learning is:

- Asking kids what *they* wanted to learn
- Fun but so trivial that *all* kids can pass without working
- Inconsistent and whimsical (not necessarily something the next teacher can build upon)
- Letting the kids decide when they think they know enough, or get bored
- How one feels about the subject is more important than the subject itself. The 'feeling focused' recommendation is also a foundation of the nonjudgmentalist philosophy that is making ancient community moral and ethical standards seem trivial (or worse) to kids.

On the surface it is difficult to argue with the author's statement that, ". . . significant learning occurs when they (i.e., pupils) see subject matter as having relevance for one's own purposes." Yet, the apparent corollary assumption that learning is not possible without significant prior interest does not follow. Besides, how many Kindergartners, or

---

86 This book was required reading in a graduate level education course at my Ed school.

even high school seniors, show enough maturity to decide these things for themselves? By the time my son had started Kindergarten, he had already had several career changes. First he wanted to be a fireman, then a train engineer, then it was a race car driver. In the 2nd grade he occasionally developed menus for a proposed pizza parlor. In the 4th grade he was to become a CEO of an architectural company, a baseball player, or a computer game tester. I wonder whether Jonas Salk was fascinated by the functions of viruses while still in grammar school, or whether he came to the study of them after being taught things about which he previously knew nothing.

Oh, I know. It is very incorrect to suggest that kids should not have choice over their own lives: "If we can send them to war, why can't we let them vote," and all that. On the flip side, when we accuse an 11- or 17-year-old of murder for which he then faces a life in prison, or worse, it is suddenly very correct to argue that, "He is only a kid and did not understand the results of his choices." In fact, National Public Radio reported on February 13, 2001, that current social science research, inspired by the plight of teens in adult prisons, has "discovered" that the thinking processes of children are "fundamentally different" from that of adults. Kids are said to be "unable" to think ahead and to process the results of their actions—"It is not that they do not think ahead, but that they *cannot*." For that reason, the report argued, it is unfair to sentence children to do "adult time." Perhaps this research will eventually help convince us that, apart from the context of prison, we should treat children as children as we once did and as common sense and tradition tells us we ought. Let us hope that this 'liberal' thinking, which is ironically, exactly what conservatives argued during the voting-age wars of the 1960s, finally gets generalized to children again, including within the contexts of school and voting. In any case, we have to decide what we want to call an adult, and stick to it. Then our laws, and our schools, would be less confusing.

The feeling-focused bullet can help us understand how Progressive research can recommend "positive and nonthreatening" learning situations and still lead to lousy scholastic results. If we ask a kid a question that translates to, "Would you rather have a nice teacher or mean one?", what answer do you suppose we might hear? How about this question; "What would you rather do in school, sit and listen to a boring teacher tell you things, or do a group activity with your friends?" If we ask kids, as has been done; "What would you do to improve your school?", the kids' consensus will almost inevitably be, "Less work and more social time." Educationists use such research to 'prove' their point and to convince themselves that relevance to individual kids is an essential component of every curricular item and that we are doing the right thing by dumbing things down. Since actual teaching is to be avoided, this sort of qualitative research does not address learning per se, but instead attempts to focus on 'readiness to learn'. If you follow the logic and the examples given, it becomes clear that 'readiness to learn' is jargon for, 'The kid has already figured it out for himself', or more to the point, it may mean, 'Someone else (i.e., a parent) has told him what it means', or perhaps even, 'He asked a question'. If the kids say that they like something, that is what we do, and if kids do not like a thing, we do not do that thing. We have satisfied the kids while simultaneously convincing ourselves that we are facilitating significant learning when we devote our instructional time to group-work activities, rather than to teaching lessons. Again, the results we achieve chronically should convince us that Progressive technique may not be all that we are led to believe.

What Are Validity and Reliability?

The truth is that many articles published as 'research' are mere opinion pieces. In fact, it is difficult to find an education research article that is more than a subjective evaluation of a subjective survey in which the validity of its methods and conclusions are explicitly ignored. If the word 'validity' is used, it is usually used as a redefinition of 'reliability'. Terms such as content validity, internal validity, construct validity, and heuristic validity are coined to camouflage the true meaning. I will show more examples of this in Chapter 6.

For instance, a favorite research tool for social science is the questionnaire.[87] With it a researcher attempts to determine how a few people (sometimes as few as one) feel about a subject, then equate the polled

---

87 For example, the 'Likert scale' is a favorite research device. Likert scales are the now-familiar surveys of personal choices that ask the subject to decide whether they, for instance, like something a great deal, like it a little bit, are neutral, dislike it a little bit, or hate it. However, the fact that a survey would verify that kids would rather play than study does not come close to proving that the way to improve learning is by allowing more play. As a mere survey of 'affect', those studies usually 'prove' nothing. They merely display the relative distribution of opinion.

opinions to universal truth. This is called "qualitative" research, as opposed to "quantitative" research. We will return to this idea of qualitative vs. quantitative research later, but for now, if you hear that a piece of research is 'qualitative' or 'heuristic', you can be assured that the research represents a thick piece of wool that the researcher is trying to pull over your eyes. Qualitative research is a favorite of Progressive researchers because those pesky numbers inherent in quantitative-statistical research never seem to go their way. As such, qualitative research plays fast and loose with the definitions of reliability and validity. Qualitative research is, "I do/don't want it to be so, so I will act as if it is/isn't so," camouflaged to look like real research. It's only contribution is to determine how the test subjects feel about whatever topic is of interest.

There is another factor that is of particular concern regarding the conclusions and recommendations of qualitative researchers. To understand this problem, we must first understand the value of having sufficient subjects from which to draw valid conclusions. For instance, if you read a research article detailing 'real' research, say for instance in molecular biochemistry, you may note that the typical number of test samples may be as few as three. Apparently this number is taken as a sort of standard by social researchers, under the assumption that, 'If it is good enough for the hard sciences, it must be scientific'. Unfortunately, if you read the whole article, in the 'Materials and Methods' sections of genetics research articles, etc., you will find the reason that so few samples may be enough. The procedures used to isolate the specific molecule of interest are often remarkably intensive. These procedures can consist of a bewildering array of procedures such as several iterations each of centrifugation, filtration, heating, electrophoresis, coagulation, oxidations, reductions, spectrophotometry, chromatography, etc., etc., which eventually purify the sample by eliminating virtually everything but the molecule of interest and some inert carrier diluent (that which dilutes the molecule of interest). Done correctly, it is only at this point that the test procedure is applied (e.g., add chemical X to see if the whole thing turns blue). Under these stringent conditions, three tries is plenty to see if it turns blue, as demonstrated by the quantitative statistical analysis.

In 'social' research, however, including education research, things are never that pure. Social answers are affected by many, many factors which cannot be filtered away. This is especially true if the answers expected are not merely factual information, such as age or gender.

Answers can vary, even from the same subject, depending on whether the subject is happy or sad, tired or rested, amused or cynical, bored or alert, old or young, on whether the answer is a guess, an educated answer, or derived from indoctrination. Answers can vary based on ideology, intelligence, political leanings, gossip, on what you once heard Uncle Ernie say, on whether you are making a joke or are serious, etc., etc., etc. Therefore, to come to any sort of valid conclusion, the competent researcher knows that he needs many, many test subjects, to adequately average out the variety of answers given into the variety of answers possible. Sets of test subjects that number several hundred are probably the minimum that should ever be used. And subject sets numbering in the thousands are even better. Herrnstein and Murray, for instance, who we will meet in Chapter 4, used a long-term sample set (subjects followed over several decades and surveyed repeatedly) of more than 17,000 persons. Unfortunately, the typical sample set in most social and educational research rarely numbers more than a couple of dozen. Some qualitative researchers make sweeping recommendations based on sample sets in the single digits, and some researchers have argued that sample sets of <u>one</u> are perfectly acceptable. In fact some have even said that the sample of one can be the researcher himself. This assumption that even opinions can be generalized to the entire population based on the answers of a single, or a very few, individual(s) is why reading only the conclusions of educational researchers is such a dangerous habit. Additionally, with no statistical evaluation possible on such small samples with multitudes of variables which cannot be diluted away, this lack of quantitative verification undoubtedly contributes to the lack of positive results achieved, even after decades of expensive attempts. Our educational system is built upon such unsupportable speculations, while refusing to consider the evidence of generations of faulty practice.

Unfortunately, problems with the sample sets are not the only procedural mistakes that our educational professionals make. Of equal concern are their mistakes of analysis (i.e., genuine critical thinking).

You may determine 'reliability' of a questionnaire when, for instance, you ask a research subject whether he likes pizza, Brussels sprouts, or homework, then ask him again some time later. If you get the same answer both times, that demonstrates the reliability of the questionnaire. However, when you attempt to argue that love of pizza somehow results in greater academic achievement, or love of Brussels sprouts *causes* you to be stupid, you need to demonstrate validity. Relia-bility merely demonstrates a consistent measure. Validity proves that you are measuring something that matters. No matter how 'intuitively' correct an idea may sound to supporters of an idea, and ideas such as self-esteem, child-centeredness, the learning styles, multiple intelli-gences, and relevance theories, etc., certainly sound right to the faithful, to demonstrate that the questions you ask *prove* a cause-effect relation-ship, you need to demonstrate validity. Reliability is not nearly enough; at least not for qualified scientists.

This may be why Progressive researches sometimes recast reliability as construct validity or heuristic validity, etc. This seems to allow the word 'validity' to be used to describe the questionnaire, despite the fact that the notions tested by the questionnaire do not rise to the level of scientific proof. As such, use of the word constitutes another example of Progressive science appropriating a word while redefining its use in order to camouflage the fact that their rhetoric is floridly turgid but heuristically flaccid (i.e., political spin is often nonsense).

I have given fairly trivial examples to make the ideas plain. How-ever, the published record is full of examples that assume, uncritically, the rightness of some politically correct doctrine, such as the distribu-tion of birth control devices to teenagers, and grade compliance with, or acceptance of, birth control distribution, as 'good' and noncompli-ance as 'bad', then conclude that it is critical (a frequently used word) to do whatever the author recommends. This is often done even when the research proves the reverse, or proves nothing at all. As we have seen in the *'Dissertation Abstracts'* section above, and will see again later, social science results often evaluate whether the experimenter abided by the arbitrary prescriptions of the dogma, rather than the effects on the subjects. In effect, they judge the results by the prediction, and do not evaluate their predictions based on the results. This is not science.

What follows is an example of how this works. Incidentally, this example is not among the seminal research articles that propelled mod-ern social science to its ideological conclusions. For that I quote some of Progressive education's prominent theorists throughout the book. This example is deliberately taken as an example of how incomplete and faulty conclusions filter their way into the thinking of subsequent re-searchers, and are used uncritically as foregone conclusions. Based on foregone conclusions, even well-meaning mainstream policymakers can make mistakes that may take generations to overcome. Nor have I chosen this example as a particularly egregious example. It seems quite ordinary. These sorts of results occur (invalid ideas filtering into common usage and common 'wisdom') because teachers, administrators, and legislators don't often read the research they depend upon to justify their techniques and procedures. Instead, they depend on the 'experts' to tell them what they should think. However, if only the experts know what is in the research, but a course of action is recommended by the experts, we can only hope that the experts have got it right. When they don't have it right, we often have significant problems. Our modern education system is an example of such a problem (as is the burgeoning litany of social problems that we are now enjoying).

Much of modern research in the various social sciences is done by use of questionnaires such as the Likert Scale. Others research instruments include the KSLI (Kolb Learning Style Inventory), and its improved versions, the KSLI II and KSLI IIA. For instance Brower, et al., used the KSLI in their study of the relation of the learning styles of candidates for athletic training programs[88] to acceptance into those programs. In other words, does a student's personal learning style seem to matter to whether that student gains admittance to a program?

The conclusions of Brower, et al., were that learning style is not an important factor in acceptance to a training program. While that result is not surprising considering that the idea of learning style has not been proven to be valid, that is not why I am quoting it here. The important thing about this study is that it takes the time to describe some of its reasoning, as all good research articles should, and thereby reveals its own logical faults. In the current example, it does not seem to matter that the concept under investigation is invalid. The mere fact that Progressive theorists want it to be true, is enough to proceed as it if were true.

The authors state that, "The Kolb Learning Style Inventory is used extensively in learning style research." They list 17 references to document this fact. With experience, workers had noticed various forms of response bias (e.g., over time, more and more responders picking the same response choice), with corresponding reductions in internal consistency (reliability) in subsequent variations to the original questionnaire.

---

88 Athletic trainers are the physician-extenders who are employed by schools, colleges, and professional sports teams to assist with diagnoses, monitor treatments, and assist in recoveries from athletic injuries, etc.

The fact that a form of response bias was noticed is a good thing. Consistency based on irrelevant factors should be addressed in any research tool if you eventually want to develop valid conclusions and recommendations based on that research. Unfortunately, this lack of internal consistency did not worry the researchers. They plugged dutifully on.

The authors then tell us that, "The validity of the instrument has not been as extensively investigated as its reliability. Construct validity of the KLSI and KSLI II has been examined, but the KLSI IIA has not been investigated with regard to validity." They also admit that, ". . . the validity of the KLSI and KSLI II is questionable," but, despite the fact that this instrument has not been proven to measure anything important regarding the effects of learning style, they report that, ". . . the instrument is considered reliable and is used a great deal in the determination and assessment of learning styles in many settings."

In their *Results* section, the authors state that, "We found no difference between the learning style distribution of the subjects who were successfully admitted to the selected athletic training programs . . ." Yet, in their *Educational Applications* (what good is this research?) section, which may be the only section of most research articles read by busy teachers, administrators, and legislators, etc., the authors say, "The findings of this study are helpful to both educators and students in demonstrating the importance of learning style identification. Most researchers agree that knowledge of one's personal learning style is advantageous."

They also say that, "By becoming knowledgeable about learning styles and assessing the learning styles of their students, educators can facilitate appropriate learning experiences based on these finding." In other words, 'We have shown our assumptions to be irrelevant, but we recommend you use them anyway.' This seems backwards, but it is a common feature of Progressive reasoning. It is child-centered theory taken beyond the public school. Of course, child-centered theory is itself a fundamental tenet of Progressive thought, but is repudiated in the research to the point that it has become a mainstay in the 'professional' and popular press. Besides, negative research results are no impediment to effective politics, so it survives, even in the minds of those who should know better.

This research should have found a place in the literature as an example of an idea that does *not* work. Irrelevancy is also important information, but recommendations for action based on ideas that do not work are dishonest, and should not be allowed. One wonders also what the 'peer reviewers' and journal editors were thinking. These worthies are the experts who are the gatekeepers charged with keeping faulty reasoning out of the scientific press. Maybe we should send them back to school to hone their slovenly critical thinking skills and replace them with genuine scientists.

I urge you to convince yourselves that this kind of research is the norm in education, by picking up any education journal and reading. If you do find research that tests results and uses appropriate controls, etc., you will find that they almost universally reject all of Progressive education's outlandish claims. Competent studies are, unfortunately, almost universally ignored, ridiculed, and vilified by our educational professionals.

To get back to our discussion of the facilitative teacher, taking the 'personally meaningful' character of good facilitated activities (p. 103) to its logical conclusions is the practice of asking the kids to evaluate their teachers. Since kids are generally after less work and more free time, which teachers would you suppose generally get the highest ratings? You guessed it, the teacher who asks the least of her pupils while giving the highest grades, and those whose classes most nearly resemble playgrounds. Teachers who genuinely try to prepare their kids for adulthood, or even for understanding subject matter, are often the ones who seem 'mean' to modern kids and who must endure pressure from administrators to realign their thinking, teaching, and/or discipline techniques. This is probably one reason why there is such a shortage of math and science teachers, as well as genuine teachers in other fields. Genuine teachers want to teach, not be playground monitors and daycare workers. Also, teachers who find their subjects to be interesting and important find it difficult to dilute their instruction to virtual invisibility. The Progressives then use the fact of this shortage to lobby for higher wages for the rest.

An example of this negative pressure was reported in the *Topeka Capital-Journal* in October of 2000.[88a] A middle school teacher in Alabama was accused "by parents and other teachers," as well as pupils, of asking far too much of her pupils. Someone had even suggested that this horrible teacher be fired for *exceeding* curriculum guidelines. A

88a Original story by Andy Acton of the Scripps Howard News Service, October 5, 2000 — Reprinted by permission of the *Topeka Capital-Journal*.

school board member had to recuse himself from Board deliberations, because he had already publicly questioned the teacher's actions and suggested that they may be "unfair." The outraged board member had written a memo to the district superintendent asking that the District investigate the teacher's lesson plans.

What is the basis of all this high emotion? This teacher had asked her 8th grade 'gifted' pupils to read Shakespeare.

Incidentally, there was no mention in the article of a spirited defense being raised by the NEA in support of this beleaguered teacher. Neither did the article explain why, nor to whom, teaching Shakespeare was considered unfair, but presumably it is to the poor, gifted pupils who run the risk of learning how to think and to experience culture through literature. Nor did the article speak to the irony of this sort of action, at a time when the nation was reported to be attempting to raise academic standards. Even the secretary of the U.S. Department of Education, Richard Riley, had *said* that he was in favor of raising standards.

Perhaps the kids to whom this is unfair are the kids who are *not* asked to read Shakespeare. Too much scholastic achievement by some pupils unbalances the Equity Wagon. No one can be allowed to get too far ahead, since everyone knows that in a perfect, 'democratic' world, everybody is the same as everybody else. Anyone who can do better than someone else must be beaten down, along with those who try to help the more capable pupils, so as not to embarrass the others. High achievement, you see, is elitist, aristocratic, and meritocratic. The fact that trying to keep up with better pupils has always inspired some slower pupils to learn more than they would otherwise have done and, by that, raise their own competence levels, is no longer considered pertinent. What is most important is that those who are not at the top may feel bad about themselves.

So as not to sound too strident, let us merely say that teacher evaluations are a bad idea and we should end the practice wherever we find it, including college, at least until pupils learn to value scholarship again, and probably not even then. Ironically, while teachers who try to teach are in jeopardy of losing their jobs, teachers who are the most Progressive often win awards for "teaching excellence." So, we have to ask ourselves, in a system that requires everyone to follow these Mad Hatter Progressive prescriptions, what does it mean for a teacher, a school district, or a book, to win an award? Is it a *good* thing for your kids to attend an award-winning school? Should you buy books that have won the Newbery Award?

Wittmer and Myrick are somewhat inconsistent in their conclusions in the same way that the kid–adult dichotomy is inconsistent in law. At the beginning of their book they put forth all of the prescriptions required by a philosophy that is not very well in touch with human nature, the nature of education, and the requirements of adult life. Yet, by the end of the book they seem to recommend some sensible things. It is almost as if they talk themselves out of Progressivism by noticing many inconsistencies and ultimately noticing that 'correct' recommendations do not result in much beyond ignorance and escalating anarchy. In the end, however, my hope that common sense might prevail crumbled.

For instance, in their comparison of facilitative (good) and normative (bad) teachers,[89] It is difficult to know what the authors mean when they report that "superior" teachers do such-and-such while "normative" teachers do not. The authors do not tell us how these teachers were identified as superior, however. Nor were we told what sorts of results they achieved to be considered superior. Were their pupils the top scorers in standardized tests or were these teachers merely popular or empathetic, or, worse, did they just act as the authors recommend, whatever the results?

The authors seem to begin to recognize their problem when they say, ". . . it has been difficult to identify 'good' or 'poor' methods. . . ." They even quote, ". . . What is essential (another overused word) is for every teacher and prospective teacher to become engaged, ". . . in the study of teaching and the acquisition of skill in the genuine 'how' of teaching, that is the interactive talk which occurs during teaching activities." This sounds as if they are referring to the discussion portion of a class using a lecture-demonstration-discussion format. Yet, then they say that knowing the subject matter only "helps." Perhaps they noticed that any particular technique, even if it is facilitative, does not work in all cases. Maybe this is because different kids require different things from school, and because different kids have different personalities and react to different subjects in different ways. It may be that a kid who eventually

---

89 'Normative' refers to a norm or standard. As used in this context, normative means teachers who compare pupils using established (i.e., traditional) standards.

becomes a modern dancer might not find the scholastic structure and requirements of a science class entirely to her liking, while a kid who will become an electron microscopist might become energized by learning the details of cell membrane structure. A Progressive theorist's solution to this apparent conundrum involves 'multiple intelligences', which we will discuss later. Nevertheless, the crux of the solution recommends that if the slowest pupils do not like something, for instance lecture-demonstration-discussions as opposed to finger painting, then that thing (i.e., a lecture) must go, even if it is the best way to teach a subject.

It is a wonder that the authors did not redo their entire book, once they seemed to understand. But then, perhaps I am the one who does not understand their conclusions. Perhaps I was guilty, in my first reading of their book, of using the definitions of words as I knew them, rather than using Progressively redefined definitions of those same words. Also, perhaps Wittmer and Myrick could not shake themselves from their nearly religious conviction that teaching is not as good as facilitating. Maybe the inconsistencies and rotten results do not concern these authors any more than they bother other educationists.

Incidentally, would it bother you to know that Wittmer and Myrick's recommendations require all teachers to be the same because all kids are unique? Wait. I thought that everybody was the same as everybody else? Hey, we have found two inconsistencies in one throw. Don't be too surprised, though. We're speaking about Progressive philosophy here. This is normal.

We ought not to specify what kind of personality *all* teachers should exhibit, or what techniques they must *all* use. Other than insisting that they *teach*, that is. We should allow people who enjoy and understand a particular subject to teach that subject. We might find that, within limits, teachers of science share certain characteristics, and teachers of languages share a different, though overlapping, set of characteristics, and so forth. Maybe we might even find that the kids who eventually emulate particular teachers share the same characteristics as those teachers. Boy, won't we be surprised if this turns out to be true? Maybe letting teachers teach, and letting kids learn the requirements of each *subject* (read, 'potential career track') would be more valuable than trying to shoehorn *all* teachers' personalities into some philosophically fuzzy mold while at the same time arguing for the essential uniqueness of individuals.

Am I suggesting that we should eliminate 'social skills' from the mix when we hire new teachers?[90] Of course not. However, unless a teacher is actively hostile to kids (or criminally friendly), personality is less important than knowledge. For instance, if we have two applicants for a teaching position who are equally qualified, hiring the cheerful and friendly guy over the sourpuss makes sense. I doubt that anyone would argue that point, other than the sourpuss. However, if we have a brilliant (or even a competent) sourpuss competing with a jolly dolt, especially if that dolt's main qualification is his acceptance of ideological, politically correct doctrine, go for the sourpuss every time. If we hire a teacher who does not know very much,[91] we do not have a teacher, at all. We have little more than a babysitter who can only lead kids in 'activities' where learning is incidental to fun. Our kids will eventually thank us for insisting on the sourpuss, or the steady competent, after they mature and earn their own promotions based on competence.

How do you tell whether you have a competent candidate or a dolt? We can check her subject-specific academic record for one thing (e.g., math for a prospective math teacher). OK, but what if they inflated her grades? Since we can no longer be assured that even college grades are not inflated, we can check her standardized test scores, even the older ones like the SAT or ACT, and her PPST and NTE.[92] Yet what if they have renormed these tests and dumbed them down? Then we can potentially develop a pre-employment test of your own. Of course this solution requires us to patch a bureaucracy of our own over the too burdensome bureaucracy that already exists.

Instead, we can finally insist that all the Progressive standards and procedures be trashed outright, and that the dumbed-down standards be 'smarted up' at least to where they once were.[93] Over time this will

---

90 Remember that traditional teachers are considered mean, too concerned with academics, and not in tune with the needs of their pupils.

91 If this condition were rare, how then can Jay Leno, and others, so easily find 'teachers' who think that George Washington fought in World War I, that the nation was founded in 1902, or that Benjamin Franklin was the first President (from a 'Jaywalking' episode broadcast in September 2002)? The evidence is everywhere. My children told me that they saw a teacher from California on the "Weakest Link" television show, who did not know that the Pacific Ocean was west of California.

92 Pre-Professional Skills Test (PPST), required in some states as a prerequisite for admission to teaching programs, and the National Teachers Exam (NTE), the teacher-certification exam required by most states. The NTE should more properly be called the PECI (Prospective Educators' Check on Indoctrination), but that is another story.

93 We may have to hire different principals, etc., as we look for competent teachers, since adherents to the Progressive philosophy do not understand what genuine teaching requires.

also save an extraordinary amount of money, which we can use to improve real learning, maintain buildings, or to raise the salaries of genuine teachers.

Keep in mind that until recently we have always measured a great teacher by the number of his pupils who have surpassed him. Great teachers are obviously very knowledgeable, articulate, enthusiastic about their subject, *and* can speak at the pupils' level. Naturally, less articulate teachers cannot hope to be as good as the great teachers. Teachers can hope to be even less effective if they do not know what they are talking about. Given the choice, I hope my kids get nothing but great teachers, but if they are not lucky enough to be instructed by members of this rare breed, I hope that they have teachers who were well exposed to that great demon of modern educational theorists, namely subject content. A step up from that would be a teacher who genuinely understood his subject, and did not merely pass tests.

I appreciated that Wittmer and Myrick eventually state that outstanding teachers, ". . . are thoroughly familiar with their subject matter." However, of their six characteristics of facilitative teachers, five characteristics deal with being pleasant, and only one speaks to curricular competence. Wittmer and Myrick write, "In general, facilitative teachers are:

- Attentive
- Genuine
- Understanding
- Respectful
- Knowledgeable
- Communicative

Notice that "knowledge," and an ability to explain that knowledge, are at the bottom of their list. In fact, an alternative interpretation could argue that an ability to explain knowledge does not appear on the list at all, and that 'knowledgeable' refers to a facilitator's adherence to the authors' prescriptions, not to subject knowledge. Traditional thinking, on the other hand, insists that developing an ability to explain the subject is vital. Therefore, I think that these authors have their priorities, or at least the balance between them, inverted. The authors' prescription might make some sense for teachers at the lowest grades. (One hopes that college graduates know more than the average sixth grader.) Yet,

as a pupil progresses through the grades, the emphasis on teacher qualifications should shift progressively until by high school, and probably
by the 4th grade, the 'knowledgeable' characteristic should be at the
top of, and dominate, the list. If a teacher does not know more than her
pupils in the first three grades, we truly have a problem.[94]

I have had teachers who were almost unbearably boring yet were
ultimately effective because they presented material to which I might
otherwise not have been exposed. In particular, I am thinking of a professor of the philosophy of religion that I had a long time ago, who looked
in our direction only by accident while he marched slowly back and
forth across the classroom dais, while droning on into a small microphone held to his lips. He needed the microphone because otherwise
even the students in the first row may not have heard his natural voice.

I am not saying that teachers with this professor's technique are
acceptable in the primary or secondary schools just because they know
their subject. Not even close. But by college, it was *my* responsibility to
review what he said, to try to make sense of it in *my* brain. The professor
already knew the stuff. My point is that if a teacher generally knows the
subject, the rest will come with experience. We would get better with
time because practice works for adults, too. On the other hand, merely
being an enthusiastic cheerleader or an empathetic activities director
will never be enough if the 'teacher' does not know his subject.

Besides all that, how are kids going to learn to deal with different
and perhaps difficult personalities if we expose them to only one 'acceptable' model of a teacher? In the end then, I would have to say that in
describing good teachers, Progressive theorists have it backwards as
usual. In preparing our kids for adulthood, knowledge is king and while
communication and explanatory skills are vital, personality is the characteristic that only "helps," especially in the upper grades.

Another problem with our supply of qualified teachers is that many
of them are not 'qualified' at all, even in the bureaucratic sense. For
instance, The NBC News *In Depth* segment aired on September 23,
1998 told us, again, that many teachers are teaching in areas for which

---

94 Yet I have heard professors, researchers, and principals justify the lack of much sensible
science instruction in grammar schools by saying that modern grammar school teachers express
"discomfort" with the subject. Mind you, this is grammar school science, not cutting-edge science
(e.g., water is a fluid, rocks are solid; spiders are not insects and neither are flowers; things fall
down when we drop them; trees are plants). Can you imagine someone who has expressly dedicated
her life to the instruction of young children, but has refused to learn the very basics of the world
they live in, being allowed to get near a pupil? Just look around.

they hold no credentials (i.e., English teachers teaching math, gym teachers teaching history, in the 8th grade my daughter's science teacher held a degree in home economics and did 'experiments' such as finding the best uses for hand soap). This is not a new problem, nor is the Progressive resistance to finding usable solutions. For instance, part of the NBC piece talked about California's decision to remedy their shortage of teachers by allowing several thousand people to teach without a teaching certificate. The superintendent of the Los Angeles schools, however, worried about the decision to allow otherwise knowledgeable people into the classroom since these people, ". . . did not know how to teach." When translated, this comment means that, 'These people might know their subject, but that is not what we want in an educator. The problem is that we have not trained them to facilitate superficial activities nor to spot nonexistent 'learning disabilities' and they may not be sufficiently familiar with the dubious benefits of dispensing unearned self-esteem.'

Since the teaching colleges do not teach how-to-teach very much anyway, but merely indoctrinate in activities facilitation and other points of Progressive ideology, this is not the worst problem. Much worse is asking people to teach subjects for which they have no expertise. The problem is worst in math and science, of course, and in particular in physics that, even at the high school level, requires some advanced knowledge of both math and science. About 34 percent of math 'teachers' do not have any special expertise in math, and we trained about 40 percent of America's science teachers in areas other than science, according to NBC.

We can lay part of the blame for all of this directly on the doorstep of the teacher's unions. Their collectively-bargained rules allow teachers with seniority to displace their colleagues with less time-in-service, from higher paying positions whether the 'experienced' teacher knows anything about the new subject or not, as Toch (1991) details. Experience may qualify these un-certified people in subject matter, as the retired industrial scientist who wants to teach chemistry, but that is clearly not enough for the modern school.

The last sentence of the NBC report asked an important question. "How can kids learn things that the teacher does not know?" That is a very good question. Maybe teacher-educators should be asking themselves that one, before we recommend accepting applicants with lower academic credentials.

On the other hand, since we ultimately require teachers (especially elementary teachers) to possess only a bit more knowledge than their pupils, and since essentially the same material is (or should be) presented each year for each new set of pupils, it should be a bit surprising that this topic of qualifying uncertified teachers is as controversial as it is. Even someone who will never get close to winning the Nobel Prize can be a 'great' teacher, if he knows things that the kids do not, and has a realistic vision of what kids should eventually know. A teacher who genuinely teaches and can discuss ideas and answer probing questions is sometimes enough to inspire a kid to future greatness. We have all heard of people who, perhaps at age twelve, decided "to become an astronomer," or whatever, after simply reading a book, seeing a movie, or getting a telescope as a gift. Of course, for a kid who eventually becomes great at something, it is possible that virtually any teacher would suffice to get him going. For kids like that, who largely teach themselves by independent study, a person who just aims him in the right direction might be enough. That is, unless the person is a facilitator who is unable to answer even the simplest questions, and turns-off the brilliant kid.

Many graduate advisors act in this way, merely pointing the way. This is exemplified in the movie *The Paper Chase* about a law school, where John Houseman tells his students, "You will teach yourselves the law. But *I* will teach you to think like a lawyer." Most normal school kids do not simulate graduate students well, though. At least not until they have accumulated enough knowledge to become graduate students themselves. Grammar school kids do not yet have the knowledge base, nor the single-minded fascination with a topic that successful graduate work often requires.

Normal kids need more help. For most kids, school itself is completely irrelevant except as a social gathering place. This is true at least until they get closer to adult responsibilities and notice that they will soon be on their own. Some kids may say that they know that school, or college, is important, but that is only because they have been told that it is. Very few kids figure this out for themselves until they get into the job market and find that they cannot be hired because they lack the knowledge required to do a particular job. For these more normal kids (the vast majority of kids), we need a teacher who will teach them something in spite of themselves and can give the kids a leg-up that they did not know they wanted or needed. Leaving a curriculum up to what the kids feel is relevant is fanciful, at best. Asking my son (while in the 2nd grade), for instance, what is relevant gave me a charming but academically useless recitation. I know I am getting in trouble again, but asking this question of a modern 14-year-old is usually just as pointless, and we can say the same of many 25-year-olds, or even of aging education professors.

I am not trying to degrade today's kids at all. This is not even a comment on today's education system, bad as it is. This is always true of all kids, on average. I recall being 18 when we were making the final political arguments about giving 18-year-olds the right to vote, and I remember looking around at myself and my friends and saying, "No way!" Even then it was clear to me that we did not have the experience, knowledge, and maturity to make decisions that obligate the whole nation. That description included the 'smart' kids in my class who paid attention to national and world events. How much more true is it with today's magnificently ignorant kids who cannot be bothered to learn anything new because they think they already know all they need to know?

I read about the proposal to accept unqualified applicants to our teaching colleges in the local paper sometime in 1997, and happily I have not heard of it since. Let us hope that the State Regents had enough sense not to study this proposal at length, but quietly trashed it, after ritual polite thanks to the presenters.

Still, how can anyone even have the gall to stand up before a State Board of Regents and suggest such a thing? Remember the bedrock thinking of Progressive educational professionals: Teaching subject matter content is the least important thing that teachers do.

Could this be a clue?

2   Ed School

"Teaching subject matter content is the least important thing that teachers do." Although this idea is a cornerstone of Progressive thinking dating at least as far back as the 1910s, hearing one of my education professors say these words astonished me. Even being skeptical about some things that I had heard regarding recent trends in American education did not prepare me for this. As I sit here and stare at this amazing statement (it has been several years now and I still cannot believe it), this phrase from *A Nation at Risk* again comes to mind: "As it stands, we have allowed this to happen to ourselves."

A Nation at Risk, and the bevy of other reports issued at about the same time, caused quite a stir when they were released in 1984. This excitement inspired the development of dozens of reform plans. By early 1985, we had more than 100 Task Forces, Governor's Commissions, Coalitions, and Blue Ribbon panels working on plans. Yet the results attained by our schools have remained uniformly awful, and even gotten worse. Schools have failed largely because instructional practices are based on seriously faulty assumptions, badly applied. For instance, how was it possible for American educators to conclude that *not* teaching is in our children's best interest? What could teachers possibly be responsible for that would send teaching to the bottom of their collective to-do lists? Let us look to see if the answers to these questions square with common sense.

This book is in part a memoir of my experience as a teaching student in a highly regarded Ed school. I will show what happened to me and my student-colleagues. You will see what they asked us to do in practice and how they taught us to prepare ourselves to stand in front of a class of allegedly bright and shining faces. What they teach in a school of education is an important thing. That is so because my colleagues working in the profession are the ones who formalize the needs and expectations of the community (and carry out legislative initiatives). Teachers help to prepare our kids for adult life and assist parents in equipping kids with enough intellectual flexibility to be ready for anything the future may send their way. Theoretically at least.

I will show what books we used and what kinds of other materials were presented to us. I will describe how they taught and tested us, and most important, I will explain the ideas that they asked us to embrace. These ideas are at the very heart of the problem. I will also include some of my experiences as a student teacher and as a substitute teacher in several middle-class suburban and rural communities. To compare eras I will occasionally mention experiences from my own days as a school kid and my experiences as a parent, and quote authorities past and present.

In the past few years several school shootings and other criminal incidents involving children have focused our attention on the problem of teen violence, teen pregnancy, the general direction our society has taken and many other changes involving teens and younger kids. We have advanced many ideas to explain the incidents. While many of those ideas have superficial merit, none of them fully explains our recent history.

We hear talk nowadays about some nebulous and mysterious 'forces' (e.g., "times have changed") that have transformed American kids from something not too different from Beaver Cleaver or John Boy Walton to something far too close to Beavis and Butthead, and is insinuating itself into 'adult' attitudes as kids age. Later, as grownups, Progressively trained kids get jobs in the media, at law, and in schools, etc., taking their attitudes with them. Yet we tell each other that, "It is the times we live in," as if the people and prevalent ideas do not define the times.

We are not victims of mysterious forces. We have done this to ourselves. We have accomplished the moral transformation of American in a very few years by taking specific, affirmative steps. If we know that *we* create and destroy our own society, we can identify the ideas most responsible for the negative changes we see. Then we can stop using those ideas, or we can at least balance the effects of using essentially good ideas to harmful excess.

Apart from mysterious forces, we hear talk about how much 'stress' our kids face now, etc. The stress kids have to face is 'very much greater' than their parents ever had to face, we say. Yet, these dark and stressful forces are not very mysterious when we look at them carefully. It is true, however, that the classrooms I taught in recently bore virtually no resemblance to what I remember as public school, even as late as 1969, when I graduated.

We have put forward many theories about this strange transformational phenomenon. These theories range from the degrading influence of television and pornography (these two are not very different anymore), through gratuitous violence in the movies and video games, to the death of shame, morality and family values and the marginalization and even demonization of religion in private and public life. All these things contribute to the problem, but they are more results than causes. These ideas do not go deep enough to be ultimate causes. Saying that family values are not what they once were does not explain why the values changed. As 'result', these factors do help maintain and promote additional problems in the society, but what was the philosophical grease that made the slippery slope slippery? What caused the marginalization of religion? What caused pornography to become an acceptable form of expression for young women? What caused the rejection of common courtesy and decency and our reported indifference to law and integrity? What teaching replaced the older ways of thinking with our 'new and improved' ideas? Why have individual rights superseded social responsibility and why are we speaking about this in a book about schools?[94a]

To answer that we have to examine what is now virtually sacred ground for many Americans, the cult of individual rights. To trespass here is to invoke immediate and outraged indignation. I know that so I ask that you bear with me. It will get worse before it gets better.[95]

94a Here is just one example of how this works. One day when in the 5th grade, my youngest daughter came home and announced that she would certainly _never_ want to be a monk. Upon questioning, it turned out that one classroom activity, said to inform the kids about life in the Middle Ages, had the kids wander around the room randomly (simulating daily life), and every few minutes drop to their knees to simulate praying. Since the kids were apparently not considered to be developmentally ready to learn why people might think it proper to devote their lives to worshiping a Supreme Being, what she noticed wasn't the devotion that the monks may have felt, but only that her knees hurt. Ergo, it's nuts to be religious because it hurts.

95 My own 'ultimate causes' undoubtedly have their own explanations, and mingle complexly with, and are effected by, many other ideas, including some ideas that I will identify as effects. One theory of these was put forth by Jacques Barzun in _The House of Intellect_. He cogently argues for an intricately intertwined intellectual battlefield pitting science against 'art', the merely trained

Self-centered thinking got an enormous boost sometime in the early to mid 1960s. Historians tell us that our problems with education started with the New Deal in the 1930s or earlier (see Ravitch, 1985, and others). *Why Johnny Can't Read,* by Roland Flesch, argued in 1955 for phonics-based reading instruction and against Whole Language instruction. Arthur Bestor published *Educational Wastelands* in 1953 saying that 1910 was the year that "educationist's" concerns began to replace common sense teaching in educational philosophy, and Mortimer Adler began publishing articles on the subject of the decay of educational philosophy as early as 1939, in which he despaired of the sophistry of contemporary Ed school professors ranging back at least forty years before that. Yet, Ravitch even says that the Progressive movement died in 1955 because many responsible academics, like Bestor and Flesch, along with disgusted parents and business leaders, unimpressed with the average high school graduates of the time, soundly discredited Progressive education's base ideas. That would make our recent problems merely a resurgence of a long-standing problem. Though that evidence is compelling, I was not in school then to recall. I *was* around, though young, when the 'Sputnik scare' in 1957 convinced schools to 'reemphasize' math and science since we had *de*-emphasized them earlier. I was in junior high school when the current devolution in education began.

Despite arguments that deny any social decay, and even interpret recent events as social progress, the recent, rapid deterioration of American society will become obvious once we see the charts reproduced on pages 126 through 128. We can see this because sometime in the mid 1960s, the graphs of dull, bureaucratic, government information collectors changed suddenly. The data, which were stable or demonstrating positive social trends, through the Eisenhower and Kennedy years suddenly showed something very different. Where there was progress on social measures, that progress suddenly stopped, or reversed itself. Where there was stability, things suddenly and dramatically turned for the worse. How and why did this happen, and why was this change so broad based and invariably negative, and what is the effect of these changes on our kids and our society?[96]

---

against the truly educated, the articulate but untutored against the mute specialist, and the newly literate but culturally gullible. "Intellect," writes Barzun, "is thus simultaneously looked up to, resented, envied, and regarded with cold contempt."

96 Since my local library did not own copies of the documents from which these charts were developed, and since the various agencies that produced or compiled these data did not answer my queries, even to the point of merely directing me to their Internet websites, which do not reference these specific documents in any case, I have resorted to adapting these charts from charts

We will get to that directly, but first ask yourselves; How could these basic trends have deteriorated so obviously and so dramatically without an attempt on our part to reverse them? Wouldn't a responsible society have ceased doing the things that were then quite new and had obviously caused the sudden changes? The answer is, that to change back, we would have had to trespass on sacred ground. Common sense, and its necessary dependence on objective evidence, lost to political correctness and exaggerated anger. Political correctness does not care what is demonstrably true. It only cares about what is symbolic of its preconceived notions.

So, to reverse the changes that began to undermine our stable, patriotic, and vibrant society, those who had recently gained political power would have had to admit to fundamental philosophic mistakes. You will agree that there is not much chance of that. Yet concerning the trespass-on-sacred-ground idea, I will not argue that we should throw away what is sacred, only rebalance things to a healthier reality.

A Bit of Recent History

Before I begin though, I need to comment on why I think our society has changed as it has so that we can judge how and whether our new teaching techniques contributed negatively to life as we know it. I make no pretense that this analysis is anything like a complete one. Still, since it seems to explain a good bit of recent history, and does so from a more fundamental point of view than "video games made me do it," it will do as a jumping-off point.

What was happening in the 1960s? Many things of course, but three things stand above the rest: The Vietnam war, and the civil rights and peace movements. Also, by the early sixties, television was becoming a ubiquitous reality in America. Prior to the 1960s, news organizations

---

published elsewhere. In the cases where there is corresponding data available for the years indicated, as in the SAT scores, those scores are 'converted' to abide by the artificial renorming formulas used now. Original raw scores are not available. The other source which tabulated the original raw scores, etc., was *The Bell Curve*, by Herrnstein and Murray, 1994. However, as I did not have the exact data which they used, I had to judge the data from its place on the published charts. Thus, my graphs are not necessarily exact reproductions (e.g., a number that was posted as a 25 into the spreadsheet that I used, may actually have been slightly higher or lower than that). Nevertheless, the general trends developed by these less-than-perfect data are still more than close enough to remain true to the originals. See Chapter 4 for a fuller discussion of the source work.

National literacy levels continue to rise until the 1960s

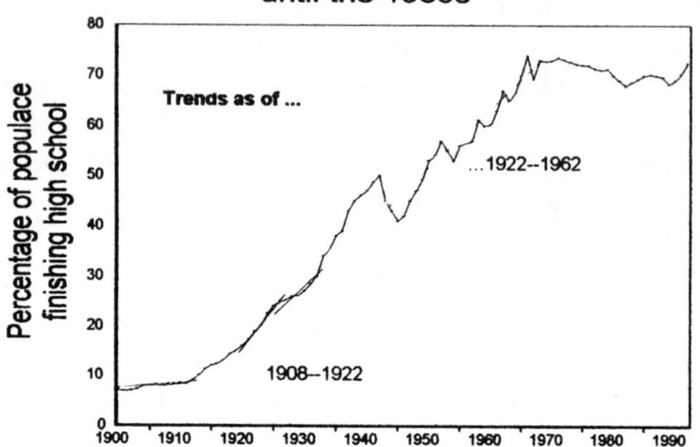

SAT scores decline after the mid-1960s

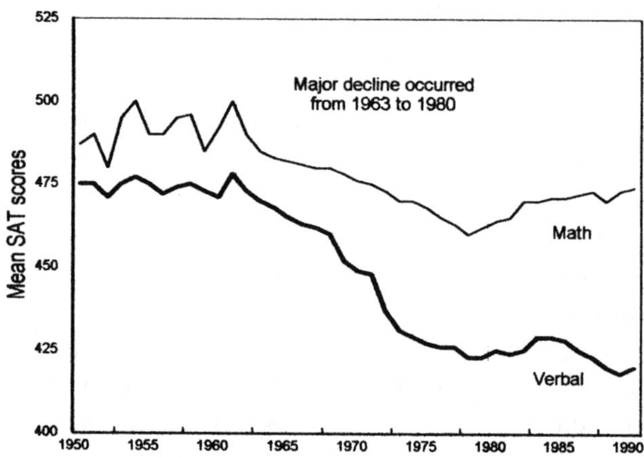

Great Society 1—Effects on Education
Chart 1—Original Data From the Bureau of the Census, 1975 and 1992
Chart 2—Original Data from the College Board, 1952–1993

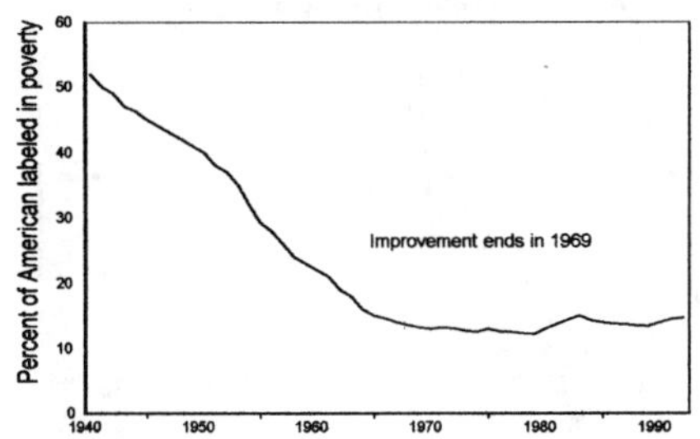

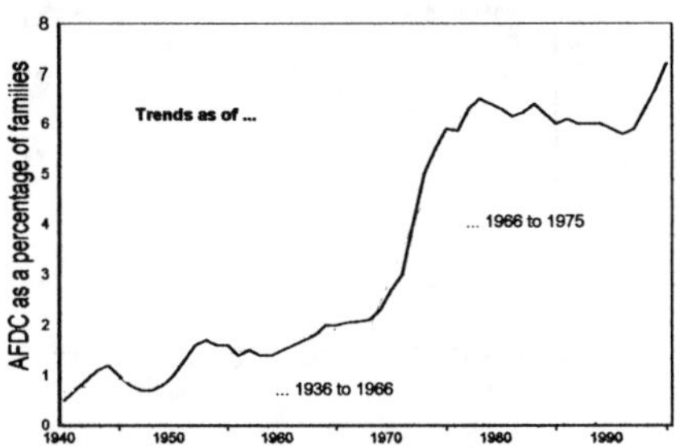

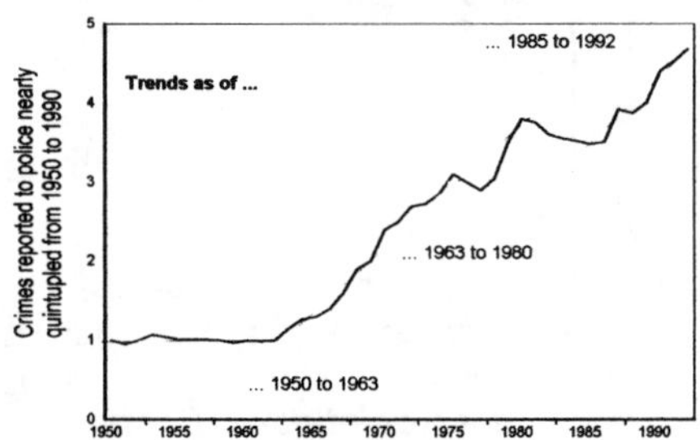

*Great Society 2—Effects
on Society*

Chart 3—Original Data from the Bureau of the Census, 1975 and 1992
Chart 4—Original Data from the Bureau of the Census, 1975 and 1992
Chart 5—Original Data from the Public Health Service

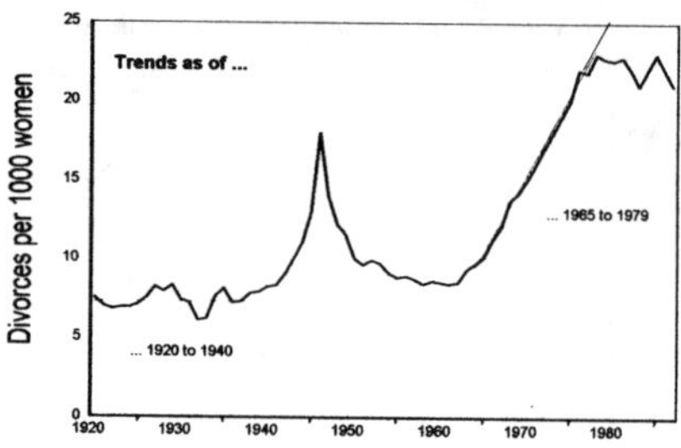

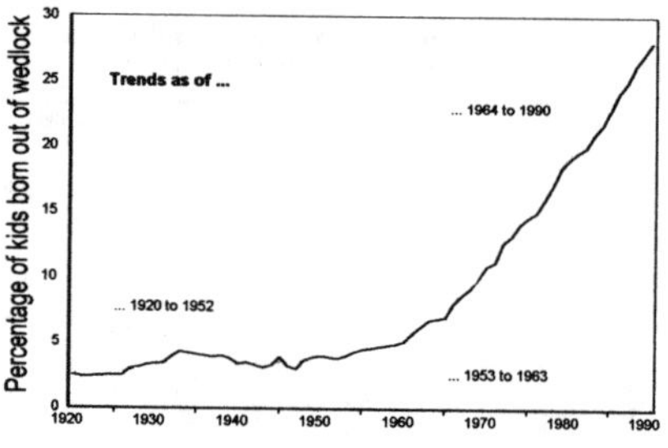

Great Society 3—Effects on Family

Chart 6—Original Data from Ross and Others, 1987

Chart 7—Original Data from the Bureau of the Census, 1975, and Annual Data Published in the *Social Security Bulletin*

Chart 8—Original Data from the *Uniform Crime Reports* of the Federal Bureau of Investigation

seemed to take the canons of journalistic ethics seriously and tried to outdo each other for 'hard' news. Two of those ongoing bits of hard news were, of course, Vietnam and the civil rights movements. Coverage of these two things did as much as anything to spur the development of the third, the peace movement.

When America saw, and not merely heard reports about, what segregation in the South was truly like, as a nation we took notice and were aghast, and ashamed. When people all over America saw Southern governors stand on the steps of school or university buildings, with National Guard troops and state policemen at their backs, they got angry and the civil rights movement got a giant shot in the arm. Thousands of new people were suddenly willing to go out into the streets to march in protest, and millions of others were willing to vote for civil rights reforms. And they meant it. Americans truly are a people for whom justice, freedom, and opportunity mean very nearly life itself. This includes 'dominant culture' Americans, without whom the various 'movements' would have remained much less influential.

Perhaps we could have weathered the storm over the civil rights movement if it were the only major national problem we had to face, but we had Vietnam, too. Many idealistic kids (kids were idealistic once, remember?) were ready to disbelieve authority figures when they saw George Wallace being George Wallace on TV. So when Lyndon Johnson told us that escalating the fighting was good for mom and apple pie, while we watched American boys kill and be killed in 'living color', it was just too much.

As often happens, outrage caused the recognition of reality to slip into a fitful slumber. For instance, antiwar teach-ins 'taught' us what our government was doing. What they told us was quite outrageous stuff. Some actions they said were standard military policy would probably have made Attila the Hun blanch, but enough people believed enough of it to conclude that, 'These folks, cannot teach us anything we want to know. They are turning good, clean American kids into monsters who eat babies, so we want to have nothing to do with them and their ideas ever again.' At least that was the thought, apparently, of many kids then in college.

The rejection of some facts and evidence, and the overemphasis of other facts and evidence, were at the heart of Great Society politics. The facts that were rejected were anything that could be identified as traditional. This included much of what had formerly been considered crucial to the understanding and propagation of democracy, such as the idea of the cultural Melting Pot. We also uprooted traditional educational ideas, such as the teaching of subject matter, in formulating new education policy. Yet this wholesale destruction of thoughtful philosophy was not a new tendency among the Progressively minded. John Dewey recognized this tendency toward ideological dogmatism in the Progressive position at least as early as 1938. In the first chapter of his little book, *Experience & Education,* Dewey writes:

> Take for example the question of organized subject matter. . . . The problem for progressive education is this: What is the place of organization of subject matter [ie., subject matter systematically presented] *within* experience? How does subject matter function? Is there anything inherent in experience which tends to progressive organization of its contents [why present a subject systematically rather than haphazardly, as you might happen to see it in individual experience]? What results follow when the materials of experience are not progressively organized? A philosophy which proceeds *on the basis of rejection, of sheer opposition* [my emphasis], will neglect these questions. It will tend to suppose that because the old [traditional] education was based on ready-made organization, therefore it suffices to reject the principle of organization *in toto,* instead of striving to discover what it means and how it is to be attained on the basis of experience.

In other words, since Progressive educationists assume untutored experience is a better way to learn in some cases, then we can dismiss traditional, systematically structured instruction (teaching) in all cases. Also, from the unscientific way it is done, we may assume that Progressive education believes that "striving to discover" (i.e., research, or finding out for sure) is suspect, too. They, therefore, found no need to conduct research to discover the causes of results. It was sufficient that the results were associated with traditional thinking to reject them. Things have not changed much in the Progressive mind, and we had already begun to see what has become of scientific research under the Progressive mantle.

However, back to the 1960s.

Older folks knew that the wildest of the antiwar claims against the U.S. were untrue. They, and especially those who had fought or lived through World War II and the Korean War, knew that most of this teaching about deliberate atrocities as national military policy was non-sense, so we felt justified in electing Richard Nixon rather than Hubert Humphrey to succeed Lyndon Johnson. The hugely unpopular war had escalated under the populist Johnson, and we hoped that Nixon would end it, which he did. However, when Nixon betrayed the trust of many more people, for many of us the scandal and inevitable resignation turned out to be the last nails in the coffin of common sense, at least for a while. Mistrust of the government grew even in many who supported the government as the traditional thing to do. As a result, more of us decided to give the Progressive point of view a try.

We had passed the Civil Rights Act of 1964, too. This law was a good thing at the outset. It was an effort that was long overdue, to try to reverse the worst of the discrimination against minorities that had persisted despite everything. Television brought that message even into communities where there was amity among all citizens and, at last, most Americans saw that official discrimination did persist in the nation, and decided that something had to be done.

Also, most people like to believe that they are normal. Therefore, most of us think of almost everybody else as very much like ourselves. So, the reports of discrimination that we heard on the radio, or read about in the newspapers, did not seem real. I believe that the thinking went something like this: "If everyone is like me and I am not a bloody-minded racist, I do not believe these reports are as bad as they say." If people are honest with themselves, they generally recognize that they accept people more quickly the more those people are like themselves. Nevertheless, we all live near, know, and work amicably with people who seem very different from ourselves. Yet, if those people do not throw their differences in our faces or insist on treating us as the enemy, we get along—we will discuss this in more detail in Chapter 5.

Also, my guess is that although Americans did, and do, travel quite a bit, business and vacation travel kept people close to commercial and 'tourist' locations, away from hidden local animosities. Hiding local animosities was in everyone's interest because if the tourists stopped coming, everyone would suffer. Additionally, folks in the South especially, who did know better, probably thought that since it has gone on for so long, you cannot fight city hall.

For some, looking back at this news might seem strange. How could a highly mobile society with national news networks and electronic communications not know what was happening everywhere? We now forget that those communications had not been as extensive, and not as visual, as they became by the 1960s. Apparently seeing (on TV) really is believing. Anyway, TV changed, or at least revealed, everything.

Meanwhile, spurred by news coverage of various social ills, President Johnson's Great Society programs had taken hold. The Wars on Poverty and on this-and-that spent lots of money but did more harm than good.[97] In its inception these programs were based on thoughtful concern about folks who were not participating in the growing prosperity since the end of the Second World War. Yet when enthusiastic implementation replaced thoughtful insight, reality took a back seat to ideology.

Once wars are over, we have always reverted quickly to familiar, individual habits. People go home and begin building futures for themselves and their families. This was also true of the Vietnam war vets. However, the feeling lingered that traditional society often creates conditions that encourage the development of baby-killers and racists, and this feeling contributed to America's new habits.

While some good came of the new political reality, newfound political successes encouraged people to push for even more. Excesses were inevitable, and quickly materialized. The self ↔ society pendulum had swung toward the 'individual' end of its range. Therefore, the Me generation was also born with its litigious you-owe-me attitude. This generation had, and joyfully promoted, catchy ideological phrases like 'If it feels good, do it', 'Don't trust anybody over 30', 'Take care of number one', and of course, 'Burn baby, burn', among others.

Eventually the former hippies got older, became the yuppies and assumed leadership roles in many areas of American life, but their anti-authority philosophy stayed with them. Some of them also became teachers, school 'administrators', 'mental-health professionals', and curriculum directors. Some of the most impatient among them became lawyers and, eventually, judges.

Inevitably, various other 'victim' groups saw the strides that the civil rights movement had made and demanded their day in the sun, too. The resulting legislation and litigations abused the basic goodness and civility of Americans and, along with bad science, turned traditional ideas on their heads. We made 'progress' through many court cases.

---

97 Read Charles Murray's *Losing Ground: American Social Policy 1950–1980* for an even-handed treatment of why our policies did not, and even cannot, work as we had hoped.

Eventually, we would begin to dismantle some of the worst of these counter-abuses, but for years most Americans were willing to try almost anything to right perceived wrongs. Many ideas were put forward and touted as essential to this effort. One of these was individual rights. This movement piggybacked on the civil rights and peace movements as an adjunct idea whose recent philosophical base was a conviction that our government ('society') was evil, and the only equitable replacement for a society-based society was an individual-based society. Ironically, although our government was considered 'bad', governmental action was considered necessary to right all wrongs.

Part of this society-vs-individual debate rests upon the familiar Nature-vs-Nurture arguments. As such, the political rhetoric quickly unbalanced far toward the nurture side of the debate. For instance, to reduce the presumed warlike tradition of our society, many people decided that we should teach kids to be peaceful. We recommended and tried many ideas. For example, some parents bought their sons dolls rather than toy guns or trucks. By the late 1990s, however, astonished sounding reports told us what we have known for millennia, that there are fundamental differences between men and women, and these differences are apparent even in infants. In the 1960s and 1970s, however, 'unisex' was the ideal that would save us all from the ravages of reality. Also, we thought judging people according to irrelevant characteristics 'caused' racism, so we asked ourselves not to be judgmental of anything that was different.

These sorts of social experiments contributed their effects, but many of our continually exacerbated social problems, such as violence, seem to stem also from the irrational extension of the individual rights idea. This is especially true of the problems associated with youth. We have now gone so far to institutionalize selfishness, at least partly by pouring unearned self-esteem on individual heads, that we are grinding our former, socially stabilizing institutions into the dirt. Much of what we once called illegal, immoral, or even sinful, we now call 'choices'. Unfortunately, healthy and stable societies require a bit more balance and a few reasonable limits to allowable behavior.

It's always gratifying when you find what may be some validation for your views. I can thank John Leo again. On October 6, 1997, he wrote a column mentioning a book by computer scientist and Unabomber victim David Gelernter. However, Gelernter is too old-fashioned to think of himself as a victim. The title of the column was "Notes of a nonvictim." Gelernter's book is called *Drawing Life: Surviving the Unabomber*. Leo tells us that Gelernter believes that we have convinced ourselves that evil does not exist in the world by "nagging one another about the allegedly awful danger of 'judgmentalism'." When nonjudgmentalism prevails, "... Truth, moral value, and simple decency all can slip away under cover of the new nonjudgmentalism and a self-congratulatory tolerance . . .," which results, as we have seen, in the ". . . appearance of so many college students who can't bring themselves to condemn even the Holocaust or any other example of genocide." In fact, ". . . Any one of the weekly stories we yawn at today would have been astonishing news a generation or two ago . . ." due to, for instance, ". . . the fact that our marriage textbooks are mostly written by people who have no special regard for marriage . . ."

"How did we get into this mess?" Leo asks. Gelernter's answer, which is ". . . bound to irritate a lot of readers (but reassure many more) . . ." is that, "The intellectuals did it . . . (since) . . . anti-bourgeois intellectuals and artists have always been outsiders with a predictable set of attitudes: opposition to 'organized religion, the military, social constraints on sexual behavior, traditional sex roles and family structures, formality or fancy dress or good manners, authority in general'." In fact, they seem opposed to anything that contains the slightest tinge of tradition or faith.

Gelernter's ideas are not exactly like mine, but you can clearly see the similarity, and the dissatisfaction with our nation's prevailing philosophy. I believe that Gelernter is right and that the 'intellectuals' include the folks who develop and nurture the ideas of our future intellectuals, our public school teachers. Of course most public school teachers merely take the word for what is appropriate, from *their* teachers, in Ed schools. The Ed School intellectuals are the ones who should know better, but apparently do not. Or they do know, but do not care.

Another problem is that we have no simple, invariably palatable way to get an education. There are no magic pills that we can take, nor any computer games that will enable us to write *The Decline and Fall of the Roman Empire*, from a standing start. There is no way that anyone can hope to become truly educated, other than by studying often difficult stuff over extended periods. This is especially true of learning useful, but, to the naïve pupil, seemingly irrelevant stuff. Facts have inspired too many discoveries considered irrelevant before the discovery, for us to know ahead of time what might prove important. This reason alone should convince us that relevance theory is irrelevant.

If the 1960s generation had its sayings and protest folk songs, the newer generation has gone one step further. For instance, there was a very popular song not too long ago, whose main lyric was, "I know what I want. And I want it NOW!" Isn't that a charming sentiment? Falls right in step with the traditional American value of 'hard work helps us create our own opportunities', doesn't it? Makes you proud to be an American today. On the other hand advertisers love it. They can sell us all kinds of things from 'gourmet' cat food and cosmetics to luxury automobiles by convincing us that, "I'm worth it." At this point they can overprice the product outrageously, and we will buy it *because* it costs a lot.

Consider again the kinds of things that we are facing today, and those that have gotten worse in recent years. The litany is long and troubling: child abuses, spousal abuses, increasing divorce rates, declining marriage rates, out-of-wedlock motherhood, single parent families, the feminization of poverty, children having children, deadbeat dad sightings, teen pregnancy, latchkey kids, recreational drive-by shootings, abortions as lifestyle choices, mothers killing their own children for sexual liberation, crime overall, teen crime and violent crime in particular, at-school shootings, drug use, road rage, date rape, murderers getting younger and younger, the lack of civility, racism, astonishing decreases in social and sexual mores, a massive decrease in integrity—both personal and official, a dilution in the definition of morality, rudeness as a virtue (attitude), an increase in gangs and nonrepentant child killers (both 'youthful offenders' and killers of children, often both in the same person), millions of kids identified as having 'special needs', psychoactive drugs by prescription, victimology, a national obsession with self-esteem and individual choice, a reduction in charitable giving, and a disastrous decrease in academic achievement at all levels. . . . The litany goes on and on. On the educational front we can also add happy and even arrogant ignorance.

How are these things related? They are all acts of selfishness. They are all different ways of saying, "I matter and you don't." One corollary to selfishness that makes sense to the so-called 'Generation X' is the conviction that, 'Don't bother me with ancient rules because they don't apply to me. I'm special'.

Incidentally, isn't it surprising how sex and/or family and other traditional relationships are central to much of this litany? Rules relating to these things must have been important to us somehow, when the society was stable. Could there be a connection between the socially sanctioned enforcement of these rules and social stability?

Our growing litany of social problems is not the hallmark of a healthy society. A healthy society balances rights with responsibilities. A healthy society maintains itself with broad and general rules that restrain behavior to within sensible limits accepted by the community. Part of the implicit agreement for living within a community has always been that if you exceed those commonly accepted limits you must then pay the price.

Don't get the wrong idea. I do not intend this as an argument that is exactly opposite to the individual rights argument. Individual rights are important for a democracy. Just ask anyone, even traditionalists. In fact they are essential. Individual rights fairly define democracy, but personal, and therefore social, responsibilities are essential too. *Both* rights and responsibilities are a part of the definition of democracy because the definition falls apart otherwise. We call those larger groupings communities, and so on, all the way up through nationhood, and beyond.

We can do few things, as responsible members of a society, without taking the needs of the family or society into account. The fact that this is exactly what our current way of teaching insures that we ignore, in favor of selfishly defined 'needs', contributes to the direction our society has taken.

The only reasonable way to reconcile those two apparently contradictory essentials is to come to a balanced compromise between the two. Fortunately this balanced compromise idea also has a name and a tried-and-true behavior. We call the idea the "Greatest good for the greatest number."

Unfortunately, this phrase seemingly leaves out some. What about those that are not a part of the "greatest number"? The first thing to understand is that "the greatest number" is not the same as the racial majority. The "greatest good" merely implies that no solution to any problem is perfect. No solution will solve every problem, but some solutions are better than others. In fact some solutions are much better than others. We must try these (almost) all-inclusive solutions to allow them to help as many of our citizens as it can, whatever the color of skin, creed, gender, or anything else. Universal education is one of those kinds of solutions. Learning the kinds of things that made "the great" great can be a liberating experience, and might even help someone from humble origins to become great. Of course, the fact that knowledge distribution has not always been perfect is a problem. Another problem is that knowledge acquisition is not always a perfectly straightforward process either., These are problems that we can address, if not always solve, but redefining ignorance as wisdom, personal feelings as knowledge, education as mere training and indoctrination as education, is not the answer.

We can label much of what now passes as our social conscience as <u>You</u> owe <u>me</u>; or, I (or my group) matter(s), and the rest of you don't. Current thinking in social philosophy, as witnessed by television, movies, self-help books, advertisements, political rhetoric, etc., rarely gets much beyond that, though, of course, it hides under the mantle of social responsibility.

We might even call individual rights the modern equivalent of the notion of the divine right of kings. The kings who grew to believe in their own divinity did so because their courtiers, whose positions depended on maintaining the good will of their political base (i.e., the king), flattered the king into believing it. The flatterers flattered the king trying to manipulate him for their own benefit. Today, political-equity rhetoric that says that everyone is the same as everyone else, flatters the modern political base, while manipulating it. We can only maintain this sort of thinking in an indoctrinated (i.e., ignorant) population that is ignorant of the lessons of history. Louis the XVI probably cried out in surprise, "But my people love me," as they introduced him to Dr. Guillotine's machine. The problem is, of course, that a democracy without a united and informed citizenry is no democracy at all.

A funny thing happens when you teach patriotism, social responsibility, and the idea that "We're all in it together." Even the slowest among us will eventually notice that we have not constructed our society out of institutions alone. America is made up of individual people, families, and progressively larger groupings of people that interact in manifold and complex ways. It does not take too long before it becomes obvious that helping 'society' involves helping individuals and that by using variations of the Golden Rule, we protect individual rights.

On the other hand, if you teach nothing but selfishness (e.g., attitude, relevance, and self-esteem that the society owes to you), and especially if you couch it in politically-correct terms, fewer and fewer people will make the connection from the individual (mainly themselves or their own group) back to society. Every-man-for-himself, and No-Limits are the working definitions of anarchy, not democracy. Some have called this recent tendency the Balkanization of America.

The range of human behavior is very wide but societies have always limited behavioral options in the interest of social stability and morality. Starting with childhood and continuing beyond that, we could eventually summarize all of the rules that are taught this way: If the range of possible behaviors is this wide (hold your hands out to perhaps shoulder width), you may acceptably do this much (hold your hands out perhaps a bit wider than your head). We have laws prescribing punishments for behavior beyond these limits.

The allowable limits still encompasses quite a range of behaviors that are available to us. The allowable range would commonly allow more than enough latitude for creatively expressing individuality. In fact, we are still able to do things outside the community sanctioned limits, because we still *do* have the choice since, as the saying goes, "This is a free country," but the further we stray from those limits, the harsher the consequences become. For instance, if we flirt with the edge of the limits, people will perhaps only smile and think of us as harmlessly eccentric, even charming, but some will begin to wonder about us. Move a bit further and people start being concerned, and may warn their kids not to emulate us. Go a little further still and eyebrows get raised and people start to avoid us and whisper about us when we pass. At this point we may think it prudent to hide our behavior from common view or, alternatively, to flaunt it in an in-your-face show of 'attitude'. Laws may already prohibit the kinds of things we do at this level, but generally people do not think it is worth the effort to prosecute, because the violation still seems minor, because the evidence against us may amount to little more than gossip, or because we are neighbors and are still given the benefit of the doubt. There is always hope that the miscreant will eventually grow up and stop 'acting the fool'. Further still and we are certainly hiding what we do because our behavior would outrage most people if they knew about it. They might fire, divorce, or jail us if they caught us. We would probably also have to find a new set of friends because even family members might turn away. Further still and we risk long prison sentences and finally, even execution. Don't do the crime if you can't do the time.

Today, usually only the final stages are considered cause for outrage, and sometimes not even then. What has become the acceptable range of individual, or group, behavior is very much wider than it once was. For instance, the idea of 'consenting adults' once generally assumed unmarried adults, or at worst, a married man and a 'working girl'. Today, adultery is considered no one else's business, even if it obviously concerns at least two families and, probably, sacred vows. Today, indignation, derision, and worse is heaped upon people who try to uphold the common cultural and community standards of only 40 years ago. These traditional throwbacks are labeled as extremist by people who call themselves moderate. Now we are even told that there are no community standards at all, because someone at the fringes of society may have his feelings hurt and because individuals must have their choices, no matter what. Another argument says there *can* be no community standard because another society somewhere, or sometime, did not think so harshly of the behavior, therefore we cannot allow American society to make up its own mind. The only thing that matters today is individual choice, and the public's obligation to fund those choices.

Did you ever hear someone say something like, "What's the matter with kids today?" and then hear someone else laugh and reply, "Don't worry. Everything will turn out for the best. This is nothing new. Kids have been like that forever. Even Queen Victoria (or Pericles, or Hammurabi, or another historical figure) was quoted saying the same kinds of things."

Go back to history to find all the references of the "What's-the-matter-with-kids-today" or the "Society-is-falling-apart" sort, and you may find that in each case kids started to act with general disrespect, often by emulating their leaders, which caused society's rules to slacken dramatically, just before that particular society crashed. It seems that if rejection of adult authority, and several other generally proscribed types of behaviors, become common or otherwise acceptable, we can take them as virtual signposts that society *is* falling apart. When this happens, societies have to tighten up their standards quickly or risk disaster. However, moving away from slack standards has always proven extremely difficult, because rich and powerful ('persuasive and selfish') leaders had personal reasons to push the social degeneration even further, and often faster, to achieve some short-term gain and soon 'common people' followed the example. Voices of moderation and tradition were mostly vilified as moribund and reactionary old fuddy-duddies who should just relax and enjoy the ride. "Don't stand in the way of progress," they were told.

As a minor example, we can still occasionally see pictures of TV shows of the 1960s that featured the rebels of the day wearing miniskirts and "Mod" clothing. Outraged folks said that this trend would come to no good, and warned us of immorality's slippery slopes. Most of us laughed off those descriptions. After all, most of the kids were still clean, well groomed, and decently polite. We thought that this was nothing more than the fashion of the day. Now look. Prostitutes are now honored as entrepreneurs and are even consulted regarding public morality and there are ongoing attempts to remove all references to religion from our social contracts and institutions.

In any case, eventually the Vandals, of whatever era, found an opening, or the people themselves finally rebelled against the worst of the excesses. Maybe both.

On occasion, however, we get a more explicit rendition of what golden-agers revere. From an otherwise forgettable and self-serving book by Alexander Cockburn, *The golden age is in us: Journeys & Encounters,* 1995, we have this excerpt:

> Golden Age? In us? Everyone has their vision of the Golden Age. My friend and neighbor, . . . thinks we're in the Golden Age of Cooking right now, and that all the greatest cooks in world history are alive today . . .
>
> In antiquity, the Golden Age was fairly specific in outline, particularly in the matter of death. There, as opposed to the successor ages of silver, bronze, and iron, death came as a pleasant sleep, followed by easy release into a spirit form which continues to inhabit the earth, attending its own funeral, dispensing wealth to its favorites. So death in the Golden Age was always incorporated into life as a sensate pleasure, followed immediately by an improved life, the way most folks would like it.
>
> Listings for the Golden Age in dictionaries of mythology are rare. But turn to 'Saturnalia' and you'll find it. These days, Saturnalia spells 'drunken sex spree', which has its element of truth, but *the rest of the older meaning involved subversion of the social order* [my emphasis].
>
> In this pre-spring festival, senators and slave owners put aside their stately togas and kindred marks of rank and donned shapeless garments, known as *Syntheses.* The prime metaphor of the Saturnalia was freedom from all bondage—the bondage of poverty, of wealth, of the laws and above all, of time. Slaves set up a mock king and were served delicious

fare by their masters. Such delicacies, given to the powerless by the powerful, were called 'second tables', because the tables were temporarily turned. Each household became a mimic republic, in which the slaves held first rank. The law courts were closed. The image of Saturn, whose ankle was bound with a woolen fetter the rest of the year, was freed. Gifts were exchanged. The Lord of Misrule reigned.

There was always something dangerous about the jovial Saturn, an element of the hooved and horned, and later he became transformed into the witch-pleasing devil of the Middle Ages. The debauched aspects of the Saturnalia became emphasized, and the revolutionary aspects began to fade away.

So the Golden Age is *subversive* [my emphasis] and it's fun, *which means that for us on the left, it should be our goal and our sales pitch* [my emphasis]. People love utopias that make sense. These days most utopias are drafted by the sort of people who drew up the plans for Pelican Bay Prison, grandchild of Quaker-inspired lock-ups of the early nineteenth century.

There are plenty of Golden Ages in my book alluring to some, though not always to me. There are the dreams of Robespierre, of Doug Lummis's 'public happiness'. There are the Golden Ages evoked by Hawaiians and by California Indians. There are Golden Ages nourished by Eastern European nationalists. There's the Golden Age of childhood innocence, frantically protected by the Satan-hunters. Sex is part of the Golden Age, and there's much in my book about the fears of those who try to keep the woolen handcuff on Saturn's leg all year round.

These days we're shy imaginers of Utopias on hold. We know we live in the age of iron, lamented by Hesiod and Ovid. All the more reason not to lose heart. There is abundance, if we arrange things differently. The world can be turned upside down; that is, the right way up. The Golden Age is in *us*, if we know where to look, and what to think.

If you read something like the biography of *Julius Caesar* by Michael Grant, you will be struck by the astonishing range, complexity, hypocrisy, and self-serving nature of political actions in Caesar's time. You will also be struck by the range of behaviors the leaders of the time allowed themselves more or less openly, from murder, theft, bribery and fraud, to various offensive sexual behaviors.

You may consider it possible to generalize this behavior to *all* times and all places. After all, the upper reaches of society have always acted this way, haven't they? No, they have not, at least not to this extent and openness. You mainly find this excess of bad behavior during Golden

Ages, just before the crash. Even in societies that do not eventually get overrun by barbarians, this laxity of standards presages a general decline during which the society loses its former grandeur and influence, as with England, France, China, and Russia. Reality raises its unwelcome head, but few care, or could do anything about it, until it was too late. Afterwards, after a period of turmoil, social standards get reestablished and stabilize the society almost as before, if you are lucky as we were lucky after the Great Depression. If the society were not quite so lucky, a civil war breaks out or some conqueror comes in to impose stability on his terms, or merely to kill, rape, and pillage. We can take rampant killing, raping, pillaging, and dictatorial or totalitarian government, as a sign that the Golden Age is over.

Incidentally, historians have been studying declining civilizations for a long time. Morris Berman summarized what we know about declining civilizations this way.[98]

- Accelerating social and economic inequality [the gap between the haves and have-nots widens]
- Declining marginal returns with regard to investment in organizational solutions to socioeconomic problems [it costs more to help the poor, and accomplishes less, i.e., the solution makes the problem worse rather than better]
- Rapidly dropping levels of literacy, critical understanding, and general intellectual understanding [this is the main concern of this book]
- Spiritual death—that is, Spengler's classicism: the emptying out of cultural content and the freezing (or repackaging) of it in formulas [i.e., political correctness tells you what you must, and must not think]

Recognize any of these as current problems?

During a society's growth and strengthening period, before the Golden Age, the rule of law was foremost. These rules could be quite harsh, but were meted out fairly equitably. At least in the early stages of growth, even the 'nobles' were not very much different from their subjects.

---

98 Berman, p. 19.

In this age of multiculturalism, which is to say, in this age where we think every white male always to have been an oppressive pig whose only true joy comes from lording it over all and sundry, stating that a 'noble' might have been little better than his household, might be taken as nonsense. An example of what I mean, however, comes from a contemporary French writer. Contemporary to the 1880s that is. We credit Guy de Maupassant with having invented the short story and being one of the form's best practitioners. De Maupassant wrote several hundred stories in the five years before his death, some of which are considered masterpiecces. In *The Story of a Farm Girl*, which is about a servant in a large farm household, who got herself 'in trouble' but managed to hide the fact, and later marries the owner of the farm, we find this passage:

> Neither could there be any scruples about an unequal match, for in the country everyone is nearly equal. The farmer works just as his laborers do; the latter frequently become masters in their turn, and the female servants constantly become the mistresses of the establishment, without making any change in their life or habits.

Typically the 'lords' were only the most successful farmers in a region.

In the realm of political lords, these were generally merely the most accomplished, or strongest, members of their respective clans. Whether the leader has intelligence, wisdom, organizational and/or military abilities all grow in importance as the clan grows in size and complexity, since the leader has to check on most things personally. Folks with this ability and ambition can be strong-minded as well, or they are unable to maintain their authority. Using the word ruthless instead of strong-minded may fit here, too.

As the clan, and its expanding group of allies (i.e., other clans), approaches the status of 'nation', some of these duties can be delegated to wise, strong, and accomplished lieutenants, but the 'lord' still holds the whole together mainly by the force of his will. These natural leaders were honored and rewarded for their wisdom, accomplishmcnt, and strength with higher responsibility, first by their own brethren, and then perhaps by their 'King', who was also the strongest, and probably the most ambitious, member of *his* clan.

In a world such as that, we award a premium to those who can work or fight the hardest, best, and smartest. To move up, ability was needed even more importantly than family connections, because life was not stable enough, and people were not comfortable enough to fully relax their guard. Another leader of ability and ambition could always be found in the next valley, or across the wine-dark sea, or even in your own family, trying to do the same as your leader. The promotion of that ambition also often led to killing and pillaging. Therefore, at least by the Middle Ages, and probably during the 'growth' period of whatever age, the expected job of young noblemen was to learn to fight.

Since we build a civilization upon its commerce and economy as well as its military might, this discussion could just as easily include the merchant class and agricultural elite with the political nobility.

It was only after they had conquered most enemies, and borders were well protected and distant from the capital (King's court), and after taxes, tributes, and commerce were extensive enough to be essentially self-sustaining (i.e., bureaucratic), that the society could begin to relax a bit. Culture, not combat, began to occupy the minds of the upper classes. At this point in a society's history, when the education of young nobles did not consist primarily of warfare, they could start thinking about less strenuous pursuits. These pursuits included a wide range of things including science, poetry, philosophy, and art. With leisure comes the opportunity to expand horizons and improve the way of life. This leisure born of prosperity leads to calling a period a Golden Age, when rich guys become patrons of the arts.

While these intellectual and artistic pursuits may be good in and of themselves, not everyone is interested, at least not all of the time. Nevertheless, some folks directed their energies at these new and exemplary pursuits with the same vigor and enthusiasm that their parents used in pursuit of war or commerce.

With leisure but little, if any, interest in the nobler pursuits, however, which encompasses most rich young men and women of any age, thoughts almost invariably turn to pursuing, and idealizing, pleasure. Since rich folks are not essentially much different from anyone else, except that they have more money, we can expect this pursuit of pleasure in any group of people with little or nothing to do, and enough money to let them do it. The fact that rich guys' excesses make it into history books reflects the fact that they are the ones who had the leisure to write or commission books and other works of art about themselves and each other. The market for books is the people who buy books, after all. It was also at these 'civilized' times when genuine ability was not mandatory in the titular leader, that extensive nepotism, which allowed incompetent and lazy men to take on honors they did not deserve and responsibilities they could not fulfill, ideas of divine rights begin to become prevalent. By the time that the people begin to think of their king as a god,[99] even his ministers, nobles, and court-hangers-on begin to think of themselves as pretty nifty and far too grand to associate with 'commoners'. At this point, societal decay is well advanced.

What examples are there? Just look at every 'great' civilization in history. Among those that we know the most about are Ancient Greece through Alexander, the Egyptians (the Pharaohs and the Ptolemies), Imperial Rome, Persia, Mesopotamia, perhaps the Aztec and Maya (It's planting time so we'd better cut out a few more living hearts), France (Louis the 'Sun King', Marie Antoinette, and all that), Imperial China, the Holy Land, etc.

For instance, on page 8 of *I, Claudius* by Robert Graves, we have Claudius describing a curse that the Sybil of Cumea prophesied years earlier, about what would happen after Rome destroys Carthage, and the results:

> "The strings of purse" are the chief instrument of this curse—a money-madness that has choked Rome ever since she destroyed her chief trade rival and made herself mistress of all the riches of the Mediterranean. With riches came sloth, greed, cruelty, dishonesty, cowardice, effeminacy and every other un-Roman vice.

To us, these sound *very* much like Roman normality, but the educated thinkers of the day knew they were not.

Is degeneracy inevitable, however? No, it is not, but you need a struggle to tighten up your standards to avoid it. Take our 'founding fathers' for instance. Before the Revolution, the standard in dress and manners, etc., was British and Continental (i.e., 'French'). We see powdered wigs, extensive jewelry and lace, etc., even in men's clothing. The fancy clothing generalized to military fashions as well, especially in Europe. This pretentious and effeminate dress was considered necessary, if you wanted to run with the big dogs of the day. Of course those big dogs had started to think of themselves as so wonderful that all their

---

99 He *must* be a god, or, he must, at least, be beloved of the gods. Look at all of the stuff he owns and controls.

subjects should simply see their greatness and be grateful for the opportunity to wallow in mud to allow the nobility to live in luxury. Yet were we grateful? Of course not. The Founders, and many other little guys, did not like that attitude much, and said so. The 'royalty' and 'nobility' eventually learned a lesson in humility, although it took an armed revolution to make the point. Then suddenly fashions in the new United States changed to something a bit more down to earth and functional (less self-aggrandizing). Suddenly we were not merely peripheral nonentities trying to impress our distant, oh, so civilized, master. We were an independent nation with a new struggle to pursue. We had work to do, to go along with new responsibilities, to ourselves and to our citizens. So we dispensed with the fluffy clothing, rolled up our sleeves and got to work.

The French and Russian nobility were taught much the same lesson as the British, for much the same reasons, though a bit more brutally, a few years later.

So, are colorful and purely decorative fashions clues to social instability that we must protect against? Possibly, but the attitude that allows us to imagine that there is nothing more important than ourselves certainly is. When we see that attitude expressing itself, along with other clues like rampant changes in sexual mores, we should begin to worry.

I wonder whether the 'Roaring 20's', that presaged the 1929 stock market crash and the start of the Great Depression, might not be a recent example of a loss of social standards, and an example of the kind of result we might expect if we allow 'rights' to outweigh 'responsibilities'. This may be true even though much of the excess of the Roaring 20s was a reaction to the Prohibition. Either way, it was an example of an unbalanced society doing harm to itself by overreacting to relatively unimportant factors.

In a very sad way it may have been a blessing that we had the Depression and World War II, if they reminded us that individual needs don't amount to a hill of beans in this mixed-up world when compared with our collective need to maintain social stability. If this idea is true, two decades of true social misery and a second World War are painful lessons to forget so quickly. "Oh, but teaching mere history is unnecessary," the educationists say. That is all just a lot of dates and useless facts to memorize. Besides, economic times are good now (late 1990s), so we can afford to forget that it is the struggle itself that makes us strong. Can't we?

I recognize that the development of the 'causes' that led up to a general upheaval like the Depression cannot be diluted to a single fact. I am not arguing that. My point is that a broadening selfishness, and the unbalancing of stable society are *not* examples of a single fact. They may however be the 'forest' as opposed to the 'trees'.

It is also interesting that no matter whether the sort of government eventually chosen by the unbalanced society, that is, whether the society unbalances in a right-wing direction (e.g., Germany's National Socialism and Japan's Imperial militarism) or in the left-wing direction (e.g., Russia's Bolshevism and Chinese Communism), both systems become repressive dictatorships. In which direction would you like our society to unbalance?

I opt for neither. I suggest that somewhere in the middle is best, where both ends of the spectrum balance each other. That sounds like a democracy to me. [With apologies to Patrick Henry—I know not what other men may say. But as for me, Give me a dull, genuinely moderate and prosperous liberty—or Give me Valium (and I refuse to take Valium)]

We will have to wait to see whether the war on terrorism results in fundamental changes.

Selfishness: Good or Bad (or Both)?

If selfishness is the root of much evil, why don't we merely stamp it out in all its insidious forms? We do not stamp out selfishness (egocentrism) because we cannot, since it is instinctive and because to try would be the kind of overreaction we have just decried.

The truth is, selfishness is not all bad. It is essential occasionally, just like individual rights. In fact selfishness is an expression of the survival instinct. We even have millions of pain receptors all over our bodies to help us decide what is OK to do and what may be harmful. We routinely try to avoid stubbing our toes and we rarely contemplate diving headlong and naked into a thorn bush; because pain hurts. Pain is a natural signal that something is wrong. We could not have survived as a species if we did not heed these warnings. Could you imagine continuing to sleep peacefully while being torn asunder by a pack of hyenas? Or, is it more likely that you would scream your fool head off, calling for help from other members in your society, asking them to put their own lives at risk? That too is selfishness, but it is necessary.

You can see the truth of selfishness-as-good in your kids, too. The attitude of newborn babies is profoundly selfish. How else would you explain all that caterwauling? A newborn human baby is completely dependent upon others for all of its needs. It can do virtually nothing for itself. A baby's crying is a signal to parents to do something to relieve some form of discomfort, whether it is hunger, a rash, cold, fever, bloat, twisted clothing, or something. As such, the crying is essentially acceptable to parents, for a while. I remember feeling amazement that I could tolerate, with no jangled nerves, the gentle and melodious beckoning of my own children, while the raucous screeching of other people's brats was, and still is, intolerable. On the other hand, now that they are beyond diapers, I am teaching my kids to desist in pointless whining. I am teaching them to modify their instinct.

How can we explain the fact of crying in an evolutionary sense? What could possibly have allowed the establishment and maintenance of full-throated, high-pitched wailing in a world filled with prowling meat eaters? Even many grazers have enough sense to hide their young. That is to say that the young go to ground and stay still and quiet while mom is off grazing alone. The newborns of species that always stay with mom must quickly learn appropriate behaviors in times of stress, such as running away. Baby birds are quite loud too, but generally only when the parent returns to the nest with a yummy grub, or something. The message to mom may be a selfish one however: "Feed me. Not them (siblings)." Yet human kids squawk whenever they feel the urge, and some feel the urge often, for extended periods, and for no discernable reasons.

The thing that allows babies to get away with; "Here I am, lions and hyenas! Come and get it!" sorts of behavior is the other end of our human instinctive spectrum; society. Though we are better in small groups, we are a social species whose members live together and help each other. We could not have survived, and many more babies would have been eaten through the ages (we might even have become extinct long ago), if parents and siblings, aunts, uncles, friends, relatives, and unrelated passers-by had not taken up sticks and stones and driven the slavering carnivores off, while risking their own lives in the process.

In a healthy extended society, its military have personified this altruistic end of the instinct spectrum, whose main function is defense, along with individual Good Samaritans and philanthropists who consider it necessary to help others in need.

However, what has all of this to do with schools today? Schools have made the maintenance and extension of selfish behavior a mainstay of their philosophy while converting altruism from a willing behavior done by friends and neighbors to an obligation of a faceless, often distant bureaucracy.

In schools, one way that the individual rights idea finds its way into the curriculum is as 'relevance theory', which is a subset of self-esteem and of child-centered theories generally. Relevance theory is also used extensively as justification for everything from Special education funding to connections to the Internet. Unfortunately, while Progressive educationists tell us that scientific research supports their ideas, that research actually tells us that the self-esteem idea shows no correlation to achievement. In fact, if there is any rule at all regarding high self-esteem, it is that, as a group, career criminals tend to have the highest self-esteem of all. That is to say: "You have what I want, but I deserve it more than you. So, I will just take it for myself, because I'm worth it." This is, of course, exactly the opposite of the Progressive predictions and rhetoric.

The fact is that humans vary widely as to self-esteem. Some, like the criminals, achieve very little despite very high self-esteem, while others, including many high achievers with low self-esteem, try harder and achieve more, *because* they are never satisfied with their own work. Low self-esteem as a precursor to voluminous and/or wonderful work should not happen according to the theory, but does as frequently as slovenly, or no, work associated with high self-esteem.

With several decades in which to slip further and further toward today's 'moderate' left, we can see progress in generational slogans, too. The more modern versions insist that everyone should have an 'attitude', and that you should not let anyone tell you what to do, because <u>you</u> know what is best, even if you are still in elementary school. Why did we slip so far to the left? Because the loose-knit coalition of all of the political victim groups, that wanted to take advantage of the new political reality, supported each other, whether the various individual ideas made much sense or not, or contradicted each other or not. Few of the victim groups could sway America alone, but by scratching each other's backs and uncritically repeating each other's lies (while touting their collective dedication to critical thinking skills), we could make 'progress' on many fronts. To defeat 'the Wing Nuts', which eventually included anyone who expressed even the mildest unease with unsupported Progressive ideas, political correctness was born.

Litigation fueled the political excesses but much of the litigation initially made sense to many people. Litigation often results in court-mandated changes in the way that schools did business. Bussing was the most prominent of these changes, but privately educationists rejoiced and resurrected their other programs. The Progressive education movement had not died in the mid 1950s. It was merely dormant. We are now debating the results of this resurrection in everything from the school achievement problem to virtually every other problem listed as our litany of woe.

When the various court and legislation-ordered changes began, educationists apparently thought, 'This is our big chance. Why not use the new politics to justify child-centered education again.' So they did. It did not matter that in promoting itself, Progressive education championed exactly the opposite causes through the 1950s than it champions today. As already stated, once upon a time, Progressive educators said that keeping girls in the home and keeping people of lesser abilities in menial jobs was the right thing to do. Today, feminism and 'college is for everyone regardless of ability' are the rallying cries. Nevertheless, the basic theories used to promote these ideologies are essentially unchanged. According to Progressive education, school is not for learning at all. School is for developing a 'better' society based on individual rights (as defined by them), and for dispensing social services.

It's a new world out there and the naïve, self-devised needs of children are more important, even when they exceed ancient limits to behavior, decency and common sense. In fact, exceeding those limits is now a virtue. Nowadays, if you are not eXtreme in some way, you are considered a nonentity. This may be good marketing for the modern youth market, but it does not qualify as common sense.

John Dewey's emphasis on using 'experience' in the classroom is used to justify the various techniques of child-centered educationists and to ridicule the efforts of traditional educators. Yet this is what Dewey said about education in his introductory paragraphs to *Democracy and Education* (1916). Briefly after describing the various uses we make of the word 'life', both in the biological sense and the social sense, Dewey goes on:

We employ the word "experience" in the same pregnant sense. And to it, as well as to life in the bare physiological sense, the principle of continuity through renewal applies . . . Education, in its broadest sense, is the means of this social continuity of life. Every one of the constituent elements of a social group, in a modern city as in a savage tribe, is born immature, helpless without language, beliefs, ideas or social standards . . .

. . . there is the necessity that these immature members be not merely physically preserved in adequate numbers, but that they be initiated into the interests, purposes, information, skill, and practices of the mature members: *otherwise the group will cease its characteristic life* [my emphasis. Translation: traditional wisdom will die]. Even in a savage tribe, the achievements of the adults *are far beyond what the immature members would be capable of if left to themselves* [my emphasis]. With the growth of civilization, the gap between the original capacities of the immature and the standards of customs of the elders increases. Mere physical growing up, mere mastery of the bare necessities of existence will not suffice to reproduce the life of the group. *Deliberate effort and the taking of thoughtful pains are required. Beings who are born not only unaware of, but quite indifferent to, the aims and habits of the social group have to be rendered cognizant of them and actively interested* [my emphasis]. Education, and education alone, spans the gap.

. . . Yet this renewal [of society's achievements] is not automatic. Unless pains are taken to see that genuine and thorough transmission takes place, the most civilized group will relapse into barbarism and then into savagery [as an example, our modern epidemic of school shootings should occur to you]. In fact the human young are so immature that if they were left to themselves without the guidance and succor of others, they could not acquire the rudimentary abilities necessary for physical existence. The young of human beings compare so poorly in original efficiency with the young of many of the lower animals, that even the powers needed for physical sustentation have to be acquired under tuition. How much more, then, is this the case with respect to all the technological, scientific, and moral achievements of humanity!

While Dewey did also reject what was seen as a rigid presentation of information (i.e., pure droning lectures with no exchange of ideas between pupil and teacher), these quotations do not sound to me as a ringing endorsement for leaving kids to their own devices, nor of ignoring "mere" facts while teaching. Quite the contrary. Though Dewey supposedly championed the child-centered philosophy, I have never read a clearer statement contrary to it. One begins to wonder how else Progressive authors have reinterpreted the ideas of thoughtful theorists to help justify modern Progressive education, and to convince us that evidence from research significantly supports Progressive ideas.

We will examine many of these ideas in greater detail, and see more examples of these deceptive reinterpretations, as we go along, but the point is that modern schools promote the idea that 'limits to behavior' are socially and educationally unjustifiable. We design limits to behavior, they tell us, to subjugate the minds of kids and to condemn them to the dreary realities of work (i.e., preparing for adulthood). Creativity and openness are the holy grail, though we cannot attain these laudable goals if we do not teach kids the things that the adults, including scientists, historians, and others, have previously learned. In fact, Progressive educationists tell us that we should not teach the rules of the various academic disciplines (like correct grammar and long division) because that, too, limits creativity. Meanwhile we spend our money on metal detectors and surveillance cameras rather than textbooks, and pundits debate whether it is time to turn our schools into prisons, to protect us from the unfettered creativity of modern children.

In fact, some schools I have seen have begun to resemble juvenile prisons. I know a high school where, aside from the normal armed policeman and security cameras, teachers are routinely scheduled as hall monitors checking hall passes and being available in case of fights or vandalism, not just between classes but during classes. The 'inmates' cannot be trusted to go to and stay in their assigned classrooms, and excuses for leaving classes cannot be trusted. Many, perhaps most, schools don't allow textbooks out of at least some classrooms at all since they know that many would be destroyed and "lost" if they did. Other schools routinely schedule classes to go to the 'media center', perhaps once per week, since their kids cannot be trusted to return library books when left to their own devices. And most Middle school educators are expected to escort their kids to and from lunch, to try to insure that they don't disrupt ongoing classes too much. Examples of this sort are numerous and routine, and demonstrate the level of integrity and responsibility that Progressive education has engendered, despite all of its lip service and cutesy posters to the contrary.

Why is teaching kids that they are not the centers of the universe a good thing and a cause for hope that we may still regain sanity in our troubled society, that schools can again be places of learning and cultural transmission rather than becoming armed camps defending the right to be stupid? Have you ever noticed what happens to a kid's personality if their parents do not work to change their babyish, selfish behaviors, but continue to accede to a kid's every whim? We have a name for kids raised that way. We call them 'spoiled',[100] Once upon a time we worked hard to avoid this condition in our kids because spoiled kids often grew up as self-centered, incompetent, and dependent. Today our mental-health professionals tell us that pursuing self-esteem is "the right thing to do." However, working hard to train kids not to be self-centered, I believe, is part of what Dewey meant by, "Deliberate effort and the taking of thoughtful pains." Today, our unhelpful reinterpretation of common sense has renamed this unwanted set of behaviors, and its prescribed treatment. Today we call it Attention Deficit Hyperactivity Disorder (ADHD) and treat it with psychoactive drugs.

On September 29, 2000 in Congressional testimony televised by C-SPAN, Dr. Fred Baughman of the American Academy of Neurology, testified that there is no medical evidence whatever for the existence of any physical disease associated with ADHD. Nevertheless, in the 20 years since we invented this ailment, we have diagnosed many tens of thousands of kids down to preschool ages, labeled them as mentally disabled, and drugged them in the name of servicing their needs. Yours may be one of them.

Mrs. Heumann, however, the Special Educator from the U.S. Department of Education, invited to testify on the same panel, sat next to Dr. Baughman and heard his testimony, yet argued passionately that the single biggest problem in education today was that educators need better training in how to identify and label problem kids, so that we could "help" even more of them. When educational and mental health professionals cannot cope with behavioral problems that they themselves created, their solution is to use drugs and blame politics or parents. Call it Spoiled Child Syndrome (SCS) if you want a fancy sounding acronym. Then treat it as sensible parents have done since the beginning of time.

Today psychologists, "counselors," and educationists admonish us to pursue and maintain selfishness aggressively in the name of teaching kids how to make proper choices. Progressive educators variously invoke parental involvement, self-esteem, relevance, and child-centered teaching theory to promote this idea.

---

100 Rousseau called flattery (artificially inducing self-esteem), "corruption by the . . . poison of opinion." *Emile*, p. 178.

This is how Rousseau handled this problem. Starting on page 79 of *Emile or On Education*, apparently answering the objections of the Progressive theorists of his era, who "incessantly project us outside of ourselves" to correct "man's bad inclinations."[101] Apparently in the middle 18th century some thought it was a school master's responsibility to correct the mistakes of nature by aiming toward a utopian vision of what human nature really is, just like today. In any case, Rousseau asks:

> And how will you prove to me that these bad inclinations, of which you claim you are curing him, do not come to him from your ill-considered care far more than from nature? . . . In case these vulgar reasoners confuse license with liberty and the child one makes happy with the child one spoils, let us teach them to distinguish the two.

Of course, parents are not getting as involved as the educationists hope. The intent of Progressive recommendations to parents is to insure that we use the educationist's prescriptions starting with the earliest years, to establish the habit of them, making the school's job that much easier. But it is not working as well as they hope. There are still too many decent kids starting school. There are still too many parents teaching kids how to read and requiring kids to do chores and to stop whining. These last two are small, homely examples of requiring the habit of responsibility to others. That makes illiterate and selfish school-trained kids feel bad about themselves as they compare themselves against more successful kids. So, what is the solution? All-day Kindergarten and other preschool programs that will allow the Progressive government to influence more kids' learning and attitude acquisition even earlier in life than they can now. We would then allow Special education to 'help' those unfortunate kids who manage to slip through the "social safety net" by being taught the traditional values that make the Progressives' job harder to accomplish.

Unlikely as it must still seem to many of us, including the well-meaning educators who recommend it, these ideas are another dollop of grease on that famously slippery slope to a Brave New World. So, it is very difficult to understand why even conservative politicians are getting on the 'fund Special ed' bandwagon. This is most assuredly *not* the right thing to do (see Chapter 6).

---

101 Progressive educators say that all learning comes from within, but they also think that nature can be improved by externally applied measures. As we can see, this weird, contradictory stuff is not new.

Modern educationists cannot understand why some kids have gotten as violent as they have, and continue to deny that ignorance is common in our pupils. They do activities in almost every class designed to teach respect for each other. We have programs galore to go along with the innovative activities, and we constantly find reasons for even more programs. Unfortunately, the main lesson that kids learn is "I can, and should, do exactly as I please. I can do no wrong. I know what is best for me, and for the world. The pursuit of happiness means never considering the long-term results of my choices. The pursuit of happiness also concerns my genitals more than my mind or how I live my life. If I am unhappy, the way to take things out on the world is not to work hard to make something of myself. What I should work hard to achieve, is another government program that will give me what I want. If there is no current government program specified to my whim, I can try to get it any way I choose, including guns and bombs (the mailbox pipe-bomber of early 2002 is a relatively benign example). I can do this because I matter and the rest of you don't."

With a psychological base like that to build upon, we should not be surprised that ever more unhappy children decide that guns are an acceptable way to vent frustration. After all, there are no rules to learn. There are no limits.

Oddly enough, the solution to all of this is quite simple. Just teach kids to read, write, and add, and tell them that hard work is a good thing. Reinforce that advice by rewarding hard work and its inevitable achievement. Along with their multiplication tables and rules of grammar, kids will learn self-discipline and a more acceptable sense of reality. A reality that includes the fact that they will be expected to act as an adult in their turn.

Of course, this advice will <u>not</u> require additional government programs and funding. In fact this advice will require the dissolution of hundreds of misguided and harmful programs, saving many $billions. Unfortunately, following the advice will also require the assistance of genuinely competent teachers, so will be unacceptable to the educationists on both counts.

Qualifying for the "Professional Program"

A month or two before starting the education program at my latest alma mater, an article appeared in my local newspaper. This is the complete text of this little article. The headline read:

Inventive spelling controversy in some school districts across nation

SAN FRANCISCO—After hearing the story "Jack and the Beanstalk," 6-year-old Pablo wrote a story of his own and read it to his summer school teacher in a halting voice:

"If I would have magic beans, I would save the beans. And when I save the beans, then I will give them away. The end."

Michelle Chabra smiled at her student's brief recital. Then she looked at what he had written:

"If i wd hf mg ics I wd save the bses and one I sav the bes then I wi g thm way the end."

Known as "inventive spelling" such creativity is permitted—even encouraged—in many American classrooms.

Although Pablo has completed first grade, like thousands of elementary school children he has never studied vocabulary lists, never used a spelling workbook and never spent a morning at the blackboard writing corrected sentences 500 times.

"The whole approach to using inventive spelling is to encourage students to become writers in the truest sense," said Chabra, who teaches first and second grade at San Francisco's Bryant Elementary School.

"When kids are limited to words they know how to spell, they write 'good' instead of 'wonderful.' They use simpler language, and their thoughts become more stilted."

The teaching of basic spelling has undergone a quiet revolution in the United States during the past 15 years. Drills are out. Learning to spell by reading is in. Teachers have become increasingly reluctant to "stifle" the efforts of young writers by correcting spelling or marking errors as wrong.

"The issue is confidence," Chabra said.

But if students are gaining confidence in writing more creatively, parents are losing confidence in the public schools' ability to teach their children the most basic academic skills. In a recent state-by-state comparison, California's fourth graders tied with Louisiana's children for the dubious distinction of being the worst readers in the nation.

Within California, fewer than half the students in grades 4, 8 and 10 achieved even basic academic proficiency on a statewide exam in April, prompting state Superintendent Delaine Eastin to call the results "alarming." She quickly appointed task forces to study the problem with math and reading.

Now a push to restore "basics" to the public curriculum is occurring in California, where "inventive spelling" has been the practice in many school districts for years. The effort has the support of Republican and Democratic lawmakers in Sacramento, who have joined together on a package of bills to require local schools to buy textbooks emphasizing basic reading, writing, arithmetic—and spelling.

I have been carrying this article in my wallet ever since I read it. I decided that if this logic, as expressed by this 1st and 2nd grade 'teacher' ever started making sense to me, I would reread the article and shock myself back to reality. The Whole Language philosophy exemplified by this article, has now made it into other disciplines, including the teaching of science, but I did not know it at the time.

Another example, out of my own experience, of how these ideas have infected teaching involves the teaching of spelling to my daughter. Happily the situation here is not quite as bad as in California in 1995. Nevertheless, when my oldest daughter was entering the 2nd grade, I went to meet her teachers and principal. The school staff described the principal to me as, ". . . Kind of an old-fashioned guy. He does not go in for all of the newer teaching ideas." I went away contented, thinking that perhaps I had stumbled into an isolated pocket of sanity in an otherwise goofy world. Although my daughter's teacher told me that she could not teach up to everyone's level because some kids were not ready to move on (a perfect argument for ability tracking rather than dumbing-down, but we will get to that later), I was also pleased to see that the teacher intended to have a spelling test every Thursday. This sounded like it was closer to genuine teaching than the California article described. The teacher prepared a short list of words for the pupils to study each week, and my wife regularly helped our girl to prepare. Our daughter did well. She rarely missed a word. In fact, by April she had still only misspelled a single word during the whole school year. That is enough to make any daddy proud, isn't it? I am afraid that I am a problem parent, however. It made this daddy nervous. One problem was that it was now nine months since school started and the vast majority of words used were still only single-syllable words. Why is that a problem? This is only the 2nd grade, and there are many words in English (or should I say in 'language arts') that have unexpected spellings. Words like 'dough' and 'cough' are not entirely phonetic and therefore harder to learn. That is true enough. However, the words on my daughter's lists were mostly words like 'have' and 'tree' though even 2nd graders use and understand words with more than one syllable. Maybe it would be good for them to know how to spell more of the words they are already using. It might even help them learn to communicate more effectively. Did you notice that the teacher in the newspaper article quoted above did not think to teach the words that her pupils did not know? She merely assumed that the kids would somehow figure them out, eventually, when their 'developmental level' allowed. It might be that if we formally instruct a 2nd grader in the use of a word like 'wonderful', she might begin to use it occasionally in preference to 'good'. My kids did.

I finally went back to the school to suggest to the principal that it may be possible that they were not challenging the kids enough. He was not around that day, but his assistant was. She told me not to worry, that all was well. She said that it was "inappropriate" to challenge the kids further, because struggling with harder words "might frustrate them."

Whatever happened to the rhetoric about challenging the kids to achieve excellence? Is that just window dressing to quiet concerned parents? It was therefore with some curiosity, not to mention trepidation, that I entered Ed school.

Applying for Ed school at my university was quite straightforward and there was little in the process that would give hints of what was to come (at least for someone as yet unversed in the political controversy). In fact, the surface indications were quite satisfactory. They gave me a sheet that listed all of the prerequisite courses needed and the names and sequences of the courses required before sitting for the teacher certification exam.

I must say that the required subject matter classes seemed reasonably extensive. The certificate that allows you to teach biology at the secondary level, as I intended, also includes certification to teach chemistry and general science. So the various science requirements totaled about 75 credits (about 63 percent of the degree requirements), and included various biology courses, chemistry, physics, geology, and math, including statistics, plus a science elective. In addition, other requirements included 'humanities' (literature courses that also discussed art and architecture), history, cultural anthropology, psychology, communications (expository writing and public speaking), and physical education plus additional electives. It was a reasonable looking curriculum, all-in-all.

The required education courses also seemed well thought out. They required a "preprofessional" weed-out course that included time spent in public schools as a 'teacher's aide' before allowing one to enroll in the education program proper. This weed-out requirement was in place not because it was so difficult (it was not). Instead it let prospective education students experience a classroom from the teacher's perspective briefly, to insure that only folks who were serious about becoming teachers applied to the 'professional' program. Not a bad idea, though I doubt that there were many who were weeded out, making the course a waste of a semester. Also, as part of my science teaching program, they required a lab-science prepare-a-class-and-practice-presenting-it course. They required the majority of these classes prior to admission to the Ed school.

The 'professional' program was also impressive, at least on paper. The description to follow refers to the 'secondary' education track, designed for those who want to teach in the 7th through the 12th grades. The specifics are a bit different for those who were pursuing careers in the primary grades, K through 6.

The education program itself was 'blocked' into three sections. Classes were scheduled within each block concurrently and each full block was programmed sequentially, because mastery of early information was considered important to understanding later instruction. Thinking back on this common sense curriculum design, it seems amazing to me that our instruction told us that sequencing instruction for kids was an irrelevant idea and that instruction should follow wherever the kids wanted to go (and did so from the very first class session) rather than preparing kids for the future, starting with the basics then demanding increasingly challenging requirements. It is this kind of inconsistency that is so maddening about this program, along with many other genuinely bad ideas passed along as wisdom.

The first block of instruction consisted of three classes, an educational psychology class, a Special education class, and a teaching methods course. The 'methods' class dealt with learning how to prepare classroom activities (pedagogy), using ideas from the other two courses to 'improve' our performance. Naturally, we also practiced presenting the activities to each other. The second block of instruction included a 'content area' teaching class (e.g., practice-teaching science, history, math, etc.) and a class-plus-'lab' dedicated to teaching reading.

Wait! Teaching reading to high school pupils? Isn't that done earlier, in elementary school so that by high school pupils can use reading to learn more advanced things? No, but never mind for now. We will find many such examples that show dumbing-down, or otherwise simply do not make sense, as we go along.

The final block of instruction was the student teaching requirement, preceded by a month of 'interpersonal relations' and 'multiculturalism' training. If there was any specific hint about the true direction that our 'professional' instruction would take, it was this third block.

Apparently, the last and most important training that we needed before they released us to an unsuspecting world, was instruction on multiculturalism and interpersonal relations (do what we tell you or you will find it difficult to become employed as a teacher). I should also have suspected something by the fact that they deeply intertwined Special education with the first block, but I am a naïve young(ish) fellow and did not, at least until we started.

In addition, there were a how-to-use-a-computer course and a foundations of education course (history and philosophy of education) that we could take as our schedule allowed. This last class was perhaps the redeeming moment of the whole program, because the professor gave a fair hearing to many controversies swirling around education today, and gave us some historical perspective as well. Under another professor, this class could very easily have been nothing but another indoctrination in political correctness. Instead, he designed the class to make us think for ourselves while providing facts from all perspectives, much as we intend traditional 'liberal' education to do. Unfortunately, that professor has now retired.

This curriculum is clearly better than the list of courses offered at the University of Massachusetts-Amherst, discussed in the last chapter, but, to paraphrase John Paul Jones, "I have only just begun to evaluate."

We had to fulfill one other requirement before admission to the Ed school. The school required the Pre-Professional Skills Test (PPST). The PPST is designed with the same basic format as other standardized college entrance tests, and is a mini-SAT, with some emphasis given to education topics. Often taken during the semester just before the junior year in college, I wonder whether it should not be more than that. We often take the SAT early in the junior year of high school, with nearly four years of instruction intervening between it and the PPST. Set side-by-side with the Graduate Record Exam (GRE), commonly required for acceptance to many graduate schools, the PPST comes in a *very* distant second.

Never having heard of the PPST at the time, I bought a study-guide to see what I was facing. This guide contained three complete practice exams, with explanations to the answers. As is usual for this kind of study guide, the practice exams were actual tests given in previous years. To show the level of attained education required by the exam, here are the three essay topics used in practice tests included in my study guide.

1) City life is criticized as being dangerous, expensive, and noisy, while suburban and country life is described as dull, culturally empty, and narrow. Explain some of the advantages and disadvantages of living where you do now. Be specific.
2) Some educators feel that students should be allowed to drop out of school after the seventh grade, age 12. Do you think this is good or bad? State your opinion and give your reasons for holding it.
3) Many people have criticized television for presenting little of value. They claim television is a "vast wasteland" and we, as viewers, are little more than a "plugged-in" generation, unable to think for ourselves. Do you agree that television has little to offer? State your opinion and support it with specific reasons and examples.

Given as the last item in a three-hour test, with a timed half-hour to read, consider, write legibly and grammatically, perhaps edit, and finally submit an essay, students may not want to face a question that requires more than this. Yet the question remains: Are we trying to find folks whom we might feel good entrusting with our kid's education, or are we more concerned about keeping things easy? Do these questions sound like much more than a Miss America question for which a quick, toothy platitude is sufficient response?

On the other hand, they do have the distinction of being at least peripherally about the kinds of things that will interest teachers of modern children, and I also work some of these same issues into this book. The test as a whole is at least an acknowledgment that there *should* be some professional standard. Whether this qualifies as a sufficient standard is a question for debate. Prepared and administered by the Educational Testing Service, the PPST includes sections for reading, mathematics and writing. Excepting the essay, all of the questions are of the multiple-choice type. At the time I took the PPST, twelve states required it, though, I am happy to report, as of 2001 my state is no longer one of them. By law, Ed schools in this state will now concentrate on applicants with greater subject matter knowledge. This is a step in the right direction.

Nevertheless . . .

Block One

Having completed all entrance requirements, I went to my first class in Ed school. What would you expect to be the very first topic of conversation in the very first class meeting of a professional teacher's college? After introductions and a short discussion about requirements, test dates, and other housekeeping matters, what would it be? A short yet impassioned lecture about the profession and the joys of seeing the light come on in expectant young faces and how lucky we were to be joining these illustrious ranks that include the likes of Aristotle, Plato, and Dewey? What about a warm, fatherly talk about how much work is ahead of us but that the profession is an honorable and venerable one that has the responsibility of being entrusted with the lives and minds of our neighbor's children and future leaders? Too hokey and old-fashioned? How about just jumping right in because there is so much to cover, and so little time to cover it? Well, we did that, sort of.

We did an activity about colors. Our own colors. Not skin color, mind you, but our psychological colors.

This first class was in the first of the three 'blocks' of our curriculum. As I said, Block One consisted of classes in educational psychology, Special education and 'methods' (pedagogy). They combined all three subject courses into one class that, with a break for lunch, met from 9:30 A.M. to 2:30 P.M., twice per week. The basic idea of a class such as this is for 'team teaching'. All three subject teachers were present for most class periods and together facilitated our activities. And they *were* mostly 'activities', not lessons. The basic rationale for team teaching is that since team teaching, and curricular integration, are the newest instructional fads ("You will see a lot of this in the future") we were to have the instructional technique modeled for us, so that we would have some basis for further experimentation when we had pupils, and colleagues, of our own.

An often used example for 'integrated study' techniques (combining the curricular needs from two or more classes into a single activity) is, reading a novel about Lewis and Clark in English class, while we study about the Louisiana Purchase in social studies. As an idea, this one has some merit, theoretically. The usual problems set in, however, when you try to coordinate starts and ends with the teachers in other subjects, and finding appropriate materials. For instance, during my student teaching time, I was involved with a group of 9th grade teachers in a version of this team teaching idea. I can even put this on a resume to impress Progressive administrators if I wish. The group consisted of biology, language arts, math, and social studies teachers and they assigned us all the same kids, for the most part, as a cohort. Generally the kids are scheduled together so that they could go from one class to another as a group. We, the teachers, met together once each week. During the time that I participated in this group, we never mentioned the possibility of coordinating instruction. Nor have I seen any attempts at coordinating instruction in any other school, before or since. Other than some gossip, the only thing the meeting was good for, was to keep tabs on our more dedicated truants. The cohort idea has now been formalized in most schools and kids are segregated into 'teams' that rarely interact. In fact, it is possible that kids can actually graduate from a school, without ever having met some of their classmates.

There is a way that integrating subjects can easily and profitably be done, at least in the early grammar school grades. Once the kids have begun to read competently enough (by Thanksgiving of the first grade at the latest), the stories that they practice their newly acquired skills upon could consist of the full range of subjects. They could read simple history, biographies, tall tales, science, myth, and books about art. All of the kinds of things that will begin their journeys through the heady worlds of fact and ideas that we will require of them, so that they may eventually become informed voters, professionals, and/or competent, thinking humans, well versed in their own nation's, and the world's culture and traditions. (Once upon a time, we expected kids to read their textbooks in the various subjects, but that happens rarely now. Not innovative enough.)

Aside: If we have to teach our youngest citizens to be good citizens, and we do, why not begin to *teach* them things at an early age? Limiting them to the modern raft of soulless, pudgy, cartoony, vapidly smiling nonentities (the kiddie equivalents of Dogs Playing Poker) that are found in modern early grade books, is denying them a chance at developing genuine interests.

Yet, while coordinating instruction might be a good idea on the surface, try to imagine the practicalities of doing it above the earliest grades. For instance, how do we coordinate the instruction of math and history? If the kids study the history of mathematics, which rarely happens, except perhaps for an occasional mention of folks like Isaac Newton and Euclid or the fact that ancient Arabs developed our numbering system (Arabic numerals) where do we go next? We do not have many novels about the development of calculus and how it relates to the use of the past participle. The same applies to coordinating English and math. We have a bit more luck with English and science where we can mention people like Copernicus, Leonardo Da Vinci, Louis Pasteur, or Alexander Fleming, etc. Perhaps science and math are possibilities, since we may introduce a unit about statistics in math while we need some descriptive statistics during a science lab. However, many kids I see could barely add a short column of two-digit numbers, so introducing statistics is an idea many high school math teachers probably do not even dream about any more. We could mention Archimedes and his bath time "Eureka" event early one year and we probably do, but where do we go from there?

We have other problems with coordinating science and English. Once we get past the mechanics of grammar, spelling, and punctuation, English classes are typically used to expose kids to our common culture, philosophy, and to the eternal social problems (at least it was once used for this purpose). That usually means reading 'literature', and *that* typically means fiction. For instance, we might ask the kids to read Austen, Hardy, Hemingway, Orwell, or Shakespeare, etc.[102] We might use an occasional biography about a famous scientist or mathematician profitably, but individual teaching units do not necessarily start and stop at the same times in cross-disciplinary classes, unless we slow instruction artificially in one or both classes to satisfy it. Trying to read a book about Linnaeus in English class at just the same time that the biology teacher mentions taxonomy, may be too much to ask. This may be especially true with the kinds of science textbooks that we have to use now. I will show this again later, but for instance, the text that I was expected to use during student teaching, *Biology: A Human Approach*, written by the Biological Sciences Curriculum Study (BSCS), was 'all over the

---

102 I will later show what sorts of books are recommended for modern pupils, as opposed to the classics. It's not pretty.

place'. In a single chapter early in the book, we had to cover basic biologic *and* cultural evolutionary theory, embryology, physical anthropology, geology, and tectonic theory. This is far too confusing a curriculum, especially for kids who can barely read and have no 'subject matter content' foundation to draw upon, to find suitable literary reading material to cover. We could perhaps tie a unit on astronomy to a reading of a *Star Trek* novel, or to watching a film about Apollo XIII, but should we? (I later saw the movie *October Sky* [about a kid who became a NASA engineer, and his early interest in rocketry] used to demonstrate the scientific method. This is a good movie, but a terrible waste of two class periods.)

Another problem with this idea is that even if we could find an acceptable book to use in the other disciplines to coordinate with sane science instruction, and I am sure we can, that puts the other teachers on the spot. Will they now have to go back to school to complete a science or math degree to be able to answer potentially detailed science or math questions? Alternatively, will we expect math, science, and history teachers to answer detailed questions about what Octavius said in Act IV of *Antony and Cleopatra?*

One other significant problem arises again. Many of our kids today cannot read well enough anyway. I will speak about this again later, too, but our overall discussion relates to the abysmal academic achievement of most American kids. Lacking competent basic reading instruction in the earliest grades, asking many of them to read anything beyond *very* basic books is a problem. This fact comes into play in many ways across the educational spectrum and is a problem that we must solve before we can think about getting fancy with our curriculum. Happily, it is a problem that is quite easy to solve, if we would only start doing it again.

As a subject area, 'English' has its own agenda, as it should, and that agenda is very different from the agendas of the other academic subjects. So mixing them may dilute the instructional purposes of each. Additional academic dilution is something that we most definitely do not need. While the notion of cross-disciplinary instruction sounds good on the surface, and we could use it occasionally, we are probably better off keeping the disciplines largely separate. The short version of this idea is that since grammar school and even much of high school instruction is, or should be, 'basic' instruction is (compared with what genuine experts in each field do), and since a pupil needs to learn to walk, academically, before he can run, and since each academic discipline requires a different set of walking skills, maybe we should teach the kids how to walk independently in each discipline first. If we can get back to doing this, and that would not be too difficult since it is precisely what teachers have done, probably throughout history, then maybe we can speak about combining disciplines later, after basic competence is back where it can be, and ought to be. However, to my knowledge, no college has ever attempted this sort of integration, so perhaps the idea should just be scrapped.

I agree that skill in combining the details of various disciplines is, or should be, an important 'outcome' of education. However, one reason that kids are now falling down intellectually, rather than soaring, or even walking, is precisely because we are trying to force too much on them at once. Pursuit of the 'cutting edge' with kids who can barely read is pressing the absurdity envelope. They are confused, and they give up.

Is this a strange argument (we're asking too much of kids) to tie to the general argument that schools are dumbing things down? Perhaps, but remember that there have now been reforms upon reforms upon reforms. Some of us are amazed at how much earlier than we remember, schools are covering some topics while we are also amazed how little kids learn. Perhaps there is a connection. I think the connection can be found in a confused and confusing, though noninstructional curriculum. An activity *about* the cutting edge is not at all the same as learning the things that got us *to* the cutting edge. As an example, I will show later how modern science instruction has accepted a version of Whole Language (whole science?) instruction and tries to put up academic roofs before pouring adequate foundations. The same idea generally applies to our current obsession with connecting schools to the Internet.

Computers and the Internet

The general argument that says that we must give *all* access to the Internet, lest they be left behind, does not make much academic or economic sense when we look at it more closely. First, what are the skills required to use modern computers that run on the Windows or Macintosh operating systems, or on the Internet? Point and click. That's pretty much it: Point and click. While a few other bits of information such as—If the machine does not do what you expect, shut it off and then turn it back on again—are helpful, point-and-click will accomplish virtually anything that they design the software to do.

We can teach the basics of point-and-click in a concentrated training session lasting approximately 12 seconds. That is about how long it took my three-year-old to catch on. Click-and-drag extends the session to 17 seconds. Once we understand the basics of point-and-click, all it takes is to find the menu item or 'hot button' that approximates what we want to accomplish, point, click, and see if it works. Almost anything beyond that concerns typewriting skills and the idiosyncracies of the specific piece of software we are using, more than with "understanding computers." Of the problems related to individual software packages, we have all seen the advertisements that feature a nine-year-old kid saying, "It's so easy, even my dad can use it," or the one where the ten-year-old kid brushes aside notions of difficulty by saying, "There are 'help buttons' everywhere."

Incidentally, we have already had a 'teaching machine' craze in the early part of the 20th century. Progressive educators touted these machines as the answer to all of our learn-at-your-own-pace dreams, too, just like computers. What they amounted to, however, were playback boxes that cycled through test questions. As such, they were useful for reviewing information only. Learning new stuff is much more effective by interaction with a teacher who knows more about a thing than we do. Even 'interactive' computers require someone, or some programmed entity, with whom to interact. Failing that, the best we seem to have at the moment are the commercial FAQ (frequently asked questions) sites which frequently don't list the questions we want to ask, or have so many unindexed questions that trying to find an equivalent to our question becomes fruitless. Unfortunately, even sending an e-mail to the 'technical support' people usually just gets us a programmed admonition to turn back to the FAQ sites which were not at all helpful.

In truth there are a few complications related to using the operating systems, but the network manager generally deals with them rather than the pupil. Yet we have a more profound concern. Jerome Bruner stated this concern succinctly in *The Process of Education* (p. 72). He was speaking generally about various visual aids before the age of computers, but the ideas still ring true, especially in the age of the couch- (and mouse-) potato. Bruner said:

> Short-run arousal of interest is not the same as long-term establishment
> of interest in the broader sense. Films, audio-visual aids, and other such

devices may have the short-run effect of catching attention. In the long-run they may produce a passive person waiting for some sort of curtain to go up to arouse him.

Thus, there is good reason to believe that the use of computers, or other systems of short-run arousal (such as facilitating activities and TV or movies in the classroom, rather than teaching lessons) may reduce creativity, rather than enhance it as Progressive facilitators claim.

We must make several points here. First about the idiosyncracies of the individual programs that we might use, whether they are word processing programs, spreadsheets, or whatever. Most software packages are still quite expensive. List price of a typical word processing program is about $495 per copy (if we do not cheat and 'pirate' a free copy), although we can often obtain them for less, especially when buying multiple copies. Also, most people do not want to take the time to learn several programs that do roughly the same things. So, software companies know that if they donate their products to schools, once those kids are ready to buy their own machine, they will almost certainly buy, and perpetually upgrade the donated company's product. There is nothing wrong with that as such, as it creates a classic business Win-Win situation (assuming that the student benefits academically too, which is not at all clear). However, despite the validity of Bruner's point above, the computer software companies argue that learning to use a computer, almost before a kid is out of diapers, will increase her happiness in life. Progressive educationists have embraced this notion whole-heartedly, and demand $billions each year to feed their habit, with no evidence to support that contention. This lack of evidence is a pattern with the modern educators, and we should not dismiss it lightly, no matter how frequently or energetically they repeat their claims.

After learning the basics of point-and-click, most people use the computer as little more than a typewriter, as a game playing machine, for 'surfing' the Internet, and for commerce, all of which generally requires little more than pointing and clicking. Overall we are not preparing kids for the 21st century workplace. We are preparing them to be mere consumers of technology products. Is that an appropriate use of our tax dollars?

Additionally, since computer advances in processing speed still are progressing quite rapidly, and being limited to yesterday's pointing and clicking speed is considered unconscionable, where are the schools going to get the additional $billions we will need to upgrade machines every three to five years? It will not take taxpayers long to think of the answer that question.

The argument that 'knowledge of computers' is necessary for success in the workplace, while now true on the surface, pales a bit when we understand that we can teach how to use a computer as an elective in the same way that typewriting was available in the past. All the kids who want to learn typing to help with college term papers, and all those who decide to become 'executive assistants', etc., can practice improving typing speed shortly before graduation. As for the others, ask yourself: Since most 'education' computer programs for kids are little more than cute bells and whistles, and programs for older kids, when they are not simply games and superficial activities, generally mimic encyclopedias, with bells and whistles, what benefits do we get to justify the extraordinary expenses? As for the more specialized business-use programs, ask yourself this: When is it necessary for a 4th (or 10th) grader, who is not yet comfortable with the concepts of long division, to learn to use a spreadsheet? We might also ask: What 9th grader would genuinely benefit from learning to use a database program?; and: What benefits do pupils get and use, from having access to the Internet?

I hope most people would quickly acknowledge that we can easily postpone use of spreadsheets and databases until a genuine need presents itself, as when the kid decides he wants to be an accountant, but I also suppose many would quickly rise to shout, "Don't you dare mess with my Internet connection!!! This is the Future!!!!" Well, maybe. I will grant that being able to conduct a real-time 'chat' with someone in New Zealand, or even Indiana, is technically quite amazing, and useful for business purposes, but couldn't kids make that contact by letter, or telephone? Kids, and their teachers, have found pen pals in the old-fashioned way for a long time, and e-mailing is just pen pals on speed. If the idea is that the Internet helps us to find similarly interested people with whom to chat, that might have some merit (although some are also using this to recruit improper liaisons with minors, and for snake oil scams, etc.). Nevertheless, is e-mail worth hundreds of thousands or even millions of dollars per year, per school district?[103]

_____

103 A corollary question related to the worldwide pen pals question is, whose language will those pen pals use? My daughter's fourth grade class had Swedish pen pals for a short time, in English. Another question comes to mind: Why is it, that the rest of the world is managing to teach their kids English plus their native languages, but we are told that American kids cannot be expected to read until the end of the third grade and that some Americans should be taught bi-culturally, meaning that English is facilitated only as a second language? This question, all by itself, should crack the armor of the Progressive educationist bastions, but there are many other

Well, what about the research we can do on the Internet? Is it truly any better than we can do in the school library? It may be a bit better now that we spend more money on computers than on library books. The Internet also can have moving pictures, but so what? As mentioned previously, having access to simplified versions of what is happening at 'the cutting edge' is nice but learning how we got to the cutting edge is more important, if our kids are eventually to get past the current cutting edge themselves.

Also, consider what we also probably get, now that 'downloading' complete term papers is possible. How much personal research writing do pupils do if they can download an article, eliminate proprietary headings by hitting the 'delete' button a few times (to hide the fact that they got the piece from a source other than their own brains), then print and submit it as their own work, potentially without ever reading the thing? We may be doing little but giving kids a new outlook on plagiarism, research, and scholastic integrity. You may have seen the television ad that encourages kids to do just that, to be able to get to a party, instead of wasting their time "doing a Dickens paper."

Besides, have you seen the Internet recently? Maybe it will settle down into a useful research tool for kids one day, but from what I have seen, we can currently describe the Internet as little more than a badly organized card catalog, with sex and snake oil. When you do a 'search' using one of the 'search engines', you frequently get hundreds or thousands of 'hits'. This sounds great until you look at the hits. Even those rated as better than 90 percent relevant to our search parameters, may have nothing whatever to do with your interest. Also, most 'home pages' that are not primarily commercial sites, are just vanity pages with hot-buttons that take us to other vanity pages, but give access to very little 'good stuff'. What 'good stuff' there is can usually be duplicated, without the moving pictures, by library books. Why not rename the 'Media Center' as the 'library' again and reacquaint the kids with books. If a paper is likely to take us more than a few minutes to 'write', we can borrow library books, repeatedly if need be, but we still generally frown upon taking a school computer home.

While I do like the idea of keeping school records on computers, except for the obvious potential for cheating by hackers (or just by kids

---

seemingly unanswerable questions. Also, now in the wake of the September 11, 2001 terrorist attacks, when our rejuvenating security agencies are begging for linguists that cannot be found, we can easily make a case against the ill-advised character of Whole language facilitation.

walking through the door when the teacher is out), if common sense reigned, schools could buy just a few machines and upgrade them less often, and potentially save $millions of dollars every year. On the other hand, my own kids' school district has recently announced that since it now has 391 computers along with local area networks, etc., it had to hire three *more* technical support employees to service them. Imagine how much good we could have done by saving all that money. School districts could use the money saved to fix their schools' leaky roofs, provide nutritious meals, remove fat-dispensing vending machines, and buy decent text and library books, give genuine teachers raises, and help recruit more genuine teachers who know their subjects.

The next point about computers again relates back to the argument that the kids need knowledge of computers for a career. This argument would have more weight if the schools taught programming (which I am sure some do in a cursory way, probably as a late-term elective) or engineering (which none do, and should not do). I have seen courses said to teach 'web design' which consist entirely of the kids following a cookbook style sequence of exercises using the precise method Progressives have ridiculed for over a century. But, we have already seen how well most 9th graders understand mathematics, or even arithmetic. Therefore, is it any wonder that the technology companies recruit overseas as much as they do at places like MIT (the Massachusetts Institute of Technology)? There *are* kids who enjoy and are good at math. In essence these kids must teach themselves, by practicing with problems and by playing math and logic games, because the normal activities facilitation methods and 'inclusion' (placing *all* kids, regardless of ability, in the same class—see Chapter 6) insure that kids who 'don't get it' slow down instruction to the point that nobody learns very much in class.

Some kids undoubtedly ask for and get special help from math teachers who are delighted that someone enjoys their subject. Yet we allow most kids to wallow in ignorance, because child-centered (relevance) theory says that we should never ask pupils to do anything they do not think they want to do, nor to pace instruction beyond what kids can already do, so as not to frustrate them. If we do not move away from child-centered facilitation, these kids will never learn anything about computers beyond point-and-click, and will never have a career 'in' computers anyway, so what is the point? We do not learn to add and subtract on a computer, so why not hire competent math teachers and buy decent text- and workbooks that teach principles and procedures, then require lots of practice instead?

I will not dwell on the subject by extensively arguing that we should ban calculators from school at least until perhaps the 11th or even the 12th grade. This seems a good idea to me since I have met *many* kids who cannot add at all without the aid of a calculator and for whom long division is an alien mystery. I have also noticed that ignorant kids have a way of becoming ignorant adults who need to know simple things, but don't. Ditto for spell-checkers, and grammar correcting programs, etc. Kids should learn to be competent writers first (this takes years of practice). They can worry about improving production speed later. Not requiring sufficient practice to approach at least basic mastery is another variation on 'dumbing-down' since punching calculator buttons is not the same as 'doing math'.

The Associated Press (AP) published a short piece that appeared in my local paper on August 19, 1998. It announced that ACT scores have held steady again. That's great, huh? The average score is now about 21 out of a possible 36. I took the SAT when I was a kid, so I do not have any experience with the ACT, but as I understand it, an adequate score for a college bound kid is about 26 or 27. Our modern college-bound kids can only manage about 80 percent of an adequate score on average. "Three cheers! We're doing the right thing!" Unfortunately, the Progressive 'right thing' again accomplishes exactly the opposite of what we say we want. The AP article also said, "A survey of those college-bound pupils also found few were choosing to become computer majors though there is strong job growth in that field and this is the computer-literate (point-and-click) generation heading to college, with laptop computers considered essential equipment on many campuses." Is anyone out there surprised?

National Public Radio picked up this story too, and added that the few pupils choosing computer majors means less than 3 percent of graduating seniors are looking at telecommunication careers. Why so few if we insist that what we do is preparing kids to work in the information age and if the potential financial rewards are so great? It may be that the kids themselves recognize that because they had previously decided that math was not relevant to their lives, and we allowed them to get away with their ignorant choices, they now do not stand a chance of landing, and keeping, a job that requires math? When school gets dumbed-down, life gets dumbed-down.

Why then, are we spending many $millions per school district to teach assisted typewriting and game playing? We could probably find a better way to spend that money. For instance, as a very minor example, I would rather not have to pay that additional tax called a 'textbook rental fee' after already paying my school support taxes.[104] Paying this fee is especially annoying since the educationists tell teachers that using textbooks pegs one as a bad and lazy teacher, so teachers tend not to use them much. Nevertheless, parents still must 'rent' the textbooks and search for and buy supplementary texts and workbooks to try to keep our 5th graders learning as close to the 5th grade level as we can, rather than at the 2nd or 3rd grade level that our schools maintain. I can say from experience that academically decent textbooks are very hard to find. I can also say that we should double the grade-level printed on supplementary workbooks available in bookstores if we want our kids to practice at approximately appropriate levels (ie., get 2nd or 3rd grade workbooks for your 1st grader, etc.). Of course, those workbooks are also written to subscribe to the activities mode of instruction, so we are still stuck, even if we do not run out of supplementary commercial workbooks by the 3rd grade. In any case, maybe the cost of supplementary work-books should be tax deductible since supplementing what the schools accept as 'good enough' is absolutely necessary if we want our kids to learn more than today's abysmal average.

Considering the preceding arguments, the ultimate 'equity' argument that states, "If schools do not buy computers, only rich kids will have computers," makes about as much sense as arguing that schools should buy every kid a car. Still, someone beat me to it. Another example of the silliness that the computers-in-school craze engenders is this. The largest school district in this city has opened several 'magnet' schools that intend to attract kids to specialize[105] in various areas. One of those

---

104 My home records show that I paid $554.11 in the twelve months prior to this writing, above and beyond taxes, for various education related expenses. These expenses included paying for school patches, birthday presents for teachers, parties, and 'enrichment' field trips, and commercial workbooks, etc. When I ask my kids what they learned on these field trips, however, they tell me, "I don't know. Nothing." I believe them.

105 Magnet school is another idea that should be reconsidered. We are asking very young kids to pick their life's work years before they need to shave. Yet, even the best 'magnet' schools are little more than a Progressive version of our old, traditional practice of ability-grouping, dressed up in politically correct clothing. That means that it costs a great deal more and accomplishes a great deal less. I suspect that most magnet schools are akin to the newer crop of 'alternative' schools, that merely separate kids for disciplinary reasons, and continue to use the sorts of facilitation techniques which did not work in the 'regular' school.

areas is computers and technology. We have a problem though. The school district admits that academic achievement in the magnet schools is "lagging" in this city, despite the usual promises to the contrary. So what is being done about it? An article in the local paper tells us that the School Board has approved another $1.7 million, from a grant from the U.S. Department of Education, to ". . . bring all schools up to (the magnet schools) level of technology." What a good idea! It does not work, even with kids whom technology supposedly fascinates, so let us bring all schools "up to" that level. Throwing good money after bad is the Progressive way. This grant will even allow the schools to give some kids computers for home use along with videophones, to allow, ". . . staff to have video conferences with parents four times per year."

If you are interested, this is school district Fifteen on the charts on pages 28 to 33 which had the dubious distinction of administering 20 of the bottom 26 elementary schools in town in 1995–1996, with similar results in other years and other levels.

My Ed school required me to take a 'computer' course too. Since I was a prospective teacher, I had to "know about computers." They taught us to point-and-click and then they gave us projects to complete, using various individual cookbook-style software programs. Still, there was no point at all to this class. Literally just silly bells and whistles. Our most extensive, end-of-semester project, required us to add various canned sounds, of bells, whistles, and animal noises, to a short presentation. We did it by pointing and clicking.

Is there anyone else out there, besides me, who thinks this does not make sense?

3   Ed School Miscellany

The masterpiece of a good education is to make a reasonable man,
And they claim to raise a child by reason!
This is to begin with the end, to want to make the product the instrument.
If children understood reason, they would not need to be raised.
—Jean-Jacques Rousseau

A teacher affects eternity;
he can never tell where his influence stops.
—Henry Adams

Child-centered Teaching

So what are psychological colors anyway? There are four colors; blue, green, gold, and orange. A set of criteria characterizes each of these colors and each color applies, to a greater or lesser degree, to individual personality types. If most of the specified criteria apply to you, as an individual, then the world sees you, and presumably you see yourself, as embodying that color. The criteria upon which we judge you, and upon which you judge yourself, can include such things as honesty, dependability, creativity, high achievement, logic, loyalty, sociability, adventurousness, confidence, autonomy, and spontaneity, among others. Very impressive stuff to roll up into a 'color'. [And they say that the concept of IQ does not make sense.] Keep this fuzzy sort of thinking in mind when we discuss the scientific bases of Progressive thinking.

As I recall, the professors gave us lists of these sorts of color-linked characteristics and asked us to evaluate ourselves, on a sliding scale (1 to 10) against the characteristics. It went something like: Serious to Fun-loving. Evaluate yourself. 'One' is serious—'Ten' is Fun-loving.[106] Then

---

106 I won't comment on the fact that someone can be both serious and fun-loving at the same time, finding vast enjoyment in very serious work. Many of the world's foremost scientists have been described in this way; Albert Einstein, for instance. Incidentally, did you notice that we can be lumped into as few as four categories, despite the fact that we are *all* unique?

we added up these grades and compared that number with a chart that identified our predominant color.

Unfortunately, I do not have any notes from which I can flesh these ideas out since they told us explicitly not to take notes; "They won't be needed," they said. The 'color' ideas were not in our text, which was almost never used anyway, but was an activity that our instructors brought to class. As you recall, this was the very first thing we did in the very first class as new 'professional education' students. To be fair, in the sense of using a set of facts to extend and teach an idea, we might call an 'activity' the equivalent of a lab. However, if we do a lab without notes we quickly lose the details, and a lab without details is essentially useless. Remember that a lab is an exercise designed to explore an idea, or concept, that is useful in the science being studied. Labs are almost never done, however, before the facts, used with the selected concept, are presented. This presentation of facts is probably done using a lecture-demonstration-discussion format. It was once common to generate clouds of chalk in an attempt to familiarize the pupils enough with the facts, so that they can understand, and eventually extend their understanding of those facts. Only then do we get to play around with, and formally practice, thinking about those pertinent ideas. Starting an activity 'cold', without the initial presentation of pertinent facts, may be fun, but we do not often get the point, or the details. This is especially true if the 'lab' is more involved that this silly colors exercise. Even if we do get the point, however, how long will we remember it? If we do remember an occasional 'point', can we reproduce the details upon which the teacher based the point so that we can explain it to our own kids, for instance? That is tough if we have never seen the details at all.

Many have noticed, and research has verified that, the first time through a subject, pupils remember very little of the stuff presented. To internalize a lesson more fully, and to retain it for future use (remember we are trying to prepare pupils for life as adults—or at least for the next grade level—not merely to entertain them), pupils must review and study the details of a subject or most of it (perhaps 90 percent or more), is gone forever within just a few minutes of presentation. This fact is also why homework is so important. The academic achievement of modern American kids and parents attests to this. For instance, a teacher recently told me that after a parent saw her daughter's homework assignment on pronouns, the parent wrote a note to the teacher saying that since she (the parent) did not know what a pronoun was, the teacher should excuse her daughter from learning about pronouns, too.

However, getting back to our 'activity'. While I did not take any notes regarding the procedures used in the 'colors' activity, I do still have the handout they gave us that summarized the characteristics of each of the differently colored pupils, and recommendations of how we, as facilitators, can most profitably 'relate to' each differently colored pupil. The summaries of each color's stated characteristics follow:

Blue. I tend to be the most talkative and communicative of all your students. I want to interact with you in a warm, caring way. I respond very well to kindness. Even though I am in school to learn, I place an even higher priority on my relationships. If you can consider some of my needs important to you, then you will be able to relate to me in such a way that I will naturally want to do well in your class. Typically, I identify most strongly with a Blue teacher who shares my True Colors. If your needs are Gold, I like your predictable style and structure. If you are Green, I enjoy your imagination and intellectual discussions and if you are Orange, I enjoy your active, entertaining approach.

Green. I tend to be the most curious and independent of your students. I will interact with you on an intellectual, conceptual, and objective level. My competence, clarity of thought and autonomy are my primary concerns in school. The secret to relating to me lies in stimulating me to utilize my mind in an atmosphere of rationality and freedom. My ability to conceptualize can be a gift to your class if you create opportunities for me to contribute, rather than make me feel out of step with a rigid academic pace or structure. I also relate well to creative Blue teachers, helpful Gold teachers, and resourceful Orange teachers.

Gold. I am the most organized and prepared of your students. I want to interact with you in a respectful, responsible way. I want you to be able to count on me, because I am very serious about doing well in your class. I place a high priority on academic achievement. I relate very well to authority, rules and procedure. I prefer a traditional classroom that provides me with detailed instruction, time to complete my tasks, due dates, and opportunity for leadership and responsibility and appropriate recognition for my performance. I identify most strongly with Gold teachers who share my need for structure. I also relate to Blue teachers who are kind and supportive, Green teachers who are knowledgeable and inventive and Orange teachers who are optimistic and resourceful.

Orange. I tend to be the most adventurous and active of your students. I want to engage you in a mutual fun-loving and energetic way.

You can relate to me most effectively when you are fraternal, active, playful, and in-the-moment. Although I am often responsible for class disruption by drawing attention to myself, I can also inject a note of spontaneity and fun into your class. When you treat me as though I have a positive, catalytic effect on the entire learning process in your class, you will see me as an ally and may find it easier to relate to me. By virtue of the energy I bring to your classroom, you will find your job much easier and more enjoyable. I relate well to Blue teachers who are patient, Green teachers who are knowledgeable, and Gold teachers who are fair.

What we find here is a good example of what is often called the child-centered teaching philosophy. Each of these descriptions seems to describe very nice kids who want to do well (and don't get caught suggesting that one of these descriptions does not apply to *all* kids) but, the theory goes, it is the teacher's job to 'relate to' each of these kids to draw out the best in them.

On the surface, again, arguing with that description seems difficult: Who is to draw the best out of a pupil, if not the teacher? Yet consider, what is the ultimate goal of a public school? We organize public schools to help parents to prepare their kids for adulthood. So, if we want the kids to become adults, shouldn't we ask the kids to emulate *adult* behavior? Toward that end, wouldn't it be a good idea for the teachers to model responsible adult behavior, so that the kids can have another set of adults from which to learn appropriate behaviors? If we read the 'color' statements carefully, we will note that in each case, educators expect appropriate behavior modifications of the adult, not the child. They depict the children as complete and perfect, within the bounds of their own colored characteristics, and in need of no further changes. They ask educators to emulate kids and to adapt themselves to the kids, not the other way around. The point here is that, if you have seen modern classrooms, including many high school classrooms, they seem to resemble a capitulation to the so-called Orange personality; loud, aggressively chaotic resembling a free-for-all, and making any semblance of directed learning very difficult. In a word, they are childish, and very frustrating for genuine teachers, and for those kids who are trying to learn the things that teachers are trying to teach.

This realization, regarding the object of Progressive behavior modifications, occurred to me again later in the semester when we did another activity. My professors designed this activity to allow us to learn about the major sources of influence in kids' lives. We were first asked to predict (brainstorm, i.e., guess) what might influence kids' thinking the most. We discussed this question and the consensus was that parents, teachers, the community, church, the media, and/or other kids were the major sources of influence. Next they asked us to guess which of these sources is the most influential. There were proponents for each item among us, but they eventually gave us the 'correct' answer; the kids themselves—and their peers. At this point we learned the major point of this activity. How could we influence kids to police themselves? How could we convince children to accept our community standards and begin to understand what we consider to be wise? Since kids supposedly exert a greater influence on each other than any of the others, one would think that we should try to reinforce the family's or community's standards of ethics, etc., so that when kids consult each other about life's problems, and pressure each other to conform to acceptable limits, they would consider the kinds of solutions and limits we would want them to consider? It seems clear that even J. J. Rousseau, would agree with that plan. He says:[107]

> I know that all these virtues [community standards] by limitation are the virtues of apes, and that no good action is morally good except when it is done because it is good, and not because others do it. But at any age when the heart feels nothing yet, children just have to be made to imitate the acts whose habit one wants to give them, until the time when they can do them out of discernment [logic and reason] and love of the good.

Yet, do Progressives recommend what their ancient guru recommends? Of course not. Instead they tell us that *we* should adopt the kids' naïve and fashionable attitudes so that we might fit in better and become more empathetic to all the stresses kids feel. Also, when we counsel the kids we should reinforce the largely uninformed Progressive choices the kids found for themselves, since their choices are what counts. Unfortunately, the choices that more kids have found acceptable in recent years include rape, suicide, mass murder, and an ever growing list of lesser acts of selfishness that were once thought antisocial, such as 'attitude' (arrogant rudeness).

'Attitude' is a good thing, they tell us, because it indicates high self-esteem, so we should never tell kids that they have made a mistake,

---

107 *Emile or On Education*, p. 104.

whether the mistake is in arithmetic, the use of verbs, or in morality. It is not *wrong* unless you get caught, the kids tell each other. For some, even getting caught does not make a vile act wrong because, 'I *chose* to do it and I learned that I have a right to do whatever I want and that anyone who tries to "legislate morality" is a repressive pig. Ergo, I think, therefore I don't care what *you* think'.

This cannot-legislate-morality idea seems to apply to any idea, except the ones favored by the Progressives, of course. In those cases, no law or level of funding is ever enough. Nevertheless, whether or not we agree with any particular law, the fact that *every* law, including the most trivial ones, legislates morality by prescribing and proscribing specific behaviors, is never considered.

The stated opposite to child-centered facilitation is teacher-centered teaching. We should avoid teacher-centered styles, they tell us, because kids do not like them. If we engage in teacher-centered teaching our classes tend to be too hard and boring for kids. Genuine teachers stress facts instead of "essential concepts" and kids just do not like facts.[108] This is where the teaching-subject-matter-content-is-the-least-important-thing-that-a-teacher-does idea rears its ugly head. They call the process of teaching, especially if we do it in a traditional lecture-demonstration-discussion format, merely "pouring facts onto kids heads," and that is a terrible waste, they tell us. We cannot draw the best out of kids unless we "engage" them on their own levels (i.e., ask them to do only the things they already know how to do, or feel like doing). As always, this is the opposite of what life requires. We cannot get the best out of kids unless we ask them to reach out beyond themselves. I suggest that maybe exposing kids to more facts is precisely what is missing in school today.

Maybe if we taught things, then kids might learn things.

Man, what a concept!

Incidentally, while 'engaging' was once a description of an entertainment, today it is educational jargon for trying to get kids to think. Of course, we design educational behavior nowadays primarily to be

---

108 By the way, I wonder which essential concept was being investigated during this 8th grade science class. The kids were asked to recognize candy advertising slogans. I asked my daughter this question. She attended the class but did not know the answer. But then her science facilitator had a degree in home economics.

fun, so I suppose, 'engage' is the right word to use after all. Yet, what are the results of all this entertainment-cum-education? The following is a typical, example of a budding, lifelong learner nurtured by the Progressive method. In March 2000, the U.S. Secretary of Education was giving his annual State of American Education speech, which was televised on C-SPAN. In it he related an education story of his own. On a family automobile trip he decided to engage his grandson in thinking about a scientific subject. While crossing a bridge over a river, Mr. Riley pointed out that the water seemed to shimmer more on one side of the bridge than the other, and asked his grandson why he thought that was. The grandson glanced briefly in both directions and answered, "Who cares?" Mr. Riley and his audience got a good chuckle out of this vignette, and the audience rewarded the Secretary with knowing nods and applause. The Secretary of all of American Education then went on to encourage educators to reemphasize the kinds of things they are already doing, since it is working so well and since it is the right thing to do. His audience, consisting largely of modern educational professionals, knows that if they keep doing the kinds of things that do not work, education will result.

What do you think? Does Progressive education 'get it' or not?

We have already discussed several reasons why allowing kids to choose their own study topics and depth of instruction does not work. If that does not work, what is the alternative? The answer is precisely the opposite of the Progressive recommendations.

We should charge responsible, knowledgeable, and experienced adults of proven competence to decide what is important for the kids to know, based on their own knowledge and experience, precisely because they do have knowledge and experience. Preferably these adults should be traditional and centrist[109] in their outlook so that the society can remain on an even keel. We then raise generations of kids to common sense, pick some of the better ones and turn them into teachers (here we will allow the new graduates to choose their own professions, of course) and keep the society strong.

How do we accomplish this simple vision? The answer is also not very fashionable right now but that means next to nothing, considering where educational fashion has gotten us. The answer is that we *want*

---

109 These two characteristics can be taken as synonyms.

kids to experience facts and ancient ideas in increasing degrees and increasing complexity, so that the kids will have an increasing variety of ideas to think about, as their teachers try to engage them intellectually. Allan Bloom, despairing of this very point but showing that there is yet hope, tells us that upon his first trip to Italy, a former student sent him a postcard that said, 'You are not a professor of political philosophy but a travel agent." Bloom writes:

> Nothing could have better expressed my intention as an educator. He thought I had prepared him to see. Then he could begin thinking for himself with something to think about. The real sensation of the Florence in which Machiavelli is believable is worth all the formulas of metaphysics ten times over . . .
>
> In a less grandiose vein, students today have nothing like the Dickens who gave so many of us the unforgettable Pecksniffs, Micawbers, Pips, with which we sharpened our vision, allowing some subtlety in our distinction of human types [everybody is *not* the same as everybody else]. It is a complex set of experiences that enables one to so simply say, "He is a Scrooge." Without literature no such sharp observations are possible and the fine art of comparison is lost [Don't be judgmental]. The psychological obtuseness of our students is appalling, because they have only pop psychology to tell them what people are like, and [about] the range of their motives. As the awareness that we owed almost exclusively to literary genius falters, people become more alike, for want of knowing they can be otherwise. What poor substitutes for real diversity are the wild rainbows of dyed hair and other external differences that tell the observer nothing of what is inside.

Another part of the solution is to progressively simulate for pupils what adulthood and employment will eventually be like. They will eventually use the knowledge they have gained to forge a life for themselves and their families. I use the word 'progressively' here in the sense that, year by year along with exposing pupils to the deep mysteries of culture and scholasticism, academic requirements should deliberately approach the kinds of requirements kids might see as adults. We should do this so that when we finally graduate them, and release them to make their own ways in the world, they can ask, "What can *I* do for my country?"

As one gets promoted through the grades, the pupil should be more aware of the fact that all his schooling is leading somewhere. It is leading to the future. It is leading to places they have not yet been and about which they know very little, or nothing. So kids, you should shut up and listen, and then answer questions based on the new stuff you just learned, *and* on what you have previously learned. You see, kids, in adult life, you will get many multiple choice exams. These exams will not always be on paper where we array the options for your simple choosing. In life, you must figure out for yourselves which choices are appropriate for each situation. You will have to make choices, the consequences of which, you will feel even fifty years later. Your life exams will be based on a wide range of potential choices and each of those choices consists of different details that work in different ways.

We must expose you to as many of those details as we can manage. If you learn how simple ideas interact, by learning about the various parts of the ideas, you might be prepared to use what you know to solve life's more complex problems. That is why we require you to sit through a variety of classes teaching a variety of subjects. To solve your life problems (that is, answer the question, "What do I do in this situation?"), you must pick among those choices that you have considered and learned about. It is tough to pick a choice that you did not know existed. Merely asking you to 'think outside the box' does not work if you have never even approached the sides of the box. To do what is best for your family, for your career, or for your country, you must know what choices you have. You must know what each choice means and whether a choice that you are considering has been used in similar situations, and whether that choice solved the problem. In other words, you have to learn stuff, and think about what you have learned.

To be able to know what each choice means, you have to know how things work, mechanically, biologically, socially, and philosophically. Your choices may involve any of a very wide variety of possibilities. You may have biological choices to make. You may have to make choices about diet and cosmetics and what to do with the wetlands and what the fuss about global warming or overpopulation means. You may have choices that involve math like, "Does buying this on credit make sense?", or "Does it make sense to buy mutual funds or CDs?", or "Should we pay off the national debt or reduce taxes?" You may have choices about artistic issues and about what you want your own children to read, see, or witness. You will have choices about such a wide range of topics that asking *you*, when you are 6 or 12 or 17, what is relevant, makes very little sense. What we do here in school is give you practice in making wise choices, while teaching you the kinds of things that adults (presumably) already know. If your teacher deems an answer 'correct', you should begin to understand *why* it is correct, and its limitations. In other words, "Why did it 'work'?", and not merely, "I'd like it to be this way." What we do in school is to give you the information you may need to understand the effects of making the choices you make.

Here, in school, we will ask you to select simple choices, usually with few variations. We know that, at your stage in life, you cannot imagine how anything could possibly be more complicated than the algebra question that you struggled with yesterday, but there are such things. In life, your choices will grow and their complexity will mount, so you have to walk before you can run. You should also know that the same decision is not always the best in each situation and that rhetoric often confuses the issues. This is especially true if you do not understand the issue to which the rhetoric refers. Being fooled by rhetoric is particularly dangerous, so it is best to know at least the rudiments of what the 'expert' is trying to convince you must be done. Also, things change, so what is the best decision at one time may also change, even if things seem to look the same on the surface. Then later, the first decision might be best again. That is why, once you understand the information from each different subject course, you will, in the higher grades and eventually in adult life, be able to evaluate, combine in creative ways, and finally use information to make the best decision for each situation. You will never have a chance of making smart choices if you remain as ignorant as you are now.

Nevertheless, not every decision will be Earth-shattering. Life requires many multiple-choice decisions every day, and many of them relate to your job, and to relating with other people. These other people may not look like you at all. That does not matter. If they are standing on the production line next to you, or are sitting in the office cubicle next to yours, they are probably more like you than not. If you want a job in that cubicle or on that production line, keep in mind that you are not alone. You are competing against others who want the same things. The funny thing about jobs, though, is that they often require you to do something. They often require the work to be done in a certain, specific way and within a specified time limit using specific data or techniques. Also, during a lifetime you may end up working for a variety of employers. Therefore, it is a happy coincidence that you can generalize your school assignment and teacher relations experiences to begin to understand how to retain employment under various conditions ('different jobs and employer personalities').

What does all that mean? It means that different teachers have different personalities and every class has a different set of requirements. It also means that it is a good thing that each subject is different, since the variety exposes kids to some of the different conditions, facts, personalities, and potential solutions, social and otherwise, that they will deal with as adults, but under conditions that will allow re-do's, if necessary. When else would we expect kids to pick up these skills if we ask all teachers to be the same cheery, though ignorant, activity facilitators.

Years ago I worked in a psychiatric hospital for 'unsocialized' kids. The average kid I see in my average modern classroom would have fit in well with the kids at the hospital. In fact, many of the kids I meet in today's schools are far less courteous than the kids institutionalized several decades ago. Schools should not be the catalysts of social decay and anarchy, especially not in the name of democracy. They should prepare healthy, happy citizens for useful, patriotic, socially competent lives.

Of course, saying something like "We should teach kids to be good workers" can infuriate some. The Progressive argument is, again, that teaching the work ethic is in reality forcing kids to learn to tolerate various oppressive conditions that enslave kids, turning them into placid, brain-dead robots who cannot think for themselves but can only follow orders. It does not seem to matter to the Progressives that a responsible society expects all kids to behave themselves, not just 'at risk' or 'minority' kids. Nor does it seem to matter that the military, who have the most experience with formalized order-giving and taking and in developing leaders from ordinary recruits, have known for a very long time that, "You cannot learn to give orders unless you first learn how to take orders." Being a good order-giver is different than merely demanding that others do what you do not want to do yourself.

Army (and I presume the other services) professional-development classes often teach that around the world the American fighting reputation is unpredictability. Other armies across the world know us as soldiers whom they can rarely rely upon to follow doctrine strictly. American soldiers improvise easily and confuse enemies who think we will do one thing, but often do another. Does that sound like mindless robots who cannot think for themselves?

Ironically, this innovative thinking works in the Army because the Army trains its doctrine relentlessly while rewarding mission accomplishment. Well-trained soldiers know very well what they, and their equipment, can do (i.e., they are well schooled in the basics) and can often improvise and innovate successfully because of it. Today's tactical situation rarely resembles yesterday's book answer, yet to be able to evaluate possible variations quickly, especially in situations with less than complete information (i.e., the fog of war), we must first know what is in 'the book'.

If this can be true in an environment that prides itself on following orders, imagine what we can achieve in other areas, if instructed properly. You do not have to imagine. Just look around. America has become the pinnacle of virtually every course of endeavor you might care to mention, and we did it in large part because the schools once taught useful, basic things placed in context, followed by increasing complexity, requiring increased skill in analysis, development, and accomplishment. Will we stay at the pinnacle however, if we honor selfishness (and bureaucracy) above genuine achievement?[110] You cannot be successfully creative unless you can predict what the result of an action will be accurately, and you cannot do *that* if you do not know the details of how things work. Yet Progressive Whole this-and-that theory (e.g., whole language, whole science, whole curriculum) literally asks every kid to try to reinvent the wheel, and the alphabet, and everything else that is known, from scratch, without instruction, even if it has been known for centuries, then accuses kids of developmental retardation if they can't do it.

'Socializing' kids is terribly hard, meaning teaching and having kids practice socially approved behaviors. It is even harder if parents teach one set of behaviors while schools and 'the media' teach that those same expectations are stupid or are designed to enslave. Allowing each kid to choose for himself which behaviors are relevant and which ones are not, makes this process harder still. It is even harder when Progressively tutored parents accept the rhetoric about individuality, and teach it, too. Allowing kids to remain 'unsocialized' (never learned, or don't care, what is socially acceptable and what is not) creates a society that looks like the one we are developing now.

Considering this sequence of truths, do you want *your* kids to be taught under the Progressive philosophy, which cannot even tell when it is drowning?

---

110 In the fall of 2000, the State Department issued 60,000 new visas to foreign math graduates, because American industry could not find enough American kids that knew enough math.

We are dealing with kids. Children. Immature young adults at best. Despite raucous protestation to the contrary and despite the rare teen who may start his own business and make a $bundle, these folks, even the smart ones, are not prepared to make what are essentially lifetime career decisions yet. Most have only a vague idea about where they want their lives to take them, and things are changing too fast for them to specialize so early. Unfortunately, this often also applies to new teachers, being barely past childhood themselves, and having spent most of that time as pupils with few adult responsibilities. This applies even to those who paid their own way through college since they have not yet had time enough to develop mature wisdom or a realistic world view (being indoctrinated to the multiculturalist world view does not count).

I do not discount the importance of pupil interest in the learning process, but left to their own devices, children will usually pick something easy, or irrelevant, or merely entertaining. We have far too much evidence of that to deny it, so sensible adults object to the "less home-work and more free time" sort of relevance.

At this point one might say that it is the teacher's responsibility to make each topic as interesting as possible, and I would have to agree, but to put the curriculum to a vote of children is nutty. We should not abdicate our adult responsibility of teaching kids what is necessary to succeed in tomorrow's world. The solution to the teaching problem (what and how do we teach?) for today is essentially the same solution that we used yesterday (historically speaking). The reason for that is that we trained yesterday's kids to survive in *their* future. Yesterday's teachers could not know what today would hold, any more than today's teachers can know what tomorrow will hold. For that reason today's kids need to know as much as they can learn about how things work today, or they will have a hard time inventing tomorrow using today's confusion. It will be harder still, if they do not even know what we knew yesterday.

Just look what yesterday's kids have invented. There are space flight, global communications, medicine, robotics, genetic engineering, and agriculture, to name just a few. Would these things have been possible if yesterday's kids were still illiterate even after a dozen years of schooling?

What today's pupils need is intensive, traditional academic variety. That is, history, English (reading and writing), science, the arts, crafts, humanities, geography, physical exercise, literature, civics, other languages, and eventually computers. In other words, our kids need an old fashioned, yet updated, 'liberal education'. They need this sort of program in high school for the same reasons that colleges offer 'survey' courses, but of course with a bit less detail. We will broaden the detail in college, if a kid gets that far. If he does not go to college to read biology, what use is the detailed biochemistry of meiosis, for example?

On the other hand, for kids who think they know that science is not for them, this will mean forcing them to learn about photosynthesis anyway, whether they will ever have direct use of that knowledge or not. The history department will force the science pupil, along with everybody else, to learn about the Crusades and the English department will force everyone to read *Ethan Frome* (gad!!!), so it all evens up in the end, gives kids information with which they can later make career choices, feeds the development of wisdom generally, and helps kids to identify personal interests. Not a bad legacy for 'mere' facts.

But, what about the argument that says that every kid is a unique individual, who needs a unique system of instruction, all his own? We will discuss this in more detail later, but when you think about the 'learning styles' argument, you realize that, prior to the Progressive devolution, we had been addressing this issue sensibly for years. Even if the requirements of a particular subject area do not match a particular learning style, you need not become a master of the esoterica of the subject matter to 'pass'. You need only get a 70 percent (a "C-minus") in a class to pass, get promoted, and graduate. That is why we accept a range of grades in the first place. Those who eventually select a career other than their school-day nemesis need not do pre–Nobel-level work to pass. They only need to develop a general, working understanding of the basics of a subject.[111] Also, when each department teaches its own subject rather than the Progressive agenda, each pupil gets a fairer understanding of what we require in that area professionally, and has a much better chance of deciding intelligently what to do with her own life. When, on the other hand, each department tries to be as easy as the others, so that *all* pupils can succeed, the main result is a homogenization of subject matter that creates boredom, confusion at the merest hint of complexity, and eventual resentment.[112] What happens when

---

111 Do our current state or national achievement averages in the 30 percent to 40 percent range qualify as a general working knowledge?

112 My second-grader told me that the only things he likes about school are recess and gym. Everything else is just too easy to be fun. This is early in the second grade and he is already on the verge of tuning out.

pupils can't find their own relevance in school? Drop out rates reach for the sky. At least 15 percent nationally, it may be more than 50 percent in the most Progressive school districts.[112a] If we then send barely literate kids to college, many of them drop out before graduation, unhappily settle for a career we taught them was unworthy of them, and demand more help for *their* kids from a bureaucracy that doesn't know how to teach kids to read, and complains that the kids cannot read because their barely literate parents do not participate in their education enough.

"Here we go round the mulberry bush . . ."

In a genuine school we allow each kid to like and dislike whatever suits them—but expect them to learn it anyway. They get to do music if they like music and they might get to blow things up if they like physics, but they each get the basics of the range of potential human endeavor. Each kid, whatever his capabilities, becomes at least functionally literate and a capable and productive member of society. This is true even if they cannot do quantum mechanics or paint as well as Leonardo. A huge benefit that we gain by this traditional system is that our kids get a wide-ranging perspective of our world and culture, rather than just an MTV view.

Maybe we will even get a reduction in perceived stress as a bonus as kids gain experience in working hard to achieve a goal. Once upon a time we thought of the desire to do well as healthy ambition. Today we say that it is a psychic emergency requiring pharmaceutical intervention.

In the end a traditional system will allow us to find the truly gifted, potential leaders. The bright kids will adapt to whatever learning style each subject requires and do well in most subjects, whether they enjoy them or not, because they want to succeed. For them, the effort, and the reward, is the point. Average-overall pupils who have a talent in some area can develop that talent and make a career in that area, though they do not get top grades in all areas. Weaker-overall students will at least be more competent at the basics, be productive citizens (rather than wards of the state) and have better information with which to make life's decisions.

112a On June 23, 2005, CNN (The Cable News Network) used an Associated Press story (Study: States mislead public with faulty graduation rates) which stated that most states are systematically inflating their graduation statistics and that the real numbers show that about a third of all pupils who enter the 9th grade never graduate at all. Three states and the District of Columbia report no graduation rates at all.

Unfortunately, if you accept the Progressive argument, we also quickly cross the other 'color' line. That is, the arguments that invoke racism at the merest hint that we might recommend teaching good work habits and subject matter content. Whoever argues these things neglects to notice a very important point. Employers (you may read 'Life' if you wish) have very different requirements than do child-centered educators. Employers depend on their employees for a livelihood. They must make money to keep their business in business. Otherwise, their own kids go hungry, along with the kids of all their laid-off workers. Especially in bad times, but always regardless, the priority of employers is not whether they are addressing their employees' psychological colors. Employers prefer happy employees, of course, and they may work to sustain a high level of contentment by supplying various employee benefits and using morale building schemes, but the primary concern of those who will pay our kids' future wages or salaries, is whether they can get the job done. This will also be your kids' primary concern, if they ever become employers in their own right. If the employee cannot get the job done, the salary goes away along with the job. It is not racism to expect employees to work for their pay, and employers expect their same-race employees to do the same. Since 'personnel costs' are typically the highest expenses in any business, by far, no thought of slavery exists, except in the minds of the politically correct.[113]

Of course, if you never learn how to do anything else, you can always enter the sex industry. It should come as no surprise that most of our modern reports of slavery arise from that Progressive, utopian lifestyle choice.

Even in semi-utopias, however (like a Progressive educator's fantasies), once you leave the cloistered world of childhood, life is not always as easy as we would like it to be. So childhood should not be as uninformed as some of us seem to want. Traditionally, in every society,

---

113 If you have just snickered thinking that this is just another conservative argument, and that the real agenda is to cushion the retirements of corporate CEOs by keeping robotic employees quiet and complacent, then forget it. I was not in favor of large corporations to any great degree, even before the accounting piracy scandals broke in 2002. I have always wondered why we would allow additional giant mergers after being burned by the last several hundred. Every corporate takeover argues the benefits of the 'economies of scale', and we nearly always buy the argument. What I do not understand is why don't the prices ever come down? Maybe a few thousand 'mom and pop' stores would be better for the economy than a few big corporate divisions. We would need fewer government bailouts of failing monsters, too. Besides, small business owners are often much more intimately involved in maintaining the well-being and happiness of their employees, who are probably family, friends and neighbors, than any personnel department could ever be. Oh, well. This is not the place for this.

culture and neighborhood, we expect people to work to survive. We should tell our kids about this early in life and we should reinforce it often. These reinforcements can be quite gentle in the early years, and if you teach this lesson early, they will not need to be harsh later since *all* will understand the lesson. Of course, the closer a kid gets to graduation and adult responsibilities, the more he should know what real life will hold in store. If we expect kids to complete assignments on time and with some semblance of competence, it is not a call to reinstate slavery; it is doing kids a very great favor. The society, and life for *all*, might just improve if its members grow up expecting to contribute, too.

All decision-making models, along with the scientific method, teach that you must periodically check your results to know if you are on the right track.[114] Our results, such as those recorded in the charts in Chapter 1, and the direction of our society generally, clearly show that what we are doing now is harming everyone, including, perhaps especially, those considered most at risk.

How can we, and schools, gently and systematically simulate life in the real world, so our kids grow up understanding that they will eventually work for a living? Simple. At home, chores are good. In school, assigning age and traditionally grade-appropriate (or higher) work in each class, with short deadlines (typically, overnight). Insist that the pupils submit assignments on time, and grade them strictly, and each year we should raise the expectation a bit, in recognition of another year's knowledge and experience accumulated. If we raise the acceptable level of work above what the average kid wants to do, we will again raise the reputation of public education to an uplifting rather than a dumbing-down experience. What we should never do is teach the Progressive ideology or the excuses that they use. These excuses include the 'learning styles' silliness, and the victory of individual choice over social responsibility. Rousseau would agree with this. Starting on page 89, he

---

114 I thought this statement was true, until I saw a poster in a math classroom that showed the decision/problem solving system as proposed by the National Counsel of Teachers of Mathematics (NCIM) labeled *Research Ideas for the Classroom, High School Mathematics*. A page reference number was given, but no year of publication. Here is the scheme: Understanding the problem; Choosing a problem-solving strategy; Implementing the problem solving strategy; and Finding, and reporting a conclusion. Note: They get all the way to 'report,' without ever evaluating the results. Happily, their website did not show a similar poster in December 2004: www.nctm.org.

A few weeks later I saw another scheme posted in a science class that also left out checking results against the hypothesis. Perhaps this helps to explain why Progressively trained 'scientists' don't bother with this step, why their results never seem to match their predictions, and why they don't seem to notice.

begins a discussion on the futility of using reason to reason with children. Along the way he says, "If children understood reason, they would not need to be raised." Later he adds, "Nature wants children to be children before being men." Then on page 91 he says, "Use force with children, and reason with men. Such is the natural order." If we follow this prescription, Rousseau tells us that, "The wise man does not need laws." J.J. knows that if we raise a kid wisely, by the time he becomes a man, the kid already knows what is right and what is wrong. <u>Then</u> we can let him choose.

What our current widespread crop of intelligent ignoramuses would be capable of accomplishing would surprise some of us, if we could dispel the ignorance. For instance, high school graduates that do not know that there are three feet in a yard, are limited in their career choices. If we dispel this level of ignorance, we expand opportunities for career choices, promotions, and advancement, and the rest of us will sleep better knowing that we were right all along. We know that we are right because previous generations managed to learn basic algebra, so why not this one? We do not need another decade of directionless research, and bureaucratic floundering based on that research, to learn what has been known for centuries.

We must also indoctrinate prospective teachers in reality. After all, it will be their job to teach things to kids so that they can have a fighting chance of surviving in an unquestionably difficult world. It is not pretty out there if you are ignorant, and we will never have, nor should we need, enough government funding to bail out everybody all the time. Besides, God loves the child who's got his own.

All of this reality sounds scary, though. Do we truly have to scare these poor children all the time? Yes, we do, though it is rendered non-frightening if they hear it from infancy. It becomes scary, however, if we surprise them with it as we hand out their unearned diplomas. In the first place, kids are much more resilient than we like to admit. In the second place, they have to know what we expect. No one ever did what was expected of them, except perhaps by accident, if they did not know it was expected. Besides that, if pupils are afraid a bit, what will they be afraid *of*? Not doing well? Isn't that what we want? Isn't that the basis of 'goal oriented' expenditures of personal energy? (Necessity is the mother of invention.) By the time that they are in high school, knowing that they will soon have to pay their own rent and fund their own vacations, will give kids a bit more incentive to qualify for a good-paying job.

Life can be simple if we keep ideological politics out of it.

With Apologies

I must apologize for the next quotation, but I want to make a point about another one of the delightful social effects of child-centered facilitation. Among the lessons that Progressive educators concentrate upon, and promise to instill in *all* pupils, is respect for others. They especially insist that their way will foster respect for those of us who are different in some way—that is for 'diversity'. At least, that is what they say in their press releases and rhetoric. The text of the following quotation is the enchanting retort that an angry 7th grader gave me when invited to sit down so that class could begin. After ignoring my instruction to sit down twice, he continued talking with his back turned to me, when I repeated the instruction a bit more firmly, he spun around and invited me to, "Come suck my ****." I submit that Beaver Cleaver and his generation would have found this outburst appalling. After the tittering stopped, this class looked at me as the enemy when I sent our hero to the office. While this response was admittedly extreme, the attitude is depressively common.

This is perhaps a mild example of the lack of respect-for-others that is found among modern children, as compared with the teachers who have been assaulted and even thrown out of windows, but it was perpetrated in a clean, 'fun', suburban Middle school, whose faculty are sure they are training the kids in sweetness and light. Unfortunately, the public rhetoric of sweetness and light has hidden a deeper truth. Other examples are still more insidious, as many parents have discovered. The irony is that, after some parents lose control of their own children, they will ask help of the school, and of their mental health professionals, to save their errant children. This is ironic because these mental health and education professionals, and their teachings, are who caused the child to get out of control.

As Thomas Sowell said, "Parents who send their children to school with the admonition to respect and obey their teachers would be surprised to learn how often these children are sent back home conditioned to disrespect and disobey their parents." The problem is that not just parents are dishonored. The kids dishonor themselves, and just about everybody else. In fact, the effort at degrading the influence of parents and our most commonly held values, takes on a sinister and wide ranging aspect. The following is an example how we make the already slippery slope of Progresesive ideology steeper. It is also an example of what many educators think is their true duty, rather than teaching. Sowell quotes from the *Humanist* magazine:

> I am convinced that the battle for humankind's future must be waged and won in the public classrooms by teachers who correctly perceive their role as the proselytizers of a new faith: a religion of humanity that recognizes and respects the spark of what theologians call divinity in every human being.
>
> These teachers must embody the same selfless dedication as the most rabid fundamentalist preachers, for they will be ministers of another sort, utilizing a classroom instead of a pulpit to convey humanist values in whatever subject they teach, regardless of the educational level—preschool, daycare, or large state universities.

On the surface, this might almost sound decent and honorable, until you discover what they are proselytizing, instead of what we are paying teachers to do. This is, however, a clear statement of the intent of the new 'internal' morality. This is the notion that I have identified as the I-am-more-important-than-anyone-else, child-centered, self-esteem philosophy. As such it is contrary to the wisdom of several millennia, which states that each of us is a part of a larger whole, that our importance stems from our obligation to be a part of that whole, all of which eventually helps to improve and strengthen the whole as well as the individual. In the Progressive religion, the individual, rather than the group, is considered supreme. Each of us is encouraged to act as if we are individually divine, in the pagan sense—that is by acting as if rules do not apply to us and that we can do anything, with little fear of a negative aftermath. Considering the results achieved, like that darling young man mentioned above, arguing that this is not the intent, should by now be falling on deaf and disgusted ears, but it is not. Instead we are accused of being 'against education' if we don't vote for still more funding.

At first, however, some of this sounded so extremely distant (along the self ↔ others continuum) that I did not expect to see anything similar in our local schools, as I suspect that you do not. All of the teachers

I have met seem to be decent people. I have met no obvious monsters or wild-eyed anarchists. In fact, I was not inclined to include this section at all, at first. Yet, based on some offhand comments my children sometimes make, I have indirect evidence that variations of this Humanist doctrine are occurring locally. For instance, during the Spring of 2002, when we had many news reports regarding pedophile priests and the supposedly pathologic effects that celibacy has on the celibate, my youngest daughter came home one day and declared that she thought that it was "crazy" not to allow priests to marry. Why they discussed any of this in the 2nd grade is beyond me, but with a few well-meaning words, the teacher had apparently taught her class full of impressionable children that priests are bad and that all religions have crazy ideas. I am no Catholic, and I have nothing but loathing for anyone who may hurt my kids, but using the news about a few who are either weak or depraved, this class of kids is now one step closer to not needing to discriminate among human variations (i.e., think) at all. Of course, the harmful effect of traditional morality is not the only topic that is the grist of modern schools. It appears that educators are not shy about indoctrinating the kids to their other concerns, either. I discovered that they asked my 7th grader to write a short opinion essay titled "My Opinion of Year-round School." My daughter was against it partly because, as she was told, "Studies show that year-round school doesn't affect [standardized test] scores. They stay the same." Of course if the intent is to affect test scores, it might help if we tested the differential effect of teaching as opposed to facilitating, rather than merely noting that using ineffectual Progressive activities for 12 months instead of 9 makes no difference. Apparently we do not want to trouble kids with that news. It might influence their opinions, and that would be unacceptably traditional. My daughter got an 'A' on her five-sentence paper.

I became convinced that it would be a mistake to leave out this section after I had a conversation with our grammar school's Special ed 'gifted' teacher. During one of our conversations, she suggested a list of books, labeled *The 50 best young adult novels of all time—So far*, showing that if our kids are not being explicitly subjected to programs such as Sowell describes, some kids are at least being encouraged to read such material. I will show some of these books in Chapter 6, and quote Sowell further, below. In any case, the list of locations and venues from which these thoroughly nonacademic educational (read "indoctrinational")[115] efforts span every State and subject area, from sex and death education to 'gifted' programs; from preschool to doctoral programs. Naturally, however, they begin in the earliest grades, when kids are most susceptible and non-critical. Uncritical pupils later fill college classes, such as those taught at Amherst, mentioned earlier. Unfortunately, we often tout these proselytizing programs, Sowell, has discovered, as, among other things, instruction in critical thinking.[116] Many training programs, often called 'values clarification' training, teach kids that they should reject their parents' views about honor, morality and—who'd a thunk it—sex, as 'old-fashioned stereotypes'. They ridicule traditional attitudes, and religious

---

115 This may be one reason why our modern school employees call themselves 'educators' rather than 'teachers'.

116 We will have a bit more to say on this topic later, but it may surprise some to know that, while on the surface 'critical thinking' sounds like one of the evaluative 'thinking skills' that are being touted constantly, 'thoughtful evaluation' is not necessarily what it means. For many Progresesive thinkers, 'critical thinking' is a recent reemergence of Marxist theory. While this is rarely stated at PTA meetings, it is occasionally admitted explicitly, as in an article published in the journal Marriage and Family called *Sociological Ambivalence and Family Ties: A Critical Perspective* (Connidis and McMullin, 2002). Copyrighted (2002) by the National Council on Family Relations, 3989 Central Ave. N.E., Suite 550, Minneapolis, MN 55421. Reprinted by permission. The authors say, "There are many branches of critical theory (e.g., Marxism, feminism, Frankfurt school [?], making it difficult to define precisely what is meant by the term." Note that critical thinking is not thought of as independent evaluation, but rather as ideological philosophy.

This is an article that generally examines why modern people have mixed feelings about fulfilling their adult responsibilities [i.e., raising kids, cooking supper, caring for aging parents] and concluded, among other things, that the institution of the family is a bad thing since it is an oppressive extension of society. The family is thought to be an oppressive thing, since, as we all know, everything can be defined in terms of power politics and the struggle of the masses against the 'privileged'. Thus, according to these Progressive thinkers, the concept of the family was invented by the privileged as a weapon in the fight to subjugate the masses. 'The family' is used to suppress our personally empowering feelings of individuality and freedom, by promoting the oppression of responsibility, obligation and love. The authors prefer critical thought to traditional thinking about familial love since it, ". . . helps to counter the more positive view presented by the solidarity perspective [i.e., families are one of society's strengths] in highlighting conflicts between family members." Nevertheless, since feeling alienated from our families is a good thing according to this view, the authors conclude that the only logical way to save ourselves from our odious obligations is to let others raise our kids or care for our ailing parents, leaving us plenty of time to do other things.

In another article by the same authors in the same issue of Marriage and Family called *Ambivalence, Family Ties, and Doing Sociology,* the authors use a subsection titled, *Theory and Ideology* to admit further, ". . . because we acknowledge our guiding theoretical assumptions and state that 'society is more accurately characterized as based on conflicting interests than on consensus', we are taking an ideological rather than an analytical position . . . We do not think that the 'truth' about the ideological bases of social arrangements, including those related to family, will be revealed through empiricism." In other words, they do not care what the evidence is, ideology is more important than reality when describing reality.

Isn't it comforting to know that your children's teachers are taught by folks who have their feet planted so firmly on democratic ground?

traditions, as 'hung up', and they teach kids that parents, 'have a hard time letting go' of 'society's moralistic tradition'. They decry parental attempts at instilling traditional values as 'going overboard' because these parents 'have serious emotional problems'.

Anything goes, and if you do not agree, you must be mentally ill or, that most heinous of all conditions, old-fashioned. This is hardly the kind of education most parents would support. Sowell calls it brainwashing, and I can see no reason to gainsay him. I have, for instance, overheard kids' conversations that featured the ridiculing of parents' concerns as "too churchy." If it is not brainwashing, it is at the very least a refusal to teach a sense of community, even with the kids' own communities. Another generation of this kind of education and we may run out of genuine educational controveries. No one will be alive who can remember what an education can, and ought to be. No one, that is, except a few aging curmudgeons (made that way by their disgust with the 'times we live in')—and we know that no one listens to old folks anyway.

Instructions to educators facilitating these sorts of 'moral training' programs, passed on to pupils, often include warnings not to tell parents what was discussed. Sowell found that the instructions may also include hints to school boards on how to deflect parental complaints about their children's changing attitudes. Again from Sowell:[117] "Board members quickly learn to tell parents they are too inexperienced to speak on the subject of education, that all the experts oppose their point of view, that scientific evidence proves them wrong, that they are trying to impose their morality on others, and that they are the only people in the community who have raised such complaints." However, Sowell concludes, "The very fact that supporters of such programs have written tactical suggestions for dealing with parents and other critics hardly fits the claim that few people have objected." Locally, it seems that "If you don't like it, you can go somewhere else" seems to be a favorite tactic.

Apart from the kinds of 'big stuff' that Sowell writes about, more homely examples of Progressive indoctrination can probably be found in many homes. In fact, many parents explicitly attempt to extend these ideas, under the tutelage of their own teachers and as influenced by the media. For instance the individual-choice message is everywhere, from self-help books to political commentary. Our kids also learn the message

---

117 Page 48.

very early in school. Who has not had a situation such as this occur to them: Parent decides to heat some leftovers for a Saturday lunch; the child says he does not want it; parent says I am not tossing this and cooking something new when perfectly good, already paid-for and pre-pared stuff is available; the child says, "But I didn't choose this." If the parent persists, she runs the risk of alienating her own kid over something that is fully within the purview of the experienced economic and nutri-tional decision-maker in the home.[118] If she also says something like, "You have to understand that in life, you will not always get what you want," the kid may be one step closer to deciding that his teachers are correct; parents are the enemy.

Then in January of 2005, I saw a survey that my 10 year old was asked to fill out *without telling the parents*. The survey asked about the kids' attitudes and experience with a variety of things, including drug use and other illegal and immoral things. It also had questions about how well the kids 'relate with' their parents. The worst of it, though, was the fact that the school counselors are teaching kids that it is OK to hide things from parents.

I wrote the preceding passages about a small aspect of Sowell's book well after I completed the section into which I fit it, and my few, edited examples may not be enough to alarm some, until they are fit into the larger, developing picture. What comes next may seem quite mild, too, but also adds to the growing picture, as supplemented by the list of books to be seen later.

One place where we often hear versions of the child-centered argu-ment concerns 'classroom management'. While classroom management also refers to such things as how to arrange seats and desks, a significant portion of this definition encompasses what we traditionally knew as discipline. Again, Progressive ideology insists that discipline should never be more forceful than pleading with a recalcitrant child because, demol-ishing all hope of developing a positive sense of self-esteem, all we do when we force someone to do something he does not want to do is teach him that "Might makes right." If we want kids to grow up gentle and non-warlike and/or as independent thinkers, not intimidated by authority figures, and if we want them to grow up as leaders and not as

---

118 Gastronomic decisions are also one way that parents have in maintaining family and cultural traditions, though Progressive thinkers would never accept this as a healthy form of multi-culturalism. In this case, it is repression, because what the kids want is what should always be done.

followers, then let them do whatever they want to, whenever they want to do it.

Unfortunately, this is not a new idea, though as is usual, modern Progressive thinkers misconstrue the idea and leave out important, though for them, inconvenient, bits of the theory. For instance, Jean-Jacques Rousseau's *Emile or On Education*, published in 1762, is a treatise on moral and social philosophy as much as it is a book about education. In it, Rousseau presents his ideas about how to educate a natural man (directing childish self-interest toward mature social consciousness—i.e., balancing selfishness with responsibility) using nature as his ideal. His book, in the 1979 translation, is almost 450 pages long, but is often reduced to only a very few simple, though misquoted, ideas that the educators take out of context to mean precisely the opposite from what the words truly mean. One of these is the foundational Progressive idea that 'the child must always do what he wants to do'. However, as Allan Bloom says in the introduction to his translation, "What is forgotten in Rousseau's full formula is that while a child must always do what he wants to do, what he *should* want to do is only what the tutor wants him to do." This is hardly a paean to 'democratic' anarchy, unless the tutor is an anarchist. In fact, Rousseau's meaning can be understood as far closer to, 'It's a free country, but there are rules and limitations'; than to, 'Do your own thing, Man'.

On the other hand, if we could distill Rousseau's ideas on morality to any educational maxim, it would be this: "Get used to doing *good* things until they are habitual. You will understand why you should do them later. By the time that you do understand the differences between good and evil, good actions will be habitual and bad things will be odious to you, and seem unnatural." We seriously degrade this sensible prescription when we allow kids to decide what is 'good' after listening to instruction in Progressive amorality.

Despite his call for an education based on experience, Rousseau does not reject formal instruction, in favor of blind floundering,[119] as

------

119 Though 'blind floundering' hardly describes Rousseau's conception of the education of the young, the closest he gets is education for children up to the age of twelve, or so. Rousseau does this because he equates "education" with the use of "reason," but says [like the developmentalists who wrote a century later] that kids do not have that abstract capacity until that age. Nevertheless, we should very carefully structure the education of the very young to develop propriety and the habits of goodness and innocence and strength of character. He would do this primarily by modeling proper behavior and by carefully monitoring the experiences allowed kids. The tutor must always be a good, cheerful, moral, and helpful man, respected by all, including those of both higher and lower stations in life.

We should avoid explicit instruction in morality, however, said Rousseau, because the young does the theory behind Discovery learning, which is also wrongly attributed to Rousseau's (and Dewey's) call for education by 'experience'. We will explore this in more detail in Chapter 7, but the short version is this: Experience is a better teacher than books. So forget the books, and go out and experience life. We frequently hear this argument in the words, "There are more ways to get an education than books alone."

Rousseau does not forgo explicit instruction for his idealized, aristocratic pupil. He merely takes the instruction out of doors, to maintain the health and vigor of his pupil.[120] Yet, far from leaving his single pupil to his own devices, choosing to traipse merrily and ignorantly in a pastoral setting, the tutor gently, but insistently, directs Emile's education and thinking toward the tutor's conception of goodness, compassion, and love, and also toward an understanding and appreciation of the physical world (e.g., the properties of matter, the relation of the Earth to the sun, etc.), and to the learning of a trade. Nevertheless, he tries to direct Emile's learning in a way that modern educationists have seized upon as facilitation, because he also says that, in the early years at least (up to age 12, or so), we must develop this learning during play and not from books. Nevertheless, along the way, Emile gets a very considerable education in physical reality, including the sciences, mathematics including geometry, astronomy, and all the rest, to rise above and see beyond, the "errors of imagination" (i.e., old wives' tales, and other forms of ignorant, evidence-avoiding theorizing) that plagued, and threatened to destroy French society in the late 1700s. We must remember that Rousseau wrote in the years leading up to the French Revolution and saw the pretentious and pseudosophisticated vanity (i.e., self-satisfied and arrogant self-esteem) of his aristocratic clients, as leading to no good. He may have had something there, after all.

---

pupil is still incapable of understanding the abstract reasoning upon which we base our moral precepts. Therefore, the child's lack of reason can make a moral act seem odious (such as apologizing to a sibling after a fight), if that act seems irrelevant or unjust ("He started it!"). This also applies to any insistence on not doing anything that is pleasant (like kicking your brother when he richly deserves it). We do not want moral acts to seem odious. We do not want a kid to develop a contempt for the moral ideas that seem contrary to his nature. That would make it harder to break bad habits later. What we do want is for the pupil to develop the good habit first, by imitation—without explaining why it is good. Just do it! The kid will understand why it was a *good* thing to do, when he is old enough to reason.

120 Rousseau noticed that French peasants seemed sturdier and generally healthier than French aristocrats, who pampered themselves and for whom the weather was an enemy to conquer (see Book I). I, too, have a pet theory regarding our modern ideas on the use of air-conditioning and furnaces, but although it, too, is related to modern teachings (e.g., the modern epidemics of asthma and obesity), this is not the place to expand on it.

Rousseau recommends using only one book, *Robinson Crusoe*, in his ideal education. From this fact, Progressive educationists seem to have concluded that Rousseau thought that reading was of doubtful usefulness. This is not true. Rousseau merely thought, that we could learn reading as easily later in life as earlier. We now have several generations of data to suggest that Rousseau may have been wrong on this one. Yet, books or no books, the pupil has to have some source of ready facts to help him understand the world. Therefore, Rousseau expected the tutor to have an encyclopedic knowledge of virtually everything. Emile could consult the expert tutor and, theoretically, have no need for a library of books.

If you can find a tutor/teacher such as that, hire him, though ideally Rousseau expects each father to be that tutor and even calls the man who pleads 'business' to get out of helping to raise his own children, a "venal soul."[121] However, the reason that Rousseau specifies that the pupil must be an aristocrat, or better yet, the son of a nobleman is explained on page 52:

> The poor man does not need to be educated. His station gives him a compulsory education. He could have no other. On the contrary, the education the rich man receives from his station [exposure to the corruption of the fashionable life] is that which suits him least, from both his own point of view and that of society. Besides, the natural education [akin to a peasant's simple life that is necessarily close to nature] ought to make a man fit for all human conditions. Now, it is less reasonable to raise a poor man to be rich than a rich man to be poor, for, in proportion to the number of those in the two stations, there are more men who fall than ones who rise. Let us, then, choose a rich man. We will at least be sure that we have made one more man, while a poor person can become a man by himself.[122]

Failing to live up to this conception of 18th-century philosophical (and decidedly politically *in*correct) social perfection, however, we,

---

121 This sounds much like the improbable insistence of "parental involvement" that is dear to the modern Progressive heart. Keep in mind that Rousseau's parents were of the French leisure and merchant classes, not the American working classes. So, this idea is improbable because we can reasonably expect no one to know enough of the range of subjects (from literature to organic chemistry) needed by modern pupils (but largely unknown to Rousseau's contemporaries), nor to have the time and resources, to prepare lessons for their kids, after work. This is why we hire teachers.

122 This reasoning *is* like the earlier arguments of Progressive educators—before the age of college-is-for-everyone.

humble turn-of-the-millennium parents that we are, may have to make due with a humble, genuine school—then help Junior with his homework.

Along these same lines, did you ever wonder how the children, and grandchildren, of the Peace Generation, raised with the conviction that the above Progressive analysis (i.e., regarding child rearing and classroom management) is correct, could have become as rude and violent as they have? The contradictions are so stark that the reasonable person should certainly have noticed that the promises made are rarely the results achieved. Nevertheless, Pollyannaish, child-centered arguments have become so widespread and so well entrenched that we have other expectations to live up to. To listen to the rhetoric, one would think that we will soon see the arrival of *Pax Progressica*, and that the smiley face will shortly become the worldwide symbol of humanity. To accomplish this dubious ideal, all we have to do is encourage girls to become warrior princesses and boys to be more in touch with their inner beings. They also regale us with the belief that we will all somehow feel a healthy commonality with all the children of the world,[123] by insisting that everyone is different from everyone else (Unity through Diversity). These sorts of silly contradictions are among the reasons why the results are so poor and why serious debate is not very productive.

The modern conception of how to raise and educate kids is seriously out of balance. This so because it idealizes the selfish end of the social spectrum and ignores, or ridicules, the responsible end. We need only look at how delightfully gentle and polite our society has become in the past thirty or forty years to prove it. Yet this idealistic, but simple-minded, idea is not new. In perhaps the most famous Progressive failure of all, Neville Chamberlain tried a child-centered–like appeasement approach with Adolf Hitler. An apt, working definition for appeasement, which Chamberlain apparently never heard, or heard and rejected, is: Appeasement is feeding meat to a predator in the hope that he will become a vegetarian. To take the child-centered comparison one step further, Chamberlain even got Hitler to sign a kind of "behavioral contract" and declared it was ". . . peace for our time." Chamberlain's blunder is worthy of Alfred E. Newman (and is in the history books that Progresssive educators refuse to read), yet Progressive thinkers endorse variations on this theme for use in classrooms, and politics, even now.

---

123 By this time, you should be beginning to hum *We are the World*. If you are bellowing it at full voice, there is probably no hope for you.

Is that description too harsh? Does the comparison not apply because school kids are not crazed dictators of angry, militant nations? Maybe, but Hitler was a human before he was a monster. He became the way he was in the end, because he was allowed, and was even encouraged, to be that way. He had "attitude" added to his self-pitying and self-aggrandizing philosophy. Today, supposedly because we had bruised their self-esteem somehow, otherwise normal-seeming kids decide that shooting up their schools and classmates is acceptable behavior. Recall that Hitler also decided that shooting-up all of Europe and parts of Africa was justified. We are apparently manufacturing mind-sets in many of our kids that might be equivalent to the mind-set of arguably the worst human of modern times, and calling it a good thing.

Just today, as I write this, a news report told us that two brothers in Chicago, aged seven and eight, sexually molested and killed an eleven-year-old girl because the younger one wanted the girl's bicycle (three cheers for sex education!). I will not reproduce our litany of woe again, but this Progressive event is another perfect foil for my 'selfishness' argument. If we teach, starting in earliest childhood with occasional affirmative reinforcement, that there is no right and wrong, that the only thing that matters is that which you 'choose', and that it is your individual right to do whatever you choose, then your childish, purely selfish ideas will govern your thinking and actions. If we are lucky, maybe those who are caught perpetrating a particularly heinous choice, will show some remorse. Progressively raised kids may feel sorry, though they may not think that what they have done was 'wrong' even then. They will probably only be sorry that we caught them. Understanding that what they did was *wrong* is less likely.

Part of the problem is, of course, that we hardly have social outrage anymore, unless it is directed at those who try to limit the excesses of selfishness. We just wring our hands and 'try to understand how this terrible thing could happen', while unleashing battalions of counselors and psychologists upon the 'stricken' population to help them 'achieve closure'. The recent spate of teen and preteen mass-murders should convince us that it is time to move back toward a rational judgmentalism and a healthy emphasis on rational limits to behavior.[124] If it does not convince us, maybe the self-esteem research, that shows that having an

------

124 Perhaps we have done this to some extent. There have been fewer episodes of school shootings, etc. in the past few years, and 'security moms' and the 'moral right' were said to be decisive in the elections of 2004.

unrealistically high sense of self-esteem contributes to criminality, will.[125] Once upon a time spit balls and water balloons were about the most violent most of our kids ever became. Now we have to worry about sawed-off shotguns, rape, and pipe bombs. That's progress for you. Of course, our own kids are not the only ones we have to worry about. There are others in the world who profess a deep and violent hatred for Americans and for the ideas that make many of us so proud. Yet, they did not grow to hate us in a vacuum.

Perhaps one unintended consequence of the attacks on the Pentagon and World Trade Centers will be that we begin to understand again that "anything goes" gives birth to and nurtures ideas that, we tell ourselves, no rational person could justify. We are shocked that people *do* justify random terror, and call it their duty to kill us. The easy argument to make is that they are merely religious fanatics that proves we must avoid all religions. I have already heard that argument, but it is just too pat. I suspect that what the Taliban and Al Qaida were concerned about, when they vilified the American way of life and solidified a very different system to distance themselves from ours, was not only the economics of capitalism, as some have suggested,[126] but also the social and moral climate that we export through our media. Folks from other cultures see and react to, among other things, the wisdom that encourages children to take charge of their own bodies, yet manages to do little but promote obesity and prurience, or both. They saw that we now honor pornographers and prostitutes, with, for instance, televised awards ceremonies, etc. They might have noted that many of us seem to think that having succumbed to drug addiction is a necessary step in the development of celebrity for movie, sports, and recording stars, and worthy of emulation by children. They might have seen our televised competitive date and "reality" shows that pit contestants for the affections of a perfect stranger, sometimes while a panel of celebrities discusses the action and generally applauds those as appropriately modern, who seem the most voracious. They may have seen all these sorts

---

125 Though the motivation for some petty thievery (simple want) is somewhat different, the gist of the self-esteem-as-justification-for-criminality notion is that, "I deserve the 'best', and I see no reason to get a job and toil, to earn it. I will just take it. After all, I'm worth it."

126 The World Trade Center was apparently the primary target, though we do not know yet what was the target of the fourth plane, that crashed in Pennsylvania. In any case, Osama bin Laden was a child of capitalism, either as an heir of his daddy's fortune, or as the international drug mogul he is said to have become. On the other hand, commerce, multinational corporations, as well as the media, do help bring our culture overseas.

of things and said, "Not for my daughters!" What the Taliban did about it was decidedly eXtreme (which should probably delight most Progressives) and horrible, but do you know what? Although I am not a fundamentalist Muslim, I do not want that for my daughters either—or for my son for that matter. I even doubt that there are many parents, even Progressive parents, who would want to see their daughters featured in one of the "Girls Gone Wild"-style videos, or their sons practicing sodomy. The way to limit these things, is to move away from the amoral and anti-moral ideals we have developed for ourselves. Nevertheless, this is not a call to emulate the Taliban, nor to justify their murderous brethren, such as Al Qaida. Far from it. What we need is a solution that takes us back to the historically tolerant American middle. We must return to a place that can balance a responsible way of life with a sensible view of the spice of life. As an important dispenser of the ideas that form the characters of children, the American school can and should play a major role in this. If schools encouraged moderation and common sense, those who graduate from the schools and take jobs in the media, would also be more likely to dispense common sense. While calling themselves 'moderate', what we teach now leads to excess and, potentially, to the collapse of our system. We are in a Golden Age now, just like Rome was during its decay.

Yet it may be too soon after the attacks to make this argument. Perhaps in time, we could analyze, at least at the broad-brush level, some motivations of bin Laden and his cronies. In the wake of the 9/11 attacks, there are indications that traditional common sense may be making a comeback, however. The media has reported recently, that many of us have said that we have begun to reevaluate our ideas and have concluded that the political and social concerns we held on September 10, 2001, do not seem to worry us quite so much anymore. People also say that the social and racial separations that they supported (to promote togetherness), just did not seem to make as much sense anymore. Many people reportedly now smile at and speak to strangers on the streets, rather than remaining in their emotional shells, and turning away, as was previously common. Let's hope that this newfound nationalism and communal feeling lasts and grows, for all of our sakes. Treating each other as fellow citizens would be a good thing, though it will be under pressure to return to the Progressive isolation if our educators and media do not also 'get it' and change the ideas that worsened the very problems they say they are trying to solve.

In any case, adult parents know that if they are consistently loving but firm, occasional anger, including an occasional swat on the rump, helps to focus a child's mind on the moral lesson at hand and teach him which behaviors are acceptable and which are not. It may take several repetitions for any particular lesson to sink in, but if a parent is typically full of hugs and encouragement, an angry voice and face will impress on the kid that "this thing I did, is a *bad* thing." This understanding relates to the old military and/or business adage of "they do what you inspect," and is the genesis of perpetuating the parental and community standards of acceptable morality and conduct, passed on to another kid.

This idea of consistent punishment for offenses is akin to the strategy that worked in New York City under Mayor Rudy Giuliani and was used to mitigate the city's reputation as a haven for criminals. The idea was called the broken window theory of crime control. This idea theorized that if someone sees a broken pane of glass in a window, it is more likely that they would try to break the other panes of glass, than if the window was intact because if the broken window is unfixed, it is obvious no one cares. It further theorized that we should write thousands of small tickets (for such relatively small infractions as parking violations) and level thousands of small fines and penalties (for petty vandalism and spitting on the sidewalk, etc.) and fix the vandalized and defaced-by-graffiti buildings. If we do this, we would minimize the feeling that many had, that rampant petty crime, despite volumes of laws on the books, is an unavoidable fact of life, and so, it is then acceptable to contemplate and act out progressively more serious crimes. On the other hand, if a city takes its own laws seriously, citizens subject to those laws tend to be more law-abiding. The laws that we then abide are not just the acts of major criminality like theft, rape, and murder, but the crimes against civility that detractors called "trivial."

Ironically, if we spend the time and money to enforce the trivial laws, people will abide by those laws, and we will not need specific, expensive government programs aimed at combating the small crimes that we don't think we can afford to prosecute. If we teach the small things not as items of individual choice but as a requirement of our common society, we will then see the big crimes merely as extreme examples of bad behavior. We will see these extreme behaviors as worthy of harsher punishments certainly, but an incomplete, but systematically increasing example of a set of unacceptable behavior is; whining, assault, battery, battery with injury, and murder (i.e., selfishness, threats, hurting, and killing). Did the 'new' theory of crime control work? Ask the people of New York who came to see the mayor as a hero, even before his leadership in the wake of the World Trade Center disaster earned him even greater esteem.

To teach good behavior to children we must start with the small things that kids might do. Proscribed behaviors may include such relatively trivial things as, no chewing with your mouth open, no high-pitched shouts, especially in closed spaces such as automobiles and classrooms, no hair pulling, no running in the house, improper uses of flatware, do not use curse words, ask before you take something that is not yours, and dozens if not hundreds of other rules. Some of these rules are family-specific and some are more widely expected. If we teach kids these things in the home, they will generalize them to public spaces and situations, and will eventually teach them to their own kids. This is especially true if the kid sees consistency in the lesson. That is, consistency between parental teachings (i.e., the same anger for each similar instance of bad behavior), and what the community expects. We call this consistency "propagating our common culture." Much more to the point of our current discussion, we should NOT tell the kids that it is their choice whether or not they can kick or steal, smoke cigarettes or rape, attend class or do homework. However, if a parent tells a kid not to curse, but her favorite TV stars are all foulmouthed but idolized and well compensated, because we celebrate verbal ugliness on freedom-of-speech grounds, what will the kid learn? What happens when the parents do <u>not</u> teach good behavior, because they think that structure and rules impinge on their kids' personal space, *and* his role models are all foul-mouthed hedonists?

The Progressive argument of no punishments, ever, has some temporary merit only if an individual child's life is akin to a concentration camp. In this case a strong-willed, abused kid may rebel against any discipline, however mild. (A quiz: Under what philosophic regime over the past forty years have the various forms of abuse become more prevalent? Check the charts on pages 126 to 128 for clues).

I must say that mere selfishness may not have been the whole story behind some of our recent kid rampages. We have to believe that there may have been other psychological problems involved for the worst of the outrages. However, the fact that these things are happening now, while they rarely, or never, happened in the age of Dennis the Menace, supports the conclusion that social control of behavior is waning. If your next historical argument reminds us that even the pre-Progressive 1950s featured juvenile delinquents, remind yourself that most of those kids were said to be the products of broken homes. Then note that some of our modern communities feature 70 percent of births into single-parent households and kids raised by grandparents because the parents couldn't be induced to care about their own children, or because the parents were in prison. In such communities even the 'normal' kids act worse than most of the juvenile delinquents of yore.

These traditional arguments may not impress the crazies among us (or the dedicated Progressives), but for the rest of us it is not a grand leap of logic to conclude that when we allow and encourage the behaviors that traditional common sense prohibits, the prohibited behavior will inevitably increase—to the detriment of the society. So arguing that bad things have always happened, even during traditional times, so there is no point to social controls ("They will do it anyway, so let's teach them to do it safely"), is another nail in the coffin of common sense. If we then honor or protect those whom we would previously have vilified, extreme versions of that behavior will, also inevitably, increase.

Thank you, you aging hippies, you.

Yet Progressives also argue that any social control is demonic if it does not square with their own peculiar, anarchist sense of justice, so any time anyone says that perhaps spanking is even occasionally justifiable, visions of torture chambers dance in Progressive heads. In trying to stamp out child abuse, the Progressive philosophy has virtually insured that abuse and 'acting out'[127] will increase. By teaching selfishness (i.e., attitude and unrestricted individual choice) as a virtue, we insure that people act selfishly and even brutally toward others because the self-centered person's thinking rarely gets beyond, "I matter, and you don't." This may be especially true if the ones they are selfish toward are helpless and cannot fight back.

Does this mean that *all* who attend today's public schools will inevitably become household barbarians? Of course not, any more than that none will ever emulate Gandhi if we allow an occasional spanking. The range of human behaviors is quite large, encompassing both good and bad behaviors. There still are many good parents out there teaching good kids who are valiantly trying to hold back the tide of Progress.

---

127 Temper tantrums of those beyond the toddler stage.

Nevertheless, we see more people doing quite inconceivable things. Susan Smith is one example, who drowned her young sons because her live-in boyfriend threatened to stop having sex with her if the boys were around. Jeffery Dahmer, the homosexual cannibal, was another.

We also see more people arguing that selfishness is the right thing to do. Have you seen the recent ads such as the soft drink commercial that features a thirsty girl at the desert 'last chance' gas station who tells her boyfriend, "Don't come back without it" ("it" being a brand-name soft drink)? The boyfriend discovers that there is only one can of the miraculous stuff left, so he drinks it himself, leaving his girlfriend out in the dust and heat. How about the cookie commercial in which the woman hides her cookies in a cutout book because, "Sharing is overrated"? These ads offer these vignettes as charmingly appropriate behavior because the colored sugar-water and cookies are so-o-o good. Is this only advertising hyperbole that everyone recognizes as mere poetic license, or a Progressive expression of a attitude learned in a classroom? I wonder. What about the ad that encourages young women with genital herpes to use a product so that they can continue to infect others without discomfort or guilt? The point here is that we can reduce the 'bad' end of the behavioral-spectrum and maximize the 'good' end by teaching a better balance between individual demands and community responsibility.

Some people might argue that we are already teaching community responsibility when we teach multiculturalism and Progressive values. Unfortunately, multiculturalism may be the single worst version of 'community' available to us since it insists on emphasizing differences rather than similarities. More on this hateful philosophy later. Our other option, the one taught in Progressive politics and Ed schools (and then in public schools), allowed us to maximize the bad and reduce the good by telling kids, and other folks, that individuals, and insular (special interest and minority) groups, are the only important things. At this point we must again implicate the contribution of the modern media in society's problems. The media's contribution has changed greatly from its relatively healthy contribution of the early 1960s. Currently the media's obsession with shows and news reports touting selfishness as a virtue (e.g., crime, intoxication, immorality, and even depravity, as acceptable forms of self-expression, of social justice, and of 'attitude' as a charming thing the beautiful people do), helps to maintain and extend the dubious self-esteem and relevance ideas we teach kids in school.

This is an easy argument to make concerning the multitude of Generation X, 'alternative relationship', and sex instruction shows we see now. Yet even supposedly serious shows, like documentaries that purport to "get into the mind of a mass murderer," often present the monster as a repressed child to be pitied and "understood." Here we can see another example of the child-centered idea that it is 'we' who must adapt to the true victim of our terrible society. What do you suppose is the 'psychological color' of the average child-molester? They often tell us that murderers, rapists, or child-molesters struck out at their victims simply because their mean old mommies would not allow them to torture neighborhood songbirds, or whatever. So don't be so judgmental, they tell us. He has had a rough life. Fight for the rights of the relocated multiple rapist that moved in next door. Be neighborly and send your little girl over with a plate full of brownies to make him feel at home.

It might be poetic justice that the media are now feeling the effects of their support for Progressive causes. In recent years media icons such as Sam Donaldson, Bernard Goldberg,[128] and others have commented on the change in the 'news' business away from the largely autonomous, but relatively expensive, coverage of current events and foreign affairs. What we have now is an economics driven (given 'em what they want) proliferation of exposé news programs, including the so-called legitimate ones such as *60 Minutes*, etc. This also includes the 'straight news' programs, such as the network evening news shows. Ideology and corporate profit rather than newsworthiness drive the decisions made by editors.

Why is this poetic justice? As we teach people to read less, it should not surprise us that people read less, including reading newspapers less. As we limit the instruction of history to the Progressive concerns, it should not surprise us that people feel increasingly isolated and helpless, and do not become interested in the world around them. What happened yesterday to people we have never met, may not be seen as relevant to our citizens, even if the U.S. is deeply involved. Instead we commonly revert to hedonism and our own private concerns because life is too short to worry about what kind of world we leave our kids.

---

128 See Bernard Goldberg's 2001 book, *Bias: A CBS Insider Exposes How the Media Distort the News.*

The argument that the media merely reflects the world as it is, and only gives the public what it wants strikes me as quite disingenuous. Again, superficially the argument is at least partially correct, but it is the sympathetic analysis and seductive presentation of our self-indulgent and nonjudgmental world[129] that turns the corner on responsibility to the society and has contributed to the public's reported apathy and indifference to immorality, criminality, and even deviance. Besides, where does the media get its new blood? Where do we get all of our oh, so creative writers, sex-obsessed actors, directors, producers, reporters, anti-intellectual pundits, and activist judges, who provide us with commentary, analysis, and legal wisdom? Not too long ago they were schoolchildren. Some still are. 'Adulthood' should not be conferred as a simple chronological inevitability. Adulthood (being a grownup), like wisdom, is the result of genuine education and experience. Some people never achieve it.

Our generations-long concentration on making pupils feel good above all else has had its toll, too. What people want to get from the media depends on what we tell developing intellects (kids) that they *should* want. What we have told kids that they should want is fact-less knowledge, the pursuit of personal pleasure, and contempt for traditional values. The long-term result for the media is that their customers want entertainment news rather than hard news and titillation rather than information. Newspapers were the first victims of this trend but the broadcast media are now being forced to scale back foreign news bureaus, etc., to pay for 'In Depth'-style features about how people feel about thong bikinis and other relevant topics.

People have heard for a long time that, "If it feels good, do it," and we did. Of course, it is one thing to pursue this idea if we are young and naïve, and a worse thing if we are now old but still had not thought things all the way through. Yet many people now feel that judging someone else for the things that we did as kids, or still do, would be hypocritical. People think this though what we did in the full flush of our youthful rebellious period (in college at age 20 or so [as putative adults]), would not raise an eyebrow of many of today's 13-year-olds. Many very young kids have already, "Been there, done that." Is there a connection between the acceptability of philandering, the availability of partners, the unrelenting sex instruction in schools, titillation, and

---

129 Except for anything considered important by traditional thinkers.

encouragement in the media, and teen and unwed pregnancies? What do you think? Recently, in 2004, I was waiting for a school bell to ring before beginning a class, and as the kids filtered in, one girl exclaimed loudly, "Hey. You guys. Did you know that Susie is pregnant?" This was an 8th grade class. There was no embarrassment exhibited by Susie or surprise exhibited by the others. In fact another girl said, "Don't worry, Sue. I've already had three abortions, from four different guys." I didn't ask.

The problem is that as we get older and have daughters of our own (and sons too, for that matter), we often develop a very different perspective on life, sex, and propriety. It is no hypocrisy to finally understand the reasons behind traditional values and to want to retain a society where those values hold. We once considered "settling down" as an indication that a sense of responsible adulthood was developing. This sense of responsibility was not a thing we should avoid. It is not like placing 'one foot in the grave'. However, though I do not know how widely the ad was seen, it is poignant that now, at a time when we teach that 'maintaining our childlike qualities' throughout life is among our greatest obligations to ourselves, someone has deemed it necessary to pay for a local media campaign featuring kids imploring their parents to, "Grow up with me."

Lack of parental participation in kids' lives is also the main finger-pointing complaint of modern educators, when asked to explain their awful academic and behavioral results. Again they are at least partially right since today's parents were yesterday's school kids. Yet the complaint loses much of its appeal when we realize that our recent sets of graduates did not learn as much as they could and should have, so are not competent to do the job we thought we hired teachers to do. Of course, the fact that the educators we hired are loath to teach much of anything either, has a lot to do with it, too. The lack-of-parental-participation argument loses even more of its appeal when we realize that the schools blame parents not merely because pupils don't learn morality, civics, and coloring, but because they also do not learn chemistry, history, fine arts, algebra, or much of anything else. To reverse these trends, educators then continually ask those same parents, and the wider, deeper pockets of the citizen taxpayer, for more money, so they can do more of what has expanded the ignorance we see.

Even so, restructuring your moral priorities is a measure of personal maturity, not hypocrisy. So, please, be as unrelentingly 'hypocritical' on moral issues as necessary, even if kids think you are not "cool." Unfortunately, however, not all adults eventually learn about traditional wisdom anymore, because not only have they not learned about ideas that we once called the finer or nobler things, they have learned that these things are evil and racist or, at best, irrelevant. A word often used when Progressives describe actual knowledge (i.e., facts) is 'trivial'. So is it any wonder that anarchy (e.g., anything goes, No Limits! No Fear!) is now considered a birthright and woe betide anyone who tries to get between our young 'uns and their orgasms.

These are the lessons taught to our kids by the folks who, on average, score barely above those who flunked out of college.[130] Remember that the single most important ability required of a college student/ graduate is the ability to learn and analyze new information, and then to explain it to others. We make these explanations in business, as elsewhere, by planning campaigns and initiatives and by the filing of reports, etc. This ability is why most businesses require a college degree of those they hire as executives and managers. We can teach others to turn a wrench or stock inventory, etc., but we expect the ones in charge to be capable of using bigger and more expansive ideas. Consequently, we once expected college to be significantly more challenging than high school, since we intended it as a preparation for adult leadership in one of the 'professions'. It may be that many of our educators did not flunk out of college, only because their Ed school required less of them than most traditional high schools. A real college would have sorely tested their ability to think, had we asked them to evaluate the ideas we once thought important for the genuinely educated mind to understand.

The media, in its various forms, also helps to validate selfishness by modeling the adult world to kids. This symbolic responsibility extends to the 'stars' of movies and TV, too, since they become associated with the roles that they play, and as practitioners of 'the good life'. Kids take these roles as the embodiment of their hopes and dreams. Kids incorporate these dreams into the things they want, or feel are relevant in their lives. Progressive schools then use this stated relevancy as something that we must pursue and support, "for the children." The current trend of aggrandizing and justifying bad behavior rather than portraying it as self- and socially destructive, not to mention the way some 'stars' live

---

130 Koerner, p. 44.

their own lives, makes it more difficult to convince kids that immorality and crime are bad things.

Another example of this trend includes news reporters who think it their duty not merely to report what happened, but to tell us what it all means (since we, the viewing public, cannot figure things out for ourselves). For example, the National Public Radio tells us, in its promotional spots, that they will not only 'Tell us what happened, but tell us what it means'. Unfortunately, the reporters and pundits may often be speculating without data, as even some of them acknowledge.[131] Many of them grew up only recently and learned their values and their politically correct, revisionist historical perspective in school. They think that they are "doing the right thing" by demanding that the government do everything for everybody, and by ridiculing traditional thinking. They just do not know any better. For them Progress is traditional. In this sense the media did not "cause" our current social problems though they help to entrench them, by an unrelenting and uncritical indoctrination in political correctness.

On the other hand, have you heard the news reports about communities, inner-city and otherwise, that say that the community has helped to clean up a drug, gang, prostitution, or other problem? How did they accomplish this great thing? They stood up, in the face of the Progressive politicians who want to understand drug dealers, thugs, and pimps, and simply told them to get out. The communities insist that the police arrest addicts and dealers and that the courts jail them. Soon the druggies, thugs and 'working girls' get the message and go elsewhere. This stuff works since we relate it to a rational community standard firmly applied. If we, as a society, would only get rationally judgmental again and insist on 'good' behavior starting while kids are still in diapers, we could do wonders. However, we have to start teaching it early in our children's lives, and the community, and our genuine teachers must support the lessons, if the lesson is to take hold.

---

131 For instance, on March 22, 2002, National Public Radio (All Things Considered) aired a report that stated, with admissions of its accuracy from media producers, that the reporting of 'trends' depends almost wholly on finding three examples of some behavior. Three examples is considered enough evidence, in a nation of more than 300 million souls, to relate weird coincidences as relevant to modern life. The manufactured trend used as the basis of the NPR story, was an Internet search for the combination of zucchini and medical syringes. Three examples were found that ranged from using syringes to feed strained zucchini to a baby, to injecting garden zucchinis with insecticide. Once one media outlet releases this deep and relevant analysis, other outlets, including television and the national newspapers, might then relay the story uncritically, just because someone had already reported it. It would not be hard to suppose that many of these reported trend searches will have something to do with sex. After all, that is what the public wants.

"Doing wonders" does not imply perfection, of course, but if we merely reduced crime to pre-Progressive revolution levels, people would gratefully raise monuments to the folks responsible.

In the end then, it is our choice, just as the Progressives say, though we cannot make reasonable choices if we do not understand the effects of the options. It is even worse if we ignore or ridicule responsible evaluations of the results of the choices. Should we abdicate our community responsibility, and insure the breakdown of the society because our self-styled victim groups prefer an anything-goes society and because we taught our young reporters and teachers poorly? It is our community choice, but we must *all* decide individually, and then vote for the kind of community in which we want to raise our kids. We must, furthermore, do it from a historical rather than a superficial rhetorical perspective. Of course, for that to be possible, we must teach history.

We have to decide what sort of philosophy we want our schools to promote. As even Francis Keppel, dean of the Harvard University School of Education from 1948 to 1962 and later Commissioner of Education until 1966 said, "education is too important to be left solely to the educators."[132] Since we have to decide this individually, it is up to us adults to make sure that our kids understand what we believe is important. That means insisting that we stress community, not child-centered individuality. We must promote community in an American Melting Pot way, not in the Progressive divisive multiculturalist way.

The problem is that we now have many newly minted "adults" who think that anarchy is the only acceptable form of freedom.

Multiple Intelligences

What was the point to the stuff about psychological colors anyway? Besides the child-centered kinds of arguments that we hear, another of the main pillars of Progressive philosophy is that learning is not what we have always thought it to be. It seems that there in no such thing as 'intelligence' anymore, as a single thing-in-the-head that we can focus upon when teaching school. We cannot teach every kid in the traditional way anymore. We will explore this 'single thing-in-the-head' idea in

---

132 Lagemann, p. 161.

more depth in the next chapter, but we can discuss some of what we infer about it here. We call one of those inferences 'multiple intelligences'.

Those of us who have not been in school for a while may be surprised to learn that we have discovered that there is more than one kind of intelligence in nature. There are at least three. The most prominent theory, as described by Howard Gardner, states there are seven separate intelligences. The seven are:

- logical-mathematical intelligence
- verbal intelligence
- musical intelligence
- spatial intelligence
- bodily-kinesthetic intelligence
- interpersonal intelligence and
- intrapersonal intelligence.

This idea is based at least partly on brain-damage research that shows that damage to one part of the brain may affect speaking, for instance, but may not affect mathematical skill.

I do not argue with the neurophysiological research. It is interesting and important though it may merely show that different parts of the brain are organized to process specific kinds of inputs, instead of processing them diffusely through the brain. I do not even want to make that much of a fuss about Gardner's categories. If we examine them, we may notice that we are 'better' at some of these categories than others. That is not surprising since we can categorize human abilities any way we wish. It may even be 'true' that we should list these abilities as individual 'intelligences', though we are probably only formalizing the idea that different people have different talents, including various physical skills. However, as Gardner admits in the introduction to his book *Multiple Intelligences,* "Had I simply noted that human beings possess different talents, this claim would have been uncontroversial—and my book would have gone unnoticed. But I made a deliberate decision to write about 'multiple intelligences: . . .'" Even Gardner knew that this description of intellectual function was, at best, an exaggeration prompted by a marketing decision, but it inspired Progressive educators into new flights of creativity. Though there was, and still is, no evidence that their methods appropriately address 'multiple' intelligences, they now seemingly had new legitimization for their ideas.

To describe and differentiate these abilities, my required textbook, *Educational Psychology*, by Anita Woolfolk, summarizes these intelligences in a chart that I adapt below. Some pertinent factors identified were these:

- People with <u>logical-mathematical</u> intelligence might eventually become scientists or mathematicians. These people are sensitive to and have the capacity to discern logical or numerical patterns and are able to handle long chains of reasoning. [To me, this one sounds much like the traditional definition of intelligence.]
- People with <u>linguistic</u> intelligence, however, might become poets or journalists and are sensitive to the sounds, rhythms, and meanings of words as well as the different functions of language. [This says nothing, however, about folks who merely talk a lot, without saying much. Neither is there any mention why a journalist, for instance, an athlete, or musician might not need the ability to handle long chains of reasoning.]
- People with <u>musical</u> intelligence might pursue careers as composers or violinists. They have the ability to produce and appreciate rhythm, pitch, and timbre as well as the appreciation of the various forms of musical expression. [That another point on the Progressive horizon equates musical ability with mathematical skill is apparently forgotten in this context.]
- <u>Spatially</u> intelligent people might become navigators or sculptors because they have the capacity to perceive the visual-spatial world accurately and to perform transformations on one's initial perceptions.
- People with <u>bodily-kinesthetic</u> intelligence may be dancers or athletes. These people have the ability to handle one's body movements and to handle objects skillfully.
- <u>Interpersonally</u> intelligent people might use their skills in careers as therapists or salesmen because they have the capacity to discern and respond appropriately to the moods, temperaments, motivations, and desires of other people.
- And finally, <u>intrapersonally</u> intelligent people are people with detailed and accurate self-knowledge. No specific career choice was suggested, but these people are said to have access to their own feelings and the ability to discriminate among them and draw upon them to guide behavior, knowledge of one's own

strengths, weaknesses, desires, and intelligence. [Presumably these folks are mostly professional neurotics.]

This stuff sounds almost acceptable until we see the educational implications of these supposed distinctions.[133] We all know people who can claim high skill in each of these categories, and we know many people who are average in each of these categories and we all know other people in whom few if any of these skills are well developed. We also all know people for whom these abilities seem almost randomly distributed. Maybe that is a good indication, as Gardner says, that these skills are mediated more or less separately in different parts of the brain. I also suspect that we will not resolve this academic debate any time soon, but does that matter for education? Whatever the answer to the last question, which we will discuss shortly and despite the preliminary nature of these investigations, use of these ideas is common and widespread in the modern classroom. The psychological color idea is a variation on this theme. Well, so what? Well, I'll tell you.

I have been using the everybody-is-the-same-as-everybody-else idea as a generic descriptor of the Progressive way of thinking, since they closely ally it with the idea of equity. Because of this philosophy, we now have 'inclusion' in the classroom. Inclusion theory insists that we cannot separate kids by ability groups, because the low ability groups are populated disproportionately by non 'dominant culture' kids, and the mere act of grouping is therefore obviously racist. Whether this is true or not, we now have kids ranging in IQ from less than 75 up through the stratospheric, sitting side by side in the inclusive classroom. The challenge for educators is to achieve individual academic excellence in a class of very widely ranging ability, while insisting that we must treat everyone identically.

However, since even educationists have noticed that some kids are smarter than others (i.e., learn things quicker and get bored when they have to sit sometimes for weeks at a time waiting for some others to catch up), some way had to be found to keep inclusion, but dilute the effects of the differential learning ability of different kids. As one programmatic solution to this dilemma, we embraced the notion of multiple intelligence, which led us to the idea of 'learning styles'.

---

133 Isn't it odd, though, that in this context, Progressive theory revels in the Nature end of the Nature–Nurture dichotomy, while it feverishly supports the Nurture end of the scale in most other controversies?

What we have then is that "everybody is the same" side by side with "everybody is unique," "intelligence is an irrelevant, racism concept" alongside "everybody is intelligent in their own way," and "we must not track individual ability" alongside "we must 'disaggregate' the achievement statistics of racial groups." It does not make much sense as a consistent philosophy, but that has never stopped the Progressives before. Ain't semantics grand?

Try to follow this logic. Since everybody is the same as everybody else, we must put everybody into the same classroom as everyone else. Since everybody is unique, we have to find ways of teaching each individual kid individually. Therefore each educator must prepare individual lesson plans for each individual kid so that she can address each kid's individual 'learning style' individually. Each kid has a different learning style because he has a unique combination of intelligences, which proves that everybody is the same as everybody else and that is why everybody is in the same classroom . . . That sound you hear is the carousel calliope song playing as we go round and round, while telling ourselves that we are marching forward with our eyes firmly set on the future.

So, if a high school teacher has 150 pupils assigned whom he sees regularly (every day or every week), as I did, ideally he must prepare 150 different lesson plans, 150 different sets of 'activity' handouts that address different outcome criteria and perhaps 150 'authentic assessments' per activity. All of this must be done while promoting 'cooperative learning,' in order to give each child individual attention. How many seconds of individual attention per day would each child get under this regime, do you think?

Put yourself in the place of this teacher. Is this reasonable? While this scenario certainly never happens in its ideal form, ideally this is what an educator should do every day of each school year of his or her working life. It gets even less reasonable when you realize that the teacher is not expected to develop each individual curriculum to suit each kid, but is expected to be prepared to react to ad hoc curricula that each kid develops for themselves, on the fly. And all without teaching, or even being competent in, subject matter. They even tell us that a teacher who shows a sensible preference for instructional efficiency and systematic organization, by routinely using a comprehensive textbook in class, is a lazy and bad teacher because she is not addressing the needs of *all* her kids. (Textbook use equals teacher-sloth was a 'correct' answer in the

"Professional Knowledge" section of a recent NTE (National Teachers Exam) used as the teacher certification exam by many states).

My favorite example of how the multiple intelligences idea plays out is this. Suppose that your kid has a bodily-kinesthetic intelligence (concerning athleticism and coordination). Suppose further that his current classroom subject matter unit is the respiratory system, and it is time to test his learning. If you expect traditional multiple-choice, true-false, short-answer, short-essay, body-parts-identification, and/or match-the-body-part-to-its-function test, forget it. Our pupil is not logical-mathematical, therefore an objective test would not be an *authentic* assessment of his learning style, and therefore unfair to ask him to explain what an alveolus is or to know that we exhale carbon dioxide during respiration. Instead, to demonstrate his deep understanding of the respiratory system and its functions, an educator might ask our bodily-kinesthetic pupil to choreograph a little dance about the respiratory system.

I swear to you, I am not making this up. One of my professors offered the above example as an appropriate authentic testing technique, with a straight face.

Just hang your diploma on the wall, Doctor. I will unpack your rattles and feathers.

Here is an example of how we use this idea in modern textbooks. Chapter 1 of *Biology: A Human Approach* is titled <u>The Human Animal</u> and features sections about chimpanzees and what Jane Goodall discovered about them; an activity about differences in grip between the various primates (opposable vs. non-opposable thumbs, etc.); and a section relating the progressive evolution of vertebrate brains, from fish through amphibians, reptiles, and birds to mammals, as represented by sheep and humans. [This section showed that the relative positions of the various brain parts (e.g., olfactory bulbs, brain stem, etc.) remain similar in the various species despite differential evolution. The difference between fish and human brains are, therefore, merely variations on a theme, not differences in kind.]

Incidentally, the book covered all of this in only about nine picture-dominated pages, which is a separate problem. Yet have you seen what passes for textbooks nowadays? The ones that I have seen, written for grammar school, all look as if they were written for Kindergarten. Most of the pictures are cartoon-y and most of the text is short and very simple. Most of the learning activities require little more than coloring, or at best, only solving very few practice problems (e.g., no more than four or six addition problems on a page, for instance). The one from which my current example in biology comes, is intended for high school freshmen, yet looks like it ought to be used in the fifth grade. Apparently, we see kids as incapable of sustaining attention for more than a few minutes at a time. The poor babies become so stressed that we must allow them to decompress frequently, by coloring something. As such, kids do more decompressing than learning.

Anyway, on page 27, we find this. The "Criteria for Projects" chart is another example of a grading rubric, and all of the various forms of emphasis (e.g., bold letters, italics, etc.) are in the original:

Process and Procedures

1. Think about designing a project to illustrate your understanding of what it means to be a human. When you have a general idea in mind, share your ideas with your partner.

Choose a medium that you are comfortable with to create your project. Some possibilities include a poster, a diorama, a poem, a story, a report, a musical piece, a play, a TV show, or a video. As you think about and plan your project, use the criteria in Fig. 1.8 to guide your work.

Fig. 1.8 Criteria for Projects. Use these criteria as you develop your project. Your teacher also will use these criteria to evaluate your understanding of the concepts of this chapter.

Criteria for Projects

Conceptual Understanding	Your project should demonstrate that you understand the idea that even though humans somehow are different from other animals, they share many characteristics.	Worth up to $\frac{1}{4}$ of the total project points
Information Base	Your project should (1) identify characteristics that distinguish humans from other animals and (2) identify ways that humans are similar. The characteristics should include general physical characteristics, (e.g., a description of hand use and locomotion, a description of the brain) and behavioral characteristics (e.g., use of language, ability to learn, social and cultural behaviors).	Worth up to $\frac{1}{4}$ of the total project points
Creativity	Your project should be engaging for others to observe, participate in, or listen to.	Worth up to $\frac{1}{4}$ of the total project points
Connections	Your project should refer to ideas that you have explored in other activities of the program so far.	Worth up to $\frac{1}{8}$ of the total project points
Presentation	You should present your project in a confident manner, be able to answer questions, and adhere to space or time limits.	Worth up to $\frac{1}{8}$ of the total project points

2. To meet the criteria listed in the rows labeled *Conceptual Understanding* and *Information Base*, be sure that you understand and can explain the following ideas to your partner:

- how humans are structured to be bipedal
- how the human hand is similar to and different from the hands of other primates

- how different parts of the cerebrum are associated with various behaviors
- how different parts of the human brain are similar to and different from the brains of other primates, and
- how nerves transmit information

Reading this quickly, it is not a bad looking project overall, at least for someone who has some background in all of the disciplines mentioned. If they specified the mode of expression as a written report of some sort I would not have too many bad things to say about this assignment (other than the fact that it covered far too much ground while providing very little background information). Illustrations would certainly have been acceptable and informative, as would using media appropriate to the purpose. However, look again at the italicized section above. Where would we find a responsible science teacher who would accept poetry or musical composition as evidence of scientific understanding? And guess which 'medium' was picked the most. That's right, although "demonstrating understanding" of concepts in some individually creative fashion represented 5/8 of the grading scheme, 100 percent of the projects turned in consisted of a single sheet of poster board covered with pictures cut out of magazines. I got pictures of people walking or sitting and pictures of hands and pictures of chimps. This was the full extent of the 'research' done, even though each kid is unique with a different learning style, all aching to pursue the scientific cutting-edge in original and creative ways as dictated by their psychological color. Very few of the projects had even a single word of writing on them explaining what the pictures represented, much less descriptions and other required demonstrations of understanding. In fact, only a small handful of the 'presentations' showed even a cursory understanding of the requirements, although we spent four or five class 'blocks' (90 minutes each) on the project and although I got hoarse repeating and explaining the requirements time and again.

The kids had simply become accustomed to the fact that despite all the noise coming from the educator's direction, we require no real work to 'pass', so why bother? Every time I said, "Break into groups to work on your projects," they simply took it as a signal that another classroom social time was at hand and to keep it going, all the kids had to do was to slowly cut pictures out of magazines and paste them onto poster board.

Another example that school is just a game (that the kids are winning) is this. During class, whenever I had to ask a kid to quit talking, which happened frequently, the almost inevitable response was that, "I was just asking (so-and-so) a question." The kids had learned that any intimation that they were actually 'on task' and not merely socializing, even if they had talked loudly enough to make it obvious that being 'on task' was the furthest thing from their minds, was enough to get them off the hook in a Progressive classroom. They typically resumed socializing immediately, without even a cursory acknowledgment from the teacher that doing so was OK.

We did this sort of group-work project to 'accommodate' the various learning styles presumably found in the class. However, to which learning style does this poster project equate, do you think. It seems to match none of Gardner's intelligences. Unfortunately, we routinely satisfy only one learning style, for kids with Progressive intelligence. Under such conditions, how could we even identify a kid who might have the capacity to become a professional at something?

I should say, and have said, for fairness sake, that this school district was a genuine disgrace. My pupils came by their ignorance honestly. Their school district featured a middle school principal who says that his goal is to construct a system where nobody can fail. He lives up to his word. Many of my pupils had virtual straight zero's for middle school[134] academic averages, yet here they were in the 9th grade. One scary thought is that those who have not already dropped out are all graduated now and eligible to vote—if they can be bothered. Presumably, these are also the kinds of pupils that the NEA would recruit for the teaching profession. These are also the (future?) parents[135] that educators rail against as not involved enough in their own kids' educations.

Once when I was teaching in a junior-level class (i.e., 11th grade—one year shy of graduation and/or college) appropriately called

---

134 The Middle School *concept* may require some review, too. This idea was developed to address the assumption that kids at this age are particularly fragile psychologically. Therefore, it is thought, kids need more protection from the slings and arrows of outrageous fortune, than folks at other ages. The result was a curriculum that was even more dumbed-down than the grammar school curriculum, and more full of "life adjustment" instruction topped by social promotion. The idea of enhanced fragility may be as faulty as most other Progressive ideas. We should drop the middle school idea, in favor of a more academically rigorous junior high school, when we again realize that kids of this age need instruction and moral guidance, not bureaucrats, surrogate-parenting, and hand-holding.

135 About 10 percent of my freshman girls were, or had already been, pregnant at the time I was a student teacher.

ABC for the simplicity of its activities, though actually as an acronym for Applied Biology and Chemistry, I had another, more direct example of how the kids greeted our Progressive attempts to educate them. This was an 11th grade class and it was well past the Christmas break (presumably the kids had already learned some chemistry). The teacher for whom I substituted left instructions that we were to review the general formula for photosynthesis:

Carbon dioxide and water plus sunlight gives carbohydrates and oxygen.
$$6\ CO_2 + 6\ H_2O + sunlight \rightarrow C_6H_{12}O_6 + 6\ O_2.$$

Though this class was considered a review, not one of our budding chemists could identify even the formula 'H_2O' when I pointed to it. At least none admitted to it. An impressive demonstration of academic excellence, don't you think? It is difficult for a visitor, such as a substitute teacher, to determine whether the kids are truly as ignorant as they seem, but why do they insist on seeming to be that ignorant if they are not? Could it be that they have learned that someone will do the work for them if they plead ignorance, and that they will 'pass' anyway, so why bother? That could also be the reasoning behind the fact that many kids give up so easily. Given a worksheet of some kind to complete, even of work they had seen many times before, such as a pre-algebra assignment (6th grade math for 9th or 10th graders), many stare blankly for a moment, then either put their heads down to sleep, or simply resume private conversations, ignoring the work.

Anyway, during the class one of my logical-mathematical (future scientist) pupils put his feet up on a desk. When asked to remove them, he refused because, he said, putting his feet up was a reflection of his learning style. The whole thing is a joke, and the kids know it. Educationists have taught kids how to make excuses for themselves, so they make them, and they have found that the best excuses are made by throwing Progressive theory back into the faces of the educators. At the very best, continuing to use these ideas as appropriate educational theory is another example of dumbing-down. And that is the very best. Saying anything more requires that your tongue be placed so firmly into your cheek, that it might burst through the cheek.

Incidentally, this class evidently all had musical intelligence, too, which was probably why trying to teach them chemistry was futile.

Every time that I tried to advance the discussion, they would begin to hum, to drown out my voice. This class was clearly abiding by the most empathetic child-centered principles. The kids were in charge but what they found relevant was certainly not 'subject matter content'.

So what do we do in the end if the multiple intelligences idea proves to be at least partially correct in a neurophysiological sense? It should not make the slightest bit of difference to *instruction*. For instance, the muscles of the individual fingers, wrist, arm, shoulder, trunk, and legs are controlled in different parts of the brain. Proprioception (the nervous feedback system that allows one to know where the various parts of the body are in space, as well as to let us know how the various body parts relate to each other or how much pressure is being exerted on, or by, the various muscles and body parts, etc., are mediated in other parts of the brain. Despite the decentralized control of all these body parts and functions, it makes no difference to the kid learning to throw or catch. How well these parts of the brain work matters, but the fact that he must use different parts does not. The same may certainly be said about other brain functions, such as learning academic subjects.

Genuine teaching at the primary or secondary level should not have to change at all, from the traditional teaching model, because the requirements of the *subject matter* do not change depending on who is trying to learn it. Two plus two still equals four, after all. Due to individual differences in the parts of the brain used, the results may come more or less quickly and be learned more or less competently, just as in learning to throw. As with learning to throw, learning addition or who was George Washington, is not different for the logical-mathematical kid compared with the intrapersonal kid. The logical-mathematical kid may just learn it more quickly and, perhaps remember it longer, but that is all. Likewise, the literary and philosophical lessons found in Melville or Dickens are the same whether you are bodily-kinesthetic or musical. If there is any validity for the multiple intelligence idea, it would manifest itself as kids begin to recognize what sorts of things they like and which things come more easily to them. These realizations will guide kids as they begin picking extracurricular activities and later as they begin to choose careers for themselves. What they learn during school however, especially at the most basic levels, say K through 8, should not change even a little bit, once we reset the educational curriculum back to some semblance of common sense. Nor should lesson presentation change markedly, once we reset presentation to a 'lesson' mode instead of an 'activity' mode.

Incidentally, after we have dispensed the lesson-relevant information, genuine lessons often already include activities. Science teachers call their activities 'labs', but English and Social Studies teachers call theirs 'discussions', etc. Furthermore, all genuine teachers assign what should be the most common activity of all, called homework. All these are mental and intellectual activities and are designed to help produce kids that are more adept at thinking than cut-and-paste activities ever can. To teach anyone to think (i.e., use and analyze information), we must first give them information to use and analyze and then ask them to practice thinking about it. Also, if we want kids to develop a sense of reality, the information provided should be accurate and complete, that is, not consisting entirely of only one ideological point of view.

Even if we do use this manifestly simple and logical procedure, however, the conclusions reached by pupils will not always be identical. That is OK since they reflect individual differences and individual experiences. America has traditionally tolerated differential opinions. Only illegal *actions*, which may be based on those opinions, are proscribed. On the other hand, despite the rhetoric of diversity, differential opinions are often unacceptable to Progressive thinkers, as a professor at DePauw University discovered in the summer of 2002. Expressing an opinion that differed from the administration's, she was demoted and had her salary cut, as was the graduate student in New York who was dismissed for daring to discuss paddling in a paper in 2005. Ironically, while chartered as a Methodist university, the professor's contrary opinion, stemmed from religious conviction and referred to various sexual practices that have been considered illegitimate by virtually every society, including ours. While saying that they could not "tolerate the intolerable," DePauw also maintained that academic freedom is alive and well. Of course, the summer of 2002, also saw a district judge in San Francisco tell us that the Pledge of Allegiance is unconstitutional.

But back to multiple intelligences.

During the last few years before graduation, some individual specialization is possible, scheduled around the core curriculum, of course. Future dancers can take dance (perhaps in public school, but more likely at a commercial studio), future physicians, veterinarians, nurses, pharmacists, lab technicians, etc., can take more biology and the other sciences, future business owners or hopeful executives could perhaps take business law or economics, future . . . Well, you get the idea.

Does this multiple intelligences idea change the requirements for living even a little bit? Not at all. The whole thing is a solution without a problem, or should we say it is a solution that causes problems?

Self-esteem

If there is any single point of Progressive philosophy that has made it into supermarket psychology, it is the idea that developing and maintaining personal self esteem is of primary importance. We hear this idea being bandied about in private conversations, TV shows, and in news reports. We usually state it in passing, as if there was no doubt as to its validity. This mythologisation of the idea reminds me of another idea that I read while in college, around 1971. I was a psychology major once-upon-a-time, and as such was required to read a variety of authors and research studies. I started to drift away from psychology because many ideas that they proposed and used just sounded too incomplete, unsupportable, and ultimately too dreamlike to be of general use. This was especially true of the psychoanalytic ideas, but one in particular finally convinced me that there was just not enough common sense involved to learn much from the then current theories. As it was so long ago, I am afraid I cannot refer you to a specific work, or even to the author, but one mental health professional was going on about something and mentioned in passing something like, '. . . since we all know that spiders are symbols for motherhood, we can readily see . . .'

I left speculation-based psychology behind and tried to find answers based more on substantiated reality.

This sort of unsupportable, near faith-based conviction seems to keep the idea of self-esteem afloat, although research shows that it just ain't so. In fact, the self esteem notions are another example of an idea that sounds profound on the surface, and is obviously easy to sell, but is quite shallow. We might even describe it, along with other Progressive ideas, as the modern phrenology. Now that we have discredited the bumps-on-the-head idea, every perceived bump on the road of life must be leveled, or else our lives become shattered, and we must never expose our children to any form of adversity, lest their lives become unlivable.

Whatever happened to the Progressive ideal of Rousseau's experiential life?

John Leo's column in *U.S. News and World Report* on May 18, 1998 entitled *Damn I'm good!* discusses a May 5, 1998 *New York Times* article by Kirk Johnson.[136] Leo writes that the self-esteem movement has a life of its own. It goes on and on, even though its assumptions are wrong and its basic premises have been discredited by a great deal of research. Leo references some of Albert Bandura's work at Stanford University. Among other things Bandura has said that, "No study has ever demonstrated a connection between feeling good about oneself and improved performance." Also, *The Social Importance of Self-esteem*, a 1989 book of essays on the movement, contained this line: "One of the disappointing aspects of every chapter in this volume is *"how low the association between self-esteem and its consequences are* (my emphasis) in research to date." That book was published by true believers, as part of an effort to promote California's $750,000 program to make self-esteem an official state goal. Even the true believers can't find evidence to support their fundamental beliefs, though one suspects that they did not mention this during their legislative campaign. Leo's contention that: "The conception of self-esteem as a kind of commodity one can acquire by constant self-affirmation now appears to be trivial and silly" is certainly true and, at the very least, any solution that we might make to improve the public schools must rid itself of this failed notion. However, although genuine teachers are more likely to expect true learning from their pupils, we must not assume, as the Progressives would assume, that eliminating the current dogma means that all schools would immediately degenerate into emotional dungeons and intellectual torture chambers. There is no reason to believe that teachers, as opposed to educators, hate kids and believe in unrelenting denigration as a motivation tool.

What teachers believe in is *teaching*, the dispensation of knowledge and the practice of using that knowledge to improve oneself and the world around us. It is possible to accomplish this while still being deeply concerned with the well-being of the pupils. The people who come to teaching are concerned with their pupils, which is why they become teachers. What is currently missing from their educational tool boxes is the conviction that 'learning' requires active, directed instruction from teachers and effort by the pupils themselves, not grade-point handouts.

---

136 Johnson, Kirk, *Self-Image Is Suffering from Lack of Esteem, The New York Times*, May 5, 1998.

Nevertheless, while the practices of the self-esteem movement have become trivial and silly, and therefore harmful, having adopted dumbing-down as a basic premise, superficially the rhetoric sounds at least plausible. The core assumption in the self-esteem movement is that children cannot learn or develop properly unless they form a positive self-image. However, the theory cannot reconcile why some students feel terrible about themselves and become academic and social successes, while others have self-confidence to burn and do awful work. Leo tells us that the research on self-esteem has been devastating at least since 1989. That is when psychologists Harold Stevenson and James Stigler tested the academic skill of elementary school students in the United States. China, Japan, and Taiwan. The Asian students outperformed the Americans, but the U.S. students felt better about themselves and their work. We managed to combine high self-esteem with poor work.[137]

Leo also reminded us that low self-esteem has been considered a serious obstacle to black success in school and the workplace for more than 40 years now. The theory says that our racist society holds blacks back by imposing a low sense of self-worth. Yet research does not support that idea either. What has been found, at least as far back as the mid-1960s is that the self-esteem of blacks is not lower than that of whites at all. It is often higher, despite the undeniable facts of history. James Coleman summarized this in a comprehensive 1966 study called *The Myth of Black Low Self-esteem.*

We have discredited another argument from self-esteem theory, that low self-esteem is the cause of violence, hate crimes, and many other antisocial acts. As the *New York Times* article mentions, studies of gang members and criminals show that their self-esteem is as high as that of overachievers. In fact, one influential study concluded that violence is often the work of people with unrealistically high self-esteem, attacking others who challenge their self-image. Another study disproved the familiar theory that welfare mothers become pregnant to boost their self-esteem.

The *New York Times* article says that the academic debate is apparently winding down, but the theory is well entrenched in school theory, and working educators do not always have time to read new theory.

---

137 Incidentally, my academic advisor in Ed school (the science education department chairman no less) mentioned this study to me one day. He proudly used it as evidence that we are "doing the right thing" for our kids.

Likewise, educators' in-service training will rarely, if ever, contradict long-held ideological dogma, no matter what the research says. Therefore, even if Ed schools begin teaching with common sense tomorrow morning, which is not likely, it will be years before new teachers get trained to new ideas that then slowly filter their way into schools with the new teachers. Current administrators, and committed educators (those who ought to be committed), will resist all attempts to shift their faulty paradigms. Floating in what they think of as our 'traditional' way of thought is just so comfortable, even if it is entirely wrong and harmful to those we say we want to help. Old wives' tales are with us still, and self-esteem theory is a modern old wives' tale that just will not die.

Yet, it just seems to make so much sense in a utopian world sort of way; in a, "Wouldn't it be nice if everyone was nice," sort of way. This is the kind of idea that we once suggested was the result of smoking too much dope. Not one prediction has been confirmed using self-esteem theory. It is time to drop the idea and to tell the schools about it. The truth is that during school, it is not what we feel about ourselves, it is what we know, and what we discover that we want to know. Academic self-confidence grows as we master the various academic enterprises. The question is one of scholarship, not "affect." The question that English, and other, teachers should be asking kids is not, "How do you feel about this or that?" The question they should be asking is, "What does the author seem to be saying about this or that?", or, "What did the character try to accomplish when he did such-and-so? Did he succeed?, Why or why not?" History teachers can ask, "What social forces were at play in the early 19th century that led Napoleon to attack Russia?", not, "Would you be sad if you were attacked?" This could be followed with a discussion about motives and consequences, such as, "Compare and contrast the effects of Socialism and democratic republicanism on the lives of people." These are the more expansive, uplifting questions, and ultimately the most introspective questions. These are the kinds of questions that make us think. Expanding outlook and uplifting intellect is what school should be about, not dispensing intellectual and emotional pablum.

If the premises of self-esteem were enough for us to spend untold amounts of money chasing honorable but unrealistic policies, what happens now that we know that the theory has no validity at all? Maybe we should use our money in other ways.

Incidentally, allow me another word about his 'feeling' stuff. The jargon word that Progressive theorists use is 'affect', pronounced Ah (as in apple) fĕkt. If you see this word used sympathetically in a piece about education, you can assume that you are reading psychobabble, at least as used by our current crop of educational professionals, and can profitably ignore the whole thing. As used by the genuinely toughtful and observant developmental psychologists, such as Piaget, Vygotsky, and others, affect seems to be a description and a label placed on various behaviors that are related to the primordial, biological systems that meditate the various emotions and sensations. As such, expressions of hunger or fear are as 'affective' as are expressions of love or happiness. Educators, however, ignore other parts of a theory that does not coincide with their notions and restrict affect to revolve around educratically defined 'needs', such as self-esteem. This is what you would expect from those who learned their theory from Cliff Notes.

Additionally, other authors have described the multitude of cases where teachings in affect are deeply and inextricably linked with efforts to subvert commonly held values in favor of tolerance for traditionally unpopular views and behaviors. Views and behaviors that, in virtually every nation and in virtually every age, have led to social sanctions, at the very least. In so doing, we are developing a tradition of intolerance toward the views held by peoples of almost every race and creed. For instance, try to think of a single other idea that is more prevalent than the belief in some force or being that affects or influences human lives. Religious ideas occur everywhere, in every culture and across time, deep into the prehistoric eras. There is no other idea that I can think of that is more 'normal' (i.e., ubiquitous) for humans than a belief in a God or gods. Nevertheless, in the Progressive mind, being religious is so far out on the fringes as to approach lunacy. Even if the existence of a God or gods ultimately proves to be untrue (and how that could be proven is unclear), the morality and character of the average religious person would be a refreshing change from today's attitudinally challenged kids. In any case, Progressive morality-facilitation sets doubts in children's minds about such fundamental relationships as that between parents and children and right and wrong. Examples of children coming home, expressing sudden confusion, about whether stealing is bad, can be found, not to mention our changing mores regarding sexual practices. Kids felt no confusion before affective 'values clarification' training, but did afterward. This is done by teaching children that tradition itself is repressive, that no one, not even their parents, has a right to question or influence their innermost feelings and that there is no such thing as "right" or "wrong," only their own feelings (as interpreted by their educators) about their own untutored choices (encouraged by their educators). Consider what we know about the maturity level of children as you decide whether letting kids 'choose' their own moral code is a good idea or not.

Despite all this, I still agree that living is better if we are not suicidally depressed, though being dissatisfied (disaffected) with your own work is also possible without psychic devastation. In fact, it is often a good thing. For instance, in a recent *Discover* magazine (May 2002, p. 13), Jacques-Lucien Monod, who won the 1965 Nobel Prize for his work in genetics, says,

> Personal self-satisfaction is the death of the scientist. Collective self-satisfaction is the death of research. It is restlessness, anxiety, dissatisfaction, agony of the mind that nourish science.[138]

So how is it possible to help kids build their own self-confidence while doing *teacher*-centered teaching? By the current philosophy, this should not be possible, but the opposite is true, of course. In fact, we may have no way to build genuine self-confidence otherwise, since genuine, healthy self-esteem is a result of genuine achievement, not flattery. To develop genuine self-esteem we have to be capable of doing something we are proud of and can offer to our family and friends in particular, and eventually to society. If we have something to offer, and are good at it, we feel proud and happy as others come to us for the service. This 'something' can be anything that the society values. Traditionally society values any kind of service that individuals cannot do, either for themselves, because of time constraints or specific training, etc., or something that we can do better than the individual who needs the service. If you think you recognize the basics of a barter system, which has sustained humanity since the Ice Ages at least, and is undoubtedly deeply involved in the development of society overall, and wide ranging, international societies in particular, you are right. A functional barter system requires the exchange of services or products, not merely a one-way distribution of benefits. Overwhelming numbers of one-way distribution cases is not the sign of a healthy system.

---

138 A genuine expression of what it means to 'think like a scientist'.

From earliest times, when society began to allow some specialization of jobs, people developed their own worth and by that developed their own self-worth. This could have been skill in storytelling, or knowledge of the uses of herbs, skill in hunting, pot or weapon making, or a green thumb. Today as much as ever, we tie usefulness to the society and potential for making a living to what we know (few employers will pay much for skill in word search games). Knowing things that others do not, and knowing that we know things that others do not, is a great help in building self-esteem. Getting patted on the head for something we did *not* do, as the Progressives insist, loses its beneficial effects very quickly. I am sure even most Kindergartners know the truth of this, though educationists do not.

The following is an example from my high school days to illustrate the point. This is a story about Nick. Nick was not a good pupil in the book-learning sense. Nick did not have the interest or the capacity to go to college. In today's system, we would probably identify him as learning disabled (LD) though there was nothing medically wrong with Nick, any more than there is anything wrong with the vast majority of kids identified as LD today.

Nick liked cars and was very good with cars and he liked to work on car engines. Most of Nick's friends were mechanics or other people who liked cars. He also read about cars, if only in car magazines and shop manuals. He 'hung out' at a neighborhood garage and he talked about cars. Once, I was involved in a conversation with Nick and a kid who came very close to being named valedictorian of our school. This other kid, let us call him Greg, admitted to Nick that he really did not understand how a carburetor worked. Nick was amazed. I heard Nick say to Greg, who had about a 97 percent noninflated scholastic average, "You don't know about carburetors? Man, you must be stupid." For Nick as for most of us, his sense of self-worth was bound up with what he knew. I believe that this is the case with virtually everyone, because I have seen many other instances similar to Nick's over the years as, I am sure, you have too. I have seen people very proud of their knowledge of baseball or football statistics. I have known a man who walked with his head up because he was the manager of a frozen foods section in a grocery store. I have known people who have lived happy, productive lives because they found a place in society that suited them, and because they did not have to ask anyone's help to survive. These, and millions of examples like them, are the sign of a healthy society. A nation with growing numbers of litigious whiners is not.

It turns out that when teachers stopped 'pouring facts' onto kids' heads and substituted 'pouring unearned self-esteem" onto them instead, America took a turn for the worse. Isn't it interesting that since self-esteem theory came into common use, we suddenly also developed a national crisis of 'stress'? Our kids are under so much stress that more of them are killing themselves and each other than ever before, and all we can think to do is to sic 'mental-health professionals' on the survivors to convince even those who are not 'devastated' that they ought to be. After various community crises, the professionals we hustle in to 'counsel the victims' are also quite often surprised that most kids do not seem devastated at all, despite occasionally witnessing some horrible scenes. The counselors should not be surprised, of course, since they have supposedly studied human emotions, but they *are* surprised (Damon, 1995). What does that say about the fact-less speculations of our mental health professionals? They do not deal with reality, but only with what they think reality ought to be. Using their unfounded speculations when we make social and educational policy, helps lead us, along with the other silly ideas identified here, to the kind of nonfunctional and self-destructive system we have now.

I hope you will allow a short aside here, and I do not want to sound cold-hearted but I truly believe that the grief felt after such tragedies as the epidemic of school massacres we have had, as well as any number of less spectacular ones, is a private thing and none of the government's business. This is especially true if governmental policies, based on faulty, unsupportable philosophy, may have contributed to the tragedy. If folks feel the need for sustenance and moral support, they should turn to family, friends, and neighborhood clergymen, not government 'counselors' shuttled in from afar.

In any case, educationists argue that using lecture (along with its indispensable cousins, 'demonstration' and 'discussion') is like 'pouring facts' into kids heads. Nevertheless, kids suddenly stopped learning when teachers stopped lecturing (yet started calling themselves educators rather than teachers). Now we can say that educators pour self-esteem on kids' heads, using social promotions and dumbing-down to give unearned high grades, etc., and kids feel worse than ever about their lives while developing the achievement-less high self-esteem usually associated with career criminals. This is not a good record.

Maybe there is a connection. Maybe it is time to switch philosophies again. Perhaps we can relate all this perceived stress to the fact
that kids know that there is something wrong with what they know.
When they leave school, whether after graduation or increasingly before,
they expect life to be like school where things are done for them. When
they get out into the real world, reality hits them in the face and they
panic. Not only have they not been trained how to deal with reality nor
were they well-practiced at working long and hard, but they were told
since they entered school if not sooner by indulgent, Progressively
trained parents, that their own selfish whims are what is most important
in life. An example might be someone who has graduated and gets a
job, but finds that the boss expects him to come to work on time, to be
clean, to be polite to customers, to work diligently for a specified number of hours, and to do it all again tomorrow. Astonishing requirements!
The boss is obviously a traditionalist and a meanie. Yet many kids find
these requirements onerous and stressful.

Here is part of a letter-to-the-editor printed on January 6, 1997.
[Reprinted by permission of the Manhattan Mercury.] The piece was a
reply to a letter to the editor that argued that wages were generally too
low for unskilled, entry-level workers:

> Don't decry the minimum wage unless you are going to examine
> the people currently applying for entry-level openings. Some applicants
> do not know how to groom for an interview or how to fill out a job
> application properly. Most require much more training time than in
> the past.
>
> Job "qualifications" previously taken for granted are beyond the expe-
> rience of many applicants. Training now must include the basics—atten-
> dance, punctuality, proper dress and hygiene, public relations [basic
> courtesy], and taking directions.
>
> Some of them cannot equate having a job with doing work. Many
> do not understand that schedules are based on business demands, not
> employees' social calendars. Training is expensive and must be considered
> when setting wage scales.

This is one result that we get when our top educational priorities
are self-esteem, rather than learning, relevance rather than self-discipline, and multiculturalism rather than community. Yet another common complaint of Progressives against folks of common sense who try
to reinstate traditional curricula is that under such a regime, schools

would be little better than a business, run as a factory. Although a characteristic of factories is, unlike Progressive schools, that they produce what they set out to produce by following proven procedures, schools are not, and should not, be run like an assembly plant or a fast food restaurant. Nevertheless, there are significant similarities. Businesses run on schedules. Classes start and end at specified times. Business supervisors assign work and establish deadlines for its completion. Schools assign home- and classwork that must be handed in at a specified time and place. Businesses expect quality because the business cannot survive if their customers go elsewhere, and those who maintain the highest quality and/or production get the highest rewards. Schools rate their pupils and eventually pick a valedictorian based on the most consistent academic quality. Businesses maintain conduct and dress codes that include hygiene. Schools . . . Oh, well. Three out of four ain't bad.

If we demand that common standards, such as those mentioned in the letter above, are again considered routinely, rather than worrying that the kids might suffer psychic trauma by being judged by those standards, and if we punish those who do not abide by the established standards, then living by the standards will become normal behavior for the pupils. Acceptable behavior will become habitual, so corporal punishment and sedative drugs will be largely unnecessary. Letting kids decide what is appropriate behavior is counterproductive, as the letter reprinted above shows. If you do not believe this, ask local businessmen who hire high school kids what they think of modern kids and their quality as employees. You might also ask those professors and instructors in local colleges who teach freshman-level courses, what they think of the quality of their recent students. I have done that. Rolling the eyes heavenward is a common response.

Incidentally, I am NOT arguing that what we need is another set of programs to address each of these quality failures. On the contrary, I fervently hope we will trash most of the programs we have now. Simply insisting that kids behave as normal humans, on the traditional American (human) model, is enough to address these and many other of today's problems. Life can be quite simple if we keep politics, bureaucracy, and mental health professionals out of it.

Reading and Whole Language

Why on Earth, we might ask, would a School of Education mandate a class in reading instruction for all prospective high school teachers, no matter what subject the teacher intends to teach? Hasn't instruction in the grammar schools addressed most of the basic reading issues by the time the kids finish grammar school? Shouldn't high school teachers assume basic literacy and move on to more advanced topics? Shouldn't high school pupils be well-practiced, and able to use specialized reading materials, like textbooks, by this time? Have they not read social studies and science texts, and discussed outlining and other study strategies, etc., by the fifth or sixth grades? Shouldn't fifth and sixth grade teachers assume fifth or sixth grade reading ability, leaving them free to pursue fifth and sixth grade-level topics? Who could possibly expect kids to get through junior high and high school if they cannot read as well as decently instructed kids can in the earliest grades?

I guess we know the answer to these questions by now. What we have is an example of dumbing-down a curriculum, while building job security for the otherwise unemployable. Locally, reading classes are camouflaged under the title of communications, and are given at the middle and high school levels, but yours may be different.

In fairness, whether we ever genuinely understand what happens in the brain during "reading" or "thinking" is a matter for the future. Until that time, however, we will still have millions of new kids entering each grade year after year, and we know that reading is a foundation stone of further education. We have known this, almost literally, since the dawn of history. In fact we call those times before the dawn of history *pre*historic precisely because we have found nothing written, for us to read, from that time. Just when Millicent Ogg (inventor of the digging stick) scratched the first prealphabetic symbols on a rock or a tree trunk, and taught her husband Flint (the inventor of fire) to decipher the symbol, we entered the 'historic' period. Since then, it has gotten progressively harder to get ahead without reading.

Luckily, teaching kids to read is not as complicated as doing neurophysiological research.[139] We have been teaching kids to read for a very long time now. Kids seem able to pick up language-related skills quite naturally without a great deal of fuss. It does take practice though, and 'symbolic' skills (skill in using symbols) require someone to tell us what the symbols mean. We call telling someone what something means 'teaching'. The trick to teaching toddlers to speak, is to let them hear

---

139 The cover of the most recent printing of *Why Johnny Can't Read* promises that we can teach a kid to read in about six weeks with phonics. My own experience supports this claim.

people speaking and to let them imitate it while correcting mistakes in pronunciation and usage. Then, by the process of successive approximations (i.e., practice makes perfect), we reward kids for successively greater accuracy in duplicating appropriate sounds at appropriate times and in appropriate combinations.

While reading may be different from speaking in detail, just as learning to speak requires speaking, learning to read seems to require reading. To learn to read, you have to read, but Progressive reading specialists say, "No. Learning to read requires 'immersion in the language experience'." Based on their results, we can ignore their recommendations as perfect nonsense.

Before we can read for content and understanding, however, we must decipher the sounds that the phonetic alphabet symbols represent. Even the name "phonetic alphabet" tells us that we intend the letters to be read as individual sounds. For that purpose, we need some manner of phonics instruction. Using 'phonics' to teach the phonetic alphabet should not be too hard a stretch even for educationists. Yet, they vehemently deny the obvious, and some of us accept their expertise. For my kids, a very few days of, "the 'A' makes the 'Ah' sound" and "the 'B' makes the 'buh' sound," followed by a few short days of, "A is for apple and 'B' is for ball" was enough to get them started. This was done the summer before they started Kindergarten. Shortly afterwards, I taught the kids to sound out simple words and to recognize word sounds as a combination of letter sounds (e.g., the ă sound in cat, bat, fat, mat, sat, pat, . . . etc.). At age five my son was reading increasingly complicated text on his own, and enjoyed doing it. Oddly enough, I have not had to beat my brains in inventing 'innovative' and expensive new teaching programs to make that happen. All it took, as a start, was repetitive drill in the basics of phonics, and more repetition in reading, and rereading simple kids' books.

To do this drill effectively requires a very special sort of teacher, however. This drill is mind-numbingly boring for anyone who already knows the letter sounds. Yet letting kids go on to something else before they are good at it is a disservice to them, even if the kids think they know it and start to yawn (and they will). The good news is that we must use this boring repetition for only a very few weeks, and only for a very few minutes each day. During most of the day we can still play the cooperative games and teach the simple lessons that have always been a part of the Kindergarten curriculum.[140] However, as for the repetitive technique, even if the kids do it correctly (i.e., learn the letter sounds, etc.) in one or two passes, do it a few more times to solidify it into their memories, and do it without losing your temper or thinking ill of the kids who still do not get it in ten tries (or are already too bored). Then do it again the next day and the next and the next. That repetition is very difficult in the short run—for the teacher, not for the kids—but is probably the only way for the kids to 'get it'. Make a game of it to keep up the kid's interest—we can also quickly change the simple drill to reading aloud together, etc.—but do it over and over and our kids will read well before the end of the third grade. Probably four years before.

After all of that, all that the kids should do is practice reading, and they will then get better quickly and be ready to move on to the kinds of lessons that reading allows. We call the magical stuff that can hold the interest of teachers and pupils 'subject matter'. By a happy coincidence, learning subject matter, and the thinking requisite in using what we learn, is what we out-of-touch, traditional teachers like to call "getting an education."

I know. This recitation does not address the problems of underprvileged kids who do not have any books in their homes. That is true. Yet, if not having good parental reading models is a reason that some kids take longer to learn to read than others, why would we simulate that poor parental example in school? Does not teaching anyone to read because a few will lag behind level the playing field for *all* kids? If we know that introduction and repetition are the keys to reading, why not teach and drill while in school and then give reading and writing homework to continue the practice after school? If *not* teaching were a valid technique, why are we no longer justifiably proud of a record of near universal literacy? Why do we allow ourselves to regress to a national pandemic of ignorance (see pages 28–33)? Is this the educational legacy you want to leave your kids? Educationists will certainly argue that this is not happening, but once again we can ignore their protests as self-serving nonsense. If they were correct, we would not be having our never-ending controversy.

---

140 Now that what is essentially a Kindergarten curriculum is used at all the grade levels, more than 50 percent of Ed school trained teachers, and an equivalent percentage of newly hired teachers, either never see the inside of a classroom at all, or quit in the first five years. More money offered elsewhere and horror at the prospect of spending their lives in daycare, sends them away.

However, perhaps we may finally be seeing the light at the end of the tunnel. In the May 1, 2004 edition of *Biological Psychiatry*, as reported in the May 8, 2004 *Science News* (p. 291), researchers at Yale discovered that, "Good teaching can change the brain in a way that has the potential to benefit struggling readers." What constitutes good teaching? ". . . experimental tutoring that consisted of 50 minutes daily, individual instruction in letters and combinations of letters that represent speech sounds called phonemes." In other words, *teaching* kids to read actually results in kids being able to read.

What prompted this neurological study using magnetic resonance imaging in the first place was that, "In 2000, a panel of educators and scientists convened by Congress concluded that reading disability stems primarily from difficulties in recognizing the correspondence between speech sounds and letters." What a surprise, non-readers did not know what sounds each letter represented.

But this was a genuine research study, not 'qualitative' research, so there were control and variable groups. The control group consisted of kids who were competent readers and simply remained in their regular classroom. The experimental group was taught all about letters and combinations of letters (i.e., phonics instruction), as already explained. The other variable group consisted of kids who received, ". . . standard remedial reading and special education programs in their schools." To make it explicit, *Science News* tells us that, "These students didn't receive explicit instruction in learning to recognize how letters correspond to phonemes." This last group learned nothing new, continued to be functionally illiterate, and their brains did not show the positive effects of genuine teaching.

Since this was essentially a neurological study, I suspect that the startling discovery that kids learn things if they are taught those things, will not make it into the education literature, or if it does, it will be just as thoroughly ignored as all other genuine research has been. Let's hope I am wrong.

A few pages ago we mentioned that another of the Progressive educational tenets is that homework is a bad thing, and should not be countenanced in the modern school. Among the reasons that Progressive teachers refuse to assign homework is to 'allow pupils to remain children a bit longer', since they will all too soon have to deal with the dreary reality of adult life (i.e., employment) and are therefore trying to provide an environment that is "for the children." However, I suspect that part of the motivation for not assigning homework is to camouflage from parents the low level of expectations that the schools promote. If parents could understand the effects of the trivial expectations of modern schools, they might become concerned.

Despite the evidence of centuries, here is what my kids' school does to prepare kids to learn to read. [Note: They are not teaching their pupils to read. They are merely 'preparing kids to learn', as if the educators were mechanics merely doing a lube job and sealing gaskets.] Remember that my son was reading before Kindergarten and that this is the school that I called probably the single best grammar school in the area.

Every week is another 'Letter Week'. Shortly after the Kindergarten year began, they called each week "A" week, then "B" week, and so forth. In honor of the letter of the week, they introduce a new cutesy cartoon character, Mr. A and Miss G, etc. Each letter has alliterative characteristics; Mr. H has horrible hair, and the like. They also do 'activities' to honor each letter. The kids color in pictures of each character, for instance.

I write this in late October of my son's Kindergarten year. One quarter of the school-year is gone and they still have eighteen of the twenty-six letters in the alphabet (i.e., nearly 70 percent left to introduce. It is no wonder that most of the kids cannot read yet. You need *all* of the letters to read competently. If they had introduced all the letters in the first week or the second, and drilled the kids on the letter names and the sounds they represent, for five or ten minutes, once or twice a day, through the end of September, by October they could have started on simple story books and probably *all* of the kids would have been reading well before Halloween. They would not be ready for Dostoevsky yet, but they would be reading.

Once we get past the really-fast-language-learning years, however, it is much harder to learn any language. That fact also helps to explain why immigrant kids often do not read English as well as native kids, at least not at first. It also helps to explain why some people speak with culturally characteristic accents. My parents, for instance, came to the U.S. in their thirties, and they always spoke with an accent and were never perfectly at home with English. Nevertheless, they learned. They had to learn because they had to pay the rent and put food on the table. You can be sure that their English classes for immigrants did not feature the coloring-in of cartoon characters. My parents are among the many millions of examples that the method of learning to read need not change at all and can be effective quickly. This means there is hope for everyone. Even Massachusetts' educators.

Incidentally, simple phonetic instruction is also the way to get newly arrived kids (both immigrant non-English speaking kids, and kids who arrive from areas that try to facilitate Progressive reading strategies) to catch up quickly. California is an example of this. By the year 2000, after California officially abandoned its bicultural education experiment, kids who formerly spoke only Spanish, learned English very quickly, and were sorry for their friends who went to schools that did not teach it.

As far as I know, no one, since the invention of alphabets,[141] has ever successfully tried to teach anyone to read other than by this general method:

1) Learn the letters,
2) Learn the letter sounds,
3) Learn to combine letter sounds into words (phonetically sound out words),
4) Recognize 'word' symbols (combinations of letters) [This is where Whole Language starts and fails],
5) Learn to pronounce the word symbols and to associate them with meaning.

By the time that we progress to step '3', everything is happening simultaneously. Very shortly after that, we can teach and practice sentence structure, verb conjugation and tenses, punctuation, and all the rest.

No one teaches language in any other way, except of course, Progressive educators. What did we ever do to deserve Whole Language instruction?

I find it perfectly astonishing that we have had to force our so-called educational professionals to use phonics to teach the phonetic alphabet, and have had years of court and legislative battles to begin to accomplish the obvious, and even then had the 'phonics' idea mutated

---

141 See Rudyard Kipling's *Just So Stories*.

into another useless set of activities, but what is Whole Language instruction anyway? The basic idea is that kids learn to read, write, and think better and faster when they hear someone reading to them. That's it. Just read to them and kids will make new and creative connections. In fact, the proponents of Whole Language systems expect that hearing someone read will inspire every kid to invent his own language. Each kid, after hearing a rendition of *Winnie the Pooh* will, with deep consideration and a detailed linguistic analysis of the components of speech used, construct a lexicon of words and become the new Hemingway . . . You *do* recognize your own little linguist at five years old in this description, don't you? Yeah, me too. Mine were little analytic dynamos, every one of them. Kid's explanations of how things work are invariably on the money, too, aren't they? Just ask Art Linkletter (what a perfectly appropriate name). His television show, broadcast in the 1950s and 1960s regularly included a segment during which Mr. Linkletter asked questions of kids. He called this segment of his show, "Kids say the darndest things" because of the unusual, illogical connections that kids made in answering his questions. The answers were certainly creative, but they amused us because we recognized that the answers showed an incomplete understanding of reality and did not make sense.

When educationists get around to teaching words, they expect kids to learn to recognize whole words as freestanding chunks, rather than learning letter sounds with which to decode the words. Without the simplification of breaking written words into combinations of discrete sounds, teaching English has been equated to teaching Chinese ideographs. Open a book written in any language with which you are unfamiliar. Even if the letters are the same as English, you cannot decipher many words, can you? Would trying to remember each word as an individual picture sound like it help? Here is an example of the confusion that can occur while attempting this trick. The language is Ukrainian. I will give you two words; **молоко** and **молоток**. They look quite similar, don't they? Would it be fair to guess that since they look much the same, they might mean similar things, such as 'lighter' and 'lighten'? Now, would this reasonable initial hypothesis lead to confusion if you tried to make sense of a sentence if the words actually meant 'milk' and 'hammer', as they do? That is what Whole Language asks of five-year-olds. If this were an easy thing that every kid could do for themselves, why was deciphering Egyptian hieroglyphics impossible until the Rosetta Stone was found which told us what it meant in languages we already knew? Also, how can we explain the fact that no human culture had a written language for the first several thousands of generations of our existence, if this were child's play?

Even if a single Kindergartner could be found that could do this Whole Language trick (starting at step 4, above), does this sound like a reasonable theory designed to simplify instruction? Beyond that, Ed school pundits warn teachers against teaching spelling, punctuation, grammar, and the rest. Why? Because that allows another of the democratic benefits of their method to shine through. If we *do not* teach the standard rules of English, they tell us, your kids will be free of the demonic social rules of dead white guys. We will discuss this bit of logic in Chapter 5.

One of the typical 'outcomes' promised by OBE (Outcomes-Based Education) techniques is that if we use these Whole Language recommendations, then kids will become great 'communicators'. As I understand it, the ability to communicate requires someone else to receive the message and decipher its meaning. Read Pablo's story again, without the translation:

> If i wd hf mg ics I wd save the bses and one I sav the bes then I wi thm way the end.

What do you think? Is this kid on his way to becoming a great communicator? This is Pablo's invented, creative version of our common language. Under Progressive theory every kid would invent his or her own version of each word, of sentence structure, and the rest. If each of us had a unique, personal version of our language, that would make communication so much easier. Wouldn't it?

Would you hire Pablo as an advertising copywriter, or as a news reporter, or an interpreter, or a college professor? Would you hire his teacher as a *teacher*?[142] Now look again at the average State standardized test scores and at the Massachusetts teachers' competency test results. Are you ready yet to insist that we teach kids to read in the old, 'obsolete' phonetic way and not to hate themselves for being American?

Admittedly, not every school uses Whole language instruction in as pure a form as that school in California did, but how well do *your* kids spell? How well do your kids' classmates read? If you are reading

---

142 Surprise! You probably already have. Or maybe as your district superintendent.

this book, chances are good that you are concerned enough to insist that your kids read and perhaps write more than the schools require. Why is that? Are you not satisfied with the results coming from your public schools? Why did we build those schools if the educators working there cannot even teach perfectly normal kids to read? "Perfectly normal" describes the vast majority of kids, including almost all 'at risk' kids.

On the other hand, while parents should be involved in their kids' education, as our educators insist, should they have to unteach the stuff that the schools do teach? Also, should a parent have to try to teach third grade stuff in the third grade, because the kids may not find third grade stuff relevant until the sixth grade, if ever?

What happens if the kids gets all the way through the really-fast-learning years without being exposed to correct spelling, good grammar, and accurate pronunciation? He will be learning standard English essentially as a second language.

Is English as a second language too harsh a characterization? Maybe, but consider this—from my own best-in-the-city school district. During a "Kindergarten Roundup," a parents' information night for parents of incoming Kindergartners, a Kindergarten educator stood up and announced that they, the educators, did not intend to correct *any* of the language usage mistakes of their pupils. The reason given was that telling the kids that they did something wrong would destroy their delicate, developing psyches or kill the joy of learning forever. All they intend to do is to gush profusely, to build the kids' self-esteem. In pursuit of short-term contentment teachers as early as Kindergarten back away from teaching in favor of excuse making. This misguided empathy thus places an early nail in the coffin of learning for many. Making excuses, along with an obsessive devotion to discredited theory, has become the norm in all the grades, and in the end, the average high school pupil needs to guess at most test answers because he does not know very much; then go to college.

After I heard this loving, compassionate announcement at the Kindergarten Roundup I wrote a letter to the principal and included a copy of the John Leo column mentioned above. Later I went to see him. The letter and the conversation concentrated on the twin notions that self-esteem theory is a crock, and that if we do not correct mistakes as pupils make them, especially during the really-fast language-learning years, those mistakes become learned as correct. Later, when (if) we finally do present the correct version of grammar or spelling, etc., the kid is already in the hole because he must now unlearn previously reinforced bad habits. The principal agreed with me and gave me a statistic. According to the principal, unlearning and relearning is at least *six times as difficult* as learning it correctly from the start. The mistakes have in effect become the kids' first language. Kids must then learn correct usage as a second language. Have you noticed that we have also raised a generation for whom "Where are you *at*" or "I was, like, Wow!", does not tear at the ears? We even hear it pass the lips of young news 'anchors' and school principals from time to time. Another example is what we have touted as the freedom of the casual use of language in e-mail and other forms of computer communications. Since many examples of this type of communication are not merely colloquial, but hold grammar and spelling, etc., to be optional, it could be that it is not merely breezy and carefree, but ignorant and careless. And, of course, there is always eubonics. Am I stretching just a bit on this point? You decide.

The final theoretical prediction that Whole Language makes is that kids will become more creative as they are freed from the bondage of restrictive grammatical rules. This idea dovetails with the idea that we should no longer teach facts in history and science classes, etc. However, have you ever noticed that the most creative people are the ones who actually know things? Genuinely creative people are the ones who can take disparate bits of information from a wide range of sources, combine and rearrange them into something completely new, and not merely trashy or goofy. For trashy, we need to look no further than TV, the movies, popular magazines, and the music industry. An example of goofy Progressive creativity is an exhibit developed recently by the museum curator at the M. H. de Young Memorial Museum in Golden Gate Park. The exhibit featured food as clothing, for instance a handbag that looks like a loaf of bread. The curator says, "I would like people to take away some of the deeper subjects but also to really be able to kick back and say, 'Holy cow! A hat that looks like a head of lettuce'. "

This bit of silliness aside, to be genuinely creative we must have bits of information to draw upon—and the more the better. I find it significant that periodically, during a Nobel Prize acceptance speech, and the like, the one accepting the award will humbly repeat variations of, "If I have seen farther than anyone else, it is because I have stood on the shoulders of giants." What they mean, of course, is that they have studied the facts and ideas developed by those who came before, often with decades of concerted effort, then perhaps added a piece of personally discovered knowledge and realized something absolutely new. *Not* learning facts and rules would have left them nowhere, starting from scratch, as if they had never been to school at all.

Guiding Readers through Text by Karen Wood, et al., was the required text for my "Reading" class. It is a compilation of several different strategies developed to help kids learn to read textbooks. The guides include ways to show kids how to outline the text for future study; how to try to teach 'content' by analogy (e.g., give kids straws to show how trees take up water and nutrients); how to try to find cause-effect relationships in the text (e.g., England enacted laws considered unfair, therefore Colonists refused to pay the taxes); and perhaps twenty others.

Some of the strategies seem OK and some seem self-evident and therefore pointless to me. I will not evaluate them one-by-one, however, since it would take too long. My main complaint is that Wood, et al. recommend most of them for nearly all levels of school, rather than for middle primary school (perhaps grades 4 and 5), with implicit reintroduction for a year or two. By the time kids are in junior high school, they should be old hands at reading textbooks. Yet, only one guide bothered stating that it was most useful in the lower grades, and use in the high school should be limited to remedial and 'resource room' classes. Resource rooms are rooms set aside for Special educators, when even they find it necessary to take kids out of 'inclusive' classrooms.

The other general complaint I have is that the book generally recommends, by example, that reading assignments be limited to one or two pages at most. I thought that Wood gave these short examples mainly for the sake of space, but I mentioned it to the professor anyway, and he argued that: "No. That short length is appropriate, so as not to tire the kids." I then stated my opinion that it was shameful that they do not recommend these strategies mainly for 4th and 5th graders. I wondered aloud why anyone would say that it is appropriate *not* to teach kids how to read a textbook until they were seniors in high school. The reading professor gave no answer to that, only his conviction that this is the right thing to do.

One more point about this class before we move on. Our 'term project' in reading class amounted to collecting many of the handouts the professor gave to us during the semester and compiling them into a 'portfolio'. We did have to do a small bit of additional work, usually consisting of variations on filling-in-the-blanks exercises, but more than

80 percent of our term project was merely giving his own handouts back to the professor. This must have been another example of the faculty modeling appropriate, academically challenging testing . . . Oops, I should say 'assessment' techniques.

Here is an example of one the handouts, although this one was not a required hand-back. Few of us truly understood what an 'outcome' was at that point in our training, so we asked. Oddly, that included the students who had just graduated from high school within the previous three years or so.[143] The professor tried to explain the word, but we still did not understand (being a great communicator himself, this professor was notorious for his unenlightening explanations). So, at the next class meeting, without further comment, but with a self-satisfied smile and nod, as if to say, *this* will explain everything, he gave us this handout to clarify the idea:

Come as a Specific Process

come abroad	come home	come to grips
come across	come home to roost	come to Jesus
come again	come into	come to life
come alive	come into one's own	come to light
come a long way	come into play	come to naught
come apart	come off it	come to pass
come at	come over	come to stay
come away	come round	come to terms
come between	come through	come to that
come by	come to a head	come true
come clean	come to blows	come up
come forward	come to grief	come upon

Does it help you to understand? Me neither.
He alphabetized it though. I guess that's something.

Methods

'Methods' was the name given to our pedagogy (prepare-a-class-and-practice-presenting-it) class. I must admit that 'Methods' fits much

---

143 I went back to my student-teaching school to collect another copy of their exit outcomes since I could not find the copy I had at the time. No one at the high school office knew what I was talking about. Not the kids who were earning academic credit being bored sitting at the main office desk, nor the secretaries, nor the gym teacher who was hanging out in the principal's

better on a class schedule than Prepare-a-class-and-practice-presenting-it. In any case, they scheduled this class with the educational psychology and Special education (Teaching Exceptional Children) classes. We occasionally had to make group presentations in the full class, though we were rarely expected to relate these presentations to the subject we expected to teach after graduation. The full class was also broken down into smaller groups for whom we prepared individual lesson plans, in our own subject areas, and presented them. We then critiqued each other.

One would think that most of an Ed school student's education would concentrate on teaching proven techniques. The how-to aspects of presenting a specific subject seem reasonably important, if only as a confidence builder, for speaking in front of a group. In fact, considering that the results our educators have achieved in the past several decades are so poor, one would think that someone would have noticed a discrepancy between the promises made and the results attained, and tried to do something about it. Since the ideologies that assure us that kids will be academic superstars if we do not teach them anything have missed the boat, perhaps someone should have been working on modifying the current recommendations. One would also think that a professional school of education would be interested in improving its record.

Ed schools are often one college among many in a university. We expect universities, and they generally expect themselves, to be at the forefront of research into whatever field they profess to teach. One of a genuine researcher's baseline tenets is that progress in research depends on how closely the researcher has come to describing reality. Failure to describe reality is also important, as a signpost highlighting what *not* to do, but success in discovering truth depends on nurturing the blossom of reality among the brambles of bad ideas. The blind, protracted pursuit of ineffectual ideology not only does a disservice to the field studied, but does damage to the very idea of scholarship and dishonors the professional craft of scholars. Publishing dogmatic editorials as 'research' should be an ongoing scandal on college campuses, and in the scholarly press. In the name of scholastic integrity, Ed schools should be forced,

---

secretary's assistant's office. None of the 'administrators' was in the building at the time I came and the principal's secretary was out to lunch, but it does seem strange. I had to go to the school district offices to get the copy. Aren't the *kids* the ones who are charged with achieving these outcomes? If they are, shouldn't they be informed? They probably were informed, however, but sensibly considered the outcomes irrelevant, and promptly forgot them. Yet, if they are not informed, could the whole thing just be a smokescreen for the true agenda?

since many explicitly reject the notion, to pursue research that validates their theories and *proves* with demonstrable and reproducible results, that if a theory expects Action A to produce Result A, then that is what happens. If it does not, Ed school X should not tell teachers that it will. Furthermore, a class in how-to-teach should help student teachers in perfecting their presentation methods by critiquing and redirecting their efforts from pedagogical wheel-spinning to what has been proved to work.

Therefore, while, on the surface, Methods classes are exactly what one would expect schools of education to offer, ours did not come up to professional expectations. They did ask us to prepare presentations and to practice presenting them. However, no one ever got less than a perfect evaluation from the professor. We (the students) were harder on each other than the professor was on us, and we even occasionally complained about that during our full-class discussions. We said we wanted a better idea about how we were doing, and some better idea of what portions of our presentation technique we still had to improve. Very reasonable requests, don't you think? Just the kind of thing that one would have thought a school of education would want to do. No dice.

What we got was yet another example of an Education professor wanting to impress us with an 'appropriate grading' method. They apparently thought that, even as adults, they may damage our self-esteem beyond repair if they told us that we were less than perfect at something. In the end, we had to rely on each other's evaluations. It is too bad that our professor forgot the simple wisdom that says: He who praises everybody praises nobody.

Why did we bother paying the tuition? With this sort of instruction, why are "professional credentials" for teachers dependent upon completing this course of study?

Cultural Anthropology

My Ed school required a class in cultural anthropology because it supposedly taught us all about the great diversity of pupils that we were likely to encounter in our classrooms. Cultural anthropology is a descriptive 'science' that, in its broadest expression, aims to document the social and cultural practices of various groups around the world and to characterize them according to similarities. The ideal practice in anthropological fact gathering is to observe without being seen, so as not to influence in any way the practices observed.

That is the ideal, but it was not always practical. The "Don't mind me. Act as if I'm not here" approach did not work as well as they originally hoped. Sitting silently, taking notes from under a nearby bush, or in the corner of a room during a wake or a wedding, etc., while never interacting with the others present, would likely elicit comment and/or suspicion. People may stop doing what they were doing, thereby ruining the earnest anthropologist's data collection plans. Also, merely observing an action or ceremony, etc., may not allow us to get to the bottom of the symbolism expressed. To find out why an eagle feather was used in the ceremony rather than a roadrunner feather, or why people would ritualistically mutilate themselves, we have to ask questions. Consequently, anthropologists had to begin interacting with, and perhaps become accepted as, members of the group they observed. The natives must at the very least think of the anthropologist as a very close and trusted neighbor.

To become a trusted neighbor, the dedicated anthropologist has to live among her subjects for extended periods. She must learn their language and learn, and follow, their customs. She must, in short, become one of her subjects as much as possible, and she must do this without judging the actions and customs that she sees. If she is judgmental, even toward what to her own sensibilities are abominable practices, they may not trust her enough to explain cultural subtleties. Even in situations where the subjects ask the anthropologist what she thinks about an action or tradition, or if they ask her how her people do a thing, the anthropologist must answer in a way that assures her subjects that while she may do things differently, their way is OK with her. In effect, subjects must see the anthropologist as 'just folks'. Once she establishes this essential trust, the anthropologist could question her subjects, and she might even get straight answers.

Eventually, after documenting many field expeditions and detailing the normal lives of many groups, anthropologists compare and evaluate the similarities and differences of the various cultures. They study the various strategies and patterns of living and they tease out similarities from the jumble of individual cultural differences found the world over.

Here is an example of the kind of summary that anthropologists make. This one refers to patterns of living. Specifically, where does a married couple live, with the husband's family, or with the wife's, etc.? Naturally, anthropologists give each category a name.

- Patrilocal—with the husband's father.
- Matrilocal—with the wife's relatives.
- Ambilocal—may choose either one of the above.
- Neolocal—apart from either of the above. These start their own village.
- Avunculocal—with the husband's mother's brother.

Each of these patterns of living is associated with the particular type of economy prevalent in that society. Since this is not primarily a cultural anthropology text, I will not detail all of the variations used around the world. However, a short list includes: economies based primarily on animal husbandry (herding livestock) and/or intensive agriculture (plows pulled by livestock or machinery, not mere digging sticks). These economies, where much heavy lifting is required, tend to be patrilocal, patriarchal (the man is considered the head of the household), and patrilineal (inheritance passes from the male to his heirs). Another example is economies based primarily on horticulture (gathering and light agriculture). These societies might be matrilocal, matriarchal, and/or matrilineal. There are a variety of others, but the main point is that cultural patterns are often (always?) based on the primary ways that people in that culture earn a living. This includes traditionally hunting-gathering → heavy agriculture → industrial societies like our own.

Why did I make this digression from what is seemingly the main point of this book? Because these dusty and technical ideas are used to help justify Progressive educational ideology, though not exactly as one might think. As is routine with Progressive thinkers, they either redefine evidence to square with the ideology, or the bits that do not support the favored theory, are swept aside leaving incomplete data to appear as the truth. This might be an acceptable ploy in politics (at least it is common practice), but it is shameful in a scientist. Unfortunately, this is probably why cultural anthropology is a required course at my Ed school.

I would like to make two main points, and a third, subsidiary point. In the description of a successful cultural anthropologist above, you read that nonjudgmentalism is a very important characteristic that must be maintained, otherwise subjects would not likely trust the anthropologist.

Some anthropologists go as far as to marry into the culture they study. I do not intend to imply that there is anything sinister or devious in the motives of the anthropologist who does this, only that there is little that can show acceptance of a group more than marriage into that group. In any case, even after dedicating his life to "When in Rome, do as the Romans do" an anthropologist should probably remember that he is not a "Roman." That is to say, he should remember that the culture that he entered has reasons for the behaviors expected of its members. Those reasons may or may not be 'reasonable' to members of other cultures, but whether they are or not, those reasons, and the behaviors that result, are the things that define the culture that expects or requires them. That is also true of the culture that the anthropologist came from.

Generalizing this dedication to nonjudgmentalism, to the point of requiring members of another culture (ours for instance) to accept anything that anyone else does, whether cultural or merely selfish, is forgetting that there were good reasons for our culture to adopt practices that might be different from another's way of doing things. Furthermore, those reasons may go back many generations, even many millennia, and are certainly related to what the culture has accepted as wisdom. However, Progressive educationists now expect modern educators to teach absolute nonjudgmentalism to our kids (with the exception that European culture is often considered irrelevant and unworthy of discussion in schools), and do so from the earliest grades. When kids learn that we are all different, but we are all OK, they often mistakenly decide that they cannot criticize or reject any ideas, because any idea has universal validity.

What is the result of all this unqualified acceptance? Before very long it becomes clear that the person with such a philosophy has no ideas with which he can identify and no firm convictions and therefore no culture of his own. The result is a society that a strong leader can manipulate as he sees fit.[144] The result can be a perfectly mindless, though self-satisfied, population rife for manipulation by the kind of strong, socialist, central government that Progressive politicians prefer.

Have you seen the original movie based on H. G. Wells' *The Time Machine?* Do you recall the 'idyllic' society of the future that Wells depicted? Yvette Mimieux and all her young, beautiful buddies willingly

---

144 See also, Adler, pp. 15–16.

accepting their fate of being herded into subterranean roasting pits because all their other "needs" were met. They did not know how to do anything for themselves. Is this vision too far to jump from a philosophy of nonjudgmentalism? Perhaps life in Aldous Huxley's *Brave New World* is more likely to your mind, where everyone is brainwashed into thinking that they are happy because they no longer have to, or are allowed to, think for themselves. Neither is very satisfactory.

I admit that the possible culture outcomes described in those two novels are unlikely if the only change made to our traditional cultural teachings was nonjudgmentalism. Unfortunately it is not.

The second major point about how the Progressive ideology uses cultural anthropology is this: Anthropologists know that societies based on similar economies tend to develop similar cultures. This is true at least in the large forms that they adopt, i.e., patrilocal residence, etc. (see above). They also know that the major societal organizations that are prevalent tend to determine other cultural characteristics. For instance, patriarchal societies honor the economic contribution of males more than they do females in economies that depend on dangerous action (hunting) or heavy labor. This is true in every similar society, not merely ours, and there are many patriarchal cultures around the world based on one or both of these economies. Anthropologists can also write, as William Haviland did, in *Cultural Anthropology*, the required text for my class, that, ". . . in all societies, the kin of both mother and father are important components of the social structure." Nevertheless, since political correctness and multiculturalism generally, and feminism specifically, are *de rigeur* just now, they tell us that the 'Western dominant culture' invented and brutally maintains the only culture that belittles the contribution of women.[145] This is an idea that can only have life in a greatly exaggerated political context. Our formerly stable society did not have a widespread problem with this idea until the Progressive movement overstated it.

The third point about societies the world over that can be gleaned from a book such as our required text, is that in all cultures, marriage between people of the opposite sex is considered necessary. It is necessary for many reasons, from determining inheritance to legitimizing births

---

145 Of course, we must also export our ideas to other cultures whose practices do not come up to our advanced sensibilities (such as deploring the 'women's rights abuses' of traditionally Muslim nations). I do not say this in support of this Muslim tradition. I only want to point out the inconsistency in fervor.

to transmission of the culture. No cultures legitimize the so-called 'alternative lifestyles', at least not for long. Some cultures tolerate them to a greater or lesser degree (usually lesser if at all, and if toleration begins to increase to open acceptance [as during Golden Ages], those cultures tend to collapse in short order). Yet no cultures allow them legitimacy, or the explicit sexual activity they imply. Why not? It could be because apparently every society since the beginning of time realized that destroying the fundamental basis of the family, inevitably destroys the society, as John Dewey warned. In fact, perhaps the most telling proof that everyone considers homosexuality as unnatural, is that no one wishes it for their own loved ones. Try to remember a single person, including the most ostentatiously tolerant who profess to delight in their gay friends, ever saying about their own developing pregnancy, "I don't care whether it is a boy or girl, so long as it is homosexual."

We (and our children) are told, however, that 1) we must be non-judgmental at all costs (because nothing is worth believing), and either 2a) there is no such thing as Western culture (because it is a combination of many immigrant cultures), or 2b) Western culture alone is evil (though it acts exactly like every other heavy labor economy on Earth) because it is purely Anglo [sometimes 2a and 2b in the same breath], and 3) the family is dead and anything goes (if we want a just and equitable society). Oh, yeah. I almost forgot. We always also have 4) Send money (to help us do 'the right thing').

Lots of inconsistencies in that last paragraph, but you are probably getting used to that by now.

Here is another. Wouldn't you think that the folks who are working 'for the children' would be glad of the support of the folks who work for 'family values'? Those two camps sound like they should be natural allies, don't they? Yet the Progressives call the family values folks evil and reactionary and scary right-wing extremists. Why? Because some of them profess a belief in religion. Who could have guessed that simply believing in something other than self would be considered extreme, or that we would call belief in the validity of time-honored moral values mean-spirited and out of touch. Of course, other-than-dominant-culture mystical religions, including such things as voodoo, are apparently OK.

What is it about Western culture religion that the Progressives do not like? At first they said it was because Judeo-Christian, and now Muslim, theologies supposedly hate women. More recently, they sneer at people for merely being religious. Could that be because religious people believe in something? Could there also be a tie-in to my 'selfishness' argument in that Christianity (and virtually every other religion in the history of humanity) professes a belief that the individual is less important than some deity, less important than the group, less perfect than some ideal, or professes some combination of the above? Furthermore, religions often profess the idea that, though we may not be perfect, our personal behavior and effort can improve our standing in life and in eternity. The effort and prescribed behavior required to attain 'grace', 'salvation', 'nirvana', or any other cultural variation, are often quite specific. Unfortunately for consistency, that includes most, or all, mystical religions. In other words, there are rules to learn. 'Anything goes' is not an idea that sits well with most religions, nor with most cultures. However, the ideas of grace, etc., that must be achieved by effort, are anathema to committed Progressives. For them, the best things in life are bureaucratically dispensed 'benefits' for which misery is a prerequisite. Being miserable (or being ignorant, in the case of education) is the preferred condition, since it qualifies us for the benefits that constitute happiness. Even if you do not practice your religion religiously (and are, therefore, seemingly a candidate for Progressive thinking), perhaps pursuing misery in the name of an artificially dispensed happiness is exactly the opposite of what your mature reflection approves?

My ideas are not very new, of course. I came across a reference to a book called *The Rise and Fall of the Athenian Republic* written in 1787 by Scottish history professor Alexander Fraser Tyler in, of all places, a letter to the editor which complained of the inequitable access to legislators afforded to large political contributors, which included this:

> Great nations rise and fall.
> The people go from bondage to spiritual faith;
> From spiritual faith to great courage;
> From courage to liberty;
> From liberty to abundance;
> From abundance to selfishness;
> From selfishness to complacency;
> From complacency to apathy;
> From apathy to dependence;
> From dependency back again to bondage.

Can you recognize threads of our civilization in this? We seem to have reached line 8 at least, and Progressives are working hard to 'take it to the next level'.

I am sure that there must be responsible cultural anthropologists out there somewhere, but they were not required reading at my Ed school. The anthropology textbook we used was very annoying to read. After reading a chapter or two of the required text, I began to note each example of how the author made subtle, and not so subtle, digs at our society. I did this by writing "We're stupid" in the margin whenever I found what I thought was an ideological comment about the U.S. or Western culture. I just opened the book again to a random chapter, and counted eleven of those notes in that single chapter. Here, as an example, is just one from page 301:

> A major difference between Mundurucu and traditional European society is that, in the latter, women have not had control of their own economic activities.

While the statement itself is only marginally true in only some cases, the worst chicanery inherent in this statement stems from the fact that the Mundurucu are a horiticultural (gathering and digging-stick agriculture) people from the Amazon forest and thus naturally matrilineal. Western culture is a heavy agricultural and industrial society and quite naturally patrilineal. We are comparing apples with oranges, and Haviland knows it—since he wrote the book. However, the author liberally sprinkles these kinds of comments throughout. Americans are evil because we do not do something as the ¡Kung! Bushmen of the Kalahari Desert, the nomadic pasturalists of the Gobi Desert or the headhunters of Borneo, do! Done long enough, this mendacious 'education' results in examples of cultural pride such as the girl in California who achieved her 15 minutes of fame when she refused to recite the Pledge of Allegiance in school. Her reason? "We are a 'bad' culture."

Three cheers for modern social studies!

Outcomes-based Education

I should acquaint you with the basics of Outcomes-based Education (OBE). I will try to keep this section short, because it is here that we must wallow in educational bureaucracy, and that is not much fun. However, when thinking about bureaucracy, I enjoy keeping this insightful description in mind: If the government were in the beer business, a six-pack would be unaffordable.

I believe that OBE is another incarnation of a philosophy developed to counteract the complaints of back-to-basics, and other folks, who notice that kids are not learning very much anymore. Variations of this idea have been in place during each historical Progressive teaching period. Since learning seems to drop off precipitously during Progressive educational pendulum swings, and since the Progressives want to stay in control, they know that some political eyewash is necessary to camouflage the fact they are not truly interested in pursuing academic excellence. The Progressive's main emphasis is on developing a Utopian society by indoctrinating us to unrelenting niceness and Progressive assumptions. The hope is, as the Marxists hoped and as the leaders in *Brave New World* hoped, that mere repetition of an ideology, along with a government that could provide for all of a citizen's needs, would eventually overcome the 'darker side' of human nature.

Outcomes-based Education tries to outflank genuine education by building bureaucratic obstacles to genuine reform, while saying that they only want to document everything for research sake. 'You say you can't see any true learning in modern ______ (fill in the blank; math; reading, etc.)? Well then. We need a program to study the problem.' 'What did you say you think we should teach the pupils? Why is *your* version of ______ (fill in the blank) better than mine? We should form a committee of *all* the teachers and administrators so we can take several years to debate the complicated issue of, 'What do kids *really* need to learn when we teach them to add? Meanwhile, we must take time each month or two to have a teacher 'In-service' where we can tell teachers how wonderful multiculturalism and inclusion and self-esteem and child-centered techniques, and all the rest, are for kids, or why tests or homework are bad ideas. We can also tell teachers why no one should get through life without the help of Special education.

In any case, for a while now OBE has required that 'outcomes statements' be developed, which must then be used by schools to develop curricula and individual activities. An 'outcome' is a statement of a general educational goal that each level of the educational bureaucracy must develop. The goals developed at each level, from the national, state, and local school board to the individual classroom, must incorporate the goals of the bureaucratic level above it (all of which Ed school trained 'scholars' control). The ultimate stated goal is for every pupil to incorporate the skills inherent in the 'outcome' into his or her intellectual make-up. To accomplish this superficially laudable goal, we must incorporate these strategies into every activity and class to address these goals explicitly.

The goals ultimately must be extensions of the Federal goals as established by the Department of Education and the Federal Goals Commission. As one might guess, though they are never very precise, the farther we get, bureaucratically speaking, from the classroom, the more general the outcomes become. For instance, a State-adopted 'outcome' may say that, by the time of graduation, "*All* children should be creative thinkers." Under Progressive tutelage, however, kids today have become so creative that they cannot even seem to organize their own games. As you drive around town, do you see kids riding bikes or playing pickup games of baseball? I don't either. Kids still participate in 'recreational activities', but only as part of an organized program. Once upon a time we could count on kids to find ways to amuse themselves. Now, they seem to require the assistance of an adult, preferably a public employee hired as a 'recreation specialist' to organize things for them.

Another example of the state of creativity in our kids can be seen in probably every classroom in the nation. Keeping in mind that one practical definition of creativity is a state of intellectual flexibility which allows its possessor to see and use new information and/or to adapt to new situations easily. Since this is another example of my own experience as a substitute teacher, I have to set the scene a bit.

As a substitute, one frequently enters a classroom without having met the teachers being replaced. Therefore, you frequently don't know the specific routines used by the teacher regarding routine matters, such as handing out tests and worksheets, etc. However, being unimpressed by the effective use of time generally and the time-on-task found in most classrooms (kids bounding about the room on personal errands, etc.), and in an attempt to keep some control over the chaos (since disruptions are disruptive), I have found that allowing kids to pass things out themselves results in more chaos and more time wasted. Therefore, I generally try to pass things out by counting out the number of whatever handout is needed per row of pupils, giving that bundle to the kid in the front row, and telling them merely to take one and pass the rest back. Here is where the example begins. When one does this, you will frequently get great variations to the simple instruction given. Papers may be passed sideways, or not at all. I have even seen a kid get up and impersonate a basketball player making a jump shot, throwing papers to the next seat. When questioned as to why the instructions weren't followed, the usual response is; "That's the way she (the normal teacher) usually does it." This lack of adaptation to novelty may occur several times in a classroom, even after a correction is made to the first, and subsequent, miscreant(s). The point here is that, even if the response regarding routine procedure is true (it often is not, but is a substitute-mode behavior, trying to put something over on the stranger) then the intellectual flexibility exhibited by the kids is pretty weak. They are slaves to habit, as are most of us. Habit is a normal human response, but then we are speaking of a system that promises to instill creativity in *all* its pupils, but is failing.

Sit back for a second and try to imagine exactly what we would do in the classroom to insure that our pupils became creative thinkers. Also, and much more importantly for the educrats, how would we document what we do? Keep in mind that every school department and classroom must have highly detailed plans that show how your second grade math unit will address this problem, how the seventh grade social studies class will revise history to improve their pupils' creativity, and how tenth grade typing class will help.

This process literally takes (read, 'wastes') years because even Progressive educators have other things to do. For instance, they must spend hours each day counseling unruly pupils. Also, administrators and school boards cannot discuss new policy initiatives until the administrators have enough data to analyze. So, after they exhaust the teachers with the bureaucracy, the administrators have to take over. Each school must prepare its Outcomes documents by consolidating all of the different ideas from each department. Then the school district must consolidate the reports from all of its schools. After completing a project of this magnitude, no one wants to touch it again for years, but of course if the latest educational fad is strong enough, we must revise and re-approve the whole mess because accreditation depends on it. Accreditation does not depend on academic results, by the way, only on whether they have the paperwork straight (i.e., have documented enough Progressive rigmarole). The ones with the most rigmarole, are the schools that win awards for educational excellence.

Go to your school superintendent and ask to see the district's outcomes alignment documents. These documents make sure that everything that we tell kids is politically correct and have components of self-esteem and multiculturalism and child-centered theory, and a few other ideas, included in every subject taught at every level. You will be amazed at the volume of it all. But what is it good for? All of that brain power used over all of those months and years can identify many nuances and 'unfilled' educational and psychosocial cubbyholes. If we try hard enough, we can continually develop new ideas for new government programs that we must then fund if we are ever to achieve academic excellence.

If everyone is working so hard to achieve educational excellence, why then is the whole thing failing so miserably? Because we are now not only missing the forest for the trees, we are trying to fill the spaces between the trees. Yet trees need only a few vital nutrients to thrive and they need air and they need sunlight. Burying a plant under too much fertilizer will kill the plant. Life and education, like horticulture, need not be that encumbered. So, we should ask ourselves: Since we did not even think of or deem these programs necessary at the time that kids easily learned how to read, add, write, and think, but since they are considered 'essential' now, when even some sixth grade 'teachers' do not know on which continent they were raised, does it make sense to continue?

Nevertheless, take another look at the 'alignment' documents. Are they that complicated? There certainly are many categories and subheadings and stuff. My kids' school district made a chart that filled a conference room wall with tiny print. Yet if we stand back from the chart and try to find some semblance of unity, what will we find? Self-esteem and multiculturalism and child-centered theory, and a few other common, though scientifically unsupported ideas. If this were a cop show, we could call these ideas 'the usual suspects'. So, in effect there is only one subject matter no matter what class our children attend, and the subject matter is always the Progressive agenda. Those of us who try to use valid research results when planning future actions have problems with this. Different trees need different nutrients, as different kids need different intellectual challenges. 'One size fits all' ultimately does not work, even if the cloak of mirrors called the Progressive agenda covers it. Does this agenda help in raising academic achievement in even one of the traditional subject classes? There is no evidence that it does, but we should not worry because, "We're doing the right thing and will challenge *all* pupils to achieve academic excellence!"

Here is an example of a set of 'exit outcomes'. This set happens to be those adopted by the school district where I presently enroll my kids, but I assume that these are a fairly standard set since every one that I have seen was not very different from any other. I also used this set of Outcomes because the school system that developed them is one of the better ones in the area. Using the Outcomes of a system that I have characterized as 'disgraceful' may lead some to think, "This is terrible, sure, but *my* school does not do things that way." Unfortunately, within certain limits, you would almost assuredly be wrong.

School District Mission and Exit Outcomes

The XYZ Learning Community exists to empower all citizens to participate fully in a rapidly changing world.

We will accomplish our mission for XYZ High School graduates when all students are:

1. **Effective Communicators** who have the skills necessary to live, learn and work in a global society.
2. **Complex Thinkers** who make reasoned decisions in developing divergent and convergent solutions to complex problems in a variety of contexts.
3. **Collaborative Workers** who work effectively independently and who use appropriate leadership and group interaction skills to be productive contributors in a variety of cultural and organizational settings.
4. **Wholistic Individuals** who demonstrate capacity for enhancing and sustaining physical and emotional well being.
5. **Self-Directed Learners** who draw directly from their learning experiences to create a positive future vision for themselves, prioritize options, develop and monitor achievable goals that support career/life role successes, and assume responsibility for their actions.
6. **Quality Producers** who create intellectual, artistic, practical and physical products which reflect originality, high standards and the use of advanced technologies. (Local Outcome)
7. **Community Contributors** who demonstrate connectedness and responsibility for others in their families, communities and work places by contributing time, energy and talent to improve the quality of life in these diverse communities. (Local Outcome)
8. **Responsive Learners** who demonstrate skills in adapting to and creating personal and social change. (Local Outcome)
9. **Reflective Individuals** who use historical perspectives to analyze and make decisions about contemporary cultural issues. (Local Outcome)

In spite of the touchy-feely language used that gives these Outcomes the disreputable feel of a political snake oil sales pitch (which is a clue all by itself), most people could agree that some of these are honorable and even lofty goals. "Live, learn and work in a global Society"; "Draw directly from their learning experiences to create a positive future vision"; "Demonstrate connectedness and responsibility for others." How can we possibly argue with that?

We can argue with it because these are not necessarily the outcomes that come out of pupils' facilitated learning experiences. The results do not come close to matching the promises. While the school district's marketing brochures inform parents where in the clouds they think kids should fly, the perennial results show that most kids are still wallowing in the mud. Things are still mightily confused in River City.

For instance, what about the Wholistic (*sic*) Individuals outcome that promises that pupils will, "demonstrate capacity for enhancing and sustaining physical and emotional well being." How does a pupil do this exactly, and can a school establish a standard for how to 'demonstrate capacity for well being'? If it can, what does that mean for individuality?

In the Complex Thinkers outcome, we find Convergent and Divergent solutions? What do they mean? Is it jargon for deductive and inductive reasoning, two very important 'thinking skills'? Why not call them by their proper names? Will they ask us now to diverge rather than to deduce facts? Will we now have to converge rather than infer properties by induction? [After carefully examining the evidence, Holmes diverged the solution?]

Perhaps the true goal of the Progressive agenda is, as the Responsive Learners and Reflective Learners outcomes tell us, to change the society? Change to what? Change to a society where anyone with an alternative and selfish idea can feel at home, and receive government benefits? How can that be done? Community Contributors are asked to demonstrate "responsibility for others." Could this have been included because individuals no longer need to take responsibility for themselves? Will pursuit of this ideal accomplish exactly the opposite than the words superficially imply, by increasing rather than reducing the number of folks who need someone to take responsibility for them? 'But, that is unfair,' one might say. Other outcomes specifically tell kids to take responsibility for themselves; Self-Directed Learners, for instance. Of course that outcome also tells pupils to make achievable goals. What kind of example is this for kids to follow if the Progressives have been working for so long toward the previously achieved goal of an educated citizenry, but are now further from their goal than when they started?

Progressives could easily accuse me of reading in much more than is there, couldn't they? Perhaps. I will even admit that some characterizations I make are essentially speculative. Except for the awful results attained over recent generations, I do not have any sort of 'smoking gun', or videotape of a group of sinister looking types drinking herbal tea while cooking up a vast left-wing conspiracy, though the literature is full of such descriptions. James Koerner's book would positively curdle your innards, for example, and it was published in 1963. For example, on page 205, Koerner quotes a dean of education regarding the withdrawal of schools of education from the normal academic rigors that the rest of a typical university regards as essential:

> Educationists "who worship their own Gods, without admitting their colleagues of other faculties into their congregation, are in danger of becoming fanatics . . ."

The pamphlet, from which Koerner took this quotation, was published in 1937, as the controversies surrounding the slow degeneration of American education were heating up. I leave it to you to decide whether we can regard the quotation as prophetic.

Nevertheless, as I have said, most of the people who carry out these policies truly seem to want to help kids. The problem that I am trying to address with my argument, and with this book, is the undeniable fact that the Progressive approach simply does not work. Not if we truly want a nation based on academic and professional achievement. If we do not believe that individual professional competence is the goal, then the goal must be something else. The Progressives have been telling us how well they have done for a long time, despite the results they achieve. If they are truly happy with the ongoing results, the only conclusion I can draw from this is that their goal is not what they say.

The following is another example of modern writing expectations and an indicator how Progressive philosophy is used in the classroom. This one is not from a California classroom before the elimination of bicultural education. I pulled this from the "Kindergarten Parent Handbook" given to me at the first 'Parents' night after my son began school. The following is a 1st grader's letter to a friend and two interpretations of its worth, as described by a Progressive educationist:

Tasha's Letter: Der Gog. can. I kom. hows. and tac you pSnt. LoVe, Tasha

Translation: Dear George, Can I come to your house and take you a present? Love, Tasha.

Tasha's letter as seen through traditional eyes . . . What do traditional forms of assessment tell us about Tasha's writing? Well, her spelling is inaccurate, for one thing. The punctuation is arbitrary—and confusing. Words are omitted. The whole thing is difficult to read. It's short. It doesn't say a lot. Such assessment reflects a host of traditional expectations about what writing is or should be. But do those traditional expectations give us a true picture of Tasha's writing skill? Not really . . .

Tasha's letter as seen through new eyes, putting *content and voice and purpose* before conventions, and viewing early conventions developmentally . . . What's really going on here? Tasha is recognizing the power of print. She knows you can get attention through what you write, and that one appropriate form of communicating is with a letter. Her letter follows traditional format with an opening or salutation a body and a closing. She also uses left to right orientation on the page, plus up to down orientation which makes her writing easy to follow. She has spaces between her words. A few words are omitted, true enough but we can easily infer what they are. The spelling may not be conventionally correct, but Tasha captures so many of the sounds of her language that the text is really quite readable; that's real developmental progress for a first grade writer. She starts names with capital letters. Notice that the comma in the closing is used correctly; Tasha has indeed been paying attention to how letters begin and end. The periods are tossed about at random, yes, but this writer knows periods are important—and that in itself is a beginning. Her message is direct, purposeful and very understandable. Short, yes. But length will come with practice and confidence.

Are you impressed? Tasha writes from left to right. That is certainly enough for any 1st grader, isn't it? Oh, yeah, she also writes her letters in an "up to down orientation." She even has spaces between her words!!! My, oh my! What excellent expectations the school has for our kids. Go ask your grandparents whether they would have been satisfied if your parents wrote only this well in the 1st grade. This is why the best elementary school in the city only manages to produce a low "D" as an average standardized test score for its 4th graders.

Did you also notice that there is *not one word about teaching* in this assessment? Tasha is left to "notice" on her own that proper names start with capital letters. We once hired teachers to point out little things like that, and to get kids to practice using their newfound knowledge. Not any more. *Educators* will tell us that, "Teaching is NOT telling." Instead, we hire educators to facilitate learning activities, hoping kids will analyze written text like an experienced adult, while they develop their own private languages. We also hire educators to identify kids to swell the ranks of the programs we must pay for by law, to prove how much the programs are needed. Otherwise, an educator's job is to wait until kids' "development" reaches the point at which kids are "ready to learn."

We can find examples of this readiness-to-learn idea in modern kids' books. For instance, have you noticed that most books intended for Kindergartners do not start paragraphs with indented lines? If we are lucky, a book might at least add a line space between the paragraphs, but some do not even do that. Kids are not considered ready to handle the deeply esoteric concept of indented paragraphs until later in their neurological development. Until then (which may apparently be several years), we must protect our kids from the dangerous encroachments of this simple convention, lest their little brains overload.

Kids would notice the common forms of our common language sooner, if those forms were formally presented (i.e., taught). Perhaps, kids could then internalize the concept of a paragraph sooner, along with sentence structure, grammar, and all the rest. If it turns out to be true that instruction improves a pupil's ability to notice things, and if we could convince our educators to experiment with this radical idea, maybe more of our kids would graduate knowing how to read and add.

The explanation of Tasha's developmental genius, seen "through new eyes," is a good example of what dumbing-down looks like. Low expectations coupled with a teaching philosophy that disdains teaching, producing awful results. We will discuss this next point in more detail in Chapter 6, but this is also an example of what the Special education revolution has done to school standards. Though there is almost certainly nothing wrong with Tasha, the logic, tied to the everyone-is-the-same-as-everyone-else idea, says: Since this is as much as we could expect of the slowest kids, we should 'assess' *all* kids against this depressing standard.

How much would Tasha have learned, if we had taught her the rudiments of our common language, and not allowed her to flounder ignorantly? She demonstrated her 'readiness to learn' by trying to use punctuation, etc., but waits in vain for a teacher to tell her how to do it correctly. What Progressive theory gives us is a refusal to build on the potential for language that a kid brings instinctively to the classroom. For example, telling kids that periods are used at the ends of sentences is among the easier conventions to teach. Yet our educators wait for our kids to notice that "periods are important," then gush congratulations for using them poorly. Tasha seems to want to learn so that she can communicate. She notices that we write letters in an "up to down orientation," and she emulates it. What she does not get is any rational instruction in the very basics of her language.

Do you think that Tasha's letter shows "real developmental progress"? Do you find it "very understandable" when even the educationist who wrote the handout deemed it necessary to include a translation? Do you think that Tasha and Pablo would have a very long run as pen pals? The fact that educational professionals can print this into a parent's handbook, in the best school district in the city, shows how deeply Progressive theories have penetrated—and why the best school is not nearly good enough.

On the other hand, if our standards are as low as this, we can say with a straight face that we are achieving our educational goals. At least we are above the State average. Yippee.

Ironically, and maddingly, I also found this on the wall of the elementary school computer room:

> We are what we do repeatedly. Excellence, then, is not an act, but a habit.
> —*Aristotle*

And this, printed on a middle school report card:

> Great things are not done by impulse, but by a series of small things brought together.
> —*Vincent van Gogh*

Are these attempts to go against the Progressive grain, or are they just more eyewash to put parents off the scent?

In my opening pages I said that we have to look beyond the words used by any philosophy, to the results obtained. Ideological dreams are not enough. To consider ourselves successful, we must also achieve our goals. I also said that we have to look at actions and results to learn the meaning of the words used. Since we have seen that academic excellence is the furthest thing from the Progressive mind, what do they consider excellent? "Excellent" are kids, and future adults, who agree with the Progressive agenda, who do not 'judge' people (unless they are people who do not agree with the Progressive agenda), who are convinced that America's success is purely the result of racist policies, greed, and aggression, and who think that the primary solution to every problem is money flowing out from a bureaucratically controlled money pot.

I also asked that we evaluate the results that flow from those actions and policies for their status as excellent. We have discussed that issue at length. The list of Outcomes is important because this is where the rubber meets the road. These are the ideas that they require educators (activity facilitators) to hold dear and upon which to base their classroom strategies. They see the current controversies regarding their results merely as a justification for writing more outcome statements and establishing more programs.

A Partial Solution

So what should teachers do to teach?

Step 1, of course, is to stop doing all of the silly and unproductive things we are currently doing and to retool our thinking away from surrogate grandmothering back to teaching. To do that in the early years we will have to drill and slowly teach facts, along with cultural literacy. We cannot teach trigonometry if the kids are still counting on their fingers, and we cannot teach Shakespeare if the kids cannot distinguish 'cat' from 'mat'. Neither can we teach the genuine benefits of democracy if the kids are never exposed to the failures of other systems throughout history. Recent man-in-the-street interviews that revealed that, when asked, some guesses about who fought in the Civil War found graduates to profess having "no clue," or harboring the belief that George Jefferson wrote the Constitution, should be enough to convince us that there has been a significant failure in education.

Later, drill some more while we teach more facts and more cultural literacy. Later still, build on what was learned and increase the pace of the teaching of facts—along with asking kids to think, and write, about the facts they have learned. Mix it all up by teaching art, music, and physical fitness, but teach subject matter content above all else, and consider adding foreign languages to the grammar school curriculum.

Finally teach more facts along with practice in using the facts for making decisions, coming to conclusions, and analyzing situations. In a phrase, do it much as we did it in the single room classrooms of old and again how we did it at times, and in schools, not considered Progressive. [You will find a more extensive list of recommendations in the final chapter.]

'If the answers are truly as easy as you say,' one might ask next, 'why can't we fix them without a big fuss'? The answer to that is at least twofold. First, we have to realize who benefits if we keep, and strengthen, the Progressive agenda, since it is clear that neither our kids nor our society wins. The groups that benefit are, as already stated, the so-called community leaders and consultants who now earn a living convincing us that we need their help. The other major beneficiaries are the teacher's unions; the NEA in particular since it is the largest and can afford the most lobbyists. How does the NEA benefit? The Progressive agenda has created an artificial 'need' for many more dues-paying members—and they are working hard to increase the need even more by lobbying for smaller class sizes, all-day Kindergarten, after-school programs, and earlier access to the victims of their own policies. While they are still working hard, they have not done badly to date. For example, the high school I attended, of approximately 1600 pupils, had two principals, *the* principal and one assistant, but my student teaching high school, of approximately 1,300 pupils, had nine 'administrators'. My high school had two guidance counselors, but my student teaching high school had five. My high school had no need for an armed policeman either, but my student teaching school did. Finally, my high school had no Special education department at all (though the district did—employing one), but Special education was the largest single department in my student teaching high school, and they argued for more.

Incidentally, about the only time anyone ever saw a guidance counselor while I was in high school was once per semester, when the counselor had to approve course selections. Even while I was in high school this did this not seem enough of a reason to keep even two of them on the payroll, but that was the mid to late 1960s, and things were already beginning to change. Today, in my student teaching school, battalions of 'behavior-disordered' pupils that had to be counseled daily, overwhelm the five counselors and the stable of administrators.

Michael Apple, in his book *Cultural Politics & Education* (1996, p. 55), which we will discuss a bit later, while trying to make a point unrelated to this one, mentions a school district that had almost 600 employees, but only "half of whom were teachers." This should help to show the extent of the problem. If we multiply this level of staffing by all the schools in America (and do not forget to include the psychologists, social workers, para-professionals, teachers' aides, secretaries for all of those administrators, and other support personnel—otherwise known as dues-paying members), we can see why the NEA is so passionate about their agenda, and why they have the political clout to influence politicians so much. Since on the surface the NEA seems to be "in" education, they can wrap themselves up in the mantle of motherhood and apple pie while the basic political message is always, "If you stand against us, we will make you look like you are a child hater and we will not reelect you." The only problem is that they are now only peripherally in the business of education at all. They are in the business of collecting dues and lobbying for more programs employing more educational professionals.

The second reason that the Progressive agenda has proven so slow to reform is that it has become so astonishingly bureaucratic. Even the working educational professionals can see that there is a problem with the achievement of modern pupils. Speak with any administrator and they readily admit that there is a problem and tell us, that, "We are working hard to fix it," (or, have they just been trained to agree with traditional parents, to get rid of them more quickly?). Still, if we ask what they are doing, we will discover that, to find the best solution to any particular problem will take years of studies that can only involve one, or perhaps two subject areas at a time. It seems that we cannot merely tell all teachers to teach, because the data collection and analysis required to determine, recommend, and document the curricular changes required for such an extreme solution would be too onerous on the administrators to fix everything at once. Therefore, each school or district picks one or two subject areas to 'improve', takes several years to develop, implement, and analyze new programs, based on current educational fads. They surprise no one that the improvement program does not help at all, since even the research that spawned the fad said that its ideas are not valid. Meanwhile a new educational fad takes hold, after which they blame lack of progress on not having incorporated the unsubstantiated precepts of this newer fad into their plan, and must repeat the process.

If the act of teaching is this complicated, and requires so many expensive resources, how did anyone ever come out of a single-room schoolhouse knowing how to read? It has now been so long since the beginning of the present Progressive era, that educators who have never actually taught anything, have already retired. All the while, of course, we get further away from the common sense academic approaches that we used earlier in our history. As we teach fewer prospective teachers how to teach, fewer teachers are left who can remember how to teach.

As I said though, many teachers can see that the new ways are silly at best, and deadly dangerous at worst, and would love to teach a subject they love, but the laws on the books, and the policies based on those laws make it impossible to genuinely do the right thing.

Unfortunately, there are other roadblocks, too.

4 IQ

One of the most important factors that determines academic success is the intelligence of the individual pupil. Hardly anyone would deny that. However, many people do deny that. In fact many argue that the mere mention of intelligence in the context of schooling is inappropriate because it is an indication of racism. How can that be?

We consider it as politically incorrect to label anyone as anything less than anyone else, especially regarding intelligence. Furthermore, a significant portion of the Progressive agenda rests on the assumption that anyone can learn anything as well as anyone else, if we devise enough innovative programs to deal with the individual 'learning disabilities' and social and cultural disadvantages that are currently holding them back. Of course, if we factor reality into the equation, we might rephrase the preceding sentence this way: If things were not different, they would be the same. Sameness is the ideal,[146] yet an ideology based on a statement as weak as that is just as meaningless.

We have already discussed the idea of multiple intelligence as a means to bypassing reality but another translation of this common, though misunderstood rhetoric, means, "Give us money." As I said in the previous chapter, a corollary meaning is: With that money we will hire many people to help confuse the issues and to do many pointless bureaucratic tasks that collectively harm kids, families, and the nation, but we *will* build dependency and indoctrinate a constituency.

Am I being too judgmental?

Oddly, those who adamantly refuse any deviation from the Progressive ideology but cannot teach kids to read, write, or add, currently call themselves moderates, while those who argue that both social equity

---

146 Though the fact that another Progressive ideal is 'individuality' does not seem to bother anyone.

and educational quality are possible, necessary, balanced, and just, and can show us how to achieve them, are labeled as extremists.

Go figure.

Quite a bit of evidence exists that shows that Progressive ideas simply do not help kids, and in fact accomplish exactly the opposite. The ideas do not help kids because they are based on faulty assumptions and twisted logic. However, arguments advocating changing these ideas and purging them from educational practices are inevitably met with howls of protest and charges of racism, mean-spiritedness, or being an enemy of education, etc. The next section is a case in point.

Oh, No! Not *The Bell Curve*

Part of my argument uses information that has had a recent public incarnation in *The Bell Curve,* by Richard J. Herrnstein and Charles Murray. I realized that to be able to use this data, which had needlessly become the object of a firestorm of politically correct indignation, I would have to try to counteract the massive emotionality that has swirled around this book since its publication in 1994. To try to do this in as concise a way as possible, I will refute the analysis Progressive critics call, "The definitive refutations to the argument of *The Bell Curve,*" a book by Stephen Jay Gould called *The Mismeasure of Man.*

My main reason for bringing Gould's views on intelligence into the text was to make a point that has an impact on current educational theory and practice. Gould's book is quite influential with many folks, including some in the news media who are often the arbiters of what people read and think. Of course, many parents and teachers do not have the time to read the scholarly journals, nor do they read book-length arguments such as this one. However, they may read magazine articles that, even if they are several pages long, generally treat subjects quite superficially. While Gould says very little specifically on the topic of education, many arguments used in the current education debate are similar in their details to the arguments that Gould uses in his book. Gould's arguments about intelligence are used in various forms by the proponents of inclusion, Special education, self-esteem theory, relevance, multiculturalism, and others, whether they learned them directly from Gould or not.

Gould's *The Mismeasure of Man,* for instance, is simply wrong in its assumption that any mention of 'intellect' concerning people has no validity and is necessarily racist. Gould was not perhaps the foremost, but was certainly an articulate and passionate advocate for the entirely fallacious, although politically powerful, notion that we can somehow reduce the obvious intellectual differences among humans to the point where the educational 'playing field' is ultimately leveled. So spend your money, do-si-do.

For these reasons, meeting Gould's analysis head-on, discussing its shortcomings is an efficient way of answering many Progressive concerns.

Imperfect knowledge about intellect has found its way into social and educational policy in the past (one point that Gould argued). Of that there is no question and is not part of my argument. It does <u>not</u> automatically follow, however, that differences in intelligence do not exist and should not be used to formulate useful and intelligent policy. Useful policy, for me at least, will include provisions for *all* pupils, but the policies we have now do not qualify as useful or intelligent if they deny the influence of arguably the single most important factor in determining academic success and appropriateness of instruction.

Gould has a well-earned reputation as a prolific and insightful essayist on many topics within biology, paleontology, and the history of science. In this case though, his politics got the better of him. His argument about intelligence and the uses of intelligence data, despite the voluminous nature of his examples, may be little more than an emotional/political one. We may summarize Gould's argument as, "I do not want it to be true, so I will act as if it were not true." 'It' of course is genetically mediated differences in intellectual function, (i.e., Nature in the Nature—Nurture controversy). His scientific objectivity falls short on this one. Happily (I guess), Gould gave us good clues about what was truly on his mind.

First let me give an example of what I mean by Gould's objectivity going south. On page 375 of the W. W. Norton paperback edition of *The Mismeasure of Man,* Gould ridiculed the fact that Herrnstein and Murray did not use the statistical, multiple regression concept of R^2 ('are-squared,' the measure of 'goodness of fit'[147]) within their main text, but discussed it only in an appendix. Yet Herrnstein and Murray explained that to make their book accessible to nonspecialist people (those

---

147 R^2 is the square of correlation factors and measures the strengths of linear relationships among variables.

not intimately familiar with statistical procedures and concepts) they placed the more technical aspects of their arguments in appendices. This kept the discussion more general yet made the technicalities available for those who were interested. Gould's implication, however, was that they were trying to hide the fact that the R^2s are quite small and therefore unconvincing.

However, Gould did not dispute Herrnstein and Murray's statistical findings. In fact he did not even dispute that there are differences in 'talent' among individuals. On page 377 he said, parenthetically, "Lord knows I would like to see more attention paid to talented students . . .," but he argued that the correlation factors that Herrnstein and Murray found were too small to be convincing. Yet the statistics attributable to intelligence are usually much higher than those found for the other 'determinants' of academic, professional, and social success, such as parental income, etc. If the statistics for IQ are not convincing, what can we say about those used by educationists and Progressive politicians? Keep in mind that Progressive social scientists rely extensively upon these other 'determinants' when they work to convince our elected officials to increase funding for their favorite programs. Leaving out demonstrably more important factors may be deceitful, but it supports their spin.

The truth is that ignoring the contribution of intelligence as irrelevant when doing school and related social research is like studying plant growth and ignoring, and even holding as evil, any mention of the contribution of sunlight. Is it any wonder then, that all of our highly touted social and school improvement programs do not work? Does it make any sense to fund programs justified solely by these less, and sometimes much less, relevant factors? Wouldn't it make more scientific and economic sense to trash those programs and concentrate on what is most important and on what works? Incidentally, I am not saying, as has been charged of others, that what we want is to "Teach the best and forget the rest." Recall Chall's findings that traditional teaching techniques work best for everybody, and are especially helpful for those whom Progressives consider to be 'the rest'.

Take another quick look at some justifying factors used by Progressive social science: Whether we were raised in a middle or lower class home; whether or not our parents went to college; how much money our parents earn; what kind of job we have, etc. Do not most, or all, of these ideas sound more like results, rather than causes? In its simplest variation the argument says: We do not become academically capable *because* our parents earn lots of money. Instead, people tend to earn more money when they prove themselves academically, and then professionally, capable. And if your parents are smart, you are quite likely to do well academically, too. Being afraid to state the obvious, so as not to admit what everybody already knows, we have put the educational cart before the horse, leaving us with programs that achieve an effect exactly the opposite of what we say that we want.

The Cart Before the Horse

To further understand the differences between the two concepts of validity and reliability that were introduced previously, and the expected effect on how Progressive research is conducted, as well as the recommendations that may be based on the results attained by that research, we can use an example that does not rely on an understanding of professional jargon. This is important because, as stated earlier, some professional educators redefine common words to the point that the logic of arguments becomes impaired.

Look at how they twist the simple idea regarding intelligence to confound us. Again from the unnecessarily and unprofessionally insulting *The Manufactured Crisis*,[148] Berliner and Biddle describe the results of two other researchers (pg. 48):

> They found that school achievement was a *major* factor in the prediction
> of intelligence-test performance. In contrast, measured intelligence was
> only a *weak* predictor of school achievement.

This is typical of Progressive put-the-cart-before-the-horse logic in that it is absolutely backwards. What it says is that if we take kids with a record of having done very well in school and give them an IQ test, we find that most of them have high IQs. "In contrast," if we check whether those who scored high on IQ tests as little kids do well in school and throughout their lives, we do not always get as strong a

---

148 Berliner and Biddle 'nominate' Herrnstein and Murray for their invented BIAS (Bigoted Ignorant Annual Sham) award. This sort of name calling is apparently acceptable for the Progressive sensibility, but only if they do it.

correlation. This should not be surprising, nor a point of outrage. Progressive policies are frequently the causes of these results. When we take a very bright kid and bore him to tears, as dumbed-down instruction surely does, refuse to assign homework (practice in thinking about ideas), or allow him to work for pay,[149] or to stay out late at night (as in midnight basketball leagues), so that he does not have the time to study, etc., we do reduce his measured achievement. We do the same when we structure our curricula to resemble a child-centered fun-instead-of-learning day camp.

This inverted logic is presented as evidence that the concept of IQ is invalid. Among the problems with this analysis is that schools do not have a historical record of future performance to draw upon, when placing kids in classes or programs. Though an IQ test is a weaker predictor of achievement than previously recorded achievement, it is far better at predicting future success than factors that are results, not causes.

The Manufactured Crisis is an astonishingly bad book using scandalously poor reasoning, yet many of Progressive education's shining lights have praised it. Among them is John Goodlad, Director of the Center for Educational Renewal at the University of Washington, who called it ". . . one of the most important books in education in a long time." Jonathan Kozol also called it, "A very important book" and Jane Stallings, former President of the American Educational Research Association said, "Berliner and Biddle have made a significant contribution to the knowledge base by reinterpreting educational statistics that have painted a dire picture of the state of American public education."

Before I show another of these important reinterpretive contributions, know that Berliner and Biddle repeatedly made a fuss about how they are the only ones to look at evidence with open eyes, while right-wingers merely try to ignore or turn back the 'advances' made in recent years. These advances include average academic achievement across the nation measured in the blind guesswork range.

Even when the authors say something that makes sense, their analysis makes your head spin. Among the things that Berliner and Biddle say that makes some sense is their "Law" of student achievement:

---

149 The 2000 census shows that 26 percent of kids 15 to 17 years old hold at least part-time jobs.

The *opportunity to learn*[150] is the single most powerful predicator of student achievement (pg. 55).

The authors realize that if we teach a pupil about a thing, he has a better chance of learning about that thing than if he had never heard of it. Incidentally, this "Law" clearly contradicts the Progressive understanding of learning as always coming from *within* each learner, but they have so far only mentioned the findings, they have not yet begun to reinterpret them.

Although they noticed the obvious, Berliner and Biddle's message is that *not* teaching is OK, and that we should not blame educationists if untaught kids do not learn. Clearly, pupils must be learning-disabled if they did not learn what we did not teach. On page 56, for instance, while reinterpreting the data that shows how badly American kids fare in international math competitions, Berliner and Biddle say:

Nobody at the time [of the competition] seemed to notice that Japanese schools were then *requiring* (their emphasis—i.e., this is a bad thing) eighth-grade students to take mathematics courses that stressed algebra, whereas we typically offered these courses to American students a year or two later. [Note: offered, not required, i.e., always give pupils their 'choice,' though we know that normal kids will almost always take the easy course and work as little as we allow.]

After this beginning they described another researcher's findings:

(He) identified four contrasting math curricula to which eighth-grade American students had been exposed: (1) Remedial classes (30 cases); (2) Typical non-algebra classes (174 cases); (3) Enriched pre-algebra classes (31 cases) ["enriched" probably means that these classes were not exclusively arithmetic, but had innovative, newly developed activities added]; and (4) algebra classes (38 cases). Only the later two types of classes were in any sense comparable to those required of Japanese students, and when (the researcher) examined student achievement for those classes, he found records that matched or exceeded those of students in the Japanese schools.

Let us reexamine this refutation: Saying that American kids trail the Japanese educationally is wrong because, when we *do* teach algebra,

---

150 Also remember that 'opportunity to learn' is jargon for facilitated 'learning opportunities'. That is a child-centered activity, like a word search game.

American kids prove they can learn algebra. In other words, the 8th graders to whom we offered the knowledge learned it, while those we did not teach, did not learn.

The question remains; If our kids *can* learn algebra, and if algebra is training in logical thinking (a higher-level thinking skill), and if training in logical thinking can improve a pupil's subsequent academic achievement and employment prospects, why not teach algebra? Another question is: If the rest of the world still considers algebra as age- and grade-appropriate for 8th graders, and if America once thought of algebra as age- and grade-appropriate for 8th graders, why are today's 8th graders not 'developmentally ready' to learn algebra? Maybe they are. Maybe all we have to do is teach them.

Another example of the author's reinterpretations is on page 10. To attempt to refute reported findings of growing illiteracy in America, Berliner and Biddle argue that calling someone illiterate is fraudulent if they "merely" missed most of the questions on a basic test of reading comprehension. They then cap this line of reasoning by saying that, "only a few [illiterate high school graduates] needed to rely on family and friends to interpret prose material." This argument might have some force if the statement referred to 'only a few 2nd graders' needing someone to read street and grocery store signs for them rather than people whom Progressive schools had 'educated' in the higher-level skills for more than a decade and whom the law recognizes as adults and voters.

The Progressive's own evidence repeatedly disproves their case, yet Keith Geiger, former President of the NEA calls *The Manufactured Crisis*, "A powerful piece of truth-telling."

What do you think? I also ask that you recall this Mad Hatter use of "reinterpretation" as we discuss Special education in Chapter 6.

Another example how other authors have misunderstood and misused the point of *The Bell Curve* is found in the book *Raising Your Child To Be Gifted*, by James Reed Campbell. As a set of prescriptive recipes for parents (and schools) to follow, in their quest to get the most out of children, this book is wonderfully useful. I find much good sense here and I recommend it for anyone who is concerned about their children's education. However, there is one philosophic aspect of Campbell's writing which must be corrected. In his Introduction, Campbell writes, "The title of this book (*Raising Your Child To Be Gifted . . .*)

reflects the importance of the nurturing environments, exceptional parents provide, in contrast to the genetic capabilities that children inherit from their parents." Campbell goes on, "In (*The Bell Curve*) the emphasis is sharply focused on the dominance on the genetic side of parents' influence. The implication is that genetic capabilities are 'set in cement' at a very early age and cannot be easily changed." He goes on, "My focus is the opposite—parents that use appropriate nurturing strategies promote optimal growth in their child's academic potential throughout their school-years."

Campbell very clearly comes down on the side of Nurture over Nature. The author makes the contribution of Nature ("genetics") seem insignificant compared with Nurture. He says this, although in his conception "natural ability" contributes 70 to 80 percent to measured achievement.[151] Chapter 2, for instance, presents charts that segregate kids into the traditional ability tracks by showing how various parental nurturing strategies, labeled 'Effective', 'Neutral' and 'Dysfunctional', may affect their kids' achievement.

According to his charts, Campbell says that kids of "High Natural Ability" and "Neutral Parental Influence" will normally achieve A's and B's in school, but Effective Parental Influences can raise that achievement to straight A's while Dysfunctional Parental Influences can lower academic achievement of these bright kids to B's and C's. Similarly, kids with "Average Natural Ability" would normally achieve B's and C's under neutral influence, but we can raise the scores to A's and B's or lower them to C's and D's because of parental influence. Finally, kids with "Low Natural Ability" under neutral parental influences earn C's and D's and will range up or down from there in response to parental influence. Campbell even provides a pie chart labeled "Proportions Of Your Child's Ability" that graphically displays that "Natural Ability" (Nature) accounts for 70 percent to 80 percent of total ability while "Parental Influence" (Nurture) accounts for 20 percent to 30 percent of total ability.

Concerning human intelligence, Nature vs. Nurture is not an either-or proposition (see the *Agile Gene* (2003), by Matt Ridley). Nature gives each of us capability potentials, while Nurture (i.e., upbringing, education, etc.) takes that potential and either enhances or shrivels it. The malleable genetic template upon which Nurture acts is "set" by

---

151 Note also that this reliance on Nurture is completely contradictory to the Progressive conception of a late-developing "readiness to learn."

Nature only to the extent that learning is either relatively easier or harder for each of us and to the extent that embryonic and developmental changes may become evident earlier or later, but are largely optimized sometime during late childhood.

I have absolutely no quarrel with the notion that positive environments, parental encouragement, and appropriate instructional methods can positively affect the achievement of pupils. Nor do I insist that negative influences like these cannot affect kids negatively. One wonders, however, why we must deem it necessary to dismiss the influence of Nature on the one hand and then use that idea to make practical points on the other. Why must it be either-or? Intelligent school and social policy would consider both factors roughly in proportion to their influence. Schools can do nothing to change the genetics of their pupils but must take whatever 'raw materials' we hand them, in the form of their registered pupils, and try to help parents provide "effective" influence to make the most of what they get.

We will discuss the philosophy of "inclusion" some more in Chapter 6, but if natural ability accounts for anything like 70 percent to 80 percent of a pupil's academic success, then teaching *to* that ability seems a logical thing to do. Placing everybody into a single instructional group, whatever their ability, as 'inclusion' does, seems irresponsible at best. Therefore, referring to the results we currently achieve, we can equate current educational practices with Campbell's "Dysfunctional" influences since they reduce academic achievement precipitously. In fact, if average kids would routinely earn Cs and only a few Ds while under the influence of dysfunctional parents, as Campbell states, what can we say about the influence of Progressive schools that produce average results so deep into the F range? Progressive theories and practices are not merely dysfunctional, they are actively damaging.

Despite the well-known charges of racism, most of Herrnstein and Murray's book dealt only with the data for those test subjects ('people') who identified themselves as 'white'. The authors did not consider the 'nonwhite' data at all, until they had finished their basic analysis. Only then did they compare the nonwhite data, to see if there was a match. Indeed there was. What they found was that 'race' per se is not a factor in whether or not intelligence matters for successful living. Instead, relative intelligence matters for everyone in the same way and to the same degree, whatever the race.

Interestingly, Gould did not refute this claim either. In a short discussion of 'cultural bias', Gould writes:

> . . . Lack of S-bias[152] means that the same score, when achieved by members of different groups, predicts the same consequences—that is, a black person and a white person with an identical IQ score of 100 (or 80, or 140) will have the same probabilities for doing anything that IQ tests are said to predict.

Gould goes on, again parenthetically,

> I should hope that mental tests aren't biased, for the testing profession isn't worth very much if practitioners can't eliminate such an obvious source of unfairness by careful choice and framing of questions.

To understand why this is important, we must understand Herrnstein and Murray's basic thesis. Despite the reports in the press, the thesis in *The Bell Curve* was not that nonwhites are inferior. The main thesis is that IQ *matters*. No matter their race and whatever their occupation, those people who score higher on intelligence tests typically do better at their chosen occupation, and at life generally, than those who score lower. Big surprise, huh? Horribly racist idea, right? No matter the race, those people who score equivalently on IQ tests do equivalently well in life and in their chosen occupations, which are also equivalent. People with similar IQs get similar jobs with similar salaries and live in similar circumstances, regardless of race. Intelligence is a major factor in predicting future success, no matter their race. Measured intelligence is often the most important factor, by far, in many measures of social adaptations, like success in school, choice of occupation, poverty, criminality, and many others.

Deliberately ignoring intelligence (Nature) as a potential factor in understanding society and individuals, leaves us with other 'determinants' of social condition, all based on the idea of Nurture. These factors, again, include things such as whether we were raised in a middle-class or lower-class home, whether our parents went to college, how

---

152 S-bias is an idea that Gould devised for his book. He described it as 'statistical bias', as opposed to V-bias, that he called 'vernacular bias' which "agitates popular debate." Gould said that statisticians sometimes confuse these two ideas. S-bias can be reduced or eliminated mathematically and *The Bell Curve* worked hard to do that. Progressive V-bias is what my book is attempting to reduce.

much money our parents earn, what kind of job we have, etc. While these factors can influence eventual success in life (along with ambition, effort, and appropriate education), they are not 'determinants' as any number of Horatio Alger type stories attest. On the other hand, high IQ is not a chiseled-in-concrete determinant either, as any number of highly intelligent failures attest. Yet higher IQ makes it easier and more likely to achieve success, as measured by choice of occupation, salary, social condition, etc., by making it easier to qualify for higher-paying, more prestigious careers.

The main technique that Herrnstein and Murray used to explain their thesis was the statistical technique known as 'multiple regression', a method that Gould admitted, again parenthetically, is ". . . the most appropriate technique." Likewise, the source of the data analyzed is, in Gould's words, ". . . the *best* (my emphasis) source of information—the National Longitudinal Survey of Youth," consisting of many thousands of subjects, questioned about many aspects of their lives and followed over years as their lives changed.

Multiple regression is a statistical technique that can compare the tested effects attributable to 'intelligence' with the tested effects attributable to other hypothesized determinant factors and can show which factor, if any, had the greater effect. What Herrnstein and Murray found was that while there was a small correlation with various measures for those other 'determinants', the correlations for intelligence, against those same social measures, beat the 'nurture factors' handily and consistently, much as Campbell showed in his charts. Herrnstein and Murray's data show that intelligence does matter. It matters a great deal. Nevertheless, Gould still wrote:

Nothing in *The Bell Curve* angered me more than the authors' failure to supply any justification for their central claim, the *sine qua non,* of their entire argument: the reality of IQ as a number that measures a real property in the head, the celebrated "general factor" of intelligence (known as *g*) first identified by Charles Spearman in 1904. Herrnstein and Murray simply proclaim that the issue has been decided, as in this passage from their *New Republic* article: "Among the experts, it is by now beyond much technical dispute that there is such a thing as a general factor of cognitive ability on which human beings differ and that this general factor is measured reasonably well by a variety of standardized tests, best of all by IQ tests designed for that purpose."

Several things come to mind here. First, it was not Herrnstein and Murray's objective to explore whether IQ does or does not 'exist'. Others have debated and studied the question extensively and we continue to study and debate it.[153] Next, even if the existence of differential 'mentality' were not a controversial idea, testing a hypothesis based on an idea is a standard practice in science. Studying an idea is the way that science tries to resolve controversy by exploring the truth, or the reality, of an idea. Debate and rhetoric are not enough. Therefore, they concluded correctly that considering the fuss made about the subject, this is an idea worthy of study, so they went ahead and studied it. Pillorying Herrnstein and Murray for conducting a reasonable scientific-statistical experiment is a little strange coming from a scientist, even if their hypothesis were wrong. The fact that the hypothesis was shown to be significantly correct should have quieted most debate, but of course, it did not. *Feelings* about reality are far more important in the Progressive mind than reality itself. The fact that reality contradicts Progressive hopes and assumptions merely inflames political outrage.

Secondly, Herrnstein and Murray are perfectly correct when they say that there is little doubt that there is 'something' in the head that largely defines individual capabilities. Despite outraged rhetoric, this knowledge is truly common knowledge, and has been used to good effect probably since prehistoric times.[154] Even one of the most politically correct groups of all, Special educators, uses IQ tests when determining whether a child has 'special needs'. For instance, one part of the definition of mental retardation is an IQ below 70, and 'gifted' pupils are tested, too. Also, the definition of learning disabilities includes the differences between 'expectations' and achievement. We base expectations, even when we call it 'readiness to learn' largely on Nature (i.e., IQ and neurological development).

If Special educators can use IQ tests to set Special educational needs, why couldn't it help determine everyone's education needs? The

---

153 I have found a book called *The Bell Curve Debate: History, Documents, Opinions* that, according to the back cover blurb, "... (gathers) together both the best of recent reviews and essays, and salient documents drawn from the curious history of this heated debate." I have not yet read this 677-page book, and I am not altogether sure I will, but a quick perusal of the book shows that both sides of the debate are included, in their own words. The authors who support Herrnstein and Murray seem to present arguments similar to mine, that there is something to 'intelligence' and that it is a fit and necessary subject for study. The arguments against *The Bell Curve* are politically polemic and even frantic denunciations of evil, scurrilous science, though I suppose that there are calm and thoughtful essays on this side of the question as well.

154 Though some ancient conceptions of intelligence may have placed it in other organs, such as the heart.

answer is, of course, that it can. Gould did argue, however, in his chapter about Alfred Binet,[155] for the exclusive use of IQ tests in Special education cases. Unfortunately, the Special education philosophy has become so pervasive in educational theory (we call it 'dumbing-down') as to make this argument unconvincing.

Let us review: If the statistics in *The Bell Curve* are done correctly, the data source is "the best" (we cannot say the same thing when discussing Progressive data), the results are predictive as intended, the results apply to everyone, and are not biased, then what is the problem? In popular rhetoric, the problem is that test results are not as 'equitable' as some of us would like, because some groups do not score as well as other groups, on average. Therefore, we are told, the results must be invalid and racist (i.e., "I do not want it to be true, so I will act as if it were not true"). As a philosophy undergirding policy decisions for an entire nation, that is just not good enough.

While average IQ scores, when grouped by race, are not equal, and we have no reason other than political correctness to suppose that they should be, we have not yet found the reasons for these discrepancies among groups. We have not exhausted the charges of racism and deficient environmental influences yet, however, if these things are the ultimate source of the discrepancies then, again, a logical course would have been to teach everybody the kinds of things that enhanced the success of the highest scoring groups, and to teach it in much the same way as we taught the highest scoring groups. This could have been done to try to bring *all* groups up to the highest American standards while also addressing environmental differences as well as is reasonable.

While this idea is not new, generally it was not done. Apparently teaching everyone the kinds of things that helped raise America to greatness is not politically correct. Instead what *was* done, at the insistence of the Progressives, was exactly the opposite. At least since the mid 1960s we have dismantled the educational system piecemeal, installed unwieldy and needlessly expensive layers of bureaucracy, taught relevance, self-esteem, multiculturalism, and all the rest. Then, while not teaching very much, we only 'exposed' kids to something vaguely like readin', writin' n' rithmetic, in much the same way as Progressives might teach the lowest scoring groups. Is it any wonder kids don't learn?

---

155 The French psychologist, whose work spanned the turn of the twentieth century, and who developed one of the first intelligence tests. His test was later imported to America, modified and released as the 'Stanford-Binet' test, which is still used.

'Mind Stuff' Is More than a Single Gene

The theory of biological determinism states, in Gould's words, that mentality is a, ". . . theory of a measurable, genetically fixed and unitary intelligence." In short, the theory complains; You are what you are, and you're stuck with it. We will explore this set of ideas in some detail shortly, but first we must look at the things that Gould was against to understand why he took the positions he did. His positions were political and personal and they forced him to shoehorn reality into a cubbyhole for which we did not intend it. Based on the evidence, it is not at all clear that his thinking went the other way around, allowing scientific inference to flow *from* the data.

As stated earlier, Gould had two things in mind when he argued against 'biological determinism'. First, Gould was against social science that seemed to lay blame on him and his wife, for his son's autism.[156] Gould did not want to feel guilty about possibly having contributed genetically to that condition. There is no need to feel that guilt, but saying that does not change anything for the parent who feels that way: On page 22 he said:

> As the father of an autistic son, I also celebrate the humane and liberating value of identifying inborn biological bases for conditions once deemed purely psychogenic, and therefore subtly blamed on parents (especially by professionals who swore up and down they harbored no such intent, but merely meant to specify sources in the interest of future prevention; autism, at different times and by various psychologists, became a result either of too much, or of too little, maternal love).

Gould clearly suspected that the 'professionals' secretly do harbor thoughts of blame for parents who bore autistic children. Individually, maybe they do and maybe they do not. Either way, the state of knowledge on the topic was, and I suppose still is, very cursory.[157] We can see

---

156 Here I must extend an apology to Dr. Gould. Using an argument as seemingly personal as this, might be viewed as unacceptable, especially now that he has died, and under normal circumstances I would agree. Two things convinced me to use these arguments, however, which I began long before his death. First, Gould himself put the information in the public domain, in this book and elsewhere. By itself, even this may not be enough to invade his personal life. However, due in part to his notoriety as a regular columnist in several national magazines, Gould was justifiably a well-respected commentator on scientific topics generally. People took his word for ideas related to science. I felt that showing that his judgment was not always as objective as one might expect was necessary.

157 We have already discussed pop psychology in our present educational problems. I must agree with Gould about the harmful contribution of speculative mental health 'experts'.

that the knowledge is still cursory by the contradictory causes suggested. Even finding a 'gene' that seems to affect expressed behavior is a far cry from understanding how biochemistry manages that effect.

Ironically, Gould thought it OK that one expression of 'mind stuff' (autism) can have "inborn biological bases," but not OK that another expression of mind stuff (intelligence) may also have biological bases. I will not speculate about what autism truly 'is'. I do not have any idea. Yet, was Gould's annoyance at the early state of knowledge about a specific expression of mind stuff enough to eliminate a characteristic as important as intelligence from scientific consideration? It is, apparently, if we assume that we can never trust humans to use the information wisely.

I do not read the technical medical and genetic research regarding intelligence routinely, but as far as I know, we do not yet know nearly enough to say what combination of things 'causes' autism, or any of the other diseases that we think, or even know, to have a genetic component. Unfortunately, we seriously misunderstand the contributions of molecular biology and genetics, as such statements (or even implications) as "the gene for autism" show. Genes are the biochemical code for producing individual protein catalyst molecules needed by the individual producing them. Other than mutations, and a short list of other ways to change the DNA molecule itself, genetic 'problems' may occur because inaccuracies in the production of the various proteins compromise the integrity of those proteins, which then don't do the job for which they are needed.

I know of no single proteins that have been identified for things as complicated as behaviors. If there are such, they probably mediate such simple on-off behaviors as a particular function of one part of individual cells, such as the behavior happens (e.g., a specific molecule passes through a cell membrane) if one specific protein is present and doesn't happen if that protein is absent.

Additionally, we know too many possible extraneous causes, including many potential environmental reasons (e.g., cigarette smoke, aspirin too early in life, lead from old paint flakes, unusual exposure to radiation, to name some of the most common) that might affect how we construct the genetic end-product molecules[158] for anyone to feel personally guilty

---

158 Perhaps stray molecules of the foreign stuff get 'caught' in the jumbled beads-on-a-string structure of newly assembled proteins, deforming them and rendering them useless, or worse, making different, harmful molecular products possible.

about a rare occurrence of a genetic disease. Only if we know ahead of time that we are a 'carrier' of a harmful gene, and conceive a child anyway, should we feel guilty.

The second thing on Gould's mind as he considered intelligence and IQ, was that he, oddly, equated use of the worst aspects of the intelligence debate with membership in the Republican Party[159] and with Progressive conspiracy theory: "Can anyone be surprised that publication of *The Bell Curve* coincides exactly with the election of Newt Gingrich's Congress, and with a new age of social meanness unprecedented in my lifetime?" (pg. 29) To his credit, Gould wondered whether he was, ". . . caricaturing," but he nevertheless continued to level political barbs regarding "meanspiritedness."

For me, the crucial point in social policy is at least twofold. Does it work?, and, Does it achieve the greatest good for the greatest number? That is to say, does the policy accomplish what it sets out to accomplish and is it good for people generally? A policy that achieves what it sets out to achieve, but is bad for the society, is bad policy. The record on those measures is clear; Progressive socialism is a disaster despite its loving rhetoric. We need not be meanspirited to oppose these policies. Quite the contrary. We need only be concerned about the effects upon our kids and upon our society to question the rigidly harmful positions of the Progressives.

Gould made the same politically motivated mistake as other Progressive thinkers. He seemed to reject the idea that there are many points along a continuum, not merely two ends, widely spaced. He was so far out on the left end of this question, in fact, that his horizon reached only as far as the center, so he equated the common sense views of the center with right-wing extremism.

This no-space-in-the-middle idea is not Gould's alone, of course. Dewey was familiar with it, and called it the principle of either-or. But, we also come across it in the unlikeliest places. For instance, in a review of the movie "Disturbing Behavior" (Excerpt from "Disturbing Behavior, Could Stand to Have More Of It," by Renee Graham, July 24, 1998. Reprinted courtesy of *The Boston Globe*) that appeared in my local paper in July 1998, I found this:

Perhaps Paul Lynde said it best in "Bye Bye Birdie" when he posed the musical question, "What's the matter with kids today?" It's a question

---

159 In case you are wondering, I have never joined any political organization or party.

as old as time. Think Adam and Eve didn't spend evenings fretting about Cain's unruly behavior and his inability to make nice with his brother Abel? It's no different for today's parents who wring their hands over children who smoke pot, listen to rude songs, pierce themselves in all sorts of ungodly places and generally refuse to live up to their potential. Given such harsh realities, what parent wouldn't welcome the chance to turn their terrible teen into an upstanding, well-groomed straight A student? So what if their personalities are sapped, they storm around like the Hitler Youth, and they have a tendency to kill when they become sexually aroused? At least they'll get into Harvard.

"Disturbing Behavior" is a mildly amusing teen trifle, but one that *dares to have a bit of a brain* (my emphasis). It is less a slice-and-dice movie than a lightweight contemplation on the price of conformity over individuality, as well as the desperation of parents who want a productive child at any cost.

Besides supporting the contention that wanting your child to be a decent and self-supporting citizen is a bad thing, the reviewer pans this movie, which is intended for children, because, among other things, it does not have enough murder and mayhem. It also offers the opinion that, if we are not 'cool', we must be a storm trooper in disguise. No middle ground is possible. This is, unbelievably, the 'brainy' version of reality that also merely comments on the fact that parents have allowed 'unruly' behavior (by raising their kids to the Progressive standard—i.e., no standard) and are then at wits' end to understand how it could have happened. This kind of thinking might be acceptable if it were only creative license, but as a basis for social policy or scientific debate, it is a disaster.

Perhaps you have noted that the reviewer assumes that too much conformity rather than a too self-conscious individuality ("Gotta do your own thing, Man") results in rude behavior of all sorts? No doubt most Americans today are becoming increasingly annoyed with the views and tactics of what many think of as our true right-wing extremists, like neo-Nazis and 'skinheads'. So, being arrayed alongside and equated with these sociopathic nut-cases because we notice that a childish conception of freedom eventually leads to repression and not to happiness, is annoying to me, and I suspect to most others.[160] My hope is that America

---

160 I must say, however, that the skinheads, etc., are not the true end of the right wing. Their philosophy can in no way be equated with, for instance, William F. Buckley on speed. They are merely ignorant bigots and criminals. It is the label of bigotry, of course, that Progressives want to lay on everyone who does not agree with them.

is also beginning to develop an equal annoyance for the intractability and intellectual dishonesty of the extreme left end. Nevertheless, Gould compounds this mistake by failing to connect the socially abominable results to the "humane and liberating" policies that he liked.

Oddly enough, the people who are hurt most by *non*-meanspirited, supposedly socially compassionate policies are exactly the ones whom Progressives intend to help the most. When the distance between the haves and have-nots spreads, the ones at the bottom suffer more. When a perfectly normal kid becomes convinced that he is learning-disabled, we undoubtedly affect his self-image, and this leads to the conviction that the society owes him something because of his nonexistent condition, causes a greater gap to develop between that kid and his neighbors, who might have helped without prompting. Of course, non-meanspirited policies are more democratic. They hurt virtually everyone, individually and as groups and as a society. The stated intent of these Progressive policies is equivalent to the famous cry attributed to Robin Hood. "Take from the rich and give to the poor." Unfortunately the results and accomplishments are exactly the opposites of their intent and we can summarize them as, "Take from everyone and give to a few." Those "few" are generally only the folks who can make a living espousing the philosophy, since it does not include many kids. Any promised short-term benefit for the intended benefit-recipient that occurs based on these policies is quickly overcome by longer-term harm. An example from education is dumbing-down, where instruction gets simpler, but leaves the pupil ever more ignorant.

Our objectives as a society should be to take the supposedly mean-spirited policies, which actually produce a society far closer to a decent conception of social justice and universal prosperity, and fine-tune them to be more helpful for everyone, not just for the richest among us, nor just for the poorest. Thomas Jefferson and Ben Franklin had some ideas like these that we once used, and as a result became great as a society. We will get to them by-and-by.

Now that we have a clue about Gould's state of mind, let us see what upset him so much.

Biological Determinism

I am far from a historian of the topic of 'biodeterminism', so I gladly stipulate to Gould's recounting of the facts relating to this controversy.

Unfortunately, however, in his mind we can summarize these facts as: "Let's find ways to justify our racism." Since, based on its results, I find that political correctness is almost inevitably wrong in its assumptions and recommendations, however, I have to take exception with his analysis.

While the history of speculation about intelligence is replete with self-serving justification of one sort or another, many of which range out toward the horrendous and beyond, one fact remains: Everyone who has ever lived cannot have helped but notice that there are differences among people, including differences in 'mentality'. Everyone knows people whom they consider to be smarter than themselves, and everyone knows people whom they consider less smart. Keep in mind also that most people are most familiar with people who are largely very much like themselves, so even in similar groups the fact that differences exist is obvious. *Everybody* cannot be that far wrong. There *are* intellectual differences among people. That is certain.

If we can see differences, and especially if those differences can be so obvious that everybody notices them, surely we can define and measure the differences. If we can measure them, then we can array the differences along some sort of continuum.[161] This measure-and-array scenario applies to all gross physical characteristics like height, weight, color of hair, speed of locomotion, intelligence, and many others. Intelligence, for all of its metaphysical hype, is still a physical characteristic or set of characteristics.

We do not yet know exactly how to describe intelligence in neurophysiological terms, however. Maybe it has something to do with the richness of specificity of dendritic connections. Maybe it has something to do with the tightness, pattern, or function of glial wrappings. Maybe it has something to do with the kind, variety, placement, and efficiency of neural membrane or cytoplasmic proteins and/or hormones. Maybe it is something completely different and maybe it is a combination or all these things and then some. We do not know, but what we do know, and what everybody can plainly see, is that differences in ability are real. There is no justification for righteous indignation at the mere mention of them.

---

161 Gould also took exception to the use of a singular continuum, preferring to speculate in the direction of what has been called 'multiple intelligences'. As we discussed, this idea may be correct in some sense, but even if it is correct 'in some sense', it is probably irrelevant to how we should educate kids.

In truth, Gould did not deny that there are intellectual differences among human individuals, but he did take passionate exception to the 'arraying along a continuum' part of the debate, though everybody does it, including himself. In the third paragraph of the Introduction to the 1996 edition of his 1981 book Gould stated (this was his central argument) that, *"The Mismeasure of Man treats one particular form of quantified* (his emphasis) claim about the ranking of human groups: the argument that intelligence can be meaningfully abstracted as a single number capable of ranking all people on a linear scale of *intrinsic and unalterable* (my emphasis) mental worth." Gould argued that genetic expression is not necessarily rigid and that genetically mediated functions, including behavior, are malleable and changeable. Well, of course they are.

I am not sure that my glib "of course they are" is universally believed (which is one thing that set Gould off), yet a quick survey of other common, physical, genetically mediated processes should convince us that it is so. Take for instance height, or body mass. Go to a history museum and look at the clothes or armor of the big bruisers of the Middle Ages. A normal, modern 12-year-old would have a hard time fitting in many of them. I have read that Charlemagne, apart from his political power, intelligence, and leadership ability was a "giant among men." Charlemagne was about six feet tall. Six feet tall is now quite common. In fact I am six-foot-one or so, and I am beginning to feel hemmed-in among today's kids. How did this happen? Have we evolved into something entirely new? Of course not. Genetically we have not changed significantly in many thousands of years. Neither do we have any evidence that I know of, suggesting that we are at the cusp of an evolutionary change that would punctuate the normal evolutionary equilibrium.

What has changed then? Nutrition, most probably, and perhaps how we process our foods, prior to consumption. Gourmets (and probably most others) will cringe at this, but eating is no more than the intake of appropriate chemicals for bodily growth and maintenance. The operative term is 'appropriate'. Clearly we can sustain human life with a wide range of diets, yet for optimum growth, we require an optimum balance of appropriate chemical types (e.g., carbohydrate, fat, protein). We require other chemical mediators (e.g., vitamins, minerals) and protein catalysts, often in trace amounts, for optimizing health and growth. Seemingly we have modified, upward, the human 'instinct' to grow to approximately five feet tall by identifying many of the nutrients needed for optimal growth, and deliberately including them in processed foods and supplements. We have grown bigger on average and have undoubtedly gone past the optimum balance between nutrition and exercise since we are too fat now, on average, as well. I have even heard it suggested that human girls are reaching menarche years earlier than 'normal' because of the hormones, steroids, and antibiotics used in producing our food. The appropriate age of menarche, and the physical development that accompanies it, is another 'instinct' that seems to have changed.

This may be an unusual use of the word 'instinct', but I think we can use it here. Most people probably equate the word 'instinct' with some form of preprogrammed behavior. What we commonly think of as 'behavior', is the intricate combination of actions from the smallest cellular constituents to combinations of systems expressed as an action or actions of the whole body (i.e., something we can see someone do). Many people may also add that the actions are deliberately done. Simple growth, therefore, is a behavior of individual cells (and is far from simple), while menarche is a behavior of the female genital system with the participation and mediation of bits of the neural and endocrine systems, etc.

Behavior need not include the whole body, however, nor must it be conscious, intentional, or outwardly visible. The production of saliva is behavioral too, as is the breathing of capybaras, but we cannot assume that these rodents consciously chant, 'In with the good air, out with the bad'.

'Instinct' on the other hand, is the genetically mediated behavior of the individual bits and pieces of living things. These 'bits and pieces' can be as small as individual molecules or they can encompass the whole body and all of its many parts and systems. Body parts do what body parts do precisely because we have built them to do things in precisely that way. Behaving body parts often also require the help of specific proteins built for their roles upon the templates written in the genetic code. The range of behavior ultimately allowed by the form and function of specific body parts can be quite remarkable, even for individual body parts. For instance, you may be able to restrain a butterfly in your hand without damage, and break a stack of bricks with the same hand, although probably not at the same time.

You might be capable of those two very different actions because, aside from practicing brick-breaking, your genes provided the templates upon which were constructed the biological machinery (e.g., proteins, ribosomal-RNA, transfer-RNA, etc.) that built catalysts and other specialized molecules needed to de-construct (digest) food, and to build other molecules that then rearrange those newly de-constructed molecular food pieces into other molecules and tissues (e.g., cell membranes, endoplasmic reticula, etc.) used to construct larger body parts (e.g., bone, muscle, glands, blood cells, etc.) These, in turn, are organized and arranged to build the parts of your hand, arm, torso, and so forth.

It is, however, the instinct ('behavior') of human genes to construct and direct the specific molecules, etc., that eventually build arms and hands rather than building wings or flippers. Thus, we build a great deal of species-specificity into the system. We should all be quite pleased about that fact, since our kids then look more like us than like woodchucks. Kids usually look like their parents because, within the constraints of species specificity, we restrict the genomes of individual progeny to the genetic contributions of specific parents. 'Designer genes' are controversial precisely because they break this ancient, natural rule.

As we can see, instinct is not simply the bonding of baby geese to friendly researchers nor the continual copulation (often with increased enthusiasm) of male mantises after beheading by their lady love, although those behaviors are instinctive, too.

How we modify 'thinking' and by what genes we produce it, no one knows. Yet, despite all that we have written about the mind-body dichotomy, thinking is another, albeit specialized and very complicated, physical function[162] the components of which were built and maintained on the template of the genetic code. So it is a good bet that proteins are involved in 'mentality' too.

Since we build each individual on the combined model provided by two specific parents, and since genetic actions produce 'molecular machinery' that has uniquely specific functions, it is no wonder that kids largely resemble, but are not identical to, their parents. The parents' genetic templates are halved, mixed, and reconstructed into the kid's unique genome, but the individual genes passed on still produce the same physical products that they did within the parent who provided them. In other words, while we are not exactly like our parents, the

---

162 The *mind* is a descriptive concept, not a 'thing'.

protein catalysts our body produces, should be virtually indistinguishable from theirs. Yet we have all heard of cases where, for instance, two bright but not truly exceptional parents produce a genius offspring and other cases where two other parents produce a so-called idiot savant. Naturally, these variations are not the only ones possible, nor are all births unusual. We have, however, implicated many factors in unusual births, but what causes these discrepancies from expected parental norms are also not known, at least by me, but they do show that significant discrepancies in mentality are possible.

Everybody is *not* the same as everybody else.

Hydra kids act much like their hydra parents, and not like wolves. Kittens look and act much like their parents too, yet cats have a wider range of behaviors than hydras. That is because their genetic templates are more extensive. The more extensive and complicated any 'machine' is, the greater the chance for mistakes in construction and therefore the greater the chance for variations in structure and function. This is especially true in machines as fluid in their construction, and in their components, as a genome and its products. This variation is the very essence of evolution, of course. However, the biological, genetic machinery also has an extensive and active quality control system built in that attempts to preclude and/or correct 'copying errors'. Also, since the environment tends to 'weed out' poorly performing (i.e., badly adapted or incorrectly copied) variations, the behavior within species remains quite similar, at least under similar conditions.

It is when conditions change markedly that a previously useless, or even harmful, variation, that happens to be adaptive under the new conditions, becomes expressed. 'Becoming expressed' does not mean to imply that the *individual* necessarily switches genetic expression (e.g., changes tooth patterns from grazer to browser; sheds scales and grows fur). Rather, individuals who already harbor a suddenly useful genetic variant may survive while those with the previously adaptive, yet currently maladaptive genetic variant, may die young without offspring. When this happens, the concentration of those individuals within the population with the 'new' genetic variant increases while the 'old' variant dies off.

Mutations (nonidentical copies) do occur, however. Nevertheless, these copying mistakes cannot be very far from the norm or the function intended for that genetic product would be corrupted and death could quickly result. This is especially true if the 'product' of that part of the genetic code is embryonic and developmental in nature. For example, if the embryonic cell that will become the heart is defective, the heart does not develop and function as it should, and the embryo dies. If however, the mutations are not immediately lethal, like an enhanced ability to withstand cold or a new skin color, they can sometimes produce and maintain similar and potentially useful variations. These non-lethal but currently useless variations are then maintained within the population and are available to the species in case conditions change.

Probably the most famous example of the potential for specific modifications, is that of the dark and light-colored, speckled moths that 'changed' their protective coloration in response to the English Industrial Revolution. Briefly: Smokestack soot killed speckled fungi upon and darkened the bark of trees downwind of early English factories to the point that the normally speckled moths that camouflaged themselves by imitating speckled fungi were more easily found by birds, etc., and eaten. For most animals, being eaten is not adaptive.[163] The only moths that survived were the rare darker variants of the same species, since they could now hide themselves on the dark-colored bark. Previously, dark-colored moths were eaten preferentially since they could not hide on light colored trees with speckled fungi. Later, when England reduced its smokestack emissions, and the fungi again colonized the tree bark, the speckled moth variant reemerged as the dominant type. This showed that the moths maintained both variants in the population but that the more useful one predominated depending on external circumstances. In other words, genetics *are* malleable.

The more complicated the inherent machinery and resulting behaviors are (perhaps involving more bodily systems and therefore involving many more physiological, biochemical, and genetic reactions and involving many more chances for copying errors) the more variation we are likely to see in species that can exhibit those variations. Take for example the finches that Darwin found on the Galápagos Islands. These birds were, presumably, descended from a single pair of birds (or even from a single gravid female) brought to the islands by a storm. On the islands, the finches found many untapped survival opportunities and with time, they radiated into many environmental niches (and into

---

163 Gould wrote about just such an example, where "being eaten" is adaptive for an animal. An Australian frog, *Rheobatrachus silus*, actually swallows its tadpoles. The tadpoles then exude something that shuts down the digestive functions of the parent's stomach. The stomach is used as a brood pouch until the tadpoles are fully formed, at which point small frogs are vomited out.

many new species) by changing the size and shape of their beaks and by changing their digestive systems to be able to subsist on the available, but very unfinchlike, fare.

Therefore, since 'mentality' is arguably the most complicated behavior of all, and since tiny variations (i.e., mutations, etc.) in intellectual capabilities are rarely fatal during embryology and development, we would expect humans to exhibit a large range of possible mentalities.

Not surprisingly the range of intelligence possible on the generic, human model is quite large. That we can measure that range numerically and array it by relative position is also not surprising. This measurement and relative ranking has been done, of course. We call it the IQ scale. The normal distribution graphically depicts that range, along with the relative occupancy rate of all the measured 'levels' of intelligence. The fact that the range of intelligence displays a perfectly ordinary bell curve shape also shows that intelligence is a perfectly normal physical characteristic.

That being said, I should also say that I agree with Gould that the self-serving habit of some to equate individual placement along this continuum as relatively more or less 'worthy' is often not helpful, although understandable. This behavior is understandable given social norms. All societies, including non-'dominant culture' societies, designate 'worthiness' with respect to many things, including behavior. For instance, some societies value gold or an elongated neck while others may value the symbolism of eagle feathers, or pigs as money. This is the nature of societies. Whether any particular social designation of worthiness is agreeable to an individual is an individual decision (though influenced by what the rest of his society thinks).

So individual characterizations of inherent worthiness can, and do, range down to the reprehensible and worse, as Gould's book amply describes. This is particularly so when we lump entire groups into categories and make social policy based on characteristic, but irrelevant properties, like skin color. One thing to which I object, however, is the usual Progressive practice of assuming (and complaining interminably) that any mention of these facts immediately pegs you as a Nazi and all-round bad guy. I will have more to say on this topic in the chapter on Multiculturalism.

I must also comment upon the idea of an individual's 'place' on the IQ continuum. An IQ number, which is the designation of this relative placement, is not a solid and immutable, chiseled-in-stone, kind of number, even in its basic designation. It is a statistical number. As with any statistical enumeration, each individual IQ number has a range of probabilities, a margin of error, associated with it. Even the margin of error numbers do not have stone barricades built around them, to which the occasional unexpected genius or idiot savant attests. So using that single IQ number as a bureaucratic marker for placement in 'programs' or classes would necessarily be an incomplete exercise. A wider range of achievement scores, including school cumulative averages, etc., are necessary to place children more accurately in ability-grouped classes, etc., not just the single IQ score. Still, it is a valid place to start.

In this sense, the single IQ score number is even less useful as we get further from the mean, since fewer people are populating those regions and the range represented by the margin of error is therefore effectively much wider. Let us say that a kid scored a 130 on an IQ test and let us also say that we have a ten-point margin-of-error—5 points above and 5 points below the graded score. This gives a potential range of from 125 to 135 as the 'true' IQ. Some people have suggested that an IQ score of 130 is approaching the genius level. My own preference on this issue is that we should not contemplate genius at least until we get beyond IQ 160,[164] but even so, the school has a problem with this kid of IQ 130 (125–135). Where do we place him? Do we put him in 'advanced' or 'gifted' classes or do we place him with the majority in 'regular' classes? If we are speaking about elementary school, we have far less of a problem since none of the kids know very much yet and all of them require a solid grounding in the basics before they can hope to achieve much, regardless of potential. However, the problem gets progressively more acute as we move up through the grades. More than likely, however, this kid would fit in and do well in either group, so the principal must use other criteria, including parental wishes, perhaps stated ambition, certainly documented achievement, and interest.

Alternatively, what do we do with a hard-working kid with a tested IQ of 100 (95–105), who gets A's and high B's in all his classes? What do we do with the same kid if he gets D's and F's, or refuses to work at all? My own preference, in the name of academic opportunity, would be to encourage this kid toward the upper end of the scholastic range.

One perfectly ordinary and legitimate use of the IQ score would be as a check against other results. For instance, if we find a significant

---

164 The current standard for inclusion in a 'gifted' program is an IQ of 128 or higher. This standard has been reduced from IQ 135 in recent years. Dumbing-down the gifted programs.

mismatch between IQ scores and general scholastic achievement, this could alert parents and teachers to the existence of some problem. Without an IQ test score, or something very much like it, all that a modern teacher has is achievement based on dumbed-down assessments, behavior, or even simply whether she likes the kid or not. The relatively objective IQ score could even act as a partial arbiter to a teacher's preferential tendencies. We would not have to rely merely on the report of the classroom teacher, no matter how knowledgeable, about a kid's potential. This partial arbitration would also help to weed out unjustified and potentially racist teacher reports.

The single number that upset Gould so much is not one number at all, but a range of numbers. I am sure that Gould knew this, however, so he must have told himself something like, "But range or no, even this probability-set implies that we have some relatively finite 'place' upon the intellectual continuum that we can use in some sense to define each person. This placement may not be razor-sharp but even using the shotgun-spread approach limits the 'worth' of each person." I cannot argue with that, though I have just suggested a partial explanation and will propose it again with more detail later. Most, if not all people, do these sorts of evaluations. We evaluate, and are evaluated by, others all the time. We evaluate people on their looks, on what kind of clothes they wear, or their sociability, on who their friends are, and what kinds of music they like, on what they contribute to their communities or their families and on many other measures, both objective and useful, or fanciful and pointless. We have no way to avoid it. It is part of being human, and not everything that humans do qualifies them for entry to the 7th Level of Heaven. The best we can hope for is to keep the preposterous noise down to a dull roar. Traditionalists in this society are trying very hard to do that. We are having trouble, however, because the preposterous noise is loudest from those who refuse to acknowledge reality (which is why the noise is preposterous).

If you have read the new Introduction to *The Mismeasure of Man*, you will know that Gould argued very passionately against codifying the Nature–Nurture dichotomy, making a very strong point that folks who try to do so are nuts. For instance, on page 34, he says:

> . . . May I emphasize again, as the text of *The Mismeasure of Man* does throughout, that all parties to the debate, indeed, *all people of good will and decent information* [my italics—I just love this phrase], support the

utterly uncontroversial statement that human form and behavior arise from complex mixtures of genetic and environmental influences.

Errors of reductionism and biodeterminism take over in such silly statements as "Intelligence is 60 percent genetic and 40 percent environmental." A 6 percent (or whatever) "heritability" for intelligence means no such thing. We shall not get this issue straight until we realize that the "interactionism" we accept does not permit such [specific] statements as "Trait X is 29 percent environmental and 71 percent genetic." When causative factors (more than two, by the way) [often, in fact, many, many more than two] interact so complexly, and throughout growth, to produce an intricate adult being, we cannot, in principle, parse that being's behavior into quantitative percentages of remote root causes. The adult being must be understood at his own level and in his own totality.

So far so good [though clearly others disagree]. But then he says:

> The truly salient issues are malleability and flexibility, not fallacious parsing by percentages. A trait may be 90 percent heritable, yet *entirely malleable*," [my emphasis—Herein lies the problem].

The implication in the preceding statement, is that we can modify intelligence across its entire range, from brain-dead to genius, by externally applied factors (i.e., pure Nurture), and perhaps, that we can effect this change at will. Gould's example of full genetic malleability is a pair of eyeglasses 'fixing' the heritable trait of bad eyesight. However, use of spectacles is no more an example of full *genetic* malleability than self-esteem theory is an example of intellectual malleability. Eyeglasses do nothing to fix the genetic problem that caused the eyeballs to be less than optimally round (which may be the true cause of poor[165] eyesight), and self-esteem theory (or any Progressive practice that I can think of) does nothing to make us smarter. Corrective lenses and political philosophy only make things look different to us. Like badly ground eyeglasses, Progressive theories distort reality more than they clarify it. Of course, the people who use this argument also say that reality is what we *think* it is.

The fact that people with less than perfect eyesight can survive at all is itself a proof that a genetically mediated range of variation on the

---

165 Please note the use of another common statement of physical 'worthiness', based upon a characteristic's variance from optimum function.

generic human model can exist. If this range can exist, how can anyone argue that a range in intellectual function is not possible? This whole line of argument is inconsistent in any case, since Gould has also concluded that 'multiple intelligences', or a range of intellectual function along multiple tracks, is possible.

Those who agree with Gould's idea of malleable intellect (nurture over nature) often argue, for instance, that we should send *all* kids to college, whether they qualify academically or not. Consider the logic: 1) Everybody is the same as everybody else. 2) You cannot get a 'good' job without college. 3) People who go to college get higher salaries (the only acceptable definition of a good job). Therefore, 4) Everybody should go to college so they too can get a good job and be smart, and [by implication] 5) The job, or the salary, somehow confers the higher intelligence. If all of this were true, then anyone could do what Gould could, for instance.

A terrible example of how the complete malleability of genetic inputs idea had been used was discussed on a National Public Radio *All Things Considered* segment aired May 12, 2004. This segment was a conversation with John Colapinto, about his book *As Nature Made Him: The Boy Who Was Raised as a Girl.*

David Reimer was born 38 years ago as an apparently normal boy. But after a botched circumcision his parents were referred to a psychiatrist at Johns Hopkins, who was the world authority on gender adjustments and seized the opportunity to demonstrate his malleability theory that sexuality could be flip-flopped with no problems. He convinced David's parents to allow him to conduct an experiment whereby David would undergo a sex change operation and be raised as a girl. David would also have to undergo hormone therapy after puberty, to help alter the appropriate female body parts. The problem was that David was not a girl and did not want to be a girl. In an interview at the age of 17, after he had been told his history and had insisted on reversing the damage done to him, stated that throughout his life he had been told all of the kinds of things that made a proper girl, including all of the sorts of feelings characteristic of girls that he was supposed to feel. Except that he did not feel those things. He said that he was becoming convinced that he must be insane. He tried to lead a normal life after his reversal operations and even married and got a job as a butcher. Eventually, however, his past apparently caught up with him and in May of 2004 he killed himself. The psychiatrist, who is apparently still at Johns

Hopkins University, did not return NPR's calls. Genetics may be malleable, but they are not entirely malleable.

Next is a sample of a more 'normal' version of this idea from a local newspaper piece appearing August 27, 1999.[165a] Under the heading "Federal grant may encourage children to pursue additional education," the local school district's 'grant specialist' said that, "Sixth graders from 'impoverished' homes [i.e., kids of parents with blue collar jobs], who have no family history of college, think it is an unreachable goal." The grant specialist then goes on to say, "Some bust the paradigm and go on to school, but the far greater number give up on going on to a *successful* (my emphasis) career." Apparently it is inconceivable that life as a hardware store clerk or a fireman can be as satisfying as that of a grant specialist. So as not to damage his self-esteem, we will not mention the fact that any competent 8th grader could easily learn to do his job of filling out forms.

Incidentally, the point of this new $3.9 million grant is, "The grant will include intensive reading interventions, mentorships, goal setting for students, professional development for teachers, college visits, and structuring courses to maintain both difficulty and accessability," though apparently no teaching.

The translation of that statement is: We will spend lots of money trying, again, to determine whether these near-graduates are developmentally ready to learn to read yet (using the same methods that did not work the first hundred years we tried it). We will hire people as surrogate parents to continue to pump self-esteem onto the kids. We will continue to indoctrinate facilitators to failing techniques. We will take more 'enrichment' field trips, and we will continue to 'eyewash' the public by telling people how difficult the program is, but if it proves too much for the college bound, we will dumb-it-down so they can pass anyway.

Teaching kids to read in the 1st grade, at the latest, and teaching at an appropriate level of difficulty in every classroom would undoubtedly negate the need for this kind of program. That being so, it makes us wonder whether the education business is now little more than a jobs program for administrators and Special educators, that provide for their own needs by manufacturing 'helpless' kids, so that they can create new programs to solve the problems they themselves created. It might

---

165a Reprinted by permission of the *Topeka Capital-Journal*.

be that this is what the education unions mean when they accuse their detractors of being "against education." If this is true, we may find a parallel between the results recently obtained by business and what we might expect from a sea change in educational thinking. A few years ago businesses felt the pinch of bloated bureaucracy, downsized to an 'alarming' extent, but promptly fueled what we have called "the greatest peacetime economic expansion in history." I suspect that schools might achieve an equivalent result if 'education' would drop the "poor baby" attitude regarding our kids that spawns the various bloated intervention programs, downsize by sweeping away the many thousands of pointlessly expensive and nonfunctional Progressive programs, and simply teach.

Also, the can't-get-a-good-job-without-college argument should insult most of us, but we often make it and, worse than that, we widely believe it. No less a personage than our former President who was famous for 'feeling our pain' has said that the government should fund college for *all* kids, at least through the first two years. Keep in mind that the current practice of colleges is already to require remedial courses in the first two years, so that students who have not yet learned to read and write well, after a dozen or more years of public school, can catch up. College was once considered *higher* education which required qualifications that were significantly above the norm, so even the words 'remedial classes' and 'college' should be a contradiction in terms. Yet today it is the norm.

Also, it occurs to me that this dream of sending everyone to college so that everyone can be as smart as everyone else is inconsistent with the you-cannot-establish-intrinsic-worth part of the argument. If higher intelligence is not a measure of some intrinsic worth, then why is sending everyone to college to increase intelligence such a priority? It's tough when you try to have it both ways.

One might say that I missed the point in this debate because I define things in terms of the *exhibition* of intelligence, rather than as some immutable 'mind factor' which is how people in the nineteenth century defined it, as Gould described. Yet that is the essence of progress, isn't it? Research begins when someone proposes an initial hypothesis, like 'mind factors', phrenology, or perhaps Alfred Binet's original assumption that absolute brain size would correlate positively with intelligence. If the idea ultimately becomes unsatisfactory because it does not explain all of the observations made, we either scrap the idea entirely or modify it to account for the new information. Knowing even what little I know about the workings of genetic biochemistry, and I am no specialist, it seems unlikely that 'intelligence' can now be viewed as a fixed and monolithic thing. Unfortunately, this may have been one of Gould's mistakes. He listed many examples of overt and perceived racism in his book, and we can hardly deny that these ideas were used to justify self-serving policies. Yet one way that he tried to accomplish his goal of the political destruction of the reality of differential intelligence is to quote people from previous centuries, and then say that those ideas are still in general favor or currently influence scientists and other 'mean-spirited' people.

For instance, on page 380, in his added chapter, <u>Critique of The Bell Curve,</u> Gould wrote, "Gobineau's[166] ideas served as a foundation for the racial theories espoused by Adolf Hitler[167] . . . [and were] published between 1853 and 1855." Farther down the page he writes, "J. C. Nott of Mobile, America's most active popularizer of anthropology in the racist mode, wrote a long appendix . . . in 1854." To imply, by omission, that we have seen no change in the attitudes of people toward others since 1855 is to deny a great deal of American history. Still, revisionist historians do that all the time. The revisionists conveniently forget that America went to war about five years after those books were written, and we went at least partially to free the slaves. We forget that these were the arguments of the losers of the Civil War. The American 'dominant culture' has now largely rejected these arguments, along with slavery. Then America's dominant-culture types led the effort to free all of Europe and parts of North Africa from other dominant-culture types and then went again to free Europe and large parts of Asia and North Africa (populated mostly by non-dominant-culture types) from genuine Nazis and their buddies, and again to free Korea and again trying to keep Vietnam free . . . and again . . . Lebanon . . . Grenada . . . Kuwait . . . Somalia . . . Bosnia . . . Kosovo . . . Afghanistan . . . Iraq, and others.

Going to war often, to combat oppression with its inevitable result of our own children dying in the effort, seems very good evidence that the vast majority of us are not Nazis at heart, even those of us who want decent schools for our kids. Unfortunately, Gould seemed to make the

---

166 Joseph-Arthur, Comte de Gobineau (1816–1882). A French 'aristocratic-royalist' and sometime diplomat.

167 A Nazi and all-round bad guy.

multiculturalist's mistake of equating any divergence from his own ideals and prescribed methods with evil (i.e., meanspiritedness).

To my mind, the exhibition of intelligence is clearly alterable. For instance, the achievement and performance of a lazy genius can be mediocre or worse, and the achievement and performance of a highly motivated and ambitious 'average' guy can be, and often is, higher than average. Also, despite advertisement claims for various nutritional supplements, I have not heard that good nutrition (or use of any drugs or medications) can definitively increase intelligence, but at least behaviorally, being chronically hungry can reduce mental concentration and therefore reduce achievement. It does for me.

On the other hand, can we modify intelligence to the point that everyone is a genius? That seems unlikely at best. Even if increasing 'intelligence' is ever possible with some yet undiscovered therapy, can we afford to destroy our society due to disappointment that it cannot be done now? Maybe we should switch some funding that currently goes to pointless and damaging dumbing-down programs to research in genetics and neurophysiology.

We can raise achievement above individual expectations, sometimes remarkably above expectations, which are the result of ability and effort, only by working and studying longer, harder, and more persistently than the norm. On the other hand, achievement can very easily be lowered well below expectations by working less and by accepting less from pupils. No amount of unrealistic thinking, political theorizing, or Government funding will ever change those truths, and it is pointless to try. That, I hope, was the point behind Herrnstein and Murray's recommendation not to waste our money on additional 'programs'. Typically, however, the charge that was immediately howled in their direction was 'racism'.

After 40 years and probably $trillions of dollars, I think we have given the self-styled 'socially compassionate' point of view the old college try, don't you? It does not work in the ways that we have tried it, and over the past several decades at least, we have tried it in every variation the Progressives could dream up. In fact, as often as we have tried it unsuccessfully, in the U.S. and the various Communist and Socialist countries, we should finally recognize that Progressive social philosophy truly is, what a recent black thinker has called, the 'compassion that kills'. Time to go back to a balanced common sense that says that everyone, regardless of capability, is necessary and can be a benefit to the society, by doing what they can to help. We must acknowledge differential capabilities, and devise an educational system that acknowledges them in people, because the reality is that, while there are broad similarities in people that can be grouped for educational efficiency, everyone is different from everyone else.

Nevertheless, we should also guard that the pendulum does not swing too far back in the other direction. It would not hurt my feelings if the pendulum stopped entirely somewhere in the middle; somewhere within that great American middle ground of common sense and practical outlooks that we once called the 'silent majority'. In fact, the last time I looked, a working definition of democracy was that 'the majority rules', not 'the loudest crybaby rules'. Of course, we also have a saying that, 'the squeaky wheel gets the grease', and if we do not mind all of this metaphor mixing, we can update that saying to, 'if the greased wheel does not stop squeaking, it should be replaced'.

While there are exceptions even now, I would like to summarize what Progressives ignore about us and our history: All of us are immigrants or descendants of immigrants and many of us, or our ancestors, came here either to escape some sort of persecution or to find a better opportunity,[168] or both. What we found in America were many people, not entirely like ourselves, around whom we have adapted our behaviors, to get along and prosper. Therefore, Americans generally live by a very decent, inclusive moral code and a sense of fairness that eventually includes *all* of us in "us." In the end, all that we ask in return is that everyone work hard and try to move in roughly the same direction.

Gradually We *Will* Refute Gradualism

Another of Gould's refutations of the idea of intelligence is very strange because it, too, is ultimately so unscientific. Gould passionately used arguments that he calmly chided others for using in their refutations of his (Gould's) other work. To describe how Gould's arguments are inconsistent with his arguments against others, we must briefly describe his other work.

---

168 I will address the obvious complaint about this statement, which is that some of us were brought here against our will rather than coming here by choice, in the chapter on Multiculturalism.

Two instances for which Gould is renowned come quickly to mind. We credit him, along with Niles Eldredge, of the American Museum of Natural History, for describing an idea that fine-tuned the Darwinian idea of evolutionary gradualism. Gradualism is the idea that says biological evolution apparently mimics the geological reality of very slow changes over immense periods of time. Darwin initially argued that species change over time only very slowly. Tiny changes in a species eventually result in its evolution from one form to another, as the Galápagos finches changed. Gould, and others, had noticed, however, that there were very few intermediate forms called 'missing links' found in the fossil record. When species did change, they seemed to change very suddenly. For a long time, we merely took this lack of missing links as evidence that the fossil record was simply incomplete. If fossilization were more common, it was argued, we would find all the missing links we could care to see. Eventually though, speciation clearly seemed to occur quite suddenly, geologically speaking, after long periods of little change, much like the difference between an earthquake and erosion. Eldredge and Gould called their idea 'punctuated equilibrium' to emphasize these quick changes punctuating long periods of evolutionary stasis.

Some scientists did not agree with this new idea, and said so in print. Therefore, Gould and Eldredge published a response to the criticism in 1977. In that response they said:

> ... the two most frequent criticisms of our paper (Eldredge and Gould, 1972) are methodological. In both cases, we feel that we have been misunderstood:
>
> Some critics (e.g., Harper, 1975) have seen our work as restrictive in scope—as an attempt rigidly to exclude gradualism by establishing a new dogma for evolutionary tempos [speed of evolutionary change]. Lespérance and Bertrand (1976, p. 610) charge that we have, "in effect denied the existence of phyletic [course in evolutionary development] gradualism in speciation." We have never understood punctuated equilibrium in this light. We see it as fundamentally expansive—as a more adequate picture that should extend the range of paleontological activity by valuing types of data previously neglected. We never claimed either that gradualism could not occur in theory, or did not occur in fact ... Nature is far too varied and complex for such absolutes; Captain Corcoran's "hardly ever" is the strongest statement that a natural historian can hope to make.

Slightly later they add:

> Our unhappiness with gradualism arose from *its* status as restrictive dogma. For it has the unhappy property of excluding a priori [based on hypothesis rather than on experiment] the very data that might refute it.

Hear! Hear! I say. Yet how can the scientist who wrote these words be the same rigid politico who will not under any circumstances, allow a more expansive and adequate picture of intelligence, and therefore human nature, that should extend the range of educational methodology, among other things, by valuing types of data currently neglected. Our (the American parent's) unhappiness with the Progressive philosophy arose from *its* status as irrefutable dogma, and the widely unhappy results it has engendered in large part because *it* excludes *a priori* the very data that would easily refute it. This exclusion, of course, does not stop with the data on intelligence, but includes much of what was once thought of as common sense. Things like; 'We learn from our mistakes', and 'If you want to learn how to do a thing, ask someone who knows how'.

The other example of Gould's contradictory usages involves his long time dispute with Creationism and creationists. Gould had long fought the good fight against intellectual blindness and emotionality, arguing that Creationists refuse to recognize mountains of supporting evidence for evolution due to their insistence upon an idea that cannot be disproved, namely that the words in the Bible are quotations taken directly from the mind of God. The most ardent Creationists will not even unbend so far as to allow that God's word may have been intended as instructional allegory rather than literal truth. This is a controversy of long standing.

In <u>William Jennings Bryan's Last Campaign,</u> an essay in *Bully for Brontosaurus,* one of Gould's books of collected essays, Gould tried to explain how and why Bryan, the famous lawyer, three-time Presidential candidate, prosecutor in the Scopes Monkey Trial, and a great advocate for many reform movements around the turn of the 19th century, could have advocated the removal of the teaching of evolution in schools. In the early part of his essay, Gould sets up the problem: Bryan was a tireless advocate for many causes of his day and an implacable Progressive thinker, yet he somehow managed to support the then reactionary idea that evolution was an invidious and harmful notion that we must stamp out. Today, of course, the political tables are turned on this issue. Gould asked, how could Bryan's thinking, in essence advocating book burning and censorship, have been so inconsistent with his previously brilliant (Progressive) career? Even Bryan's supporters noticed his inconsistency and apparently asked about it. In explaining himself in 1923 Bryan stated: "There has not been a reform for 25 years that I did not support. And I am now engaged in the biggest reform of my life. I am trying to save the Christian Church from those who are trying to destroy her faith."

In trying to answer this conundrum about Bryan that he posed to himself, Gould wrote:

We must acknowledge, before explicating the reasons for his shift, that Bryan was no intellectual. Please don't misconstrue this statement. I am not trying to snipe from the depth of Harvard elitism, but to understand. Bryan's dearest friends said as much. Bryan used his first-rate mind in ways that are intensely puzzling to trained scholars—and we cannot grasp his reasons without mentioning this point. The "Prince of Peace"[169] displays a profound ignorance in places, as when Bryan defended the idea of miracles by stating that we continually break the law of gravity: "Do we not suspend or overcome the law of gravitation every day? Every time we move a foot or lift a weight we temporarily overcome one of the most universal of natural laws and yet the world is not disturbed." (Since Bryan gave this address hundreds of times, I [Gould] assume that people tried to explain to him the difference between laws and events, or remind him that without gravity, our raised foot would go off into space. I must conclude that he didn't care because the line conveyed a certain rhetorical oomph.) He also explicitly defended the suppression of understanding in the service of moral good:

"If you ask me if I understand everything in the Bible, I answer no. But if we will try to live up to what we do understand, we will be kept so busy doing good that we will not have time to worry about the passages which we do not understand."

This attitude continually puzzled his friends and provided fodder for his enemies. One detractor wrote: "By much talking and little thinking his mentality ran dry." To the same effect, but with kindness, a friend and supporter wrote that Bryan was "almost unable to think in the sense in which you and I use that word. Vague ideas floated through his mind

---

169 A speech called *The Prince of Peace* that Gould told us ranked second only to the *Cross of Gold* for popularity and frequency of repetition.

but did not unite to form any system or crystallize into a definite practical position."

"Almost *unable* to think," (i.e., think = consider, evaluate, and analyze evidence) because, "vague ideas floated through his head." Remember that Bryan was a Progressive thinker. Perhaps *all* of his ideas were the result of this mode of unrealistic rhetoric building? Maybe modern Progressive advocates have taken their lead from Bryan's apparently Orwellian notion that if we say something long enough and often enough it does not matter that what we say is absurd, people will eventually believe it. Then we can manipulate them. Perhaps this is why multiculturalism and educational equity and inclusion and self-esteem and relevance and everybody-is-the-same-as-everybody-else and individual choice, etc., sound good as rhetoric, but fall flat in practice. Yet, despite falling continually flat in practice, Progressive thinkers continually recommend them. Could "a certain rhetorical oomph" be enough to build a career on, at the expense of those we purport to help? Perhaps this can explain how modern Progressives can see the disastrous results of their recommendations yet convince themselves that they are doing 'the right things' and continue to recommend them, even while we and our children fall victim to our 'mysterious' cultural forces? It may be, further, that the folks that denigrate the teaching of 'facts', scaled appropriately to kids of differential intelligence, do so because they have a profound disregard for the truth, preferring vague ideology and rhetoric?

I am not here to debunk evolutionary theory, or even Gould's support of it. He helped convince me years ago that even if other ideas eventually augment or replace natural selection as the mechanism of evolution, the theory was on the right track. Nevertheless, I would like you to see his words used in support of Bryan. Gould's answer to Bryan's evolutionary foibles starts with this:

Bryan's long-standing approach to evolution rested upon a three-fold error. First, he made the common mistake of confusing the fact of evolution with the Darwinian explanation of its mechanism. He then misinterpreted natural selection as a martial theory of survival by battle and destruction of enemies. Finally, he made the logical error of arguing that Darwinism implied the moral virtuousness of such deadly struggle.

Gould chided Bryan for the same sorts of logical errors that he is guilty of, concerning the intelligence question. We could just change a word here and there to describe Gould's approach to intelligence. For instance:

> Gould's long-standing approach to intelligence rested upon a three-fold error. First, he made the common mistake of confusing the fact of intelligence with the Social-Darwinian explanation of its mechanism. He then misinterpreted modern explanations of thinking as a martial theory of survival by battle and destruction of enemies. Finally, he made the logical error of arguing that *The Bell Curve,* or anything else that notes intellectual differences, implied the moral virtuousness of such deadly struggle.

In the intelligence debate, Gould's mind is as set as any Progressive educational professional. Although Gould did not have very much to say about education per se, his approach to this question is very similar to the way modern educationists approach education and learning. It is a shame, really.

It is more than a shame. The ideas have contributed to considerable bad feeling and have been used to justify much bad educational theory, among other things.

Multiculturalism is one of those other things.

5 Multiculturalism

A house divided against itself cannot stand.
—*Abraham Lincoln*

Education then, beyond all other devices of human origin,
is a great equalizer of the conditions of men
—the balance wheel of the social machinery.
—*Horace Mann*

Unfortunately, this chapter is necessary because much Progressive educational theory and practice are at least partly predicated on the proposition that traditional education is a racist enterprise at heart, in the political sense. The arguments exactly parallel the kinds of arguments Gould used (see the previous chapter) and the answer to these arguments parallels exactly my arguments about balancing selfishness (survival) and responsibility (sociability). We must address this balance in the clear light of day and not by the preposterous obfuscation of political correctness. In that spirit, I promise to limit my use of the word obfuscation.

Racism is as natural as breathing. Furthermore, it is a good thing.

My guess is that the preceding statements will require some explanation. What I mean is almost certainly not what you think. For starters, my definition is not political. The word 'racism', moreover, carries a great deal of emotional and political baggage that interferes with sensible discussion so much, that I have tried to think of a different word to describe what I mean. I have even consulted professors of dead languages to see if I could adapt another root word to my needs. So far no luck. 'Xenophobia', the fear of anything foreign, may be the best alternative word currently available, but it also has an unsavory, political smell about it that I would just as soon avoid. What we need is something brand new that can start life with no baggage to unload. I try out two or three possibilities in an upcoming footnote. They are, perhaps, a bit heavy, but perhaps they need to be. Anything too familiar will have familiar overtones that might compromise the intent.[170]

How can I say that racism is as natural as breathing? For a start, when I think of this phenomenon, I think of biology, not politics. For my definition to have any meaning, you must accept the idea that humans are members of the animal kingdom. This is not the place to describe all of the many and varied lines of evidence, which span nearly all of the sciences, for human inclusion in this ancient and ubiquitous group. The evidence is so overwhelming, however, that not to accept it is tantamount to deliberately wearing intellectual blinders. Nevertheless, if you do not like to think of humans as animals, you may use the term 'biological creatures'. Furthermore, you may define the 'creator' of these creatures as whoever or whatever you like. Biologically speaking, it is the same in the end.

In any case, Mother Nature is an essentially conservative lady. She rarely changes things just to be changing them. If humans are members of the animal kingdom, then we can expect to have reactions and internally moderated processes that are similar to, and often identical to, other animals. In the previous chapter we briefly examined the idea that while Nature continually accumulates nonlethal variations in the genome, those changes do not express themselves unless there is a survival benefit to do so, or at least no devastating survival detriment to keeping them. The processes of reproduction and growth try very hard not to change anything because any random modification to an adaptive gene is more likely to be harmful than otherwise. Similarly, once a structure or instinct has been embedded in an animal's makeup, and especially if the structure or instinct ('behavior') is adaptive (i.e., has survival value), it remains, though perhaps in modified form, beyond evolution to a different creature. Survival need or evolutionary advantage may be necessary, however, before Nature changes which of the accumulated alleles (i.e., gene variations) will predominate. Mother Nature was the first to live by the maxim, "Don't fix it if it ain't broke."

The March 1999 issue of *Scientific American* (SA) magazine features an example of this. Within an article about how pregnant human mothers optimize the initiation of labor within the uterus, was a side feature labeled, <u>An Evolutionary Clue from Toads</u>. The same corticotropin-releasing hormone (CRH) that is the focus of the full SA article

---

170 If after reading the following explanation you can think of a word that will serve, please let me know somehow.

about human mothers, has also been found in the western spadefoot toad, and seems to have a role determining when to allow tadpoles to develop into adult toads. Development into adult toads depends on how quickly mama toad can lay her eggs in the rain pools where the toads breed, before the pools dry up. Sheep also use CRH for the same purpose as humans.

If CRH has been around since amphibians were young (perhaps 350 million years ago), filling the same role in many creatures, including humans, it seems hard to deny there is something to evolutionary ideas. This is also the case with territoriality.

Many living things, including plants, animals, fungi, bacteria, etc., defend a territory in some fashion. We may take the fact that defensive behavior in general spans the biological Kingdoms as one of the many demonstrations that all living things on this planet are related. Perhaps the various genome projects that are, and will be ongoing over the years, will eventually show that the various genes that influence specific defensive behaviors are somehow similar. Time will tell. If behavioral controls turn out to be genetically similar, along with similarities in the genes that build bones and sebaceous glands, etc., perhaps more folks will finally begin to think that since all living things are related this profound similarity amid profound diversity, is somehow a part of God's plan. When that happens, we can begin to resolve the philosophic arguments that confuse and hurt the education of our kids.

In the nonanimal Kingdoms, defense strategies are most often chemical in nature. Plants, etc., produce various antibiotics or other poisons that they spread into their general area or incorporate into their tissues. They use the poisons to limit competition for rare resources (e.g., food, space to grow, etc.), especially in the immediate neighborhood (territory) of the individual in question.

In the Animal Kingdom resource hoarding also often takes the form of defense of a specified territory, which is, of course, why we call it territoriality. The animal, or band of animals, stakes out a place large enough to provide all that it requires to live and raise young. These necessary resources include water and a food source, access to mates, perhaps shelter from the weather, and nesting or brooding places, etc. Even animals such as migrating grazers, that do not keep a permanent territory, often keep a fluid territory within which they maintain what precious resources can come with them, such as their mates and offspring, etc. The literature is full of examples of variations of this behavior. It would therefore be strange if the human genome did not contain some provisions for protective behaviors, too.

Before advanced technology, including stone tools and digging-stick agriculture, allowed human bands to increase their numbers beyond the norm, humans and protohumans lived lives that we could not describe as different from other animals, except for the details of how we earned our living and what we required for that living. We typically lived in small bands, the normal size of which was perhaps five or six to twenty or thirty individuals. A routine day consisted of searching for anything edible and eating it in place; the original fast food. Alternatively, if the food item was not rooted to the ground, and if it also objected to becoming lunch, we required active hunting. Finally, since we see few peoples today living truly primitive lives, and since even those people's lives have now been touched and perhaps irrevocably modified by contact with 'civilized' settlers, researchers, and tourists, one mode of deducing what prehistoric human life might have been like, is to study animals. As hinted at earlier, apart from its intrinsic interest, the main point to doing animal behavior studies is that we can generalize many findings to human biology. Yet, trying to pull some defining truths out of observations of recent human behavior alone, is fraught with problems. This is so because of the cacophony of human intellectual acrobatics that obscures the truth. These intellectual acrobatics include philosophy, even if we do not base it more on unrealistic or impossible hopes than on reproducible facts. Cultural variations, politics, symbolism, superstition, mistaken causal relationships (i.e., old wives' tales), and even gossip can also confuse our understanding.

Animals represent a variation on the natural, perhaps even universal, theme. Therefore, it makes no difference that the capacities for intellectual acrobatics may be what makes us different from the other animals. Even that difference is merely one of degree, not an absolute difference.

"Biologie. Biologie. Toujours biologie."

E. O. Wilson, the biologist and author of *Sociobiology* has written a new book that he calls *Consilience: The Unity of Knowledge* in which he argues that genes and culture have coevolved, an idea apparently similar, or at least in some sense partially related, to mine in that it concerns itself with the biology of the 'mind'. While I have not yet read his full book, Wilson has recently published an article in *The Wilson Quarterly* (no relation as far as I know) that is something of a 'plug' for his book. In this article he states that:

> . . . all mental activity is *material* [my emphasis] in nature and occurs in a manner consistent with the causal explanations of the natural sciences. During the past several decades, that hypothesis has gained considerable support from four disciplines that succeed partially in connecting the great branches of learning. The first is cognitive neuroscience, also known as the brain science—the once but no longer "quiet" revolution of neuro-science—that is physically mapping the mental process. The second is human behavioral genetics, now in the early stages of teasing apart the hereditary basis of the process, including the biasing influence of the genes on mental development. The third bridging discipline is evolution-ary biology (including human sociobiology, often referred to as evolution-ary psychology), that attempts to reconstruct the evolution of brain and mind. The last is environmental science, that describes the physical envi-ronment to which humanity is genetically and culturally adapted.

With this broad scientific assault on the question, we will gradually understand the relevant mental processes more clearly. Meanwhile, since humans also engage in resource-hoarding behaviors, we can as-sume that the behavior cannot be merely the result of our lofty reason overcoming a uniquely human adversity. It is instinctive. Yet, specific resource-hoarding behaviors can change over time, and this possibility of change again shows that instincts *are* malleable. On the other hand, much as we might like to, we cannot swoop down on an interloper like a hawk with wings, so instincts while malleable, are not *entirely malleable*, unless we can afford to wait a very long time, and probably not even then.

Other animals eat, sleep, fight, and make babies just as we do, and it is precisely because they are only a variation on a theme, and not something completely different, that truths learned from animal and other biological studies are useful to understanding humans and their behaviors. What makes an animal behavioral model useful is that it is set at a more basic level than humans, without the interference of intel-lectual acrobatics. Also, since we saw that behavior is ultimately 'mate-rial', we can use animal models to research behavior just as we use them to research medicines and cosmetics.

One way to maximize the usefulness of the comparisons of any animal social model to the behavior of early humans, is to study them in the same environment as used by early humans. Schaller and Lowther put it this way, ". . . since ecological conditions strongly influence social systems, it seems that it might be . . . productive to compare hominids with animals that are ecologically but not necessarily phylogenetically similar, like the social carnivores. The group dynamics, dominance hierarchies, land tenure systems, cooperative hunting techniques, and the like of the wolf, wild dog, hyena, and lion were compared with those of contemporary hunter-gatherers and, by inference, those of early hominids." Often comparisons with these carnivores seemed even more pertinent than similar comparisons to our closer kin, the nonhuman primates. Therefore, a good model for inferring at least some aspects of early human life is lions.

Lion behavior is a good model for some early human behaviors because lions had to solve the same kinds of survival problems as our early ancestors. Not surprisingly lions evolved some of the same solutions to those problems as humans.

African lions live on the East African plains and woodlands and they are meat eaters. Early humans lived on the East African plains and woodlands too, and ate meat, at least part of the time. The plains are wide and mostly grassy, although large tracts may be swampy or brushy. The savannah offers few places to hide from predators or dangerous browsers and grazers like elephants or water buffalo, or from other dangers, such as fire, except in the rare tree or perhaps on a kopje, which are even more rare. Kopje are outcrops of bedrock found in East Africa and pronounced like "copy" (kä-pē).

Two of the main strategies that both humans and lions used were to live in groups, which is very rare among cats, and to defend territories. Living in groups allows a greater efficiency in hunting and allows some specialization of effort, while maintaining territories allows enhanced control of required resources.

For humans, as for other animals, it is a very natural extension of these two facts to predict that due to the emotions-exhibited in defending territories from other groups of humans, an antipathy may develop between competing groups whose territories border each other. This is especially true during times when resources are diminishing or when populations are rising, or both (just look at the history of the human world). This is the same as two lion groups fighting in border disputes. These border disputes can occur even if the lions in the different groups are related to each other.

A very cursory summary of lion society shows that lion prides are composed of a resident group of related females (mothers, sisters, aunts, cousins) and their cubs, and, usually, a group of related brothers or male cousins that take up residence by ousting the previous group of males. These males stay in residence until they, in turn, are also ousted. The males defend their new territory even if the neighbors are their own kin. There is something about having access to food, as opposed to starving, that can make even relatives antagonistic.

Even so, this sort of antipathy between human groups is clearly more than simply being disappointed with someone for not sharing. As such, it can easily develop into a full-blown and seemingly irrational hatred. As the dispute becomes extended through generations, the hatred of competing groups becomes transferred from individuals in opposing groups to the groups themselves. Racism in the political sense is born of the affiliation with one's own group combined with the often brutal competition with others, fed by the need to survive.

Both the survival instinct and sociability are considered good things, and so they are. Yet together they can manifest themselves as a dislike of those who make life harder, either by competing for needed resources or by forcing us to put ourselves in deadly peril, or both. In the 'lower' beasts, this competition may be no more difficult to understand than an empty belly, or raging hormones, etc., that cloud the mind and induce one to consider oneself, or one's group, above all other considerations in an effort to survive. In the 'higher' animals, including man, association of specific individuals or groups with stressful situations may allow transference of a vague, generalized animosity to those individuals or groups. A vague animosity sharpens specifically over time, even beyond the alleviation of the conditions that spawned the argument in the first place. The famous feud between the Hatfield's and the McCoy's is a case in point, as are the seemingly traditional wars the world over of, to us, seemingly identical neighbors. The various attempts at 'ethnic cleansing', and fights over resources in southeast Europe, the Punjab, the Middle East including northern Iraq, Cambodia, Indonesia, various areas in Africa and others come quickly to mind.

The problem with this argument, of course, is its directionality. The wording of the argument assumes that each animal can make logical connections and that the growing hatred is a consequence of that logical thought. In reality my argument is essentially the reverse of that. Since we can easily see that these general sorts of behaviors do exist, even in species to which we cannot attribute logical thought (i.e., plants, etc.), then the behavior, at least in its broad form, must be mediated from within. We call behavior that is internally mediated 'instinct'.

Resource hoarding behavior, and especially its ancillary behaviors (for instance how residents stake out and mark borders, how, and how often, they patrol the borders, how they notify the group and react to border crossing, etc.), are all accomplished in species-specific ways. Yet the fact that species with resource-limit problems also have resource-hoarding behaviors of some sort, suggests that these behaviors must be instinctive. To engage in a specific behavior, the individual must have the structures and the biochemical mechanisms that allow that behavior (e.g., trees do not run from browsers because they do not have the requisite locomotor systems). If we then add the human intellect and ego to the mix, which can manifest themselves as ambition, we can see that it would not be difficult to talk oneself, or one's followers, into a rational hatred of those who are "Not like us." [Don't get excited that I called this hatred "rational." We are not done yet.]

I started with a discussion of territoriality, saying that humans have instincts just like other biological creatures. Behaviors passed along from species to species cannot be entirely cultural in nature but must, by definition, be instinctive (heritable). What we call racism, in the political sense, is a human manifestation of territoriality. The way that racism manifests itself in everyday life is by making people suspicious of other people who are not in their own intimate group. Just like the lions that fought ferociously to keep their control of the resources they need to survive, early people staked out, maintained, patrolled, and defended borders very fiercely. We still do. These borders do not have to be very extensive. Remember the saying, "A man's home is his castle"?[171] Even our laws reflect this ancient and rudimentary understanding, giving us significantly increased rights in the home, including use of deadly force, that we do not have in public places. Can the fact that we still energetically defend borders be a result of reason alone developing a reasonable strategy to overcome a uniquely human problem? Doesn't seem likely.

However, I also said in my opening paragraph that racism is a good thing. We would agree, for example, that starvation is not a good thing

---

171 The more politically correct, "a person's home is their territory," just does not have the same ring to it.

for individuals. Since resources are ultimately limited in any area, and since territoriality is an ancient and rudimentary method of balancing resources with the population that depends on it, anything that limits the population within such an area, while allowing the species as a whole to survive, is a good thing (the greatest good for the greatest number). Since Mother Nature has used racism/territoriality for a much greater space of time than the history of *Homo sapiens*, we cannot say that we invented it. Any method that could be found that will keep "Those others—Not like us" out of "our" valley, helped us to survive. Therefore racism/territoriality, being instinctive, is as natural as breathing. So, since racism, or whatever term we eventually coin to describe it, helped us to survive, it is a good thing, by its very definition.

Of course most of us do not live in bands of five to thirty, separated by great distances anymore, and modern manifestations of racism are not always such a good thing. Hating others 'just because' is not very helpful in a world as interconnected and crowded as ours.[172] That does not matter. We cannot shed our instincts as easily as that; not even in response to Progressive proscriptions.[173] They are buried deep in our genes after all. On the other hand, it is a very good thing that our instincts are not as immutable as some fear. The resolution to this dilemma is my stilted phrase; "Those others—Not like us."

Our instinct instructs us to keep anyone at arm's length whom we do not recognize and who is "Not like us." On the other hand, we do not seem to have an instinct for or against specific individuals nor about whom 'us' should include. Under certain circumstances even the closest relatives can have deadly fallings-out, and people who have many superficial differences can be friends and partners if they all identify with the same things. These 'things' can be almost anything; a job, a hobby, a sports team, a nation. Even the Progressives can recognize this truth.[174] For instance, in the textbook *Educational Psychology*, we find this (pg. 160): "... upper-class Anglo-Europeans, African-Americans, and His-panic-Americans typically find that they have more in common with each other than they have with lower-class individuals from their own

---

172 This may be an example of what Paul Ehrlich, in *Human Nature*, calls "evolutionary hangovers"; that is, ancient behavioral repertory that interferes with current needs.

173 This is why "respect for others" programs mixed with "I matter and you don't" training, does not achieve its desired goal.

174 Though, of course, they ignore the effects in favor of the divisive interpretation that just happens to provide a living, advocating for their favorite victim group.

ethnic groups." We may not have any limit to the variety of things that can bring people together, since 'coming together' is yet another instinct. We are a social species after all.

As an example, in some sense all lawyers have more in common with each other than with other people. Their shared education, professional requirements, and trained modes of thinking set them apart; no matter the membership in which race or creed each individual lawyer happens to hold. We can say the same thing for carpenters, piano players, English professors, and high school kids, too, and many other manifestly interracial groups. Whom we include in our 'social race' is at last a matter of our own choosing, and not genetically defined. This idea may not be good taxonomy, but it is reality for social structure. This may also be used as a clue in describing a new word for racism.[175]

I submit that our patently malleable racism is precisely why the Melting Pot idea, that assimilated so many different peoples into a single proud nation, is so powerful. Multiculturalists should take note: stressing differences does not bring people together, as you claim, but does exactly the opposite. The NEA slogan, "Unity through Diversity," apart from the telling fact that its central emphasis has little to do with teaching ("the least important thing"), the presumed object of a teachers' association, also stresses differences that ultimately lead to disunity, a result that is exactly the opposite of the rhetorical sentiment. All we have to do is to look around to see that stressing differences convinces people they *are* different. When people see their neighbors as different enough, political racism and warfare may result.

On the other hand, I am not naïve enough to argue that all we have to do is to become a Cubs fan and peace and harmony will reign across the land. That, of course, is too simplistic. Hatred of other groups is still a very powerful rallying cry, and almost certainly will always be. It will always be because, while the territoriality/racism instinct is modifiable, the object of the instinct is still a very personal thing. Each of us makes those choices for ourselves, sometimes in total contravention to instructions. Each of us is taught who and what to love. Routinely this includes the people and things our relatives and childhood friends love. Yet many of us then end up loving something very different. Neither instinct (nature) nor education (nurture) is the final arbiter of

---

175 Unisociality—associate only with one's own group? Heteromisosocialism—hatred of other groups? Heterosociophobia—one who fears different groups? What do you think? Not as quick and catchy as the incumbent? Maybe making the last two into acronyms will help—HMS and HSP?

everything, although each is important. Ultimately, personal experience might be the most important thing.[176] Working side by side with, "Those others—Not like us," and seeing that they *are* like us, and are OK, is probably the only thing that will modify what most people think of as racism.

Of course, the 'Other' has to *be* OK. If someone we know is human detritus, (i.e., a thief, liar, back-stabber, whiner, [fill-in-the-blank with what you do not like]), or if he treats us like an enemy, then we will not like him even if he is of our own race, color, creed, or family. Since humans do like to pigeonhole others, we may generalize the fact that we do not like *him* to his other characteristics, be they cultural, ethnic, racial, or anything else. Yet if we find that we do like him, and he does not treat us like an enemy, we may generalize our friendship to others like him. This last bit has been happening all over the U.S. for generations now, and would be much easier, and would approach universal harmony much quicker, if it were not for the rhetoric of separation used to bring us together.

Back to Ed School, for a Moment

Some of what passes for 'ideal' nowadays is quite strange. The last 'academic' course required of us before we began our required ten weeks of student-facilitating, was Multiculturalism. What is it about this topic that qualifies it for such a significant placement in the professional development of a prospective teacher? Multiculturalism is in effect the summation of all of the dumbing-down, history revising, 'Euro' hating instruction that came before. In addition, it has some peculiarities all its own. As a condition of student-teaching, we were required to incorporate the basic precepts of multiculturalism into whatever classes we taught. We also had to document how we intended to do it. It made no difference what subject we teach, be it math, science, 'Language Arts', or gym. By this time in our training, they expected us to accept that learning "2 + 2" is different to differently cultured children. It should also be clear that gravity works differently in Uruguay or Mongolia than

---

176 Let us not have the modern advocates of Rousseau's educational theories jumping for joy just yet.

in Oregon. So, to accommodate children from all of those places, instruction in this topic should be done differently depending on an individual pupil's ancestry (you never know when a headhunter's child might enter your class). The rules of dodge ball are differently understandable if you are Sioux or Irish, black or Hispanic, even if . . . But I am getting ahead of myself.

Unfortunately, multiculturalism is difficult to debate against because it often presents itself with a surface veneer of respectability. Furthermore, the rhetoric of multiculturalism is ultimately very simple ("they" are out to get "us" [note the similarity to political racism]), while explanations of modern intercultural reality require more time and multiple lines of thought. Unfortunately, one of the criticisms of the American educational system is that many high school graduates cannot follow an argument that requires more than one logical step. That is to say that many of us are now rife for indoctrination, but not prepared to note the inconsistencies, reason through the propaganda, and decide for ourselves. This characteristic is helpful to multiculturalists and Progressive ideologues, however, because when we listen to dueling rhetoriticians, one-issue multiculturalism often wins the day. The audience has been primed for it with revised and dumbed-down history that makes the complications of reality much more difficult to comprehend.

Nevertheless, while there are several problems with it, Alan Singer's article, *Reflections of Multiculturalism,* represents the respectability I mentioned. These quotes from Singer, who in 1994 was an assistant professor of social studies education at Hofstra University, decry his position in the middle, between the "rock" of the uglier aspects of multiculturalism, generally called ethnocentrism (and in particular the proponents of afrocentrism), and the "hard place" of traditional ideas on the teaching of history. In Singer's words, more traditional historians, like Arthur Schlesinger and Diane Ravitch, accuse multiculturalism of ". . . substituting 'ethnic cheerleading' for scholarship and of engaging in 'social and psychological therapy' instead of teaching history." The phrase that is often used in discussing this predilection of multicultural instruction is feel-good history. While Singer calls himself a multiculturalist, some afrocentric multiculturalists, refuse to acknowledge Singer as a kindred spirit at all. Singer is a white man who must therefore be a part of a conspiracy to perpetrate "cultural genocide" on blacks. This is a very nice application of the promised equity and interracial harmony, don't you think? What was that line from Mel Brooks (playing a very Yiddish sounding Indian chief), to Cleavon Little in *Blazing Saddles*: "If you can't even recognize a brother, how will you ever recognize a friend?"

In any case, Singer identifies ten ideas that add up to multiculturalism. They are:

1) "... Multiculturalism is a way of looking at the world that is rooted in scientific exploration, that challenges the cultural limitations distorting our vision ..." He says that multiculturalism's obvious place in school is in the social studies curriculum as well as instruction in literature, art, music, and other areas.

2) "... Multiculturalism is based on the idea of 'multiple perspectives' that there is more than one way to view and understand an event, an idea, or an era." He points out that the losers of wars, and those who come under the influence of different cultures often had a point of view, too, and that they did not always think that the changes they had to endure were good ones.

3) "Multiculturalism is a call for 'inclusion' in the curriculum. It says, 'I should be visible in this classroom, but so should you, and so should all the people that inhabit this nation and world'." Singer tells us that everyone should know, and be proud of, the history of their own ancestors since that will help them to understand how the world developed. Sounds like the study of history to me, but of course one can detect a subtle hint of relevance theory. Left as subtle, I have no argument with it, and can wholeheartedly support the idea. We *do* have an interest in ourselves. As you read history, haven't you made particular note of events that just happened to occur on your birthday? Relevance in balance with reality, (i.e., the world does not revolve around us) is not completely irrelevant, it just should not be the focus of everything.

4) "Multiculturalism insists that we see the world in all its global complexity. There are billions of actors on the world stage, and a viewpoint that ignores most of them leaves us unable to understand the forces that are shaping our planet." This, to me, also sounds like the traditional reason to study history and geography.

5) "A multicultural perspective requires dialogue between people of different points of view, acknowledgment of different experiences and respect for diverse opinions. . . . Multiculturalism values creating knowledge through research, analysis, and discussion."

6) However, Singer also recognizes that, "Proposed multicultural texts and curricula often offer one event, work of art or cultural manifestation to represent the sum total of a people's experiences." This is a problem because, "Students need to understand that African history did not begin with the Atlantic slave trade, that Jews existed between the times of Jesus and Hitler, that Native American civilizations flourished before Europeans arrived, and that Egypt did not disappear when Cleopatra died." He notes that the way history instruction is done currently, as opposed to the way we are told it is done, does not work. Therefore:

7) "As educators, I believe that we are responsible for the confusion between what Afrocentrists do and the study of history. We teach history as a collection of isolated and seemingly random facts to be memorized. The Afrocentrists' response to the traditional curriculum is to ask, 'Why your "facts" and not mine?' If we want students to understand the differences between multicultural history and Afrocentrism, we are going to have to abandon our reliance on lectures and allow students to discover patterns and create connections through their own thinking and research." Again, please note that this article was published in 1994, a full three decades after we were promised that the study of history would become more inclusive. It is now 2005, and things haven't changed yet. To counter this problem that he identifies, Singer tells us that we should abandon the lecture method in order to allow kids to become "active learners [and] participate in shaping the future." This recommendation, of course, is the same one made at least since the mid 1960s, and amounts to asking kids to develop a historical perspective without the guidance of responsible and experienced historians, or teachers of history. This idea can be called Whole History, and is just as faulty as Whole anything else.

8) "A key precept for a multicultural education should be respect for the richness of difference. . . . I become conscious of who I am and what I am as I compare myself with you. Without difference, identity has no meaning." Singer then notes another theoretical mistake made by our anti-intellectual intellectuals: "Some educators are concerned that valuing cultural difference contributes to moral relativism and requires us to accept oppressive practices because they are part of another group's culture." He refers to such practices as genital mutilation and female infanticide and notes that: "When 'outsiders' challenge a group's cultural practices, it can have the undesired consequence of reinforcing the practice by transforming it into a symbol of national opposition to imperialism. This is one of the factors that contributes to the growth of fundamentalist movements in a number of countries."

9) "In the United States, an expressed goal of education is the creation of an active citizenry committed to democratic values." I get the

impression that Singer's democracy is not the relabeled anarchy we find with other Progressive theorists. This is probably why he has had trouble fitting in with the club.

10) Unfortunately, he continues to say: "The notion of multiculturalism that I have described here points to a different way of organizing our classrooms. In most classes, the teacher is the expert, the conveyor of all knowledge and the job of the student is to absorb passively what the teacher presents. In the kind of multicultural classroom that I envision, everyone is an active learner, sharing different insights into people and curriculum subjects." Singer concludes this because; "Over the years, a number of African-American students have mentioned in class that they resent always learning about slavery and how their people were oppressed. They also have not really been interested in learning about the glories of ancient African civilizations." This can also be said about pupils of Austrian or Swedish descent and European history. Never mind, they should know it, so we should teach it, whether they find it less relevant to themselves than next weekend's baseball game or not.

Singer concludes with this: "When I explain these ideas about multiculturalism to groups of teachers, they generally respond that 'it seems so reasonable', and they don't understand why it has generated such intense controversy. I think the reason for the controversy is that most of the debates about multiculturalism have little to do with the nature of history, the relative merits of different types of art and literature, or the most effective ways to teach about them. They are political debates about who will hold power and shape education policy in American society."

If we discount some seemingly hidden parts, this description of multiculturalism does, indeed, seem "so reasonable." In fact, if we replaced the missing parts this could almost describe what I remember as 'Social Studies' before the Great Society reforms took hold. It is a thoughtful, considerate, and nearly inclusive rendition of the sort of program that we can design to produce good citizens.

So what is missing? I will get to that in just a moment. First I want to show what is Singer's single worst theoretical/practical mistake. While arguing that multiculturalism allows a ". . . process of comparing similarities and differences" in practice it concentrates on the differences. The differences are used to further the power struggles mentioned at the end. As a result the practices of multiculturalism divide and segregate us into contentious groups. Need I say again that multiculturalism achieves exactly the opposite of its advertised goal?

We can identify some of the many reasons for this result in Singer's description. Singer tells us that afrocentrism is, ". . . neither a study of history nor an approach to historical understanding. It is a political and religious movement that uses historical information for the creation of unifying cultural symbols." Afrocentrism is "not a search for historical understanding but rather an attempt at reconstructing culture and creating a collective consciousness." In other words, it is indoctrination that they expect us to swallow whole, without the balancing study of history, and they expect us to tax ourselves to pay for the privilege of destroying ourselves. Furthermore, we should use the public schools to accomplish this cultural reconstruction. Afrocentrists, therefore, have a goal of "reconstructing culture" and "creating (a) collective (African) consciousness" while rejecting "the religion of science"[177] and the systematic study of history because they do not embrace the traditional African 'humanistic and spiritual viewpoint' " with its ". . . traditional gods and traditional ways of knowing and are major reasons why afrocentrism and multicultural education are not the same things." The problem is, of course, that many people think that they are the same thing but do not consider how difficult layering traditional tribal ways of knowing onto a technological society would be, especially if we reject the systematic study of history and science. Ironically, the cultural anthropologists are the ones who show us that this is not possible. However, that does not matter, people do it anyway, and wonder why things just do not seem to work well. (Santayana, where are you when we need you?) Doing these things uncritically, while arguing that it is the result of critical thinking, is a bit backward, too.

Revising History Must Be Fun; Everyone Is Doing It

Afrocentrism is not the only variation on this theme, of course. I will shortly show another, but the modus operandi is much the same. Meanwhile, I said several paragraphs ago that Singer's conception of

---

177 I cannot let this religion-of-science comment pass. The most important thing that some 'Godless scientists,' as well as scientists of every faith, have against religious explanations of everyday events, is precisely the fact that religions, especially fundamentalist religions, do not require reproducible proofs to validate their beliefs. They are content, and even proud, that their faith is blind faith. To call science a religion, which changes constantly in response to discoveries, when the various Progressive ideologies never adapt even to their own research results, is disingenuous to say the least.

multiculturalism is missing some things. While Singer's version of things is more honestly *multi*cultural than other versions, it leaves out an important one. What is missing is the U.S. culture and our national stake in maintaining a nation born on the premise that, "United we stand. Divided we fall." Singer, and other thoughtful multiculuralists, would probably argue that their conception does include *all* cultures, but that is not always what happens in practice.

The practicalities of any teaching enterprise are that we do not have enough time to cover every subject under the sun, nor can we cover the subjects that we do choose in as much detail as each subject requires. For that reason significant ideas must be trimmed from the discussions, perhaps hoping for a chance to resurface the topic for a fuller discussion later.[178] Yet perhaps not. Political correctness has been such that the main emphasis of revisionist history is to insure that we see white guys in as bad a light as possible. There has been considerable talk about this in recent years, in some political debate and even in stand-up comedy routines, so I am sure that you are familiar with some of the rhetoric. This idea has gone so far that we find strange omissions of well-known history in surprising places.

For instance, E. D. Hirsch, Jr., has written a book called *Cultural Literacy. What every American needs to know.* His basic argument is that cultural literacy is waning in America for many reasons. He defines cultural literacy as, in my words, knowledge that authors can expect readers to be familiar enough with so that they do not need extended explanations about a reference. In other words, if a writer, including newspaper reporters, etc., mentions Superman, Plymouth Rock, Happy Meals, the Manhattan Project, *The Last of the Mohicans*, or Grover Cleveland in passing, you would not scratch your head and say, "Huh? What's he talking about?" The idea of cultural literacy does not require the reader to have a specialist historian's understanding of the topic referenced. Only a general recognition and 'some' knowledge of the topic and, perhaps, its context. Hirsch includes a nonexhaustive and fluid list of 5000 items, compiled after consultation with many literate people, that he and those he consulted think should be immediately familiar to every literate American.

These concerns are not merely quaint or academic. They get to the heart of who we are as a nation. I can again use the education of

---

178 This, if it were done routinely, is what was once known as building on prior learning.

my children as an example. I have begun to intensify my efforts to supplement my children's instruction because the school has neglected the study of American history, among other topics, to an alarming degree. My daughter's fourth grade class, for instance, spent most of the second half of the year reading the novel, *Little House on the Prairie*, rather than reading a grade-appropriate history text. She could recognize the name of George Washington, and knows that he was our first President, but little more than that. The name Patrick Henry was completely unknown to her and the only thing that she could guess about Benjamin Franklin was that, ". . . he lived a long time ago."

Since this sort of education is common now, Hirsch has written a series of kids' information books, pegged to each of the elementary grades (K to 6) where he includes stories, poems, songs, and other culturally relevant information. He intends these books as a resource for teachers or parents to insure that we can continue to talk with each other with a significantly similar cultural base. The point is that we can neither speak with each other nor feel community with each other if we don't all know the same things. We have all heard stories of uncouth Americans going to other countries and committing unwitting yet deadly insults upon their hosts because they did not know that, in that culture for instance, showing the bottom of one's foot, or flashing the "OK" sign, is insulting. Hirsch argues that all Americans should be familiar with our own cultural constants if we are not to seem foreign to each other and if we are to communicate effectively with each other. His arguments are more extensive than that, but you get the point.

John Dewey would undoubtedly agree with Dr. Hirsch. In his *Democracy and Education*, Dewey writes: "To have the same ideas about things that others have, to be like-minded with them, and thus to be really members of a social group, is therefore to attach the same meanings to things and to acts which others attach. *Otherwise there is no common understanding, and no community life* (my emphasis).

In his, *What your first grader needs to know*, Hirsch includes sayings like "An apple a day keeps the doctor away," stories like <u>Jack and the Beanstalk</u> and <u>Pinocchio,</u> several of Aesop's fables with recognizable and widely agreeable morals, some history and geography, some math facts, songs like *La Cucaracha* and *On Top of Old Smoky*, and so forth.

Anyway, we would expect someone who argues for a common cultural literacy not to fall into the mistakes that political correctness requires of us and to leave out significant information. Yet, for example, here is what Hirsch includes in a section of short pieces about the coming of the Spanish, including Hernando Cortés and the Conquistadores, to the New World. In this sequence we find this:

The Spanish Conquerors

> ... The leader of the Aztecs at this time was named Montezuma [mon-the-ZOO-mah]. You may also see Montezuma spelled Moctezuma. Have you heard the song that beings, "From the halls of Montezuma"? It's the song of the United States Marines. Montezuma had terrible dreams that something bad was going to happen to his people. That something bad was Cortés. Cortés and his soldiers captured the city Tenochtitlán, and took the gold and other riches ...

Why Did the Spanish Win?

> The Aztecs were fierce warriors; they had conquered many people around them. . . . And there were many more Aztec . . . people than Spanish soldiers. So why did the Spanish win?

Hirsch mentions better weapons and the fact that the Aztecs had never seen horses, then goes on:

> But something even more powerful worked against the Native Americans. They caught diseases from the Spanish ...

Did you notice something? When the Aztecs were "fierce warriors" he calls them 'Aztecs'. Yet suddenly they are the victims of the Spaniards, and are demoted to "Native Americans," so that we may feel sorry for them. Also, we have to wonder, why is it OK to honor the Aztecs for conquering, ". . . many people around them," but being conquered is not OK for them, and reflects badly on us? Additionally, why did he leave out the fact that Aztec mythology (expecting gods and/or rulers to come from the East as the Spanish did) worked against the Aztecs or the fact that almost everyone for miles around gratefully helped Cortés in his march to Tenochtitlán because they hoped to oust and punish their Aztec conquerors? How does it happen that he does not tell us that Montezuma's subjects might have been unhappy because the Natives at the time had the delightful habit of ripping out the living heart from the chests of their slaves and captives, and then eating them (for which purpose the slaves and captives were kept in pens and deliberately fattened up like livestock)? Hirsch has also not told us that Montezuma had a taste for the flesh of young boys.

Not exactly a complete story, is it? Imagine if Cortés, or the Spanish generally, had not insisted that cannibalism stop. What would the Alamo have been like if Santa Anna had been an Aztec? Therefore, while the Spanish were certainly not purveyors of sweetness, light, and human rights every time, as a dishonest telling of history in the opposite direction would do (i.e., uncritically glorifying the Spaniards), but which traditional history instruction did not do. Maybe rather than revising history in the Progressive, and equally dishonest way, and teaching our kids to hate themselves by affiliation with the Anglo's,[179] we should *all* say a silent, '"Thank goodness" that the Spanish did come and promoted a different morality and spread different cultural constants among the Indians. A balanced telling of history in its context, with a healthy dose of morality thrown in, would teach our children the lessons of history, along with the things that we consider to be good and bad and would, if done properly, go a long way to easing the tensions that the supposedly peace-loving Progressive rhetoric inflames.

What we have then, is the juxtaposition of the U.S. Marines with poor Montezuma's sleepless nights, possibly nervous about losing his cushy job, though we would not establish the Marines for several hundred years. We also have Aztecs as proud and honorably fierce one minute, and as victims of ravaging handfuls of diseased white guys the next, with nary a mention of what has become known as 'Montezuma's revenge'. Bernal Díaz, who served under Cortés tells us that in the first month after landing in Mexico, about 10 percent of the expedition was already dead either from wounds or disease. I do not intend this as a glib trivialization of small pox, but as a recognition that dysentery is also a frequently deadly disease that was not reliably curable until we developed antibiotics in the 20th century. Small pox has since been eradicated.

While the facts presented by Hirsch are all correct, the context and the omission of other pertinent facts, paints a far different picture than the historical reality. This is true even if Cortés embarked on his adventure primarily to gain wealth and influence, which he did (as did the Aztecs).

---

179 OK. So the Spanish were not Anglo. What does it matter? They were white, weren't they?

Yet, featuring the advent of small pox in the Americas as an intentional act of genocide, as some of the worst versions of history do, can also be seen as a deliberate act of revisionism. One wonders why the Black Plague, which is thought to have originated in central Asia and brought to Europe as unwanted cargo on trading ships, is not also seen as an attempted genocide by Asians against the poor, defenseless European. After all, more than 40 million Europeans died as a result. One may say that, 'We cannot expect first graders to understand the subtleties of political discourse yet, so why burden them?' Quite true, but it is this truncated sort of presentation of history, that is proudly associated with multiculturalism, that eventually helped to inspire that girl to refuse to say the Pledge of Allegiance, and her parents to "understand her personal choice." If we get this sort of history from someone like Hirsch, should we suppose that a dedicated multiculturalist, who explicitly rejects the systematic study of history, would do any better?

Here is another example of multiculturalism in action. A fellow student who was training to be a social studies teacher, told me that she intended to teach 'the truth,' rather than American 'myths' to her pupils. She was going to make sure that her pupils knew that George Washington never chopped down the cherry tree, that Thomas Jefferson merely took credit for the Declaration of Independence because someone else actually wrote it (i.e., an evil, upper class white guy takes advantage of poor working stiff),[180] and that we should belittle, or expunge, Benjamin Franklin's contributions to America, because Franklin was a 'womanizer'. Multiculturalism in practice is not the multiculturalism of the ivory tower and political rubber chicken circuit.

That brings us to another point that we can extrapolate from the "don't bother first graders with political details" comment above. Have you noticed that a variety of teaching reform techniques, including multiculturalism, seem designed for a college discussion class and seem to assume that the pupils are not products of a dumbed-down curriculum but are informed, thoughtful, and academically inclined, despite the fact that we frown upon teaching facts? Have you also noticed that they generally recommend these same techniques for kids in *all* the lower grades, even those who have not yet developed the capacity for true rational thought? Since young kids usually just remember ideas

---

180 What she apparently mistook to be a hired ghostwriter was probably George Mason, another Virginian, who had published a Declaration of Rights for the Virginia legislature just weeks before Jefferson published the United States Declaration of Independence, using very similar words.

told to them by adults, without understanding them, for these kids the "discussion" can be considered indoctrination. We can see this in Singer's ideal of getting away from teaching through the lecture mode (Item 7). I will bring this point up again in the chapter about teaching science. For instance, Singer achieved his epiphany with his college students. This is not to say that high school pupils might not have made the same complaints, but the sorts of leaps of intuition that educationists assume children will make, seem to be based on an assumption that Hirsch's culturally literate America exists by osmosis. Somehow telling first graders about what Cortés was *really* like assumes that they already knew the other facts, and we are now merely setting the record straight.

The problem is that if we do not teach a thing, chances are good that pupils will not learn the thing. What we are left with is raising millions of kids to hate whites, though most of them are white. This strange 'ideal' pushes its way through the kids' experience with their friends and neighbors. The friends and neighbors may be normally wonderful folks, but since no one is perfect, the kids see an occasional bad deed, hypocrisy, lie, or act made out of a bad mood. (I believe that the chances of witnessing such a thing are increasing with time, too, since we have been teaching selfishness as a virtue for so long.) Regardless, a steady diet of "white guys are invariably bad" convinces many kids of the multiculturalist dream, to "reconstruct the culture" in a deformed and ugly image. The result would not be recognizable to Norman Rockwell.

This "in their own image" idea brings us to yet another point. If we can no longer recognize and celebrate the major influences to our common culture, then whose images do we use? If Western Civilization, with its explicitly recognized, multiple influences from dozens of very different European countries, the Near East, Asia, Moorish Africa, Latin America, and the rest of the world for that matter, is not multicultural enough, then which other one do we choose? Which minority, of the literally thousands represented in America will come into the ascendancy? Will we have a different '-centrism' for every individual American based on individual heritage, requiring schools to teach thousands of different victim-oriented variations of history? Or is dumping on white guys enough? Isn't it odd that America and Europe are the immigration destinations of choice for the rest of the world, despite the fact that white guys are 'always' repressive? Can any other nation of modern times anywhere come even remotely close to matching America's record as a "dream" to be attained? The Islam city of Mecca probably comes close, at least for Muslims, but then the pilgrims all go home again. Emigrants come to America intending to stay. Besides, why are all of those emigrants leaving their home lands where they are in the majority to come here as minority immigrants? It may be because America has always been a place seen as better than wherever the immigrants came from? Of course 'better' is not always perfect, but it is better. All of those immigrants brought their cultures with them. They could hardly help that. Yet they come, and continue to come, seeking for freedom and opportunity. With effort and perseverance they find it, too.

The schools should not be used to 'reconstruct' history. We should use schools to *teach* history, and to perpetuate what is essentially good with America by teaching kids to be proud to be American. If we have to choose what to teach because we cannot teach everything, we should teach patriotism and national pride because all of us made America what it is.

Why are we doing the kinds of self-defeating things described above? Among the strongest reasons mentioned is the historical fact of segregation, and worse, in America. As stated previously, the various *des*egregation and integration strategies gained momentum because of our collective conviction that racism is bad, reinforced when we saw undeniable evidence of it on TV in the early 1960s. The stated goals of the desegregation and integration-of-schools movements are to overcome the clear achievement deficits of many minority pupils and to develop positive interracial contacts among kids. As political ideals, how can we argue with that? Unfortunately the current atmosphere of animosity and distrust between some minority communities and the 'dominant culture' is fostered and maintained by the very policies that we advertised as necessary to achieve harmony. Ironically, we designed these divisive policies with the deep involvement of the same minority members who called for equity.

I will try to avoid the problems with the welfare system and the so-called 'entitlement mentality' which is produced as much as possible, but education policy alone clearly cannot fix all of American society's problems. That education is no panacea is largely true, though it could do much to alleviate our social problems, and to move toward the normalization of academic results, as we see in Japan.[181] For example, an

---

181 White, 1987.

intelligent, and natural, form of desegregation, which is seamlessly possible in public schools, would go far to get us moving forward again.

This is America. America was founded on the principle that everyone is entitled to live his life according to his own needs and abilities. Among the few things that America traditionally asks of its citizens in return, and those who would become its citizens, is that they contribute to the common good: "Ask not what your country can do for you, . . . etc."[182] This means that each of us must work to share the burdens of citizenship as we provide for our individual families. Notice that there is a balance between individual needs and social responsibility implicit in that statement. This tradition is developed and maintained in large part by what we teach kids at home and in school. Furthermore, what we teach in school is often (or should be) a variation of what we teach at home, and vice versa. Since we expect our schools to reinforce our common values to our kids, the kids learn values at home and in school that they then teach to their kids. It is no coincidence that our system is falling apart at just the time when our schools and politicians are emphasizing individual selfishness in the guise of individual rights, multiculturalism and group segregation in the guise of freedom, and Special education that defines *all* people based on the handicaps of a few (see the next chapter). We should strongly reemphasize the idea of the greatest good for the greatest number if America is not to disintegrate and relinquish leadership in the world.

However, many people feel disconnected from America's traditions. We now sometimes teach that there are no "American" traditions at all, although some also teach that *Amerika* insists that immigrants strip ethnicity off at the border crossing. The feeling is that the 'Melting Pot' imagery is invalid as we move away from white (European ancestry) society. People forget that there is considerable diversity in Europeans and that it sometimes took quite a long time for each of the various European nationalities to integrate themselves into America precisely because of those differences and animosities carried over from the supposedly homogeneous 'old country/continent'. These animosities diminished only as each immigrant nationality accepted local ways of doing things while influencing local customs as they assimilated into the Melting Pot, and were perceived by the earlier arrivals as not so different

---

182 How did this phrase come to imply a socialist style government? Could the rise of the Great Society have anything to do with it, with its emphasis on services provided for a helpless populace?

after all. It also seems significant that Europeans in America were melding into a united nation for 200 years before the idea took hold in Europe.

Each newly arrived ethnic group becomes the 'minority', even if they are white, until its members learn to become American. Under the influence of revisionist histories people choose to forget, or to resent, that the influence and amalgamation of European thinking, which is greatly influenced by oriental, including Arabic, philosophy is what led America to its dominant place in history. It is precisely that place in history, and the economic opportunity that comes with dominance, that still convinces people to come here. Once, when Rome was the superpower, all roads led to Rome. Now most roads seem to lead here. Besides, no law I know mandates that immigrants relinquish all old-world traditions at our borders. Quite to the contrary, even our Constitution, including the Bill of Rights, mandates that citizens are left largely alone.

Integration is a two-way proposition, however, since integration also changes the group that accepts a newcomer, and the newcomer must be willing substantially to join the resident group and abide by its ways, or the group will never completely accept him. Because both the accepting majority and the applicant minority resist full integration, since neither group is eager to change their ways, some groups have had considerable difficulty blending into the American population despite long residency.

We distinguish blacks from many others as to difficulty of integration in at least three significant ways. The first way, of course, is skin color and its associated other physical characteristics. The second way is that while most immigrants come here hopefully and eagerly, many blacks were originally brought here against their will. More recently, however, the fact that the 'boat people', including many blacks, have been willing to risk their lives in unseaworthy craft to get to our shores shows that there is 'something' here that they now want desperately. Finally, the achievement of blacks in school, and afterwards, has been poorer on average than other groups. [I might add a fourth way; the adamant refusal to fit in by some of the most vocal 'community leaders' and fringe groups, despite a growing acceptance by the 'dominant culture', but I will not since I would be immediately subject to charges of recognizing reality and called a racist for my trouble.]

The first 'problem' is relieved to some extent by intermarriage, though it will take a long time, if ever, before it disappears. Thinking of a more complete acceptance than marriage is difficult, but I should note that interracial marriage is still widely controversial and causes animosities to the general idea of integration, from both sides, whatever the races or ethnic groups involved. We cannot change or deny the second problem, the historical fact of American slavery, but it is an emotional barrier that blacks must cross themselves. Even now we often mention slavery, which ended in the mid 1860s, as a reason blacks should get special treatment today. Nevertheless, we can find much more recent examples of *de facto* slavery, even involving my own family (in Stalin's USSR and Hitler's Reich) and perhaps in yours, than in the American black experience. Black-on-black slavery is still a widespread problem in Africa, however. On the other hand, the fact of continued segregation despite emancipation must be considered. Yet if everyone's stated goal of integration is ever to become a reality, we would all do well to put these emotionally charged facts behind us and emphasize our similarities, rather than our differences. There is little chance that we will ever see each other as equals otherwise. We must all learn from the past, but living in the past has rarely proved helpful.

This brings us to the third way that blacks are distinguished today, lower average achievement, in school and in the workplace, than other racial groups. The notion that this result is caused exclusively by prejudice is, of course, a principal reason for ongoing black anger and resentment of American culture and has undoubtedly contributed to the idea of afrocentrism. This anger is based on the premise of indistinguishable potential among racial groups (everyone is the same as everyone else) coupled with undeniable prejudice (Those others—Not like us) that resulted in a diminished set of opportunities for blacks. If we accept the ideas that there are no important differences in the average capabilities between blacks and others, then there is no defensible reason for the position blacks often hold near the bottom of our society. The problem is that we have not yet proven the average intellectual equality of blacks. What evidence there is has been forthrightly developed by Thomas Sowell, a black academic. Others give many reasons for the disparity of academic accomplishment, none of which can be fully explored, however, unless all black pupils make a concerted effort to improve their achievement. Remember, achievement = capability + effort. Achievement is not a birthright, it is earned.

Of course, obscure academics are not the only people to have noticed this. What is probably the single best example of this strange failure of Progressive and liberal thinkers to acknowledge reality occurred in late May 2004. During a speech celebrating the 50th anniversary of the U.S. Supreme Court's Brown vs. Board of Education decision, which acknowledged that the practice of 'separate but equal' educations for whites and blacks is unjust and unconstitutional, Bill Cosby, a very well-known and widely beloved black actor and comedian, found himself embroiled in a strange controversy. In his speech which he, as a well-known philanthropist, was invited to make, he "shocked" his audience by stating the obvious making essentially the same points that I am making here, and was rewarded for his comments by the usual knee-jerk commentary of the Progressive community. There were even suggestions that Cosby may, in fact, be a closet anti-black racist. 'Thoughtful' Progressives and black politicians allowed that Cosby was "probably" not a racist, but concluded that he has "lost touch with the black experience," despite the decades he has spent in community service projects and the money and time he has thrown away on Progressive ideas trying to improve conditions of blacks in this country and elsewhere. What Cosby was apparently reacting to, was the sense that he is beating his head against a wall, trying to change a community culture that refuses to acknowledge its own problems, but is determined to remain as adolescent and self-centered as modern politics will allow, by blaming others for their own faults.

For instance, many black leaders and parents tell black kids, and the kids then tell each other, that they should not even try to succeed in the 'white world', because there are just too many obstacles for them to overcome. One result of this sort of advice is that black kids pressure their peers who are trying, to stop "acting white."

Based on what we know about black politics today, this sort of reaction should not be at all surprising. It is quite common, after all. But what does surprise me is the concurrence of the traditionally very strongly religious black culture, both Christian and other, with virtually every edict of Progressive thought and politics, despite the bedrock assumption of Progressivism of the stupidity and repressiveness of religion in general. One would have thought that black church/mosque goers would have noticed the incompatibility of these assumptions and the differences in life before and after the advent of the Progressive revolution, and cried foul.

We can see this sort of negative self-pressure in other ways, too. Public television and other venues frequently produce documentary-type shows about many different groups. These shows are usually, I presume, produced specifically by members of the groups depicted. This would mean that Irishmen produce programs about the Irish experience in America, Jews produce shows about the Jewish experience in America, blacks produce shows about the black experience in America, and so on. If the producer is not necessarily 'of the blood', then the show is probably at least based on a book about the experience by someone who is. If you watch these shows, you may notice a very great difference in tone. While all of the shows explain that groups' early hard times in the New World, including general and even institutional prejudice arrayed against them, most concentrate on their successes despite the hard work and extended periods required for the group to 'make it'. Most of the shows have an upbeat tone born of pride in overcoming adversity. Often there is a 'Horatio Alger' type of story embedded within the wider story. You know the kind of thing: Local immigrant boy springs from humble beginnings to own most of the known universe, or becomes president of this or that. This proud identification with success is not necessarily true of the 'black' shows, however. Most of the ones I have seen never seem to get past the message that life is impossible because of what others have done to 'us'.

No educational policy or technique can overcome hurdles like that. Furthermore, a social policy that actively encourages such thinking can be called counterproductive. Under these conditions they doom even well-meaning governmental policies to failure, especially if the governmental policies support the depressing sentiment by assuming that permanent assistance is necessary. Yet, since a great deal of educational policy is predicated on the notion that everyone is the same as everyone else, it seems that it is in everyone's interest, including the blacks themselves, to find out why there is an 'achievement gap'.

One of two things will occur if they allow us to try. The first is that blacks will prove themselves on a par with the rest of society, or perhaps even higher. I suspect that blacks would not have a problem accepting this result. If this happens then we can move toward a future that is as productive as the past. I do not mean to belittle the challenges that would arise in a transition of this sort, especially in overcoming the negative inertia of the past several decades of black rhetoric, but stability would eventually return. The other possible outcome is that on average, blacks would not be found equal to other groups. Most blacks must also accept this outcome, as whites have apparently accepted their secondary placement to Asians in scholastic achievement, for any subsequent progress to occur. While acceptance is unlikely in the current climate, a logical interim solution might be to equate *all* people, regardless of race, based on their tested intelligence and to note that there are many whites, Asians, Hispanics and others, who fall within the same tested ranges. In fact, based on their status as the 'majority', there are as many, or more, white poor people as black poor people. Every one of these people is subject to the same economic pressure exacerbated by high taxes and rising prices. We are truly 'all in it together'.

Would an unequal intellectual result mean that we doom every black kid to a life in a dumpster while every white kid immediately moves into a Park Avenue penthouse? Of course not. People of all capabilities would get and keep jobs appropriate to their capabilities and achievement, as they are already doing. We must drop the divisive, diversity labels we currently use and insist on the inclusive label of "American" (without modifiers or hyphenations) and act as if we mean it. If we did that, then either tested result makes little real difference for the society. For instance, politicians whose ancestry happens to be Italian, are not considered to be Italian community leaders. They are thought of simply as community leaders. "The various civil rights bills, and the acceptance of the idea of equal opportunity by most 'dominant culture' Americans have already largely removed the only other real obstacles to full integration.

Aside: Perhaps the first step that we could take to remove the divisiveness from our everyday educational thinking is to stop *disaggregating* educational statistics. Disaggregating refers to reporting results by reference to each ethnic group. That is, 'white' (or worse, "white, non-Hispanic") kids earned this score on average, 'Polynesian, non-Asian kids earned this, and so forth. These categories are divisive precisely because they divide us. Minority 'leaders' want these categories because they think that by using the categories there will always be a way to find fault and demand reparations or special treatment, of the dominant culture (and because they would not have a job otherwise), but most of us are sick of them. We are sick of them, or we are confused by them, because each of us can legitimately check more than one category. Most of us are already multicultural by heritage but prefer to be called simply "American," even if we are proud of our pre-American heritage and active in that ethnic community's life.

Ironically, my Ed school Multiculturalism professor gave our class a handout, part of which detailed the labels that various folks prefer being called, in response to a 1995 U.S. Department of Labor questionnaire. Here it is (Note: Asians were not included in this survey.):

Black	%	American Indian	%	Hispanic	%	White	%
Black	44.2	American Indian	49.8	Hispanic	57.9	White	61.7
African-American	28.1	Native-American	37.4	Of Spanish origin	12.3	Caucasian	16.5
Afro-American	12.1	Alaskan native	3.5	Latino	11.7	Anglo	1.0
Negro	3.3	Some other term	3.7	Some other term	7.9	Some other term	2.0
Colored	1.1	No preference	5.7	No preference	10.2	No preference	16.5
No preference	9.1						

Isn't it odd that in every case, the majority of Americans preferred not to be called a hyphenated American? We can assume that "no preference" means that they want to be known simply as 'Americans'. In fact, if these were the results of elections, the pundits would say that we have landslide defeats for hyphenation, yet political correctness demands that we do it anyway? That's democracy the Progressive way.

I have nothing to prove the next thought, but it may be that the changing fashion of monikers may be nothing other than a check of political correctness. When a particular way of identifying a group becomes too common and universally accepted (as labeling "Negroes" changed from "colored" to "black"), it can no longer be used to distinguish political friends from enemies and neutrals. Nor can *not* using the newly updated appellation be used as an excuse for political intimidation.

Perhaps that is an unworthy thought. Perhaps not.

However, getting back to sane educational policy, we must recognize that our society cannot maintain itself if significant portions of our citizenry see themselves as unwanted. We do this *to* them whenever someone says, "You cannot get a *good* job without college." Whatever else we do, we must stop demeaning the occupational choices to which average and low intelligence limits some people, of whatever race. We permit the genuine destruction of self-esteem when we insist that any job that does not require a college education is worthless.

Ironically the people who are the most vocal in demanding desegregation and integration (while insisting on disaggregation and racial preferences) are often those who demand college for everyone. They should stop that. College for everyone has the effect of qualifying unqualified people to do jobs that can significantly affect our lives, such as counselors and others, who then help us make personal decisions, such as lawyers, and politicians, doctors, and especially educrats, mental health professionals, and social workers. It is even possible that some unqualified people become education professors (but we cannot be sure of that because the mountain of evidence can still be ignored with impunity).

America needs its bakers, truck drivers, mechanics, secretaries, plumbers, store clerks, carpenters, and laborers of every description. The nation would fall just as surely without the contribution of these people as it would under an overwhelming invasion. None of these jobs require college although, ironically, advancement in many trades requires an understanding of an increased body of job-specific knowledge (facts and ideas). This is ironic because the supposedly lowly trades require licenses, based upon fact-based credentials, for permission to practice the trade. This is done due to the recognition that allowing anyone to become, for instance, a master plumber, despite ignorance and lack of experience is not a good idea for the trade or for their customers. Yet many insist that we allow anyone to enter, and even graduate from, college regardless of qualifications. I have even heard an argument in which someone angrily expressed outrage that a "seriously retarded" man was not allowed to graduate from college, since it was his right to develop his self-esteem. Who is smarter here, the tradesmen who require specific knowledge and experience for advancement, or the Progressive intellectuals who cannot find the Atlantic Ocean on a map, but run our education establishment? If we again see these noncollege jobs as worthy of a life's work and not merely something to settle for after we have flunked out of college, and if the jobs could give families a living wage again as they could in the past (before the War on Poverty, etc., helped increase the have–have-not distance), our kids can then be prepared to face life proudly and contentedly, by doing something they can do and hopefully enjoy doing, and we can begin to act like a united nation again.

The schools should be at the forefront of insisting that all of our kids get the best and most appropriate fact-based education and/or training possible. In the end, if we do not rediscover the way to reintegrate our various groups. America may fall, to the detriment of *all*.

Biculturalism: A Chip Off the Old Block

I promised an example of another "-centric" groups' attempt to reform America. Here it is.

Toward the end of my class in multiculturalism, they required us to make a no-more-than-five-minute presentation detailing some aspect of the theology. We were assigned a topic, at random I assume, from a handout that the professor gave us titled, 'Glossary of Terms: Multicultural Awareness'. The terms included such things as abuse, assimilation, curriculum, instruction, de jure segregation, ethnocentrism, melting pot, stereotype, and a dozen or two more. It was never explained why words such as 'abuse' and 'instruction' belonged in a glossary specific to multicultural awareness, however.

Incidentally, the professor also graded this class in a way that modeled 'appropriate' grading practice. Although we were now within three or four months of being college graduates and fully qualified and certified professional educators (and presumably, adults), and were training to teach near-adults at the secondary level, he awarded us colorful stickers that said things like, "Awesome" and "Out' a sight" as rewards for work. They were just like the 'bluebird' stickers that my second grade teacher used. Also, everybody got these bluebirds whether the 'work' was good or not. For instance, one presenter defined "Pedagogic Style" as "Pedantic formality, a narrow often ostentatious concern for book learning and formal rules," and still got his bluebird although pedagogic style merely means teaching, or instructional style and does not imply any style in particular. The presenter was absolutely wrong in his facts but politically correct in ridiculing learning itself. No one, least of all the professor, corrected his mistake. I guess no one wanted to be judgmental.

My assigned topic was 'bicultural education' and I got a 'bluebird' too, although I stood up and said, in effect, that despite the respectable face presented for public viewing, in practice bicultural education, like multiculturalism generally, is a duplicitous sham that we should erase from our collective memory.

We see the 'respectable face' that bicultural education uses to address the world, however, in its definition. "The purpose of bicultural education," they tell us, "is to produce learners who have competencies in, two different cultures." How can we argue with that? This is a restatement of the justification for learning French or Spanish, etc., that

I heard as a kid, since bicultural education is most often used with its first cousin, bilingual education.

Although typically the research required to complete this Glossary of Terms assignment could consist of nothing more than a quick look into a dictionary, I went to the library to discover what competent researchers thought of my topic. I quickly found a review of literature published in 1984 by Margaret Gibson.[182a] Nineteen eighty-four sounds like an old review, according to our current standard of change-every-thing-twice-a-day-before-it-gets-obsolete, but I chose this review because it *was* a review and therefore covered much ground. Also, it was written at the time that bicultural education was 'getting big'. I thought it would be interesting to see what contemporary researchers thought of bicultural education in its formative years.

Gibson identified five approaches to multicultural education and her review covered all five. I got my 'respectable' definition of bicultural education from this article as well. Her description of bicultural education continues thus:

> Many if not all of these programs . . . seek to foster and maintain pride in the native culture, to develop a fuller understanding of one's heritage and traditions, to strengthen identity, to increase motivation and academic success, to reduce prejudice and discrimination, to increase educational opportunities and social justice.

The formal, academic presentation of bicultural education is described as consisting of several assumptions. They are:

Assumptions regarding values:

1. One's native culture (including language) ought to be maintained and preserved.
2. The mainstream culture (if different than the native culture) ought to be acquired as an alternative or second culture.

182a Originally published as Gibson, M. A. "Approaches in Multicultural Education in the United States: Some Concepts and Assumptions," *Anthropology & Education Quarterly*, Vol. 7, No. 4 (Nov. 1976): 7–8. The version that appears here was edited and abridged, and subsequently republished as Gibson, M. A. "Approaches to Multicultural Education in the United States: Some Concepts and Assumptions," in *Anthropology & Education Quarterly*, Vol. 15, No. 1 (Apr. 1984): 94–120. © 1976, 1984 by American Anthropological Association. Used with permission.

3. Students whose native culture is the mainstream culture also will profit from the acquisition of competencies in a second culture.

Assumptions regarding strategies:

1. Just as it is possible to provide instruction in two languages, so too, it is possible to provide instruction in two cultures.
2. Bicultural education is a strategy for providing instruction in two cultures.
3. Bicultural education, as an approach to formal instruction, parallels and is adapted from the methods and techniques of bilingual education.

Assumptions regarding outcomes:

1. Bicultural education will enhance a sudent's ability, to function in both the native culture and the mainstream culture.
2. Competencies in a second culture will be acquired without rejection of the student's native culture.
3. Bicultural education will lead ultimately to full participation for non-mainstream and mainstream youth alike in the socioeconomic opportunities that this nation offers.

Assumptions regarding target population:

1. Bicultural education is a reciprocal process.
2. If bicultural education were recommended only for those students whose mother tongue is other than English it would collapse into a compensatory program for the culturally different.
3. Therefore, bicultural education is aimed, at least ideally, at all students; all students will benefit from competencies in two cultures.

In reading this technical article I got the impression that Gibson was largely sympathetic to the stated goals and assumptions of bicultural, and multicultural, education. Nevertheless, she concluded that,

. . . the literature on multicultural education lacks clarity with regards to key concepts and abounds with untested and sometimes unsupportable assumptions regarding goals, strategies and outcomes.

"Lacks clarity." "Untested." "Unsupportable." This is a very genteel way of saying that the whole thing is a fuzzy-minded and speculative crock. Multiculturalists generally and biculturalists specifically, like the good Progressive thinkers that they are, merely present their convictions as fact, and move ahead in the face of evidence that their ideas will not accomplish what they say it will.

Some of the reasons for this can be inferred from the assumptions above. I cannot argue with the idea that immigrants should remember where they came from, but when did it become the host country's duty to preserve the immigrants' native culture? Has any other nation in the history of the world ever done, or even considered, doing that? For instance, my parents were very proudly Ukrainian. Could you imagine my school system assuming a parents' responsibility and hiring someone to teach me to be Ukrainian, Norwegian, Thai, or Bantu? Me neither. This idea is so nutty that I am sure that it never occurred to my parents, and it would never have occurred to any other reasonable person in the 1950s. No one that is, unless they had a political agenda in mind. Which brings us to the *practice* of bicultural education.

To discover the way that our educational system addressed bicultural education, I found a report by The Little Hoover Commission, a California think-tank that is frequently asked to research topics for members of the California government, including the Governor. Report #122, entitled *A Chance to Succeed: Providing English Learners with Supportive Education,* was released in 1993. (Little Hoover Commission, July 1993, *A Chance to Succeed: Providing English Learners with Supportive Education.* Sacramento, CA. pp. 2 and 7. My comments are in brackets.)

Dear Governor and Members of the State Legislature:
More than one million children in California today do not speak English well enough to understand what is going on in a classroom—and the number is growing daily at a rate that far exceeds overall school population growth.

[How can that be? Are even native English-speaking kids falling behind grade expectations in their use of the language?]

For almost two decades, the State Department of Education has perpetuated the myth that language and academic needs of these students could be met if all schools adopted a single program approach and if adequate resources were committed to teaching English learners.

[One-size-fits-all programs address *all* pupil's individual needs, so long as you throw enough money at it. Recall again the achievements of one-room schoolhouses with essentially no resources.]

The result of the Department's single minded pursuit of the method known as native-language instruction has been divisive, wasteful, and un-productive.

[During this time California sank from one of the best States academically to tied for last, with Louisiana.]

Students, trapped in the middle of a political and academic tug-of-war, have suffered the brunt of this failed policy direction.

["It's for the children".]

And from the Executive summary:

For the better part of two decades, bi-lingual education programs—in California and elsewhere—have been as much a problem as a solution for the education of children who come to school speaking little or no English.

But what has begun as a well-intentioned and urgently needed ef-fort—to provide teaching appropriate to the needs of children who had too often been neglected—calcified into a self-serving machine that paid less and less attention to the real children it was supposed to serve. Frequently it became an ideologically based program more concerned with the intrinsic virtues of bilinguilism and biculturalism—and with keeping children indefinitely in those programs—than with its supposed mission: getting them into the English-speaking mainstream as quickly and efficiently as possible.

Not surprisingly, the results have often been precisely opposite [I'm glad I'm not the first to notice] to what had been intended—locking students into separate programs for years on end. And sometimes they run to the absurd: Native English speakers who, because they tested poorly and had Hispanic names, were placed in bilingual classes con-ducted largely in Spanish; children from Chinese and Russian families who were assigned to the programs but who, since no classes in their language were available, ended up in Spanish bilingual class. [So much for the "needs" of the pupils.]

California's experience is a case in point. By 2000, after California had abandoned its failed experiment, parents, and the kids themselves, were pleased to see that kids taught exclusively in English became truly bilingual[183] while those trained to biculturalist standards were merely illiterate in two languages.

Some Theory (Ed School Professors Love This Stuff)

To show some of the ideological and theoretical underpinnings of multiculturalism, I will acquaint you with the book *Cultural Politics & Education,* by Michael Apple. Apple is the John Bascom Professor of Curriculum and Instruction and Educational Policy Studies at the University of Wisconsin, Madison. I read this book as a requirement to a graduate level course that I took before I left my Ed school alma mater. The jacket blurbs on the back cover include these items from some of Progressive education's heavy hitters. Paulo Friere, a Brazilian educationist, calls Apple a "distinguished scholar . . . involved in the struggle to build a critical and democratic education." We already know that "critical and democratic" actually means "Marxist and Anarchist" (see footnote 116). Geoff Whitty, Karl Mannheim Professor of Sociology of Education, University of London says, "Apple draws upon contemporary social theory to show how education policy relates to broader social issues." And Maxine Greene, Teachers College, Columbia University says, ". . . he sharpens and further develops his insistence that we consider 'educational reform' within a carefully wrought social context . . ." His context is a world from which he sees both major American political parties as 'right-wing.' Finally, Carlos Alberto Torres, Professor and Director of the Latin American Center, UCLA, tells us that the book is a ". . . contribution to our understanding of the complex interactions between culture and power in education."

Apple's primary theme is that the American "main group" invariably attempts to subjugate and repress the peace-loving natures of people at the lower end of the human spectrum. Apple is also trying to forge an alliance with every category of people who could possibly have the slightest beef with the main group.

---

183 Learned and spoke the native language at home.

To develop his primary theme, Apple tells us that the only way to achieve a society that is fair and equitable for all, is to teach the repressive political history of "winners and losers" in the society. His secondary themes are that the neo-liberals are now interested in turning the schools over to the market forces that govern trade and that the neo-conservatives are interested in what he says is a dangerous return to government control of morality. Apple also says that these two groups have recently entered an alliance that will result in continuing repression of democracy and make the pursuit of social equity more difficult; he recommends that we defend, and even extend, "progressive gains."

His reasoning is a classic example of a system that starts with false assumptions and by that creates a logical image of life that makes little sense when evaluated against reality. Unfortunately, a great deal of social and educational policy written in the past forty years or so, is based on these same faulty assumptions.

One thing we can say for Apple is that he hangs his biases out for all to see. He is for the little guy, and against 'the state'. Of course, since he rejects the current thinking of both political parties, whose combined ideas generally encompass the vast majority of our citizens, the 'little guy' turns out to be the economic low end of our society. Apple is a Marxist and a Communist who tries to unite the downtrodden masses to rise against the forces of the 'main group' and its unreasonable insistence on 'property rights'. Of course Apple is also against anyone who comes to agree with the main group. He does not see that American society is an amalgam of many diverse groups, and that each has contributed to our culture. In reading this book, I got the impression that for Apple, apparently once we have joined the 'main group' we become part of a kind of cultural Velveeta, fully homogenized with no further individuality. Being more than the sum of its parts is an idea unfamiliar to Apple. Only those still outside the main group are real. On the other hand he argues for a national common sense. Can he have it both ways?

You may have noticed that Apple is not a multiculturalist in the sense that most people would recognize. For instance, he does not specifically argue for the legitimacy of immigrant cultures or other-than-dominant-culture ways of doing things. Apple's orientation is mainly the view from the bottom of the economic ladder without reference to parental heritage, but his arguments are similar to those used by many more traditional multiculturalists.

Unfortunately, Apple's common sense does not make sense and he cannot, or will not, see his own contradictions. For example, he spends a great deal of time complaining that teaching either the practicalities of the working world (i.e., life-adjustment instruction), or traditional subjects for that matter, to pupils is repressive, unjust and racist. He says that this is especially true regarding those who will eventually be blue collar workers. Apple also says the government fiscal policies are hurting poor people. Then he proclaims that the only just way for our society to act, is to bring new taxes and establish a new bureaucracy to insure that we train paid workers in the basic worker needs including the gamut of social services, and, at long last, the sorts of things we would expect of a public school education.

We have to wonder, however, why it would not be wise to begin in grammar school, to teach the knowledge that will prepare pupils for a high school diploma and to continue that instruction through graduation? If we do this, maybe our graduates would then be far more likely to be self-sufficient and would require far fewer social services. Nope. The first 18 years of your life should be spent hearing how someone has done you wrong. Then, since no one has yet taught these working adults grammar and high school level knowledge by the time they have completed high school, the only "just" course of action would be to build another expensive bureaucracy to meet the educational needs of paid workers after they reach adulthood. Those needs of workers are, not surprisingly, precisely the things that Apple refuses to teach in grammar and high school: basic language and math, self-discipline, a basic understanding about how the world and life work (history, science), a realization that life gets easier if we cooperate with each other (civics in a patriotic mold), and an understanding that poor individual choices will affect their lives (e.g., having babies alone, refusing to learn to read and write [morals aiming at eventual wisdom]). For some, an understanding of mechanics and/or electronics will be useful. Some may need basic business skills (typing, bookkeeping, etc.) and/or an understanding of basic business precepts (i.e., supply/demand and if it costs more to make it, you must charge more when you sell it), etc., etc.

We can call all the things that Apple hates, along with the practice of new habits, like lifelong learning, as the 'work ethic'. Instilling some of these ideas and habits into kids at an early age would also make the teacher's job much easier and more enjoyable since teachers could then

do the job that they presumably love doing (teaching) rather than playing the policeman or social worker. Not for Apple though. All this work
ethic stuff sounds too much like the powerful elite trying to keep the
little guy in his place. Of course, since the powerful and elite in America
often rise from the lower classes, and became powerful and elite despite
very humble beginnings by working hard, they realize that working hard
is a way to rise and to stay on top. So the powerful and elite also teach
these things to their own kids, hoping, as most parents do, that their
kids will be successful too. So if public educators do not teach it to all
kids, and the only kids to learn a work ethic are the kids of the powerful
elite, guess who has the better chance of being the powerful elite of
the future?

Trying to wind my way through Apple's pretzel-like logic was quite
a challenge, but then Apple warned us he would make it so (p. 20):

> I'm less interested in arcane academic distinctions or the mobility politics
> within the academy that makes such distinctions 'important', [concern
> over neo- and post-modern interpretations of things, as opposed to the
> genuinely historical] than I am in understanding the limits and possibilit-
> ies of critical actions surrounding cultural politics and education.

In other words, rational discourse is irrelevant, sticking-it-to the 'big
guy' is all that matters. Of course, sticking it to the big guy backfires
(since to abide by all of our government regulations or to pay massive
legal judgments and stay in business and provide employment for the
little guy), we oblige the big guy to raise his prices, fueling inflation
and ultimately hurting the little guy most of all.

That result is no impediment to Progressive leaders though. It only
gives them a spate of new problems to blame on someone.

Apple's central assumption is his absolute refusal to acknowledge
that there are differences in the ability or interests of pupils. He places
the blame for everything that he says is wrong with our society on
differential access to power and resources.

What may be another of his central assumptions is found in his
use of the words 'democracy' and 'democratic'. For most of us these
words connote 'government by the will of the people' and 'the majority
rules'. Since Apple thinks that both American political parties are right-
wing, he sees a shift in political outlooks among the American people
but cannot accept the notion that most people may have had enough

of 'Progressive gains' that destroy whatever chances their children may have at occupational competence and the pursuit of happiness (not to mention that the national debt had reached the thirteen figure stage by the middle 1990s). For most of us *democracy* means some variation on 'we vote and the majority decides on the rules'. For Apple, democratic means each of us makes our own rules (so long as we agree with Apple). He uses the word 'democracy' only in reference to critical (of the norm) thinking. Clearly, Apple also uses 'critical' in the sense of complaining rather than evaluating, and expects kids to learn how to find fault with traditional American thinking—because it does not adhere to Marxist ideology. In this Apple rejects the traditional notion of majority rule and insists that <u>his</u> way is the only just way. Reinterpretation, à la Berliner and Biddle, is the Progressive way. Apple states this quite explicitly. On page 21, Apple says, ". . . this is part of a conscious collective attempt to *name the world differently* (emphasis in the original), to positively refuse to accept dominant meanings, and to positively assert the possibility that it could be different." In other words, 'we don't want the world to be as it is, so we will act as if it is the way we want it to be'. In another interpretation, it means, 'dealing with reality unrealistically will force reality to conform to our unrealistic notions'. Of course, making social and educational policy based on this sort of conception of reality may justifiably be described as crossing the line into insanity.

Apple's corollary assumptions flow from his central assumptions. He may not have always used the words that I use, but I feel sure that this is what he means. The assumptions include, but are not limited to:

- A common culture in America is a myth, and even if it is not, it is a bad thing
- 'Democracy' means anarchy
- All perceived differences among humans are a result of prejudice [since everyone is the same as everyone else]
- Any attempt to categorize people [other than his own categories of course] is repressive
- Only unsuccessful people understand life
- Teaching traditional subjects is 'training', not 'education'
- Teachers must be 'socially critical' [Marxist] and the only legitimate curriculum contains little beyond education in 'democracy' [unrestricted individual choice, repression, and anarchy]

- Life/politics are very complex and do not reduce legitimately to 'grand narratives' [except his own version of course]
- Anybody who is in charge is necessarily evil [though *he* would be different, if put in charge]
- Corporations [the elite] have full control of their own destinies, and governmental rules do not influence policies or procedures

On occasion Apple does make some sense. When he is quietly trying to analyze what he dislikes in neo-liberalism, for instance, he states quite well that reducing schooling to a matter of market-like choices (e.g., vouchers, etc.) is not likely to solve very much [at least in a balanced society] and might segregate our society even more. He is quite right, and I agree that school vouchers would be a mistake. Vouchers would be a mistake, that is, unless we cannot bring reality back to our system another way. We may need more direct means to upgrade academic quality, such as vouchers or Charter schools, etc., to get the attention of a system that accepts Apple-like thinking as reasonable. However, my main problem with vouchers is the conviction that where government funding goes, strings will inevitably become attached. If government ideology embraces the Progressive agenda, as it has, even private schools that accept vouchers will inevitably become educationally corrupted. (I have already written that I have interviewed at least one private school principal who would not assure me that all of his ninth-graders could spell 'they' correctly.)

Apple also makes sense when he argues that there are things in the schools today that should be enhanced rather than changed. Yet my hope that he might start to listen to himself never lasts. The very things that he would save are precisely the things that reasonable people would quickly purge. Things like the self-defeating emphasis on 'woe is me'. In contrast, most of us would agree that we should strengthen the things he would purge. For instance academics <u>and</u> a Jeffersonian and Franklinian understanding that most kids will enter the work force immediately after high school, or even sooner, would lead most of us to expect schools to help kids develop job skills.

Apple says that he is very much *for* teachers. In one of his other rare lucid moments Apple says, and here I agree with him, that the attempts by some to blame all of the world's problems on teachers are a mistake. He says that we must look beyond the simple blame on one part of society for problems that affect everyone. (I say this because I agree with criticisms such as Sowell and Koerner level at education professors like Apple.)

Yet his lucidity never lasts. Apple argues that a personal sense of dependency is a good thing. He argues that falling standards, high drop-out rates, and illiteracy should not concern as unduly. He argues that the family is not and *should not* be considered a "... guardian of social stability," and on and on. According to Apple, teachers should be the arbiters of social norms. They should be the agents of "critical" thought regarding those norms and quietly subvert what the majority (and the pupils' parents) think they need, in favor of Apple's anti-majority vision. In this way we will achieve social justice and everyone will be equally rich.

Many educational professionals think this bureaucratic parent-sur-rogacy, in the form of all-day Kindergarten, Special education, child-centered teaching, etc., makes sense and expect teachers to agree. This raises a serious question: Would you let Apple or anyone taught by Apple, near your kids?

The short version of any evaluation of Apple's evidence has to include that his rejection of common social standards has taken him to analytical flights of fancy from which he loses sight of reality. Turning kids into whiny incompetents is not a parent's fondest dream. In the often cold, hard world of real life, kids need to prepare themselves for adulthood to the best of their abilities. Apple's vision of social homogeneity just does not, and cannot, exist. It even contradicts his own most ardently held ideal, the diversity of humans. People *are* different. Trying to shoehorn everyone into a mold of Apple's making is not any more possible than using the Puritan's mold. The natural diversity of humans is precisely why the American 'Melting Pot' works and 'ideal' or utopian visions invariably fail. Unfortunately Apple (very much like Gould) uses history only to say: 'See! These guys said bad things in the otherwise forgotten past. That proves that everyone is rotten; except me."

Another thing we can say about Apple is that he can sling an 'ism' with the best of them. His neo-this, and postmodern-that, possibly only makes sense to his buddies and himself.[184] However, for a self-proclaimed 'educator', he has very little to say about teaching. Also, many of his 'neo'-conceptions turn reality on its head. For instance, did you know

---

184 Apple is another example of Gelernter's 'intellectuals'.

that neo-liberals want a weak state while neo-conservatives want a strong one? I wonder if Al and Dubya knew that?

In one of the great schisms of intellectual preference (splitter vs. lumper), Apple aligns himself squarely with the splitters. He seems quite manic about it. No 'grand narratives' for him. Apple sees so many ghouls and demons that even the common sense of the majority is unacceptable.

Apple ignores the fact that a nation founded on the idea of 'united we stand, divided we fall', has a stake in preserving freedom. For him even nationhood is somehow evil. On page 15 he expresses shock and horror that our society, ". . . relies on *winning consent* [his italics] to the prevailing order, forming an ideological umbrella under which different groups who usually might not totally agree with each other can stand." Would you agree that is this a bad thing? To me this sounds quite inclusive, reasonable, and an excellent working definition of Melting Pot democracy. Moreover, it sounds like a way to preserve order and peace among the citizenry while explicitly accepting each other's warts and differences. For Apple, however, it is 'hegemonic'. Despite what else he says about why he uses the term hegemonic, which simply means 'pertaining to leadership', he seems to use it merely because it rhymes with demonic. As he also says, ". . . in some circles it makes people nervous."

Apple apparently cannot see any positive changes in the attitudes of American society over the years. Despite some notable bumps, the movement of American political philosophy is an incremental assimilation of various groups into the 'main groups'. Moreover, as time goes on, we Americans seem to have ever more difficulty with wild-eyed attempts at excluding groups. From the new immigrant's point of view, after a perfectly normal initial reluctance with new ideas and/or new people, individual members of each new group accept the mainstream way of doing things and prove that they too are 'just folks' ("When in Rome, you do as the Romans do.") In return, the only thing that the American mainstream eventually asks is that the newcomers join, be friendly, and work hard. For Apple, these homely attitudes are signs of conservatism, which he equates with elitist power politics.

The fact that the familiarization period for new immigrants has often taken all of a generation, and sometimes more, had not permanently bothered immigrants in the past. Coming from countries where they may have had no rights at all, most arrived with the deep conviction and hope that their own hard work and perseverance would result in their children living a life that they (the parents) could only dream of. Today, multiculturalists argue that everything must be in place at the border crossing, or we are guilty of injustice.

If there is a general movement to the right in America today, away from an Apple-like vision, it is merely a rebalancing movement back to the center. In the 1960s we took a giant skip or two to the left, and we are just now realizing that pie-in-the-sky idealism does not answer life's recurring questions. If there is a movement toward the political right, inspiring some to suggest solutions to educational problems based on market forces (e.g., vouchers) or religious convictions, etc., it could be that people are merely trying to rediscover, and attempt to use, the kinds of ideas that worked for them in other situations. These efforts will eventually sort themselves out and, in the process, maybe we will remember that despite differences, members of a functional and contented society identify with each other.

We have seen several versions of multiculturalism and we have seen that, no matter what reasonable face is presented to the world, the fundamental theology of multiculturalism is in reality no more than a political ploy to increase political power for one group or another at the expense of everyone else. The use of 'education' as the venus is a deceptive exercise since their immersion into these loving 'educational programs' invariably harms kids and the society. Unfortunately, if we immerse kids in these programs and indoctrinate them to dependence, they grow up thinking there is no better way.

If we are to indoctrinate kids to anything, and there is no question that any social instruction does that, then let it be that it is good to be an American, and that Americans of all creeds are all in it together.

Even 'traditional' social instruction teaches a vision of what life should be like. Realizing that, we must decide which common vision we would want our children to share. Do we prefer a bleak vision where everything is stacked against them and the only way out of their travail is either revolution or subjugation to an all-powerful, bureaucratic government that doles out 'benefits', along with unearned 'self-esteem' leavened by psychoactive drugs?

The various Communist experiments tried variations on this idea. They did not work.

Or would we rather have our kids grow up into a vision that tells them that everyone has access to whatever opportunities they can qualify for, but that their own effort will help to determine their own success? You may recognize this as the American experiment. This can work if it is allowed to.

Despite this ultimately reasonable view, the multiculturalist society does not seem to see the success stories in its own midst. For instance, how could the other-than-dominant-culture multiculturalist leaders (e.g., lawyers, politicians, business executives, small business owners, etc.) have gotten to their leadership positions if they did not have access to our educational system that prepared them for life in the fast lane? Cynics might say, however, "But look at all these others." True enough, not everybody makes it big. Yet if we simply count noses, and line them up according to income, we will find there are as many, or more, fully dominant-culture folks who are in the same economic boat as are members of minority groups. And the gap between the haves and have-nots is growing, in every group, because we have stopped teaching genuine thinking in favor of 'critical' indoctrination. For that we can thank multiculturalism.

I suppose that Booker T. Washington is now out of favor with multiculturalists generally, because his message to his fellow blacks was so reasonable sounding, since he recognized the essential truth that most reasonable people see:

> For my race, one of the dangers is that it may grow impatient and get upon its feet by artificial and superficial efforts rather than by the slower and surer process which means one step at a time through all the constructive grades of industry, mental and moral development and social development, which all races have had to follow that have become independent and strong.

This is much too reasonable and realistic (read, 'racist'), I guess.

Anarchy Means Never Having to Say You're Sorry

A somewhat more traditional multiculturalist is Joel Spring, from the State University of New York at New Paltz. Spring champions the cause of the American Indian and his method is scarcely less inflammatory, and perhaps just as uniculturalist, as Apple's. The primary theme of Spring's book, *Deculturalization and the Struggle for Equality* (also required reading), is very clearly that American culture is unrelentingly racist and has a long and continuing history of oppressive discrimination against anyone or any group that stands in its way. Spring seems to think that Americans generally favor the extermination or subjugation (deculturalization) of everyone else. On the other hand, a secondary theme of Spring's book is that while white Americans have tried their utmost to kill the spirit of dominated cultures everywhere, the dominated cultures have fought the good fight and are winning in their attempts to rise above hatred and subjugation to live in peace and harmony and multicultural bliss.

On the surface Spring's evidence, which consists of many examples of clearly racist statements and policy decisions, seems to support his main contention that white American society has conducted a determined and protracted campaign of subjugation and repression against everybody else. Yet many facts within his stated evidence plainly show that the single-minded racism that Spring assumes was not so single-minded at all. Still, there are enough examples in history to make his case seem valid, especially if his audience is not truly interested in the long-term lessons of history, but are merely interested in making an exaggerated political point.

Spring's biases are evident in almost every paragraph. For instance, even the chapter title for his opening chapter includes the words, ". . . Superiority of Anglo Americans." His point is that immigrants who arrived from England have dominated American culture and that 'Anglo' people are unrelentingly racist in everything that they do. For example on page 3; "Reflecting the attitudes of English colonists, the 'founding fathers' rejected the idea of a multicultural society and advocated the creation of a unified American culture." Spring is clearly attempting to use our current present-minded, history-ignorant attitudes to convince people that the recent ideas of multiculturalists were available and fully developed during the American colonial period, and would have been universally adopted had it not been for the repressive domination of the Anglos. Blessedly they were not.

Spring also uses the same sentence to imply, as Apple does, that, ". . . creation of a unified American culture" is somehow a bad thing and a racist idea as well. Yet, for me at least, it is difficult to see how unifying disparate groups into a proud and powerful nation that is interested in "justice for all" could be considered a reactionary and racist idea. Still, we have already seen many ideas in Progressive thought that do not stand up in the light of reality. Having said that, however, there is no question that we did not always pave the road to the Melting Pot with sugar and spice.

"Deculturalization" (in the title and elsewhere), which for Spring means the, ". . . stripping away of a people's culture . . ." is a second major theme. Spring documents many examples of attempts to force people to 'conform fully' to the American culture as it was at the time of the attempt. Again like Apple, Spring is not as eager to point out the diminishing number of these attempts over time, nor the diminishing vehemence with which we prosecute these attempts, nor with the growing percentage of Americans (now grown to a vast majority) who feel at least annoyance, if not worse, at the attempts. Spring does sometimes mention early attempts to incorporate native, still stone-age groups into the developing mainstream and to help them survive and prosper in the changed environment of the day. Nevertheless, he couches each of these efforts in the rhetoric of racism rather than accommodation. For instance, after starting with anti-Anglo rhetoric, Spring quickly switches his anger from "Anglo" to "Anglo-Saxon," then to "European-Americans" and at last to the "dominant culture," as one new group and then another group, initially reviled and feared by the previous settlers, adapted themselves to the realities of the evolving American culture, were accepted, began to prosper, and identified themselves as 'American' (without a hyphen) while retaining their own essential old-world culture. These adjustments and accommodations changed both the settlers already there and the new arrivals.

On the other hand, it is not yet clear that any culture, no matter how acculturated, can have all of the answers for the education of children, and Spring does present evidence to show that other methods worked well at certain times in history. The strongest of these is the example of the Choctaw and Cherokee Indian schools that resulted, in the case of the Cherokee with a ". . . literacy rate in English . . . higher than the white populations of either Texas or Arkansas."

Some of Spring's efforts range to the preposterous, however. For example, in the early 1600s, the Virginia Colony was still trying to hang on by its fingernails, and it was not necessarily certain that it would not disappear, as its predecessor colony did. The education of Indians was not in the forefront of everybody's thinking, even if the Indians had agreed to it eagerly, which seems unlikely. Nevertheless, on page 8,

Spring writes, "In the early seventeenth century, the *meager* (my emphasis) efforts of the Virginia Colony to educate Indians in colonial homes and to establish Henrico College for the education of Native Americans was doomed to failure . . ." You should know that Henrico College was established on a tract of land of 10,000 acres set aside specifically for the purpose, and was planned for nearly two years. Money, books, and other materials, including articles for a chapel were donated by the nearby settlements of blood thirsty Anglos. This experiment in Indian genocide failed when, on Good Friday morning, March 22, 1622, the local multiculturalist Native Americans rose up in a coordinated attack and killed 350 settlers along both banks of a 140-mile stretch of the James River. What would have been Henrico College was torched (Urban, et al., p. 19). Plans to rebuild the College were, understandably, not immediately renewed.

The fact that some colonists tried to establish a school for Indians at all, while the school for white kids was not yet complete, and that the attempts were not immediately quashed by the dominant majority, is astonishing if we accept Spring's basic premise.

Despite these little setbacks, there were many efforts, as Thomas Jefferson put it (pg. 13), ". . . (In) bringing together their [Indian] and our sentiments, and in preparing them ultimately to participate in the benefits of our Government, I trust and believe we are acting for their greatest good." Other examples giving the lie to Spring's arguments appear throughout his book. For example, page 115, "These core [Anglo-American Protestant] values . . . include mutual respect, individual rights, tolerance of differences, and individual participation in government," and on page 17, "I did not doubt then, nor do I now, the capacity of the Indian for the highest attainments of civilization . . .," and " . . . there were now several missionary schools already in operation, though on a small scale, all of them furnishing proof that a plan commensurate to the object, would reform and save, and bless this long neglected, and downtrodden people." These are not the sentiments of a blood thirsty and depraved people intent on cultural genocide. Yet surprisingly, Spring uses them to advance his own arguments.

What is most striking in Spring's book is that he is so taken with his own arguments that the final few pages of the book can be full of recommendations for "ethnocentric" education and examples of American democratic principles, all of which demolish his assumptions, yet he adds them to his own litany of woes without further commentary.

His final sentence merely states that the idea of Anglo cultural superiority was, ". . . seriously challenged by the great civil rights movement and the new immigration"; as if this explains everything.

Spring's scholarship seems typical of a multiculturalist in that it is genuinely shabby. Spring accuses white America simply of having a culture and of having the audacity to think that it is good. Apparently, American culture is odious while everyone else's is wonderful. The fact that every other culture promotes its own ways of doing things when they manage to become dominant does not slow Spring down for an instant. For example, on page 7, Spring references Axtell and Jemison in describing what a wonderful life white women had after being "captured by Indians," yet he fails to describe any Indian holidays and ceremonies that allowed the white women to 'celebrate their whiteness'. On the contrary, they required the captured women to act like the Indian women of their tribe. Why was this not a bad thing?

I certainly do not think that absolutely everything in our culture is perfect. Far from it. Yet like it or not the New World did change when Europeans came to America, just as it did previously when Asians crossed the Bering land bridge to become 'native' American, spread across the continent, and then warred against each other continually. That each group continued to resist other groups' demands is expected, and that some attempts at forcing conformity to the new way were brutal and unjust is regrettable, but the ongoing historical reality is that the American experience after the "Anglo" invasion, is one of continual accommodation of both dominant and immigrant groups, to the eventual benefit of *all*.

The fact that we are having this debate at all is a tribute to the sense of justice inherent in most Americans' thinking. On the other hand, the fact that this debate continues, despite obviously incoherent arguments that selectively eliminate and misrepresent the very facts used to advance it ('use political spin'), shows that many of us were not educated well enough to recognize a faulty argument logically. "Feeling-focused" arguments may be used to confuse an ignorant constituency, or as a rabble-rousing diatribe, but it is intellectually dishonest and ultimately undemocratic. The fact that we now teach teachers to extend and promote this ignorance, in the name of democracy, is shameful, if not actively seditious.

Spring's arguments may have been much more to the point during the Indian wars of two centuries ago, but to complain continually about injustice, when the dominant culture had recently spent 40 years and several $trillion dollars in a new concerted effort at achieving social justice (the Great Society, and beyond), and damaged itself in the process, is annoying to say the least. Additionally, Spring seems to imply by omission, as most multiculturalists do, that European whites were the only group that was ever mean to anyone. History and current events are replete with examples of one group or another's unkindness to others and includes each group's unkindness to members of its own group. Since we are all human and since we have blessedly not yet developed a Meanness Quotient (except in economics and weather reporting with their Misery Indexes), we must assume that the tendency toward unkindness is spread equally across the races, nations, tribes, clans, and families, as is the tendency toward kindness.

As stated earlier, racism, Spring's central theme, is an attitude that I believe is of a genetic origin but is modified individually. To expect quick acceptance of a minority view, by every member of a majority, especially in contradiction of its own deep-seated traditions, is unrealistic at best. In any case, which minority view should *all* Americans accept? Are we now to progress into the future chanting what might be the multiculturalist's theme, "United we fall, Divided we stand?" The National Education Association thinks so. Remember their recent motto, "Unity through Diversity."

America is an amalgam of hundreds of minorities, just as each of us is an amalgam of many nationalities. Take me for example. I have already said that I am Ukrainian. Yet I am only three parts Ukrainian, if we count grandparents and divide by four. The other part is Russian and that is not the end of it. Based on the position in geography of my ancestors, the history of the area, and the characteristic, although subdued fold along my son's eyes, you might guess that we have Mongol in there somewhere. Apparently a member of the Golden Horde, a nonwhite group long renowned for its pursuit of multicultural harmony, honored an ancestor of mine with multicultural bliss and by that became another one of my ancestors. Besides that, and for some of the same reasons, it is very possible that there is Viking in my blood, and Greek, Macedonian, various Slavic groups, Persian, Ottoman Turk, and a host of others. My guess is that you too can describe a similarly varied genealogy. We are all multiculturalists in the flesh, but identify mainly with the folks with whom we were raised. We typically do not identify with another group unless we live nearby and get to know and like members of the other group. Tell my father that he is half Russian and he would recall his delightful childhood under the heel of Stalin's multicultural charmers, and perhaps blacken your eye. Of course Stalin was not a Russian either, but Georgian.

Each human must accept individual others into the group with whom he identifies, in order for the predominant, cultural attitude to switch to the acceptance of the other group. This takes time and it is true that some individuals never do learn tolerance, often because of unpleasant incidents with the other group. Spring even mentions a few examples of dominated group racism without voicing any outrage. For example, in a quotation from Margaret Szasz; ". . . the powerful Powhatan Algonquian saw their culture as superior to the colonial culture." I have no doubt at all that this statement is true. It would be strange if it were otherwise, yet for Spring this example of perceived cultural superiority is not a bad thing, it merely points to the wisdom of the dominated group in fighting to maintain their traditions. For Spring apparently, "When in Rome, do as the Romans do" should read, "When in Rome, expect the Romans to do it your way." That, apparently, is the route to multicultural harmony. Incidentally, as with the Aztecs we discussed earlier, why do we think of the Powhatan Algonquin as powerful, if they had not conquered, subjugated, or otherwise dominated other, weaker groups, and why is that not a bad thing?

Although he describes himself as an anarchist in a biographical blurb in *Contemporary Authors CD-ROM 1997*, Spring does not mention anarchy as a goal. However, we can begin to understand why he likes multiculturalism so much if we know that the ultimate goal of anarchists is the dissolution of society and its institutions.

Unlike any responsible historian, but very like multiculturalist revisionist historians, Spring tells us that we should evaluate all history from the perspective of the present. This sort of thinking allows the idea that even attempts by white Americans to bring dominated cultures to parity with the rest of society are actually attempts at oppression. For Spring, as for most multiculturalists, "American" schooling is, and always has been, intended only for the education of the white elite. He is also convinced that "dominated" cultures can do a better job of preparing their own children for modern life than "Anglo" schools can, and, of course, multiculturalism is a good thing and has always been a goal of every society, other than white societies.

I think I will stop here. Although my Ed school required very little academic research (the articles that they asked us to read were chosen for us), I can bring in other examples, but the examples are monotonously similar and generally inflammatory. For instance, they asked us to consider role-playing prejudice games, to show kids how awful racism is. I think that reasonable people would agree that practicing racism would foster racism, but role-playing democracy games was not on our agenda.

My suggestion is that we teach history in large part the way it was taught in an earlier part of our history. It was based on the assumption that being an American is a good thing. It intended to create pride in belonging, and it did acknowledge the contributions of other cultures (e.g., the Arabs in math and science, the Phoenicians for our alphabet, the Chinese in gunpowder, the Babylonians in law, and almost everybody in commerce, to mention only five). My education also included some civics and democracy training that discussed liberty and freedom for all. Nor did traditional education stint on the facts that Americans were joyfully imperialistic at times, just like every other culture in the history of the world that could be, and spoke about some injustices that were done in our collective names. So when I left my old neighborhood cocoon, I was willing to listen to and accept anyone who had a good idea. I think that the multiculturalism that I was taught was about right, although we never used that name then and should stop using it now. It did both fill us with pride and patriotism and made one willing to adapt. Contrary to their stated goals, the modern versions merely solidify differences.

Multiculturalism, with all its variants, is simply not working, in school or in the wider society. To insist that we continue to pursue this failed philosophy is counterproductive at best. Also check to see who is hurt the worst under this system and we will find that it is the people who are specifically targeted for help.

I do generally agree with one statement that multiculturalists, and others make, that modeling is among the most powerful strategies in teaching. However, the multiculturalist intention is to get kids to model themselves after the more radical minority leaders, in terms of their hatred, and to foment new revolutions. If we truly want a tolerant nation, willing to accept the good ideas of others no matter where they arise, what teachers should be modeling of course, is the community and American standards of dignity, knowledge, and hope. Teachers should also model the 'culture' of their content area and they should model general adult behavior that deals with adversity in constructive ways. Multiculturalism makes these things difficult because it denies that there is an American culture, and insists that it is somehow demeaning to be asked to learn the kinds of things that helped make America great. The multiculturalist philosophy creates a solution that exacerbates the problems it is intended to solve.

Trying to shoehorn multiculturalism into every subject area, thereby turning every class into a sociology activity is similarly counter-productive and is contributing to the burgeoning American ignorance, especially since multiculturalism relies on an ideologically revised version of history to advance its agenda. It does not matter what culture we were born into, the teaching of algebra is the same everywhere, save for the language used to explain the ideas and procedures. The basics of understanding erosion are no different for Zaireans than for the Swiss and objects react to gravity in much the same way in Korea as they do in Indonesia, Peru, or Arizona.

All of this being true, it occurs to me that the only true multiculturalism that schools should be promoting is the individual 'culture' of subject content. Requirements are different in biology class than they are at band practice. History class requires different things of pupils than English or French class. We require a different mind-set in each, along with different facts, ideas, and actions. Some kids are better in art than they are in physics and some kids do better in literature class than in social studies. This is undoubtedly at least partly because they have different interests and perhaps because they have different learning styles, but "So what?" Some kids do poorly in all subjects for reasons having nothing to do with culture. This is even true of some of the children of 'old money'. Some kids do well in some areas but not others, but for a pupil to excel in all of the different classes that a school requires shows great adaptability, that is also unrelated to the culture that saw them first. These folks prove that they can adapt to whatever requirements life throws at them. It is the school's job to throw a wide range of requirements at kids, to help determine their strengths and weaknesses. We *want* to find and cultivate these well-rounded kids as our future leaders. Yet, since our society also needs people to fill every job, not just leadership jobs, we also want to help *all* kids determine the range of occupations to which each might be suited. To homogenize all of this wonderful diversity into a self-centered orgy of fuzzy thinking is disgraceful at best, and it had helped turn the U.S. from an educational leader to an educational laughingstock in less than fifteen years.

We should prepare kids to be productive in careers that they enjoy and for which they are well suited, not teach them ways to find fault with each other based on irrelevant factors, such as skin color or parental ancestry.

Similarly, Singer unfortunately supports certain ideas that are educational myths, such as all 'lectures are bad' by saying that lectures, ". . . condition students to accept the status quo." Even if that were true, and I hope that it is, what is wrong with the traditional status quo, anyway? Something takes on the mantle of status quo in an educated democracy as it gains acceptance as demonstrable truth. Traditional American values and philosophy, which are amalgamations of widely diverse but useful ideas, along with the creative development of new ideas, took the U.S. to supremacy in virtually every field of endeavor imaginable. It took us to the moon and beyond the outer planets and it made much of the rest of the world try to emulate us. We can be proud of that. We have no reason to wring our hands in shame. We can, and should, fine-tune our attitudes from time to time, but we should not have 'fixed' what wasn't 'broke'. Now of course, our culture is broken, and we must work to save our society. One of the first steps is to relegate 'multiculturalism' to the historical scrap heap and let it rot, right alongside eugenics.

Status quo can be a very mild, happy and peaceful time, if it is done well. Peace is what everybody says that they want. The following is an example of what we can expect within a period of status quo. After near a century of upheaval, during which Caesar was assassinated and a series of increasingly depraved emperors reigned, including Tiberius, Caligula, and Nero, the subsequent emperors, while maintaining ultimate authority, at least tried to maintain the forms of the Republic and did not actively attempt to extend the empire beyond its current boundaries. As a result (from Edward Gibbon's *The Decline and Fall of the Roman Empire*—pg. 64–65):

> Domestic peace and union were the natural consequence of the moderate and comprehensive policy embraced by the Romans. If we turn our eyes toward the monarchies of Asia, we can behold despotism in the center, and weakness in the extremities; the collection of the revenue, or the administration of justice, enforced by the presence of the army;

hostile barbarians established in the heart of the country, hereditary sa-
traps usupring the dominions of the provinces, and subjects inclined to
rebellion, though incapable of freedom. But the obedience of the Roman
world was uniform, voluntary, and permanent. The vanquished nations,
blended into one great people [melting pot?], resigned the hope, nay
even the wish, of resuming their independence, and scarcely considered
their own existence as distinct from the existence of Rome.

Dedicated multiculturalist will likely gag at the previous sentence,
however:

> The established authority of the emperors pervaded without an effort
> the wide extent of their dominions, and was exercised with the same
> facility on the banks of the Thames, or on the Nile, as on those of the
> Tiber. The legions were destined to serve against the public enemy, and
> the civil magistrate seldom required the aid of military force. In this state
> of general security, the leisure as well as opulence both of the prince and
> people were devoted to improve and adorn the Roman Empire.
>
> Among the innumerable monuments of architecture constructed by
> the Romans, how many have escaped the notice of history, how few have
> resisted the ravages of time and barbarism! And yet even the majestic ruins
> that are still scattered over Italy and the provinces, would be sufficient to
> prove that those countries were once the seat of a polite and powerful
> empire. Their greatness alone, or their beauty, might deserve our atten-
> tion; but they are rendered more interesting by two important circum-
> stances, which connect the agreeable history of the arts with the more
> useful history of human manners. Many of these works were erected at
> private expense, and almost all were intended for public benefit.

The Roman melting pot worked while the barbarian version was
despotic at the center and weak at the extremities. United they stood.
When they eventually divided again, they fell. And the rich guys were
philanthropic. We would not expect anything at all like philanthropy if
we believe the multiculturalists. Pop philosophy, as personified by the
baboon in *The Lion King*, has told us repeatedly that "Change is good."
Just as in our genes however, random change is not always as good as
we are led to believe. Sometimes a little stability goes a long way; but
we have to identify with each other first.

6   Special Education

I wish to propose for the readers' favorable consideration a doctrine which may, I fear,
appear wildly paradoxical and subversive.
The doctrine in question is this: That it is undesirable to believe a proposition
when there is no ground whatever for supposing it is true.
I must, of course, admit that if such an opinion become common,
it would completely transform our social life and our political system.
Since both are at present faultless, this must weight against (my proposal).
—*Bertrand Russell*

If school budgets need to be cut, and even if they do not, Special education funding should be cut by <u>at least</u> 90 percent. We should not eliminate it, because a very few pupils can benefit from the help, suitably readjusted, but Special ed has done more damage to 'normal' kids and to our society than almost anything else anyone could have thought of, short of shackles and chains. Special educators decry what they see as the traditional practice of denigrating and ignoring the less capable, describing it as "Teaching the best and ignoring the rest." Yet their assumptions have led us to designate millions of kids as learning disabled and to reset *all* teaching to a level where "*all* can learn." They have made these 'improvements' although the legal mandate for Special education may not include instructional manipulations. As a results, the normal confusion of the untutored, previously thought to require the instructional intervention of a genuine teacher, is now thought to be a medical emergency requiring drug therapy. Progressive educators have changed the basic educational premises so much that its rallying cry of "level the playing field" can be thought of as don't-teach-*anyone*-anything-that-*anyone*-else-might-find-challenging.

Despite the rhetoric of excellence, Special education teaches kids, and their parents, that they are so helpless and mentally defective that someone else has to read to them their already below grade-level materials, that they are so incompetent that they must take easier tests than 'regular' pupils, or that they should be evaluated using 'authentic assessments' instead of tests of knowledge. Authentic assessment caters to the 'learning styles' theories that in practice, allow kids to paste up a collage of magazine pictures, for instance, and accepts that as proof of a deep understanding of evolution, mathematics, or about the system of government in Spain. Mere word search exercises or the viewing of movies are the norm in many of today's classrooms and educators provide kids test questions ahead of time, and the kids still fail.

As an educational theory, Special education is a disaster and is destroying the souls of our kids. Special education is the welfare system (identify 'victims' and give them 'benefits') extended into the schools and it has done as much harm there as its big brother has done in the rest of society.

By the way, had you noticed that when we at least partially reformed the welfare system and no longer officially considered people chronically helpless, but expected them to do much more for themselves, the employment rate went up to record levels, the economy swept to record levels, and the crime rate dropped significantly? The fact that we suddenly had surpluses in federal and state budgets makes us stop and think, too. It makes us think that similar improvements are likely in the schools when Special ed excesses are brought to heel.

Additionally, the fact that we have seen a sensible 'back-to-basics resurgence' in the past few years, although we have indoctrinated our kids to dependence and victimology for the past few decades, shows how bad things have gotten. To go against what has become a tradition for most of our population is significant.

Yet what is wrong with Special education, apart from my angry words above? Isn't Special education designed to help kids with learning disabilities cope with an increasingly technological world? That is the rhetoric certainly, but that is not what is happening in practice. In a phrase, the thing that may be most wrong about Special education is its penchant for massively overdiagnosing the so-called 'learning disabilities' and for requiring educators to facilitate activities, rather than to teach lessons, as if everyone, not just those diagnosed as learning disabled, were in Special ed.

As I stated earlier, in the 1950s and 1960s my entire school district identified perhaps a handful of kids who needed special help. Today, a common *percentage* of kids officially identified as disabled reaches into double figures. The classes that I taught, in all of the schools where I taught, had an average Special ed roll of 12 percent to 14 percent. I have heard other school systems report 18 percent and even 50 percent. Extended to all the schools in America, this amounts to millions of kids identified as mentally disabled in some way. Just imagine: Millions of kids deemed so helpless that the whole educational system tries to redefine downward what is grade- and age-appropriate instruction, and is succeeding. Does this square with your vision of a vibrant and growing America, or even with your idea of how to develop high self-esteem?

Since there are that many kids officially identified as needing Special help, and since we have all come to believe that 'inclusion' is the law, this means that the teaching of *all* kids is affected by the dumbing-down that we require teachers to make in all classrooms. So, even if 'only' 12 percent of kids are 'in' Special education, Special education dominates *all* of education.

Well, OK, but why is this a bad thing? Aren't the Special education folks good people who want what is best 'for the children'? Generally, the answer to that question is 'yes'. All of the Special educators that I have known genuinely seemed to want to help kids. Nevertheless, as with so many variations of the Progressive philosophy, what is released for public consumption (and the public includes most teachers) is different from reality, and the results attained never match the promises made. Unfortunately, people believe the party line because an 'expert' said it was so, and because the political rhetoric tells them that anyone against Special ed, or against more funding for Progressive school programs generally, is "meanspirited" and "against education." Yet what is happening to the average kid if we teach him according to the Progressive method? He is earning 'Fs' labeled as 'A's and 'Bs', and feeling very good about it.

The Progressive rhetoric has been used for so long by now that we have a generation or more of people who have been raised under, and indoctrinated to, superficially compelling but substantially silly, intellectually dishonest, and ultimately harmful ideas, and we call the use of these ideas 'essential'. These ideas are all of these things (harmful, etc.) probably because the ideas have been developed either by people who proudly call themselves anarchists [see the previous chapter], or by many of the slowest 'experts' among us.[185] The public, however, believes that the current Progressive reality is real because they literally do not know

---

185 Bestor, 1953; Bruner, 1960; Sowell, 1993; and others.

any better and because we taught them that thinking anything different is evil (despite also teaching that change is good).

As we look at another sampling of the kinds of research said to support their conclusions, which I will shortly provide, we may no longer have to ask ourselves: Why and how did we come to a level of national scholastic incompetence that is so astonishingly high, and how did we become convinced that this level of incompetence should not concern us? I suspect that it may be because we listen to modern 'mental health professionals' and because our modern intellectuals support the analysis of all those pop psychologists, counselors, self-help book authors, and victimologists of all stripes. There is so much of it around that we may think that the experts know what they are talking about. They do not. Yet, because we think the law requires us to treat every kid identically (because every kid is unique), since the faulty 'learning styles' ideas are so immensely impractical, and since each teacher is dutifully trying to 'level the playing field' for *all* pupils, we focus lesson plans at the lowest end of the achievement continuum.

"So what do you want to do," one may ask, "teach every kid as if he were Einstein?" Of course not. We should teach each kid according to his individual capabilities. As we do it now, however, despite the rhetoric that we are teaching individual kids individually, the vast majority who are 'average', as well as the slower pupils, and especially those who are very bright, are *all* getting a raw deal by being asked to read the equivalent of Dick and Jane books, if they are asked to read at all, when they could read Stevenson, Kipling, or Dickens. Instead, our kids are asked to read modern, Progressively approved books (see page 418) because we are told that the classic books of Western culture have no relevance to modern Americans. Yet, if you have read Hemingway, Carson, Shakespeare, Orwell, Twain, and many others typically used in traditional liberal education, you will remember that many themes explored by those authors are the very ones that Progressive folks say are important to explore. Themes such as equity, conformity, human qualities, the injustice of slavery, the contributions of other cultures, love and sex, the pain of war, the hypocrisy of some of the religious, even corporate malfeasance, and many others. So why aren't we asked to read them? Probably because traditional education also has the disturbing habit of discussing things such as honor, patriotism, fidelity, integrity, loyalty, morality, the professional and social benefits of learning things, fairness, self-reliance and self-discipline, altruism, differences in capabilities, diligence, sacrifice, perseverance, faith and, perhaps worst of all, of attributing positive characteristics to some people of European ancestry. Another possibility is that all the topics listed can be far too difficult and not relevant enough to the lives of our facilitated children. Unfortunately, ignoring these items from the responsibility-for-your-own actions end of the self-and-others continuum, places far too strong an emphasis on the "Me" ends of things. Then, even though a bureaucracy cannot be flexible enough to adjust to genuinely individual needs, the 'responsibility' aspects of society are covered by assuming that all problems can be solved by impersonal help from the government. The lesson that the kids learn is that "I cannot get through life without outside help," but "You have the responsibility to help me." Once again the Progressive solutions help to destroy what is good about America, and substitute self-disdain for genuine self-esteem, victimology for self-reliance, and separatism for community.

Also, the intellectually dulling influence of not reading responsible and challenging textbooks is a related problem, and we will touch on that again in the next chapter.

So what *is* Special education anyway? There is no way of telling, by reference to my Ed school textbooks. In fact, we used no text at all in the Special ed portion of our classes, only handouts. Also, there is no mention of Special education in *Educational Psychology* at all. There is no mention in chapter and section headings, nor in the index. Isn't that odd? I even tried to find it under "Education, Special" and could not. The educational history text, lists only six page references to special education in the index.

Special education started as several educational sub-specialties primarily concerned with kids with genuine problems; autistic kids, profoundly retarded kids, and kids with various combinations of deafness, dumbness, and blindness, etc. Today, however, Special education is a combination of essentially all the various flavors of the Progressive ideology. It has embraced all of the relevance, self-esteem, child-centered, educratic, and multiculturalist ideals, and it has invented a few wrinkles of its own. Joy in the power of coalition politics has replaced the needs of children. Of course, maintaining power requires money. How many $millions are budgeted for Special education and its programs in your school system? How many McGuffey Readers[186] and "Jolly Numbers" workbooks (an arithmetic title that I remember from my grammar school days) do you think that would buy?

Instead of decent textbooks that teach things, we now have learning disabilities (LD), behavior disorders (BD), and the bureaucratic delights of Quality Performance Accreditation (QPA). Special ed has also laid claim to a variety of medical conditions, e.g., epilepsy, cancer, having a club foot, polio, etc., whether the condition has any relevance to instruction or not, if some sort of procedural 'accommodation' is deemed necessary. Usually we would require no routine changes at all in *teaching* kids with these conditions, but if a teacher has to make up a special homework packet, etc., for a bedridden kid, suddenly that is Special ed territory, though of course the 'regular' teacher has to do it.

Special ed has even annexed the education of 'gifted' kids, who they tried to label as 'intellectually challenged"[187] alongside kids with brain damage. Thank goodness that label did not catch on. Political correctness has also encouraged us to think of normal kids as 'non-disabled'. Defining the whole nation in terms of race, or even nonexistent handicaps is an idea designed to encourage teachers to challenge *all* kids to academic excellence, I guess. According to this point of view, disability is normal and they seem to use that view to justify diagnosing more pupils into Special ed.

Equating disability with normality is just half-a-step away from thinking that being disabled is the preferred condition. Educratically speaking it *is* the preferred condition, if the disability qualifies you for some special assistance. Does this match your hopes and dreams for your kids? Do you think America would have grown as fast and gone as far as it has with such a strong emphasis on handicaps? It does suggest the mind-set of ivory tower Special Educators, however.

How much farther should Special ed cast its net? My class notes (reproduced below) tell me that approximately 7.6 percent of school aged children have some 'exceptionality'. Can we expect LD to become LE (learning exceptionality) soon?

---

186 Used by generations of "school ma'rms," starting in the 1830s. Many kids learned to read using these remarkable books, which featured patriotic and moral tales written at a level that today would be considered fit only for very 'gifted' kids, yet were once used in one-room schoolhouses, for every grade. Yet through them, America perpetuated its 'justice for all' ideals because kids were taught them early and consistently.

187 Mentioned during a class dedicated to teaching us the only acceptable, politically correct labels to use with the various 'exceptionalities'. For instance, 'disabled' is preferred over 'handicapped' and we must not say, 'the diabetic kid'. Instead say, 'the kid with diabetes'.

Exceptionality	Percent of school aged kids	
Learning disabilities	3.90	
Speech & language disorders	1.70	
Mental retardation	0.96	
Behavior disorders	0.69	
Hearing impaired	0.11	
Other health impaired	0.10	
Physically impaired	0.09	(Orthopedic impairments)
Visually impaired	0.04	
Intellectually challengcd	0.01	(Includes autism and brain damage)
Total	7.60	

If this adds up to only 7.6 percent of school aged kids, how can all the perfectly ordinary schools where I had taught average 12 percent or more? Could there be a teentsy little bit of data fudging going on across the nation? Or are the textbook data just starting to age while life in these Educratic States of America have become more Progressive?

I make no claims for the next set of facts, but I find the coincidence intriguing. A few days ago (late 1998), I watched C-SPAN while a Republican Member of Congress argued passionately for more money for Special education generally, and in particular for increasing the percentage of funding of Special ed costs that the Federal government now makes. In his speech, the Congressman mentioned these facts:

- In the early 1970s, the Feds funded about 6 percent of all Special costs. (This was at a time when we identified about 7 percent of kids as having a disability of some sort.)
- Today Federal taxpayers pick up about 12 percent of the tab and we list about 12 percent to 14 percent or more of kids with disabilities.

The Congressman argued that the Federal government should "do the right thing" and help the States more in insuring that *all* the poor, disabled kids achieve a good life. What I wonder is, if we increase the percentage of federally mandated coverage again, to the 40 percent that they ask, will the percentage of kids officially identified with special handicaps rise again to match it? We have already been told that more than 20 percent of Americans are mentally defective in some way. Is that just more fraudulent, political folderol aimed at convincing us that more funding is needed. This would be the equivalent of the previous announcement, several years ago, that homosexuals amount to more than 10 percent of us, and the claim, which I will detail soon, that about 10 percent of us suffer from Tourette Syndrome. The smart money says, "Yes!"

Here is a quotation from Rita Kramer's book, *Ed Schools Follies*, printed in 1991. Kramer quotes from a professor's lecture on the Exceptional Child in the Regular Classroom, from Michigan State U.:

> There has been a 365 percent increase in LDs, the mildest level. *It's leveled off because the government stopped paying* [my emphasis]. There's great variability in who we are talking about—is it a kid who can't read or do math or is it one who is failing social studies? It started out as a program to provide special help for a small group—now it's up to 3.4 million. The government has pulled out, that pot of money hasn't been increasing. We have to ask, Are the ones with the worst disabilities being served? There are no exit criteria established for these kids—they're lifers. They never go back to general education. It's a McDonald's ethic—more people are served every year. The special ed people want to keep them there.

The professor goes on:

> Who is learning disabled? The school imposes the label. The aim is to reduce the child's difficulty in adapting to society. But there are . . . two problems. First, the category is too inclusive. Are they all really disabled—or are some of these children *instructional casualties* [my emphasis]? Secondly, to be eligible for services the child has to be classified—referred and evaluated. And unfortunately the system doesn't work, it's not very accurate. It costs three to four thousand dollars [*circa* 1990] to declare a child eligible, *and afterwards we can't distinguish the LDs from others* [my emphasis]. We have only a 50 percent success rate in telling the difference—about as good as tossing a coin.

Referring to 'mainstreaming' (placing retarded kids into regular schools), he continues:

> Can we really do this—teach heterogeneous groups of kids in the classroom? Yes—to a limited extent. And we get better at it by trying. You folks [his class of ed students] will make it happen. It's not going to

happen at the university level. There are things you can use to integrate some of the kids some of the time.

This professor is a true believer, so he has hopes that academic learning and intellectual equality will improve slowly, though more than a decade later there is still no evidence of it at all. Yet, when we read between his lines, and take into account his deep doubts, we can tell that even the Special ed community knows that they are overreaching, do not really know what they are doing or where their ideology is leading, and are deliberately ignoring the needs of most of the population in their pursuit of invariant outcomes (i.e., equity).

I suppose we should be pleased by the candor, though the professor assumed he was preaching to the choir. Yet, because his words have been ignored and largely forgotten, it is not a comforting vision. Normal kids who have not managed to learn what we have not taught them, are trapped in Special Ed—space, forever. The only way to get them out again, is to cut off the funding for all but the genuinely handicapped.

On a practical level, however, apart from ideology, this particular professor knows of what he speaks. He recommends that kids be allowed to practice the things that we want them to learn ("If they only spend six minutes per day reading, you can't expect them to get good at it"). His other sensible recommendations attend to things such as the physical arrangement of the classroom. Desks should be in rows facing the blackboard and away from windows (no campfire circles), to reduce distractions and allow easy supervision and flow of traffic. Most good ideas have a simple, unpretentious feel to them, and these recommendations qualify.

Alphabet Soup

When you question the validity of the Special education methods, as I have done, they will tell you that there is a great deal of "research" in the scientific literature that supports the use of their methods. Here is an example of how research supports the Special ed cause.

Another of the few papers they asked us to write in Ed school involved picking an exceptionality, finding several journal articles and writing about it. I picked Gilles de la Tourette Syndrome (TS), primarily because I did not know very much about it, though what I did remember suggested a genuine physical condition. I quickly found several articles and began reading them.

The etiology of TS is still in doubt, with speculation ranging from neurology to genetics, but the outward manifestations are often pronounced and involuntary 'tics'. These tics can be either muscular or vocal and cause embarrassment and physical discomfort, especially while trying to control them. One of the noticeable vocal tics may be an involuntary or "inappropriate" shouting of obscenities called coprolalia (literally, fecal [or pornographic] babble).

I discovered that the history of Tourette Syndrome is short and 'progress' in the field is a very recent thing. Until the early 1900s TS was thought to be a physical disorder. Then early in the century, Freud's ideas changed it to a psychological problem somehow akin to mental retardation.[188] That is where things stayed until the 1970s when we discovered that certain sedative drugs seemed to help control the 'tics'. This new discovery seemed to place TS in the realm of the neurological diseases. In the 1980s significant co-occurrences were noted with other disabilities. The most common of these were Attention Deficit Hyperactivity Disorder (ADHD) and Obsessive-Compulsive Disorder (OCD), which are themselves newly invented. By the 1990s things came full-circle with the reported observation that there was a genetic component to the disease. We again thought of Tourette-Syndrome as a physical, perhaps genetic, disorder when researchers noticed that families could have "more than their share" of the disease. A reference to Tourette Syndrome in an unrelated article in *Discover* magazine (June 2002, p. 49) suggests that too much of the neural transmitter dopamine, is the culprit.

To summarize: As late as 1972 doctors thought TS was very rare. In fact *there were only 50 cases ever recorded* before the onset of the new Progressive era. By 1993, however, the thinking on the prevalence of TS got confused and confusing (or deliberately misleading). Some authors reported that as many as one million people in the U.S. show symptoms although many are mild. If true, this may mean that as many as 1 in 300 people may have TS. Other reports range from 1-in-2000 to 1-in-1000. This lower figure (1-in-2000) equates to about 1-in-400 children in school, which means that perhaps every grammar school in American should have at least one.

---

188 Categorizing mental retardation as a purely psychological problem does not make sense to me, but apparently did to Freud.

Various authors have described the prevalence of individual symptoms as well. Some say that 5 percent to 10 percent of us show some tics (i.e., upwards of 30 million Americans, based on current population figures, and 600 million worldwide). These tics may manifest themselves as eye blinking, shrugging, grimacing, or vocalizing, for instance. Several authors report that coprolalia occurs in about ⅓ of all persons with TS (10 million Americans) and one author reported "self abuse" in ⅓ of her subjects. Anderson (1993) says that 50 percent to 56 percent of people with TS have some Learning Disorder (LD), 50 percent have ADHD while Harris, Silver, and Sekhon (1993) report that 26.8 percent had dyslexia as opposed to only 4.2 percent of the controls.

In truth many of these results are quite suspect, as the widely disparate estimates may suggest. This is especially true of those reported by Harris, et al. (1993). Harris reports data *based on samples as small as 13 people.* The largest study quoted by Harris, et al. had only 100 subjects and, the authors tell us, most of their data were drawn from a subset of only 21 subjects. We can infer very little from such small samples and much of that is likely to be misleading and useless. The fact that Harris reports statistics to the ¹/₁₀ percent is unwarranted, implying far more precision that the scanty data can justify.

It is astonishing that these sorts of "research" makes it past the editorial and peer review boards of what we, the lay public, are expected to believe are scholarly journals. Unfortunately, this level of scholastic integrity may be common. Many other authors I read do not state the basis of the findings of the authors that they quote, but if they are as bad as Harris, perhaps all these data should be withdrawn until they can gather more comprehensive information. What we have now seems not to be 'research' at all, but mere ideological editorializing and marketing.

Apart from these irregularities in statistical method, I wonder why finding research subjects is such a problem if so many people suffer with the disease? If the prevalence is as large as reported, we would all know many people who show at least some symptoms and it would be a simple matter to collect enough test subjects to do more definitive work. College introductory psychology classes, the traditional source of subjects for many psychology researchers, would be brimming with them, eager to participate in exchange for academic credit and millions of concerned parents would be beating the doors down of neighborhood physicians everywhere. As a layman's check on these figures we can do our own sample collections. If as many as 1 in 300 of us have TS, a high school as large as mine, for instance, would have had perhaps five or six pupils who showed some significant symptoms. Of those, we would have known two (1-in-3) to exhibit coprolalia. I can assure you this was not the case. In the age of Ozzie and Harriet, if even one kid had wandered around the school habitually shouting 'inappropriate' obscenities, we would have known about it. Of course, they would be harder to spot today.

How many people of your acquaintance show signs? In my life I can think of only one person who showed any tic pronounced enough to be remarkable. Oddly enough it was my high school biology teacher, who would stretch his neck (point his chin up and to the side) perhaps once or twice an hour. I think he just wore tight collars at a time when we still expected male teachers to wear a tie.

So, what we have are only 50 cases ever recorded in history, until shortly after the onset of the Great Society and the rapid rise of victimology. Suddenly, based on stastistical samples as small as 13, they tell us that there may be millions of sufferers.

Similarly, until the early 1960s, schools had only a handful of kids in any community thought to need 'special' help, and now we near 15 percent of the pupil population nationally, and the list is progressively growing. The 1997 *Information Please* Almanac © states that 21.3 percent of the population of the United States was school aged (age 5 to 19 years) in 1990. If we had about 295 million citizens in the year 2000,[189] it means that we had approximately 59 million school-age kids then.[190] Fifteen percent of that makes about 8.85 million kids identified as needing the assistance of Special education.[191] Are these kids truly that helpless and defective that they cannot learn to read or add, or are we just using them to squeeze money out of the government? Perhaps the battle cry, "for the children," is starting to have a hollow ring to it.

The following chart, also from my class notes, shows the prevalence of the various exceptionalities within the Special education rolls:

---

189 The year 2000 census indicates this revised number.

190 Official Census Bureau figures for the year 2000.

191 Forty percent of 59 million is about 24 million kids potentially annexed by Special education, if my previous speculation regarding percentages increasing to match funding is correct.

Exceptionality	%	
Special learning disabilities	49.9	
Speech and language	22.2	
Mental retardation	12.3	
Behavior disorders	8.9	
Multiple disabilities	2.2	
Hearing impairment	1.3	
Other health impairment (epi-lepsy, cancer, etc.)	1.3	
Orthopedic impairment	1.1	
Visual impairment	0.5	
Autism	0.1	
Deaf and blind	0.0	(less than 0.05%)
Traumatic brain injury	0.0	(less than 0.05%)

Half of all 'exceptionalities' are the newly discovered 'learning disabilities' (increasing since teachers stopped teaching and began listening to our self-styled mental health professionals), and about 9 percent are 'behavior disorders' (increasing since 'discipline' became a bad word).

One of our classroom activities in Ed school included the visit of a respected Assistant Superintendent from a nearby school system. He spoke mainly about behavior problems in his district and what had been done since the shooting that occurred in the school cafeteria a year or two earlier. One thing that I distinctly remember him saying was that he thinks perhaps 90 percent of the kids identified as "behavior disordered" (BD) actually suffered from what he called "conduct disorder." In other words, they were merely spoiled kids who were not taught to mind their elders when they were young. In the same way, I believe that most, and perhaps all, of the kids identified as 'learning disabled' (LD) are in truth TD, or "teaching disabled."

For the sake of argument, therefore, we can largely eliminate the so-called learning and behavior disabilities from the Special education lists on pages 375 and this page as essentially nonexistent Progressive inventions. This description is not just a fantasy of mine. Other wide ranging reviews have said almost as much. For instance, in *In the Name of Excellence*, Thomas Toch quotes several Special ed teachers and administrators regarding the "misclassification" of pupils. An administrator in New York City, for instance, admitted that, "the bulk of youngsters [identified] . . . aren't handicapped [in any clinical sense]." A teacher in suburban Florida said, "If kids aren't achieving up to par, or they are difficult to teach, teachers try to push them to learning-disabled classes. Even Madeleine C. Will, the U.S. DoE's Special ed administrator from 1983 to 1989, acknowledged that the misclassification of learning-disabled pupils is now a "great problem." And, of course, the education professor from Michigan State quoted above, assumed that most Special ed kids are actually "instructional casualties."

We can also drop the 'multiple disabilities' category to avoid double counting and drop the various physical impairments because the true bailiwick of 'regular' education is the distribution of knowledge based on intellectual function, not whether a child has a club foot, epilepsy, or cancer. If we do this, we are left with mental retardation, brain damage, and autism, at roughly 1 percent of the population, as subject to Special education. This is about what I would have guessed, based on the number of kids that seemed not to be included in our regular classrooms when I was in school. Of course this low number is now used as an indication of discrimination.

I do not mean to imply that the various physical impairments are not a hardship to a growing kid, or to an adult for that matter, but they are not within the mandate of 'education'. Handicaps such as deafness and blindness do require special techniques to assist learning or even to make book-learning possible, using for instance, books in Braille. Accommodations such as allowing a kid in a wheelchair to leave class two minutes before the end-of-class bell rings, and placing a partially deaf kid close to the front of the class, are perfectly acceptable as well. These techniques are essentially compensations for impaired bodily functions that hinder the accumulation of information or make navigating school halls during 'rush-hour' inconvenient or even dangerous, etc. Once in the classroom, however, learning may proceed routinely. Some of those sorts of accommodations may be within the purview of Special education, but we should not dumb down *instruction* in these physical-handicap cases any more than we should dumb down instruction for the rest of the pupil population.

Common sense, and centuries of experience, tells us that if we start teaching the basics to kids, they will learn basic skills and will largely resolve what learning problems they have, as they drill and practice their newfound skills. A pupil cannot move on to 'harder' stuff until he understands the simple stuff, but once he knows the simple stuff, not moving on is doing the pupil a disservice. Comparing the awful results attained by the Progressive philosophy to genuine education, is a perfect demonstration of this simple truth.

The Progressive philosophy preaches that every kid will somehow get deeply motivated to become a 'lifelong learner' if we only leave him alone. They tell us that actual 'teaching' is unnecessary, and even harmful. We should merely depend on the kid's natural curiosity to lead the way toward intellectual nirvana. How, then, can we reconcile the statistics that tell us that now 60 percent of adult Americans (the percentage is growing) do not read any book of any description during the course of a year and that even the comic book industry is suffering?

The lifelong learning idea implies that superficial classroom activities are so much fun and intellectually inspiring that kids will naturally demand to learn more and/or will seek out the additional knowledge on their own. There are at least three problems here. First, many teachers today explicitly tell their pupils, and parents, that they do not believe in homework because kids work so hard in school that they need a chance "just to be kids." (Of course if no homework is assigned, then there is no homework to grade. However, it would be unfair to mention that, so I won't). Second, if homework is assigned, schools often provide time during school to do it, as I was forced to do while student facilitating. I am not referring to regularly scheduled 'study halls' that might help to fill out a schedule (i.e., seven scheduled classes in an eight period day).[192] What I am referring to is that since kids now routinely choose to ignore homework assignments, many educators use normal class time to complete assignments so that they will have something to grade. Not surprisingly, however, the kids' routine ignorance slows the learning process and, not coincidentally, convinces kids that school itself is about 'activities' rather than about learning. Finally, when pressed, educators often blame parents for asking educators not to assign homework since it interferes with after-school activities. These parents are those who educationists have indoctrinated over the past several decades, and are convinced that all life is about organized activities. After more than forty years of intensive Progressive efforts, lifelong learning may not be catching on. In the end the most likely habit to be formed is the lifelong habit of not learning outside school. Or inside school either.

---

192 In my kids' school "study halls" are used as a punishment. Other schools call this practice "in-school detention." This, too, is undoubtedly thought of as a way to associate learning with pleasure.

Educationists have to respond to the growing complaints of parents, teachers, employers, and college professors that kids are not learning as much as they once did. Since organizing elementary schools as if they were little more than daycare centers is not affirmative enough to satisfy the growing army of complainants, we are forced to tinker with the system. While this tinkering presents us with an apparently moving target (the rhetoric calls this, "We're working hard to improve the system"), the best that Progressive facilitators can think to do is to 'create learning opportunities'. We are told that these improvements will let kids experience life to its bountiful fullest, 'empower' them to think 'outside the box', and move them into the future. Sounds so sweet, doesn't it?

We have already discussed our Kindergarten educator's refusal to correct early language mistakes, and how that makes it six times harder to unlearn incorrect information and relearn the correct spelling and grammar, etc., but variations on this Whole Language–like technique hinder learning of higher-level knowledge as well. The way that 'creating a learning opportunity' is accomplished, often consists merely of scratching the surface of a topic, asking kids to guess what it all means, telling them that they are wonderfully creative even if there are long established conventions that contradict the kids' ignorant inventions (i.e., if kids think of anything at all, they often suggest ideas proven unworkable perhaps centuries in the past [but do not kill their self-esteem by telling them so]), then moving on to the next 'essential learning experience'. I will expand on this bit of wheel spinning in Chapter 7.

Just think of what Progressive systems imply about kids, however. This is important because the assumptions of any system determine the sorts of methods used to achieve stated goals. This is also another example of educationists telling parents things what they want to hear, but absolutely failing to deliver.

In order for Progressive ideas to make sense to us, we must assume that kids are capable and eager to investigate deep, philosophic ideas by an extended and single-minded pursuit of some topic. We will shortly see that educationists explicitly emphasize learning in "depth rather than breadth." Does this sound like many six-year-olds that you know? Or even many of our modern, Progressively raised 18-year-olds?

We should not develop learning strategies as if kids are miniature graduate students, determined to make a name for themselves by saying something new and original. As I asked previously: What is intellectual 'creativity' if not an attempt to reshuffle the things we know into combinations that are new, unusual, and perhaps demonstrably useful? How can any of these things happen, even if a rare kid has the personality to attempt it, if the pupil does not know much of anything yet? In written language, for instance, the unusual (i.e., "creative"—Progressively defined) is evident only in comparison to standard usage, spelling, etc. However, true intellectual creativity, as opposed to mere deliberate bad spelling, etc., reorganizes *facts and ideas*. How can anyone, much less an untutored kid, reorganize facts and ideas of which he is completely unaware? Where is all of this creativity going to come from and what will it use as its fodder? If we sit and think about and accept this dilemma, we are almost inevitably drawn to Plato's idea that learning is merely the memory of things already known and somehow passed to children at conception. In other words, we already know everything there is to know, from birth. We need education only to help us remember it.

I doubt if anyone today, other than those who partake of funny weeds, believes this metaphysical pap. Pap it may be, but it also is the basis upon which they build Progressive educational ideology. Remember: all learning comes from within. It is for this reason that educationists can say with a straight face that 'teaching' is not what teachers do, and why the practical definition for 'academic excellence' (i.e., what educators do as opposed to what they say they do) does not include things academic.

When we look at what is actually done in the classroom, we find very little to support the ideological rhetoric. The theory implies that all kids are miniature post-docs pursuing intellectual fulfillment. Perhaps they are, or will be. However, genuine research and common sense tell us, for instance, that interruptions during a lesson hinder learning. Yet the typical day in the typical classroom is full of changing activities, because attention spans are deemed too short to spend a whole class period on one topic, even though they tell us that learning must be in depth rather than in breath. Additionally, there are the constant comings and going of paraprofessionals, volunteer parents, various Special ed facilitators and 'study buddies', kids going to and coming back from various 'enrichment' activities, etc. Frequently, schedules even break a class into two parts, with lunch in between. These classes also have their occasional tests. Just imagine what that would be like to try to insure that test takers do not collaborate under this sort of a system. Many schools interrupt classes with PA announcements and, of course, there are the incessant interruptions perpetuated by the kids themselves, who use school as a social gathering, interrupted only by the periodic requirement to move from one classroom to another. Therefore, finding the time to fit all the various innovative programs mandated by all of the various reforms that are active in the average school may reduce learning as much as the intrusive programs themselves. If we then factor in the hope that untutored kids will learn things by themselves (perhaps dressed up as revealing 'developmental readiness to learn' or teaching 'responsibility for one's own actions'—another use of society's complaints to camouflage a lack of basic instruction by telling parents what they want to hear), what we produce is widespread ignorance, not academic excellence. A good example of this is the recent spate of quiz shows, such as The Weakest Link, that rely mainly on questions about movie stars and popular songs for their easy, early questions, but often use traditionally school-like questions to eliminate contestants and find winners.

What little kids need are facts to build on, and enough practice to internalize those facts. While they are trying hard to "think," their untutored brains have very little yet to think *about*. A young kid's major attempts at idea reorganization and analyses have to wait for the facts, and additional mental development, before they can proceed profitably.

We will see this idea again in the next chapter as we discuss 'Discovery Learning'. Yet, as Sherlock Holmes in *A Scandal in Bohemia* tells us:

Dr. Watson: "What do you imagine it means?"
Holmes: "I have no data yet. It is a capital mistake to theorize before one has data. Insensibly one begins to twist facts to suit theories, instead of theories to suit facts."

The other problem with leaving kids to discover things on their own is, of course, that kids would rather play.[193] Accumulating wide ranging though useful knowledge is not necessarily on their personal agendas. They might become fascinated for periods of time with one topic or another. For instance trains, race cars, or mazes; but these fascinations are usually quite superficial and are not enough to sustain them for long. So they soon move on to the next toy, game, or activity. They move on because what interested them originally was some surface

---

193 We can use Tom Sawyer as the model of a normal, energetic, kid.

characteristic inherent in the previous toy, game, or activity. They might have liked the look of a locomotive or the noise or the billowing smoke or the fact that wheels are turned by visible push rods. However, if you try to explain the internal workings of a coal-fired steam engine, you lose them. They do not know enough yet to begin to understand what you are saying. Yet how did they become interested in mazes, or fire trucks in the first place? Kids become interested in things because someone exposes them to those things. This is where a genuine teacher starts. Progressive facilitators end here.

My recommendations of repetitive drill in the earliest lessons match what Direct Instruction recommends because it works. It works at least partly because as you may have noticed, kids *like* repetition. My kids asked me to read them the same stories repeatedly. I will bet yours did, too. Maybe their brains are trying to tell us what works best for them at that age. Perhaps they are, quite naturally, reviewing previously learned information for new ideas, trying to learn a thing in breadth rather than in depth. To examine this idea we must examine how kids learn.

Let me beat you to the punch. I know that for me to answer this question in any definitive way would be preposterous. 'Learning' is such a large and difficult subject that many illustrious neurophysiologists, philosophers, psychologists, and others have spent entire careers attempting to unravel this pertinent riddle without ultimate success.[194]

Nevertheless, the generalities of how we answer this question are central to determining how we structure an educational system and what teaching techniques we use. We can also judge the effectiveness of any methods based on an educational theory, by looking at the results attained. I will give a descriptive version of reality that makes sense to me. As you read this, ask yourself if it seems closer to reality than Progressive politically correct and utopian metaphysics.

---

194 Read Jerome Bruner's *The Process of Education,* 1960, as a brief but judicious beginning. Bruner was a psychologist at Harvard and director of a conference on this very topic. Notice ideas that Progressive educators have taken to excess, and thereby rendered nonfunctional. These include ideas such as 'discovery' learning, learning concepts by superficial activities, and the importance of interest or curiosity in learning (i.e., child-centeredness generally). You may also see some of the ideas that I have used, such as asking genuine subject matter experts to help with curriculum development, learning facts in context as the road to conceptual understanding, the need for sequencing information with increasing complexity as stepping stones through the grades, the need for teaching differently-abled students similarly but with varying content complexity, and not devolving teaching to the obsessive use of teaching machines. As usual, a balance is needed if useful ideas are to come to fruition.

How Do Kids Learn?

Pupils learn in different ways at different stages of their lives. In fact pupils learn *to* learn as they grow and mature. They layer each new learning strategy upon the strategies that they learned earlier and each new strategy probably modifies the strategies that are already in place.

At first, kids (babies) learn purely sensually. While the potential for a moral existence is built into the makeup of newborns, the behavior that is most evident is completely self-centered in that absolutely everything they recognize relates directly to their own needs; hunger, too hot, too cold, sleepy, discomfort in the bowels, diaper rash, etc. This is true since at first kids probably do not associate the sounds, smells and sight, etc., that they experience to anything specific. Probably the first thing that they 'learn' is that squalling loudly gets some attention to their perceived needs. Blessedly, this stage lasts only a short time, although the selfishness often lasts a lifetime, especially if we teach them that they should always 'take care of number-one'.

Eventually kids begin to learn the rudiments of the language used in the home and their expression of needs begins to become a bit more sophisticated. Along with learning the language, kids start to have names to 'call' things. This, along with the rules of how to relate ideas using language, is important if they are to think about the things in their lives with any sort of efficiency, or to express their thoughts to others. At this point their learning is not abstract, but it is becoming symbolic. Parental do's and don'ts related to specific actions and situations begin to impinge on a kid's psyche. For a while, it may seem as if kids are deliberately trying to provoke parents by continually repeating forbidden actions. Though there is evidence that infants attend to their parents' voices, the reality may be that, the first few times a parent says "No," it does not register on a kid's consciousness. The words can be just so much background noise to the kid's thoughts. At the very least, the meaning of the sound "no" is not yet understood. It is not until the parent makes an affirmative impression, that the lesson begins to get through. Perhaps raising a voice or a mild swat on the hand may help this impression, if other methods do not work. Like it or not, however, one result of this affirmative impression is that kids learn that someone out there decides things for them. This is a good thing at this early stage. After all, the reason that we call thoughtless self-centered and unwise actions "childish" is that children are characteristically guilty of them.

While children may complain, often loudly, about not getting their way, most kids are happy to let someone else be responsible, especially if we teach them very early that there are consequences attached to their actions. A young kid's reticence to try something that we consider to be routine, such as saying "Hi" to grandpa on the phone, demonstrates this.

(This suggests another idea. Perhaps, as adults we should reclaim responsibility for life's major decisions and enforce our laws and traditions that say that kids must defer to their parents, until they achieve adulthood themselves. Just a thought. If we do, of course, we can again expect schools to make sensible curricular decisions and to enforce discipline in the classroom. That will give us another problem, of course. We must insure that those we accept as teachers have been properly prepared for their roles as adults and teachers by others who know what they are talking about. But back to the topic at hand.)

Soon, the world begins to expand for kids because they have developed physically to the point that they can now walk, talk, and think a little bit more as they eventually will. At this point kids need more information to help flesh out their world. Kids play and explore and then do it all again while continuously adding to their sum of knowledge.

While many workers have described some more detailed and subtle changes in brain function related to learning, I think my short summary is accurate, if nonspecific. Kids remain in this stage through most of their 'formative' years and possibly well beyond. This is so because they subconsciously realize that they do not know very much. At first simple tasks such as "Say, Hi to Grandpa" on the phone is a nearly insurmountable challenge, but it eventually gets solved. Then, putting on your own socks, crossing a street, paying for a candy bar, asking someone for a date, and so forth are all addressed in their turn.

At this point many would say that the best way to learn these 'skills' is to experience them, and so it is. However, preparing to try each of those actions for the first time, especially the much more intellectually challenging 'actions' required of a pupil, such as reading and addition, requires specific information that the neophyte does not have. Since successful life after high school is a bit more complicated than putting on your own socks, and since the requirements of life as an adult are far more mysterious but essentially equivalent to early simple lessons, it requires a great deal of specific information and many ideas of which the Kindergartener is completely unaware.

Therefore, genuine teachers 'pour' information into kids' heads (exactly as horrifies Progressive educationists), and at first the kids remember only a small portion of it. Kids therefore need the initial drills and seemingly endless repetition to help memory (I will bet many adults still use that little alphabet song to recall many relative letter positions). We must also remember that we are dealing with developing brains with an incomplete set of neurons and neuronal connections. One thing that we know about brain development so far is that the brain reacts to inputs and makes connections based, at least in part, to what it is exposed to. If we don't challenge a developing brain with academic challenges, it may not develop the capacity to handle the challenge. We not only get better through practice, but lack of practice may actually hinder the ability to practice.

After they have drilled the most basic basics to the point of nearly unconscious recall, teachers try to get pupils to 'learn' a larger proportion of the needed information. To do that, teachers begin to ask kids to think about new information provided while considering the knowledge they already have, and about how it relates to other things, such as today's lesson. Happily, kids' brains are ready for this stage when they enter what Piaget called the Preoperational stage, where they can, ". . . think operations through logically in one direction." While drill and repetition of new information continues for a while, very quickly (by the second or third grades, if not sooner), the sheer volume of information required makes pure repetition less and less practical, although it is still occasionally useful, such as while learning the multiplication tables, memorizing a poem or song, learning the periodic chart of the elements, or studying for specific subject-matter tests. Therefore we dispense ever more, and more detailed, information to the youngsters and singsong group repetition is replaced by the teacher teaching about new things, supplemented by simple homework assignments that allow repetition ('review' or 'practice') of information after a period of rest. This repetition reinforces the habits that a kid will need if he is ever to become a lifelong learner and encourages independent thought in using newly learned skills. It does this by forcing kids to make their own decisions about the lesson contents. There is no one to ask, "Do I have to write this down?"

Finally, perhaps shortly after the arrival of puberty, abstract thinking starts to rear its welcome head, and in this sense the learning task begins to be easier at last, for pupils and teachers. Unfortunately, learning must also get much harder at the same time because the volume, variety, and depth of learning required of the pupil is increasing all the time. Additionally, the information, as facts and ideas, must be a great deal more detailed, if the pupil is ever going to become a knowledgeable, responsible, and productive adult. (You may have noticed that life gets more, not less, complex as we get older.) Practice in handling large amounts of detailed information is especially important in a modern, technological society like ours. If we do not practice thinking, we never learn to think.

The problem remains, of course, that while the kid is now increasingly receptive to complicated stuff, he has little experience with which to decide what information may become important to him eventually. Evaluative maturity, which we can define as knowledge of what works, (i.e., wisdom) is lacking as well, since wisdom arises from evaluating experience, including other people's mistakes—e.g., reading history. Teaching kids to think is vital, but letting them decide what they 'need' is like asking toddlers why Socialism is such a bad thing, even if it sounds so "fair." They simply do not know. Furthermore, there is no logical reason we should think that they would know. The idea is another example of modern education trying to build roofs before they lay the foundation. We will explore this a bit more in the next chapter, too.

The way we teach kids to think is to give them simple new things to think about, then ask them to evaluate, or to manipulate mentally, the simple ideas. For a preschooler this might mean an exchange such as this, "Look at this picture of a bus in the air. Do you think it can fly?" "No. It has no wings." A ninth grader, however, should be capable of dealing with, "Compare and contrast the governmental systems associated with a democracy and a monarchy." We should not expect that a ninth grader's answer to such a question would be in any sense complete, but we should expect a thoughtful and reasonably informed essay. My ninth graders, however, could not spell "they" consistently.

As stated earlier, Art Linkletter once used the charming and innocent ignorance of children to entertain us and in the process showed what lack of experience would produce, if we put kids in charge. If you would like to see childish ideas in action today, look at our schools, even the 'good' schools, and you may get an idea.

Learning, then, is intimately related to memory, and to what the brain is 'wired' to do. At first learning might be almost pure sense and memory. As we recognize similarities, associations begin to help memory. The combination of memory and the ability to generalize can eventually produce symbolism. At some point generalization and abstraction start to fill the gaps in a kid's sum of knowledge, while checking against what is already known helps to focus thinking in productive directions. Interest, either personal or imposed, is also needed. Unfortunately, 'interest' begins life primarily as self-interest and, if left undirected, can remain almost entirely sensual.

In life however, kids, especially modern kids, need a great deal more knowledge than "I'm OK. You're OK." We must each learn many things for which we have no inherent interest. Proper grammar and long division are two examples. How many third graders do you know who would ask to study long division, or who care when to use 'who' and when to use 'whom'? In the end kids must learn what we as adults have noticed is generically useful, even if acquiring that knowledge is difficult or even sometimes boring.

Trying to convince the poor, beleaguered pupil that personal knowledge about how we transcribe proteins is relevant to them will probably be futile with most kids, though most competent high school biology teachers will try. On the other hand, kids who develop an interest in biology will eventually thank us for teaching them. In fact, I am sure that the detail (facts) of a subject is the true 'hook' for the kids who *get* hooked on a subject. Keeping instruction in the preconceptual stages, without pouring facts into their heads, is doing a disservice to the kids who may otherwise never feel the hook. How many physicists, astronomers, geneticists, engineers, and anthropologists, or shop foremen and craftsmen for that matter, did we lose in the last four decades because well meaning but politically correct educators never exposed them to the delightfully difficult challenges of those disciples, thinking they were helping *all* pupils by keeping things simple? ["You mean I have to be good in biology to be a veterinarian? Forget it, then. I'll teach second grade for a while instead. Then I'll become an Ed school professor. I already know all I will need to know to be that."]

One other imperative responsibility of teachers is to find out which of those kids with bright shining faces (or more typically, sullen, world-weary, or self-satisfied faces) could become a leader, or even a competent worker, in various fields. We need scientists as well as laboratory technicians in today's world, not just consumers. Teachers also have the responsibility to train their own replacements. Those with little or no interest will complain and quickly forget the detail of a particular subject. No matter. Having the capacity to learn the details of meiosis, however, will be a signal that we may have a bright kid on our hands, even if she eventually becomes a caterer rather than a cell biologist. Even if a pupil becomes something other than an academic, being pushed to work in an intellectually disciplined way, while learning that self-discipline is a good thing, will eventually convert that intellectual discipline into another lifelong habit, work for its own sake. We can do this by giving kids good grades when they have done the work well, and poor grades, tempered by encouragement, when they do the work poorly. Also, developing the habit of self discipline reduces a kid's dependence on others, as is knowing that self-reliance is a salient characteristic of adulthood.

Learning Disabilities

What are learning disabilities anyway, and why have they contributed to the deplorable educational state that we have? We have gotten to our current educational state because of the conviction of Progressive educationists that "Self-esteem" is the end-all and be-all of existence. Therefore, despite the 'fact' that everybody is the same as everybody else, since we cannot expect some kids to progress as quickly as others, we should allow no one to make the less talented feel bad. This is equity in action.

Before we discuss learning disabilities, we should understand why self-esteem became so important. If you graduated from high school before the 1970s you will probably recall that some category name generally designated academic classes. This type of system is called 'ability tracking', and is currently considered a bad thing. You probably recall an 'advanced' variant, a 'regular' version of some sort and a 'slower' class. These may not have been the names used in your district, as some of them were not in mine. I went to school in New York State where the ability tracking groups were designated 'Advanced,' 'Regents' and 'non-Regents'. The Board of Regents of the State of New York produces standardized exit-competency exams every year for each of the core subjects at every secondary grade. As I recall, we had to take these tests from the seventh or eighth grade through the twelfth. Success on these tests may also have been used as criteria toward earning a Regents Scholarship, payable if you attended a college within N.Y. State. Unfortunately, I have heard recently that these tests are now under fire for unrestrained political correctness. Reportedly, the tests have been purged of any reference, no matter how trivial, that might upset anyone in some way. There are now no references to race, creed, color, national origin, or belief. If this is true, then along with dumbing-down, they have undoubtedly purged the soul from those tests to abide mindlessly to the Progressive agenda.

Nevertheless, in the good old days, the Regents level was the standard (average) teaching level that we expected the vast majority of pupils to attend. Oddly enough, the middle portion of the educational normal curve contains the largest number of data points ('pupils'). These kids either went on to college or did not, depending on their desires, college acceptances (based largely on grades and other accomplishments), and finances. Kids in the non-Regents classes were not required to take the Regents exams, though I think they could if they wanted. Few kids were taking non-Regents classes in my high school, and relatively few kids took Advanced classes. Yet there were more kids in the Advanced classes than in the non-Regents classes. That is an indication that if a system honors achievement, the normal curve for achievement skews toward higher achievement, beyond the native abilities of the population. We can see that in a population of normal kids, our school's average scores were probably in the nondumbed-down high 70s or even low 80s, depending on the subject, rather than the 30s and 40s, as we see today. I suggest that, appropriately instructed, our current pupils can do it again. Today, however, the achievement curve is skewed significantly to the low end, exactly the opposite of what we can expect of our kids, and need I say it again, exactly the opposite to what Progressive educationists promise.

Imagine if you were at the low end of the achievement curve, however. Did you feel bad about it? Possibly. I am sure some did, as I felt bad that they did not include me in all Advanced classes. It is often a good thing to feel bad about a lack of achievement. It is an incentive to work harder, improve, and move up. Therefore, some, and possibly all, non-Regents kids did feel bad to some extent. Still, since Progressives feel that no one should ever feel bad about themselves, they had to devise a way to eliminate 'negativity' and achieve universal contentment. By 1975, Public Law 94-142 (PL 94-142), the Education for All Handicapped Children Act was passed, which mandated a variety of provisions. According to my class notes, they were:

- Free 'appropriate' public education
- Notification and procedural rights for parents
- Identification and services rights for parents
- Necessary related services
- Individualized assessments
- Individualized education plans (IEPs)
- Least restrictive environment (LRE)

Again, on the surface, this list looks benign and just. Left to itself it might have remained so. Yet the educationists charged with writing the regulations that carried out the law, interpreted the law in very Progressive, which is to say, expansive and expensive ways, and you will note that there is *no* provision for instructional modifications of any kind.

Another handout that told us that PL 94-142 was passed in 1976, titled, "Where does it say we have to *do* inclusion?", tells us (I quote):

The term *inclusion* does not appear in any federal or state law. Inclusion is, rather, the term used to describe our *current interpretation* of Least Restrictive Environment (LRE).

PL 94-142—1976

- [makes] Special education a federal mandate
- [gives *all* students the] . . . right to free, appropriate public education in the least restrictive environment.
- established a continuum of special education services (regular classroom—resource room—special ed room—home)
- concept of *mainstreaming* developed

[Mainstreaming (placing retarded kids into the 'regular' school) was not part of the law, it only *developed as an interpretation*, yet it was included as a bullet item implying mandatory implementation.]

Also, on the same handout:

1990—Individuals with Disabilities Education Act (IDEA) [provided that] . . .:

- Children with disabilities are to be educated with children who are not disabled, to the maximum extent appropriate
- Special education, in the form of supplemental aids and services, will be provided along with regular education instruction

[Note: supplemental aids and services, *not* instructional modifications]

- A student cannot be removed from the regular classroom unless the supplemental aids and services are proven unsuccessful.

[The fact that they have proven almost uniformly unsuccessful, and even harmful, has certainly not been revisited, other than to ask for more of the same.]

- The concept of inclusion developed.

We must understand some of the terms used. 'Mainstreaming' is the process that places handicapped kids into the 'regular' school, rather than being segregated elsewhere. 'Inclusion' takes it one step further and places retarded kids into the regular classroom, rather than into special classes in the school. In the early 1960s educational 'handicaps' referred mainly to kids with very low IQ scores and achievement, and, to a lesser degree, to those with the kids of physical impairments that interfered with the acquisition of knowledge (e.g., blindness, etc.).

The 'least restrictive environment' idea implies, for instance, that if a kid does not need institutionalization, we should not institutionalize him. Fair enough. Both terms also imply that bussing retarded kids to some separate location, as if they could somehow pollute the normal kids, is unfair at best and made the retarded kids feel bad and achieve less by being isolated. Kids need peer role models and if retarded kids were to learn to function in society, they had to be *in* society. Again, fair enough,[195] but setting up a separate classroom within the regular public school building still stigmatizes the kids in the special class since the 'normal' kids make fun of the retarded kids. Despite this inevitable teasing,[196] mainstreaming was deemed an appropriate first step because

---

195 Some (Sowell, 1993) have questioned the assumption that role models similar to the pupil are needed to enhance learning, saying that no believable evidence of it has ever been presented in support, but I will grant it for now, for the sake of argument.

196 I suspect that these kids were originally isolated to separate buildings precisely because of the teasing. Aside: Several local school districts have recently built separate "alternative high school" buildings, for those whose "needs had not been met by the regular high school." It's

the rhetoric that proclaimed that 'separate but equal' was not any more possible for the retarded than it was for the races. Of course in education, 'equal' must also contend with relative intelligence, but we have already seen what Progressive education thinks of that idea. Therefore, although it does not say anywhere that inclusion is the law, only to include disabled kids in regular classrooms "where appropriate," the idea of inclusion developed next. Inclusion is the practice of not merely placing the 'special' kids in separate classrooms in the regular school building, but including the special kids in the same classrooms with the 'regular' pupils. Dismantling the ability tracking system was sold as an equity issue.

The problem is, if we do not set up a special classroom for these kids, the logical place to include them would have been with the lowest groups in the regular school. Of course placing the retarded kids in with only the 'non-Regents' kids, in a traditional ability-tracking system such as we had in the 1960s, would stigmatize the non-Regents kids since we would seem to equate them intellectually with the retarded kids. So ability tracking was dismantled *in toto*, and the kids were scheduled into classes more or less randomly instead.

We still have another problem. Even if *all* kids now sat together in the same classrooms, we were still teaching the lessons more or less traditionally in the 1960s, and it was clear to everyone that there were significant differences in ability represented in the class. That was the point to inclusion, and to dismantling ability tracking, after all. The argument now was that virtually everybody felt bad because they were not as smart as the top few kids, and had daily reminders of it, since they sat in the same classroom.

How can we make the slower kids feel good about themselves, while in the midst of brighter kids, in a system that honors academic achievement, as we once did? Since turning everyone into a genius is not possible, advocates could only think of two ways to try to make *all* kids feel comfortable. One is to gear all instruction to the slowest pupils and to stop honoring academic achievement and the competition that encouraged it. In this effort 'merit', and 'meritocracy[197] became bad

---

getting tough to get around the mulberry bush. It's getting crowded and traffic is now going in opposite directions.

197 A system where those who can do specified work are entrusted with doing that work, and those that cannot do the work, were not. That is to say, a system developed and maintained by common sense and used everywhere and throughout time. Variations on this system, e.g., nepotism (especially where the appointed ones are incompetent), contribute to its own downfall, are the exceptions that prove the rule.

words and the encouragement of individual distinction was replaced by an emphasis on "cooperative learning." This is the primary rationale for the mechanisms of dumbing-down. However, once we decided to stop honoring academics, but are constrained by the fact that parents and the rest of society expect a school to pursue academics, our descriptions of what we do, and our rationalizations for why we do it, become ever more twisted and nonsensical over time. I have already given many examples of this, and will continue to do so.

Another way of making everybody comfortable in the inclusive classroom was, unfortunately, to manufacture more mentally deficient kids (remember, the retarded kids, the original object of the whole exercise, comprise less than 1 percent of the population), and to make enough of them to make deficiency seem 'normal'. I believe that this is why 'learning disabilities' were invented. We know this in modern educational and political jargon as "levelling the playing field." Recall at this point that self-esteem theory, which is at the heart of all these adjustments and 'reforms', has no validity in research, predicts precisely the opposite of what it delivers, and is ultimately harmful, both to individual pupils and to society generally. Recall also that medical testing has found no physical evidence for any disease characteristically associated with these newly defined disabilities.

So what is a learning disability, how are learning disabilities identified, and how do they achieve Progressive goals? Well, they clearly do not achieve the publicly stated goals of improving learning. They do exactly the opposite, but here it is, again from my notes. A learning disability is a:

- Disorder in psychological processes that results in
- Difficulty in learning that is
- Not primarily due to other causes (retardation, brain damage, etc) and shows
- A severe discrepancy between potential and achievement

Quite vague, isn't it? Even the U.S. Department of Education definition is little help;

- A disorder in one of more psychological processes involved in understanding or using language spoken or written

During our class discussions we attempted to pin the definition down a bit. We were told that a learning disability could be almost any discrepancy between expectations and achievement. Incidentally, 'expectations' were once based largely on what was deemed necessary for academic success (i.e., the 70 percent passing score). In current practice, however, if we have problems with math and do worse there than in other classes, they could label us LD. You say that you did not like writing book reports, blew them off until the last minute and slapped something together after quickly skimming the book and earned a D-minus rather than your standard "B"? You could be LD. Having trouble conjugating verbs in French class? Clearly LD.

During our class discussion, I commented to the Special ed professor that under these conditions, LD could describe virtually everyone, at one time or another. With a smile, she agreed.

Do you feel that Special ed casting net closing around you? How do you suppose your self-esteem would have fared had they identified you as LD? Would you have aspired to the career that you have if you had thought of yourself as mentally disabled?

Of course, the 'regular' teachers of the day could not work with such a fuzzy definition. So the educationists have developed a formula, making the designation of LD seem like a scientific exercise. In this State, for instance, the official definition of LD is a 24-point discrepancy between IQ and achievement (even if IQ tests and Achievement tests are the proverbial apples and oranges, measured by different scales). Therefore, according to the example in my notes, if a kid's tested IQ is 115 and his 'achievement test score' is 85, subtract 85 from 115 to get 30. Since 30 is greater than 24, we have ourselves an LD kid, though he tests 'above average' in intelligence.

Looking at the definitions again, we see agreement that there is no physical disease process at work. This is a 'psychological" process. It is a learned response to the things taught. It is, therefore, a manufactured problem. If we teach kids to respond in a certain way, and they can learn the correct response, calling that response a learning disability is shabby science.

Incidentally, do you wonder why merely discussing IQ is a huge *faux pas* for the rest of us while Special ed can use the idea openly for its own purposes? If IQ is a useful idea, perhaps it should be included as a criterion in all aspects of pupil evaluations. In any case, think back to the first chapter where we discussed the recent, alarmingly low achievement of the 'average' kid. These poor results create lots of potential for perceived achievement discrepancies. Therefore, whether or not they specifically intended our current system to achieve its current abysmal results, Progressive education in a nutshell means: Don't teach kids facts, but rather fill their heads with academic pablum and damaging psychosocial nonsense and presto-change-o we have ourselves, "The Nation of the Learning Disabled." Still, everyone feels good about themselves—tra-la.

This thing reads like a B-movie plot doesn't it?

It gets worse.

You will not get designated as learning disabled after a single achievement discrepancy calculation. Before the school system can 'help' you, you must endure another procedure that results in an Individual Education Plan (IEP). The process that results in an IEP is essentially a combination mega parent-teacher conference and intellectual due process hearing that might include a dozen or more 'experts'. After someone notices some achievement discrepancy (usually a teacher who does not truly understand the technical [read 'fuzzy psychobabble"] definitions) they schedule an IEP. Parents or legal guardians are asked to attend since our mental health professionals have not yet been able to annex parental responsibility fully, and parents still have the right to refuse 'placement'.

Unfortunately, since our kids' achievement is generally abominable now, parents often arrive at the IEP 'deeply concerned' and willing to try almost anything to get Junior's grades up. Parents are already adults after all (usually) and realize that an F-minus average will not qualify Junior for a very lucrative career. The panel of experts show the parents their kids' test results, which were administered before the formal hearing, and the parents see the 'professionals' concerned and understanding faces, listen with growing consternation and confusion to additional impressive-sounding psychobabble and leave thinking that these people represent Junior's last hope.

Of course they intend IEPs to be 'positive experiences' for everybody (self-esteem first and last), so they also show parents a list of their kid's "strengths." During this phase of the program, parents may learn that their child, "writes letters in an up and down orientation." Imagine what you would think if the best thing your kid's teachers and counselors can say about your child is that he writes letters in an up and down orientation? The school has just justified the provisions of PL 94-142 that state that parents have procedural and notification rights. Another result is, of course, that the school has just earned the additional funds that placement in Special education brings, and the best part is that it will not cost the parents a thing, since PL 94-142 also says that your kid has the right to "free, 'appropriate' public education." _All_ of us pay this cost, not the parents.

How can I dispute the opinions of all these 'experts'? Because their opinions are just opinions unsupported by competent research, and because their results are so poor. Read the supporting research that I have read and you will see nothing but ideological editorials. I will show some more samples shortly. Remember that even the textbooks state that Progressive techniques show little or no positive academic effects attributable to their techniques, yet "educational professionals" and "observers" insist we do them anyway.

In one sense, though, we have to give them credit for consistency. If facts are unnecessary burdens when teaching children, why should the results of genuine research affect classroom recommendations.

If you want to read about some of the genuine research of various social scientists about what kids are like and the potentials they truly have, if only we would teach and encourage them, try _Greater Expectations_ (1995) by William Damon of Brown University. The subtitle of his book is _Overcoming the Culture of Indulgence in our Homes and Schools._ Here is a social scientist for whom evidence is important. His conclusions are based on facts, not ideology with blinders on. As such, he inevitably recommends a balance between the two ideological extremes because even Progressive thinkers occasionally say something that has merit. When we find it, accidental though it may be, we must use it to help our kids move forward. Damon references many other researchers who respect reality. It is a shame that calm and thoughtful consideration does not make for quick and exciting sound bites. If it did, common sense would be much more common.

Unfortunately, after indoctrinating kids from the earliest grades in Progressive ideology and the wisdom of fact-less recommendations, some modern kids became mental-health professionals. We have now trained battalions of psychologists, social workers, self-help gurus, family counselors, educators, and administrators. Typical training over the past several decades stressed the philosophy that expects kids to fail, so they see failure everywhere they look. Still, they call it success, or worse, say failure does not matter because feeling good about ourselves is more important. However, it does not hurt the professional's feelings that they can also draw a paycheck and feel good about 'helping' these poor babies, too. Of course, we have now accepted massive academic failure as the norm, even as IQ scores remain the same, so it is OK, because we are doing the right thing.

To tell you the truth, this analysis does not seem to square with the nice, apparently committed people I know who work as Special educators and counselors, and that bothers me. I am not therefore trying to suggest that the nice, smiling lady that you know is a monster in disguise (even if they feel compelled to tell your kids to keep things from you). Yet the facts do support my analysis, so my best guess is that most of the working people have been as duped and indoctrinated as the rest of us, including the politicians and judges who let loose this travesty upon our kids.

We can summarize much of the Progressive philosophy in the phrase, "Poor baby!" Whenever somebody has some slight problem with anything, the immediate assumption is that their internal perception of the problem is so traumatic and would leave psychic scars of such depth and importance, that normal life could never go on happily for the 'victim' without official propping up. One indication of this is that no one is merely sad about anything any more. The lowest level of sadness that we hear about today is 'devastation'. Also, it is now considered the government's duty to reassure us and to insure our happiness, so we always send in counselors to help us 'achieve closure' after some disaster makes the news. It may not be as sexy but, apart from being far less expensive, after an appropriate period of grief I suspect that it is psychically much healthier for family, friends, and local ministers to tell someone who has suffered a loss that, "Life goes on. Snap out of it. There are living people who depend on you." Left to their own devices, the people we know generally help us manage our emotions adequately. Bureaucratic strangers should stay out of it. Still, that is just my opinion.

Are you angry yet? You should be, but you should also be frightened because 'progress' marches on. Apart from the never-ending, misguided calls for increased funding for Special ed costs, one of my final exam questions for the Special ed class proposed the idea that since IEPs are individualized plans, and since we all want to do what is best for *all* kids, perhaps requiring IEPs for everybody might be useful.

Apart from the impossibility of asking teachers to develop individual lesson plans for each lesson for each pupil, some of my own experiences positively scream about how bad an idea this is. In a previous life, in the Army, I had a job that periodically required me to attend sessions that sound very much like an IEP, though those sessions were more properly designed for bad conduct cases rather than LD. We tried to decide whether we should 'substantiate' charges of various sorts of abuse against people. Abuse is certainly a serious matter, but they absolutely appalled, and even frightened me, by how little information was required to decide what to do with someone. Even the courts have "hearsay" rules. But not here. Proof was often incidental or nonexistent. Often a simple accusation was enough (much as in the Salem trials of the Colonial era). Decisions made by this official body could then follow a person forever because various regulations required that reports must be filed with named agencies. A finding of 'substantiated' is the equivalent of an indictment and the names of people thus identified, whether there is any proof or not, get posted to a national database where potential employers, police, and others can find it.

Other final exam questions, designed to give prospective educators experience in making decisions about kids based on simulated "real life" situations corroborated my experience as well. (Keep in mind that educators were, on average, college students with the lowest scholastic qualifications, and have no training in medical or psychological processes, other than their Progressive indoctrination. That description also includes many of their professors.) These situations provided only the most cursory details about, for instance, achievement deficits or the situation at home, etc., but expected us to select a course of action for the child. Not surprisingly, the expected decisions would swell the Special ed rolls.

One real example of the frightening possibilities was the case of two professional parents (Mom and Stepdad) and their fourteen-year-old daughter, which I witnessed in my former life. The daughter was a normal, modern girl, described to me later, by Mom, as ". . . fourteen going on twenty-one." The daughter had been invited to a party with 'college kids'. Dad sensibly said "No." Daughter became angry and, with the encouragement of a self-styled 'radical feminist' educator, accused Dad of sexual abuse. Dad is in a profession with very strict scrutiny rules and might have been rendered permanently unemployable had the report gone forward as "Substantiated."

Had the reports been filed, Dad would have had a problem because it is very difficult to argue with a committee of 'experts' once it files a report. Very little in our society today resembles Big Brother more than a 'panel of experts' in psychologically-based disciplines. But what do you do if the government requirements are mindless and you are just a little kid? I have no doubt that most of those experts are well-meaning, but the harm they often do in the name of building self-esteem can be irreparable. Just listen to the news on any given day.

Apart from the selfishness issues that we have discussed, one manifestation of this harm is that, if we mandate an IEP for every pupil, it is virtually certain that the folks who would get that mandate would be government employees. With access to taxes, the government is the only body that could possibly afford to set up and maintain such a bureaucracy. The government also has subpoena powers and the authority to compel compliance with its dictates. In no time at all, this system would get overwhelmed and they would issue new, less restrictive guidelines about who can sit on these panels, perhaps mandating that a certain percentage of the panel be trained in Special ed. Very quickly colleges would respond to this new 'need' and qualify unqualified people to do the work that consists mainly (other than deciding what is best for the helpless, ignorant population, of course) in filling out forms and filing reports. The folks who fill in the required forms would do that with little useful information since all 'authentic assessments' are inflated, subjective folderol (see Chapter 7), but they would file their reports and would potentially ruin another life.

Another inevitable outcome of such a bureaucracy is that, since the system becomes overwhelmed, they would devise procedural shortcuts. Someone would likely develop a checklist of acceptable outcomes or appropriate transitions to life after high school, or some such thing. This has probably already been done to some extent within the Special ed/counseling community. I contend that it is a very bad idea to ask anyone, much less overworked government employees, merely to use a checklist that tells us what to do with the rest of our life, especially if we become obliged to do what the checklist demands, as a court order does. This obligation is another possible Big Brotherish outcome, yet would be sold as an adjunct to freedom (choice).

All of this may sound a bit overblown, but we have all seen many bad ideas take on a bureaucratic life of their own, rarely to the benefit of anyone, including those they intend to help. One case in point is Special education.

Is this characterization unfair? Perhaps. I have asked Special ed folks about that and about the proliferation of 'educational services', at the expense of teaching, and they protest that, "We are not responsible for the need for educational services. The parents are demanding these services (because of an IEP)." "It's the right thing to do." "For the children." "Hike!" But achievement keeps going down," we say. "Why are you concerned?" they reply. So pony up your taxes, Bunkie, and if you dare to vote against us, we will brand you as "Against Education" and mean-spirited besides.

For the past few pages we have been following a trail that took us away from Progressive research, as exemplified by the Tourette Syndrome and Bicultural Education papers shown above. You may have wondered how I can complain about small sample sets in Progressive research when I only found six articles, or so, for each of these. Isn't that too small a sample, as well? Ordinarily your wonderment would be justified. However, here you should look at the facts from the flip side. These were the first articles I came to. If these kinds of articles were rare, how could I find them to the exclusion of responsible research? Am I that lucky that I can just go straight to the stuff that just happens to support my positions? If I am so lucky, why haven't I won the lottery yet? The truth is, this stuff is the rule, not the exception. The journals are filled with them.

Special Ed Classroom Recommendations

Let us look at the kinds of recommendations that Special education makes for improving your kids' understanding. These recommendations come in lots of very similar variations and each State undoubtedly has its own version. I have one set related specifically to Tourette Syndrome but I will not use those because while many recommendations for this disability are similar or even identical to those for all Special ed kids, with only 50 genuinely documented cases of TS in history, hardly anyone could argue that the specific recommendations are applicable to everyone.

Instead, here is another of my classroom handouts, that I have modified with my comments, etc. This handout details how teachers might modify classroom procedures to "accommodate" learning disabilities. The higher the "Level" of modification, the deeper we delve into Special 'education'. Remember that the law specifies that Special ed is required to provide "aids and services" only. Quoting the handout:

Adaptation Modification Options: Level and Descriptions

When considering the question <u>What do we do now?</u> Teachers have many options available to make instructions relevant and meaningful to *all* students.

Notice that 'relevance' is immediately invoked. Incidentally, the emphasized word *'all'* was originally used to imply that it was not right that regular education wanted to exclude retarded kids (and, in the multiculturalist's version, non-dominant-culture kids) from regular classrooms. It has more recently evolved to have a more inclusive meaning. Over time, everybody has become targeted by Special education and they indoctrinate prospective 'regular' teachers to use techniques designed to fit the slowest kids, but which get used with *all* kids. This annexation of all of education is quite conscious and deliberate. For instance, in a recent issue of *Teacher Education and Special Education*, Fisher, et al. write, "In the last decade considerable attention has been paid to the identification of the skills, knowledge and dispositions that enable all teachers to embrace and successfully implement inclusive education practices. For example, in a comprehensive review of practices that foster inclusive education, Udvart-Solner and Thousand state that 'the innovative changes occurring in general education *are the same kinds of changes required for effective inclusion*' [my emphasis]." The general idea is that what is good for the slowest among our pupils, is appropriate for all pupils, regardless of ability. In other words, teach everyone as if they were retarded. The authors then tell us which practices are the most appropriate for our children: "These initiatives include outcome-based education, multicultural education, Multiple Intelligences Theory, constructivist learning, interdisciplinary curriculum, . . . authentic ways of assessing student learning, multi-aged grouping, instructional technology, peer-mediated instruction such as cooperative group learning and partner learning [i.e., study buddies; kids taken from one class/grade to help kids within another grade] . . ." Most of these items should be quite familiar to you by now.

In planning and delivering student instruction, all or part of one level, alone or in combination with other levels, based on the individual needs of the student or students, may be used.

One lesson plan is never enough. Not if you are a *good* teacher.

Level 0—No Adaptations/Modifications needed.

This level is a bit deceptive of course, since everything has already been changed ('dumbed-down') over the past several decades, to conform to Progressive dictates. As we have just seen, however, none of these specific changes are mandated in law. Federal and State Departments of Education or well-meaning administrators who 'interpret' what is appropriate, instituted all of them.

Level 1—Reinforcing the Activity or Content.

'Activities' come before 'content'. *Good* teachers do not teach 'lessons' with subject matter content, of course, but they were forced to include content (against their better judgment) because the bureaucracy of QPA (Quality Performance Accreditation) requires all teachers to participate in developing 'outcomes', etc., and there are still genuine teachers out there who are gamely trying to stand their ground.

1. Help students with class requirements

    In its general outlook, this set of recommendations looks a lot like school as I knew it. Of course, the way all of this is done in practice (because teachers cannot prepare more than one lesson plan per lesson) is closer to the upper end of this chart (see Levels 3 and 4).

2. Pre-teach or re-teach material

    I am not sure what "pre-teaching" refers to but it may be as simple as introducing and defining new words at the beginning of an activity. "Re-teaching," of course, involves reviewing, etc., and is quite normal practice. Remediation, however, is the likely meaning here. We know it as; do not teach today what we can hold off until tomorrow (or next year). The results produce 9th graders proudly achieving at the fourth-grade level.

3. Develop aids and advance organizers for class requirement

    This might mean anything but this single item may be the closest thing to the original intent of PL 94-142, trying to help kids with genuine handicaps by producing large-text material, audio notes, or Braille materials, etc.

4. Add extra practice or enrichment

I like #4. To me it means homework and, presumably, meaningful extra-credit work. Unfortunately, it now also means giving extra time in class to complete homework that the pupils chose not to do at home. We will speak about other games that pupils play shortly. Other 'enrichments' that can, and are being used, include frequent field trips (i.e., kids use these as a social outing) or taking 'advanced' kids out of their own class to help teach kids in lower grades. Helping lower grade kids sounds very nice, but when are the upper-grade kids expected to learn their own material if they are rarely in their class? Why do we need teachers if we can just draft kids?

5. Develop study guides

We have discussed study guides previously. They are OK for late grammar and, maybe, early junior high school, but are just a way to dumb down lessons, if prepared by high school teachers. By high school, a kid can make her own study guide as she reads each assignment, if she wants one. We once called this practice "taking notes" and "studying."

6. Develop discipline plan

A discipline plan is necessary of course, even if it is not expressed as a formal document, but the way Progressives say we must develop one is not what most of us have in mind. One of the favorite group of methods is the "Behavioral Contract" where the kids get to make their own rules and, in theory, are expected to abide by them. The contracts are an invention designed to counteract the decaying self-discipline of modern pupils. The idea fits very well with giving kids choices and with relevance theory, but as a rule, this should not be done, especially in the early years. If the school acted as if adults ran it, these contracts would not be necessary at all. Kids would already know what we expected and what is unacceptable behavior. Additionally, these school-day experiments in choice do not affect the individual kid alone. They affect the whole class, and may contravene the kinds of things that parents are trying to teach their kids, especially in ethical and moral choices. The point at which kids become adults is soon enough to allow them to mess with the rest of society. The school should merely reinforce what has already been taught at home, including what we once called the community standards, not allow the whims of kids, influenced by the politically correct, to reinvent society every few months.

7. **Use alternative instructional methods**

This means 'mix it up' a bit. Despite my defense of the lecture method, and especially the lecture-demonstration-discussion method. I do not say that lectures are the only allowable instructional method. On the contrary, many other methods may and should be used under appropriate circumstances. For instance, watching an occasional short video can be done if the video shows detail that can be seen in no other way. Labs are good methods and have been used for a long time. Other examples might include an occasional mock debate, or oral report, etc., when appropriate and for a change of pace. Therefore, #7 is not necessarily a bad thing, unless a 'regular' method does not exist, or is uninstructive, and every class is a new alternative. Even genuine teachers frequently use instructional variety. What you do and how you do it depends on the lesson. The sorts of alternatives that we will read shortly should not be available, however.

Level 2—Adapting/Modifying the Activity or Content

Here is where the Special ed fun really starts. From this point on we will see no more recommendations for increased work, as in Level 1, #4 above. Practice apparently does not make perfect in a Progressive world. On the other hand, we *will* see an increasing number of recommendations that reduce and dumb down the work load.

1. **Select appropriate unit outcomes or reduce number of unit outcomes.**

Carefully choose which of the school's general outcomes, or subject requirements, your target 'poor baby' will have trouble with, and get rid of them.

2. **Change mastery requirements/level**

If they complain that it is still too hard, cut back even more.

3. **Alter the pace of instruction.**

This one is generally acceptable even in genuine schools, but it should not be slowed to the extent that kids do not get exposed to grade-level requirements, as is happening now. Speeding up the pace should be as common as slowing it temporarily. Unfortunately, speeding up is virtually unknown nowadays, unless we include elimination of topics, or, conversely, discussing 'cutting-edge' topics with little or no preliminary instruction.

4. Adapt or modify class work.
   A) Highlight texts/reading material
        Do the pupil's reading, thinking, and note-taking for them.
   B) Write or rewrite worksheets
        Worksheets are common tools, and have been used for a long
        time. The problem here is that the main emphasis is to dumb-
        down, not challenge or instruct. Word search games are the
        order of the day, not lessons that instruct. Word search games
        include such things as crossword puzzles that list the words
        that must be used. As such, these activities are little more
        than pattern recognition exercises that may be appropriate in
        Kindergarten and 1st grade, but I was preparing to teach high
        school science and was told that they are acceptable and
        necessary even at that level. Another modern use of work-
        sheets is as tests. Kids are given a worksheet, shown how to
        fill it out, then later a blank copy of the same worksheet is
        used as the test of the subject matter.
   C) Make or modify study guides
        See above.
5. Use alternative activities and projects
   Allow cut-and-paste and artsy activities and choreography, etc., to
   replace thinking.
6. Adapt or modify tests.
   A) Change the administration
        Read it to the pupil and let him ask questions during the test;
        Let two or three kids take group tests, etc. In effect, read 'may
        allow cheating', Also, see 2 above. An example of the results
        of this idea is this: I was proctoring a test in a 'block scheduled'
        class one day. Block scheduled classes were double the usual
        traditional length, (one and a half hours) but given every
        other day. This meant that everyone would finish the test long
        before the class ended, and required that additional activities
        in the form of worksheets be available to fill time while every-
        one finished the test. One pupil handed in his completed test
        and began doing the additional worksheets. Later, something
        occurred to him and he asked to get his test back. I said, "No.
        That's not the way it works", at which point he opined that I
        was "F____ing retarded" for not allowing him to cheat openly.
        He could not have known that, aside from my traditional
        opinions, I was reluctant to return his exam since I had already
        graded his open book test. He scored a 57 percent.

B) Change the content

Ignore the State's grade level requirements. Dumb it down.

7. Design alternative assessment activities.

Allow choreography to replace paper and pencil tests.

Level 3—Develop Parallel Activity or Content.

Parallel activities are those that are similar to what the regular pupils are doing, but not the same. For instance, if the class is working on some sort of presentation about the plight of whooping cranes, the LD kid would do another cut-and-paste exercise featuring birds.

1. Make or use more appropriate or functional materials that parallel the regular curriculum.

   I do not recall discussing what a 'functional material' might be, but based on #2 below, it may be that they intend that we develop new 'outcomes' on the spot to 'meet each pupil's needs'. It also sounds as if this recommendation requires us to reevaluate what the lesson (activity) "really means" and cut out the parts that are not relevant (too hard) to a kid.

2. Determine the functional value of regular class activity and use authentic activity and assessment.

   Notice that there is not even a cursory nod to 'content' anymore? Since 'authentic activities' are a sham and almost perfectly useless, this recommendation might mean, "Just give up. They're not learning anyway, so why bother? We are in full daycare mode now." But then, with their unrelenting focus on "activities" rather than lessons, many schools are little better than daycare centers anyway.

Level 4—Developing Alternative Activity or Outcome.

This is an even deeper use of the idea of 'functional value', as in Level 3, #2, above. It means: Ignore State-mandated requirements and content standards, though they are already dumbed-down. Although genuine research has shown that distractions and interruptions make learning more difficult, we should do it anyway. We should do it anyway, they tell us, to decrease confusion and increase instructional focus in the classroom.

1. Incorporate skill listed on IEP in the regular classroom environment (may or may not relate to regular class activity).

   Let him 'write letters in an up and down, orientation', and pat him on the head like a puppy. Then send him on to college.

2. **Task-analyze regular class activity and define step(s) as new activity outcome.**

> Do the work for the kid, then give him an "A" for effort (i.e., being present occasionally). Task analysis expects the teacher to break every lesson (activity) into easily reproducible steps. On the surface, this sounds like a traditional fourth grade science 'lab', but they intend it as an option for every class at every level. Imagine task-analyzing a literature, history, or science lesson. Also, this is another example of the Progressive lack of consistency. If task organizing is appropriate, why do educationists argue so forcefully against phonetic reading instruction? Phonics expects teachers to teach kids to break words down into their constituent sounds, as symbolized by letter and groups of letters. Additionally, you should keep this argument in mind when you read in Chapter 7 how Progressive education argues against multiple-choice tests *because* they focus on easily reproducible steps.

I suppose some of these recommendations may be appropriate for the truly mentally retarded, especially Levels 3 and 4, but to use them with kids who are intellectually similar to their ancestors and can easily earn genuine passing grades in a non-dumbed-down world, is simply disgraceful.

An indication that this dumbing-down occurs regularly and not just for the so-called learning disabled is this. My daughter's fourth grade teacher, a bright and sensible woman who recognized that the current philosophy is not good for children, had organized a modified form of ability grouping. She and other fourth grade teachers regularly swap kids so that they can bring together a few of the kids whose 'math skills' are more advanced[198] (probably because their parents used flash cards, etc., to practice at home). The teacher told me, shortly after the State sponsored standardized tests were administered, that her advanced group was "several chapters" ahead of the other kids but that the standardized test asked for skills that she had not presented yet. So even the fourth grade 'advanced' group was not instructed in what even the State educationists consider to be average fourth-grade-level work.

---

198 I should give kudos to the principal as well, for allowing this modified step in the right direction.

How does all this dumbing-down affect kids? Other than learning little or nothing, you mean? The kids are smart enough to see through the sham. School becomes a game to see how little work they can get away with and still pass. Many kids now do not care if they pass or not, of course, but from the point of view of the kid who does, the scenario goes like this:

Kid: "It's too hard."
Educationist: "Don't worry, we'll dumb it down."
Kid:: "It, like, still too hard."
Educationist: "That's OK. We'll put you in a program."
Kid: "It too *ha-a-ard*!!! I don't know where you're *at*."
Educationist: "Don't sweat it. You'll graduate anyway and the President says we will pay for your college, too."
Kid: "We, like totally, wan' mo' free time, y'know . . . Totally. That would be awesome."

Once the kid has been in the system for a while, they get very good at this game and beat Progressive educators at it handily. This scenario also goes a very long way to explaining why relative academic scores fall as kids progress through the school levels, and why the drop-out rate is so high as the kids decide that school is irrelevant. Recall from Chapter 1, the typical grammar school average math score is "D," the middle schools score "D minus" and high schools score "F."

As adults we should be wise enough to recall that old salt, "If you give 'em an inch, they'll take a mile." As it is, we have abdicated our responsibility as adults trying to insure that kids' fragile psyches are not bruised by occasionally telling them that they made a mistake and that they have to learn to correct their mistakes if they want to pass in school and succeed in life?

This idea rings true in the Progressive mind since for them identifying a child's mistake is the same as deliberately pursuing a program of psychological torture and personal denigration. Theirs is a vision of meanspirited right-wing monsters with hatred oozing from every pore, who delight in repeatedly calling kids 'morons' and telling them nothing but that they are stupid and will never amount to anything. If a teacher like this is found, right-wing or otherwise, fire him, but I suspect we would find very few chances to do that because the people who become teachers generally seem to like kids. Used judiciously by a teacher that kids perceive as strict but fair, mild bruising of egos is often just the thing to get a pupil motivated. My guess is that most of us can relate a story of our own along these lines (perhaps a story about your all-time favorite teacher), but I will show an example of self-motivation, based on ego deflation, in a few pages.

Rather than motivation, the next example shows what Special education does for pupil morale and love of learning.

I helped to judge a science fair once. It was a small, local affair and featured the projects of grammar school kids. As we might expect, the projects were not cutting-edge science, but at least the kids showed some willingness to try. Of course, no kid beyond the fourth grade entered the fair. Maybe this is a clue too.

We judged the fair over two days. The kids were present only on the second day. The first day allowed judges to examine each project at leisure to see which ones were the most original, best tried to answer the question they posed, and were complete according to the rules, etc. The rules specified a format that required each project to consist of several parts including an introduction, some explanation of samples, procedures and methods, and a summary of results and findings, and also a few other items such as references [i.e., prior knowledge is required]. Since these were early attempts at science, and since science is a content area that is considered 'hard' and therefore not much like party games, and especially since the judges' evaluations counted for nothing in the school grade, our job as judges was not to criticize too harshly, but to encourage. In other words we were asked to simulate genuine grammar school teachers. So we did.

The budding, young scientists were present on the second day of judging so that we might question them to see who seemed to have been most deeply involved in the project. For several entries, the project was clearly more Mom or Dad than Junior. That is not necessarily bad, of course. The kid needs considerable guidance at this age and doing a project together is 'quality family time' of the best sort.

I remember one conversation in particular, however. I was still trying to encourage continued participation on one of the 'Mom' projects when I asked the fourth grader, "Well, did you enjoy doing the project?" I got a noncommittal shrug so I asked, "Do you think you will do another one next year?" The answer was, "No. I don't have to. I'm gifted."

Judging a national education system based on one short exchange is probably unfair, but it seems that those two attitudes just do not mesh somehow. Where could this child have learned that ability precludes continued effort if not at school? Knowing what we know about Special ed and its current philosophy, would you want your kids in a 'gifted' program administered and taught by 'Special ed'? In truth, I can barely imagine it. It is a modern educational oxymoron. There are only two possible justifications for agreeing to take your kid out of 'regular' class. The first is if they managed to get at least a little bit more subject matter than the other kids do, or if it was organized to actually teach things. But then, that should be done in every class.

There's Literature, and Then There Is . . .

When my son was identified as someone who could 'possibly benefit from the enhanced educational opportunities' that a gifted class could provide, I went to speak with the Special educator. She seemed a bright woman, who told me her own kids had done well in school, but, it turned out that if I agreed to allow her to help my son, she mainly intended to allow him to do more puzzles than in the regular classroom. This enhanced educational opportunity still did not consider that teaching things is pertinent, only presenting him with "problem solving" challenges in various puzzles and games.

I had asked her to have some samples of evidence supporting the idea that what she recommended is appropriate fare for the gifted kid, and she had several photocopied items waiting for me when I arrived for our appointment. It may have been a coincidence, but the one on top was a one-page article from *Helping Hand* magazine titled *Gifted Children and Their Emotions*, that postulated that gifted kids are more "sensitive" than regular kids, so teachers should be especially ready to recommend psychological therapy and parents should be encouraged to accept it. At the time my wife and I were informed of our son's perceived gifts, we were also told that he may need speech therapy. Apparently the fact that his speech was just fine while he still had his two front baby teeth was not considered relevant. I declined the speech therapy. The article, which was written by the director of the National Hospital for Kids in Crisis, listed no references to prove its claims. It amounted to advertising for the hospital, camouflaged as teacher education.

I had asked for proof of appropriateness for their 'enhanced' instructional methods, but what I got was more unsupported and fatuous psychobabble. I had no expectation that this teacher would have a research library at her fingertips in her grammar school classroom, yet she undoubtedly speaks with many parents who have questions. Some of those parents must want more than restatements of unsubstantiated ideology as proof of appropriateness. She even told me that many parents refuse her help so as not to label their kids as nerds. Today's parents have apparently been educated to fear the social stigma of high capability. This is quite a change from the past when being 'left behind', and being thought of as ignorant, was a source of embarrassment.

Another handout shown to me was a "teacher nomination form" used to identify kids for the gifted program. It listed, and was titled, <u>Characteristics of G/T</u> (gifted/talented) <u>students, including negative problem traits.</u> Among the listed traits was being bored by the typical classroom fare, and making the boredom known. This is considered evidence of a potential need for therapy.

Stapled to the *Emotions* article was another one page article called *Tips for Identifying and Working with Children Who Are Gifted.* This one was originally published in *CEC Today*[199] and written by CEC's "Information Specialist, Gifted Education," who flirted with common sense when she said, "Some gifted children approach a topic so broadly that they exceed their ability to anticipate the steps necessary to complete the task *they have chosen* (my emphasis). They can imagine the finished building design, but they don't know how to get the materials they need. They can visualize the puppet show being performed, but they don't know the names of the materials they need to create the puppets. They may need help to visualize their tasks in small steps that can be managed easily." Yet the flirtation was not consummated. This author can see that kids don't know important, basic things yet, but does not recommend teaching them anything. The discovery of specific information is still left up to the kids themselves. Her recommendations were full of the same fluffy-sounding 'open-ended' solutions that are being used in classrooms today. Some of her recommendations actually made some sense, as words, but, of course the implementation of those recommendations somehow did not involve instructing the kids. They merely restate, over and over, the 'need' to be left alone.

---

199 The magazine of the Council for Exceptional Children.

For example, another of the handouts I was given is a list of <u>Needs of Gifted/Talented Students.</u> The sheet listed 14 "needs," not one of which involved instruction in anything. Here they are:

- Freedom from the restrictions of structured requirements and time allocations
- Flexible program which includes a differentiated curriculum involving the higher level [*sic*] of thinking
- Time to experiment and explore
- Opcn acccss to needed learning resources whatever and wherever the [*sic*] may be
- Confrontation with societal problems and issues for which there is no single predetermined solution [Values clarification training tied to, "Do your own thing, Man."]
- Opportunity to brainstorm
- Encouragement to ask questions, make discoveries, pursue own interests in depth
- Opportunities to work with other gifted/talented students at least part of the time
- Wide variety of in-depth cultural experiences beyound [*sic*] the usual field trips to zoos, museums, industries
- Opportunities to help others (e.g., as volunteer reader to the blind, as companion to the elderly . . .)
- Friendly recognition and acceptance of student's giftedness
- Introduction to students to own gifts (abilities)
- Active concern for the gifted/talented among administrators, counselors, teachers

And, of course

- Teachers who are facilitators of access to learning opportunities

Clearly, what they have in mind for our local crop of bright kids could hardly be equated to an "Honors" class of old. Rather, it may be a Kindergarten with slightly more challenging toys. The item that comes closest to recommending instruction of any kind says that gifted kids need another, "Flexible program" and invokes, "the higher level of thinking." The words used are all familiar by now. Gifted kids need, "freedom from the restrictions of structured requirements and time allocations" . . . "flexible" . . . "open access" . . . "in-depth cultural experiences, for which there is no predetermined solution." The only other mention of working involves "encouragement" to pursue their "own interests." In effect, gifted kids are on their own, like "normal" kids, only more so. Teachers have no function other than to facilitate "access to learning opportunities (more superficial activities)."

To facilitate these approved opportunities, and to detail the sorts of "in-depth cultural experiences" they have in mind, along with two sheets listing Internet sites for gifted kids, I was also given a seven-page listing of, The 50 best young adult novels of all time—So far. Try to think what novels might be on a list labeled as grandly as that: *Tom Sawyer? Kim? Gulliver's Travels? Journey to the Center of the Earth? Great Expectations? The Lost World? Treasure Island? A Connecticut Yankee in King Arthur's Court? Alice in Wonderland? Black Beauty? The Call of the Wild? The Once and Future King? The Mysterious Island? The Red Badge of Courage? The Time Machine?* Perhaps Rousseau's favorite, *Robinson Crusoe?*, or even something a bit more recent and less challenging, such as *The Chronicles of Narnia* or *Charlotte's Web?* Not on your life. What we get are books to which, we are assured, today's kids can relate. Books such as, *I Am the Cheese,* and *Killing Mr. Griffin.*

Killing Mr. Griffin is about some kids who acted on their affirmative choice to kidnap a "strict" teacher, but they didn't know he had a bad heart. We also get, *When She Hollers,* which is about a girl who threatens her abusing stepdad with a knife, and is afraid of what may happen when he comes home. Another is, *Gentlehands,* about the shock of finding out that your kind and loving granddad was once a Nazi war criminal. *Midnight Hour Encores,* is about a girl and her father on a journey to trying to find the mother/wife who deserted them "so long ago." Then there is *Forever,* about a "sexually explicit, but wholesome" friendship between two teens. All these titles are on a list of books apparently intended for grammar school kids. A final example, *Remembering the Good Times,* is about three friends, until one commits suicide; then there are only two friends.

Clearly, these books were chosen to foster the culturally traditional values of a sense of community, pride in ancestry, the support of family, love of life, morality, faith, respect for elders, and to teach kids to be trustful of others and trustworthy in their own right. This handout includes short synopses of the books, all of which read like made-for-TV-movie plots, which are widely known to be designed to appeal to the nobler, more intellectual instincts, and are therefore appropriate for gifted readers and higher-level, critical thinkers of all ages. The synopsis for *I Am the Cheese* reads;

> Where is Adam going on his urgent winter bike ride to nowhere? Who is Brint the Interrogator? And why does Amy never answer the phone?

All of the excerpts read in this vapid, breathless way, except the first one for *Catcher in the Rye*, by J. D. Salinger, and this one gives us a clue. This synopsis reads, "Holden Caulfield's lost weekend in New York City. The now classic coming-of-age novel that established the edgy style and voice of young adult literature sixteen years before the genre was invented." Sixteen years after 1951, when *Catcher in the Rye* was first published, is 1967. At the start of the current Progressive era. These books seem to have been chosen, and labeled, "the best of all time," not for their deathless literary merit, or even for their reputed interest (relevance) to modern children, but for their indoctrinational value for the Progressive agenda. They even promise to continue training our gifted, future intellectuals and leaders with more of the same watery 'genre'. The title to the list reads, "The 50 best . . . —so far."

Here is another example of an effect Special education has on kids. During Ed school, they allowed us (educators in training) to interview some kids identified as learning disabled, and other kids in a gifted program. Kids in each 'condition' were brought to the Ed school during separate class periods.

The similarities were striking between what the LD pupils and what the gifted pupils told us. Both groups said that they really wanted the schoolwork to be 'relevant' and that school would be easier for them if the examples given in class related to their own lives better. They are so similar, in fact, that we got the feeling that they are not truly speaking their own minds but were mouthing the 'party-line.' This is the indoctrination I have mentioned several times touted as 'the wisdom of children'. Yet one has to wonder, if this relevance is so critically important that even the kids are indoctrinated in its need, and educators have been pursuing it for generations, why don't the kids see more relevance in their instruction? Why are they dropping out in record numbers? As Rousseau tells us, "The harm is not in what the pupil does not understand but is in what he believes he understands."[200]

---

200 *Emile*, p. 182.

Even their more personal comments were quite similar, except that the gifted kids said that they wanted to be left alone more than the LD kids, who wanted more help (i.e., more party-line). Some gifted kids said that they still needed to be forced to complete their assignments. This revelation was made quite arrogantly in at least one case, with some head-nodding from the others. One young man, who styled himself a computer nerd, said with a laugh, "My dad will figure it out one of these days that I don't have to do homework. I'll pass anyway and all I want to do is work with my computer." While he is almost certainly correct in assuming that his Progressively assigned work is essentially irrelevant to his success and that he will pass with little or no subject-related work, more than one of my classmates commented on how self-satisfied, and unambitious, the 'gifted' group seemed. This 'school is pointless' attitude is not at all different from what the LD kids said. A couple of these kids, 9th graders, said that they wanted nothing more to do with school at all. All they wanted was to work on cars. Was the common hopeful 'outcome' of developing 'lifelong learners' accomplished for either end of the spectrum, or are the loftily professed and printed outcomes just more eyewash to keep parents at bay?

The learning and teaching implications here are quite clear. Neither group of kids is yet mature nor experienced enough to know what life will hold for them. Both are in for a rude awakening when they enter the 'real world', at which point their "stress" levels will assuredly skyrocket (providing continued employment for many therapists).

On the other hand, teaching the traditional course of reading, writing, 'rithmetic, with some history, science, civics, music, crafts, physical exercise, and extracurricular activities thrown in, would undoubtedly stand both groups in good stead. We can instruct the gifted kids with more detail and eventually with more analysis required when their brains are ready, while we can teach the average kids a bit more concretely with a bit less analysis required. We would distribute the kids we now designate as LD to the various ability groups as their individual potential allowed. Otherwise, genuine good teaching practices should apply to all.

My final example also contradicts the Special ed and self-esteem philosophies by showing someone who developed a bit of wisdom because of a mild, though perfectly ordinary, psychic bruising. The story has a happy ending. The one bruised did not require counseling or medication as a devastated and broken man. He became stronger, and better educated, because of the experience. In fact, he became a life-long learner.

On July 20, 1998 Theodore Hershberg, a literature professor from the University of Pennsylvania, gave a speech that was broadcast on C-SPAN. In it he recounted his own experiences as a young college student at the University of Illinois and the University of Chicago. He told of his early days when he felt very much out of his league because he had not yet read some books that some of his classmates could already quote, occasionally in the original French, etc. Hershberg also remembered that he did not know anything about some authors that were 'required reading', and that some of his classmates seemed to have read them already. He also said that he distinctly remembered thinking that he disliked that feeling of relative ignorance and determined to fill all of his own educational gaps.

That was then, this is now.

Hershberg spoke of former reading requirements that modern colleges do not even consider imposing on their students anymore, because the modern students would not stand for them. He spoke of the former educational philosophy that provided suggested-reading lists that asked students to read long, and often dry ancient books, that at first flush did not seem to have any direct relevance to the students' lives at all. No one was 'forced' to read those books. You would not be tested on them, at least not directly. The point was that since even college classes could not cover everything, if you wanted to have a 'good' education, real professors deemed it important at least to have read, and better still, to have understood the thoughts and ideas presented in those older books. Furthermore, understanding the works that were covered required that you be already familiar with the ideas that the current authors took for granted which were influenced by the ancient writers, whom they quoted. Therefore reading the great works in some semblance of chronological order is generally best, as stepping stones to modern thinking. This is often also true of the historical sequence of scientific advancement. It was understood, even by some neophyte students, that to progress, you needed a philosophic and cultural foundation from which to grow. Also, reading these ancient ideas gave students a connectedness to the past that no amount of history-less political correctness could give. Yet, the main service that history-*full* political science could give to modern thinking is as a check against over-interpretation that can debase both the original thought and its child, the modern thought. This is especially true if the modern thinker misreads the ancient thought, as Progressive thinkers seem to have done with writers like Rousseau and Dewey, etc.

Hershberg also spoke of a philosophy of "consumerism" that pervades higher education today, where college is considered, even by the colleges themselves, to be a "dispenser of services" (Special ed goes to college). No longer are universities institutions of the highest educational standards that allow you to enroll (if you pass the entrance requirements), but where it was your own responsibility to measure up if you wanted to graduate. He spoke of all the new 'consumerist' programs, and even full departments, established for no reason other than that modern, politically indoctrinated students find them 'relevant'. These programs and departments include multiculturalism, women's studies, gay and lesbian studies, etc., about which we say many things, with never any mention that they are programs of very high academic standards, since of course, they are not.

Hershberg spoke of the practice of asking students to grade their professors and how essentially useless those evaluations are, but how pervasive. His speech was very much more polite than mine would be under the same circumstances, but in the end he implied (he could not say it in so many words) that the students are not getting their money's worth in college any more. Hershberg equated many colleges to discount stores of education. We can thank Special education and the general run of Progressivism for this, too.

It's the Right Thing to Do?

Some may dislike the fact that I lump the various major victim-equity groups (i.e., "special" pupils, multiculturalist, etc.) into a single category. I understand, but in that great intellectual schism between lumpers and splitters, I am far more comfortable with the lumpers, especially when discussing large, general themes, like educating everybody. Detail does have its place. In fact I have, and will again, argue that teaching detail is vital for the intellectual and scholastic development of kids. That development includes being able to see similarities in seemingly dissimilar details. On the other hand, philosophies and government programs based on ideas with unsupported, speculative detail are decidedly unwieldy and do not achieve their goals. The detail is best left for the classroom, where its merits can be discussed, not for educratic programs. In educating kids, too many conflicting and overlapping programs merely confuse the issues, confuse the kids, and cost an awful lot more than they are worth, if they are worth anything at all. Routinely they are worth less than nothing, since they are harmful to small children and diverse societies.

Perhaps the most important reason for the acceptance and energetic support for Special education, and for Progressive programs generally, is that it sounds like the kinds of things that good people would do for each other, until one learns the details behind the rhetoric. Operationally, however, there is a huge difference between a family, or even a local charity, helping someone in need, and a national bureaucracy attempting to do the same thing. In either case, the objective is to do what is right for the individual. The difference between the two, however, is that the family has an interest in seeing the family-member-in-need get back on his feet as quickly as possible. The family/community will help its own, but wants that help to end as quickly as possible. This is not niggardliness. Instead, this is a recognition that resources are limited, and the family/community cannot support someone forever. It is also a recognition that dependence is draining on a person's character. We have known for millennia that people are stronger, and feel better about themselves, if they can contribute. They feel worse if they cannot. Therefore, the family/community wants each family member to be available to help with the next crisis by adding to its physical and emotional resources, not to be a continual drain on them. The family considers asking for outside help only for those who cannot function normally (i.e., the genuinely handicapped, minor orphans, etc.), and often not even then.

Bureaucracies, on the other hand, cannot deal with only one family member at a time. By their very nature, government programs must try to satisfy as many different people as qualify for the help. Rules about qualifications, however, cannot be all-inclusive. They should be fair enough to identify those who are in genuine need, but firm enough to encourage personal effort to improve individual conditions. So far, this is not much different from a family's rules, but there is another requirement. Unlike a family, a bureaucracy cannot adjust its rules as individual situations change, even if it is in the interest of us all to have none but productive citizens. We cannot write rules that get tougher on some clients and ease up on others in similar-appearing situations. The rules are monolithic, and therefore much less than optimally effective, because, to be otherwise, would either invite even more fraud than we see currently, would invite many lawsuits charging unequal treatment, or would encourage profligacy by case workers. Whether the profligacy is dictated by well-intentioned reasons or not, a nation could not afford to allow everyone to take as much as they wanted from the government. In the end, these sorts of reasons inevitably create a system that does as much harm as good, and eventually more harm. The underlying reality is that government programs invite permanence, while family crisis assistance is temporary. Temporary is better.

I realize that this argument is very unsatisfactory for many. Many individual examples can be brought for whom endless assistance might seem justified. I cannot argue the merits of individual need. My argument is of necessity a broad one, and an important part of the argument is that families and neighbors are much better suited to deal with their own than are governments. We know this to be true because, until people like the Marxist and anarchist intellectuals we have discussed began to denigrate the family explicitly, all of our attempts at all of the various forms of government assistance have been, in effect, attempts at reproducing families, even for those with none. Unfortunately, they do not work very well, and the bigger the programs get, the worse off we are. We now have many more welfare clients than we have ever had, even counting the reductions caused by welfare reform.

Part of the reason for the preceding is that, apart from their ineffectiveness, bureaucracies have other interests, job security among them. This means that while individual case workers may genuinely want to help people in need, to continue to justify its existence, and even to grow, the bureaucracy, as an entity, needs to keep as many people as possible dependent on it for as long as possible. We have already seen examples of this in California's bilingual education programs and the growth of the numbers of kids identified as needing Special assistance, etc. Justifications for continually qualifying more people for assistance and the expansion of parent surrogacy are also used, as is "compensatory education."

"Compensatory education" is an outgrowth of both Special education and multiculturalism but concentrates on replacing (i.e., compensating for) nonfunctional parents (often rendered thus in large part by other government programs, including the public schools). They attempt this compensation with additional government programs to gain equity for the 'disadvantaged'. I lump all these together because, whatever their object, their arguments, demands and techniques are quite similar. They feed on each other's success. If someone cannot do for themselves for one exaggerated or otherwise faulty reason or another (but just happens to make up a constituency), the government must step in to deliver happiness and to make it right. None of these ideas works because they are not based on reality, but rather on a utopian view that absolutely refuses to accept supportable evidence, and tries to change everybody because everybody is like everybody else, except white guys.

'Compensatory education' is the generic name given to the mountain of programs, of which Headstart is probably the best known, that attempts to compensate for some deficiency in the environments of disadvantaged kids trying to get them 'ready to learn'. It should be no surprise to learn that the textbook, *Foundations of Education*, tells us, that of the 1,200 programs already active between 1970 to 1972, *only 10* had "unambiguously demonstrated . . . success." I suspect that the functional ten worked because they did not rely on Progressive methods. *Foundations of Education* failed to tell us, however, that the non-functional 1190 programs had been discontinued, nor recommended that they should have been discontinued. As Rita Kramer says, quoting a candid Vanderbilt University education professor (*Ed School Follies*, p. 69): "Advocacy for the handicapped has become a way for someone to develop a constituency. It's subverting the original intent of the legislation."

Education would be much simpler, more pleasant, more effective, and less expensive if we took politics out of it.

I have used this phrase (Education would be simpler . . .), regarding life or education and politics, several times in this book and by this time I hope that you are at least beginning to equate the actions that educationists take with the awful results they achieve. I would like to add to my examples to show that I have not merely pulled my interpretation of Progressive ideology out of the air, but they are, in fact, taught to teachers as essential ideology.

Often during class, when I questioned the potential effectiveness of a technique, the professor would say that they developed the technique after years of research and practical application. Since they rarely asked us to read any of the research directly, we had to take the professor's word for it. (Keep in mind that most educator-candidates had been raised in a Progressive environment where 'activities' replace lessons, so we generally would not have thought to check the record for ourselves. That is just not the way learning works nowadays, and I expect that our professors counted on that. I must admit that at the time I did not do it to any great extent either, which only shows that assignments tied to a grade have a way of focusing your attention. If you already know that you will 'ace it' without additional work, additional work seems unnecessary.)

On the other hand, each course required us to buy a textbook or two, though they rarely asked us to read them. The texts are full of clues that the research is not as convincing as they led us to believe, much like the cultural anthropology text we discussed earlier. The 'education' text references seem to follow a pattern, once we sort through all of the item-specific verbiage. The pattern goes like this: A) Name of the program or theory described. B) Description of what they have designed the program or theory to accomplish. C) Statement that it does not work, and D) Statement that "experts," "educators" or even just "observers" recommend that we do it anyway. The flip side of this is a statement that some traditional techniques does help learning, tied to a recommendation that educators not use it.

I still wonder who those unnamed 'experts' and 'observers' might be, though I suspect that they may be Progressive politicians, NEA officers, and community leaders with a personal agenda, or parents who notice a discrepancy between promise and achievement in their kids.

If the technique described is a traditional teaching technique that the authors must prove incorrect, the sequence sounds like this example from *Educational Psychology*, p. 461; "In the 1980s several studies reported strong positive correlations between the amount of homework pupils were assigned and their grades. . . . But assigning more homework is not necessarily a good idea."

It works but don't do it.

The reason given why we should not assign homework is this: "The seat work and homework must be meaningful extensions of class lessons, not just busywork." They even tell us that, "To benefit from the seat work or homework, students must stay involved and do the work."

What insight. What a depth of understanding. However, for the Progressive educator this admonition does not mean: "Assign meaningful work and tell the kids that it will count." Instead, it seems to mean:

"Since the kids will choose not to do it anyway (and I am going to have to take the time to grade it), why bother to assign it?"

As I said, 'traditional' teaching maxims are often the targets of derision in teacher 'in-service' training and in Ed school and are not merely listed as nonfunctional techniques to be avoided. The following is the example given in the text, of a supposedly typical homework assignment supporting the contention that assigning homework is not a good idea: "Read each sentence. Decide which consonant letter is used most. Underline it each time."

Could you imagine any competent teacher assigning such a pointless exercise, even in the earliest grades? I suspect it is the creative product of a Progressive educator's mind, trying to design an innovative 'preparing to learn' activity out of a State mandated 'language arts' requirement. On the other hand, as a part of a multiculturalism activity, my classmates and I were asked to go through portions of a book and count how often the pronoun 'he' was used as opposed to 'she'. This was considered an appropriate college-level activity.

An example of this kind of exercise that is currently being used in a Progressive public school classroom is this one from my daughter's fifth-grade math class. The activity asked the kids to code the letters of the alphabet as A = 1 cent; B = 2 cents, etc. They then had to pore over the dictionary trying to discover words "worth" specific amounts of money; "Find a word worth \$1.63," and so forth. It seems inconsistent yet again that a technique is rightfully ridiculed on the one hand and used on the other. Incidentally, based on this sort of activity, they told us that our children are "doing algebra."

In another example, in support of accepting 'learning disabilities' as valid, my professors attempted to belittle the ancient wisdom that states, 'If he has trouble with a lesson, he just may not be trying hard enough'; (The underside of, "If you practice, you get better," which implies that, "If you do not practice, you do not get better.") The professor showed us a video about one educationist's humorous take on getting learning disabled kids to try harder. The gist of the video was that since the kid is already mixed up (i.e., has some brain malfunction that scrambles incoming information [probably as a result of not teaching at an earlier age with the result that the brain is now trying to use neuronal connections developed for other purposes]), trying 'harder' merely compounds his confusion. When we strip away the rhetorical translation (i.e., "Don't ask him to do anything he cannot already do"), we are left with the peculiar, but characteristically Progressive notion which says that kids can learn more if we do not teach them. Of course, teaching less does give the teachers more time to convince kids that we all need more programs to help them learn more.

Here is another example, although I offer this one not because of a pointless juxtaposition in the textbook, as in the 'counting consonants' exercise, but because of what even the Progressive textbooks say about the multiplicity of programs offered. On page 405 the author says, "Almost every study examining time and opportunity to learn has found a significant relationship between amount of content covered and pupil learning. In fact, the correlations are larger than the correlations between specific teacher behaviors and student learning. . . . Basically, students will learn what they practice and think about." On the surface traditional teachers would find this perfectly acceptable, and a sensible statement of educational reality. However, the jargon to understand here is "opportunity to learn." For most of us, this phrase means that if something is taught, the student has a better chance of learning it than if it is not taught. This is such an obvious idea that it seems astonishing that we must teach it, and even more astonishing that modern educationists ignore the advice written into their own textbooks, to opt for the hope that the kids figure things out for themselves (Discovery Learning). Unfortunately, however, they are following their own advice, once 'opportunity to learn' is redefined.

As we have seen from *The Manufactured Crisis,* 'opportunity to learn' does not assume the teaching of specific subject matter or introducing pupils to subjects about which they would otherwise not have known. Instead, it implies the facilitation of another learning activity (i.e., game or project that may or may not relate directly to the subject), leaving the discovery of relevant information to the pupil.

If you are by now developing a strong cynical streak with relation to modern educational processes, you may begin to believe that educationists do know that we have to teach, but do not teach specific subject matter, precisely because they know that kids will know less if they do not. For instance, Marxist economics and Marxist-like education have failed everywhere they have been tried, but to know that we have to know the history. Progressive education merely makes promises that sound as good as Socialism once sounded, even to intellectual people, until they tried them. To cover up this perfidy of no-instruction, educators tell the public that their pupils are learning 'higher-level thinking skills'.

Those educrats who do not ignore the obvious advice (probably because of political pressure from the sensible), turn it into another focused 'program'. For example, we have long known that reading is such a rudimentary skill that we must master it early, especially in a modern society. Many modern educators do not teach reading, however. They try to facilitate 'readiness to read' by doing Whole Language activities. As early as 1955, Flesch told us[201] why these techniques do not work, of course, but rather than insisting that teachers teach kids to read with little fuss, various groups have started programs such as "Reading in Fundamental," and "Everybody Wins"[202] that argue that adult volunteers (not necessarily teachers, or even parents) should help kids to learn by reading with them. I am pleased to see that some of these say that we should read *with* the kid, rather than merely *to* the kid, as pure Whole Language would have us do. However, while we have to honor the impulse that impels people to try to help kids, I have to wonder, why on Earth should we need programs such as this at all? Isn't this why we have schools and hire teachers? The reason may be that schools have mystified learning to read by pushing the Whole Language, 'learning disabilities' and 'discovery learning' ideas to the point that now only 'reading specialists' could possibly teach kids these manifestly simple skills. Today's parents and teachers seem to have forgotten the simple connection between phonics and reading (i.e., letters represent the sounds used in language), and because many of today's parents, whom we taught using Whole Language, can hardly read themselves and therefore do not read at home, either for themselves or with their kids.

What will we do when today's parents are grandparents, and tomorrow's kids are three generations removed from near universal literacy and academic common sense? Will the supply of well-meaning volunteers begin to dry up so that eventually the government will step in to require retired professional people to read with kids to receive Social Security? We can call the program "Older Surrogate-Parent Readers," or something. Maybe we can tie this program into the idea of "It takes a village," while giving them a modern, high-tech feel, by calling them gDOS, or "Government Designated Official Storytellers." I do not want to make too much of this idea and I know it sounds weird at this point, but just think about it. This is depressing speculation only, but given

---

201 *Why Johnny Can't Read.*

202 "Everybody Wins" ironically also has a "Plus" offshoot that "targets flagging parental literacy."

what we know about how government programs start and grow, can we say for certain that it could not happen?

Additionally, genuine educational researchers tell us that keeping classroom disruptions and unstructured movement to a minimum increases learning for kids. Disruptions disrupt concentration (which is why we call them disruptions). Therefore, kids and others (i.e., upper-class 'study-buddies', paraprofessionals, parents, Special educators, etc. etc.) coming in and out of the classroom disrupts concentration and reduces learning. Why then would we want another disruption every time a volunteer comes into a classroom to pull out one or more kids to do something that the teachers should have done routinely and painlessly years before?

One last thought. Once upon a time, when kids progressed from one grade to another based on routine academic achievement, a common refrain heard in homes in the evening was, "No, you cannot go out. You have school tomorrow." Today, well-meaning parents, encouraged by educational and mental health professionals, insure that their kids participate in multiple week-night activities. Some parents have even taken to complaining to teachers and principals that what minimal homework is assigned, is interrupting those activities. To spur this activity on, especially in disadvantaged neighborhoods where surrogate parenting is already most prevalent, we petition the government to increase our taxes to establish additional after-school programs. These programs amazingly include such things as midnight basketball leagues, based on the justification that if kids have something to do, it would keep them off the streets, and they might not do drugs, or get pregnant, etc. Part of this justification rests on the argument that, "Rich folks take their kids to activities, so we need them, too." My idea is that if kids, *all* kids, were at home, doing their homework, and then sleeping at night, we could close down most of these programs, inner-city *and* suburban, reduce taxes and walk the streets safely again. Is this idea pathologically naïve? I hope not.

Oh, yeah. I almost forgot. Doing homework helps kids learn things. That seems enough of a reason for genuine teachers to assign it.

One day while in the second grade, my son came home and said, "Lots of parents don't do very much with their kids. Do they?" While this may unfortunately be true, we can easily argue that as with many current social problems, it has burgeoned under Progressive what-I-want-is-the-most-important-thing-in-life self-esteem tutelage, and that the current crop of educationists is working hard to increase the tendency among new parents. Meanwhile, the schools are working hard to decrease the time spent teaching and increase the time spent surrogate-parenting. Already by the second grade, in a nice suburban grammar school, kids are being trained to think that activities are the object of all life, and the main obligation of parents is to schedule and transport kids to them. If parents do not insure that their kids are entertained at night, they are bad parents, and the village must then pick up the slack.

I wonder whether time spent inventing games and other ways to entertain themselves, might not help develop the higher-level thinking skills that Progressives promise but cannot provide. This idea almost sounds like discovery-learning until we recall that, in a world run by common sense, the kids spend time in school learning things, and use that learning to fuel their imaginations.

Here is another example of the gobbledegook that justifies the 'need' for new programs. It uses the 'learning facts is bad' idea as a jumping off point (page 621 of *Educational Psychology*):

> Emphasis on passive learning of low-level skills seems to be particularly pervasive in schools with concentrations of working-class pupils and low achievers. A change in this pattern will require new approaches for delivering cognitive instruction, as well as fundamental improvements in programming throughout the system.
>
> Explicit teaching [equivalent to 'Direct Instruction' mentioned earlier] frequently has been criticized [by Progressive educationists, though not by genuine teachers] for a tendency to neglect important higher-order learning (i.e., reasoning, critical thinking, comprehension of concepts) in favor of small-step learning of factual material.[203] Some critics believe that the format of explicit teaching or direct instruction [review of previously provided information, teacher presentation of new material, guided practice, feedback, and independent practice] discourages higher-order thinking. . . . Such prescribed approaches (lead) to an educational world in which "passive learners" are "fed bite-sized chunks to be regurgitated on command before the next scrap of spartan fare can be served" and in which there is a lack of concern for such themes as "individualism, individual freedom, creativity (and) analytical thinking."

---

203 Note the contradiction: Learning the factual basis of reality in small steps, especially when starting from a base of profound ignorance (as is the condition of most school children), is bad, but 'task-analyzing' activities, thereby breaking them down into small digestible chunks, is good.

We will address these "concerns" explicitly in the next chapter, but as usual, the reality is opposite to the rhetorical concern. However, here we have another example of imagining only the worst scenario imaginable, thereby insuring that the scenario occurs. This quotation is a restatement of the basic Progressive charge that traditional teaching is little better than pouring learning onto kids heads, and the less capable the pupil, the less learning is poured. Furthermore, it makes two implications. First, teaching facts precludes asking pupils to think about and use those facts and second, that there truly are no slower pupils at all, only politically deprived people, all of whom would become award winning scholars if we could only design new programs to help them (by not teaching facts).

Incidentally, we have probably all heard about the evidence that says that modern science and history textbooks are full of errors such as the history book map which placed the Equator through Florida and Texas. This is presumably due either to revising those facts to abide by the politically correct world-view or to the dilution of reality and disdain for facts that dumbing-down brings, or both. In any case, what 'facts' there are, are already inaccurate, leading to a distorted view of reality, compounding the effects we see. Also, as always, if kids do not learn to read well, we can present little to them that might help to develop those higher-level skills that we all want kids to develop.

A group of functional illiterates is likely to appear passive in their learning style, perhaps whatever their inherent intelligence. As they grow and are facilitated further, they soon decide that school is irrelevant to them, that they already know everything that they need, and that adults are just there to keep them from having fun. Under these conditions we would see decreases in genuine individuality, creativity, and analytical thinking. This is also a very good description of the kids I tried to teach. Bright, shining faces have been replaced, in a large proportion of today's pupils, with dull and listless ignorance.

Despite all of my previous comments I can report that common sense lurks just under the surface, although it is unseen and unrecognized. This is good news since the seemingly huge, systemic adjustments we need to get our schools back on track are not as drastic as it might seem (though the personnel and bureaucratic changes that would be required to carry out genuine reforms would likely be quite extensive). An example appeared in my hometown newspaper on April 19, 1999. The article rejoices with a small, rural school's 'reading facilitator' at the success of her new, federally funded (to the tune of $150,000) reading program. This school had a total enrollment of 452 in 1999, and is a combination Elementary and Junior High school.[203a]

Only a dedicated educationist with access to public funding could justify spending $150,000 to be told the obvious, however, and then gush with enthusiasm thinking that it was the bureaucratic procedure, the "program," that made the difference. The obvious advice, probably known for centuries, is to match reading ability among reading group members. However, since kids do not learn to read in a normal course of study anymore, the purchased program tells the school to match reading ability no matter the grade level. That is considered the "unique part" of this program. "For example [the facilitator said], a fifth-grader reading at the second-grade level will read with others of the same ability." Of course the other unique thing, for educationists at least, is that the program apparently recommends that we *teach* reading, and require *practice* in reading, during this reading class, in extended "uninterrupted" sessions. The reading-ability groups meet during 90-minute daily reading sessions and, as the weeks go by, "their abilities improve dramatically." Additionally, the program suggests another sensible idea to the reading facilitator; that learning to write well will reinforce learning to read well. "We are teaching English reading and writing all at once. Our children want to learn to read." The article goes on; "The cross-grade grouping is the unique part of this" and all this advice works because, for the purposes of this program, 'inclusion' is dispensed with; "Teachers don't have to teach several different reading levels at the same time."

So what is magic about this program? Why does this program work when others have failed? Ability tracking (or at least experience tracking) is one reason. Teachers do not have to teach several different reading levels simultaneously so they do not confuse their slower pupils and bore their smarter pupils while losing *all* pupils eventually. The program also tells them that if we want kids to learn how to read and write, we have to ask them to read and write. Therefore, the lessons designed for this miraculous program are uninterrupted, giving time for the pupils to practice what they learn. Instead of chopping up the day into many compensatory activities, breaking up the continuity of instruction in

---

203a From "Grades Mix to Match Reading Levels" by Maggie Lee © April 19, 1999, *Topeka Capital-Journal*. Reprinted by permission.

any one area, and sending kids here, there, and everywhere, they simply sit the kids down and teach.

The answers to the 'education mystery' are right in front of our faces, if we would only recognize them. Let us hope that the principal of that school (and of your school) decides to try genuine teaching for other areas too, like math, history, geography, civics, science, and all the rest.[204]

This common sense idea does not require Federal grants to start. If the district's teachers had routinely used this sort of strategy from Kindergarten on (if they had been taught that teaching *is* what teachers do), all but the slowest fifth-graders would be reading at the fifth-grade level, or higher, not at the second-grade level. Then *all* teachers would 'have a difficult time containing [their] enthusiasm' for the success, as this facilitator cannot. Wouldn't it be a pleasant problem to have, trying to devise ways of getting more fifth-graders to read at the sixth-grade level, rather than at the third? When this problem is again universal, maybe teachers can then ask kids to use their newfound reading skills to learn more stuff by reading academically challenging textbooks and thinking about what they read.

How can I promise that fifth-graders will read at the fifth-grade level in short order? The article also said, "this success especially is encouraging . . . because 75 percent of [the school's] pupils are Hispanic, many of whom can't read or speak English when the academic year begins." If nonnative speakers can learn to read and write English in a very few weeks, imagine what we can do with most of our native-born kids who already know most of the words they would be exposed to, but who just do not know what they look like on paper. The usual time-honored teaching techniques are no longer in vogue though. Teaching teachers that teaching is not 'fun' for kids, and is therefore useless, is.

What do we do with the millions of kids who are already too old to start over? I tried to teach my biology pupils to learn more by requiring them to take notes that they could use to study for exams. However, the kids had apparently been taught that class notes are nothing but crib sheets and that they would invariably be available during tests,

---

204 I can report that in January 2000, the largest school district in my metropolitan area (the one with all of the schools at the bottom of the rankings charts on pages 28 to 33), announced their own version of this program. Their version will still mix pupils of equivalent reading ability across ages and grades, but will schedule 2-hour sessions. Let us hope they find success, and eventually simplify and generalize the idea to other subjects.

allowing mere copying of unlearned and mysterious words from the crib sheet to the test paper. One kid tried to verify that fact, but I told him that, "No. The notes are to help you study for the test." Hearing this, the kid slung his notes toward the trash can, asking angrily, "What the f*** do I need this for then?"

My attempt did not work with this class in the week or two I had before I was forced to modify my approach, but would work with kids whom we had not taught Progressively, as it did in the 1950s and throughout history.

I have hope that genuine teaching will eventually work with the academically ruined kids as well, but it will be a longer and more emotional struggle to fight our way back up the slippery slope down which we have required schools to slide. You should know, however, that it is at least possible that effectively training previously untrained adults would be more difficult because one factor in brain development involves nerve cells making permanent connections to other nerve cells. In *Human Natures* (2000), during a discussion of the influence of genetics on development and behavior, Paul Ehrlich gives us an example regarding a different kind of learning than intellectual learning. He tells us, on page 126, when, ". . . human beings who are born blind because of cataracts have the cataracts removed between the ages of ten and twenty years (they) do not see the world in the same way as do those born with normal vision, and they have special difficulty in properly seeing what they hadn't touched while blind." Their learning-to-see system had adapted to the conditions under which it developed (i.e., cataract blindness). When the brain develops under one set of environmental cues, significant changes in that environment, even if those changes are in a more natural direction, may render the neural connections made early as less effective than they would have been, had they been made under optimal conditions. Quoting researcher John Allen, Ehrlich says, "the brain is unique among the organs of the body in requiring a great deal of feedback from experience to develop its full capacities." Apparently, sometime around the age of ten may be the time beyond which not-yet-old dogs begin to have trouble learning new tricks. During development, specific neuronal connections are made that the brain is led to believe will be needed in the future. If the brain is led to believe that certain connections will not be needed, they will not be made. Instead, developing nerve cells will be led to make other connections.

This is thought to be the reason that people with certain disabilities (i.e., blindness) often develop their other senses (e.g., hearing) to a greater extent than fully sighted people.

This reasoning may apply to intellectual learning, too. If a brain is not required to learn (i.e., store, remember) certain kinds of information, attempting to teach that information later, as in adult remedial education programs, may be much harder. This is so since the developing neurons either made their connections elsewhere and are no longer available as basic storage devices, or they are already filled with other kinds of data. This may explain at least partially why unlearning and relearning basic skills (e.g., language, pronunciation, accents, etc.) is so much more difficult than learning them correctly as kids.[205] If this is even partially true, then the traditional arguments regarding poor academic results achieved by Progressives become more than mere academic, or even political disputes. It is possible that not teaching kids to think, and not giving them increasingly complex things to think about, may render them permanently damaged (in their ability to adapt to modern requirements) and in some sense *unable* to think. This could explain 'passivity' in their learning style, too, and may explain why it took genetically modern humans several millennia to develop writing, and several millennia more to reach the "Information Age." Asking each kid to reproduce millennia of language development individually, is manifestly unfair "for the children."

The Progressives are right about one thing though. Teaching the most basic skills can be monumentally boring, if we ask kids to learn by rote, as we should. Happily, while necessary, rote learning need not last forever. However, attempting "higher-order" thinking before the brain is ready, or before the kids have much to think about, is like expecting an uninflated balloon to rise off the ground, as if by wizardry. If we try it too early, all we will achieve is intellectually flaccid confusion, and passive learning styles.

The most explicit (repetitive) form of Explicit (Direct) Instruction seems most appropriate in the lowest grades and for the most basic skills, whatever the intellectual capability of the pupils. As kids master the most basic skills (e.g., arithmetic, reading, etc.), instruction can quickly begin to move away from the rhythmic repetitions that direct instruction prescribes. Very quickly, kids would think about new things if they had

---

205 Recall that it is six times harder to unlearn bad grammar, etc., and to relearn correct language usage, then it is to learn it correctly from childhood.

new things to think about. That is why we need to teach kids "facts" in context. However, if we also neglect to teach basic, conceptual, foundation-building facts, those facts will not be available when the brain is ready to use them, since memory storage seems at least partially distinct from 'thinking'. If we further teach kids that they already know all that they need to know, by teaching 'attitude' and never saying they made a mistake, we may lose whole generations of kids to education forever since learning new stuff will seem irrelevant to them.

This is not mere speculation. We have generations of present and former pupils for whom it is a daily reality. Refusing to recognize that education consists of learning facts and requiring pupils to practice manipulating those facts, leaves the education professional confused as well. Confused educational professionals insist that what they require are, "new approaches for delivering cognitive instruction, and fundamental improvements in programming throughout the system." The fundamental improvements we need include teaching rather than facilitation, scaling Special education back to appropriate levels, and eliminating most, if not all of Progressive education's pointless and nonfunctional programs.

I am genuinely troubled to have to write the next chapter. It will show the version of reality that modern science instruction likes. One would think that scientifically trained folks would know better.

7   Teaching Science,
or any other subject for that matter

A good teacher is one who helps you become who you feel yourself to be. A good teacher is also one who says something you don't understand until ten years later.
—Samuel Johnson

It is not hard work which is dreary, it is superficial work. That is always boring in the long run, and it has always seemed strange to me that in our endless discussions about education so little stress is ever laid upon the pleasure of becoming an educated person, the enormous interest it adds to life.
—Edith Hamilton

Next year all of you will have a classroom of your own. Your year will consist of 180 instructional days, or so. How will you fill those days?

Here is a simulated copy of the State's curriculum guidelines. Here is a textbook that you may use. Here is a simulated school calendar, approved by a simulated School Board that lists days that will interfere with a smooth presentation of your curriculum. The calendar includes teacher in-service days, standardized test-taking days, holidays, and the days that grades are due, etc.

Your first assignment is to decide what topics (text chapters) you will present and in what order you will present them. Also, you must decide what chapters you will leave out, if any, and why?

Daily lesson-plan details are not necessary yet. That will come later in the semester, but a long-term plan with logical progression is necessary. Keep in mind the logistical realities of 'days available' between major holidays while you plan your year.

Your proposed schedule and justifications are due next Monday.

While our professor asked us (prospective science educators) to prepare various lesson plans and to practice presenting them, I expected the first day in "How to teach science" class to include an assignment such as the one above. It never happened. When I eventually asked my professor why not, he laughed and said that, "It wouldn't work because the students would not stand for it." While the answer squares with relevance and child-centered theory, it is an astonishing reason. What could be more relevant than having a curriculum to follow, for anyone nervous about being prepared for a first job as a professional teacher? And why would the professor defer to the ignorant desires of his students? Oh, well. What did I know?

While I was generally disappointed with the science-teacher instruction that I received, I must admit that we placed more emphasis on reading 'research' here than in my other education classes. The professor gave us a list of some twenty or more journal articles to read, and we actually discussed most of them in class.

The journal articles fell into several groups. We can call the first group of articles the "learning science is a good thing" group and could have a general heading of 'achieving scientific literacy'. With the spread of an anti-intellectual Progressive intelligencia that argues against teaching subject matter content (because all true learning comes from within) my professor seemingly used this group of articles to try to equip us with the professional and intellectual ammunition needed to stave off other Progressive inroads into the science curriculum. This is a good thing to prepare science teachers to do, especially in today's world. For instance, since equipment breaks and supplies need constant replenishment, the budgets for the lab sciences are quite high, compared to subjects such as history, math, and languages whose consumable supplies (other than the periodic replenishment of textbooks and maps, etc.) can be limited largely to office supplies and perhaps chalk. For that reason, and because we already spend so much money on computers now, some people have questioned the need for 'hands-on' labs, etc., in favor of Internet explorations.

The reasons that 'labs', and science overall, are at risk are examined to some extent in *The Third Culture* (1995), a compilation of essays about various aspects of science and about recent discoveries in the fields of biology, math, physics and cosmology, brain research, and others. One essay argues that science itself is under siege by modern intellectuals who profess beaming pride in knowing nothing at all about math and science.[206] For these modern 'thinkers' the only topics seemingly worthy

---

206 Morris Berman, in *The Twilight of American Culture*, gives many more examples of this phenomenon. In fact, Berman's examples go well beyond pride of ignorance. He documents a growing number of examples of an angry conviction, even among profit-driven university administrators, that anyone who *does* know things, is bad.

of an intellectual life are the emotional ones. Therefore, art and literature alone are the grist of an 'educated' person's thought since these are the 'essential' items. Science is too hard and is too structured to allow true creativity anyway (sound familiar?). So if scientific knowledge is not a necessary component of an educated person's life, why bother teaching labs at all? Merely discussing how we "feel" about global warming is more important than understanding what global warming is, how we know that it is occurring, and perhaps eventually developing the knowledge needed to devise ways to counteract the effects.

This sort of thinking is based on the usual Progressive arguments; Since everybody is just like everybody else, (and since everybody thinks that everybody else should be just like themselves), if I, as an educationist, never liked science, it must not be relevant for anybody else either. Besides, money is tight and "the Law mandates" Special education and a range of expensive social services. If something must be cut to help pay for the noninstructive requirements and Internet access, where are the largest pots of money in a school district's budget to be found (outside Special ed that is, which is sacred and, as everyone knows, is in dire need of augmentation)?

However, hands-on science instruction is crucial in a well-rounded, modern curriculum for many reasons. First, science is about things (e.g., creatures, rocks, air, electricity, planets, continents, etc., etc.) and how those things act, react, and relate to themselves and to other things. Science is about reality and understanding a thing is often much harder unless we see it, touch it, handle it and perhaps modify it with other things. We call these modification experiences 'doing experiments' and we expose kids to it in labs. Mere observation, as in "science enrichment activities," is useful, such as during field trips, and is a necessary step in any science, but is very often inadequate to a full understanding since the reasons for the thing's actions, reactions, and relationships are often subsurface or hidden in some way. Examples of a hidden relationship are the influence of alleles in genetics, why leaves are green, how predation helps the hunted, or whether the moon truly is made of green cheese.

"Mere observation" is the main way that "enrichment activities" are structured for some school kids. We may take kids on a field trip, and may 'engage' their curiosity, but we rarely or never follow that up anymore with detailed instruction to examine the observed phenomenon. This is especially true of the type of pointless enrichment activity such as the field trip a local school did recently, to the municipal bus barn, to watch as advertising placards were changed.

Enrichment activities are the equivalent of looking at the pictures in a magazine without reading the captions or the story for which the pictures were taken. One reason those enrichment activities, as they are structured now, are largely useless, is that the knowledge gained is not tested, so kids do not have to review (study) what they learned. If the kids choose not to listen to the tour guide, but merely use the day as a social outing, little or nothing gets retained.

Incidentally, the fact that lab instruction is considered unimportant by Progressive theorists is quite surprising when we realize that it is the kind of traditional instruction that most closely approximates the stated Progressive ideal of 'experiential' learning. It would be surprising, that is, if we did not know that teaching is the least important thing that teachers do.

Another major reason hands-on lab instruction is useful is that use of scientific equipment per se, and specimen and reagent manipulations, are among the most important learning items in science. In fact, hands-on instruction truly may be the central learning item since scientific understanding is validated only when hypotheses can be proven untrue based on physical interactions, not mere theoretical speculation. Proceeding with assumptions as if they were true, without demonstrable, repeatable, and verifiable evidence that they are true, is the most manifestly *un*scientific thing anyone can do. Yet "feeling focused" instruction does exactly that, not to mention Progressive policy legislation. Continuing to profess unproven ideas and to develop such systems of thinking even after evidence to the contrary is overwhelming, is unthinkable to the true scientist. It is, of course, the stock in trade for Progressive education. This is another reason the support of "science educators" for the Progressive ideology is so frustrating and maddening.

Hands-on instruction is just as important for the pupils who do not eventually become professional scientists and technicians as it is for those who do. The training in 'attention to detail' is worth the trouble all by itself, and careful employees are as greatly appreciated by the supermarket manager who needs an efficient stock clerk as by the college laboratory teaching assistant who helps those who major in science. Apart from teaching the 'scientific facts' of chemical composition and physical properties, etc., handling specimens and reagents teaches observation, patience, diligence, and precision and we can think of it as reality training in that it teaches that things are often not like we see them in the movies or in advertising. First-hand exposure to hands-on science will also broaden the respect for those who 'do' science professionally while, also, demystifying it. If you have handled science-stuff with your own hands, you have a much greater chance of understanding that; "I now know that this stuff is not magic but it is very intricate stuff. I know that somebody had to learn this stuff or I would never have this neat______(fill in the blank [i.e., vaccine, TV, plastic doodad, computer game joystick, etc.]). I am glad that someone is out there working on it." Better yet, for some there will be the realization that, "I can do this!" and perhaps even, "This is fun!"

Another of the objectives of schooling is, or should be, to identify kids who would be good at specific occupations, whether it is science or anything else, and to help kids to choose their life's work wisely. Art teachers like to encourage their most talented pupils to take up art professionally. English teachers try to direct their best pupils toward careers in journalism, etc. In an age when technology, including bio-technology, is so important, science teachers must also have a way of identifying talented kids and encouraging them to continue their studies. We make this obligation more difficult as science instruction, including the use of labs, is marginalized. The painstaking, procedural nature of some lab experiments causes some people to question the 'cookbook' nature of some lab work, but those who do, miss the point. Although the familiar act of practical chemistry we call 'cooking' allows us to deviate substantially from the printed recipes, yet still produce a delicious meal, attaining the correct result in a scripted 'cookbook' lab, without precise measurement and careful handling of reagents, is often not possible. Therefore, lab work is often painstaking and meticulous. Also, while scientific discovery can be very exciting, it is just as true that day-to-day scientific work can be drudgery. Kids must discover for themselves whether they are the kind of person who can tolerate the long, seemingly dull, repetitive hours in the lab or on the scorching desert plateau, etc., for the rare but ecstatic joy of genuine discovery.

We should not make school labs deliberately boring (like cutting more pictures out of a magazine). That would be defeating the purpose. Yet what can we say about the fact that test scores plummeted once the definition of 'learning' was changed to place 'fun' ahead of information, and, in fact, generally removed information from the definition altogether?

Another reason for the 'cookbook' nature of school labs is that getting a correct answer should be possible even for those who decide that they do not like science. These kids will find something else to do with their lives, and that is perfectly OK. However, getting the 'correct answer', which validates procedural precision and proves the nonmagical aspects of modern science, should also be uplifting to many pupils. Those pupils who can see past the drudgery may find the holy grail of any science, the enthusiastic, genuinely creative, and personally fulfilling pursuit of reality.

Of course, as you have noticed while reading the evidence presented, and in your own observations of life, Progressive thinkers seem to have very little use for genuine evidence, preferring inverted ideological rhetoric to reality. This intellectual disdain for reality may be behind the attempts to gut science instruction. They know that logical thought based on realistic assumptions, leading to verifiable results brands most Progressive recommendations as puerile or preposterous, so it is not in the Progressive interest for kids to learn things, or to teach kids to think clearly.

Despite charges to the contrary, many (most?) instructional experiments (i.e., school labs) do not tell the pupil what the result will be ahead of time, as is also implied by the 'cookbook' complaints. The experiment is often structured so that, with the assistance of careful record keeping, the pupil must determine and explain the result of making specified manipulations to specific things. This is not cookbook science. This is true science since the results and explanations are not known ahead of time to the experimenter, but must be discovered. The fact that these neophyte experimenters must often be talked through the procedures, and perhaps be led to the 'correct answer', is in the nature of 'teaching' and discredits the notion that all learning comes from within. Teaching pupils things that they do not yet know is, after all, the traditional reason for hiring a teacher in the first place.

As you can see, traditional science instruction has been covering all the bases, including the Progressive goal of personal discovery learning, all along.

It is therefore surprising and maddening, that my professor thought another type of article essential for our consideration. This set of articles came in two variations. The first of these kowtowed to the Progressive requirements of satisfying the 'learning styles' of *all* pupils and the 'individual needs' of LD pupils and of multiculturalism. These articles supported the preposterous notions that learning about the laws and facts of biology, chemistry, and physics are somehow different depending on your 'native culture'. As in other academic areas, the arguments advanced to support these ideas often recommend spending a good deal of time making sure that *all* pupils understand that white guys are evil, racist swine, and that nonwhites also contributed to our ancient fount of knowledge. The worst of these articles went so far as to blame even the recent drought and famine in Ethiopia on the West. Therefore that article recommended that to prepare our kids for the 21st century, we should spend time in high school science class teaching kids multicultural science, such as Babylonian calendar-making.

I will not spend any more time arguing against this silliness, except to say that these arguments are entirely contradictory to the 'Learning science is a good thing' argument. A very odd thing is that I recall my high-school science and social studies classes mentioning every one of the examples of non-Western contributions that the articles insisted could only be done through non-traditional facilitated activities. Traditional science instruction routinely mentioned the contributions of non-Westerners, so the 'problems' that educationists want to solve were already solved, and sensible, nondivisive versions of the recommended solutions were already inherent in traditional science and history instruction. It is sad, therefore, that sane science teachers could not keep this stuff out of the modern science classroom.

The second variation to Progressive science education makes a little more sense. This variation argues that since science, and the practical products of science (e.g., technology), impacts our everyday lives, and often rubs against various long-held traditions, it is a good idea to examine the effects of science on our culture, beliefs, and traditions periodically. A common example of this is to discuss how the theories of evolution cause controversy, but it can also include discussions about nuclear power, assisted suicide, contraception, pollution, vaccinations, TV, and many other possible topics. While educationists act as if they had invented this idea too, science and social studies teachers have always done this. At least in my experience.

Educationists group these sorts of articles under the basic heading of S-T-S (Science, Technology, and Society) with recommendations of how to incorporate ethics into science activities. The articles either made sense or not depending on how ideological their arguments were. There is another problem, however, that many find disturbing, but we have already discussed the basis of that problem, so I will only mention it again. That problem is that the direction of some of these potential S-T-S discussions (i.e., contraception, transsexual surgery) may be quite different from what many parents want, and may serve to undermine parental teaching.

Learning Cycles and Discovery Learning

As I said, although we did practice lesson plan preparation, etc., I was disappointed at how much time was spent insisting that multiculturalism is a valid and necessary part of any science curriculum. This insistence was done in two ways. The first way used the next set of journal articles, and the second required us to fit all of our lesson plans into a format that mandated various 'accommodational' components.

The lesson plan design format, or instructional approach taught was called 'the learning cycle'. There are several specific versions of learning cycles described in the literature, and my Ed school primarily taught us the one that our professor preferred. On paper, a learning cycle is a procedural device, using a specified lesson plan outline, moving a pupil through familiar sets of steps ultimately culminating in 'understanding'. There is nothing inherently wrong with using this method. Overall it is designed to help the teacher 'cover all the instructional bases' in a systematic way, (even if using a 'lock step' system with rules is contrary to the dictates of Progressive creativity training).

For traditionalists, the acceptable parts of the system try to use what some scientists think is true about pupil motivation, trying to develop interest in a topic to try to maximize learning, and so forth. Teachers throughout the ages have called these techniques, "Introducing a topic" and "Summarizing the day's lesson just before the bell," etc. In this sense, recommending that inexperienced teachers begin with a familiar lesson plan format, which they can modify as their experience grows, is an ancient and sensible practice.

However, these 'learning cycle' formats subscribe to, and support, the 'discovery learning' method that argues that to teach 'essentials' rather than 'mere facts', we must allow kids to discover every concept for themselves. The facilitator's role is to help pupils over the rough spots and to follow the pupils wherever their interests take them. Earlier I said that we could equate 'discovery learning' in some sense with validating old wives' tales by discounting mere facts as "easily counted but relatively unimportant." "Essentials," they tell us, "point a student to a more sophisticated use of skills or knowledge" (see 'authentic assessments,' pages 462 to 483). This language sounds good to people who want these things for their children, so again the Progressives dress their rhetoric up in sensible sounding clothing to make things seem as if they are after academic excellence.

We know that knowledge generally accumulates in very small increments. This is true both of the sum of human knowledge and in the developing brains of children. Even the currently favorite Progressive developmentalist, Lev Vygotsky, said so. That is why it took us something like 2,300 years to get from Aristotle to the Information Age, and why we ought not teach high-school level stuff (i.e., stuff that requires the beginnings of inductive reasoning and a fairly large base of facts) until high school. We also know that some kids are better than others at the various forms of data accumulation and analysis. Those are often the kids who eventually go to graduate schools to pursue very specialized analytical careers, and, perhaps, press the edge of the envelope. Yet many others do not.

Inquiry or Discovery Learning, as formulated now, in effect attempts to bring a graduate school level of understanding to the primary and secondary schools ("We are teaching your child to think like a scientist"), but tries to do it using comic book–like facilitation materials. Even this description of apparent intent may sound good to many, if we can pull it off. However, we want to develop this understanding without the requisite instruction that precedes it or makes it possible, and of course, the results achieved do not validate the rhetoric.

If you have been there, you know that rigorous graduate schools require their students to engage in a very close study of their subject field, and require independent and truly original ("creative") investigations of some aspect of their field. These independent investigations attempt to push the envelope a bit farther in a very limited and specialized area. Rigorous graduate schools can do this because their students have proven that they are capable of the sustained intellectual effort this sort of program requires, and because the students have expressed their deep interest in the field, by seeking admission to the program.

Trying to do this with ninth grade pupils who are still hardly beyond the Dick and Jane books is fanciful, to say the least, especially if we say that facts are unimportant. It may not sound nearly as sexy and cutting-edge, but we will see that traditional fact-and-idea-based instruction and objective testing does get us to these lofty heights, at least for some pupils. Progressive recommendations often limit a pupil's intellectual investigations to, "Are trees plants?"

Therefore, besides the insistence that adherence to the Progressive ideology is mandatory, by requiring authentic assessments, etc., the major problem with the way Discovery Learning is structured, is that it amounts to a method we can call "Whole Science" instruction. If you recall, in its purest version Whole Language theory insists that it can teach kids to read without asking them to read, hoping that kids will somehow individually derive creative grammar and spelling, etc., by merely listening. Whole Science seems to want kids to understand higher-level ideas without knowing the facts and lower-level ideas from which we have built the higher-level ideas. We can therefore characterize it as trying to put up a roof before pouring the foundation. How does Whole Science do this? By turning instruction on its head and starting with the conclusions.

Let us take a fact that we have already presented to see how this works. I mentioned previously that half of the kids asked in a recent survey did not know that the Earth takes a year to circle the Sun. Space-based photos aside, we can assume that the astronomical knowledge-base those kids are operating from is in some sense equivalent to the knowledge-base that contemporaries of Copernicus and Galileo had. If we do not teach a kid that the Sun is the center of the solar system, he may think that the Sun goes around the Earth. Hoping that some kid in the class had accidentally watched the Science Channel rather than the Cartoon Channel to provide a needed bit of information that might advance the Inquiry Learning activity, is too haphazard a method upon which to educate kids. If we want kids to know things, we must tell (or show) them those things. Afterwards we can discuss it and its implications. Inquiry Learning attempts to discuss topic conclusions before they are understood. Expecting a kid in high school to reproduce the thinking of a mature Copernicus is a method doomed to failure.

Of course educationists *do* know that if we would want kids to learn a topic, we must present the topic formally, and practice using the facts and ideas associated with that topic. Else why would they insist that multiculturalism's and Special education's indoctrinational topics be incorporated into every activity?

As Alexander Pope[207] put it:

'Tis education forms the vulgar[208] mind,
Just as the twig is bent, the tree's inclin'd.

Whatever else we can say, however, Progressives cannot be accused of ineffective marketing. The justifications for Inquiry Learning are another example of using the right words to sell an idea that is essentially faulty. People *want* to hear how quickly their kids will advance to 'the cutting edge' using the new, innovative techniques.

For instance, one description of what Inquiry Learning is for, says that the intent is to get kids "thinking like a scientist." That sounds very good to parents, and to the educational professionals who make the text and teaching-program buying decisions. If we ask the educationists how they intend to produce such stunning learning, however, they tell us that they can do it by teaching broad "concepts" without the dull, stultifying and uncreative intrusion of mere facts. Kids are capable of these academic feats because our new and improved techniques are designed to bring out the genius in every kid that traditional methods only entomb. As a marketing promise this is hot stuff, but the fact that it does not happen as advertised is a problem for some of us. If you are selling snake oil, however, reality only spoils your sales pitch.

Here are three of the many quotations that can be gotten from *Emile*, the supposed seminal work in Progressive education theory, regarding what Rousseau thought about teaching 'concepts' before understanding the facts that lead to the concepts. This one is on page 187 and is said in the context of a short discussion about instruction about "public opinion" (i.e., politics):

Does one know a folly when one takes it to be reasonable? To be wise one must discern what is not wise. . . . Teach him [your pupil], therefore, in the first place what things are in themselves, and you can teach him afterwards what they are in our eyes. It is thus that he will learn to compare the opinion to the truth and to raise himself above the vulgar [i.e., unreasoned opinions].

---

207 An English poet and social satirist (1688–1744), called "one of the most feared writers in English" for his biting characterizations of human follies.

208 Untutored or unsophisticated.

This one from page 239 discusses the lessons of history and the fashionable practice of substituting a "depiction of the human heart" as a moral lesson for the fact of what actually happened:

> The worst historians for a young man are those who make judgments. Facts! Facts! And let him make his own judgments. It is thus that he learns to know men. If the author's judgment guides him constantly, all he does is see with another's eye; and when that eye fails him, he no longer sees anything. . . . One has to know how to read facts well before reading maxims (concepts). Philosophy in maxims is suited only to those who have experience. Youth ought to generalize in nothing. *Its whole instruction should be in particular rules* (my emphasis).

Apparently the intellectual French fashion, just before they had their heads cut off—ending the French Golden Age—was to ignore reality and substitute a 'depiction of the human heart [emotion, feelings, affect]'. Sound familiar?

Even Rousseau's view of history is instructive, though it seems to support the modern Progressive ideas, at first. After a short comparison of the merits of several classical historians, such as Thucydides, Sallust, Livy, Herodotus, and others, he says:

> History in general is defective in that it records only palpable and distinct facts which can be fixed by names, places and dates, while the slow and progressive causes of these facts, which cannot be similarly assigned, always remain unknown.

In other words, learning the end results and assigning a moral to those end results is incomplete if you don't know what led to the end results.

Here is what Rousseau said about the processes of 'forming ideas'. From page 203:

> The manner of forming ideas is what give a character to the human mind. The mind which forms its ideas only on the basis of real relations [i.e., facts] is a solid mind. The one satisfied with apparent relations [i.e., mere symbolism] is a superficial mind. The one which sees relations such as they are is a precise mind. The one which evaluates them poorly [i.e., is convinced of the 'reality' of political spin] is a defective mind. The one that makes up imaginary relations that have neither reality nor appearance

is mad. The one that does not compare at all [i.e., is nonjudgmental] is imbecilic. The greater or lesser aptitude at comparing ideas and finding relations is what constitutes in men greater or lesser intelligence, etc.

Evaluate what we have learned about Progressive methodology against these standards. I think Rousseau would not be pleased with what has been wrought in his name. Still, he would not be surprised. There are Progressive-style (i.e., message in spite of evidence) writers in any golden age. On page 240 he says:

The philosophic spirit has turned the reflections of several writers of our age in this direction. But I doubt that the truth gains by their work. The rage for systems [i.e., simplified explanations, e.g., 10-second sound bites] having taken possessions of them all, each seeks to see things not as they are but as they agree with his system.

On the other hand, getting pupils to think like a working scientist is not the least bit different from what traditional teachers want of their pupils, though traditional teachers do not make such grand, global claims as turning everyone into a scientist. Genuine teachers realize that, like it or not, when the reality of differential pupil ability is factored in, they cannot possibly deliver on such an exaggerated claim for *all* pupils. The best that can be done is to try to train every mind to evaluate reality realistically. Also, traditional teachers hurt their marketing prospects by being honest and insisting that reading, writing, homework, and all those pesky facts must be learned first since they know that jumping from profound ignorance directly to 'higher-level skills' is unlikely, at best. A positive-minded genuine teacher might tell us, however, that learning is easy, if you work hard enough at it.

Additionally, when we look at the way any competent scientist operates, we will see that their procedures thoroughly discredit the notion that 'mere facts' are unimportant. Given a problem to solve, the typical scientist will begin with extensive library research. This is also a very large part of how scientists get to be scientists in the first place. The scientist does this research to increase his knowledge and understanding of the topic, and to suggest ideas that he can use in designing an experiment to further illuminate the problem in which he is interested. Afterwards, even when the scientist thinks that he understands a topic very well, the library research, supplemented by reading the latest research journals and books, never stops. The competent scientist knows that facts are his life's blood. In fact, the search for knowledge has become known as re*search*, precisely because each researcher must organize, in his own head, what is already known, before moving forward.

After the library research is advanced well enough to suggest an aspect of the problem that is not well understood, the first step in designing a new experiment would be to define the problem in a way that would lend itself to experimental review. It is not enough to want to cure cancer, for instance. First we must know what cancer is. We all know (because we have been told) that there are different cancers for different body organs. If there are several kinds of cancer we must find out whether the diseases are caused differently in each organ or whether the causes are the same and only the organs affected are different. Even if the causes are the same, are the results (i.e., the pathology) all the same as well, or do the causes have different results because they affect different kinds of tissues. . . .

We can go on for a while in this way, but you get the idea. This is the same characteristic of scientists which has been well known to all but Progressive educators for centuries, that Jules Verne spoke of in *A Journey to the Center of the Earth* (p. 8). The protagonist, speaking of his uncle, the choleric and original Professor Hardwigg, said:

> He was a very learned man. Now most persons in this category supply themselves with information as peddlers do with goods, for the benefit of others, and lay up stores in order to diffuse them abroad for the benefit of society in general. . . .

Nevertheless, there is another aspect of thinking-like-a-scientist that we must understand. The current methods of modern physical science are now fairly well advanced. So, defining "a problem that would lend itself to experimental review" often requires studies of things at the cellular or molecular/atomic level. Or smaller. These levels are so vanishingly small and complex that the investigation would necessarily concentrate on minute parts of detailed biochemical pathways, etc., to make any headway at all.

For instance, the perfectly ordinary phenomenon of blood clotting is initiated, controlled, and the bleeding ultimately stopped by a "cascade" of biochemicals, many of which have to be prepared on the spot from materials available. These materials are then transformed in intricate detail, one acting upon the next in perhaps a dozen specific steps, into the molecules needed to staunch fluid bleeding, and plug the wound. The general course of events begins when a tear or other wound initiates bleeding. At this point platelets rush to the site and clump around the wound. Then red cells accumulate and a chemically produced fibrin mesh binds the elements together. Teasing out one chemical step in the pathway that leads to a specific precursor molecule needed by one of the many pathways, from among the biochemical soup that is our blood plasma, is a daunting task. It would be even more daunting for anyone who has no notion that clotting is anything but blood drying on the skin and who merely 'feels' that bleeding is a bad thing.

Even the studies that examine 'macro' systems are very quickly swamped by data that require minute analysis. For instance, we all know that eyes are for seeing, but have you ever wondered precisely how eyes can turn refracted light into the electrochemical messages that our brains can interpret as shape and color and movement?

Telling kids (and each other) that facts are mere superfluous detail is so blazingly irresponsible that it is astonishing that we have not told these 'educational experts' to go back to sleep.

Remember that to maintain their in-good-standing status, Progressive facilitators must allow the <u>kids</u> to decide what they want to learn. The problems with trying to facilitate this kind of curriculum, with Inquiry Learning or any other technique, are manifold and the possibility that the teacher may not have appropriate expertise in the problem selected is not inconsequential. Of course, most high school classes would not try to delve into a problem as complex as curing cancer, but the problems with the method are essentially the same. To teach anything new, a teacher must know more than her pupils. If a 'learning activity' starts with the assumption that the kids know the early detail when they clearly do not, we doom the technique to failure. That was certainly the case with the classes that I was asked to teach. That was also the fatal flaw with the textbook that we used. So while attempting to get kids to 'think like a scientist' is the ultimate objective in any science curriculum, asking them to reach informed conclusions before they are ready, causes little but confusion and ultimate resentment, and therefore promotes ignorance rather than alleviating it.

Beyond that, by using Progressive ideas, kids can learn to believe that they are too stupid to do science, and this may damage their self-esteem, or may convince them that the knowledge is irrelevant, thereby accomplishing the very things the Progressive agenda promises to avoid. If we decide to cure cancer or learn precisely what 'learning' is, we will soon discover that we need a lot of basic information before we can go on. Doing a word-search game *about* your subject is not enough.

The school's job is to provide the beginnings of that basic information because we cannot know ahead of time what may eventually fascinate any of our entering Kindergartners (or what will be available for them to be interested in, twenty or forty years later). The foundations of knowledge (i.e., basic facts building systematically toward more detailed facts) must be made available to each of these kids so that each of them can eventually choose where to go from here. Academic "choice" therefore, is essentially for adults, not for kids. Adults in the form of genuine teachers who design and present curricula, and adults as high school and college graduates who have a good, general idea of the practical options available to them. Not providing a foundation of systematically acquired facts, and a lifetime of experience in using those facts (i.e., practice in thinking and analyzing facts), along with thousands of seemingly irrelevant additional facts that can be used as the building blocks for future thoughts, insures that a pupil's eventual choices stay limited. Failure to train kids in the use of facts, as Discovery Learning does, digs each kid into an educational and intellectual hole and then tells them that they are on their own, in the name of cooperative learning.

If we then compound the mistake of providing an education devoid of information by using assessment techniques that discourage effort and thinking altogether, or at best limit effort to attainment of some trivial or irrelevant minimal criteria, and by using Progressive motivational techniques that produce arrogant ignorance, we get average scores deep in the "F" range and have lost another generation of potential scientists, historians, novelists, and citizens with common sense.

Nevertheless, I am of two minds about discovery learning. Used on very simple 'scientific' problems based on even simpler facts that have already been presented and learned, and requiring very simple solutions, asking kids to try to predict what additional information would be helpful in solving the problem, has merit. (Incidentally, the simplicity of any lab investigation is a relative thing that we should gear roughly to the average achievement, or slightly higher, of an individual class). In fact, I recall my high school teachers asking these sorts of questions on occasion (i.e., during every lab period). *You* should recall the attempted State-sponsored science assessment I described earlier (see page 79).

Of course, the kids first have to be physiologically and psychologically developed enough to be capable of logical thought to pull this off, which is probably one reason we do not teach high school lab courses until high school. Since there is much more for a primary or secondary pupil to learn that one experiment can teach, for anything requiring more than tiny incremental steps in understanding, I can see this method (i.e., formally design your own experiment) used explicitly perhaps only as much as once per semester, but no more. In fact, once a year is more likely and perhaps as little as a single 'senior project' during a high school science career.[209] Using the achievements of the very rare, extraordinary kid who is, for instance, doing virology research in her basement, as validation and as a rhetorical template for the Progressive techniques is distinctly disingenuous. The reasons for this are simple. Developing a truly original experiment and carrying it through completely takes a great deal of time, effort, and resources. It requires expertise that the 'facilitator', or genuine teacher for that matter, may not have and of course, perhaps what is most important, it also requires considerable preliminary knowledge, all ideas that Progressives find irrelevant.

Even simple experiments done decades or even centuries ago, required knowledge that earlier pupils did not have. We have no reason to believe that any modern pupil could have knowledge that Aristotle, Leonardo, Pasteur, or Mendeleev did not have, unless we teach them that knowledge in advance. The modern pupil first has to learn the things that the ancients discovered through detailed observation and experimentation. If kids do not learn the facts that lead up to the experiment we ask them to develop, they are in the same position that Lister was in when he was a kid, lacking the information that he learned later. Newton did not discover the calculus or the laws of physics in a hopeful school activity. He did it later, after years of study and thought and "Eureka-like" inspiration—based on those years of study and thought.

In fact, if we do not teach, but hope that kids will somehow become interested enough to learn detailed things by themselves, we all regress. John Dewey understood this about the importance of genuine instruction. He said:

------

209 This can be the culmination of a high school career for those pupils who have already been accepted to college, especially if they expect to study science.

. . . these [teachings] supply a protection, perhaps our chief protection, against a recrudescence[210] of these superstitious beliefs characteristic of savages, those fanciful myths and infertile imaginings about nature in which so much of the best intellectual power of the past has been spent.

To me this sounds as if Dewey is describing Progressive education's re-emergence from the Great Society as represented by the new interest in the occult and with television shows that feature speaking with animals or with the dead.

Do you think that Newton-like inspiration could never be the stated goal of precollege educationists? Think again. During one of our class discussions, we were calmly told that it is "our job" as science teachers to develop in our pupils the kind of understanding and insight that Barbara McClintock had when she postulated "jumping genes" in corn in 1951. Jumping genes are a description of how reciprocal pieces of genetic material transfer themselves from one chromosome to another during recombination. This insight has since been proven to occur in both eukaryotic and prokaryotic organisms (organisms with and without cellular nuclei). Here is how Francisco Ayala explained it in a genetics text (p. 139) that I used during my microbiology-student days:

The evidence for exchange in both organisms consists of a correlation of genetic exchange with an exchange of cytologically visible chromosome segments. The evidence for physical exchange in corn is as follows. Corn plants heterozygous for alleles of two genetic markers, *colorless (c)* versus *colored (c+)* and *waxy (wx)* versus *starchy (wx+)*, and two cytological markers, a heterochromatic knob and a translocated piece of another chromosome, were bred. . . . From one such cross 28 progeny kernels were obtained exhibiting the four phenotypes indicated. . . . The kernels were planted and the chromosomes of each plant examined for the presence or absence of the knob and the translocated piece. Plants that were *wx+/wx+* can be distinguished from those that are *wx+/wx* by the pollen that is produced: all pollen grains of the former plants stain for starch, whereas only half of those of the latter plant do.

Do not worry if you haven't a clue what this seeming gobbledygook means, though it is a simplified description of McClintock's great insight, for which she won a Nobel prize. Like real scientists do, McClintock came to her understanding after reading hundreds of books,

---

210 To break out again after a dormant or inactive period.

thousands of research articles, conducting hundreds of her own experiments, alone and in collaboration with other experienced scientists, and after literally decades of thought and discussion on the subject of biology and botany generally and genetics specifically. Asking a high school teacher to develop this sort of understanding in kids who have trouble spelling 'they' and who do not understand a process as simple as diffusion, is unrealistic at best.

So what do we do? We "get real," that's what. We should teach real kids real facts and build slowly upon those facts. "Intuitive" and/or "cutting-edge" leaps of understanding will develop only later, if at all. If you have no idea what an allele is, much less the details of the many various alleles, you have no chance of using the "concept" of alleles in an explanation of anything.

The way this can be done is to structure a class in this general way: Lecture about the facts needed for that class (or demonstrate the properties of the items [e.g., gas, fluids, flame, etc.] as appropriate) and stop frequently to ask, and answer, questions about the newly presented information. These frequent questions will generate interest, clarify pupil misunderstandings and inspire deeper understanding, both by pupils, and the teacher. This lecture-demonstration-discussion format will allow the class to move ahead as quickly or as slowly as the composition of the class allows. If the teacher is truly a *teacher*, it will keep the focus of the class on the subject of the class, rather than on wandering off chasing the simplified interest of the moment. Whether kids eventually earn their living as scientists or not, as they are asked to think they will become better, and more disciplined, at thinking. Our kids, however, facilitated in the Progressive way, are getting worse and worse at following an argument that requires more than one logical step. Arguments of one logical step, and especially arguments based on incorrect rhetorical speculation, amount to indoctrination, not teaching (but they make good sound bites). However, an ignorant, lied-to population cannot sustain an informed, democratic debate and therefore cannot sustain a democracy for long. As Thomas Jefferson said:

If a nation expects to be ignorant *and* free, it expects what never was and never will be.

In 1994, G. E. Uno and R. W. Bybee wrote one of the 'biological literacy' articles that I mentioned earlier. Unfortunately, the authors tend toward the Progressive perspective, but since they have had some training in logical and fact-based (i.e., scientific) thinking, we can modify their core ideas into something useful, if we purge some silly, unjustifiable implications that they make.

The authors identify and describe four levels of what they call the biological literacy continuum. From the lowest to the highest, they named the levels Nominal, Functional, Structural, and Multidimensional literacy. The levels of literacy range from merely being able to identify that certain words or ideas are "biological" (Nominal) [word-search-type activities are almost, but not quite, on this level], to being able to incorporate detailed knowledge and investigative techniques (i.e., thinking) as part of everyday life (Multidimensional). The ultimate goal is to try to get pupils to ". . . think creatively, formulate questions about nature, reason biologically and critically, evaluate information, use biological technologies appropriately, make personal and ethical decisions related to biological issues, and apply biological knowledge to solve problems." The authors suggest, however, that since we cannot expect even experienced researchers to be multidimensional in all areas of biology, the goal of biology education should be one of merely increasing interest in biology for pupils (make it fun) and making biology relevant to pupil's lives. Trying to move pupils up a level on as many fronts as possible is a secondary goal. The authors briefly suggest strategies for achieving these goals that they call ". . . science as a way of knowing."

That is not too bad, other than the insistence on dumbing-down based on relevance theory, etc. In fact, I must admit that it surprised me that an article like this one appeared in such a recent issue of a scientific journal. The ideas are self-evident and I thought essentially part of the intellectual equipment that most science teachers carry with them. As I try to regenerate memories of my high school experience, I remember discussion sessions in my science class although those classes were very heavily weighted to fact accumulation and to playing with those facts (doing labs and taking objective tests). In truth, I do not recall much emphasis being placed on individual creativity, though some of us had unique and insightful explanations for why things happened as they did. We would not expect *any* creativity following a dull, mind-numbing lecture if we could believe the educationists. Yet, the reason for this lack of an explicit emphassis on an artsy sort of creativity was, again, that our teachers understood that scientific creativity requires a great deal more knowledge than is typically in the repertoire of most kids. Also, perhaps more so than in other disciplines, we have to know many, often disparate, facts before we can have any hope of saying anything 'new' and truly creative. A famous example of this is Darwin's formulation of early evolutionary theory (about living things) after reading a geology textbook and a book on economics.

These were high school science classes, not world-class labs with brilliant, experienced researchers working on cutting-edge problems. Yet creativity grew with knowledge, as attested by the 'unique and insightful' explanations that my classmates often made.

To spark the light of deeper understanding in at least a few sets of eyes, after deliberately pouring into, and then retrieving many facts from, pupils' heads, a genuine science teacher's life must consist of a plague of essay questions. That is OK, for two reasons. Short essay questions are almost as easy to grade as multiple choice questions, if we keep the topic of the essay limited and to the point. Every essay question need not require a complex and massive effort that contemplates the origins of life on Earth. It can be as limited or as expansive in scope as any multiple choice question.

The benefits of using essay questions of that type, rather than relying exclusively on so called fact-regurgitation multiple-choice questions are several. First, we allow the pupil to explain things in his own words, thereby allowing for individuality and creativity, and it also checks to see whether a pupil truly understood the ideas discussed, or merely memorized a phrase or fact. In this sense short essay questions are the necessary offspring of the more limited multiple choice/fact-recognition question. Next, a short essay question need not stretch a nonscientific soul to the breaking point. It does, however, promote the systematic accumulation of knowledge and the realization that science, at least at the high school level, is not always impenetrable and can be useful in daily living ('is relevant'). After being tested with a series of objective questions and short essays, a pupil can sit back and tell himself, "Hey. I really did understand that stuff a little bit. It was not just regurgitation. I had to think, and I did OK."

Finally, writing short essays is <u>writing</u>, and practicing writing is a vital part of learning to write well. Future adults will need to know how to write at least competently in almost any career they may choose. If you have ever done any writing, you have probably noticed that an early version of your masterpiece is often a bit cryptic. Working to make it more understandable and persuasive requires much work, thought and elaboration.[211] Not surprisingly, all that work, thought and elaboration goes a long way to teaching us the things that we would explain, and to suggesting better ways of explaining it. Almost any job that a college graduate might get, will require her to write some kinds of reports that must deal with analysis of detailed facts and to explain conclusions logically and persuasively. This applies to script writing as well as scientific and technical occupations.

Writing short science, history, and literature essays will eventually stand future managers and executives of all sorts in good stead, whether they become professional scientists, historians, and novelists or not. This is especially true if your teacher is someone (i.e., a professional who knows the stuff you are discussing) who can read your work and suggest ways to improve it, both factually and stylistically (i.e., you learn from your mistakes—if you find out that they are mistakes). Incidentally, being told that placing a comma in one place is more correct than placing it in another place, or that Grant, and not King Tut, is buried in Grant's Tomb will not mangle the average pupil's psyche irretrievably, so horror at potential self-esteem destruction need never arise.

Even if a pupil does not eventually become a manager shortly after leaving school, after some time on the job she may want to compete for a promotion. Employers often want to promote the most competent people available, to try to maximize the probability of business success. Having had analytic training would improve an employee's chances of impressing the boss, in conversation and in writing.

There are, however, other ways of practicing proving your knowledge and competence.

A Test by Any Other Name . . .

This seems as good a place as any to continue to sing the praises of the lecture-demonstration-discussion method, and then traditional testing, over any Progressive method.

The first thing to understand is that lectures are not necessarily as dry and boring as most Progressive visions imply. If we read descriptions of lectures from that point of view, the main descriptor used is, again,

---

211 For instance, when I first sat to write this book, I envisioned a pamphlet of perhaps 40 pages. Now look.

some variation on, "Pouring facts into kids' heads." This description implies that there is no attendant attempt to connect the facts into an understandable whole. They make it seem as if the lecturer invariably drones on in a dull monotone, as if he is merely reading a thesaurus aloud and is just as bored with the whole thing as anybody. This description is nonsense, unless the lecturer does not know his subject. Mark Twain gives us an example of why it is nonsense. In *Life on the Mississippi* (p. 15) he writes, "To say that DeSoto, the first white man who ever saw the Mississippi, saw it in 1542, is a remark which states a fact without interpreting it. . . . The date 1542, standing by itself, means little or nothing to us; but when one groups several neighboring historical dates and facts around it, he adds perspective and color, and then realizes that this is one of the American dates which is quite respectable for age." Only lectures and demonstrations (when appropriate), often preceded by individual reading, and discussion of that reading can give scope and meaning to bald fact. That scope and meaning are then called the "lessons" of history. Lessons are impossible without the facts that anchor them to reality. Without the facts we are left with ignorant opinion (i.e., old wives' tales).

The descriptions of a lecture as a baffling and invariably boring exercise are obviously taken from the perspective of the unprepared and unmotivated pupil. This should not be surprising. As we have seen, education students, as a group, are among the weakest students at any university. Many managed to qualify for college only because of open admissions policies that take any warm body that presents itself. This may be especially true of those who eventually "earned" a doctorate in education. Given the opportunity to institutionalize their own academic insecurities, they take it, and do another disservice to us *all*.

However, with adequate preparation before the class, including instruction in prior years and having listened and participated in prior assignments, a lecture is always an attempt to create word and mental pictures for the pupil, using the pupil's mind as a canvas for the imagination. When teachers mention 'mere' facts, as they must, there is always an attempt to explain why those particular facts are pertinent in the current context and to weave the facts into the growing description of reality. Lecture-demonstrations are attempts to bring the pupil's thinking 'into' a subject (as in, "I'm really into XYZ, man"), which is why questions and discussion are usually encouraged. Done well, even a dry topic, can be genuinely exciting. I suspect that we have all seen, on

TV and elsewhere, scientists who speak about some rare and seemingly inconsequential slug, a dusty pot shard, curly line on a graph, picture of a desolate landscape, or something, and describe their excitement when they discovered that the slug molts purple, that Aristotle may have handled that particular pot, that they have just discovered evidence of a predicted force of nature, or that the landscape is on a comet. If we knew as much about slugs, ancient pots, physics, or astronomy as those guys do, we would be excited, too.

Admittedly some people lecture better than others, and some people lecture much better than others, but the point is still the same. If we want kids to have any chance of understanding any larger message inherent in a topic, they have to know the details of the topic first. Even if a particular lecturer is a less than stirring speaker, exposure to the facts is an indispensable part of the lesson. In a case where a teacher is not exciting, which does happen, the kids will always adapt themselves to the teacher's style very quickly and learn how to listen to this teacher. They will, that is, if they know that whatever the teacher's instructional style, learning the information is required and 'doing well' is beneficial to them.

I mentioned some of these ideas in my Ed school class and in the written assignments that I turned in, and was told several times that I was "lucky" to have gotten such a well-rounded education, but, "most (90 percent+) [of kids today] have _NEVER_ (professor's emphasis verbally, and capitalized in large letters and double underlined in italic) been asked to express an opinion or thought . . ."[212]

It occurs to me that maybe there is a lesson in there somewhere. Maybe we should allow modern kids to be as lucky as kids in the 1960s were and not merely "facilitate their learning experiences" as we do today. That seems a simple observation, but is one that is fraught with political overtones, at least for educationists.

Here, again, is another simple observation. I find it decidedly strange that at a time widely regarded as the Information Age, educationists should consider information (factual knowledge) as unnecessary. Since they clearly haven't a clue, maybe we should replace the educationists and the damaging bureaucracies that they have invented, with normal humans with common sense who know and understand their subjects and who enjoy sharing what they know. Maybe if we teach kids

---

212 Quoted from the professor's comments on one of my final exam papers.

what we know, and worry less about leveling the playing field at a sub-basement level than about how to build up-escalators to the future, we would *all* be better off. Yet, it is hard to get on an escalator that does not exist.

Here is a final observation. My high school classmates and I seemed to respect our teachers much better than today's kids respect theirs, despite child-centered, let's-be-buddies facilitation. We thought that our teachers knew things that we did not, and some of us even thought that it would be a good thing to know the things that they knew.

Authentic Assessments

I said that I would speak about traditional testing methods, but maybe I should wait until after we see the Progressive version in more detail. It will provide some perspective.

We have already discussed "Authentic Assessments" briefly, but so far I have only given a quick example or two showing how weird this idea can become in practice (e.g., replacing objective tests with choreography, expecting a word-search activity to display understanding of magnetism). Since 'testing' is an integral part of any serious science class, or any other class for that matter, it is important that we understand why we <u>cannot</u> use authentic assessments as a generic testing method.

To examine this idea in a bit more detail, I will reproduce, with comments, a 'Table' entitled "Characteristics of Authentic Tests" reprinted in *Educational Psychology* on page 564. The text reprints this chart from G. Wiggins, writing in the magazine *Educational Leadership*. Any of the various methods of emphasis used (i.e., italics, quotation marks, parentheses, etc.) are Wiggins', et al.

I will reproduce the Table separately first, to show it in a consolidated way, without my comments intervening. See whether the original, which makes sense to the modern educationist, makes sense to you after I translate some of the jargon as I reproduce the Table again, with comments included. Although educationists recommend the use of 'authentic assessments', for *all* classes and courses, notice that using these ideas seem far better suited for genuine 'activity' classes such as art, drama, or music. During our second pass through the Table, I will argue that using these ideas in the traditionally academic courses is inappropriate because they are solutions without a problem and do the very opposite of what they are advertised to do. Also note that the ideas may be born of the complaints of weaker pupils, try to puzzle out the jargon, and try to imagine using these recommendations in any academic class. Will it fit into the academic classes, such as math and science, or even in the more 'philosophically based' classes, such as literature or history? Then imagine using them in grammar school. You will see that these Progressive ideas merely waste enormous amounts of time, add confusion to and dilute an already watery curriculum.

Characteristics of Authentic Tests

A. Structure and Logistics
1. Are more appropriately public; involve an audience, a panel and so on.
2. Do not rely on unrealistic and arbitrary time constaints.
3. Offer known, not secret, questions or tasks.
4. Are more like portfolios or a *season* of games (not one-shot).
5. Require some collaboration with others.
6. Recur—and are *worth* practicing for, rehearsing, and retaking.
7. Make assessment and feedback to students so central that school schedules, structures, and policies are modified to support them.

B. Intellectual Design Features
1. Are "essential"—not needlessly intrusive, arbitrary, or contrived to "shake out" a grade.
2. Are "enabling"—constructed to point the student toward a more sophisticated use of skills or knowledge.
3. Are contextualized, complex intellectual challenges, not "atomized" tasks, corresponding to isolated "outcomes."
4. Involve the student's own research or use of knowledge, for which "content" is a means.
5. Assess student habits and repertoires, not mere recall or plug-in skills.
6. Are *representative* challenges—designed to emphasize *depth* more than breadth.
7. Are engaging and educational.
8. Involve somewhat ambiguous ("ill-structured") tasks or problems.

C. Grading and Scoring Standards

1. Involve criteria that assess essentials, not easily counted (but relatively unimportant) errors.
2. Are graded not on a "curve" but in reference to performance standards (criterion-referenced, not norm-referenced).
3. Involve demystified criteria of success that appear to *students* as inherent in successful activity.
4. Make self-assessment a part of the assessment.
5. Use a multifaceted scoring system instead of one aggregate grade.
6. Exhibit harmony with shared schoolwide aims—a *standard*.

D. Fairness and Equity

1. Ferret out and identify (perhaps hidden) strengths.
2. Strike a *constantly* examined balance between honoring achievement and native skill or fortunate training.
3. Minimize needless, unfair, and demoralizing comparisons.
4. Allow appropriate room for students' learning styles, aptitudes, and interests.
5. Can be—should be—attempted by *all* students, with the test "scaffolded up," not "dumbed down," as necessary.

Here is what it means.

Characteristics of Authentic Tests

A. Structure and Logistics

1. Are more appropriately public; involve an audience, a panel and so on.

If the idea is not to destroy self-esteem, why on Earth would we insist that everybody perform some public performance art about everything, including tectonic plates, the behavior of amoebae, electronic circuits, long division, the mythology of Egyptian mummies, the proper use of semicolons, or any of the thousands of other individual topics that we might teach throughout a genuine school career? Besides, how is a science teacher to evaluate a rap song about the discovery of Radium? Is rhyming talent an appropriate criterion for proving 'content' knowledge?

2. Do not rely on unrealistic and arbitrary time constraints.

This item is complaining about an exam designed for some sort of art project. Imagine coming into an exam in oil painting, getting a blank canvas, and being told that you have fifty minutes to produce something of value.

For an academic class, however, this item considers the supposedly 'learning disabled' who are often 'accommodated' by either getting more time than anyone else to complete exams, or by being given truncated, or otherwise even more dumbed-down exams than the regular pupils.

In real life, teachers, like most humans, must always abide by schedules. Knowing that, teachers design exams to end within the time constraints. Complaining that already dumbed-down assessments are too stressful is another example of "giving kids an inch" (and then some), then having them "take a mile." The kids win in the short term, since they get out of doing the work, but they lose in the end, since they got out of doing the work.

Society loses, too.

And, of course, a refusal to encourage pupils to learn to meet deadlines is deeply appreciated by employers everywhere. Including the employers of artists, like advertisers.

3. Offer known, not secret, questions or tasks.

This is an interesting one. "It's a trick question," is the typical complaint of the unprepared pupil. For anyone who attended classes, participated in the lessons, and did the assignments, there are rarely any trick questions. Occasionally, however, teachers will add a question that requires extra insight as an additional challenge, but these are not 'secret' questions, only harder questions that require the sorts of creative intuition or logic that educationists fervently pursue, but cannot capture.

This item also harkens back to the old, lame complaints that white guys have always tried to keep secret information for their own use and power. Yet if true, wouldn't we expect those who say they want equality to hanker after that 'secret' knowledge, rather than insisting on not teaching it.

Society loses again, since the knowledge formerly thought of as rudimentary and essential, slowly recedes into the dustbin of history. At least until the next upheaval when society is shocked into remembering what is truly important.

4. Are more like portfolios or a *season* of games (not one-shot).

This is a cheap shot at another of the Progressive bugaboos; the so-called high-stakes test, and yet another artsy solution to a problem that did not exist. Despite the fact that we actually want tests to mean something, so as to keep pupils focused on them, we can already equate periodic tests, and even more frequent quizzes, to a season of games that build on the knowledge that accumulates during the year. As I understand them, however, a 'portfolio' in an academic setting, much like an artist's portfolio, deals mainly with evaluating improving technique, not necessarily with accumulated knowledge. Is that all we want of the schools? In this sense, however, improved writing technique, if used again as a criterion of essays, etc., might seem to fulfill this requirement, but, of course that is not what is wanted here, because we already know that requiring good sentence structure is too confining, uncreative, and possibly racist, don't we?

Do you see how this emphasis on performance attempts to turn *all* classes into the finger painting of academics? Do you also see how an emphasis on an artistic portfolio may be used as a check on the politically correct development of a pupil's thoughts?

5. Require some collaboration with others.

This item is designed to attempt to fulfill the typical "outcome" requirement of 'working in groups' and to imply that kids never learn cooperation under traditional tutelage and the conditions of academic competition. Competition is bad, they tell us, because someone always does worse than someone else, and then feels bad.

On the other hand, while tests should generally test individual learning, there is some value here, if we change the word "require" to "may occasionally allow." "Require" merely validates cheating, while "may occasionally allow" can refer to traditional collaborative evaluations, such as labs, etc. Of course, while labs routinely allow lab partners to share data and to work together on preparing the report, each individual pupil may be required to submit an individual report, to ensure that one lab partner didn't do all of the work, while the other merely copied.

As for learning 'cooperation', it is true that people do work in groups in real life, but we typically also expect each member of the workgroup to contribute something. No workgroup, especially in real life, likes to 'carry' an incompetent member who is unprepared or unwilling to contribute. Still, we also expect everyone to be nonjudgmental, don't we?

6. Recur—and are *worth* practicing for, rehearsing, and retaking.

Notice that we have 'practice' and 'rehearse', not 'study'. Also 'retaking' is another common accommodation for the learning disabled. Here we are encouraged to allow *all* kids to retake assessments repeatedly until they finally manage to meet some minimal 'criterion' (see C.2. below).

The use of the word *worth* implies that paper and pencil tests are not fun and that we learn nothing of value if we simply pour knowledge over kids' heads only to be regurgitated later. That can be true, if we are chronically unprepared and "cram" disconnected facts into our head just before an exam. In fact, these facts are disconnected only to the extent that the unprepared pupil did not think about them before the cramming session. Under traditional instruction, however, I believe that more kids enjoy taking tests than let on that they do. This is especially true in the upper-level classes, and even more so in college, when all that knowledge gained over the years is truly starting to come together, and increasingly improved analytic abilities begin to excite a genuine love of learning.

7. Make assessment and feedback to students so central that school schedules, structures, and policies are modified to support them.

I must admit not knowing to what this item refers. In my experience, schools have always given pupils feedback and scheduled around tests, both the standardized variety and individual subject tests and quizzes. I also recall that my teachers took time after virtually every exam and quiz, other than standardized tests that were graded elsewhere, to provide feedback by "going over the test." Occasionally that feedback consisted merely of identifying the correct answers, with little discussion, but if you were interested, the teacher was always there, to question later. Also, think back to those 'fishing for points' sessions we all witnessed, or participated in. To get additional grade points, a kid had to convince the teacher that her answer had merit, that she had analyzed the question and noticed a relationship to some information that had escaped the attention of the teacher. As annoying as those sessions could be at times (especially for the teacher), they are a wonderful demonstration of genuine creativity born of information and of 'higher-level thinking'. Also, thinking pupils helped to keep teachers on their toes by forcing them to write less ambiguous questions. Of course, they now tell us that question ambiguity is a good thing (see B.8., below).

The "structures" item has me stumped too, unless they expect us to build every classroom to include a stage, complete with limelights, curtains, dressing rooms, and all the rest. Perhaps this is a reference to the kinds of architectural recommendations that were all the rage a few years ago. At least one high school in which I work has open classrooms with missing walls, making at least some classes mere groupings of kids in various parts of a large room. I was told that this was regretted almost as soon as the school was occupied for the first time. The disruption inherent in an architecture such as this annoyed even the educators.

B. Intellectual Design Features

This entire section is an example of the educationist's requirement that educators shoehorn everything into some Progressive template, whether the template makes sense or not. It is amazing that the author came up with more items here than in the other major categories. Most of them say the same thing, namely that all tests should be child-centered and adapt to the various learning styles.

1. Are "essential"—not needlessly intrusive, arbitrary, or contrived to "shake out" a grade.

The "essential" comment in this item implies that tests of rules or other minor bits of learning, such as correct information, are too confining. Tests should be 'open-ended' to allow the kids' inherent creativity to shine through. "Don't sweat the small stuff," like mixing humans with dinosaurs, 'matching' Abe Lincoln with the Peloponnesian Wars, stating that salamanders have feathers, or refusing to use punctuation. Details do not matter. Only creativity.

I do not know what "intrusive" refers to, unless it is another jab at learning "unnecessary" facts, but describing objective test questions that are based on the information discussed in class as "arbitrary" is interesting. The first two definitions for 'arbitrary' found in the dictionary[213] are 1) determined by impulse or whim, or 2) based on or subject to individual judgment or discretion. Yet, as technical Progressive jargon, 'arbitrary' often means 'having a correct answer'. In this sense, learning that

---

213 Webster's II New Riverside University Dictionary, 1984.

$2 + 2 = 4$ or that trees are plants are examples of questions with arbitrary answers. It is easy to see the discrepancy between the true meaning and this reinterpretation. 'Good' questions, according to this reinterpreted usage, are those that allow pupils to develop their own judgments and meaning. These questions are proudly called open-ended. Interestingly, the dictionary also defines open-ended. It has several meanings, including 1) not restrained by definite limitations, restrictions or structure, 2) open or liable to change, 3) indefinite or inconclusive, and 4) allowing for an expansive or unstructured response. Defining assessment rubrics and other Progressive criteria (See C.3. below), as *not* arbitrary therefore qualifies as 'spin' of the worst kind and are more examples of saying one thing but meaning exactly the opposite. Use of this reinterpretation is not only deceitful (i.e., deliberately confusing), but wrongheaded.

Besides, what is a test if not an attempt to evaluate how much each pupil has learned? Every test "shakes out" a grade, and the average of many tests, quizzes, and other evaluations, helps to determine individual achievement. At least they do if we are genuinely interested in following through on the rhetorical promises of achieving academic excellence. Of course, if that is not our intent, we can always use 'authentic assessment'.

> 2. Are "enabling"—constructed to point the student toward a more sophisticated use of skills or knowledge.

Another touchy-feely item that assumes that every kid is a 'postdoc' just waiting to emerge. On the other hand, we design essay questions to elicit more sophisticated use of skills than matching questions. That is why we have essay questions that allow kids to grow intellectually over the years as they slowly learn to analyze situations and explain and describe what they have learned.

> 3. Are contextualized, complex intellectual challenges, not "atomized" tasks, corresponding to isolated "outcomes."

Much as items 1 and 2, this argues against 'objective' testing techniques of any kind, such as multiple choice, matching, fill-in-the-blanks, etc. Still, isn't it interesting that they equate subjective Progressive 'outcomes' to objective tests? Of course, QPA (Quality Performance Accreditation), and the other mandated record-keeping requirements, have made the construction of 'outcomes' very bureaucratic and structured, and we should avoid structure wherever it is found.

The Progressive revulsion to "atomized" tasks" is consistent with their hatred of structured lessons generally. It is, however, inconsistent with the previous recommendation that classroom activities should be task-analyzed to be more readily understandable to the supposedly learning disabled. The current argument is, of course, that traditional educational tasks are 'mere content' and unimportant. What is important is the ability to think big, contextualized ('politically correct') thoughts. Ignoring the importance of "atomized tasks" (i.e., discrete bits of information or facts, as tested by individual test questions) in favor of using nondescript, ambiguous ideas, that can in no way be termed a coherent whole, is the equivalent of trying to build a sand castle with perfectly dry intellectual "sand." The castle quickly crumbles to an indistinct hump because we cannot connect the individual grains of sand into any recognizably organized form. Besides, if each grain of sand can be equated to a separate (atomized) fact, how are we to build a sand castle at all if we are not allowed to use sand?

As you can see, Progressive thinking is consistently inconsistent.

4. **Involve the student's own research or use of knowledge, for which "content" is a means.**

Does this item require first graders to do independent research, too, or merely to speculate without information? This item is the pupils' equivalent of what we found for the "Facilitative" teacher, for whom expertise with 'subject content' only 'helped'.

5. **Assess student habits and repertoires, not mere recall or plug-in skills.**

Once more. Same as before. Accept only what the kid has already shown that he can do (repertoire) since we have no need to go on to learn new things. Of course this would also allow less academically qualified people to "teach" since they would not need an understanding of subject content. This would turn teachers in all subjects into gushing art critics ('self-esteem builders') and leave time to do the truly essential things, such as providing social services and indoctrinating kids in the Progressive ideology.

Note also the odd thinking that says that habits and repertoires are good, but recall of items of common usage is bad. How does one develop habits but by repetition, or develop habits considered appropriate if we are not told that they are appropriate, and reinforced by a requirement to develop that habit? If the repetition tested is repetition of items of common usage, such as the capitalization of proper nouns, conforming to that usage improves communication with of the rest of those who use the same language.

Confirming that pupils had been listening during a lesson, by asking questions about things said in the lesson, is also a normal habit for genuine teachers. Progressive educators apparently see the development of memory, a higher-level thinking skill, as a mere 'plug-in skill', like throwing darts.

6. Are *representative* challenges—designed to emphasize *depth* more than breadth

Here 'learning styles' again raises its ignorant head. Of course they *say* depth, but they accept collages of magazine cutouts, word-searches, crossword puzzles, and coloring-in cartoons as indicators of deep understanding. Interesting that they specifically champion depth more than breadth though. Once upon a time a liberal education implied learning a little bit of many things, to more fully understand the world and perhaps to discover what we may want to do with our life. Only then would we concentrate on any real 'depth', and even then it was not until college, where we often took another year or two of broad 'survey' courses before we were finally required to declare a major.[214] Later still, we made fun of specialists in narrow specialties as "Knowing a lot about very little." Now we expect a pupil's individual learning style to limit her understanding from an early age, and we are told that this is a good thing.

7. Are engaging and educational.

I was always told that tests are learning experiences. They are, too. I had many insights into what we were really talking about when the test question crystalized the pertinent facts for me. I wonder how much crystallization, as opposed to mental sedimentation, occurs nowadays?

8. Involve somewhat ambiguous ("ill-structured") tasks or problems.

This is another version of the 'open-ended' questions argument for which there are no 'correct' answers. If there are no correct answers, accepting any answer, or even accepting no answer, is legitimate. If no

---

214 Or was the advent of survey courses an accommodation that colleges were forced to make in the past, in response to an influx of students taught during previous Progressive cycles?

answer is correct, there is never any need to make anyone feel bad about themselves by telling them they got a wrong answer. Of course, if we are never told that we made a mistake, we cannot learn from that mistake.

Are you getting the feeling that all of this is more about proving the educator's level of empathy for the various invented disabilities, rather than anything about kids' learning?

C. Grading and Scoring Standards

1. Involve criteria that assess essentials, not easily counted (but relatively unimportant) errors.

This is yet another invocation against objective grading and in favor of rubric scoring that accepts some minimal 'good enough' rather than reaching for the heights. Recall that modern Report Cards, at least at the grammar school level, now rarely categorize achievement as higher than 'Satisfactory'. The 'relatively unimportant' part again says that rules, facts, and details are unimportant and confining.

2. Are graded not on a "curve" but in reference to performance standards (criterion-referenced, not norm-referenced).

Recall that grading 'on a curve' was a traditional teacher's way of adjusting for relatively low scores on particularly difficult exams. We kids deeply appreciated the procedure. I suspect, however, that here 'on a curve' suggests a reference to *The Bell Curve*, that we all <u>know</u> is a racist document, especially if we had not read it.

Nevertheless, for those who may not remember, here is a common version of grading on a curve. If the highest score earned on a test was, say, an 85 percent rather than 97 percent or 100 percent, the teacher granted everybody an additional 10 or 15 points. This potentially allowed kids who earned a 55 percent or 60 percent to 'pass' (i.e., 55 percent + 15 percent = 70 percent).

'Criterion-referencing', usually by use of a rubric scoring system, says that the pupil did 'well enough' against a 'performance-based' criterion. This subjective evaluation makes it an inappropriate scoring method for objective tests. Of course we are not supposed to test knowledge anyhow, only performance.

Another variation on grading on a curve was used in subjective evaluations, such as book reports and other longer writing assignments. Since it is not possible merely to mark off wrong answers and subtract from 100 percent in this sort of evaluation, a subjective way must be used to rate relative accomplishment. This subjective standard was established by the teacher early in the year and maintained throughout the year, so kids quickly learned what sorts of things the teacher considered important; whether it was precise punctuation, sentence structure, elaborate descriptions, persuasive arguments, or all of the above and then some. These structural items were then layered over the main point of the exercise which may have been a correct use of facts about the subject of the essay, but might just as well have been a creative use of ideas developed by an author. "Compare and contrast" types of essay questions require considerable creativity and understanding, for instance.

The 'curve' part of the evaluation referred to the conviction that letter grades should be distributed along a 'normal curve' centered on the expectation of what the average pupil could achieve. Most grades awarded under this procedure were typically high Cs. Relatively fewer Bs were awarded and As were even more rare, being reserved for the best efforts. However, teachers never stuck to the full 'curve' obsessively. Very few failing grades were awarded, unless a pupil's effort was clearly less that what we would expect of someone who attended classes.

In one sense the Progressives may be almost right about performance testing, but as usual they ultimately get it backwards. For instance, most math tests are performance-based, although they are not often done in front of an audience. Many types of "verbal" questions, including essay questions, are also perfect examples of performance tasks. These are the kind of questions that ask us to find and correct the grammar or punctuation mistake in a given sentence, etc. In the lowest grades, however, evaluative multiple-choice, etc., tests are rare even in genuine classrooms. That is because multiple-choice tests that require the pupil to choose among various subtle distinctions presuppose a level of intellectual or factual sophistication that is not possible in the very young pupil. The fact that all types of objective questions are not appropriate in the first several years also gives the lie to the Progressive claim that they are mere regurgitation, though we also use questions of pure recall at this level too (i.e., What did Winnie do when he found the honey pot?). In the lower classes, testing should consist of more specific performance tasks of the kind I mentioned above (e.g., math, verbal). That is to say, kids should be given arithmetic problems to solve, spelling tests, and other "structural" verbal performance tasks to do.

On the other hand, fact-based multiple-choice questions are very legitimate even in the lowest grades. If, for example, a 1st grade science class mentioned that butterflies have antennae, but whales, camels, and birds do not, asking a kid to remember what sort of animal has antennae is OK. Again, this sort of fact-based question helps to build a kid's conceptual base about the world. He will need it later in life.

We definitely have a place for performance-based tests in adult life, too. Art, shop, gym, typing, and music grades are very often based on performance. Military, and other sorts of vocational training, consist in very large part on performance. For instance, putting-on, sealing and clearing a gas mask[215] has a performance standard of nine seconds. Even if a soldier practices and can complete the procedure in four seconds, he gets the same "Go" score as the guy who limps in at eight-and-a-half seconds.

The reasons for the 'Go–No go' standard are that they intend the gas mask to save your life in a toxic environment. It either does or does not keep one safe, depending on whether you get the mask on in time. During routine performance testing, soldiers try to optimize their chances of success by practicing a few times just before we test them for the record. They also take off eyeglasses, unbuckle helmet chin straps, take off bulky, movement-restricting field jackets and gloves, take a deep breath (since 'stop breathing' is the first performance standard) and stand poised like a gunfighter ready to rip open the carrying case at the first hint of the shout "GAS," which starts the clock. With a few practice tries, four-second performances, and even faster, are quite common.

In combat, however, conditions might be less than optimal. The soldier might be exhausted and breathing heavily after sprinting for cover or after a ten-hour road march. He may be heavily clothed in winter while carrying a heavy backpack, up to his waist in a swamp, carrying a casualty on a litter, still covered by a poncho after rain or crawling on her belly under low-lying branches. Somehow, the military decided that nine seconds is usually 'good enough' to save soldiers' lives,[216] and if they can accomplish the procedure under 'ideal' conditions, they have proven that they know the actions required to complete

---

215 Forgive me, all you grunts out there. I know that this is a 'protective' mask rather than a 'gas' mask and that you 'don' the mask, not 'put it on', but I'm speaking with civilians now.

216 Maybe because most people can easily hold their breaths for nine seconds, or because even Gomer Pyle could complete the task, after the necessary training. I suspect, however, that our experience in World War I trenches had a lot to do with it.

the steps correctly, even under trying circumstances. The speed requirement emphasizes the urgency that 'doing it for real' might require, although he might potentially have a minute, or a half-hour, before the toxic cloud reaches him.

Taking a history or literature test is not much like combat, however. Proving that we 'understand' the Civil War, as discussed in class, may require more than performance of some minimal skill. It may require us to know the dates of various events, recall the names of major participants, and the sequence of occurrences, discuss how various factors (e.g., population, society, industrialization, the personality of commanders, etc.), affected events, and much more. Grading a posterboard collage, a one-page comic strip, or an original trombone piece called 'The Civil War', just does not give a good enough indication of historical understanding, deep or otherwise.

Although it is nearly as unlikely, writing or producing a short play, or something equally involved might do it, in theory, but just imagine the logistics of it all. It would take far too much time for a single group of three or four pupils to do even a cursory job of a stage production. Then, imagine how much time it would take to grade all the different productions. Also imagine that everyone in class is doing the same thing. The guys who sit through five or six 'plays' before they are 'up' may have an enormous advantage in rubric scoring. Also, how does the teacher grade all of the different plays? What if one pupil wanted to write a song and play the guitar instead? How do you grade that? Do you grade it higher than someone who merely writes a poem, because a song is a poem too, but it involves composing or adapting music as well as playing and singing talent?

The logistics are impossible and a single year in which to try to cover all of American history, for instance, is short enough without taking time to try to turn all the kids into superficial, though affective, historical thespians. In the end, trying to develop 'criteria' upon which everybody can be individually creative in the 'artsy' sense is also not possible, even if Ed schools trained the teachers to evaluate them, and we do not. So attempts at grading of this sort inevitably give superficial 'participation' grades. The kids know it and learn very little because they merely do just enough to 'check the box' on the rubric. If the pupils still do not manage to 'check the box', which is all too common, they pass anyway so that the teacher does not have to turn in many failing grades.

Incidentally, "norm-referencing" refers to comparing the work of kids with each other, rather than to some arbitrary, though downwardly fluid, minimal criteria that characterize grading-rubrics. This is because, in the Progressive ideology, competition does not inspire kids to do their best by trying to outdo their peers. Competition is, we are told, a bad thing and leads to nothing but more self-esteem destruction. Thus (as stated in B.1., above), it is interesting that they characterize objective tests as 'arbitrary' and see criterion referencing as 'open-ended' and *un-contrived*.

What a surprise. We found another delusional and contradictory, yet creative, use of words. Creative, that is, if reversing definitions qualifies as creative and ethically justifiable. Clearly, however, reversing definitions is considered acceptable when designing rhetoric and educational theory.

Allan Bloom gave an example of this tendency to redefine in his *The Closing of the American Mind*. He was speaking of the use of history and social science to promote the multicultural philosophy at the time, not authentic assessments, but the lesson is the same. He said (pg. 30):

> History and social science are used in a variety of ways to overcome prejudice. We should not be ethnocentric, a term drawn from anthropology, which tells more about the [redefined] meaning of openness. We should not think our way better than others. The intention is not so much to teach students about other times and places as to make them aware of the fact that their preferences are only that—accidents of their time and place. Their beliefs do not entitle them as individuals, or collectively as a nation, to think they are superior to anyone else. John Rawls is almost a parody of this tendency, writing hundreds of pages to persuade men, and proposing a scheme of government that would force them, not to despise anyone. In A *Theory of Justice,* he writes that the physicist or the poet should not look down on the man who spends his life counting blades of grass or performing any other frivolous or corrupt activity. Indeed, he should be esteemed, since esteem from others, as opposed to self-esteem, is a basic need of men. So indiscriminateness [nonjudgmentalism] is a moral imperative because its opposite is discrimination.

3. Involve demystified criteria of success that appear to *students* as inherent in successful activity.

The point of an essay question does often mystify unprepared pupils, but allowing those same unprepared pupils to decide how to define success in an academic setting has done great damage to the integrity of the subject and of curricula everywhere. Just imagine allowing kids to decide when and whether they have succeeded in a chemistry experiment or in the evaluation of a Shakespearean sonnet. What criteria could they possibly devise that would be more appropriate than a trained and experienced teacher's criteria? Even if a few kids would genuinely try to challenge themselves, do we grade everyone by the overachiever's criteria, or by the kid who says, "Don't know and don't care?" Or do we grade each kid by his own, individually devised, criteria? What do we need 'teachers' for then? Well, we do not need teachers; they tell us. We can get by with facilitators. Unfortunately (for Progressive theory), consistency and even efficiency are important for learning, and for the logistics of teaching. Even a poor genuine teacher's criteria are likely to be much better than this confused mess.

Also keep in mind that this prescription for the appropriate way to test kids is a one-size-fits-all template. Even if this messy sort of system made sense for college students or even 'advanced' high school seniors, and I do not for a moment concede that it does, imagine forcing this philosophic and logistical quagmire into the grammar schools. How much precious instructional time would be wasted trying to get fourth graders to decide what makes an inherently successful activity? A clear indication of time wasted is that modern instruction and learning seem to be pegged at approximately half of grade-appropriate levels. Therefore, at least half of all instructional time is already wasted. When you factor in the fact that the instruction is also dumbed-down, you will see the problem.

4. Make self-assessment a part of the assessment.

See C.3. above. This item goes to the 'affective' aspect of learning that Progressive educationists love so much. How do you feel about what we are discussing? Emotion is far more important than 'content'. Why? Because the intent of Progressive education is to make kids feel dependent on the various bureaucracies with which we have saddled ourselves and to make kids 'socially critical thinkers' (i.e., Marxists or anarchists who hate America).

Most working teachers would probably bristle at this characterization. This is not what they have in mind at all. I do not doubt that for a moment, but as I said, most of them have been as flim-flammed by the rhetoric as the rest of us. When you look at the results we have attained, however, you have to give credence to this analysis. Regardless, in the short term the main character of self-assessment that genuine teachers want kids to engage in is, "What do I have to do to reduce the number of red marks on my next paper?" The hope is that the kids' solutions to this dilemma prominently feature such things as; "I have to pay attention in class, take better notes, do the homework, read the assignments, and study more." Over the long term, competent self-assessment leads to making wise career decisions, etc. While pupils might consult parents, teachers, classmates, and others regarding these decisions, self-assessments are ultimately private and there is no need to have a public sensing session after every quiz, test, or activity.

5. Use a multifaceted scoring system instead of one aggregate grade.

Traditional educators have long used a multifaceted scoring system. We call it lots of quizzes and frequent tests. We do this so that kids do not have to study massive amounts of stuff for any single test, with the possible exceptions of semester and final exams, increasing the chances of progressive learning for *all* kids (progressive in the sense of building on accumulated knowledge). Book reports, lab reports, projects, term papers, mock trials, research reports, and so forth, are other subject-oriented forms of evaluation. Various combinations of these testing techniques, including various consolidating exams (e.g., unit, midterm, or final exams) are appropriate depending on subject matter, teacher preference, type of class (e.g., lab, art, discussion, etc.) and learning level. The traditional system is already almost infinitely flexible and "multifaceted" while staying focused on *teaching*.

However, the item, again, merely wants us to use rubrics that give credit for 'appropriate use of color' (i.e., don't color Mozart's face green) on the poster board that demonstrates our understanding of *The Magic Flute*, etc.

6. Exhibit harmony with shared schoolwide aims—a *Standard*

Let's all hold hands and sing "Kum-bah-yah." Doing everything the same way will promote diversity and individuality.

D. Fairness and Equity

1. Ferret out and identify (perhaps hidden) strengths.

Give credit for writing letters in an up and down orientation.

2. Strike a *constantly* examined balance between honoring achievement and native skill or fortunate training.

Give credit for writing letters in an up and down orientation, and
if they forget even that, lower the standard.

"Fortunate training" again implies that white guys dispense 'secret'
knowledge only to each other while demonizing the notion of learning
for *all* kids. Note once again that there is no mention of teaching any
of the good stuff. Dumbing-down is much more appropriate.

3. Minimize needless, unfair, and demoralizing comparisons.

While 'unfair' unfairly implies that any comparison is unjust, where
in life will you find a place where we believe this sentiment? Picking
sports 'superstars' as opposed to benchwarmers? On-the-job promotions?
Shouldn't we do kids the very great favor of letting them discover what
they can do well and enjoy doing, and for which careers they might
eventually qualify? The flip side is just as important. Discovering what
potential jobs are less well suited for them (based on educational requirements, interest, physical skill, etc.) would save a kid much time, money,
negative affect, and destroyed self-esteem. This is not invariably demoralizing, except to those who have been trained to expect maximal results
for minimal, or no, work. For the kid who discovers a love for an essentially nonacademic pursuit, it can be uplifting, even inspirational. This
is also true for the kid who discovers a love for one sort of academic
pursuit, for instance biology, math, history, or literary criticism, while
discovering that they hate another, such as biology, math, history, or
literary criticism. Doing anything less, like constantly looking to justify
another pointless and expensive program, is shameful. Constantly looking for the worst possible interpretation for reality, and concentrating
on trying to camouflage failure, rather than encouraging kids to "Do
your best" likewise qualifies as shameful.

4. Allow appropriate room for students' learning styles, aptitudes,
   and interests.

Kids do this all by themselves by gravitating toward elective classes
and extracurricular activities which they enjoy, and away from the things
they do not enjoy. This is an appropriate example of permitting individual choice. Nevertheless there is, or should be, an unavoidable core of
knowledge with which *all* pupils should be acquainted, whether they
find them easy or relevant or not. Turning every class into a sociology

activity is genuinely harmful for all of the reasons stated throughout the book (and I probably missed a few).

> 5. Can be—should be—attempted by *all* students, with the test "scaffolded up," not "dumbed down," as necessary.

We <u>should</u> test all kids, especially in the 'core' subjects, but that is not what this item means. 'Scaffolding up' is an apparent reference to the ideas of a Russian developmental psychologist named Lev Vygotsky who was at odds with some technical, theoretical aspects of Piaget's analysis of the development of language. The author of *Educational Psychology* interprets Piaget as leaving developing kids all alone in an almost inhuman isolation, while Vygotsky allows for social interaction and language. On page 47 the author writes, "Whereas Piaget describes the child as a little scientist, constructing an understanding of the world largely alone, Vygotsky suggested that cognitive development depends much more on the people in the child's world."[217] There is more to his ideas of course, including a detailed evaluation of concept formation, but the aspect of Vygotsky's ideas that the text highlights is his idea of 'assisted learning'. This idea may be little more than the realization that kids often take clues and suggestions from adults in their attempt to learn how to do things. I do not think that Vygotsky intended that we not teach kids anything specific, but only assist in their own discovery learning, as Rousseau was said to have done, and as the Progressives insist. Nevertheless, the word 'scaffolding', apparently coined by Jerome Bruner, is the notion that a suggestion or hint, or seeing a thing done by someone who knows how, often helps kids understand and learn.

I also doubt whether Piaget ever said that learning by the example of others never happens. Making suggestions and providing demonstrations is a common practice in genuine classrooms. We call the various forms of this practice "teaching." However, we may take the idea of

---

217 Not so oddly enough, it seems that self-esteem training manages to isolate kids by convincing them that they are all that there is. No one else truly matters. This is OK, however, so long as there are Progressive educators and paraprofessionals around to give them the answers without, at the same time, showing them their mistakes. This selfish isolation is reinforced by child-centered instruction which convinces kids that they know all that there is to know anyway, that other people's ideas are largely irrelevant, and that even if they notice that they do not know all, someone else will do the work for them. The result is that modern school kids unashamedly profess a profound ignorance and give up very easily, knowing that they will pass anyway. Again, however, employers don't see things exactly as educators do, and expect each employee to work for their pay. Not being trained to think that work is a requirement clashes with real life, causing the national epidemic of stress that we enjoy today.

'scaffolding', as used here, to mean that teachers should prompt kids' faltering efforts to explain their deep conceptual understanding that inspired their posterboard masterpieces during authentic assessments (as I had to), and then give them credit as if the teacher were not the only one in the room with a clue. Used this way, scaffolding-up *is* dumbing-down. Educationists seem to like the idea because of Vygotsky's allowance for more "social interaction" in education, leaving the philosophic door open for more 'group work' (which kids mainly use to socialize) rather than lecturing and discussing, and for a more extensive patchwork of intrusive programs and services.

Do 'authentic assessments' improve learning and thinking skills? Look back to the charts in Chapter 1 to help you decide. Use of authentic assessments, however, can help us explain how kids can be on a school's Honor Roll then score so poorly on simple standardized tests, and find themselves so deeply over their heads as college freshmen.

You have to ask yourself, for instance, would you want the folks who determine the causes of airline crashes to be trained using Progressive techniques and tested using authentic assessments, or would you want them to have specific, technical knowledge, and genuine understanding of metallurgy, polymer chemistry, electrical components, engineering, design, aerodynamics, meteorology, etc. Would you also want them to be sure of their expertise because their own testing was rigorous and to the point? What would you think if you walked past a hospital laboratory and saw the technicians toe dancing, or if you saw your accountant pasting pictures onto posterboard, to send to the IRS? Would you think that you would have gotten your education tax dollars' worth?

This seems a good place for a short discussion of the way that educators are adapting to the 'standards' and 'accountability' movements which have passed laws requiring additional testing at specified times during a kid's school career. These laws would not have been necessary if the schools had been doing a decent job, of course, but as stated earlier, once a law is passed, implementation of the law requires that regulations be written which, in turn, require certain actions of those who will carry out the provisions of the law. Those regulations are typically written by members of the government agency that will administer the law. In education, this is a State Education Department, which, as we already know is typically staffed by Ed.D.s.

The reason that these testing laws have been passed is because the American citizenry had noticed that kids are not learning very much in school, and the laws are an attempt to force educators to do better. In the minds of the educationists, however, typical standardized tests are bad things because of their insistence on requiring answers to questions to which pupils had not been prepared. Of course, limiting a superficial 'education' in favor of genuine learning is precisely the point of the new laws. Nevertheless, rather than merely insisting that teachers teach a competent, liberal curriculum, committees of educators have been established in the States that are trying to carry out these laws, to ensure that kids are tested on specific points of political correctness. This intention could be seen in a Public Broadcasting Service (PBS) *Frontline* program seen on March 28, 2002, where committees of educators were arguing for which victim group's plight would take precedence in the new curriculum designed to "insure that the tests test what kids are actually being taught in school." Unfortunately, trying to get schools to stop doing the pointless things that they are currently doing, is the ultimate point of the new laws, but, as has already been quoted: "Principals and teachers who do not want what others seek to impose on them often are extraordinarily adept at nullifying or diffusing practices perceived to be in conflict with prevailing ways of doing things. The result may be the appearance of change, but no change."[218] The same is true of Progressive State education departments.

We will discuss the original intent of standardized testing, along with the difference between standardized tests and routine classroom tests and quizzes next. Nevertheless, after diluting the intent of the newly required tests, you can be sure that within a short time, educators will begin to complain that the new tests do not do what the legislators intended, or that the paperwork required by the new laws is too onerous, which proves that tests are useless and unfair and that, therefore, all testing should be stopped.

During the previous discussion I said several times that I did not know what a term referred to. Ordinarily, that type of comment would not be acceptable. Before saying such a thing in print I should try to find out, especially if I am critical of the ideas that I say I do not understand. To try to correct that problem, I found the referenced article

---

218 John Goodlad, In *A Place Called School* (1984, p. 16).

from which I took the authentic assessment 'Table'. As you may expect by now, it was no help in clearing up the confusion but rather extended it with additional twisted and unsupported reasoning. In fact, the article was not a research article at all, but another opinion piece that sought to debunk the idea of standardized testing by presenting this hare-brained scheme as a theoretical replacement. If you read the article quickly, without thinking about what all the words mean, it almost makes sense in places, but not if you look harder.

I said earlier that authentic assessments, and Progressive notions generally, are solutions without a problem. I have also said, repeatedly, that Progressive ideas recommend doing exactly the opposite of what should be done. This article contains some examples of what I mean. For instance:

> "Reform of testing depends on teachers realizing that standardized testing evolved because the school transcript became untrustworthy."

This statement is quite true, even if the author makes it sound that recent school transcript untrustworthiness could not be attributed to the pointlessness of authentic assessments. This untrustworthiness is a recent phenomenon, based on report cards that allow social promotions, but it is also true that a different sort of problem occurred earlier in our history that initially prompted the development of the standardized testing industry. So we must ask why did transcripts seem untrustworthy to college admissions committees to the point that the testing industry developed many decades ago? This question is too large to answer in a paragraph or two, but let us hope that this abbreviated description of history is sufficiently complete to lead us in the right direction.

Why Standardized Tests?

Once upon a time there were few colleges, and they were expensive. Only relatively well-off people, or parents who made extensive sacrifices and made them for extended periods, could send their kids to college. Occasionally whole communities pitched in to send an especially worthy kid to college. However, this did not happen very often, because even middle-class people did not always see college attendance as inevitable. The kid had to have specific interests and he had to be clearly superior to the other kids in the community if the community were to help one kid when they could not help all. It did not hurt if he were also the town quarterback, or something. Specific interest was a requirement because colleges often tended toward the same instructional content, which was heavily weighted to the teaching of dead languages and either the law, medicine, or preparation for the ministry. A few also taught science or engineering.

As the population grew and agricultural markets expanded beyond the local area, we established "Ag" colleges that mainly served a single State. Entrance requirements became known by the teachers in the State and they instructed accordingly, looking for qualified pupils to recommend. Most kids did not go to college, regardless of ability, but either did what Dad (or Mom) did, or 'moved to town' to work in a factory, store or office.

Eventually, as America's economy started to change from agrarian to industrial, and as the population ('tax base') and interests grew to include other than agricultural or industrial needs, more pupils began to go out of State for their postsecondary education, and colleges established their own entrance exams based on their needs. Engineering colleges wanted students who were ready to learn advanced math, physics, and chemistry, etc., and may not have cared whether a particular student could dance nicely. On the other hand, schools of fine arts did not care whether you could do trigonometry in your head or whether you knew the gestation period of a milking goat. In either case, what was taught in each local classroom around the nation may or may not prepare pupils for the kind of school that particular kid wanted. There are kids who grow up on farms who are more interested in iconography than husbandry, but schools in agricultural communities stressed the natural sciences, especially botany and the animal sciences. The valedictorian of such a school, who perhaps wanted to study electrical engineering or physical anthropology, may have been well behind his classmates from cities with many factories and museums.

However, colleges wanted a diverse student body, and they did not want to have to flunk out anybody who did not want to flunk out. Yet, what happens if the valedictorian of a particular school in a particular year did not have the academic background to allow immediate immersion into the intricacies of cell biology, astrophysics, or comparative literature? Was it fair to accept this pupil based on his valedictory transcript alone, only to have him flunk out after having used up his parents' life savings? I suspect that is one important reason that standardized testing became so important.

Now, of course, when the stated ideal is to send *all* kids to college no matter their knowledge or capability, maybe standardized tests are no longer valid. Still, we have to reenter the twisted logic of the author. He says,

> To regain control over both testing and instruction, schools need to rethink their diploma requirements and grades. They need a clear set of appropriate and objective criteria, enabling both students *and outsiders* (author's emphasis) to know what counts, what is essential—what a school's standards really are. Until we know what students must directly demonstrate to earn a diploma, they will continue to pass by meeting the de facto "standard" of being dutiful and persistent—irrespective of the quality of their work. And standardized test makers will continue to succeed in hawking simplistic norm-referenced tests to districts and states resigned to using them for lack of a better accountability scheme.

We have a lot to talk about in this simple sounding quotation. Let us start with the end of the quotation. As we do, however, note that he specifies a need for objective criteria, just as sensible people would require. Then see what his criteria are.

We have already met the term 'norm referenced'. It means that we judge and rate a pupil's academic achievement in reference to other pupils' academic achievements. In a norm-referenced system, typically consisting of objective tests, you can eventually rate the pupil as better or worse than his peers and to what degree this pupil mastered the required material. If the level-of-knowledge "norm" against which we judge a pupil is realistically considered age- or grade-appropriate, we can see how well our kid does against similarly prepared pupils of the same grade. Further, if virtually every kid in the State or country of the same age-grade was tested against the same level of knowledge, we can evaluate the achievement of those students who completed a particular course of study [i.e., graduate from a particular college], against other students who did, and did not, complete that same course of study. If we do, we can get a clear indication whether our kid has the capacity or prior knowledge needed to complete a particular course of study.

As a bonus, which is currently being ignored, the information gained from this sort of countrywide comparison shows that there are bright kids everywhere, not just in prestigious Eastern boarding schools. As a result, more kids from more diverse backgrounds were offered admission than ever before. This is what the original versions of tests such as the SAT and ACT have done for us,[219] and for college admissions committees.

Another great benefit of entrance exams with a national scope, is that, if they are done well, they can act as the long sought after *de facto* national educational "standard." If there is any benefit to establishing a national level of academic expectations, and I believe that there is, then it would be an additional benefit to establish that standard without the machinations of a national bureaucracy. These standards should be driven by academic and intellectual concerns, not by political fashion. This academic standard would then be used by schools when they develop their curricula, establishing minimal expectations for promotion to each grade, thus insuring that their graduates have been exposed to, and proven competence in, the 'skills' required for completion of a course of genuinely higher education. Also, since properly designed standardized tests do not presuppose instruction in any specific prior knowledge,[220] other than the purely "structural" kinds of knowledge as proper punctuation and the multiplication tables, they can give college admissions committees objective evidence of the likelihood of success.

Therefore, let us say that a particular college finds that pupils who score a composite 900 on the SAT, or a 25 on the ACT, almost invariably fail to graduate for academic reasons. That college's admissions committee would then be justified, all other things being equal, in not offering other pupils with similar scores admission to their college.

Similar reasoning applies for schools primarily interested in specific academic knowledge. You may recall that generic "College Entrance" standardized tests include two major parts; math and verbal. These tests also have add-on exams that test knowledge, reasoning, and/or competence in other areas, such as the various sciences, calculus, American history, French, etc. Schools of engineering are typically more impressed with high math scores while schools of journalisms look more closely at the verbal scores. This system seems sensible, and since many kids see these tests as 'difficult', calling them 'simplistic'[221] is missing the point

---

219 Now that these tests are also being 'renormed' downward, they may not be as valid or useful.

220 Unlike the new tests being designed for the new spate of State-mandated tests.

221 Like 'arbitrary', as jargon 'simplistic' means that they have questions that require specific factual knowledge or that they are not open-ended.

by a country mile. The quotation above, however, implies that objective tests do not test anything 'essential', of course, but we will get back to that directly, too.

Moving up the quotation; to me, "dutiful and persistent" sound like two characteristics that I want my kids to develop, but even so, I cannot allow the ". . . irresepective of the quality of their work" comment to pass. Passing kids despite poor, or no, quality has only reappeared as a problem of national proportions quite recently. In fact, you may have recognized it as an important theme of this book.

It is delusional, however, to say, as the author does, that the way to prove a pupil's qualifications to everyone, including outsiders, is to have a diploma dependent on a 'performance' seen by no one other than the pupils themselves and their own teachers. This does not come close to passing the "Huh?" test. This is, however, the criterion the authors call "objective."

Elsewhere in the article the author also complains that under a traditional grading system:

An "A" in "English" means only that some adult thought the student's work was excellent. Compared to what or whom? As determined by what criteria? In reference to what specific subject matter?

In a traditional classroom, grades are based on the criteria that each classroom teacher defines. The author tells us that this is a bad thing. Then he says that *his* scheme is a good thing because it is, ". . . essential—and teacher designed."

Are you getting as tired as I am of these nonsensical and duplicitous contradictions? Also, are you sure you still want people who accept this stuff as wisdom to be responsible for teaching your kids?

So what should a high school diploma be based on if not on demonstrated competence in subject matter content that might prepare kids for lifelong careers? On a performance, of course:

. . . a repertoire, the judgment and skill to 'put it all together' in one central challenge, repeatedly tried.

In essence, what they require, is some personal project that the pupil perfects over time. Schools would grant a diploma when the kids, at long last, manage to achieve the minimal criteria they themselves have helped set. The author grandly equates this to an oral defense of a graduate thesis. If it is similar to that, it mainly requires technique rather than content. However, if a kid wants to be almost anything besides an actor or a Progressive educationist, he must know things before he gets to college or on the job.

My father tells me (from personal experience) that in Stalin's time, the ideological educational professionals in the USSR tried some of these same ideas. They went so far as to say that, since everyone was the same as everybody else, only one pupil per class needed to be tested at the end of a school-year. One poor kid was picked and tested, and everybody in the class got the same grade as him. The Communist Chinese also attempted to further their cultural revolution by using such ideas, until they noticed that their pupils learned less, not more, than their parents did.[222]

Even the Communists gave up on this sort of philosophical hoo-hah. Why can't we?

Now let us try to get back to common sense. As we have discovered, learning occurs in small increments, building fact upon fact until we can easily paraphrase Hamlet speaking to Horatio, and say, ". . . There are more things in Heaven and Earth, Progressive educationists, that are dreamt of in your philosophy."[223]

We once had a sentiment that no one hears much anymore. That sentiment was that, 'Once you begin to know how much you do not know, you are on the threshold of wisdom'.

Relax, guys. This does <u>not</u> mean to imply that traditional education insists that the best way to educate kids is to tell them constantly how stupid they are. The understanding that there is more to learn is one of those personal, genuinely 'affective' moments that Progressives love, but rarely achieve. Traditional educators know that once enough knowledge accumulates to support a level of understanding that is beyond the ordinary, it becomes clear to the earnest pupil that there is a great deal more to know before he can hope to reach the next level of understanding. I suspect that once upon a time, this genuinely empowering and energizing realization came to many more people than now. The main

---

222 Klitgaard, 1986.
223 Shakespeare, *Hamlet*, Act I, Scene V, lines 166–167.

realization that seems to occur to many of today's kids is that knowing little or nothing, is no impediment to self-esteem, but that they need bureaucratic help with all aspects of their lives. This sense of dependency plays well into the hands of the Progressive ideology, inspiring them to design yet more pointless and debilitating programs, but it is the opposite of what we want.

Teaching to the Test

Let us discuss objective testing and 'teaching to the test'. We have already spoken briefly about short essay questions. Essay questions, by their nature, are opportunities to express your understanding of a topic with more individuality and creativity than is possible with other, more objective test questions. As a bonus, you get better at writing descriptions and persuasive arguments the more you write descriptions and persuasive arguments.

The arguments against objective test questions usually stress how limited their scope is and how 'uncreative' they are as a consequence. They are called 'regurgitation' questions. The truth of the matter is that objective questions are far better at generating high-level thinking than an open-ended assessment based on a performance criterion that expects only that the effort is a dumbed-down, or even an irrelevant, 'good enough'. Far from being trivial questions of mere recall or recognition, objective questions are almost infinitely flexible tools that can range from a preschool matching of pictures of objects with pictures of similar objects, to an almost hideously difficult question requiring detailed, semantic distinctions and esoteric understanding that would challenge the best of us.

It is also true, however, that the more a question reaches for subtle distinctions and analysis of complex thoughts, the more it is likely to become vague and to permit more than one answer. Where this begins to happen, is the place where essay questions of all sorts begin to take over, which is why most responsible teachers include both types of questions in their tests. That transitional 'place' between the specific knowledge (often multiple choice) questions used for that particular test, and the analytical understanding required of essay questions, may be quite short, however, and leads to the main criticism of multiple choice questions; that is of their relative triviality. Though the facts being tested may or may not be trivial, until pupils learn enough stuff, these questions are useful and necessary. Perhaps some rigorous graduate schools can dispense with them altogether, using essay questions exclusively, though I doubt it, but grammar and high schools cannot. They cannot because they are useful tools in leading our pupils to true understanding. Once they have discovered thinking for themselves, if they ever do, then they can teach the rest of us something new, usually by developing a new fact or facts.

Another aspect of the testing controversy revolves around standardized tests generally. The complaint is that if teachers know that a standardized test, or tests, are 'hanging over the heads' of their pupils (i.e., are "high stakes" tests), teachers tend to 'teach to the test'. They tell us that this is a bad thing because, as usual, if kids are asked to practice with a certain kind of test question, they do not get to express their individuality. Once you see that objective tests accomplish exactly those things that Progressive rhetoric says they do not accomplish, you will readily see that teaching to the test is a very good thing. In fact, standardized tests, and their country cousins—the standard classroom quiz or test—help teachers to teach kids to think.

Unfortunately, the kinds of solutions I will recommend do not always work in modern practice. Over the last decade or so, many State legislatures, under pressure to raise academic standards, have passed legislation requiring school systems to be more "accountable" for their results, and, of course, we now have the national No Child Left Behind law. This is a good thing in a system that ignores objective evidence. In practical terms, the way this must be done is to establish objective testing procedures by means of legislation. Passing legislation, however, is only the first step and is complicated by the fact that what educational professionals of the test-writing variety, consider to be grade-appropriate knowledge, is not what it once was, or should be. Dumbing down has occurred for so long that the intellectual inertia of those who are responsible for developing the tests pulls their expectations down. So even the standardized tests are now dumbed-down.

We also have significant costs involved in developing standardized tests. Therefore, many States buy commercially prepared standardized tests. As we might expect, as a commercial enterprise test preparation companies need to sell their product if they are to survive. Since educational professionals are the customers of such companies, the educationists exert considerable influence on the characteristics of the tests. Then, since schools are under increasing scrutiny, by the public and by legislatures, many school superintendents merely tell test companies, "Just sell me a test that will make me look good."[224] Therefore, modern standardized tests reflect Progressive expectations and practices more than they reflect the intellectual requirements of competent adulthood.

Also, and for the same reason, to pass as many pupils as possible, schools today often spend considerable time cramming for the purchased test. Some schools even give academic credit for the cram classes. This should not be the reality of standardized tests that we evaluate when we must decide the benefits of the various testing options. Unfortunately, this is what we have, so standardized testing is already weakened as an option. This weakness is the result of the educationist's ministrations, and is not inherent in the tests themselves.

You must also realize that when I say "teaching to the test" I am not talking about giving kids the answers to the test questions, or giving them the test questions themselves, or both, and simply trying to get pupils to memorize answers to questions they do not understand. Progressive education does that.

Spending a month or two trying to cram 12 years of previously undispensed knowledge into pupils' heads, is likely to be ineffective, even if the classes include shortcut test-taking strategies, as many do. This is true, of course, since the cram sessions do not give pupils the time to explore, question, think about, and understand the nuances of the instruction that they were never given over the previous 10 to 12 years. Actually *teaching* subjects would have allowed that understanding to develop and grow, but of course our education professionals were more interested in other things. Ironically, these are the same education professionals who then complain that standardized tests, and the last minute cramming techniques resorted to, do not seem to work very well, and give norm-referenced tests a bad name. It is also these cramming techniques that are generally known as "teaching to the test." Cramming is not what I mean by teaching to the test, and school superintendents and principals who resort to it, should be replaced.

The short explanation of the apparent contradiction that norm-referenced tests teach kids how to think, is that, norm-referenced tests, both the standardized and/or routine classroom variety, have been known for a very long time to correlate with success in college and

---

224 Sowell, 1993.

eventual success on the job and in life generally. This should not be a hard idea to grasp. If you have been exposed to and know many things, and especially if you were successful at learning and working with many or all of those things, you have proven that you can easily adapt to changing situations, and the more you know, the easier dealing with variety is for you. If this 'correlation to success' is so, and it is, then 'objective' kinds of questions must have something to offer. The object then is to discover what that can be.

Considering the fact that virtually everything that Progressive theorists have said over the years is contrary to reality, let us see what they do not like about objective tests. Then we can do exactly the opposite, and help our kids prepare for the future.

Objective test questions are too limited in scope, they tell us. They are not 'open-ended'. They require specific knowledge, and the ability to discriminate between sometimes subtle distinctions, and they are easy to grade. Also, they do not teach higher-level thinking skills.

In fact, these very things are the strengths of objective tests (except of course, that they do train higher-level thinking).

Objective questions can be very limited in scope. That allows kids to construct and understand simple ideas, and parts of ideas, that they can then build on over time until they become large concepts. Objective tests get harder as kids learn more. We call this 'challenging kids to academic excellence' and, ironically, is the only truly progressive system of testing yet devised. It works precisely because learning occurs in small steps. One of the tragedies of Progressive instruction is that upper level classes are often nothing but a rehashing of already dumbed-down lower level classes. For instance, my *sixth* grade daughter came home one day with a math test that had asked her to "write 'four thousand' as a number." Another question asked her to add and subtract three two-digit numbers. Of course they were laid out "like" algebra (e.g.,. 65 + 34 − 27 = ____), so this must have seemed like a higher-level thinking skill to her educator.

My daughter was capable of these 'higher-level math skills' in the first grade. Yet she said that only two of her sixth-grade classmates maxed the test, and one kid got a 58 percent.

'Teaching' the same subjects repeatedly, to progressively sinking results, does not display the ability of Progressive educators to teach higher-level skills very well. When even high school math classes consist mainly of arithmetic, or at best unused algebra 'concepts' such as identifying a variable as opposed to a constant, and high school biology classes expect little more than word recognition skills, it is hard to see that modern educators can teach anything.

Teachers who write grade-appropriate objective tests (after teaching the grade-appropriate material to be covered) allow kids to learn as slowly or as quickly as their individual talents and abilities allow. This is especially true if you group kids by relative ability so that the instruction provided closely approximates the capabilities of the pupils, so they progress at approximately the same speeds. Objective test questions can be very easy, or they can be very challenging. This flexibility makes it possible for a teacher to tailor test questions to the pupils in his or her class, thus addressing the genuine academic needs of pupils while systematically leading them toward an adult understanding. Either way, the information they seek to retrieve from pupils are the bricks with which we construct ideas. Not teaching the facts that we already know to affect a question, forces the pupil either to speculate ignorantly, or to retrace steps needlessly.

If multiple-choice, matching, true-false, and the other types of questions that seek after 'facts' are the bricks, then an essay question is the mortar that creatively ties the facts together. Asking a kid to construct his own reality without established structure, as Whole Language or Discovery Learning do, is doomed to failure since the kids do not have anything to hang their theories on. Without objective milestones to return to when an idea does not pan out, we reduce kids, and theorists, to postulating unrealistic thinking and even magic, and to discussing their feelings about things they do not understand. (Had you noticed a recent [late 1990s] increased interest in 'psychics' and Astrology supplemented by Brazilian power crystals?) If we then refuse to acknowledge or identify mistakes in fact or in the use of ideas (in the name of self-esteem), we end up validating the pupil's ignorant speculations. If we also teach little beyond personal selfishness and multicultural ideas, we should all just go home and stock up on ammunition and canned goods.

I have already characterized modern science instruction as Whole Science, and while searching for the 'authentic assessment' article discussed earlier, I saw another article that recommended "Whole Curriculum." Considering the burgeoning ignorance that is the result we get with educated Whole anything, this is a genuinely scary idea.

You have to remember two things about test questions, and about the classroom full of kids that must submit to them. First, the classroom is full of individual pupils. Those pupils are most assuredly not identical. Even if we group kids by ability, we will see a range of abilities within each group. It should not be a teacher's concern to any large degree, but within each group, we will also see a range of preparedness for the test that may or may not have anything to do with native ability. For those reasons, genuine teachers write test questions across a range of difficulty. They deliberately write some questions to be very easy. They often place these questions near the beginnings of exams to be used as 'ice breakers'. Even well-prepared, brilliant kids can have some test anxiety. Up to a point this is a good thing. It helps to focus the attention and study habits. Teachers know this and give kids a break by easing them into the test. Once the first few questions are 'under a kid's belt', they can settle down, relax, forget the grade they want for the moment, and just let their accumulated knowledge flow out, onto the test paper.

Therefore, if the teacher establishes a standard of "You must keep up because we have lots to cover," and then teaches at an appropriate level, kids will meet that expectation. Yet, this type of classroom standard is a great deal more effective if the pupils do not differ from each other too much, and is the main reason for ability grouping.

Of course you do not want a test to be too easy. I have noticed, for instance, that if a test seems too easy for me, I often do worse than on 'hard' tests, because I get careless. Anyway, the format of 'easy' questions can be just the same as harder questions. That is to say, they can be multiple-choice, matching, short answer, fill-in-the-blank, true-false, identification, short essay, and longer essay questions. Beyond that are even longer essays such as book reports and research papers, etc. What makes test questions easy or hard depends on any number of factors. The most important of these are the class's average ability and the level of previous instruction and individual preparedness.

Incidentally, if my comments seem to imply that multiple choice, and other fact-based questions cannot be used to test for understanding, as opposed to simple memory, rest assured that I do not mean that at all. Their flexibility is the true beauty of objective questions and clever teachers can use them in limitless ways. Of course teachers must also be good at writing good test questions, which is another reason that today's standardized tests are not what they could be. The way that teachers learn to be good test question writers is, you guessed it, to write test questions and see the results. "When you practice you get better" applies to teachers, too.

What do objective questions have in common, and what are they good for? The answers to those questions are simple. What they have in common is that they test a kid's memory and understanding of the subject presented in class and in the required reading, at a level that challenges most of the class most of the time. That seems an important point and brings us to "teaching to the test." This phrase means that teachers try to teach and test at approximately the same level of difficulty as the standardized test that is hanging over their pupil's heads, assuming the standardized test is written at a level appropriate for the grade. At the high school exit level this usually refers to the common college entrance exams, such as the SAT and ACT. However, it may also mean State-mandated exit competency exams, such as the New York State Regents exams once were. Previously administered standardized tests are widely available from companies who prepare study guides. Teachers can easily check the degree of difficulty used in these tests, but the appropriate level of expectations should be reflected in the curriculum guidelines in any case, and should also be dictated to the test writing companies. In the olden days (the early 1960s) teachers could also choose decent, challenging end-of-chapter questions in textbooks to help challenge kids at grade-appropriate levels. If teachers then require a similar, or higher degree of accomplishment from their pupils on a daily basis, and if they write their own test questions to match the level of factual knowledge and analytical understanding required by the standardized tests and textbooks, the kids get to practice thinking at the level of the high stakes test we are teaching to. This is a _very_ good thing.

Dare I say it yet again? If you practice, you get better.

Taking a College Entrance exam would not be a psyche crushing event if the kid already knows that he can pass, because he is well practiced at that level of questioning, and has consistently succeeded at grade-appropriate tests, or higher. Therefore 'teaching to the test' is not only a good thing, it is a necessary thing. Surprising pupils with a level of expectation that they never experienced, nor been asked to attain in the classroom, is the Progressive tragedy, and one reason that standardized test scores have fallen so dramatically.

Stated a bit more simply, if we teach and routinely test 10th graders at the 5th grade level, do not be surprised if they achieve at the 5th grade level. To get kids to achieve at their own grade level or higher, we must teach and test at grade level or higher. It truly is this simple. Therefore, to achieve a decent education for *all* pupils, we must reestablish grade-appropriate levels of knowledge for all the grades. This will be difficult because petulant modern educators do not want to. Possession (of the system) is nine-tenths of the problem. The other tenth is that most kids would rather play. That is the easy tenth.

However, let us get back to the tests. Another of the complaints about objective tests is that they require specific knowledge that is "culturally dependent." The argument goes that kids raised in ghettos cannot compete because they have no knowledge of the country club life. Of course, neither do the vast majority of our other citizens, so that argument falls flat quickly. Sitting in the same classrooms and participating in the same lessons equalize the culture in the classroom for all pupils present. Whatever else can be said about the sociology of poverty, etc., *not* teaching kids while in the classroom, is not the answer.

In any case, for the standardized tests at least, specific knowledge is not necessary, excepting three types. The first is the 'math' portions of the test, which require knowledge of specific mathematical ideas and techniques. Next is the 'verbal' portions of these tests that ask kids to identify and correct mistakes in spelling, punctuation, usage, etc. Teaching standard English from the earliest grades, and asking kids to write using standard English, and then grading strictly, would quickly solve most of the basic competence problems that we have. The third place where specific knowledge is required is in the 'add-on' exams for specific subject areas (such as math, American history, or chemistry, etc.).

The math tests, of course, are fairly straightforward and are difficult, or not, based, at least in part, on a pupil's exposure to, and understanding of, the specific procedures required, such as addition, dividing by fractions, squares and square roots, use of coordinate planes, etc. The solution is to teach these things *before* testing (i.e., teach to the test).

Despite the fuss made by multiculturalists about the content of standardized tests being heavily geared toward the dominant culture, in the places where the content varies from one test to another, standardized tests always give you the information you need to answer the questions. I refer to the 'reading comprehension' sections of the tests. They ask you to read and understand the short essay presented. They do not ask pupils to remember things they were not taught.

Reading comprehension tests, however, generally present you with a series of short essays regarding topics that are generally not well known by any of the pupils, including the dominant culture pupils, and ask them to read the essays. Then we ask the pupils a series of questions based on the presented essay. Doing well on this sort of test depends on the pupil's basic preparation in reading and understanding written material and on practice in evaluating what is read. It requires experience with, and understanding of, the nuances of vocabulary, word usage, and punctuation, etc., and in analyzing written material, not any specific knowledge other than what is in the essay itself.

How does a pupil gain competence, and perhaps expertise, in analyzing written material? By analyzing written material, of course. If you practice, you get better. By the way, this, too, may be counted as the educational 'experience' that educationists say they value so much, but cannot seem to achieve. 'Teaching to' the analysis of the language portions of the test requires teachers merely to use essays, and the various other objective questions, regularly and at appropriate levels of difficulty, in order for the pupils to gain experience in using their heads. If over the years the questions used are at the same, or slightly higher, level of difficulty as the standardized test questions for each grade level, all will be well. Kids over the generations have proven that they can handle the difficulty level, if they are asked. The problem is that in recent years we have not asked, to the point that we now think it is unfair to ask.

A local grammar school teacher even told me that a principal told her that standardized tests are deliberately made at a level that is unattainable by the average pupil. It is sad that she might have believed that, when even State testing officials admit that they are only "using [tests] to identify kids who lack basic skills and who need remediation,"[225] but it is a travesty that someone she respected told her so. Perhaps her respect was misplaced.

---

225 Toch, p. 210.

8   Conclusions: Genuine Education

A child miseducated is a child lost.
—*John F. Kennedy*

The object of teaching a child is to enable him to get along without a teacher.
—*Elbert Hubbard*

Let's review. We have discovered that the American public school system began a long, dramatic, and catastrophic downward slide beginning in the 1960s. This slide corresponds perfectly with the most recent ascendency of the Progressive ideology. We have gotten to the point now that the average American kid is an abject academic failure, but is happy about it. We have also discovered that the educational professionals have not paused an instant in their insistence that all is well and getting better, and that we should sleep easy (after we write another check) since they are on the job. Many other positive aspects of life in America began to deteriorate along with the school system.

We have found examples everywhere we look, that show that Progressives routinely say one thing but do the very opposite, and promise one thing but accomplish the very opposite. They also insist that the only reforms possible should be based on their own obviously faulty, but very expensive, assumptions. We have also discovered that the people who know professors of education professionally, i.e., those academics who work with them on university committees, etc., consider schools of education to be "academic slums" and many professors to be "breathtakingly ignorant."

Before I go on, I must make a brief comment about these statements. I believe that these statements from the colleagues of our education professors must be considered very significant. Where have you ever heard its like? For normally collegial academics to say such things in public, much less to print them, is quite beyond belief. For them to appear in print in some numbers must surely be taken as 'the tip of the iceberg' regarding how our schools of education, and their products, are seen by the rest of the academic community. As our public school teachers are instructed by these folks, it's no wonder kids don't learn.

The Progressive agenda, created by these worthies and their protégées, with all of its wonderfully expensive programs, has created a nation that is progressively forgetting helpfulness, civility, intelligence, and patriotism and is replacing all that with selfishness, arrogance, individual and collective ignorance, helplessness, and mental defect. Maybe the 9/11/2001 attacks have been a catalyst that will begin our return from the abyss, but only time will tell.

Nevertheless, the schools have had help in their efforts "for the children." Multiculturalism has promised a new resurgence of patriotic, community feeling while teaching how evil we are, and have always been. Special education is converting a proud, forward thinking nation to a nation of dependent whiners who are afraid to read a book without psychiatric and pharmaceutical support, and is constantly telling us that they need more money to 'help' even more kids. They have done this by subverting the honorable, founding cry of, "All men are created equal" into the mewling complaint that everyone is the same as everybody else, and we just cannot live without more bureaucrats.

Promoting national ignorance and destroying the feeling of community in the pursuit of a receding equity is not helpful. We should *all* find it astonishing that anyone has to describe these inconsistencies and objections, and that some 'professionals' reject them as revolutionary, racist, elitist, meritocratic, and "against education." A nation that values common sense, and refuses to use its children as political pawns, would have turned its back on such arguments long since.

Thomas Jefferson and Education

Thomas Jefferson thought that having a say in their own lives would be best for the governed. He also realized that it takes intelligence and knowledge and a social conscience to govern well and justly. Obviously, therefore, for our citizens to have any hope of doing a good job at our grand experiment in self-government, many more people would have to have access to knowledge and be able to think clearly (i.e., competently analyze) about that information. Even as early as the 18th century, the power of decent information was self-evident.

Jefferson thought that we should afford our citizens an education that prepared each citizen to earn the kind of living that suited them by inclination and talent, and that would help to improve society overall. Jefferson also wanted the citizens to know enough to follow the issues of the day and to make useful contributions to the ongoing social debate. Of all of those average, informed citizens, we would then identify the most able, educate them to wisdom and social responsibility and ask them to lead for the common good.

For Thomas Jefferson, unlike our current social philosophers, democracy meant a representative government under which we could hear the voice of every citizen and, where we needed consent of the majority to make substantive decisions. It was this 'substantive decisions' point that required an informed and literate populace.

His idea of democracy was probably not identical to modern common notions, however, but then neither was the reality of daily life in the 1770s identical to modern life. For instance, while Jefferson thought that everyone should get a basic education, consisting of reading, writing, some arithmetic, and history, to be able to understand and to develop perspective concerning the debates about current events, he generally recommended that higher schooling and the responsibility for social leadership be limited to men. This idea of democracy is not nearly as oppressive to women as it sounds to the modern politically-correct ear, of course. Apart from the practical considerations of cost, prohibitive to a new nation populated largely by subsistence farmers and small craftsmen, I think that Jefferson truly meant democracy to be representative, right down to the household.

The following is an excerpt from Section I of *The Bill for the More General Diffusion of Knowledge*, which Jefferson proposed to the Virginia Legislature in 1778. This proposed bill, which Virginia did not adopt probably because of the expense, would have established a state-supported school system. Before that time, individual families provided schooling for their own children, as did some 'public' schools established by individual communities and churches. The *Bill* would also have established basic guidelines regarding responsibilities for construction, maintenance and staffing of the public schools:

And whereas it is generally true that the people will be happiest whose laws are the best, and are best administered, and the laws will be wisely formed, and honestly administered, in proportion as those who form and administer them are wise and honest; whence it becomes expedient for promoting the public happiness that those persons, whom nature hath endowed with genius and virtue, should be rendered by liberal education worthy to receive, and able to guard the sacred deposit of the rights and liberties of their fellow citizens, and that they should be called to that charge without regard to wealth, birth or other accident, condition or circumstance; but the indigence of the greater number disabling them from so educating, at their own expense, whose of their children whom nature hath fitly formed and disposed to become useful instruments for the public, it is better that such should be sought for and educated at the common expense of all, than that the happiness of all should be confided to the weak or wicked:

Doesn't that sound like what we want in our schools? Who should be educated best? Not just anybody, but all those, ". . . whom nature hath endowed with genius <u>and</u> virtue." Why should virtue play a part in that selection? Because these future leaders would then, ". . . be rendered by liberal education worthy to receive, and able to guard the sacred deposit of the rights and liberties of their fellow citizens." This is a very heavy burden to shoulder, so we certainly want kids whom we can trust with our rights and liberties, to compete for the honor because, ". . . the laws will be wisely formed, and honestly administered, *in proportion as those who form and administer them are wise and honest.*" Where would we find these excellent kids? Anywhere that they can be found, ". . . without regard to wealth, birth or other accident, condition or circumstance." Well that sounds very good, but how can the kids of poor people compete, who do not have the resources to go to fancy schools? That describes most people even today, and that is why we set up public schools in the first place, because, ". . . it is better that such should be sought and educated at the common expense of all, than that the happiness of all should be confided to the weak or wicked." Even Jefferson could recognize that some guys *are* wicked and untrustworthy, and that wealth had no monopoly on morality.

Jefferson lived in a time when education was not universal, though there had been some movement in that direction. In the colonial period many people were either totally uneducated or only minimally literate. He knew that it would require a massive and expensive effort to achieve true universal education. Since the U.S. (or the Virginia) government was not a superpower in the 18th century, and was almost destitute after the Revolution,[226] fully educating only the smartest of the men was a sensible compromise.

Why the men? Like it or not, fair or not, Western civilization is, and was, a male dominated world. As stated earlier, this is a fact explained by cultural anthropologists. Cultures which subsist by specific types of economies whether they are agrarian, pastoral-nomadic, etc., usually opt for similar familial arrangements. Whether a specific culture becomes paternalistic, maternalistic, or another variant depends more on the kind of economy used than on politics. Western civilization was also a world that had organized itself around families as far back as prehistory, and was comfortable with that idea. With exceptions, nearly all women supported this arrangement.

I think that women's movements start in patriarchal societies only after conditions move from hard through tolerable and into the comfortable range. For instance, the current ongoing movement in the U.S. gained momentum after the rise of the middle class. This new arrangement relieved many women of the need to help with the family business or farm, moved the principal breadwinner to an industrial job, and began to isolate 'housewives' (a new idea) away from extended family homesteads and into nuclear family homes and apartments. Most women originally embraced staying at home warmly. Women applauded these developments with the expectation that it would reduce the hours of labor they would have to endure. They greatly appreciated not needing to walk behind a plow or toil endless hours in the family shop. They saw it as a step toward simulating the kind of lifestyle that rich women led. Women eagerly sought convenience and further reduction of their workload. We can see this by the rapid rise of the household appliance industry. We can still occasionally see the early TV ads, and even earlier mail-order catalog ads, that are now used as evidence of a subtle oppression of women. However, as the media is very fond of telling us, they only give the public what it wants, and women *wanted* better stoves and refrigerators, etc.

Nevertheless, women soon noticed, perhaps because the multigenerational home was no longer common, that they were often bored at home and that the principal breadwinner was making more decisions on his own. This shift in decision making resulted from the fact that

---

226 For instance, the Army was reduced to approximately 700 men after the Revolution, yet there was a near mutiny of the Army, for failure to pay salaries.

the man was in the business and political community while the housewife stayed home.

Of course, further industrialization also forced ("change is good")
many single women into the workplace, and these women noticed
quickly that they did not have independent representation since they
did not yet have the right to vote. Women merely wanted a say in their
own lives again.

Despite recent, social, political, and economic changes, from prehistory at least to the time when Jefferson wrote, the titular heads of
families were almost universally men. However, the primary function
of any head man is to solve his family's problems. In practice, this
worked, and still works, this way. Whenever a problem of any sort arose
within a family, there would be a discussion. Any member of the household, including wives, children, and even servants, if there were any,
might initiate the discussion. They might discuss when to take the geese
to market, how to adjust planting schedules to this year's weather,
whether the family bakery should build a new oven, whether the family
could afford to take a sick child to a physician rather than treating him
at home, or any countless other situations. Anyone who had a stake in
the decision would have a say, and a wise head man would listen. He
might also consult others who had experienced similar situations, and
in the end the family would decide. If there was any serious difference
of opinion about the options available, the head of the household would
then arbitrate and decide what he thought was in the best interest of
the family. If he made a bad decision, the whole family would suffer,
so it was in his interest to take the best counsel available and make the
best decision possible.

Obviously there were, and are, variations on this scenario. Some of
these variations are not as moderate as my example implies. Variations
include domineering individuals of either gender. Yet I am trying to
find an average middle ground that applies to the majority, of any race,
not develop an argument dedicated to uphelpful extremes.

It is much the same for the nation. Though Jefferson's *Bill for
the More General Diffusion of Knowledge* did not specify household
arrangements, I think that it was something like my example that Jefferson had in mind when he drafted the *Bill*. In that spirit, having the
head of the household act as the household representative to the government, as a voter, was an efficient and equitable way of having everyone's
voice heard. It makes sense, then, that if you cannot educate everyone

fully, you should educate everyone as much as possible, educate those who were destined to be the heads of households even more, and educate the most capable, from among the prospective heads of households the most. Jefferson made little distinction regarding class or creed or anything else but scholastic aptitude, achievement, and virtue regarding who would qualify for the highest schooling. Section XVI of the *Bill* discusses how qualified children of poor parents would be selected for additional education at the public expense; ". . . after the most diligent and impartial examination . . . whose parents are too poor to give them further education, . . . of the best and most promising genius and disposition, to proceed to the grammar school of this district . . . without favor or affection."

One characteristic of the candidate for public assistance that Jefferson continually specifies is that he should have "virtue." Just imagine; Jefferson also requires virtue, along with "eminen(ce) for . . . learning, integrity and fidelity" of those who would administer the schools. This is very different from some of our current educationists, who may be trying to subvert our traditional teachings and are considered "breathtakingly ignorant." Education, then, was not a right to be abused, but an opportunity open to all, to be sought and for which to compete. This is the very essence of democracy and equal opportunity.

Being a Jeffersonian liberal meant holding as a self-evident truth that all of us are created equal and have the right to pursue their own lives, liberty, and happiness. The conservatives of the time (King George, et al.) took exception and tried to restore what they thought was a better way. In a sense though, it may be true that there is no such thing as a liberal at all. Everyone merely has an individual idea of what they would conserve. Despite the often repeated rhetoric that, "Change is good," anyone who is dissatisfied with a situation generally prefers that the other guys should change. Everyone prefers that life may continue according to their own ideals. If you are comfortable with the way life is, and are used to it the way it is, then doing something different often requires a significant effort. Often we expend considerable emotion before any recommended change can go forward. People like stability. Change is uncomfortable. Few people recommend real change if it makes their own lives unstable. Revolutions occur not merely at times when we see a disparity between the 'haves' land 'have-nots,' but when the 'haves' get too arrogant, believe their own press, and start to think of themselves as divine and above the struggles of the rabble. A benign and helpful aristocracy ('government') has always been acceptable, whose primary responsibility was the common defense. It is mainly at times of relative peace, featuring conspicuous consumption on the one hand (during Golden Ages?), while 'regular folks' are 'eating cake' on the other, that emotions run high. At times like these we have known people to cut off the heads of their self-serving governors.

While Jefferson did not decapitate anyone, he did foment and support a revolution. However, when the revolution was over and the new system was launched, Jefferson promptly became a conservative based on his notions of the greatest good for the greatest number. In this way he helped invent an American common sense and establish a stable life for American citizens. We can see his recommendations for public schools in that light.

Ironically, having rebalanced common sense a bit to the left, he made possible the eventual preposterously logical step of demanding that we should treat everyone identically. Treating everyone identically is not a democratic idea at all. It is Marxist idea and goes well beyond common sense. You may recall that after the American experiment was launched, others saw the benefits and decided that if some is good, more is better. The French Revolution and later Marxism, modern socialism, and communism were ideas that came after democracy and took the ideas of equality too far. Following those failed ideas farther to the left is a prescription for the excesses common to them. Consider the two sides side by side:

> **Marxist:** No one is any better than anyone else. Everyone should have only what he needs to survive, no more and no less.
> **Progressive:** Everyone is the same as everyone else. It is our responsibility to level the playing field so that everyone can achieve at the same level as everyone else.

I doubt that Jefferson had this in mind when he wrote the Declaration of Independence. Democracy allows everyone to compete for the 'brass ring'. However, it tries to insure that, "... those children whom nature hath fitly formed and disposed to become useful instruments for the public..." and "been... endowed with genius and virtue"... "should be rendered by liberal education worthy to receive, and be able to guard the sacred deposit of the rights and liberties of their fellow citizens."

"Worthy to receive . . . the sacred right and liberties of their fellow citizens." I don't know about you, but this idea of what education is for sounds a whole lot better to me than, 'Let's pass them whether they learn or not, or we will have to deal with them in the courts later'.

I think that we would genuinely appall Jefferson by the state of our public education system today. He would probably think that the asylum is now in the hands of the inmates. In his conception of 'education for citizenship' he assumed a civil return to the government that made possible an education and the subsequent improvement in living conditions that education often allows. It is no coincidence that the current generation is the first generation in American history that is less well-off than its predecessors. Also, as George Will has recently noted and many others including E. D. Hirsch at least imply, this is the first generation that is less well educated than its parents. We're now well into the second such generation.

For two hundred years, with a few notable downturns like the worldwide Depression, our system, based largely on the Jeffersonian model, did improve the living conditions for our citizens, whatever their occupation may have been. Not too many years ago, an unskilled and uneducated immigrant laborer could provide for his family on a single wage. His income did not provide many luxuries, but it did provide a family home, enough to eat, and even occasional vacations. The laborer could also dare to dream that his kids would be better off because we were educating them. Now look.

Jefferson probably never heard or thought of the words 'melting pot' or 'multicultural', but he noticed that we have populated American with many different folks. He also noticed that more than one group had good people and useful ideas to contribute. He therefore recommended that everyone be allowed to contribute their individual talents and capabilities, ". . . without regard to wealth, birth or other accident." Jefferson assumed and hoped that there would be an effort made by everyone to advance the ideals of the new nation and that everyone would benefit by it; and he was right.

Also, although even in his day political debate was quite raucous and the notion of States being individual and sovereign was common, he would be unable to understand why a nation that understood the ideas of, "United we stand. Divided we fall" would deliberately try to divide itself into contentious bands. He would certainly not support the notion that the public schools should aid in our own destruction.

Jefferson would applaud our current system because it provides a more nearly universal education than was economically possible in his time. However, he knew that education should be uplifting, Jefferson would be dismayed that we now have a system that looks for the lowest common denominator in *all* kids because it wrongly assumes identical, low capabilities. Jefferson wisely argued that we should prepare all kids for productive self- and community-supporting, patriotic lives while actively trying to find the smartest, most virtuous kids to prepare for leadership. The result of our search for the lowest common denominator, along with the attendant notion that we should instruct all kids identically, drags all but the slowest kids down. Our modern, technologically advanced system produces pupils who have spent twelve years or more (including Kindergarten and/or Headstart, etc.) in our tax-supported system, yet can barely read, but are still eligible for advanced schooling. Seeing this strange and inconsistent amalgam of disparate ideas, Jefferson would rightly think that we are all nuts.

Updating Jefferson's ideas a bit is necessary since it is not the 18th century anymore, but the core of his thinking is still as valid as it ever was. This is because the challenge of educating kids has not changed. The cutting edge of technology may be moving forward at an alarming pace, but the five-year-old ready for Kindergarten does not know any of that. He or she just wants to play with all their new friends. On the other hand, they are also supremely curious and will absorb a great deal of basic information easily, if only they are presented with it. Young kids like to repeat things often to learn them. We can use that to advantage by starting their education by using some version of Direct (repetitive) instruction for the basics of reading and writing and arithmetic. Yet this "rote" instruction need not last forever. Very quickly, when they have learned the basics, they can move on.

Life is simple if you recognize fundamentals, and take politics out of it.

Benjamin Franklin and Education

Benjamin Franklin was known for many things. He was a successful printer, publisher, and businessman, a scientist, a diplomat of distinction, and a practical philosopher who acted to improve life as he saw it. Despite a paltry formal education, consisting of one year at the Boston grammar school and some writing and arithmetic lessons with private tutors, Franklin was the driving force behind the establishment of what eventually became the American Philosophical Society. The Society was a group dedicated to spreading the latest thinking and learning among learned people from each colony and Europe by means of personal letters. As such, it was the original American information superhighway. Franklin also organized and arranged for funding America's first lending library and an academy that eventually became the University of Pennsylvania. His ideas relating to that academy, properly updated, are just as relevant to schooling today as they were in his time.

Franklin is credited with a far more practical and down to Earth idea of education than was prevalent in the 18th century. This reputation seems to stem primarily from two ideas. The first is that Franklin argued forcefully against counting anyone as educated if they had only learned Latin and Greek. He valued the learning of languages, but not as an end in themselves. Language needed to be useful to the person learning it. Franklin agreed with Jefferson that a free citizenry needed access to much more knowledge than was common at the time. This implied that many people should be schooled since most people had neither the vocation nor the inclination to become lawyers or ministers of religion. The language that was of most use to the people who would become known as "the backbone" of America, was English. Various modern foreign languages were also useful, especially for those in the law, diplomacy, and commerce. Yet usefulness was the single most important criterion for learning a language, or any other subject for that matter. If you had a need to learn Latin or Greek then please learn them. Still, Franklin argued that even if you have a need to learn other languages, learning proper English grammar was necessary first, so that you would not sound like a bumpkin to the people you most needed to impress.

[Note: in this section all forms of emphasis, particularly italics, capital letters, and spelling are in the original. Bracketed comments, however, are mine.]

The second reason Franklin is considered a practical educator, which has given him something akin to the mantle of Father of the American vocational education movement, is an extension of his ideas relating to language. Arithmetic, for instance, was not merely necessary as a precursor to abstract mathematics. Franklin sensibly thought everyone should learn arithmetic because it is also essential for bookkeeping and accounting, whether for business or the household. Quoting from John Locke, the philosopher and political theoriest, "Merchants Accounts, he says, if it is not necessary to help a Gentleman to *get* an Estate, yet there is nothing of more Use and Efficacy to make him *preserve* the Estate he has." In other words, if you wanted to get ahead in the world, whether you inherited or whether you had to work for a living, you'd better know the details of your business if you want to keep it. One can hear the echoes of *Poor Richard* telling us that "a fool and his money are soon parted."

Still, it takes more than English grammar and arithmetic to get an education. In his, *Proposals Relating to the Education of Youth in Pennsylvania* (1749), a piece that established the need for his Academy and set out the basic proposed curriculum, Franklin wrote this often quoted passage; "As to their Studies, it would be well if they [the pupils] could be taught *every Thing* that is useful, and *every Thing* that is ornamental: But Art is long, and their Time is short. It is therefore propos'd that they learn those Things that are likely to be *most useful* and *most ornamental*, Regard being had for the several Professions for which they are intended."

The definition of "ornamental" in the quotation above seems to mean those things which may not be strictly necessary for an occupation, but are nice to have. What is "nice to have" would, of course, vary greatly whether you were planning to go into the diplomatic service or open a hat shop, but the point is made.

This emphasis on "the several Professions for which they are intended" included the "Carpenter's, Shipwright's, Engraver's Painter's, Carver's, Cabinetmaker's, Gardiner's, and other Businesses." It is this listing of potential occupations, along with his emphasis on learning what is "useful" that may be the most direct evidence for Franklin's identification with vocational training, but he mentioned these professions in a footnote detailing the second of his proposed curricular items, drawing, as useful to anyone, including these named occupations. I have seen nothing, however, that would make us think that Franklin thought a school system should replace the apprentice system then in common use.

"Drawing" was in Franklin's proposed curriculum because it is useful in making a point. Again quoting from Locke and in the spirit of 'A picture is worth a thousand words,' Franklin writes; ". . . as that which helps a Man often to express in a *few Lines* well put together, what a *whole Sheet of Paper in Writing* would not be able to represent and make intelligible." In other words, you need not be a master draftsman or professional artist when you enter your chosen profession, but some understanding of perspective and how things go together would hold you in good stead. It is, at least, quicker than long-winded explanations, and quick, concise instructions are very useful in getting things done, or in selling an idea to a customer or investor.

Franklin's proposal for the academy was unlike Jefferson's in one important respect. Probably realizing that public funding was not available, his was not a call for a publicly funded school system but rather, was to be a privately subscribed enterprise intended to become self-sustaining, so that the original trustees would not have to continue to provide funds indefinitely. Also, the academy was envisioned as a tuition charging school. It was, in fact, a private school. Nevertheless, Franklin also intended to provide for at least some indigent pupils. In the original *Constitution of the Publick Academy in the City of Philadelphia*, he writes, "When the fund is sufficient to bear the Charge, which it is hoped, thro' the Bounty and Charity of well-disposed Persons, will soon come to pass, poor Children shall be admitted and taught gratis . . ."

No matter how pupils were admitted, the curriculum taught would remain the same. Listed in the order that Franklin mentions them in his *Proposals*, the curricular items include, swimming, drawing, arithmetic, accounts [bookkeeping], geometry, astronomy, the English language, reading the classics, writing letters, pronunciation, history, geography, chronology [what happened in what order and who were contemporaries in time], ancient customs, morality, natural philosophy [biology—including gardening, planting, grafting, and inoculating], mechanics [how things work], and good breeding.

While "good breeding" was listed last, in a sense it is the whole point of education for Franklin and his contemporaries. Franklin quotes a Mr. Hutcheson, a professor at the College of Glasgow and thought to have written a two volume *Dialogues on Education*, "The *principle End* [objective] of Education is, to *form us wise and good Creatures, useful to others and happy ourselves*. The whole Art of Education lies within a narrow Compass, and is reducible to a very simple Practice; namely, *To assist in unfolding those Natural and Moral Powers with which Man is endowed, by presenting proper Objects and Occasions; to watch their Growth that they be not diverted from their End, or disturbed in their*

Operation by any foreign Violence; and gently conduct and apply them to all the Purposes of private and public life."

"Good breeding" therefore means more than simple politeness. It is a way of living that most people today, probably including Progressives, would value, despite their insistence that morality is a separation of church and state issue. Yet how would this good breeding be developed? Should we leave kids to (perhaps) discover it while telling them they can do no wrong? Not according to the folks who helped develop the practical American sensibility. Instead we should,

> . . . assist in unfolding [every kid's] natural goodness [shift the balance from childish selfishness to social responsibility], . . . by presenting proper objects and occasions [teach by example and ask kids to practice], to watch their growth that they not be diverted from their end [tell them when they have strayed from the accepted path and reward them for keeping to it], . . . and gently conduct and apply them to all the purposes of . . . life.

Why is this so important? Because,

> Without it, his [the pupil's] other Qualities, however good in themselves, make him pass for proud, conceited, vain or foolish. Courage . . . in an ill-bred Man has the Air, and escapes not the Opinion of Brutality; Learning becomes pedantry; Wit, Buffoonery; Plainness, Rusticity; and there cannot be a good Quality in him which ill-breeding will not warp and disfigure to his Disadvantage.

Furthermore, Franklin quotes M. Rollin, ". . . whose whole Life was spent in a College; and wrote four Vols. on Education, under the Title of, *The Method of Teaching and Studying the Belle Lettres, . . .* "

> . . . the *End* of Masters [the objective of teachers] should be to *improve their* [pupil's] *Hearts* and Understandings, to protect their Innocence, to *inspire* them with Principles of *Honor* and Probity [integrity], to train them up to good Habits; to correct and subdue in them by gentle Means, the ill Inclinations they shall be observed to have, such as Pride, Insolence, and high Opinion of themselves, and a saucy Vanity [attitude] continually employed in lessening [deprecating] others; a blind Self-love solely attentive to its own Advantage; a Spirit of Raillery [anything goes] which is pleased with offending and insulting others; and Indolence and Sloth, which renders all the good Qualities of the Mind useless.

In other words, we have known for a long time that unless curbed and molded with instruction in decency, 'attitude', far from being a virtue, makes you ugly, and 'self-esteem', as opposed to self-confidence, offends others and does you no credit. Unfortunately, despite the archaic phrasing the above description can easily describe today's *Progressively* instructed kids.

In a letter to Samuel Johnson in 1750, Franklin extends his ideas about the importance of instruction in virtue. He writes:

> I think with you that nothing is of more importance for the publik weal [welfare], than to form and train up youth in wisdom and virtue. Wise and good men are, in my opinion, the *strength* of a state: much more so than riches or arms, which under the management of Ignorance or Wickedness, often draw on destruction, instead of providing for the safety of a people. And though the culture bestowed on many should be successful with only a *few* [not everyone will learn the lessons equally; there are no magic bullets], yet the influence of those few [the eventual leaders] and the service in their power, may be very great.
>
> I think also that general virtue is more probably to be expected and obtained from the *education* of youth, than from the *exhortation* of adult persons; bad habits and vices of the mind, being like diseases of the body, more easily prevented than cured. [This means that it is better to teach the young early than erect ineffectual adult education programs (and prisons) after the fact. In other words: An ounce of prevention is worth a pound of cure.]
>
> I think moreover, that talents for the education of youth are the gift of God; and that he on whom they are bestowed, whenever a way is opened for the use of them, is as strongly *called* as if he heard a voice from heaven: nothing more surely pointing out duty in a public service, than *ability* and *opportunity* of performing it. [That's a pretty nice description of a genuine teacher.]

Rollin preceded his above passage with a description of what he considered another of the main objects of education. He said that all learning is useful as *means* rather than ends. Each topic in the curriculum should be included because it promotes, supports, and leads us to greater learning and to the love of learning and especially to useful knowledge. Franklin gave good and sensible reasons for each of his proposed curricular topics and deciding whether the *specific* reasons given are as useful today as they were in 1749 would seem to be a more useful debate than dismissing them merely because a dead white guy said them. I expect that Franklin would certainly agree that allowing kids to decide what is good, moral, and necessary is genuinely silly, and that abdicating our responsibilities as adults has created the ongoing controversy over education, and the need for books like this one.

So how do we proceed with instruction in decency? Remember, we are discussing schools, not churches or families. School-instruction in decency would be accomplished primarily by teaching history, according to Franklin. Quoting again, Franklin reproduces Rollin's "Rules for Studying History." My interpretation will appear in parentheses after each 'rule.' They are:

1) To reduce the Study to Order and Method. (Do it systematically so that teachers in later classes can build upon what the teachers in lower classes taught.)

2) To observe what relates to Usages and Customs. (Don't judge actions in another era or nation by today's standards. This may also mean: Find out why a particular action was taken at a particular time and place.)

3) To enquire particularly, and above all Things, after the Truth. (Do not judge actions in another era or nation by today's standards, and certainly not by political correctness that ignores the findings of genuine research. In other words; Don't use the political debate of today to interpret reality.)

4) To endeavor to find out the Causes of the Rise and Fall of States, of the Gaining and Losing of Battles, and other Events of Importance. (Do not judge actions in another era or nation by Progressive reinterpretations, but rather by evaluating the words used at the time of the important event. This will give you instruction on motives, both good and bad, from both sides of a controversy/war. This will also provide instruction on the results of the actions chosen. Evaluating results, whether you like them or not, will give instruction in practicalities, and in morality. Afterwards we can discuss whether we think it was a good thing to do and perhaps even how we feel about it.)

5) To study the Character of the Nations and great Men mentioned in History. (This is an extension of the previous rule and goes even deeper into training in morality. Franklin's own words relating to instruction in morality are: "by descanting and making continual Observations on the Causes of the Rise or Fall of any man's Character, Fortune, Power, &c. mention'd in History; the Advantages of Temperance, Order,

Frugality, Industry, Perseverence, &c. &c. Indeed the general natural Tendency of Reading good History, must be, to fix in the Minds of Youth deep Impressions of the Beauty and Usefulness of Virtue of all Kinds, Publick Spirit, Fortitude, &c." (Note again the repeated emphasis on "telling" kids what is right and wrong, on "showing" kids by examples from history what is right and wrong and by "impressing" on them why these things are either right or wrong. By doing this, the object is to raise kids to know right from wrong, not merely to hope a few might eventually discover it for themselves, or to inevitably choose to follow failed, but politically correct, courses of action.)

6) To be attentive to such instructions as concern moral Excellency and the Conduct of Life. (Everybody uses this next quotation for their own purposes and I will do the same. It seems oddly appropriate. "Those who do not learn from history are doomed to repeat it." If a society does not teach its most hard-learned truths, it will forget those truths and the relearning will again be hard, if not bloody.)

7) Carefully to note every Thing that relates to Religion. (At this moment in history it probably matters little which religion you choose, discounting genuinely extremist variations, since most of them seem to espouse roughly the same things—Peace, faith, love, harmony, and good works.)

Like Jefferson's vision, Franklin's seems to reflect a much more positive view of human nature and a more practical vision of how to bring kids into their adult birthright than the one prevalent in education today. While seemingly archaic in language, it would be good to note again that kids come to school with little knowledge and their basic educational needs are little different now than they were 250 years ago. While there were missteps in social policy over those past 250 years, if we concentrate on the things that worked, adapt the subjects taught to modern times, and try to expand the range of those who were afforded access to those things, we seem more likely to arrest and reverse the recent problems that our schools and our society have seen.

I, for one, find the emphasis the Founders placed on virtue, service, and merit very refreshing, after my recent immersion in the self (in Ed school) and instruction in the virtues of aggressively pursuing mediocrity. I have said it more than once already, but it bears repeating; while nothing in life is a perfect solution to everything, using the solution that works best, most of the time, is better than aiming at unattainable utopian dreams of universal anything, including equity, that inevitably harm the very ideals pursued. Emphasis on self and the personal perfectness of individuals sounds good as rhetoric and may gain you the votes of those you have convinced are victims, but it also seems to harm the society called upon to help, making the ideal harder to accomplish, both in depth and in breadth. In other words, our current Progressive path seems to have created more people who need help and fewer people who can (or want to) give it.

How Do We Fix It?

How do we restructure our failing system? Again, we could go and ask the successful and responsible old-timers who taught before the Great Society began to ruin almost everything, for the details of successful instruction, but the basics are simple. Incidentally, by recommending that we seek out the old, retired geezers, and despite everything else I have said, I do not mean to imply that no one in schools today could possibly have any good ideas or common sense upon which to build effective schools. My thought is that getting back to a system that worked well would give our future attempts at fine-tuning that system more historical credibility than tinkering with a system that currently seems designed to fail, and is failing. However, this updated system should be developed with the deep participation of academic specialists outside the Ed schools. If you read descriptions of what many public schools are like, mind and spirit-numbing places where teachers pretend to teach and pupils just mark time, it becomes clear that the current educational well has all but run dry. Left to educational professionals and administrations established by the politics-first-and-last, money-above-all-things teachers' unions, even good ideas are quickly converted to bureaucratic tar pits that kill incentive and smother scholastic enthusiasm.

Considering these things, it is very likely that any idea worthy of the name, has little chance of success in our modern system. Even thoughtful people have soured on good ideas, concluding that they cannot work, after witnessing how they were handled by educationists. Yet it was not all that long ago that schools did teach, pupils did learn and children did grow up excited about living. The way it was all done was by teaching. It worked because learning things is the grist of any intellectual mill. Learning things is what eventually excites minds to learn even more. Superficial activities might engender a desultory "gee whiz" reaction, but the reality is that it does not last, as our drop-out rates and average achievement show.

For any future system to have any hope of success again, we must sweep away the byzantine tangle of laws, regulations, and union rules that we have now, and start afresh with a class full of kids and a teacher who knows things and is eager to share that knowledge. We need principals and curriculum developers who know that there is a place, an intellectual level, that must be reached before additional movement can be expected. We must research to find what accomplishes these things in as simple a way as possible. We must search the literature for the nuggets of reality among the dross of ideology, and we must then do those things simply and systematically. However, we must first stop doing the things that work against our simple aims.

The goal must be clear and beautiful, but not utopian. To get from here to there, we must realize that work is required. Teachers must teach and pupils must study. An ancient wisdom tells us that nothing worth doing is ever easy. That may apply to kids most of all.

We must also train our teachers to reality and common sense. To do this, we must reshape our vision of kids. We may even have to embrace ideas we know not to be entirely correct to do it. If we view kids more as firm and eager blank slates and less as seething cauldrons of neurological and psychological weaknesses, we will get more done, and use fewer drugs doing it.

Our teacher's colleges have lost their way. This has happened because they are trying to get our children to The Emerald City. Yet the Wizard of Oz was a fraud. His presentations were bombastic multimedia extravaganzas, but there was no real magic there at all. The sad thing is that we already know it, but continue to listen to the intellectual Munchkins who control education today. Recall that the Munchkins called on the Good Witch to guide them. We shall note also, that for all the Witch's vaunted goodness and wand-waving magic, she did not know that the Wizard was a fraud. Let us allow her to flit around in her own fantasy world by herself. The rest of us have work to do, and so do our kids.

Genuine science in our Ed schools will lead to genuine learning in our public school classrooms. The better our future parents become, the smaller our social problems will become. We must continue to work to alleviate whatever misery we find among our citizens, but the long-term solution is not a morass of short term programs. Especially if those short term programs never die.

Life can be fairly simple. It is an unrestrained bureaucracy, led by undereducated Munchkins with attitude, that makes it complicated.

We must also get the word out to the public, and especially to working teachers.

Elementary education should be quite similar for everybody, since what we need is grounding in the rules of the various disciplines, the basics of reading, writing, arithmetic, and observation, physical activity, art, music, and the rules of the society (civics eventually tied to history). These societal rules are an extension of parental and community expectations (e.g., be polite, learn to share, do not kill or steal, etc.) and are also the limits of behavior to which we must all abide, if society is to function well at all. We must also train our kids to the idea that we will expect <u>them</u> to contribute brains and sweat to our society, rather than teaching them to expect society to give them everything and make life easy. Despite all of our hopes, dreams, public funding, technology, or toys with Happy Meals, life is not easy or $free and kids should know it. The current mental health perspective of protecting kids from every curve that life throws at them is wrong. We should not protect kids, except from the things they cannot avoid by themselves, like child molesters and educationists. Instead, we should teach our kids how to deal with things. As Dewey puts it, "Being merely sheltered by others would not promote growth. For it would only build a wall around impotence (the lack of capability, incompetence)." The best, and perhaps only way, to avoid incompetence may be by teaching rules and facts, what they mean, and how to use them. Learning plus experience, eventually leads to wisdom.

On the academic side of life, we must tie the knowledge dispensed in each grade to the grade levels before and after, by knowing what was taught the year before and knowing what is expected in the following year, rather than asking kids what they think is relevant. In that way, remediation would be kept to an absolute minimum at each level, rather than being a cornerstone of the whole system. We should aim the difficulty level at a bit above average to, occasionally, quite a bit above average for each ability-grouped class. This will make things continually challenging for the mass of pupils and will pull everybody up, rather than dragging them down by aiming at the bottom, as we do now. This method will also help us begin to discover which of the kids is likely to go farther academically than their peers.

No real sorting by ability is necessary in the earliest grades, but the indications of differential ability will be there, and we should not ignore them. One purpose of an educational system, which is politically incorrect to mention, is that it allows a society to begin to nurture future chiefs as well as all of the Indians.

Since grade school kids do not know enough to know what they will need, or what they will be interested in as adults, we should allow very little choice to kids at this level. Instead, we should expose everyone to everything, academic, artistic, physical, etc. This varied exposure is also the very basis of scholastic equal opportunity.

Late grammar school and junior high school kids are still ignorant, too (even the smart ones), so junior high school is a transition from elementary basics to advanced basics (e.g., arithmetic to preliminary conceptual mathematics—algebra, etc.). This is so because kids at this age, the physiologists and developmentalists tell us, are finally developing the capability for genuine reasoned thought. Therefore we must intensify our attempts to teach kids to think while continuing their basic accumulation of data. We do this by asking them to explain what they have learned (i.e., lots of essay questions, and math word problems). What we should not do is assume that kids are in such psychological turmoil that they need to be coddled academically and psychologically.

Accumulation of data, however, is a lifelong process, because without it, our thinking can be limited to little more than what we learned in Kindergarten or in gossip. However, even in junior high school, we should still allow little choice of academic classes (except possibly for which foreign language to learn, what required shop class to take first or what musical instrument to take up, if they hadn't started years earlier). Even these choices might be the parents' choices, rather than the kids'. If a parent allows his kid a say in the decision, as I did, the kid should decide in consultation with the parent.

In junior high school, the beginning of explicit ability sorting during the school day could begin, because true reasoning ability is beginning to show itself at this age and because potential occupational interests are beginning to make themselves known. The occasional elective course, and also extracurricular activities after the normal school day, will allow kids to continue to sort themselves by interest.

High school coincides with the final push toward adulthood. Most kids will not go on to higher education, nor should they. We would never know it by listening to modern educationists, victim-community leaders, and politicians intent on building a dependent constituency, but many good jobs do not require college, and others that do require college do so only because the employers cannot depend on a high school graduate being sufficiently literate. By high school, kids should know very well whether they are cut out to be physicists or foremen, executives or clerks. Yet we attempt to provide a one-size-fits-none education on the misguided notion that anyone can be anything with very little real effort. The current ideas are terribly democratic though, just like the Progressives envision—they hurt everybody.

We have perpetuated the college-for-everyone myth for so long that the reputation of the trades, and of those who work with their hands has suffered. There is honor and even a majesty in being a carpenter or a welder or a housewife, even if these occupations do not require stratospheric IQ levels. Yet neither do they preclude high IQs. What they do need is basic knowledge of techniques and skills, and time to practice, to perfect and extend those skills. Very much like any other job. We should encourage kids to be proud of their abilities whatever they are, and to follow those abilities into whatever occupation suits them and their interests best, because the society literally cannot exist without them.

Ability group sorting is therefore essential at the high school level, but with considerable flexibility built in. A few kids, faced with impending adult responsibilities, will suddenly grow up and get ambition, so we should establish a way to give a kid who has not yet shown much scholarship a chance to try higher-level (college bound) work. On the other hand, we should also have a very strong program designed to send kids competently and confidently into the workplace.

Incidentally, 'college bound' kids also need these same working skills as anyone else, so we will still see lots of mixing among the ability groups during the school day, instead of the rigid segregation that Progressives fear. Besides, the core academic stuff will still be essentially the same for everybody, though taught according to capacity. We should require everyone to take English and literature and probably other languages, social studies (including basic economics), the sciences and civics (on the patriotic model), etc. By this time, the kids will have sorted themselves artistically (chorus, orchestra, band, art, drama, dance, etc.)

and athletically. The basics of the trades (e.g., wood, mechanics, electronics, home economics, and 'office technology', including computers), should also be available.

It is probably in the core academic courses that we will sort kids by ability most visibly. A kid who will drive a truck does not need a course in particle physics, but he does need to know a bit about how things work to be a competent citizen and voter and to care for his truck, so two levels of physics should be available. A kid who will work in a flower shop or hardware store does not need detailed molecular genetics, but he does need to know a good bit of general science so as not to be taken in by outrageous advertising claims, and to be a competent citizen and voter and to understand the basics of his livelihood. Therefore, we should offer basic biology.[227] A kid who will work on a factory floor does not need to understand margin investing or organic chemistry, but she does need to know how the different parts of our economy and government fit together and may need a general understanding of chemistry for her livelihood, or so as not to be taken in by outrageous advertising claims. On the other hand, the future architect also needs to understand economic basics, and the future orthopedic surgeon would benefit greatly from wood shop. Also, athletic or artistic ability is not limited to one academic ability level. So again there will be a natural mixing among ability groups. This natural mixing is the best available method of promoting integration too, since it is neither political nor contrived.

Pointing these things out for those who are obsessively concerned that college would become an elitist enclave under this sort of system is necessary. College _would_ be an elitist enclave, but not elitist by race or connections necessarily, but by academic ability, as it should be. We intend college as 'higher' education after all, but if we also train everybody to understand that they have personal responsibilities in the society, we must necessarily train the future leaders that they also have the responsibility to lead and maintain fairness, not merely grab, as self-esteem training does.

This finally brings us to postsecondary education (college). I see postsecondary education as a variety of things, each of which is simultaneously elitist and democratic. It is elitist in that we train the most

---

227 I taught in a school that offered molecular biology, oceanology (that's what they called it), botany, and several other courses purported to be advanced, but had no course in basic biology. The reasoning was that the kids would pick up the basics as they learned the higher-level concepts. I saw little evidence of it.

capable of the folks interested in specific disciplines in the intricacies of those disciplines, whether it is genetics, anthropology, literature, or managing a manufacturing plant, etc. College is also democratic in that anyone else, including housewives, factory workers, hospital lab technicians, janitors, and taxicab drivers, etc., who enjoy and want to learn more about philosophy, the classics, experimental psychology, the history of film, or anything else, can do so, even if only on a non-degree-seeking basis. Taking one course per semester at night should not be prohibitively expensive, even if your local college happens to be one of the nation's flagship private universities. The possibility of earning a degree to enhance prospects for a promotion, or to qualify for another job, would also be available.

College (university) should be for the academically best qualified students, who intend careers at the high end of the various disciplines. We should pay for this on a needs basis. Smart middle-class kids would pay with savings, scholarships, summer jobs, and loans. Very bright but poor kids could be subsidized by the State or by businesses who identify very good potential and appropriate ambition in their employees. Standards should be quite high, to the point that dumb and/or lazy rich kids would have real trouble getting in. Perhaps even some of these slugs might slip through if their parents essentially also paid for x number of smart but poor kids. The price of these subsidies is that students admitted to college should continue to be taught that their gifts, intellectual as well as monetary, carry a responsibility. College kids must be brought to understand that, as our future leaders, they have an obligation to continue to structure our system in a way that is best for everyone. They should eventually lead, not merely grab what they can and complain that it is not enough, or not provided fast enough.

Community service may not be necessary as a structured obligation (personal choice still counts for something despite everything I have said), although requiring two or three years of military training or the Peace Corps, etc., may have merit. If we teach kids responsibility from early childhood, helping would again become the kind of thing that people do routinely for their neighbors and their nation. Once upon a time, the wives of local community leaders and businessmen, often organized under the auspices of a local church, etc., were the ones who organized the local charities, etc. I am sure that still happens, but the local charities are typically now overwhelmed by the national charities, and also by how much work is needed in the aftermath of the Great

Society. As I said earlier, news reports of a disaster should not sound surprised that people helped others they did not know. Instead, people who do not help should individually feel some guilt that they did not help. Unfortunately we cannot get to this point if we teach nothing but woe-is-me, 'individual rights', and 'choices' based on nothing but ignorant and often immoral selfishness. Of course churches, parents, and neighbors must start this teaching very early in life, and schools must reinforce it throughout life if the lesson is to 'take'.

The odd thing is that if we teach individual *responsibility* (including the responsibility to try for good grades) and respect for others, then individual *rights* follows naturally in the minds of most. And communities feel good about themselves, too. What we do now, teaching and even institutionalizing selfishness, may have somehow become politically correct, but it destroys the very ideals that it intends to foster. These ideals include personal equity (including self-esteem) and a quality education for everyone.

Responsibility instruction would not require a new bureaucratic program. None of these ideas would require a new program or innovative new venues, such as 'magnet' or 'alternative' schools. Everyone can accomplish every bit of it in old-fashioned neighborhood schools and homes. Responsibility would merely become normal, habitual behavior, as we expected kids to do their homework on time, be polite, and mind their teachers, etc. Vandals would be appropriately punished by detention, repayment, and so forth. If we want kids to be more like the Flintstones, and less like the Simpsons, we must structure the society to expect the one and reject the other. That is an adult, community responsibility, mediated by standard limits to behavior and appropriate judgmentalism.

Junior Colleges would be for the next tier of students; those who made it through high school easily enough but did not make the grade for university. Many of these kids will eventually make up the bulk of the shop foremen or department managers or will own their own neighborhood businesses. This group may also include the smart but lazy kids with average grades and test results. The best of these students, especially those who suddenly grew up in the face of the realities of independence, might then move on to universities. The State (community) would largely subsidize these schools. Another source of subsidy could be businesses who identify good potential and appropriate ambition in their employees. This kind of local subsidy would also foster identification with and loyalty to those businesses, who could then require x number of years of subsequent work to justify their expense. The military already does this, training doctors, nurses, and others. This kind of community subsidy would improve social stability too, as it would promote more local employment, nearer to the extended family. Today, many young adults leave their hometowns for the 'perfect' job, leaving siblings, parents, and grandparents unhappy that they rarely see their siblings, kids, or grandkids. While an argument that the resultant cosmopolitanism is a good thing can be made, it comes at a price. This dispersal contributes to the dilution of the stability and supportive strength of families and lifelong friends.

Another tier of postsecondary education would be the trade and/or technical schools that expand on specific skills and knowledge (e.g., electronics, medical and veterinary technology, woodworking or secretariat skills, computer maintenance, automotive repair, etc.) for those who want and need those skills and that knowledge. While ultimate licensing may still be the prerogative of the State, these schools also certify basic and/or advanced competence, or at least instruction, in those trades. This is a good thing for their eventual customers.

This two or three tiered postsecondary system would not cause frantic competition across levels for students to any excessive degree, since different people would be going to different schools for different reasons. Yet we must allow movement between levels as individual circumstances allow. It all would be much less expensive than our current system, too, because we would not be subsidizing millions of kids who do not need and, if the truth is known, do not want college but currently clamor to go in the mistaken impression that college is necessary for everyone.

We can then also stop turning our undergraduate schools into what the high schools once were; our high schools into what the grade schools once were; and our grade schools into daycare centers whose 'teaching' consists of little more than scratch-the-surface activities at all levels.

You want to know a secret? We have the remnants of much of this system already in place. Unfortunately, the head is confused. Our Ed school professors are convinced that education does not involve teaching anyone anything, and sensible efforts to expose that fact are met with howls of protest and political invective. The politically correct have taken control of every level of this system and have been systematically turning the brains of pupils into a nondescript, homogenous mush for

so long that we have deemed 'adjustments' and 'interventions' necessary
at each level. These adjustments include terrible damage to curricula
and even to the perceived purposes for education. This includes even
the good ideas, layered upon, and themselves ruined by the bureaucracy
perhaps needed for other good reasons (such as accountability). As the
computer nerds say, "Garbage in, garbage out." With appropriate modifications for technology and the changes it brings, education should
revert to the way it was at least 40 years ago, before the Progressive rot
set in. We should trash Progressive reforms wholesale and then fine-
tune a system that works. Let us not merely tinker with what has become
a disaster. It can never be anything but a disaster, if the Progressive
ideology is in control. For instance, there have been recent reports (Feb.
2001) that California is considering eliminating the SAT as its primary
college-entrance tests, in favor of, ". . . a test that is more closely tied to
the actual high school curriculum." The arguments are depressingly
familiar: ". . . standardized tests are 'unfair'; preparing for standardized
tests (teaching to the test)[228] demands too great an effort and takes away
from what is truly needed, appealing to the 'needs' of the students."

These arguments made little sense before we had generations of
evidence that prove their lack of prediction, they make no sense now
that we know they are patently absurd. We should redo school policies,
teacher certifications, and school accreditations keeping in mind what
works, not to the senseless ideology that does much harm and little good
and misleads us into thinking that destroying the educational system
somehow improves kids' prospects in life.

Toward that end, we should repeal virtually all current educational
legislation, back to about 1960, or even 1910. This recommendation is
not intended to imply that the broad thrust of the various laws aimed
at equity be abandoned, as would undoubtedly be charged. I agree fully
that no child should be left behind, nor be denied the basic right to
an education. My argument is that what we have wrought denies an
'appropriate' education to virtually everybody. Progressive don't-teach-
facts techniques leave more kids behind that anything thing else we
could do, short of don't-let-them-into-the-school-at-all. I hope that this
result was not the intention of those who crafted the laws we must
now dismantle, but designing curricula based on ideological politics

---

228 Since this phrase, like so many others, has been misappropriated and mis-redefined, we
might need another new word. Perhaps 'genuine teaching' will suffice.

and unsupportable speculation, as we have done, is not the answer. A curriculum should be based on the subjects themselves. What are needed are high academic standards, and the effort and attitudes required to achieve them as well as teaching perseverance, the personal benefits of hard work, and the thinking skills that seem so foreign to our kids. Finally, decency and achievement will follow largely on their own accord. As they once did.

The mid 1960s are about the time that the current educational philosophy came back into its ascendency and we have now given it a fair try. Forty years, trillions of dollars wasted, and a society seemingly on the leading edge of implosion, is evidence enough. Progressive socialism does not work. It promotes ignorance and arrogance rather than competence and love of learning. Let us truly go back to the basics and teach our kids how to be respectable, competent adults who have a role to play in the society. The cult of individualism, which many of our schools support and which our social laws have made possible, is destroying us. Kids will do as we teach them. If we teach them to make excuses for themselves, they will do well at that. If we teach them that life requires effort, and that the effort is worthwhile, they will again become good at that.

To help redirect the education of our children to a responsible direction, I offer the following list of general suggestions. This list is not intended to be comprehensive. In fact, much of it concentrates on suggestions relating to themes, to be filled out by the intelligent, knowledgeable creativity of teachers, principals, and school boards within the confines of a sane and solidly academic curriculum.

A main focus of the list is that it concentrates on the lower end of the grade-level scale. If we build a solid foundation, the rest will almost take care of itself by mere extension of the ideas (but we will need to keep a sharp eye out for the inevitable infiltration of educational nonsense). Instruction in the higher grades will necessarily grow upon the early foundation, as it, unfortunately, does now. So we need sane themes upon which to build the foundation. Building even a solid foundation upon quicksand will doom the strongest house to fall, even with little apparent stress on the house (the society is dying, although the economy seems good). On the other hand, if we build a flexible foundation upon bedrock, the only thing that will topple a solid but flexibly built house is an earthquake, and maybe not even that. Progressive ideology is clearly a quagmire of pseudointellectual quicksand, and child-centered facilitation and multiculturalism are perhaps the weakest foundation imaginable upon which to build. Even their own philosophical icons and research say so, though not very loudly.

The ground we must build on is the bedrock of the American Melting Pot and the diverse natural abilities of our children. The foundation we must build depends on the work ethic and the academic basics. These two themes have taken the U.S. to dominance in most areas. To squander that position is a shame.

- First and foremost, we must stop diagnosing nonexistent Special ed disabilities. This, all by itself, will eliminate the tendency to dumb down. Also, pouring undeserved flattery (self-esteem) upon heads while telling pupils that they are mentally disabled or psychologically vulnerable (i.e., the sensitivity of giftedness, etc.) is characteristically inconsistent, and obviously damaging. Then, when we follow up the dismantling of the excuse factory by teaching for genuine excellence rather than aiming at the lowest artificial denominator, our kids will surprise us with their capacity. If we take our current academic averages of about 40 percent as the baseline and compare it with the non-dumbed-down averages of 75 percent to 80 percent that previous generations earned, we can see significant improvement is easily possible. An additional benefit to dismantling these programs is freeing up $millions, and perhaps $billions of dollars that can be used for decent textbooks, teachers' salaries, paying down the debt, etc.
- Reserve Special ed help for the seriously mentally retarded and those with undeniable physical handicaps (e.g., the blind, the deaf, kids with cleft palates, autistic kids, kids with Down syndrome, etc.). This special help will consist of assistance in overcoming or mitigating those physical handicaps, not dumbing-down academics.
- If we wanted kids to do nothing but play, we would not need schools at all. Therefore, what virtually everyone needs is solid, traditional instruction based on facts, not feelings. This instruction should be done by lessons aiming at learning and understanding, not superficial activities that aim for mere fun and political indoctrination. 'Activities' are still acceptable, especially in the lowest grades, but they should transition, probably no later

than the end of the 3rd grade, if not sooner, to being supplementary rather than the meat of the instructional day. Additional hands-on lessons, such as science labs, should also be solidly academic. 'Solidly academic' should not imply 'dull for dullness' sake. Nevertheless, life is not merely about recreational activities, so school should not be either. This is why we hire and pay teachers. The way one finds entertainment in a lifelong occupation is to find a job that features tasks one likes to do, yet is still needed by an employer. Potentially, we could hire ourselves. Extra-occupational play is our own business.

- If an activity is truly instructive, like a decent workbook exercise, call it a lesson or an exercise, not an activity. Then grade it with an eye toward learning. No one gets 'empowered' by doing pointless activities. Additionally, school should be systematically more difficult as kids mature and move through the grades.

- All instruction is age and grade-appropriate (or slightly higher), not dumbed down to accommodate the now nonexistent disabilities or 'inclusive' classes. The basic model for instruction is an updated, but old-fashioned liberal education that includes the basics of the academic disciplines, music, physical exercise economics, civics and patriotism, mediated by ethics, morality, and community standards.

- Subsequent instruction in mathematics is rendered pointless if kids cannot read or do arithmetic easily. Therefore, very early instruction in both arithmetic and English should be largely drilled or repeatedly practiced, at least until the kids begin to read, and the basic addition and subtraction facts and concepts are memorized. Then, after a year or two of practice (mere rote repetition will not be necessary beyond the first few days or weeks if we assign enough seat- or homework), do it again for the multiplication tables and division, fractions, etc. Call this instruction "arithmetic" until we begin the transition to conceptual "math" in the 6th or 7th grade. Leave the calculators and word processors for later—usually much later.

- Historical instruction is based on history in the patriotic mode, not on multicultural rhetoric. While patriotic, the instruction should not deny reality by any means, but neither should it dwell on our historical warts, unless we want to perpetuate them. To balance these two, we must teach kids to do as responsible historians do. That is, to evaluate, and teach, history from the perspective of the period being studied, not against modern political correctness. Stress the lessons of history, to include why particular actions were done and what were the consequences of those actions. Stress also the reasons that particular actions were deemed necessary, and the moral lessons of 'good' and 'bad' actions, but undergird the whole by teaching a preponderance of facts. Concepts are learned best when the preponderance of evidence leads inevitably to them.

- Science instruction should be based on teaching facts and the uses to which scientists put those facts. Science is the intellectual pursuit of physical reality. Everyone should learn the basics of science so that, apart from gaining an understanding of how the natural world works, our children will understand that even politically motivated changes must depend on reality, not ideology.

- Early English instruction is based on the rules of standard English and the phonetic decoding of letter sounds, not the fantasy of Whole Language. English topics to drill and practice are spelling, vocabulary, sentence structure, etc., etc. Drill is supplemented with *many* directed exercises and homework assignments since the point is to render this learning as second nature. 'Thinking' is difficult to achieve if you cannot explain your thoughts, even to yourself.

- Homework should be a familiar friend to all kids, introduced early and made routine. Homework should not be so trivial that kids can routinely complete it during class or on the school bus, yet they need not be oppressively long and difficult, especially in the early years. The idea is as much to set the habit of independent learning, as a way to practice with newly instructed skills and ideas. Homework is the way to promote lifelong learning by forcing kids to think about things they would ordinarily ignore, and to extend personal knowledge and understanding.

- In Kindergarten, homework assignments could be limited to once or twice per week and completed by the average kid in only 10 to 15 minutes. First and second grade homework can be assigned two or three times per week, to last perhaps 15 to 30 minutes, and it should be at least at a grade-appropriate difficulty level. Duration and difficulty increase through the 4th grade to perhaps 30 to 45 minutes, and should now frequently include more than one subject assignment per night. By the 5th and 6th grades, if not sooner, homework should routinely include reading text pages and answering questions based on that reading. Keeping in mind that a school day is typically only six hours long, not counting the lunch hour, homework should not be so extensive as to be overwhelming, but by high school an average of ½ to 1 hour per subject amounting to two to three hours per day should be routine.

- School books should be grade-appropriate with a 'feel' of aiming even higher. Cartoon-y picture books should probably not be used much beyond Kindergarten. Reading books should in some sense be 'literature' or historic, not today's bland and vapid kids' books. Unfortunately, as a category, 'inappropriate kids' books' might be as difficult to define as pornography, and I hesitate to identify any titles in particular. However, what I have in mind are the souless, culturesless, feel-good, politically correct books that have proliferated in recent years.

- Grading, whatever the level, subject or assignment, should be at least at grade level, or slightly higher, (i.e., teaching to the test).

- Most of the day in Kindergarten still can, and should, consist of socialization training, work on eye-hand coordination (e.g., use of scissors, crayons, etc., learning to write letters legibly, including cursive writing) and games. Socialization training (i.e., learning society's rules, obeying elders, "there's a time for playing and a time for quiet learning," etc.) may consist of games and group-work but should support cultural and community expectations about behavior and morality. Relativistic morality should never rear its ugly head. What I mean, of course, is training in un-restricted choice, that ethical expectations are different (or non-existent) for different people, that relevance to their childish expectations is all-important, or that they can expect to have things done for them because their learning style makes even simple things too difficult. Additionally the solidity and stability of the traditional family should be reinforced as a good thing. After all, virtually every culture in history was organized around one of several very limited variations of it. 'Alternative lifestyles' should not be presented as acceptable. Instead, while resisting any urge to be Puritanical, we should teach the stabilizing normality that works best, since the modern rhetoric of tolerance is used merely to justify anarchy. Our society has developed a logical variation of the extended family over many generations and through the many swings of fashion and philosophy that we have experienced. The point at which kids finally become independent adults themselves is soon enough to allow them to make lifetime choices. Until then the idea that 'Under my roof we live by my rules' should prevail, as it should in the home.

- Kids should be taught that effort and achievement are important and linked, because achievement depends largely on effort. We can do this by grading strictly and professionally and by rewarding good work and encouraging improvement. For those of a Progressive bent, who will immediately assume that the extreme opposite of spoiling kids is expected, let me assure you that I suggest nothing of the kind. I am <u>not</u> saying that we should browbeat, terrorize, or humiliate kids regularly for being different or less capable, only that whatever they eventually become, they will be better at it if they learn to work hard, and to enjoy it. Each will get the identical educational opportunity, since they are all sitting in the same class participating in the same lessons. What they make of that opportunity is up to their own interest, capability, and effort. Encouragement is necessary and should obviously be given, but the precepts of undeserved flattery should be taught only as an idea that we should not teach.

- Pupils should not be given reasons, or training, in making excuses for themselves, sociological or otherwise. Therefore, child-centered teaching should be eliminated as unproductive. Self-esteem, relevance, learning styles, and all the rest should be taught in Ed schools only, if at all, as examples of what not to do. Do not ask kids what is relevant. Tell them what the next assignment is, when it is due, and what the standard is for doing well.

- The bulk of the 1st and 2nd grades will consist of English language,[229] arithmetic drill and practice, and the beginnings of fact

---

229 Teaching an additional language from earliest schooling is also perfectly OK, especially in communities predominantly consisting of non-native speakers. These parents cannot be expected to teach their kids the fine points of the language, with exercises and tests, any more than predominantly English-speaking parents can teach their kids. But biculturalism should not be the driving force. Teaching foreign languages, and perhaps teaching Latin (as the basis for many other languages) should be done because our small world is populated by people speaking languages other than English. Yet English, as the overall predominant language, would be used to tie the nation together in shared experiences and knowledge. The Melting Pot, not multiculturalism.

accumulation in history, science, the arts, etc. This instruction will support the community standard regarding behavior, ethics, and morality. Therefore practice-reading should include many stories that have a moral, such as Aesop's Fables, etc. The moral may be discussed in the context of the kids' lives, but with little in the way of thinly veiled political rhetoric included. Though it can start far earlier, discussions within the context of kids' lives should eventually transition (probably by late grammar school and certainly by junior high school) to more expansive and universal, and therefore more literary, treatments of the themes of honor, diligence, sacrifice, friendship, love, loyalty, injustice, power, fidelity, magnanimity, the benefits of knowing things, respect for law, government excess and mismanagement, integrity, war, joy, crime, tolerance, despair, religion, honesty, the 'wages of sin', death, and the meaning of life, etc., etc. Only the politically correct will be surprised that this treatment is much more inclusive and diverse than the PC recommendations, and allows kids to feel a kinship with people, cultures, and history much different from their own, while learning patriotism, ethics, morality, analysis of wide-ranging ideas, and concise and persuasive communications. If we ask a kid to use his brain, he has a much better chance of learning to use his brain than if we spoon-feed him on intellectual pablum and a nonexistent social homogeneity.

- Again, multiculturalism (i.e., hate America first) should be avoided like the destructive plague it is, and its many divisive manifestations should be removed, such as disaggregation of achievement data. On the other hand, fables other than Aesop's and some literature other than books from 'Western Civilization' may be used. We may assume that Pakistani parents want their kids to be as good, smart, decent, helpful, cheerful, and hard working as Colombian, Thai, Korean, Australian, Finnish, Moroccan, South African, and Greek parents. We can assume that because people from all those places, and more, have come to America and seem to want those things for their kids here. If there are moral stories similar to Aesop's, Robert Louis Stevenson's, or Kipling's from around the world, by all means use them, but we must somehow get the kids to feel a community with

531

each other. ("No matter where we come from, we are *all* Americans here.") If we do not, we will destroy ourselves with internecine squabbling, and worse. Probably the way to do this is to find some decent, central ideas, such as the Golden Rule, the Ten Commandments (perhaps suitably secularized, or internationalized [i.e., God is God, by whatever name or conception you know him, not just the Christian god]), the work ethic, and others, that most Americans (most humans) agree with, and make this the new status quo. Then we can do as Franklin recommends; use the lessons of history to show the overall usefulness of leading a moral life, etc. The Melting Pot changes people, of that there is no doubt, but sensible immigrants expect to change. That is why they emigrated in the first place. An American standard is certainly no worse, and may be considerably better and stronger than any other, precisely because of its diverse and multinational nature. 'Hybrid vigor' is what biologists call this tendency for combinations to surpass individual inputs. Hybrid vigor is what the Melting Pot is all about. We have a saying that is appropriate for the effects of multiculturalism too. It is: Cutting off your nose to spite your face.

- The lecture-demonstration-discussion format should be the primary mode of instruction in the academic subjects and should start with the basics of each. For example, do not teach molecular biology in high school, if at all, unless we have taught basic biology first. Variations to lecture-demonstration-discussion are subject specific. For instance, arithmetic and math instruction will primarily show and explain technique, then practice, practice, practice, including the 'word problems' that crystalize the concepts being used. History (social studies) will consist of descriptions of a topic (e.g., event, period, social and economic context, etc.), consisting of many interwoven facts and discussion about how those facts affected each other, the event's participants, and the course of subsequent history. Literature will involve extensive reading at night and subsequent explanations and discussion, both verbal and written, of themes, while grammar instruction will mimic arithmetic and math; explain the rule, then practice using it. When mastery/competence of a technique is achieved, use it to explain the next, more advanced technique. Then practice that newer technique. Science will consist of much explanation of facts and procedures, along with some history of the development of those facts and reasons for the procedures, followed by fact and procedural playtime (lab). Starting at least in the second grade, testing will include answering many essay questions.

- Testing is done objectively to the greatest extent possible using age and grade-appropriate means. Subjective testing is perfectly acceptable, even unavoidable, for written work, within the context of the classroom, but should still be strictly based on the rules of standard English, logic, use and explanation of ideas, etc. Grading rubrics, as currently formulated, should be generally eliminated. Teaching-to-the-test, and slightly beyond, should be routine and expected. The curriculum should be genuinely challenging, intellectually and academically.

- By junior high school, ability-tracking based on achievement, etc., can be explicit. Admission to any 'track' is based primarily on scholastic achievement up to that point. The highest track should consist of college prep work, possibly with small Honors classes for the best pupils. Since the basic requirements of college prep work are exposing kids to an ever increasing array and complexity of facts, and training kids to analyze and use those facts (i.e., think) and are the same basic requirements necessary for 'mere' citizenship and daily living in the Information Age, we should do the same things for average pupils. 'Average' classes will, therefore, enroll most pupils and should mimic the college prep curriculum, though taught at an appropriate level of difficulty and detail to genuinely challenge the average kid. Kids with improving achievement can move up to the advanced classes, if wanted and warranted. A variation of tracking can be used in the grammar school, too, though it may be unnecessary due to the basic nature of the subject matter being taught. Teachers can schedule subject lessons at the same time each day, and trade kids to form ability groups. Teachers can also trade assignments based on expertise, or familiarity with a subject. 'Concern about labeling' should be replaced by honoring achievement.

- Other electives should be advanced academic classes, for the most part. Life-adjustment style classes should be very few and far between, and preferably nonexistent. The wild proliferation of electives that we see today should be curtailed as diluting the time spent teaching the core subjects. The reason we have time for them now, is that the core subjects are currently addressed using silly activities, just as they were in Kindergarten. There are just so many word search puzzles you can do before even the kids realize that you are simply marking time. Genuine teachers know that there is never enough time available to explore their subjects adequately, and are loath to give up what time they have, even if some kids would choose other things. Kids will discuss the thread of civilization and the behavioral and social options previously attempted in history and literature classes, or as they have always done, in private conversations with parents and friends. As needed, the ideal situation will exist if teachers note extreme variations from society's norms, by referring to the norm of the period discussed, and the damage done to the society as a result. Teaching that an unrestricted 'Change is good' is an anarchist's dream. The rest of us want stability in our lives and the lives of our children. Therefore we should teach kids to fine-tune society as appropriate, but not to throw the traditional baby out with the extremist's bath water. When future adults decide that removal of future extremism is desirable, moving to the opposite extreme should not be the logical alternative. Instead, kids should be taught political and social balance, not ideological extremism. Politics of any stripe should be left to discussions after kids have enough information to see more than one side of an issue, after they are capable of true analytical thought, and after they have had some exposure and experience with the pros and cons of different positions. Prior to that, political instruction, if any, is a parents' business.

- The basic vocational classes (shop, home economics, computers) will be a part of the core curriculum since everybody could bene-fit from the skills. Nevertheless computer and Internet use will be de-emphasized from the pointless, obsessive, and economically unjustifiable levels it has attained, and save us more $billions of dollars.
- Advanced vocational classes should be available as electives for everybody, while the core curriculum is satisfied. A vocational track might be developed with a coalition of local employers to teach appropriate skills. These might include higher-level technology skills, but should not include school credit for paid work at the plant.

- Teachers should be required to prove and maintain expertise in the subject areas they teach, and in the effective presentation of that material. Continuing subject matter education should be mandatory. Teacher in-service training should often take the form of subject matter seminars, not mere indoctrination in child-centered pedagogy. The more a teacher knows, the more interesting she can make a discussion, and the more inspiring she can be. And, not coincidentally, the more a teacher knows, the less they will be impressed by ideological arguments, whether those arguments come from the left or the right.

- While we are on the subject of teachers and their professionalism, we should again require them to dress the part. This is school, a preparation for adult life and responsibilities, not a daycare center. Baggy T-shirts, jeans, gum chewing and flip-flops (all items I have seen) are not a good example to set for the kids. While exceptions could be granted for gym teachers, etc., men should wear a shirt and tie and probably at least a sport coat. Women should wear equivalent clothing. Individual districts can debate whether to require some sort of uniform for the kids, but as a minimum boys should be required to wear a shirt with a collar, decent pants and shoes, and girls should wear the female equivalent; the kinds of clothes we once called 'school clothes'. This, along with our other changes, will begin to raise the kids' notions of pride in the schools, and in themselves. And we could then pull down all of the thousands of posters and signs touting 'respect' and 'character', etc. that are seen as just so much white noise and ignored by the kids.

- We should also begin putting our buildings back in order. As one step, we should follow the nutritional guidelines of sensible folks and remove the candy bar and soft drink dispensers, etc. Our mania for giving the kids what they want (and to get more money for pointless and damaging programs) has caused us to allow many bad habits to creep in, including the habit to bribe the kids for doing less than they should. Many schools have 'incentive' programs that, for instance, tell kids, 'Turn in this required assignment, and you'll get a cookie'. Casualness in all things has allowed food in the rooms and this should be reversed. I have seen kids bring in full bags of chips, spend a class eating candy bars, and one kid even brought a breakfast taco into the classroom, and made sure everyone saw that he was eating it. These sorts of rules should be scrapped.

- Ed schools should at least be overseen, if not Chaired, by genuine academics, scientists, historians, classicists, mathematicians, etc. [A Ph.D. in some rigorous, scholarly field (not education) should also be an absolute, unwaiverable requirement for superintendents of individual school systems. This Ph.D. may be in business or management. Several years of university teaching experience could (should?) be an additional requirement.]. Curricula and research in Ed schools should be subject to the same academic scrutiny as any other legitimate academic discipline. Unsupported and unvalidated fuzzy thinking (without benefit of demonstrated scientific validity) should be purged wherever it is found. Instructional recommendations based on the unsubstantiated, fuzzy thinking should be vetoed out of hand. These academic overseers should <u>not</u> be reassigned from departments with an ideological ax to grind and scholarship as shoddy as the Ed schools themselves, such as feminism and multiculturalism, etc.
- A possibility that should be seriously considered is that Ed schools be disbanded altogether, as the University of Chicago did after 1909. Their function might be parceled out to the various academic colleges as Departments of Pedagogy. Prospective teachers would then major in the academic discipline they propose to teach and merely take additional classes in teaching that subject. These additional classes must be based on proven techniques, not dogmatically romantic opinions. This might be the best way to eliminate the possibility of yet another Progressive resurgence in the future. As Ellen Lagemann said (p. 244), "If professional educators are trained in settings where they can learn to read, criticize, and themselves engage in research, they are more likely to become intelligent consumers of research (and perhaps participants in it) than would be the case if they are trained in "ed school" where there is little or no research. . . . What is more, I believe that in addition to immersion in professional knowledge and concerns, educators-in-training as well as their faculty mentors need more exposure than has traditionally tended to be available to the people and ideas associated with other university faculties." It is true that Lagemann was arguing for more genuine research within the currently organized ed schools, but since that

is not working, until our educational professionals can learn to become responsible scholars, they need adult supervision.

- We should consider repealing all school related legislation that is currently in force, back to perhaps 1960, if not as far back as 1910. This will force school boards to research the laws written earlier, which are suddenly back in force, when school was used for education rather than indoctrination, and to re-institute policies that address teaching sensibly. Statewide, or lower, laws and regulations will also be written reimplementing genuine teaching practices. Except for laws with genuinely archaic provisions (e.g., requiring pupils to provide fodder for the school-bus horses, or something), no new legislation should be written until a settling-in period of several years has elapsed. The settling-in period will allow the old, but resurrected policies, to become normal again and will give teachers some time to gain experience teaching rather than facilitating. Additionally, this period will allow a realistic renewal of in-service training to be designed, based on the details of effective instruction. Later, fine-tuning adjustments can be set up to perfect a system that works.
- Textbook publishers should be required, by responsible schools (i.e., the marketplace), not by government edict, to publish books that elevate the academic standards at least to age- and grade-appropriate levels. Using books written well below grade levels insures that kids achieve well below grade levels. These books could be written, or at least reviewed, by the Departments of Pedagogy mentioned above.

I continued to read and add to my book as I waited for a publisher to make an offer, and the more I read the history of our educational system and the more classes I witness, the more angry I become. Therefore, this next recommendation is admittedly uncharitable, and will in all likelihood be considered a bit excessive (though perhaps not if you read Koerner and Sowell). The idea is this: Since our War on Drugs is almost as big a flop as our education system, and since the vast majority of those jailed over the past few years have been nonviolent jerks who hurt few, other than themselves and their immediate families, maybe we should let them out. This would reduce the prison population by a reported 50 percent. That would leave just about enough room to incarcerate all of the committed educationists who may yet, if not stopped, reduce our schools and our brains to mush and our society to smoldering ruins. Aside from perpetrating an intellectual and fiscal fraud lasting several decades and garnering trillions of dollars from State and federal coffers, the charges can be 'contributing to the delinquency and ignorance of minors' (not to mention sedition, treason, active anarchy, educational malfeasance, dereliction of duty, support of pornography, and spitting on the sidewalk). 'Hard labor' would be a just sentence, too. Merely firing these folks, as they so richly deserve, would release hordes of angry, otherwise unemployable but politically connected intellectual rapists onto an unsuspecting nation. That might be messy.

Instead, incarcerating all of them would keep them feeding at the public trough, as they have done lo these many years, yet would keep them off the streets where they could do little additional harm. The more I think of it, the better I like it. Even the new inmates would be happy. They would finally enter a world where they are fully dependent on government sponsored social services and could live out their days debating among themselves who has the most profound learning disability, who would require the most intensive pseudotherapy, and who is responsible for the quality of the prison media center. Maybe their parole could be contingent on them teaching some number of inmates to read? That requirement would likely keep them in the big house for life.

The rest of us would have to clean up the mess they left us, but it would be worth it. After all, it truly would be "for the children."

Oh, well. It was a good dream while it lasted.

Unfortunately, these ideas, even the ones with a snowball's chance of being enacted, will do little to mitigate the self-serving hypocrisy of the teacher's unions. These organizations, and their massive public relations systems, would try mightily to abort any real improvements in education, as they currently do. They will probably succeed too. They have almost always done so in the past, primarily because, after any sort of reform is enacted into law, who do you suppose is left to make it work? The educational professionals, of course. It is a real shame that tarring and feathering is no longer considered acceptable behavior. If parents truly understood what is being done to their children, they might want to resurrect that practice. One way to reduce their influence, however, is not to allow new ones to be trained. So while we heat the tar for use against the current crop of noneducating teacher-teachers and politicians, we have to do something about insuring that future teachers know what they are talking about.

What we need are people who can remind our educationists what education is for, and help install procedures and teacher-training recommendations that do not merely spin our educational wheels. When education is again about training kids to think, and history and science instruction, etc., are again about history and science, etc., we will see a resurgence in intelligence and competence in all walks of life that will make us all proud. In this way also, the entire university will also have a say in the preparation of its applicants, and of the nation's citizens. Of course, it is now a common complaint that our universities are overrun with extremist intellectuals as well, so there is a lot of work to do. On the other hand, once sane education is again the norm, we will spawn fewer of these folks too.

Educationists will complain about 'placing limits on intellectual and academic freedom", etc., but that should not worry us unduly. We are not speaking about an academic debate on an esoteric question of little practical importance to any but a few specialists. We are speaking about our kids. When our kids and the entire society are at stake, as they clearly are, common sense should override the right to be stupid. Everyone does have that right, but when they insist, and have the power to assure, that their own brand of stupidity be spread nationwide and perpetuated down the generations, the rest of us have the right, and the obligation, to stop them.

Besides, we have evidence that habitual drunk drivers harm more than themselves, and we brush off their complaints that we unfairly limit their freedoms, with no loss of sleep. It is a little different with the Progressive ideology overall, and educationism in particular, however. While we also have clear evidence that Progressive education, for all of its loving rhetoric, damages others, namely the rest of society overall and kids in particular, unlike drunk drivers, they clearly always manage to help themselves. Under these conditions we should have no qualms whatever of putting them on a very short leash, at most. Our educational system should be used to prepare our citizens for independent and productive lives, not merely to prepare our kids to be either wards of the state, or wardens. Parents, and anyone who depends on humans for their business and/or livelihood, should be storming the doors of school districts and legislatures, demanding major revisions in practice and curriculum.

Still, do not be concerned, because educational professionals are on the job and they know that all true learning comes from within and that teaching is an unnecessary burden that should not be in a teacher's job description.

Remember to pay your taxes.

Bibliography

> He that teaches us anything which we knew not before
> is undoubtedly to be reverenced as a master.
> —*Samuel Johnson*

> Teachers are more than any other class the guardians of civilization.
> —*Bertrand Russell*

Adler, Mortimer, *Reforming Education*, MacMillan Publishers, New York, 1977.

Alvarez, Yadhira, *How Teachers Can Help Stop Racism*, Creative Classroom, September 1992:108–115.

American Association for the Advancement of Science, *Benchmarks for Science Literacy*, Oxford University Press, New York, 1993.

American Association for the Advancement of Science, *Science for All Americans, Project 2061*, Oxford University Press, New York, 1990.

Anderson, D. J. *Identifying the child with Gilles de la Tourette syndrome.* Preventing School Failure, 37 (Spring 1993); 25–28.

Anderson, Hans O. (1978), *The Holistic Approach to Science Education, The Science Teacher*, Jan. 1978:27–28.

Andrews, Lori B. and Dorothy Nelkin (1996), *The Bell Curve: A Statement*, in *Science*, Vol. 271, 5 January 1996:13–14.

Apple, Michael W., *Cultural Politics & Education*, Teachers College Press, New York, 1996.

ARCO Editorial Board, *PPST, Pre-Professional Skills Tests*, MacMillan, New York, 1990.

Atwell, Nancie, *In the Middle, Writing, Reading and Learning with Adolescents*, Boynton/Cook, Portsmouth, 1987.

Ault, Charles S. Jr. (1985), *Concept Mapping as a Study Strategy in Earth Science*, JCST, Sept.–Oct. 1985:38–44.

Ayala, Francisco J. and John A. Kiger, Jr., *Modern Genetics*, 2nd Ed., Benjamin/Cummings Publishing, Menlo Park, 1984.

Bacon, Francis (1620), from *Novum Organum*, in *Galileo's Comandment*, E. B. Bolles (Ed.), W. H. Freeman, New York, 1997.

Bacon, Francis (1597–1625), *The Essays or Counsels Civill & Morall*, The Easton Press, Norwalk, 1980.

Banks, James A., *Multicultural Education: For Freedom's Sake*, Educational Leadership. Dec. 1991–Jan. 1992:32–36.

Barzun, Jacques, *The House of Intellect*, Harper Books, New York, 1959.

Barzun, Jacques, *From Dawn to Decadence*, Perennial Books, New York, 2000.

Berger, Sandra, *Tips for Identifying and Working with Children Who Are Gifted*, CEC Today: Dec. 1996.

Berliner, David C. and Bruce J. Biddle, *The Manufactured Crisis, Myths, Fraud and the Attack on America's Public Schools*, Addison-Wesley Publishing Co., Reading, MA, 1995.

Berman, Morris, *The Twilight of American Culture*, W. W. Norton & Co., New York, NY, 2000.

Best, John H. (Ed.), *Benjamin Franklin on Education*, Columbia University Press, New York, 1962.

Bestor, Arthur (1953), *Educational Wastelands: The Retreat from Learning in Our Public Schools*, University of Illinois Press, Urbana, 1985.

Binford, Lewis R., *In Pursuit of the Past, Decoding the Archeological Record*, Thames and Hudson, New York, 1983.

Biological Sciences Curriculum Study, *Biology: A Human Approach*, Kendall/Hunt Publishers, Dubuque, 1997.

Bloom, Allan, *The Closing of the American Mind*, Touchstone, New York, 1987.

Boyd, Robert F., *General Microbiology*, Times Mirror/Mosby, St. Louis, 1984.

Bracey, Gerald W. (1996), *Asian and American Schools Again*, Phi Delta Kappan, May 1996; 641–642.

Brescia, Frank, John Arents, Herbert Meilisch and Amos Turk, *Fundamentals of Chemistry*, 4th Ed., Academic Press, New York, 1980.

Brock, Thomas D., *Biology of Microorganisms*, 3rd Ed., Prentice-Hall, Englewood Cliffs, 1979.

Brockman, John (Ed), *The Third Culture: Beyond the Scientific Revolution*, Touchstone, New York, 1995.

Bronhelm, S., *An educator's guide to Tourette syndrome*, Journal of Learning Disabilities, 24(1): 17–22 (1991).

Brooks, Douglas M., *The First Day of School*, Educational Leadership, May 1985:76–78.

Browder, Leon W., *Developmental Biology*, Saunders College, Philadelphia, 1980.

Brower, Kelly A., Catherine L. Stemmans, Christopher D. Ingersoll and David J. Langley, *An Investigation of Undergraduate Athletic Training Students' Learning Styles and Program Admission Success*, Journal of Athletic Training (2001) 32(2): 130–135.

Brown Center Report on American Education, *The Nation's Achievement, Part I*, Brookings Institution, 2004.

Brown, Theodore L. and H. Eugene LeMay, Jr., *Chemistry, The Central Science*, 2nd. Ed., Prentice-Hall, Englewood Cliffs, 1981.

Bruner, Jerome, *The Process of Education*, Harvard University Press, Cambridge, 1960.

Burden, Paul R. and David M. Byrd, *Methods for Effective Teaching*, Allyn and Bacon, Boston, 1994.

Burke, James and Robert Ornstein, *The Axemaker's Gift: A Double-Edged History of Human Culture*, G. P. Putnam's Sons, New York, 1995.

Bybee, Roger W. (1995), *Achieving Scientific Literacy*, The Science Teacher, 62(7): 28–33.

Bybee, Roger W. (1987). *Teaching about Science-Technology-Society (STS): Views of Science Educators in the United States.* School Science and Mathematics, 87(4): 274–285.

Campbell, James R., *Raising Your Child To Be Gifted*, Brookline Books, Cambridge, 1996.

Chall, Jeanne S., *The Academic Achievement Challenge: What Really Works in the Classroom?* Guilford Press, New York, 2000.

Charles, C. M., *Building Classroom Discipline* (5th Ed.), Longman Publishers, White Plains, N.Y., 1981.

Cheney, Lynne V., *Telling the Truth*, Touchstone Books, New York, 1995.

Cobern, William W., Adrienne T. Gibson and Scott A. Underwood (1995), *Valuing Scientific Literacy*, The Science Teacher, 62(9): 28–31.

Cockburn, Alexander, *The golden age is in us: Journeys & Encounters*, Verso, London, 1995.

Connely, C., *Mindy has Tourette's syndrome*, Learning, 20(5): 42–45 (1992).

Connidis, I. A. and J. A. McMullin, *Ambivalence, Family Ties, and Doing Sociology*, Marriage and Family, 64(3): 2002.

Connidis, I. A. and J. A. McMullin, *Sociological Ambivalence, Family Ties: A Critical Perspective*, Marriage and Family, 64(3): 2002.

Cooper, Jim, *Cooperative Learning and College Teaching: Tips from the Trenches*, The Teaching Professor, 4(5), May 1990:1–2.

Cothron, Julia H., Ronald N. Giese, and Richard J. Rezba, *Students and Research, Practical Strategies for Science Classrooms and Competitions*, Kendall/Hunt, Dubuque, 1993.

Crawford, M. H. and P. L. Workman (Eds), *Methods and Theories of Anthropological Genetics*, University of New Mexico Press, Albuquerque, 1973.

Davis, Bernard D., Renato Dulbecco, Herman N. Eisen and Harold S. Ginsburg, *Microbiology, Including Immunology and Molecular Genetics*, 3rd Ed., Harper & Row, Philadelphia, 1980.

Defore, Daniel (1719), *Robinson Crusoe: His Life and Surprising Adventures*, Everyman's Classics, Knopf, New York, 1993.

Delaney, Kathleen R., and Frances Belmonte-Mann, *Identifying the Mental Health Needs of Preschool Children*, Journal of School Nursing, 17(4); August 2001: 222–226.

de Maupassant, Guy (c. 1884), *The Story of a Farm Girl*, in *The Tales of Guy de Maupassant*, The Easton Press, Norwalk, 1964.

Dewey, John (1916), *Democracy and Education*, The Free Press, New York, 1997.

Dewey, John (1938), *Experience & Education*, Touchstone, New York, 1997.

Díaz del Castillo, Bernal (c. 1555), *The Discovery and Conquest of Mexico*, Da Capo Press, New York, 1996.

DiGisi, L. L. & L. D. Yore, *Reading comprehension and metacognition in science: Status, potential and future directions* (ERIC Document Reproduction Service No. ED 356 132 (1992).

DiTulio, Benigno, *Horizons in Clinical Criminology*, New York University Press, New York, 1969.

Dobzhansky, Theodosius, *Mankind Evolving*, Yale University Press, New Haven, 1962.

Doyle, Arthur C. (1892), *A Scandal in Bohemia*, in Six Great Sherlock Holmes Stories, Dover Publications, New York, 1992.

Eccles, John C., *The Physiology of Nerve Cells*, The Johns-Hopkins Press, Baltimore, 1968.

Eccles, John C., *The Understanding of the Brain*, McGraw-Hill, New York, 1973.

Ehrlich, Paul R., *Human Natures*, Island Press, Washington, D.C., 2000.

Eiseley, Loren, *The Immense Journey*, Vintage Books, New York, 1957.

Engelmann, Siegfried, *War Against the Schools' Academic Child Abuse*, Halcyon House, Portland, 1992.

Evans, Elizabeth D. and Rita C. Richardson, *Corporal Punishment, What Teachers Should Know*, Teaching Exceptional Children, Winter 1995:33–36.

Finn, Chester E., Jr., Marci Kanstoroom and Michael J. Petrilli, *The Quest for Better Teachers: Grading the States*, Fordham Foundation, Washington, D.C., 1999.

Fischer, Douglas, Nancy Frey, and Jacqueline Thousand (2003), *What do Special Educators Need to Know and Be Prepared to Do for Inclusive Schooling to Work?* Teacher Education and Special Education, 26(1), 42–50.

Flesch, Rudolf (1955), *Why Johnny Can't Read—and what we can do about it.* Harper Bros., New York, 1986.

Fort, Deborah C. (1993), *Science Shy, Science Savvy, Science Smart*, Phi Delta Kappan, May 1993:674–882.

Franklin, Benjamin, *Poor Richard's Almanack*, Peter Pauper Press, New York.

Galbraith, John K., *The Great Crash*, 1929, Houghton Mifflin, New York, 1988.

Gardner, Howard, *Multiple Intelligences: The Theory in Practice*, Basic Books, New York, 1993.

Gibbon, Edward (1776), *The History of the Decline and Fall of the Roman Empire: The Turn of the Tide*, Vol. 1, The Folio Society, London, 1983.

Gibson, Margaret A., *Approaches to Multicultural Education in the United States: Some Concepts and Assumptions.* Anthropology and Education Quarterly, 15:94–119 (1984).

Ginsburg, Herbert and Sylvia Opper, *Piaget's theory of intellectual development. An Introduction,* Prentice-Hall, Englewood Cliffs, 1969.

Goodlad, John I., A *Place Called School: Prospects for the Future,* McGraw-Hill, New York, 1984.

Gould, Stephen J., *Here goes nothing,* in *Bully for Brontosaurus,* W. W. Norton, New York, 1991.

Gould, Stephen, J., *The Mismeasure of Man,* W. W. Norton & Co., New York, 1996.

Gould, Sephen J. and Niles Eldredge (1977), *Punctuated Equilibria: the tempo and mode of evolution reconsidered.* Paleobiology, 3:115–151.

Gowlett, John, *Ascent to Civilization, The Archeology of Early Man,* Alfred A. Knopf, New York, 1984.

Grant, Michael, *Julius Caesar,* M. Evans and Co., New York, 1992.

Grant Wood Area Educational Agency, *Multicultural Education,* The Summer Linker, 1996.

Graves, Robert (1934), *I, Claudius,* Vintage Books, New York, 1961.

Gribbin, John and Jeremy Cherfas, *The Monkey Puzzle, Reshaping the Evolutionary Tree,* Pantheon, New York, 1982.

Gross, Martin L., *The Conspiracy of Ignorance: The Failure of American Public Schools,* Perennial, New York, 1999.

Harris, D., A. A. Silver and H. Sekhon, (1993, February), *Tourette's syndrome and learning disorders,* Paper presented at the Learning Disabilities of America Conference, San Francisco, CA.

Haviland, William A., *Cultural Anthropology,* 8th Ed., Harcourt Brace, New York, 1996. (Plus Study Guide and Workbook)

Heider, Karl, *Grand Valley Dani, Peaceful Warriors,* 2nd Ed., Holt Rinehart & Winston, Inc., Fort Worth, 1991.

Herrnstein, Richard J. and Charles Murray, *The Bell Curve, Intelligence and Class Structure in American Life,* The Free Press, New York, 1994.

Hill, Winfred F., *Learning: A Survey of Psychological Interpretations* (Revised Ed.), Chandler Publications, Scranton, PA, 1971.

Hirsch, E. D. Jr., *Cultural Literacy, What Every American Needs to Know,* Vintage Books, New York, 1988.

Hirsch, E. D. Jr. and John Holdren (Ed's.), *What Your Kindergartner Needs to Know, Preparing Your Child for a Lifetime of Learning,* Delta Books, New York, 1997.

Hirsch, E. D. Jr. (Ed.), *What your First Grader Needs to Know, Fundamentals of a Good First-Grade Education,* Delta Books, New York, 1998.

Hodkinson, Harold L., *What Should We Call People? Race, Class, and the Census for 2000,* Phi Delta Kappan, October 1995:173–179.

Hodson, Derek and Reg Dennick (1994), *Antiracist Education: A Special Role for the History of Science and Technology*, School Science and Mathematics, 94(5):255–262.

Huelskamp, Robert M. (1993), *Perspective on Education in America*, Phi Delta Kappan, May 1993:718–721.

Huxley, Aldous (1932), *Brave New World*, Harper & Row, New York, 1969.

Huyvaert, Sarah H., *Reports from the Classroom*, Allyn and Bacon, Boston, 1995.

Inhelder, Barbel and Jean Piaget, *The Early Growth of Logic in the Child*, W. W. Norton, New York, 1964.

Jacoby, Russell and Naomi Glauberman (Ed.), *The Bell Curve Debate, History, Documents, Opinions*, Times Books, New York, 1995.

Jefferson, Thomas, *A Bill for the More General Diffusion of Knowledge*, in Thomas Jefferson, Writings, The Library of America, USA, 1984:365–373.

Johanson, Donald and Maitland Edey, *Lucy, The Beginnings of Mankind*, Warner Books, New York, 1981.

Johnson, Kirk, *Self-Image is Suffering From Lack of Esteem*, The New York Times, May 5, 1998.

Johnson, Otto (Ed.), *Information Please Almanac*, Houghton Mifflin, New York, 1997.

Johnson, Roger N., *Aggression in Man and Animals*, W. B. Saunders, Philadelphia, 1972.

Jolly, Clifford J. and Fred Plog, *Physical Anthropology and Archeology*, 3rd Ed., Alfred A. Knopf, New York, 1982.

Keogh, James, *Getting the Best Education for Your Child, A Parent's Checklist*, Fawcett Columbine, New York, 1997.

Kerman, Sam, *Teacher Expectations And Student Achievement*, Photocopied handout, Journal, etc., not indicated.

Kernan, Alvin B., *In Plato's Cave*, Yale University Press, New Haven, 1999.

Kessler, Jane W., *Psychopathology of Childhood*, Prentice-Hall, Englewood Cliffs, 1966.

Kipling, Rudyard (1903), *How the Alphabet was Made*, in Just So Stories, Konecky & Konecky, New York, 1991.

Klitgaard, Robert, *Elitism and Meritocracy in Developing Countries: Selection Policies for Higher Education.* Johns Hopkins University Press, Baltimore, 1986.

Koerner, James D., *The Miseducation of American Teachers*, Penguin Books, Baltimore, 1963.

Kramer, Rita, *Ed School Follies: The Miseducation of Teachers*, Excellence in Education Series, John M. Ashbrook Center for Public Affairs, Ashland University, Ashland, OH, 1992.

Lagemann, Ellen C., *An Elusive Science: The Troubling History of Education Research*, University of Chicago Press, Chicago, 2000.

Lawson, Anton E. (1991), *Exploring Growth (& Mitosis) Through a Learning Cycle*, The American Biology Teacher, 53(2):107–110.

Lawson, Anton E., Michael R. Abraham and John W. Renner, *A Theory of Instruction: Using the Learning Cycle to Teach Science Concepts and Thinking Skills*, National Association for Research in Science Teaching (NARST) Monograph No. 1, 1989.

Leakey, Richard E. and Roger Lewin, *People of the Lake, Mankind & Its Beginnings*, Avon, New York, 1978.

Lehninger, Albert L., *Biochemistry*, 2nd Ed., Worth Publishing, New York, 1975.

Leo, John, *Damn, I'm good!*, U.S. News and World Report, May 18, 1998:21.

Leo, John, *Dumbing down teachers*, U.S. News and World Report, August 3, 1998:15.

Leo, John, *Notes of a nonvictim*, U.S. News and World Report, October 6, 1997:11.

Leonard, William H. (1981), *Laboratory Instruction is on Trial!* The American Biology Teacher, 43(8):445–447.

Levi, S. L., *The Tourette Syndrome Association, Inc.*, Journal of Learning Disabilities, 24(1):16 (1991).

Levin, James and James F. Nolan, *Principles of Classroom Management, A Professional Decision-Making Model* (2nd Ed.), Allyn and Bacon, Boston, 1996.

Little Hoover Commission (1993), *A Chance to Succeed: Providing English Learners with Supportive Education*, Report #122, www.lhc.ca.gov/lhcdir/122rp.html.

Mandell, Herbert E., *Gifted Children and their Emotions*, Helping Hand; 7:3, Dec. 1996.

Matthews, A. (June 24, 1990). *The Poppers on the plains.* The New York Times Magazine, Section G: 24–26, 41, 48–49, 53.

Matthiessen, Peter, *The Tree Where Man Was Born*, E. P. Dutton, New York, 1972.

McCandless, Boyd R., *Adolescents, Behavior and Development*, The Dryden Press, Hinsdale, 1970.

McLaughlin, Barry, *Learning and Social Behavior*, The Free Press, New York, 1971.

Miller, William F. Jr. (1993), *Present and Future Nuclear Reactor Designs, Weighing the advantages and disadvantages of nuclear power with an eye on improving safety and meeting future needs*, Journal of Chemical Education, 70(2):109–114.

Montessori, Maria, *The Absorbent Mind*, Henry Holt & Co., New York, 1995.

Mooney, Carol Garhart, *Theories of Childhood: An Introduction to Dewey, Montessori, Erikson, Piaget & Vygotsky*, Redleaf, St. Paul, 2000.

Morris, Richard B., *Witness at the Creation: Hamilton, Madison, Jay and the Constitution.*, Mentor, New York, 1985.

Murnane, Richard, et al., *Who will teach? Policies that matter*, Harvard University Press, Cambridge, 1991.

Murray, Charles, *Losing Ground: American Social Policy 1950–1980*, Basic Books, New York, 1984.

National Assessment Governing Board, *Science Framework for the 1996 National Assessment of Education Progress*, U.S. Government Printing Office, Washington, D.C.

National Commission on Excellence in Education, The, *A Nation at Risk, The Full Account*, USA Research, Inc., Portland, 1984.

National Education Goals Panel, *The National Education Goals Report, Building A Nation Of Leaders*, U.S. Government Printing Office. Washington, D.C., 1997.

National Research Council, *National Science Education Standards*, National Academy Press, Washington, D.C. 1996.

National Science Foundation, *Science and Engineering Indicators*, 1998.

Nei, Masatoshi and Richard K. Koehn (Ed.), *Evolution of Genes and Proteins*, Sinauer Assoc., Sunderland, 1983.

Nemko, Martin, *How to Get Your Child a Private School Education in a Public School*, Ten Speed, Berkeley, 1989.

Nevin, John A. (E), *The Study of Behavior, Learning, Motivation, Emotion, and Instinct*, Scott, Foresman and Co., Glenview, 1973.

Noddings, Nel, *Educating for Intelligent Belief or Unbelief*, Teachers College Press, New York, 1993.

Ornstein, Allan C. and Daniel U. Levine, *Foundations of Education*, 5th Ed., Houghton Mifflin Co., Boston, 1987.

Ost, David H. and Robert E. Yager (1993), *Biology, STS & the Next Steps in Program Design & Curriculum Development*, The American Biology Teacher, 55(5): 282–287.

Ostlund, Karen L., *Science Process Skills*, Addison-Wesley, Menlo Park, 1992.

Ottenheimer, Martin, *Marriage in Domini, Husbands and Wives in an Indian Ocean Community*, Sheffield Publications, Salem, 1994.

Page, David S., *Principles of Biological Chemistry*, 2nd Ed., Willard Grant Press, Boston, 1981.

Pang, Valerie O., *Why Do We Need This Class? Multicultural Education for Teachers*, Phi Delta Kappan, December, 1994:289–292.

Pindiprolu, Sekhar S., Stephanie M. Peck Peterson, Sarah Rule and Benjamin Lingnugaris/Kraft, 2003, *Using Web-Mediated Experiential Case-Based Instruction to Teach Functional Behavioral Assessment*, Teacher Education and Special Education, 26(1):1–16.

Popper, Karl (1974), from *Replies to My Critics*, in Galileo's Commandment, (E. B. Bolles, Ed.), W. H. Freeman, New York, 1997.

Ratner, Joseph (Ed.), *Intelligence in the Modern World, John Dewey's Philosophy*, Modern Library, New York, 1939.

Ravitch, Diane, *Left Back: A Century of Battles over School Reform*, Touchstone, New York, 2000.

Ravitch, Diane, *The Troubled Crusade: American Education 1945–1980*, Basic Books, New York, 1983.

Research & Education Assoc., NTE, *National Teachers Examination*, Research & Education Assoc., Piscataway, 1995.

Ridley, Matt, *The Agile Gene: How Nature Turns on Nurture*, Perennial, New York, 2003.

Rousseau, Jean-Jacques (1762), *Emile or On Education*, Basic Books, New York, 1979.

Routman, Regie, *Literacy at the Crossroads: Crucial Talk About Reading, Writing and Other Teaching Dilemmas*, Heinemann, Portsmouth, 1996.

Samples, B. (1994), *Instructional Diversity, Teaching to your students' strengths*, The Science Teacher, February 1994:14–17.

Schaller, George B. (1972), *The Serengeti Lion: a study of predator-prey relations*, University of Chicago Press, Chicago.

Schaller, George B., and Gordon R. Lowther (1969), *The Relevance of carnivore behavior to the study of early hominids*, Southwestern Journal of Anthropology, 25(4):307–341.

Scharmann, Lawrence C. (1991), *Teaching Angiosperm Reproduction by Means of the Learning Cycle*, School Science and Mathematics, 91(3):100–104.

Scharmann, Lawrence C. (1993), *Teaching Evolution: Designing Successful Instruction*, The American Biology Teacher, 55(8):481–486.

Scharmann, Lawrence C. (1994), *Teaching Evolution: Past and Present*, (Ed.), Censorship: A Threat to reading, learning, thinking, Chapter 15:148–165.

Scharmann, Lawrence C. and T. D. Block (1992), *Teaching evolution: Understanding, concerns, and instructional approach alternatives*, Kansas Biology Teacher, 2(1):13–15.

Sheridan, Charles L., *Fundamentals of Experimental Psychology*, Holt, Rinehart and Winston, New York, 1971.

Singer, Alan, *Reflections on Multiculturalism*, Phi Delta Kappan, December 1994:284–288.

Smith, Roger (1999), *The Timing of Birth*, Scientific American, March 1999:68–75.

Solomons, T. W. Graham, *Organic Chemistry*, 2nd ed., John Wiley & Sons, New York, 1980.

Sowell, Thomas, *Inside American Education: The Decline, The Deception, The Dogmas*, The Free Press, New York, 1993.

Spencer, Thomas D. and Norman Kass, Ed., *Perspectives in Child Psychology, Research and Review*, McGraw-Hill, New York, 1970.

Spring, Joel, *Deculturalization and the Struggle for Equality, A Brief History of the Education of Dominated Cultures in the United States*, 2nd Ed., McGraw-Hill, New York, 1997.

Stenesh, J., *Experimental Biochemistry*, Allyn and Bacon, Boston, 1884.

Stevenson, Harold W. (1992), *Learning from Asian Schools*, Scientific American Dec. 1992:70–76.

Stossel, John, *Philosophy of Teaching*, ABC News, 20/20, (video c. 1996, no date indicated).

Strickland, Guy, *Bad Teachers, The Essential Guide for Concerned Parents*, Pocket, New York, 1998.

Sturluson, Snorri (translated by Magnus Magnusson and Hermann Pálsson), *King Harald's Saga*, Dorset Press, New York, 1966.

Sullivan, Bridget (Ed.), *Teachers: A Tribute*, Ariel Books, Kansas City, 1996.

Swanson, David W., Philip J. Bohnert and Jackson A. Smith, *The Paranoid*, Little, Brown and Co., Boston, 1970.

Tanner, Nancy M., *On Becoming Human*, Cambridge University Press, Cambridge, 1987.

Tattersall, Ian and Jeffery H. Schwartz, *Extinct Humans*, Westview Press, Boulder, 2001.

Teitelbaum, Philip, *Physiological Psychology, Fundamental Principles*, Prentice-Hall, Englewood Cliffs, 1967.

Thomas, Elizabeth Marshall, *The Harmless People*, 2nd Ed., Vintage Books, 1989.

Thompson, Richard F., *Foundations of Physiological Psychology*, Harper & Row, New York, 1967.

Toch, Thomas, *In the Name of Excellence, The Struggle to Reform the Nation's Schools, Why It's Failing, and What Should be Done*, Oxford University Press, New York, 1991.

Tolstoy, Leo (1869), *War and Peace*, Signet Classic, New York, 1968.

Towle, Albert, *Modern Biology, Annotated Teachers Edition*, Holt, Rinehart and Winston, Harcourt Brace Jovanovich, Austin, 1993.

Treiber, Frances, *Ineffective Teaching: Can we learn from it?* Journal of Teacher Education (Photocopied handout—Additional information not indicated).

Trent, Stanley C., *A Case for multicultural teaching: "On the birth of a man-child—a grandfather's letter,"* The Holmes Group Forum, VII(3), Spring 1993:19–22.

Twain, Mark (1883), *Life on the Mississippi*, Signet Classic, New York, 1961.

Tyack, David and Larry Cuban, *Tinkering toward Utopia, A Century of Public School Reform*, Harvard University Press, Cambridge, 1995.

Uno, G. E., & Bybee, R. W. (1994), *Understanding the dimensions of biological literacy.* Bioscience, 71(8): 553–557.

Urban, Wayne and Jennings Wagoner, Jr., *American Education, A History*, McGraw-Hill, New York, 1996.

Verne, Jules (1864), *A Journey to the Center of the Earth*, Signet Classic, 2003.

Vygotsky, Lev S., *Thought and Language*, The MIT Press, 1962.

Walker, Alan and Pat Shipman, *The Wisdom of the Bones, In Search of Human Origins*, Alfred A. Knopf, New York, 1996.

White, Merry, *The Japanese Educational Challenge: A Commitment to Children*, The Free Press, New York, 1987.

White, Richard B. and Mark A. Koorland (1969), *Curses! What can we do about cursing?*, Teaching Exceptional Children, Summer 1996:48–51.

Wiggins, Grant (1989), *Teaching to the (Authentic) Test*, Educational Leadership, 46(7):41–47.

Willis, C., *Tourette syndrome and associated features and the school aged child*, Paper presented at the 25th Conference of the National Association of School Psychologists, Washington, D.C. (April 1993).

Wilson, Edward O., *Resuming the Enlightenment Quest*, The Wilson Quarterly, Winter 1998:16–27.

Wilson, Edward O., *Sociobiology*, Belknap Press, Cambridge, 1975.

Wingrove, Allen S. and Robert L. Caret, *Organic Chemistry*, Harper & Row, New York, 1981.

Wittmer, Joe and Robert D. Myrick, *The Teacher as Facilitator*, Educational Media, Minneapolis, 1989.

Wolfe, Stephen L., *Biology of the Cell*, 2nd Ed., Wadsworth Publications, Belmont, 1981.

Wood, Karen D., Diane Lapp and James Flood, *Guiding Readers through Text: A Review of Study Guides*, International Reading Association, 1992.

Woolfolk, Anita E., *Educational Psychology*, 6th Ed., Allyn and Bacon, Boston, 1995.

'XYZ' State Board of Education Outcomes Education Team, *Curriculum Standards for Science*, Revised June 14, 1995.

'XYZ' High School Agenda 1994–1995. (Where I did my student teaching)

Yager, Robert E. and Pinchas Tamir (1993), *STS Approach: Reasons, Intentions, Accomplishments and Outcomes*, Science Education, 77(6):637–658.

Index

A clever quotation proves nothing.
—*Volatire*

('fn' indicates a footnote)

Meritocracy, 77, 112, 397, 499
Mexico, 332
Michigan, xxxviii
Michigan State University, xlvi, 376, 382
Mill, John Stuart, ix
Minnesota, xxxviii
Minority, xxxix, 46, 131, 185, 209,
    334–335, 337, 341–342, 358, 363,
    365
Missouri, xxvii, xxxviii
Monod, Jacques-Lucien, 233
Mort, Paul R., xxxvii
Motorola, ix
Multiculturalism, (found throughout
    but especially Chapter 5)
Multidimensional literacy, 457
Multiple regression (R^2), 275, 284
Murnane, Richard, 102
Murray, Charles, 94fn, 107, 124fn,
    132fn, Chapter 4
Muslim, 205, 255fn, 256, 335
Myrick, Robert, 103, 113–114, 116

Napoleon, 231
National Aeronautic and Space
    Administration (NASA), 165
National Assessment of Educational
    Progress (NAEP), xvii, 23, 40
National Center for Educational
    Statistics, 1
National Commission on Excellence in
    Education, xxviii
National Counsel of Teachers of
    Mathematics, (NCTM), 191fn
National Education Association (NEA),
    xiii, xl, 15, 98fn, 112, 224, 270–271,
    280, 322, 426
National Education Goals, 40
National Geographic Society, 2
National Hospital for Kids in Crisis, 415
National Longitudinal Survey of Youth,
    284
National Public Radio (NPR), 104, 172,
    214, 302
National Science Foundation, 2
National Socialism, 147

National Teachers Exam (NTE), 115,
    220
Native American, 326, 331, 361
Nature–Nurture, 27, 34, 133, 218fn,
    275, 281–283, 300–302, 322
NBC News, 2, 117
Neandertal, xxxii
Newbery Award, 113
New Deal, 124
New Mexico, xxxviii
New Republic, 284
Newton, Isaac, 164, 454–455
New World, 331
New York State Regents exams, 394, 495
New Zealand, 169
Nixon, Richard M., 131
Nobel Prize, 1, 18, 52, 119, 188, 233,
    247, 455
No Child Left Behind, 490
Norm-referencing, 464, 472, 476, 485,
    491

Objective test, 16, 39, 63, 220, 447, 457,
    462, 468–469, 472, 476, 485, 487,
    489–490, 492–493, 496, 533
Obsessive-Compulsive Disorder (OCD),
    378
O'Connor, Flannery, 1
October Skies, 165
Office of Education, xxxi, xxxviii, 11, 13
Opportunity to learn, xxxiii, 279, 428
Oregon, xxxviii, 10, 324
Organization for Economic Cooperation
    and Development, (OECD), 18fn
Orwell, George, 164, 311, 372
Outcome, xxxiii, 19, 74, 84, 87fn, 166,
    219, 245, 249, 255, 269, 340, 346,
    377, 404, 406–407, 409, 411–412,
    420, 463, 466, 469
Outcomes-Based Education (OBE),
    245, 258–264
Ozzie and Harriet, 380

Pablo, 156, 245, 268
Paddling, 58, 60–61, 227

Parental involvement, xiii, xx, 80, 153,
201fn
Pasteur, Louis, 164, 454
Peace movement, 125, 129, 133, 202
"Pedagese," xxxfn
Pedagogy, see "Instruction" above
Percentile ranking, 23, 37–38
Phonetic alphabet, 239, 243
Phonics, xv, xxxiv, xl, 55, 124, 238fn, 239,
241, 243, 412, 429
Photosynthesis, 188, 225
Physics, xlivfn, 95, 118, 158, 189, 366,
439, 444, 454, 461, 484, 520
Piaget, Jean, 11, 65–66, 232, 390, 480
Plague, 333
Plato, 162, 385
Pledge of Allegiance, 227, 258, 333
Political correctness, xliv, 15, 125, 143,
150, 160, 214, 255, 286, 292, 313,
329, 330, 342, 374, 394, 421, 482,
513, 528
Poor Richard, 59, 273, 509
Pop philosophy, xxvi–xxviii, 368
Pop psychology, 182, 287, 372
Pope, Alexander, 448
Portfolio, 248, 463, 466
Pre-Professional Skills Test (PPST),
115, 160–161
Private school, xi, xix, 20–21, 47, 354,
510
Problem solving, xxxiii, 12, 26, 29, 31,
33, 44, 63, 191fn, 415
Progressivism, (found throughout)
Prohibition, 146
Project method, see "Instruction" above
Prosser, Charles, xxxvi
Protestant, 325, 361
Psychological colors, 162, 175, 177–178,
190, 210, 218, 223
Public Law 94–142, 374, 395

Quality Performance Accreditation
(QPA), 374, 407, 469
R^2 (Multiple regression statistic), 275,
284

Racism, (found throughout but
especially Chapter 4)
Raising Your Child to Be Gifted, 280
Ravitch, Diane, xxxv–xxxviii, 93, 124,
324
Reading is Fundamental, 429
Reimer, David, 302
Relevance theory, xxi, 47–48, 108, 135,
149, 408, 457
Reliability, 105–110, 277
Religion, 56, 117, 123, 134, 140,
194–195, 204, 256–257, 508, 514,
531
Christianity, 256–257, 310, 339, 532
Creationism, 20, 309
God, 192, 232, 265, 309, 315, 331,
512, 532
Humanism, 194
Islam, 335
Jesus, 249, 326
Judao-Christian, 256
Protestant, 325, 361
The Ten Commandments, 532
Renorming, 18fn, 41–42, 115, 124fn,
486fn
Report Card, xv, 20, 22, 25, 39, 60, 69,
83, 268, 472, 483
Republican Party, 289
Research, (found throughout)
Construct validity, 105, 108, 110
Content validity, 105
Heuristic validity, 105
Internal validity, 105
Reliability, 105–110, 277
Qualitative . . ., 105–107, 241
Quantitative . . ., xliv, 106–107
Validity, 3, 6, 105–110, 226, 228, 231,
277, 398, 536
Resource hoarding, 315, 320
Revolution,
Chinese cultural . . ., 92, 488
American . . ., 145–146, 502
French . . ., 146, 200, 505
Industrial . . ., 63, 297
Russian . . ., 146, 505

Third International Math and Science
    Study (TIMSS), 1
Thorndike, Edward L., xliv–vlv, 93
Three Rs, xxi, 25
Title 1, 12
Toch, Thomas, xxxviii–xxxix, xlviifn,
    102fn, 118, 381, 497fn
Tolstoy, Leo, 9
Torres, Carlos Alberto, 349
Tourette Syndrome (TS), 376–380, 405
Trinity Evangelical Divinity School, 96
Tucson Early Education Model, 11
Twain, Mark, 372, 460
Tyler, Alexander F., 257

U.S. News and World Report, 90, 229
UCLA, 349
Unabomber, 133–134
United States,
    . . . Bill of Rights, 337
    . . . Declaration of Independence,
        333, 505
    . . . Congress, xxviii, 8, 153, 241, 289,
        375
    . . . Constitution, 269, 337
'Unity through diversity', 15, 202, 322,
    363
University of Chicago, xliv–xlv, 78fn,
    421, 536
University of Illinois, 10, 421
University of Iowa, 44
University of London, 349
University of Maryland, College Park, 96
University of Massachusetts-Amherst, 90,
    160, 196
University of Memphis, 96
University of Oregon, 10
University of Pennsylvania, 421, 508
University of Sarasota, 96
University of Washington, 278
University of Wisconsin, Madison, 349
Uno, G. E., 456
USSR, 338, 488

Utopia, xx, xlii, xliv, xlvii, 7, 50, 61, 68,
    141, 154, 190, 231, 259, 355, 387,
    425, 514, 516

Valedictorian, 89, 134, 237, 484
Validity, 3, 6, 105–110, 226, 228, 231,
    277, 398, 536
Vanderbilt University, 425
Van Gogh, Vincent, 268
Victimology, xii, 122, 132–135, 149,
    210–211, 215, 235, 311, 321fn,
    331–332, 334, 370, 372–373, 380,
    402, 422, 482, 515, 519
Vietnam, 125, 129, 132, 305
Vincent, William, S., xxxvii
Virginia Polytechnic Institute and State
    University, 95
Voltaire, 553
Vygotsky, Lev, 232, 346, 480–481
    Scaffolding, 464, 480–481

Wallace, George, 129
Walton, John Boy, 122
War on Drugs, xxi, 537
War on Poverty, xxi, 343
Washington, Booker, T., 358
Washington, George, 115fn, 226, 330,
    333
Western Civilization, 36, 334, 502, 531
Western culture, 256, 258, 372
White, Merry, xxii, 335fn
Whitty, Geoff, 349
Whole Curriculum, 186, 493
Whole Language, xxv, xxxiii, xxxv, xxxix,
    10–12, 14–15, 65, 124, 157, 166,
    169fn, 186–187, 243–245, 247, 384,
    429, 447, 493, 528
Whole Science, 166, 186, 347, 493
Will, George, 506
Will, Madeleine C., 382
Wilson, E. O., 316–317
Whitman, Walt, 63
Wittmer, Joe, 103, 113–114, 116
Wood, Karen D., 248
World War II, 130, 146, 328

About the Author

Konstantine Turkalo is a retired officer in the United States Army and a teacher. He earned his undergraduate and graduate degrees from Syracuse University, Colorado State University, Kansas State University, and Webster University, with fields of study in education, psychology, mass communications, management, and microbiology. Mr. Turkalo lives in the Midwest where he continues to do some substitute teaching, and enjoys time in his woodworking shop when not writing.